Economic Geography

———◇———

Economic Geography

———— ◇ ————

Third Edition

James O. Wheeler
University of Georgia

Grant Ian Thrall
University of Florida

Peter O. Muller
University of Miami

Timothy J. Fik
University of Florida

Cartography by
Thomas W. Hodler
University of Georgia

JOHN WILEY & SONS, INC.

New York   Chichester   Weinheim   Brisbane   Singapore   Toronto

ACQUISITIONS EDITOR	Nanette Kauffman
MARKETING MANAGER	Catherine Beckham
SENIOR PRODUCTION EDITOR	Jeanie Berke
DESIGNER	Ann Marie Renzi
PHOTO EDITOR	Hilary Newman
ILLUSTRATION EDITOR	Edward Starr
COVER	Designed by Rafael H. Hernandez; Photo © Pablo Bartholomew/Gamma Liaison.

This book was set in 10/12 Times Ten by University Graphics, Inc. and printed and bound by Quebecor Fairfield. The cover was printed by Lehigh Press.

This book is printed on acid-free paper. ∞

The paper in this book was manufactured by a mill whose forest management programs include sustained yield harvesting of its timberlands. Sustained yield harvesting principles ensure that the numbers of trees cut each year does not exceed the amount of new growth.

Library of Congress Cataloging-in-Publication Data

Economic geography / James O. Wheeler . . . [et al.]. — 3rd ed.
    p.   cm.
    Rev. of ed. of: Economic geography / James O. Wheeler, Peter O. Muller. 2nd ed. 1986.
    Includes bibliographical references and index.
    ISBN 0-471-53620-2 (cloth : alk. paper)
    1. Economic geography. I. Wheeler, James O. II. Wheeler, James O. Economic Geography.
HF1025.W48 1998
330.9—dc21
                                        97-45934
                                          CIP

To our wives, Emily E. Wheeler, Nancy L. Muller, Susan Elshaw Thrall, and Denise E. Fik.

PREFACE

We are pleased for the opportunity to revise *Economic Geography*, to update the statistical materials, and to add the findings of new research and perspectives to this third edition. The major change to the earlier Wheeler and Muller editions is the addition of two new coauthors, Drs. Grant Ian Thrall, and Timothy J. Fik, Department of Geography at the University of Florida. Professor Thrall was responsible for totally rewriting the energy section, Part Five, and for updating and revising the agricultural chapters, Part Six. Professor Fik has revised the two industrial chapters, Part Four.

In addition, Professor Wheeler has added a new chapter on the global economy (Chapter 4), and Professor Muller has revised his chapter on "The Changing Economic Geography of the Restructured Metropolis," which now appears as Chapter 9. Professor Wheeler has revised all of the other chapters. The last chapter of the previous editions, by Professor Wheeler, has been made an appendix in this revision, as this chapter on techniques will hopefully serve students and professors better as a reference chapter.

The organization of this book, as with the previous editions, is intentionally somewhat different from that of most textbooks in economic geography. Rather than progressing from a discussion of the primary, the secondary, the tertiary, and the quaternary sectors of the economy, this book—after an introductory chapter describing economic geography—treats global population patterns and problems, and the worldwide distribution of technology and economic development. The book then turns to the analysis of global interdependence, and to spatial interaction patterns (transportation). After the analysis of transportation, we discuss the city and its economic activities, including retailing. One chapter is devoted to the changing economic geography of cities (metropolitan areas) in the 1990s. We then review the industrial location process, including basic location theory and the problems of industrial regions. The next part of the book examines the economic geography of energy production and consumption, both at the world scale and the U.S. level. After the treatment of energy, two chapters are devoted to the economic geography of agriculture. The appendix provides an introduction to locational indices and techniques. Although we feel this organization provides a logical progression, the book has been prepared in such a way that an instructor may assign the chapters in any order deemed appropriate.

We are grateful to the many people who assisted in various ways in the development and preparation of this book, many of whom we thanked in earlier editions. We thank the several reviewers of the manuscript chapters in the different stages of their preparation for their helpful suggestions for improvements. We especially thank Dr. Thomas W. Hodler, Department of Geography at the University of Georgia, for preparing all of the new graphics and maps and for improving many that appeared in the earlier editions. Professor Muller wishes to thank Dr. Mary

M. Sapp, Director of Planning and Institutional Research, University of Miami, for her assistance. We also thank all of the staff at John Wiley & Sons, Inc. for their considerable help in overseeing the many facets of the production of this book.

James O. Wheeler
Athens, Georgia

Peter O. Muller
Coral Gables, Florida

Grant Ian Thrall
Gainesville, Florida

Timothy J. Fik
Gainesville, Florida

CONTENTS

Economic Geography

———◇———

PART ONE

Introduction

CHAPTER 1

The Study of Economic Geography

⬦

No single parts unequally surprise,
All comes united to the admiring eyes.
—ALEXANDER POPE

INTRODUCTION TO GEOGRAPHIC ANALYSIS

The field of geography arises out of two fundamental human qualities. One is the need to know something about the local geography in order to carry out economic, social, and political activities, whether—gathering in the Amazon rain forest, growing wheat in twentieth-century Kansas, or robbing banks in modern suburban St. Louis. This geographic knowledge of the local area, although commonly taken for granted by an individual, is nevertheless an important part of geographic analysis. It is important to know how individuals and groups behave within their local geographic environment and why. Knowing the local geography is not merely a convenience to an individual, but a necessity to the functioning of society and the economy. Taxi drivers need to know their local city geography, and so do city planners.

The second human quality leading to an interest in geography is the natural curiosity people have about distant places. Since most of us, astronauts and traveling diplomats apart, are relatively fixed geographically in our day-to-day activities, we see and know firsthand only a minute fraction of all there is to know about other places. When we do travel, we all too frequently gain merely a passing flavor, seeing the proverbial tip of the iceberg. A tribesman listening to storied legends of far-off places, a family member scanning issues of the *National Geographic* magazine, a salesperson discovering a new regional market area—all are reacting to and are interested in the geography of other places. With the quickening pace and widening influence of technology, the distinction between local and distant geography is becoming blurred. The World Wide Web allows the opportunity for the most geographically remote locations to connect in global cyberspace with world-wide places in virtual reality. I cannot go to Manhattan Island in less than four hours, but I can go there immediately in virtual reality.

Before fixing on what economic geography is, we must say a few words, by way of setting the stage, concerning the discipline of geography in general. We may usefully approach geography by considering two continua: a human-physical continuum and a topical-regional continuum (Figure 1.1). Any geographic study treats, in varying degrees, the physical environment and the human (cultural and social) environment. Economic geography, emphasizing human pro-

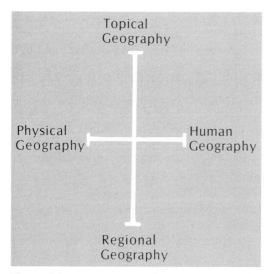

Figure 1.1 Two fundamental continua in geography are the human-physical and the topical-regional. All geographic studies may be located somewhere on this diagram, depending on whether the study falls more toward the human or physical end or toward the topical or regional end of the scales.

duction, distribution, and consumption activities, naturally falls toward the human end of the scale. Even here, climate, terrain, soil, and hydrology, for example, will play a critical role at some level of analysis.

The second continuum represents an approach to the analysis of the spatial variation in human and physical elements.[1] This approach may be through examination of the geography of a *region*—the state of Wisconsin, the Ohio valley, or San Diego, for example. Conversely, the emphasis may be on a particular *topic* of geographic significance, such as areal variation in income, soybean yield, or incidence of violent crime, all of which vary from place to place and help characterize places. One might study the economic geography of a region, a second region, a third, and so on, until all the world was covered. On the other hand—and more sensibly—one could

[1]The term *spatial* is used synonymously with *geographic* in this book.

decide on the major topics of economic geography and describe the principles involved in the distribution of various kinds of economic activities. Basically, such a topical (or systematic) organization is followed here. The regional approach focuses on a large number of variables or locational characteristics in a limited area, whereas the systematic approach analyzes a smaller number of functionally related characteristics over a wide area. At the extremes, the regional emphasis leads to intensive case studies of minute areas that have little general applicability; the topical approach can lead to highly generalized conclusions that do not apply very well to particular localized geographic problems.

Since these two continua exist in time, the study of geography may be approached from a third perspective—the continuum extending from the most faded past to the present. All four end points of the two continua may be approached historically, although physical changes through time are generally slower, though not without occasional flooding and erosion followed by dormancy and drought. Most historical-geographic studies are either longitudinal or cross-sectional. Cross-sectional studies treat geographic conditions as they existed at some point, or "slice," in time—say, the geography of Eu-

The teaching of geography is becoming more common at the primary, secondary, undergraduate, and graduate levels, as more and more people appreciate its value in their lives.

rope. Longitudinal studies seek trends over a period of time, such as the development and spread of the tractor as an agricultural technique across the U.S. Midwest. Historical-geographic studies tend to be on the human side of the scale, longitudinal research is usually systematic, whereas cross-sectional analyses are commonly regional.

Geography is that discipline that analyzes variations in phenomena from place to place on the earth's surface. Although many more-convoluted definitions could be quoted or concocted, the bases of geographic study, as defined here, are (1) the **description of locations** on the earth (of whatever phenomena are deemed significant and at whatever scale or level of generalization is appropriate) and (2) the **understanding of why** these locations were selected and how they relate to other locations. The distribution of locations can be displayed easily by mapping, as with cities, coal mines, or highways. The interpretation of locations, a goal of this book, can be achieved less readily, for several kinds of explanations may be used.

The task of explanation in geography comes under the general heading of **spatial analysis**, as the term has come to be used in contemporary geography. Spatial analysis is closely tied not only with cartographic techniques, but especially with more elegant statistical and mathematical models and geographical information science (GIS). Although the interest is in explaining empirical spatial patterns, the approach is frequently theoretical, in which general principles are developed and tested with regard to particular real-world data. For example, rather than explaining the location of a grocery store merely in terms of a sequence of specific historical changes in land use, one might call on appropriate elements of spatial-marketing theory dealing with the location of competition, changing modes of transportation, or changing neighborhood characteristics.

The basic distinction between **site** and **situation** is used in explaining geographic phenomena. "Site" refers to the characteristics inherent in the parcel of land on which the location occurs (the land occupied by the grocery store, a residential dwelling, a farm, and an office building). Each site has advantages and disadvantages for different locational purposes, such as degree of slope, swampiness, percent of area in trees, soil productivity, or simply size of the land unit. Understanding geographic distributions at the local level is accomplished through site analysis. "Situation" has to do with the relative location—the relationships of one location with all other relevant locations. Through the analysis of relative location, the greatest achievements are made in geographic understanding. It is also here that the greatest difficulties are encountered because the first law of geography is that what is located at one place has an influence on what is located at a prodigious number of other locations, the nearer ones, generally showing greater influence than the more distant ones. Sorting out the strength of these influences is a broad research goal with which all geography is concerned.

Economic geography focuses on the distribution of production, distribution, and consumption activities. The economic geographer wishes to display the spatial distribution of these economic activities and to understand why they are located as they are. A significant part of this understanding lies in recognizing how economic activities are interrelated in particular areas and how the activities are tied to other economic activities at other locations. For example, one may examine the situation (relative location) of a manufacturing plant through analysis of the linkages with raw-material sources and with market locations. At a different level, the economic geographer may wish to understand why this same manufacturing plant or advertising firm selected its specific site from the several alternative sites available. When the same basic questions and approaches of the geographers, as outlined here, are focused on the spatial patterns of **economic activities**, we are dealing with the broad field of economic geography.

What is the relationship between economic ge-

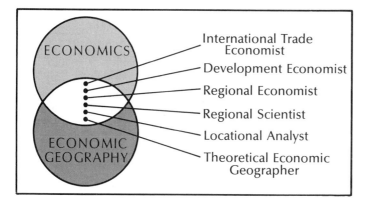

Figure 1.2 The relationship between economic geography and economics. *Source*: Taaffe, 1974.

ography and the field of economics? Edward Taaffe answers that question by the illustration in Figure 1.2, which shows an overlap zone between these two fields. At the core of economics is economic theory. Part of the overlap zone is *regional economics*, in which economists use economic theory better to understand regions. Locational analysis, though based in the spatial perspective, is also of interest to economists, who have made major contributions in this overlap zone. Thus, the two fields, economics and economic geography, have separate core interests—economic theory and spatial economic analysis, respectively—but share certain common research concerns. The result is that, in this overlap zone, research in regional economics and locational analysis draws from the ideas and approaches of both economists and economic geographers. The field of *regional science*, represented by a number of professional scholarly journals, for example, is a fertile area of overlapping interests between economic geographers and regional economists.

SUBFIELDS OF ECONOMIC GEOGRAPHY

Just as human geography may be subdivided conveniently on the basis of subject matter into such areas as, for example, political, population, urban, and economic, so, too, may economic geography be reduced to its components. Figure 1.3

depicts a traditional breakdown of economic geography into topical clusters. ***Primary economic activities*** involve the extraction and utilization of resources, as in mining, forestry, hunting, and agriculture, in which humans and the environment come into direct physical contact. Secondary activities are those that process, transform, assemble, or otherwise manufacture a wide range of goods and encompass everything from handicraft industries (basket- and quilt-making) to large, modern automobile assembly lines. The tertiary sector makes available to consumers all kinds of goods and services. A fourth, or quaternary, sector has also been increasingly recognized in the industrialized nations, with the explosion of knowledge and the growth in consumption of information-related services (from tax consultants to research "think tanks"). The quaternary sector in the most highly developed countries has increasingly replaced manufacturing as the basis for economic growth. In addition to these main sectors of the economy, transportation and communications cut across and connect all four sectors. A final category of activities needs to be recognized. Although not strictly, or ever primarily, economic in purpose, governmental and institutional activities (including nonprofit organizations) expend large sums of money. They influence and are influenced by many kinds of economic activities.

The service activities, the largest and fastest

growing employment component in the industrialized world, cut across the tertiary and quaternary sectors. Included in the quaternary sector are the producer services, comprising planning, management, legal, financial, marketing, and accounting services for large corporations and governments. The producer services are among the most rapidly expanding employment categories in a country such as the United States or Canada.

APPROACHES TO ECONOMIC GEOGRAPHY

Research in economic geography in the 1990s may be characterized by three major philosophic approaches. The first, *positivism*, employs the scientific method to interpret and understand issues in economic geography. The scientific approach is based on empirically verifiable and commonly agreed upon evidence through replication of analytical results. It involves informed hypothesis testing leading to empirical generalizations and lawlike statements. It is closely associated in eco-nomic geography, and indeed within the social sciences, with use of statistical and mathematical techniques. GIS is central to analytical and positivist approaches to geography in general and with especially numerous applications in economic geography. Positivism gained its greatest following in geography during the 1960s. In fact, today it continues to represent the mainstream of research as reflected, for example, in articles published in geographic journals and in related fields.

A second philosophic approach to economic geography, *structuralism*, posits that what we see in the world does not reveal the *causes* of what we see. For example, the enjoyment of eating a California-raised grapefruit should not be seen merely as a function of the shipping distance and price to the consumer (à la positivism), but rather as the economic, social, and political plight of the lowly paid immigrant and migrant labor force contributing to one's dining pleasure. Thus, the structure of the economy cannot be directly ob-

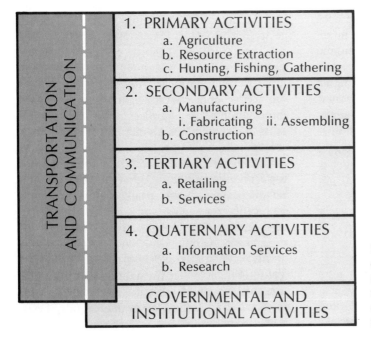

Figure 1.3 The subfields of economic geography cut across the primary, secondary, and tertiary, as well as the quaternary, sectors. Transportation and communications cut across each of these subfields and, in fact, connect them.

served, and we should therefore develop ideas and theories that will help us understand what we see and experience. While there is no way to directly test such theories, we can debate them to achieve better understanding. One important strand of structuralism is known as Marxism, which essentially entered economic geographic thought during the 1970s, and focuses in particular on the social class structure and struggles between the forces of labor and capital. Marxist and structuralist geographers in general emphasize studies in industrial geography, where conflicts between management and labor have traditionally been keen.

A third approach is *humanism,* which evolved in the late 1970s and the 1980s in part as a critique of positivism. Humanism values subjective experience and disdains so-called scientific objectivity as an impossibility. Knowledge is gained personally and individually, and the focus is on human thinking and feeling. Humanistic economic geographers object to both positivism and

structuralism on the basis that these approaches view people as responding mechanically to spatial and structural forces. A humanistic geographer wishing to study a city's central business district, for example, would seek to understand it by gathering first-hand experience rather than by collecting precise data on sales volume by store location (positivism) or by theorizing about the role of capitalism in central city decline (structuralism).

Recent technological developments in large-scale data storage, manipulation, and display (mapping) have had a beneficial impact on research in economic geography, as in all fields of geography (Figure 1.4). Geographic information science (GIS) allow the input, storage, analysis, and output of spatial data, with either point or area coordinates. Large data sets comprising numerous variables, when viewed in overlaid fashion, frequently lead to new hypotheses and keen insights into geographic relationships that have not previously been noted or understood.

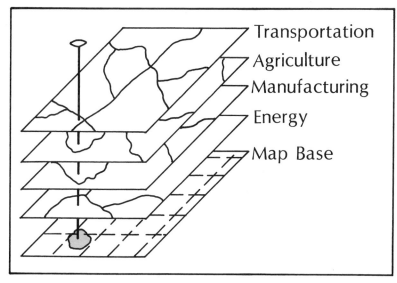

Figure 1.4 Geographic information science (GIS) is a set of procedures designed to store, retrieve, analyze, and map spatial data from many different sources and represents an extremely rapidly growing area of geographic analysis.

ECONOMIC LOCATION THEORY

Economic geography, then, is an extremely broad field in the sense that it examines a wide range of activities. This breadth is shared, of course, by the discipline of economics, and the social sciences in general. Like economics, economic geography is unified as a body of knowledge that is not so much identified by the subject matter studied as by a set of interlocking principles or theories, which are constantly evolving. In the case of economic geography, these principles and theories are those of the location of economic activities, known formally and collectively by the term *location theory*.

Location theory seeks to explain the basic, universal factors that determine and influence the location of all kinds of economic activity. Like all bodies of theory, it attempts to offer *general* explanations and cannot apply exactly to all locational decisions. All theories are based on assumptions, and when the assumptions in a theory do not correspond to reality, the reason is not that the theory is necessarily wrong, but rather that the theory does not apply well in that particular situation. In addition, different facets of location theory are in various stages of development and at different levels of verification. Location theory is constantly being modified through both deductive and inductive analysis. Many areas of location theory are only partly tested, and other areas are only imperfectly stated at all. From the body of location theory arise many hypotheses that need to be tested with respect to particular manufacturing, agricultural, and transportation systems, as well as increasingly to the locations and spatial linkages of research, management, and administrative (quaternary) functions. Location theory provides a conceptual framework that helps us to understand particular and individual elements of the economic landscape.

Figure 1.5 displays the outlines, somewhat idealized and greatly simplified, of how location theory develops and is modified. We must start at

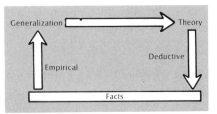

Figure 1.5 Economic geography may be approached both empirically and theoretically. Many studies combine elements of each approach in an attempt to understand spatial patterns and processes.

the base—at the level of "geographic" facts or data. This qualifying adjective is used to emphasize the distinction between geographic data and other kinds of data. Very simply, if a piece of information (datum) is geographic, it must be associated with a place or a location. "Twenty tons of wheat" is not meaningful geographically unless we know that it refers to a *place* where it was produced, processed, or consumed, or the *places* between which it was shipped. It must be mappable. Thus, in addition to data value or magnitude, there must be some type of locational coordinate system describing the place or places these data refer to, such as the familiar latitude and longitude system. Geographic data can, therefore, be extremely "coarse," pertaining to such broad regions of the earth as population densities by continents, or "fine," depicting local conditions with a high degree of detail. Obviously, different levels of understanding will emerge depending on the *scale* at which data are observed or collected.

Having a base of data, either *area-specific*, as for counties, or *point-specific*, as for individual households, or both, one may proceed empirically, or *inductively*, by going from detailed facts to a single generalization. These methods may consist of simple data-mapping to discover areal patterns, or statistical analysis to determine relationships among data sets. The theoretical, or deductive, procedure, as widely recognized in the literature on the scientific method, proceeds from a general statement to one that applies to a great many specific facts. A deductively generated theory, if it is to have empirical usefulness, must be brought into contact with appropriate facts where testing will help verify or discredit the theory. Location theories are not created in ivory-tower isolation.

Since the locational process is highly complicated, the location theorist, in setting forth a theory or extending an existing one, relies on a storehouse of generalizations that have been built up and sifted from a broad factual base. Although the arrows in Figure 1.5 show the typical directions that theory development takes, they do not show the circuitous and tortuous paths, including dead ends encountered along the way.

A useful way of viewing the content and approach of economic geography may be seen in Figure 1.6, derived from Brian J. L. Berry.[2] The rows in the matrix represent places, which may be points (shopping malls or farmsteads) or areas (counties or census tracts). Places are depicted from a single place (one) to infinity (or a very large number, N). Economic attributes of places are shown as columns in the matrix, and these economic attributes include manufacturing, retailing, wholesaling, agriculture, services, and transportation, representing groups of columns. An individual column, for example, may represent median family income or board feet of timber harvested. Thus, any study in economic geography may be viewed as relating places with economic attributes.

If we were to examine one particular attribute, say, retail sales over a large number of places, such as metropolitan areas, we could think of the result as a single map depicting the magnitude of retail sales figures. Here we would have an example of a systematic analysis of one feature of economic geography. It is likely that we would wish to relate this single feature, retail sales, to one or more additional features, perhaps popu-

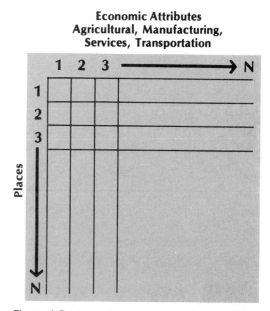

**Economic Attributes
Agricultural, Manufacturing,
Services, Transportation**

Figure 1.6 Places (points or areas) are depicted as rows in the matrix, and economic attributes are shown as columns. Examples of economic attributes are agriculture, manufacturing, retailing, services, and transportation.
Source: After Berry, 1964.

lation size and median family income, to improve our understanding of the distribution of retail sales among metropolitan areas. When the economic geographer studies one of a limited number of columns in the matrix over a large number of places, he or she is using the **systematic** or topical approach to spatial analysis. Suppose an economic geographer is interested in the economic geography of a single county in New York or a small group of counties. With reference to the matrix, the geographer will examine one or a small number of rows but will include a large number of attributes characterizing the economic geography of those rows. Now the approach would be following the **regional** method. The economic geographer typically uses both the systematic and regional approach to research, the systematic providing generalization and principles and the regional providing information

[2]Brian J. L. Berry, "Approaches to Regional Analysis: A Synthesis," *Annals of the Association of American Geographers* 54 (1964), pp. 2–11.

on relationships among attributes in particular places.

PAST TRENDS AND MODERN FOCUS

As indicated, the field of economic geography has both an empirical and a theoretical side, and these should be viewed as complementary approaches to the fundamental questions of the field: Where? and Why? Before 1960, most empirical research in economic geography emphasized the factual, or descriptive, approach: studies focused, for example, on a particular manufacturing city (or region) or on a selected industry. In agricultural geography, a common subject breakdown was by type of farming, and a long list of studies was compiled on cotton, silk, jute, cacao, tea, sugar beets, and almost every other type of farming ever attempted. By undertaking many regional case studies or studies of many industries based on occupational types, it was therefore assumed that generalizations could be derived and that the parts, when eventually put together, would form a coherent whole.

Instead of bringing unity to the field of economic geography, however, this approach often produced increasing fragmentation as researchers became overly specialized in more and more esoteric industrial and agricultural occupations, such as lead mining in southeastern Missouri. Experts in tobacco geography became estranged from colleagues studying Manila hemp production in Luzon or potash deposits in Germany. No one could be an expert in the entire field of economic geography defined in this way, so scattered and minute were individual areas of interest.

At the same time that research in economic geography was rushing to fulfill the task of describing every occupational type, no matter how obscure, and every region, no matter how small or insignificant, a countertrend was developing, slowly at first, but gathering momentum as its value became more widely recognized. Just when it was becoming most fashionable to define wor-

thy research by its novelty or outlandishness (e.g., olive production in the heel of Italy), publications on economic spatial analysis and regional science began appearing in the literature from disciplines outside geography. Thus, the initial steps in establishing a theory of location for economic activity were stimulated in part by those in academic territories outside geography. But within a short number of years in the 1960s, economic geography changed in focus from an essentially descriptive to an increasingly theoretical subdiscipline.

Increasingly, statistical and mathematical techniques have been employed in the contemporary era. The research designs have frequently been described as **nomothetic**, searching for lawfulness in geographic patterns and processes, as opposed to **ideographic,** emphasizing what is unique. In the 1970s, a much greater concern with the economic **behavior** in space of individuals and groups was added. And, finally, economic geography today is characterized by the application of location theory to specific real-world problems. A problem-solving approach, including a sharper focus on the societal impacts of the economic system, has replaced, in surprisingly quick measure, the purely ivory-tower philosophy. And it has been widely recognized that solutions to economic location problems, of which there are many in both metropolitan-dominated industrial societies and poor, rural, developing economies, must be undertaken with

Adult college student doing geography homework.

a solid foundation in the principles of locational theory. More and more, empirical work is undertaken with a conceptual basis. This broadened conceptual basis has provided the foundation, starting in the late 1970s, for a great flood of applied research in economic geography, and with it, outstanding opportunities for those trained in economic geography to obtain employment in the private and public sectors.

Other trends in economic geography have involved a so-called *behavioral* focus, in which the emphasis is placed on how locational decisions are actually made. It is one thing to describe a region as producing a particular crop or combination of crops; it is another to understand how the farmers in the region have come to decide what crops to raise. Another recent trend in economic geography is the emphasis on the *societal impacts* of economic activities, ranging from the effects of environmental pollution from a manufacturing plant on the surrounding area to the increase in neighborhood accessibility from the construction of an urban freeway. Contemporary economic geography also is increasingly interested in the *policy implications* of economic activities. It is recognized that the role of government is fundamental in affecting the level and location of economic activities. This role is carried out not only by the federal government, but also by state and local governments. Alternative public policies lead to different—sometimes quite different—locational patterns. Another trend in modern economic geography is referred to under the general label of *applied geography*. Since many professional geographers are employed in planning organizations, government agencies, and business and industry, the training of geographers at the bachelor's, master's, and doctoral levels has come increasingly to involve how geographic concepts and techniques can be applied to a wide range of practical problems. A recent M.A. in economic geography obtained employment with the Gwinnett County School Board (suburban Atlanta)—one of the fastest growing counties in the United States during the 1990s. He supervises the optimum routing of school buses to link students' residential locations with their schools. (Updates in the routing system were needed on a weekly basis.)

Closely related to developments in applied geography is the contemporary concern with *problem-solving approaches* in economic geography. A background in mathematics, statistics, and computer programming and location analysis is useful. Practical skills such as cartography, air photography, remote sensing, computer graphics, and geographic information systems (GIS) are extremely helpful in the analysis of spatial problems.

GLOBALIZATION TRENDS[3]

The concept of *globalization* has spread throughout the social sciences, including economic geography. Although the concept goes back to the 1960s (McLuhan's "global village"), only in the 1980s was the term widely accepted, in both the academic and popular literature. This new outlook on geography is challenging the traditional approaches to economic geography and much debate exists on the precise definition of the term.

Such phrases as "the global shopping mall," "the global workplace," or the "global city" attempt to capture the essence of globalization. This concept is based on the new communications technologies and their impact on the local and global economy, as well as on social, cultural, and political life. Local communities are "embedded" within the global economy, as decisions made in far-away places impact localities. At the same time, localities compete with one another for a niche in the world system. As Amin and Tomaney (1995) state, "It would appear that a new era is unfolding in which governments and global firms bargain with one another on the

---

[3]This section is based, in part, on Peter Dicken, Jamie Peck, and Adam Tickell, "Unpacking the Global," a paper presented at the annual conference of the International Geographical Union Commission on the Organization of Industrial Space, Seoul, Korea, August 1995.

world stage for a favourable position within the international division of labour, rather than in pursuit of national economic interests."[4]

Globalization may be understood in terms of five characteristics:

1. Capital has become more globally mobile, so that investments are more footloose.

2. The market has become less regulated, breaking down governmental and political control.

3. Powerful multinational firms are the principal agents of change.

4. The nation-state or national political forces have been weakened, giving way to multinational corporations.

5. Dual trends have been set in motion, the one trend toward more homogeneous global conditions as a result of widespread competition, and the other toward enhanced differences as localities strive to maintain their identities.

Thus, globalization represents a complex set of processes, which economic geographers have only just begun to understand.

SPATIAL PATTERNS

The distribution of economic activities over the earth's surface or within a region may be viewed as forming a *pattern*, or spatial distribution. Such a pattern may be explicitly recognized when the category of economic activity in question is represented on a map. For example, Figure 1.7 depicts, by a series of *nodes*, or points, the distribution of grain elevators in an area of the Canadian Great Plains. Such a map describes a *point pattern*. It answers the basic question *where* with considerable cartographic precision, and it provides a starting point for spatial analysis. Geographers today are fond of conceptualizing a great many phenomena as if they occurred only at a single point, even though they, of course, occupy some space in reality. A house may be mapped as a point, as may be a factory, a shopping center, an office building, and even a metropolitan area extending over many square miles. A point pattern implies that relative location is to be emphasized in the description and analysis and that the actual area (site) that the phenomenon occupies is not significant at that level of spatial analysis.

Other categories of geographic patterns may be noted. Another glance at Figure 1.7 reveals *linear patterns* representing railroads used to transport the grain. These linear patterns are not independent of the point patterns in location and layout. Any type of movement or connection between places may be viewed as part of a linear pattern whether or not there exists an observable physical facility connecting the places. For instance, the frequency of telephone calls, FAX messages, and overnight mail delivery among the offices, manufacturing plants, and warehouses of a large corporation may be mapped to form a linear flow pattern.

Combining the linear and nodal concepts, one may define a *nodal region*, which is useful in many kinds of geographic analysis. A nodal region consists of an area in which the activity (the orientation of the linear pattern) focuses on a single node. A major city will "organize" the activities of the surrounding area, for example. To delimit the extent of a nodal region, one must know where the intensity of focus or the magnitude of movement drops below a defined threshold. Thus, each grain elevator forms the focus of a small but separate nodal region, from which it obtains a greater share of grain than does any other elevator. Similarly, Chicago, for example, is the focus of a nodal region based on motor truck transportation, the extent of which is based on the average maximum mileage that 18-wheelers roll away from "Chi-town" (as the truckers call it) in a 24-hour period.

Another commonly encountered type of spatial pattern is depicted on the *choropleth map*.

[4]A. Amin, and J. Tomaney (1995), "The Regional Dilemma in a Neo-Liberal Europe," *European Urban and Regional Studies*, Vol. 2, p. 172.

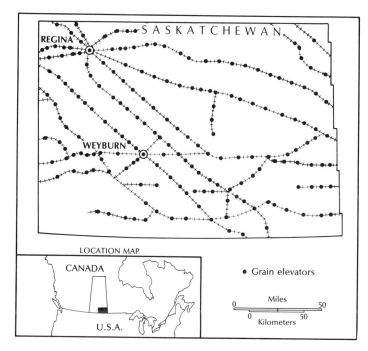

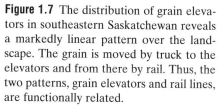

Figure 1.7 The distribution of grain elevators in southeastern Saskatchewan reveals a markedly linear pattern over the landscape. The grain is moved by truck to the elevators and from there by rail. Thus, the two patterns, grain elevators and rail lines, are functionally related.

On such a map, entire areas, such as states or counties, are recorded as having a single value, indicated by a single color or shading. A land-use map of a city may be shown by a choropleth pattern. At another scale of analysis, the United States and Canada might be divided into agricultural regions on the basis of dominant kinds of agriculture pursued. Thus, choropleth patterns may represent what geographers have called *uniform regions*, where the element defining the region (such as dairy farming, cash grain farming, or goat herding) is more or less evenly spread within the region, but weakly represented outside the region.

A fourth, and final, general category of spatial patterns is the *surface*, which may be illustrated cartographically in a variety of ways. As the name implies, a geographic surface, also known as a statistical surface, shows a continuous distribution of some feature over an area. The most intuitive example is the landform surface, in which elevations above sea level are shown to form a pattern of hills and valleys. Perhaps the

most common method of surface mapping is by use of *isolines*, as in Figure 1.8b. These are lines connecting points of equal magnitude. Many kinds of phenomena for which data exist only at points may be generalized into a continuous surface, as for a median-income surface of a region. In such a case, lines are drawn to connect all places with a specified median income to give the overall pattern of regional income variation. Computer programs draw three-dimensional representations of geographical surfaces, as in Figure 1.8a, in which the peaks show location with high median income and the valleys the poor places. These programs can be placed north or south, in whatever direction, in order to obtain the best visual perspective for a particular spatial surface.

Spatial patterns often combine to form *hierarchies*, interlocking sequences of patterns ranging from small to large scale. Such spatial hierarchies reflect the extent and dimensions of an *economic system*, where a system consists of a set of elements with functional relationships and

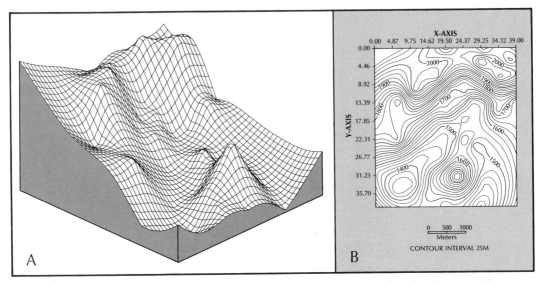

Figure 1.8 The isoline map (*b*) depicts a continuous distribution, such as elevation, by use of lines connecting points of equal value. Where lines are closest together, the slope is steepest. In (*a*) the identical information is represented by a three-dimensional surface drawn by a computer plotter, that is, a computer moving an ink pen.

with interdependencies among the elements defining the system. A system is, then, defined by a disciplinary perspective, and geographic systems are seen from the perspective of the location of the system elements. Take the example of a commercial agricultural system, looking first at the smallest components in the hierarchy. At this level we may note the role of the farmstead as an organizational node around which the farm operates—a small-scale nodal region. This nodal region in fact consists of fields in which different crops are grown, the fields constituting an elemental type of uniform region. In this area, numerous farms will act as nodal regions, thus defining a uniform region. Scattered over the uniform agricultural region will be a series of small agricultural and marketing centers acting as collectors of farm products and as distributors of goods and services required by the rural population. These centers, of course, function as nodal regions. As a group, however, these centers may be said to form a uniform region of marketing centers. This example could be extended

further up the economic system, to the level of metropolitan areas. The main points are clear, however. We have described in terms of spatial patterns a functionally related group of economic elements constituting a hierarchical pattern of alternately uniform and nodal dimensions. Beyond description and mapping, of what further interest are these patterns?

SPATIAL PROCESSES

To answer this question, we turn to spatial *processes*. The word *process* implies something happening over time. A spatial process, then, involves change within some or all of the elements of a system. Since we are dealing with spatial economic systems, spatial processes are mappable as they may occur at different rates or take on different characteristics at different places over time. The term *pattern* has been used to describe an activity distribution frozen at a point in time, and to that extent a somewhat artificial situation is reflected. The concept of spatial process is used to "explain" spatial patterns, as it refers to a causal chain of events that produces change over time. A pattern existing at one moment of time is the result of the operation of processes that have had differential spatial impacts. Geographers are concerned with the interplay between pattern and process, and these two concepts are avenues geographers use to analyze spatial economic systems. In the simplest sense, pattern answers the question *where*; process answers the question *why*.

Since spatial economic patterns are a result of human decisions, many approaches to the analysis of economic systems involve studying behavior as a spatial process. Economic patterns change because of human decisions, which may be based on different economic goals, different perceptions of economic alternatives, different preference and cultural systems, and different methods of solving problems or making choices. Locational decisions may be based on various levels of information. A locational decision made within the constraints of a particular strategy will affect the pattern of locations in some given way, whereas another decision maker, following a different drummer, may generate quite contrasting locational changes. For example, an entrepreneur who believes his or her customers are unanimously price-conscious may locate near a supplier to reduce cost, which can be passed on to the customers through lower prices that undercut competition; he or she may be indifferent to the location of the customers. A second entrepreneur may locate with maximum convenience to customers. The point is that the two entrepreneurs will create contrasting spatial patterns on the economic landscape.

Different processes operate on the economic landscape at different times. The observed cross-sectional pattern is a composite of influences, some continuing to operate and others having ceased far in the past. Economic geographers view the spatial economic system as it exists at the present, as well as a kind of artifact, created largely in the past and only slowly responding to

Manufacturing is classified as secondary production. Here is a view of a modern automobile assembly plant.

more current influences. The present spatial pattern at any particular place for any specific economic activity, through a feedback mechanism, helps shape the next stage of the process unfolding. The task of explanation is to unravel the varied spatial processes as they acted in the past and continue to act in the present.

In addition to human behavior as a direct spatial process, technological change brings about conditions broadening or reducing the range of human choice. And technology, as we will explain more fully in Chapter 3, has had a snowballing effect over time, increasing geometrically. To illustrate how a given spatial pattern may be the result of many past and present spatial processes, consider the distribution of manufacturing in metropolitan areas today. On the one hand, the distribution of manufacturing shows clustering near the center of the urban area; on the other, much of it is spread widely throughout the suburbs. Two different kinds of spatial processes have been responsible for the development of this pattern. One, occurring principally in the past, was a centralizing influence, having to do with accessibility at a given level of transportation technology (the railroad, river, and canals). The other process, of considerable current impact, is a decentralizing factor, related in part to the motor truck as a transport agent. This example is of two contrasting processes affecting metropolitan manufacturing location, and the explication of the pattern is fairly straightforward. In most other cases, the geographer faces a much more complex challenge.

The principle of *locational inertia* must also be considered in spatial studies of economic systems. Economic location inertia is a time-lag effect that activities experience in the adjustment to new locational influences. The inner-city manufacturing plant might be one such example. Here is a plant that located in the past because of one set of locational factors. Other factors now operating would suggest the plant should select a different kind of location. However, because of capital sunk into building and equipment, it is no simple matter to move, since the building, perhaps old and needing repair, has limited economic value except to the firm occupying it.

SUMMARY

Geography is one of the most ancient disciplines in human recorded history; economic geography, the study of how human earn their living in different locations and the patterns and processes reflected in this geographic variation, forms a sizable part of the field. To the centuries-old methods of description and synthesis, modern research in economic geography has been aided by developments in the social and behavioral sciences, in computer science, in statistics, in mathematics, and in GIS. The use of the scientific method to study economic spatial systems has permitted new ways of understanding old questions. The principles of economic location theory have formed a core around which economic geography is focused. These same principles act as a guide to applied economic geography, such as the spatial planning of economic establishments. A large body of empirical research has been developed over the years, and a complete and balanced treatment of economic geography must present both the theoretical and the empirical contributions.

Further Readings

Abler, Ronald, John S. Adams, and Peter Gould. *Spatial Organization: The Geographer's View of the World*. Englewood Cliffs, N.J.: Prentice-Hall, 1971.

Amedeo, D., and R. G. Golledge. *An Introduction to Scientific Reasoning in Geography*. New York: Wiley, 1975.

Berry, Brian J. L. "Approaches to Regional Analysis: A Synthesis." *Annals of the Association of American Geographers* 54 (1964), pp. 2–12.

Chorley, Richard J., and Peter Haggett. *Models in Geography*. London: Methuen, 1967.

de Souza, Anthony R. *A Geography of World Economy*. Columbus: Merrill Publishing Co., 1990.

Dicken, Peter, and Peter E. Lloyd. *Location in Space.* 3rd ed. New York: Harper and Row, 1990.

Gaile, Gary L., and Cort J. Willmont, eds. *Geography in America.* Columbus: Merrill Publishing Co., 1989.

Haggett, Peter. *The Geographer's Art.* Cambridge: Basil Blackwell, 1991.

Hartshorn, Truman A., and John W. Alexander. *Economic Geography.* 3rd ed. Englewood Cliffs, N.J.: Prentice-Hall, 1988.

Johnston, Ron J. *A Question of Place.* Cambridge: Basil Blackwell, 1991.

Johnston, Ron J. ed. *The Future of Geography.* New York: Methuen, 1985.

Sauer, Carl O. "The Education of a Geographer." *Annals of the Association of American Geographers* 64 (1956), pp. 286–299.

Schaefer, Fred K. "Exceptionalism in Geography: A Methodological Examination." *Annals of the Association of American Geographers* 43 (1953), pp. 226–249.

Sheppard, Eric. "Modeling the Capitalist Space Economy: Bringing Society and Space Back." *Economic Geography* 66 (1990), pp. 201–228.

Taaffe, Edward J. "The Spatial View in Context." *Annals of the Association of American Geographers* 46 (1974), pp. 1–16.

Taylor, Peter J. "World-Systems Analysis and Regional Geography." *Professional Geographer* 40 (1988), pp. 259–265.

CHAPTER 2

Global Population Processes and Pressures

———— ◇ ————

Do you know that numbers of your fellow-creatures are starving, for want of what you have too much of?

—J. J. ROUSSEAU

THE DISTRIBUTION OF PEOPLE

Of the tens of thousands of maps geographers have created, none is as fundamental as the map of world population. An essential starting point in economic geography is with the distribution of people because the occurrence of economic activity at a place is obviously dependent on humans being at that place. Furthermore, the kind of economic activity occurring at a given location depends, among other things, on the density of population. Wheat farming on the Great Plains is consistent with a scattered rural population; the concentration of heavy industry in the Ruhr Valley in Germany is related to the clustering of workers and their families.

Glancing at the map of world population, we immediately notice the uneven distribution of people over the earth. As striking as where the people are bunched together are the immense areas where people are not found. We might well think of world population as forming **human continents**, complete with peninsulas and islands, separated by vast "oceans" of nearly uninhabited spaces (Figure 2.1). Removing the land continents and watery oceans and replacing them with human continents and nonhuman oceans give a more realistic and graphic presentation of where human beings are located on the earth. It also shows more dramatically the distances isolating one human continent from another, and, especially in historical context, it goes a long way toward explaining cultural differences.

Let us begin in East and Southeast Asia. Of the 5.8 billion humans on the earth, over 34 percent live in the East and Southeast Asia cluster. The People's Republic of China alone, with over 1,200 million people, has over one-fifth of the world's population (Tables 2.1 and 2.2). Japan has another 126 million. The density of population (i.e., the number of people per square mile) drops off in general as one leaves the flatter, lower-lying coastal areas in China and proceeds westward into the both more rugged and drier interior. In southern China the density of population is highest along a strip fringing the coastal area, declining into the hilly areas. Even here, however, densities are high, ranging from well over 100 to over 200 people per square mile. Extending southward into Southeast Asia, densities in general decline further except for certain "islands" of very high density. The most notable exception is in Indonesia (201 million people), on Java, the most densely settled island on the earth.

High concentrations also occur in the Philippines, Taiwan, Vietnam, Thailand, and Myanmar (formerly Burma). In all of these cases, the high densities occur along coastal areas and in major river valleys. Despite the existence of some of the world's largest cities in East and Southeast Asia, the area is dominantly rural, and the majority of people earn a living from agriculture. Only Japan, with its highly industrialized economy, is an exception.

South Asia forms a second human continent, separated from the East and Southeast Asia cluster culturally as well as by the high arm of the Arakan Mountains in western Myanmar. After the People's Republic of China, India, with its 950 million people, is the second most populous country in the world. Split off from India in 1947 were Bangladesh (formerly East Pakistan; 120 million people) and Pakistan (formerly West Pakistan; 134 million people). Again, the distribu-

tion of population is highest along the coastal areas and in the fertile river valleys, the Ganges of India being the best example, followed by the Indus in Pakistan. Several large cities are found in these areas, and yet once again, the majority of the people are engaged in agricultural activities.

The third human continent is Europe, which extends eastward in peninsula form into Russia, where it narrows until finally ending near Lake Baykal, in Siberia. In contrast to the agriculturally based population in South and East Asia, Europe and the former Soviet Union support a dense population with an industrial system. Russia, the sixth most populous country in the world, has 148 million people. The rest of Europe's population has been growing slowly. After Russia, the leading European countries in population totals are Germany (82 million), Italy (57 million), the United Kingdom (59 million), and France (58

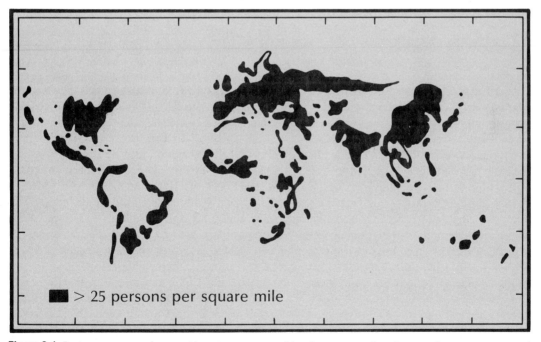

■ > 25 persons per square mile

Figure 2.1 Just as one may view continents as masses of land, one may also view continents as masses of people, forming human continents. Human continents constitute only a small portion of the total earth. *Source*: after Bunge, 1969.

Table 2.1 Leading Countries in Population Size, 1996

Country	Population in Millions	Rank	Percent of World Population
People's Republic of China	1,218	1	21.1
India	950	2	16.5
United States	266	3	4.6
Indonesia	201	4	3.5
Brazil	160	5	2.8
Russia	148	6	2.5
Pakistan	134	7	2.3
Japan	126	8	2.2
Bangladesh	120	9	2.1
Nigeria	104	10	1.8
Mexico	95	11	1.6
Germany	82	12	1.4
Vietnam	77	13	1.3
Philippines	72	14	1.2
Iran	63	15	1.1
Subtotal	3,816		66.1
World Total	5,771		100.0

Source: World Population Data Sheet, Population Reference Bureau, 1996.

Table 2.2 Population of Major World Regions, 1996

World Regions	Population in Millions	Percent of World Population
Africa	732	12.7
Asia	3,501	60.7
East Asia	1,443	(25.0)
Southeast Asia	496	(8.6)
South Central Asia	1,385	(24.0)
Western Asia	176	(3.0)
Australia-New Zealand	29	.05
Europe	728	12.6
Northern Europe	94	(1.6)
Western Europe	181	(3.1)
Eastern Europe (includes Russia)	309	(5.4)
Southern Europe	141	(2.4)
Latin America	486	8.4
North America	295	5.1
World	5.771	100.0
More Developed	1.171	20.3
Less Developed	4.660	80.7

Source: World Population Data Sheet, Population Reference Bureau, 1996.

million). Other European countries, about which a great deal is heard in world affairs, have surprisingly low population totals (Greece, 10.5 million; Sweden, 8.8 million; Denmark, 5.2 million).

Continuing our westward journey among the human continents, we come to the fourth and final extensive area of high population densities on the earth. This is eastern—and especially northeastern—North America. The densities here, however, are generally lower than in the other three areas, for this area has been intensively occupied historically a much shorter time than the others. Like Europe, of course, these parts of the United States and Canada are highly urbanized and industrialized. Of the several areas of the world colonized and settled by Europeans from the seventeenth century on, eastern North America is the most populous and, along with Australia and New Zealand, economically

the most advanced. It is also an area in which the native population, the American Indian, has been almost completely displaced. The United States and Canada comprise only 5.1 percent of the world's population.

Looking beyond these four human continents, we see only scattered islands of people. Southern California is one such island, representing perhaps the most rapid buildup of concentrated population resulting so fully from human migration in human history. Another island is peninsular Florida. The Pacific Northwest of the United States and the adjoining Pacific Southwest of Canada comprise another human island. Looking southward, high human densities can be seen in central Mexico and along the coasts of the Central American countries. Most striking of all is the coastal location of people in South America. In fact, only three coastal portions of

South America lack noticeable densities. One is a narrow strip along the coast of northern Chile (roughly, latitudes 20–30 degrees south) extending from the coastal Atacama Desert inland into the nearby Andean Mountains. The second coastal area of sparse population is likewise along a desert strip, in Argentina, from about latitude 40 degrees south to latitude 50 degrees south, including the southern tip of the continent, and running back along the wet west coast in southern Chile. The third coastal area is in northeastern Brazil, encompassing the broad estuary of the Amazon River and extending through French Guiana and Suriname. The most important gap in South America's population distribution, however, is the massive hole in the South American doughnut, centered on but extending beyond the huge Amazon valley. The countries with the largest population in Latin America are Brazil (160 million) and Mexico (95 million).

This coastal distribution of population holds only partially for Africa. Population is almost entirely absent where deserts join the Atlantic Ocean, as along the Sahara Desert (latitudes 20–30 degrees north) and the Namib Desert (latitudes 15–30 degrees south). Unlike South America, however, Africa does have a significant interior population: (1) in East Africa (centered around Lake Victoria), (2) along the Nile River in Egypt and the Sudan, and (3) in most of Nigeria (the largest African country, with 104 million people). Several other, smaller concentrations of people are scattered throughout the interior. The Sahara Desert, already mentioned, has large uninhabited tracts. At present, just over 12 percent of humankind lives in Africa, a continent where the human race probably originated.

Australia, the smallest of the land areas known as continents, also has the smallest population, just over 18 million (or less than 1 percent of the world total). Here, again, we see the Latin American pattern of peripheral coastwise distribution of population. Antarctica, covered with ice, has no permanent population.

Vast areas of the earth, then, are very sparsely inhabited. These areas include wide latitudinal—and therefore temperature—extremes, from the treeless tundra landscape in northern Canada and Eurasia to the tropical rain forests of the Amazon and Congo basins. Wide precipitation differences characterize these sparsely in-

Two combines harvesting wheat, an example of land in extensive, rather than intensive, cultivation.

habited areas, ranging from the extremely dry, extensive deserts of Australia and of the Sahara to the humid, tropical river basins. In general, most heavily populated areas coincide with fairly flat plains, although dense populations exist at high elevations, especially in the tropics, as around Lake Victoria.

Because of the diversity of densely inhabited climatic and landform regions on the earth, it is clear that climatic and geomorphic factors play no direct role in man's settlement concentrations except perhaps in areas of environmental extremes, as with aridity (in deserts) and frigidity (in permanent ice cover). Even in these environments, however, it is the restriction in earning a living that discourages settlement concentration. Although technology exists to permit humans to survive in these environments, the costs of implementing and maintaining these technologies are prohibitive. Thus, to comprehend the distribution of population on the earth entails an understanding of the economic foundations of the population, and to know something of world economic geography necessitates a knowledge of where humans are located on the earth. The role of technology, treated in Chapter 3, is a critical intervening variable.

POPULATION TRENDS AND CHARACTERISTICS

Human beings have only recently become the dominant species on the earth—but even now, as we have just seen, not everywhere. For tens of thousands of years the human population was incredibly small, no more than several thousand. Life expectancy was short, the deathrate and the birthrate were both high. The very survival of human beings as a species was uncertain. Dispersed over the landscape, owing to the need for land for collecting and hunting, the number of humans did not equal the current population of Kalamazoo, Michigan, or of Athens, Greece, at its peak in classical times. For approximately 98

percent of human history, people gained their basic livelihood from gathering food, hunting, and fishing. It took a rather large amount of land to support one person in such an economic system.

The human species dates back about 2 to 4 million years according to various anthropologists. The Pleistocene, the period in which at least four separate advances of glacial ice spread over large areas of land in North America and Eurasia, goes back 1 million years. The most recent ice sheet melted back from North America and Eurasia only about 10,000 years ago. The limited and sketchy data from archaeological findings make mapping of the distribution of early human population difficult and subject to a high degree of generalization. For example, although evidence points to the existence of pre-Pleistocene peoples far removed from Africa, one does not know whether such evidence represents an isolated handful of humans or a large group.

One geographer, William Bunge, attempted to trace early human populations.[1] He developed maps, based on very sketchy information, of human populations during the early Pleistocene, the Pleistocene, and the early post-Pleistocene. More and more evidence points to the origins of the human species in Africa, and Bunge shows humans, representing a single race, spread over southern and eastern Africa during the early Pleistocene. By the Pleistocene, people had dispersed over the whole of Africa, much of Europe, and large sections of southern and eastern Asia.

As people spread ever wider across the earth, they split off into a growing number of tribes or nations, each with an essentially self-sustaining economy based on the gathering of food within a particular territory. As more and different environments were encountered through human migration, several different kinds of economic

---

[1]William Bunge, *Field Notes* (Detroit: Discussion Paper No. 1, The Detroit Geographical Expedition, 1969).

systems developed, depending on the opportunities available on the physical landscape and, even more importantly, the nature of the human culture and technology. Probably fundamental to all these subsistence economic systems, whether based on hunting, fishing, collecting, or some particular combination of each, was the need to protect and control a territory.

Also during the Pleistocene, again following Bunge, the differentiation of humans by racial characteristics began to be seen over large areas of the earth. (We only wish that archaeological data could as easily present us with a map showing types of economic activities predominating on different parts of the earth.) Congoids were dominant throughout sub-Saharan Africa, Capoids in northern Africa, Caucasoids in Europe and Southwest Asia, Australoids and Mongoloids in Southeast and East Asia, respectively. By the early post-Pleistocene, human beings had occupied all the continents (except Antarctica), though in a settlement pattern that was geographically most uneven. The diversity of racial characteristics also continued, through human migration and breeding. The growth of population was slow and uneven until only a few thousand years ago.

Population totals in early human societies depended on the success of the economic system and its adaptability to the environment. Human migration meant adjustment to different environments and contacts with alien cultures and technologies. Even primitive economic activities, such as root gathering, pottery making, spearfishing, or nomadic hunting, required the cooperation of human groups and necessitated some kind of division of labor. The social system was largely coincident with the economic system.

Economically, early people existed in a *subsistence* state. Each group, tribe, or nation essentially consumed only what it produced, whether that production consisted of simple gathering, hunting, or, later, growing plants and domesticating animals. Trade, though it no doubt occurred even in very early times, was not an important component of economic life. The territory inhabited—or controlled, as the case may be—provided all the economic resources. Since such resources as were perceived to be important at that time varied geographically, some human groups prospered relative to other groups with less useful resources. Societal organization and culture were additional factors in economic efficiency, and the level of the primitive technology was more critical in the utilization of resources.

Sometime between 10,000 and 12,000 years ago, humans domesticated both plants and animals. This technological breakthrough, whose consequences are known as the ***Agricultural Revolution***, dwarfed all previous human technological achievements, including simple toolmaking. Its impact on population was direct and momentous. Surplus food was now more readily assured, save for disease and insect devastation or the unreliability of precipitation. Although such agriculture was highly labor-intensive, a surplus nevertheless meant that not all working members of the group had to devote full time to raising food; rather, other kinds of economic (as well as social) activities became possible.

The Agricultural Revolution brought about profound and fundamental changes in the economic way of life. One of the most important of these changes was the greater leisure time it afforded, which was often directed to subtle and minor technological improvements. These more inconspicuous changes, lost forever to recorded history, had a cumulative effect in creating even more efficient agriculture. For example, the so-called hoe culture gradually advanced over a period of time from the use of the digging stick to that of the metal hoe. With each technological advance, fewer hours were required to produce a crop, again permitting greater leisure from the direct food-producing activities. The fruits of the Agricultural Revolution eventually led to a new human settlement pattern, the city, and to a new economic system associated with urbanism, about which much will be said in later chapters.

Pottery manufacturing plant at Coalport, United Kingdom, illustrating the beginnings of the Industrial Revolution.

Agricultural improvements meant surplus production above the subsistence level, and some 7000–9000 years ago the first cities appeared, although smaller settlements of course preceded them.

Even with the development of cities, human population rose gradually but irregularly, because, quite naturally, not all areas of the earth developed the same level of agricultural sophistication simultaneously and because of the unpredictability of the deathrate from disease and plague. Nevertheless, total population rose from an estimated 10 million people in 8000 B.C. to approximately 20 million in 6000 B.C., a doubling in 2000 years (Figure 2.2.) (Note that the total population of Australia and New Zealand today is approximately 20 million, consisting only 0.5 percent of the total human population.) After 6000 B.C., population rose even more irregularly and perhaps even more slowly, owing in part to the inadequate sanitation in the early cities and the paucity of medical knowledge. Cities frequently were unhealthy places where people were jammed together to perform nonagricultural economic activities and where disease could spread rapidly.

By the time of Christ, there were still, at most, only about 300 million people on the earth, a number not much larger than the population of the United States and Canada today. The figure rose to about one-half billion by 1600. Since then, it has spiraled fantastically to more than 5.7 billion within a mere moment, as it were, of human existence. The basis for this incredible growth is

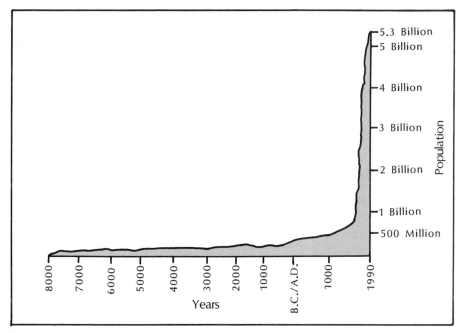

Figure 2.2 Overpopulation is a recent phenomenon in human existence, as illustrated by the incredibly long time in human history during which population was at extremely low levels.

associated with the ***Industrial Revolution***, the factory system and all it has brought with it. The Industrial Revolution, with its use of steam power and machinery, brought about gigantic leaps in productivity, attracting massive migration to cities. Once again, these industrial developments created a new and different economic system, one that was urban-dominated. Whereas after the Agricultural Revolution cities provided an alternative way of life to a small percentage of people, following the Industrial Revolution urbanization became the way of life, directly or indirectly, of everyone in an industrial society.

Whereas industrialization resulted in world population growth, the industrializing countries themselves began to grow more slowly because of a drop in the birthrate. To understand this seeming paradox, one must recognize that the Industrial Revolution was part of a larger technological revolution that simultaneously brought about major medical advances. These medical advances meant reductions in the deathrate and, thus, in population growth. Perhaps the ultimate curse of colonialism was the export of medical technology to virtually the whole world, but *not* the export of industrialization to these same areas. The medical technology permitted population growth but, lacking industrialization, not economic development.

The Demographic Transition
Since population totals and trends historically have been closely connected with different kinds of economic activities, it is useful to outline the demographic sequences that typically have occurred as a result of economic development in general and of the Agricultural and Industrial Revolutions in particular. Furthermore, demographic trends relate to levels of economic well-being, to the size and growth of markets, and to labor availability and its substitutability with au-

tomation. In fact, knowing at what stage a country is in vis-à-vis the demographic transition reveals much about the overall level of present economic development, as well as about past conditions and future projections.

The ***demographic transition*** is divisible into four stages. Although shown in Figure 2.3 here as occurring over equal segments of time, these segments are highly variable, depending on the particular country and how rapidly the many ingredients associated with economic change have been taking place. Historically, it is clear that Stage 1 is the longest and, in fact, has characterized the human condition from its earliest beginnings up until the recent historic past. This stage probably represents 98 percent of human history. In this stage, both the birthrate and the deathrate are high. Although both rates fluctuate, typically the deathrate is more highly variable. In any case, the growth of the population, if it occurs at all, is quite slow. A high birthrate in Stage I is necessary for group survival, given the high deathrate. The high birthrate, historically, not only occurs "spontaneously" but also as a matter of economic necessity in order to maintain labor-intensive subsistence activities, whether food gathering or food growing. A primary cause of the high deathrate in this stage is the high incidence of infant mortality.

Suburban sprawl and spillage into an agricultural landscape: residential housing development on former farmland in Grayslake, Illinois.

Rapid population growth occurs during Stage II, in which the birthrate continues at a high level, but the deathrate is markedly reduced through medical technology. The deathrate declines only slowly, but as it does, natural increase (the difference between the birthrate and the deathrate) brings about considerable growth. Migration, of course, is not considered here. One reason for the high deathrate in Stage I is that food-gathering economies frequently exist at the margins of starvation. Even after agriculture becomes widespread, plentiful food supplies are not always assured, and starvation or caloric and

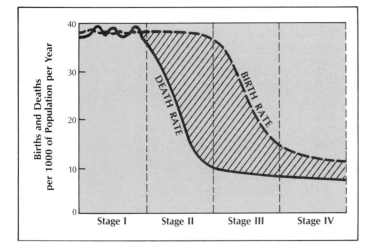

Figure 2.3 The demographic transition is one theory that attempts to associate changing population characteristics with changing levels of technology. The demographic transition results from the forces molding birth- and deathrate changes.

protein deficiencies are all too common. With gradual improvement in agricultural and medical technology, the deathrate drops.

In Stage III the deathrate, already at a low level, continues to decline at a slow pace. The most notable change, however, is a rather precipitous fall in the birthrate. This drop coincides with the maturation of the industrial system and concomitant urbanization. Whereas a large family is an economic asset in a labor-intensive agricultural system, in an urban-industrial society it becomes a liability. As infant mortality decreases, the need to have many children declines with the high level of survival. With a high degree of labor specialization, individuals' aspirations take on greater economic dimensions and lesser social-status significance. In fact, social status becomes more tied to income than to pride in family size. Historically, the desire to reduce family size was conveniently achieved through the employment of more effective modern contraceptive techniques, first developed in nineteenth-century Europe.

We now come to Stage IV, where both birthrate and deathrate are low. This stage is characterized by slow rates of population growth in a number of industrialized countries, including the United States. As these lines converge, zero population growth occurs. Attaining Stage IV necessitates a highly urbanized economy and the shift to a *postindustrial economy.* At present, only a small proportion of the world's population has achieved this stage, presupposing as it does a mature and sophisticated industrialized economic system with increasing employment in the service sector. Such an economy also relies heavily on international trade, as well as on intensive trade, transportation, and especially communications, within the borders of the country and around the world.

The association between population characteristics and the economy serving that population is quite strong. As a country progresses from Stage I to Stage IV, its level of economic development, as measured, for example, by gross national product, increases. In Figure 2.4, (see Color Plate I) countries are divided roughly into the four demographic stages, and these stages provide considerable insight, as we will see more fully in Chapter 3, into the degree of economic development in the four areas. The portion of the world in Stage I is largely confined to Africa, but even here the African countries are transitional between Stage I and Stage II, as the deathrate in this area has already fallen and population growth is accelerating. Although the death rate has been somewhat reduced in recent years, it still remains extremely high—on the order of 25 to 30 deaths annually per 1000 people. Infant mortality accounts for a large number of these deaths. This area of Africa, where typically less than 30 percent of the population over 15 years of age can read and write, is also among the very poorest economically of any part of the world.

The second and third stages of the demographic cycle are transitional economically between the more primitive agricultural activities and highly industrialized, urban-dominated economic systems. Countries in the second demographic stage are located in Africa and southern and southeastern Asia; there are also a few in Latin America. The gross national product is low in these countries, but typically not as low as for countries in Stage I. Whereas the countries in Africa in the first demographic stage are engaged to a large degree in primitive subsistence agriculture, those in the second stage generally have a somewhat more important commercial component superimposed on their traditional subsistence economy. (By subsistence farming, of course, we mean the production and consumption of food by the same people, whereas commercial agriculture implies production for profit and thus an exchange of products, or trade.) Among the countries in the third demographic stage are those in Southeast Asia and several in Latin America. Although subsistence farming remains important in many of these countries, the commercial element of the economy is of growing significance and stands in marked contrast to the traditional agrarian subsistence way of life. Both second- and third-stage countries are sometimes referred to as *pluralistic societies*, because a modern commercial class exists side by side with a traditional subsistence group. The two societies differ not only in economic well-being, but also in social value systems, as reflected in language, dress, religion, and other customs. A wide range of economic activities, in both subsistence and commercial agriculture, characterizes the diverse group of countries in these intermediate demographic stages. In certain cases, pluralistic societies resulted from colonialism or the remnants of colonialism (as in the case of the United States in Vietnam in the late 1960s).

The economies that support populations in the fourth demographic stage are often referred to as advanced or developed. These include the countries of Europe, Russia, Japan, Anglo-America, Australia and New Zealand, and Argentina and Uruguay. In each of these countries, the percentage of people living in rural areas and engaged in agriculture is relatively small. Manufacturing, tertiary, and quaternary activities are dominant; the mobility of people and commodities through modern transportation systems is high; and communication flows and the dissemination of information are intense. In the past few years, the People's Republic of China has moved into Stage IV as a result of an intensive governmental effort to reduce population growth.

Turning back to Figure 2.3 and its geographic expression in Figure 2.4, we will not be surprised to find that those areas of the earth in the first three demographic stages are growing the most rapidly (Figure 2.5 [see Color Plate II] and Table 2.3). This is not surprising because the greatest gaps between birthrate and deathrate occur in Stages II and III, which encompass large areas of the earth. Stage I, largely (though not exclusively) confined to Africa, is also growing rapidly, owing to the extremely high birthrate (between 40 and 50 births annually per 1000 people). Only in the fourth demographic stage, corresponding to areas of the developed world, is population

Table 2.3 Average Annual Rates of Population Growth by Major World Region, 1996

World Region	Average Annual Growth Rate
Africa	2.8
Asia	1.6
East Asia	1.0
Southeast Asia	1.9
South Central Asia	2.1
Western Asia	1.9
Australia and New Zealand	0.8
Europe	−0.1
Northern Europe	0.2
Western Europe	0.1
Eastern Europe (includes Russia)	−0.4
Southern Europe	0.1
Latin America	1.9
North America	0.6
World	1.5

Source: World Population Data Sheet, Population Reference Bureau, 1996.

growing slowly, generally on the order of less than 1 percent per year, compared to the world average of 1.5 percent. The growth countries of Latin America, having reduced their deathrates below the world average but maintaining birthrates well above the world average, are the fastest-growing of all countries.

POPULATION AND FOOD

Over 80 million people are now added to the earth's population each year. This is nearly the equivalent of adding the population of Mexico to the earth each year or that of the United States in less than three years. If present trends continue, it will take only 46 years for the population of the earth to double; it will take less than 36 years, however, for it to double again. Population is thus growing geometrically, although faster in some areas than in others. For example, Brazil, which already has over 160 million people, will double its population in the next 41 years. At the present growth rate it will take Great Britain, by contrast, nearly 385 years to double its population (Table 2.3).

We are, then, confronted with an alarming fact. The countries of the world that are least able economically to absorb population growth are precisely those that are growing most rapidly in population. Put another way, those industrialized countries that through technology have become most efficient agriculturally can most easily feed their population, whereas the large populations of Africa, parts of Latin America, and South and East Asia are faced with a most critical food shortage. The paradox is that the countries with the highest proportion of the labor force engaged in agriculture are often those not able to produce enough food for their population. These are the countries characterized by subsistence agriculture, a low level of technology, inefficient agricultural methods, and a scarcity of additional arable land. In sum, the world's agricultural economies are limited in productivity by traditional social and cultural heritage, by technologically constrained economic practices, and by physical environmental restrictions.

Just over 43 percent of the world's population was classified as urban in 1996, the other 57 percent being rural (Figure 2.6, see Color Plate III). The percentage of urban population, reflecting primarily the degree to which agricultural population can produce surplus food beyond its own needs to support the urban dweller, varies from a high of approximately 90 percent in the United Kingdom, Israel, Australia, and Iceland to a low of 25 percent in parts of Africa (Table 2.4). International food flows are, of course, vital in this equation. A certain correspondence exists between the percentage of urban population and the stage in the demographic cycle, with higher urban percentages relating to later demographic stages. The correspondence, however, is not perfect. The most striking exceptions are several countries in South and East Asia, including the People's Republic of China.

Table 2.4 Urbanization of Major World Regions, 1996

World Regions	Percent Urban Population
Africa	31
Australia and New Zealand	85
Asia	33
Europe (includes Russia)	74
Latin America	71
North America	75
World	43

Source: World Population Data Sheet, Population Reference Bureau, 1996.

As seen in Figure 2.6, several countries in this part of the world are in the lowest percentage category of urban population—less than 30 percent. In the demographic cycle, however, most of these countries are in the second, third, or fourth stages. One explanation for this discrepancy—a lower rate of urbanization than expected from demographic structure—is the intensive nature of the agricultural system. Whereas commercial wheat farming on the Great Plains is described as "extensive agriculture" because it requires an extended area in which labor is not intensively utilized, the agricultural practices in South and East Asia are commonly referred to as "intensive." Each operator is responsible for a limited—sometimes extremely limited—area that is utilized very intensively, whether in a subsistence or a commercial fashion. Multiple cropping is common, and every square foot of land is used. The intensiveness of land utilization, to the extent it is combined with subsistence activity, means that the population is more closely wed to the land than in most other areas of the world.

A number of attributes correlate strongly with the concept of "development," which is treated in greater detail in Chapter 3 (Table 2.5). Sharp contrasts exist between the more developed and less developed countries of the world, most notably in per capita Gross National Product

Table 2.5 Correlates of "Development"

Attributes	World	More Developed	Less Developed
Birth Rate[a]	24	12	27
Death Rate[a]	9	10	9
Natural Increase (%)	1.5	0.1	1.9
Projected Population in 2025 (million)	8.2	1.3	6.9
Infant Mortality[a]	62.0	9.0	68.0
Percent Urban	43.0	75.0	35.0
Per Capita GNP[b]	$4,740	$18,130	$1,090

[a]per 1000
[b]U.S. dollar, 1994 (Gross National Product)

Source: World Population Data Sheet, Population Reference Bureau, 1996.

(GNP), over $18,000 to almost $1,100. Associated with these differences are various demographic contrasts. We have already noted the demographic transition, with low birthrates in the more developed nations, though little differences occur in the death rates. These contrasts lead to differential rates of natural increase and in world population projections in the year 2025.

In all parts of the world, the urban population is growing faster than the rural, putting added pressure on the world's already precarious food supplies. Whereas the world's urban population has been increasing about 40 percent each decade, rural growth has been only between 10 and 15 percent. Great disparities exist in these growth rates among the major world areas, with the fastest-growing areas (in both rural and urban categories) being the poorest economically and the lowest in caloric and protein consumption. Countries in the developed world typically have a daily per capita intake of about 3000 calories and 90 protein grams, compared to figures of around 2000 calories and 60 protein grams per capita per day for much of the rest of the world. These averages, of course, conceal much lower values for sizable numbers of the population.

Countries in which per capita dietary energy supplies do not meet the levels required to carry out normal, active, and healthy lifestyles are found throughout much of Africa, Latin America, and South and Southeast Asia (Figure 2.7, see Color Plate IV). Protein deficiency can result in a long list of physical impairments and in mental retardation. Thus, a vicious cycle is established in which a low level of agricultural productivity results in inadequate food supply, leading to malnutrition, which in turn curtails human energy available for labor-dependent agricultural productivity.

Migration is attributed both to "pull" factors (attractive features of destinations) and "push" conditions (negative evaluations of a present origin). The rapid growth in urban population in the developing world is often not so much the pull of cities as an attractive economic alternative as the push off the land. The result is known as **hyperurbanization**—that is, more people coming to the cities than there are jobs to accommodate them. The consequence is all too often "squatter settlements" and, in the case of Egypt, for example, people subsisting off garbage dumps.

The Malthus Theory

Since the publication of *Essays on the Principle of Population* in 1798, Thomas Malthus's famous statement on population growth has been widely debated by both scholars and laypeople. The essence of Malthusian theory is the equation between population growth and food production. Malthus argued that population growth is in fact a function of food supply. Population tends to grow geometrically unless it is checked by starvation, war, or disease; food supply can grow only arithmetically. In addition to the checks on population growth resulting from war or disease are the preventive restraints exercised by society (abortion, infanticide, and, much more recently, various contraceptive devices). However, the result is almost inevitably an imbalance in which population threatens to outstrip food resources.

A vicious cycle is set in motion, and any increase in food supplies simply leads to greater population growth, and population growth is limited only when the living standard falls near the subsistence level. The Malthus principle, everyone agrees, is a depressing one—though by no means does everyone agree with this theory.

Let us examine some applications of the theory. Although Malthus, an Englishman, was writing just as the Industrial Revolution was accelerating in Great Britain, his critics have accused him of not giving sufficient attention to the role of technological change. A wide variety of agricultural techniques have permitted considerable growth in food supply. Moreover, in industrialized societies the growth in the standard of living has been associated with changes in attitudes toward birth control and family size. Although Malthus by no means ignored the role of technology or of attitudes, he could not completely foresee modern developments in the economically advanced countries of the world. Epidemics of typhus, malaria, and smallpox, for example, are today widely controlled, and medical facilities are widely available. Nor could he foresee the massive consequences of birth control techniques, which did not become available until about 35 years ago—and then by no means everywhere. His theory has not correctly described conditions in the economically developed world during the nearly 200 years since he wrote, for a higher standard of living has not led to a faster rate of population growth.

The Malthus theory may better apply to the large and growing populations of the developing world because these populations more nearly meet many of the conditions Malthus set forth. For example, Malthus assumed as a starting point in his theory that people were already living at a subsistence level at a population density near the maximum supportable by the land. In fact, we may only now be reaching that critical ratio of people per unit of land in many of the developing countries. With population density at its maximum with respect to land for cultivation,

A crowded street scene in Calcutta.

a direct link may be made between food output and population growth. Since medical technology has spread more rapidly than agricultural technology from the industrialized countries to the developing economies, population growth in the developing countries has been rapid because of the reduction in the deathrate. As already noted, food is in short supply in many of these countries, as measured by caloric and protein intake. Starvation has been a longtime problem in countries lying along the southern fringe of the Sahara Desert because of unreliable precipitation. Have we now arrived at a critical threshold in many parts of the world in which population growth will so exceed food supplies as to result in widespread starvation, as a next step beyond malnutrition?

The answer depends on a number of factors. How much more land can be placed into cultivation? What techniques of food production, along with the associated cost and efficiency, will be applied to the land? Since in a commercial economic system not all countries or regions need to be self-sufficient in food production, will patterns of trade emerge such that all the world's peoples will have access to enough food and be able to afford it? Will agricultural and other technology spread itself more or less evenly throughout the world so that all land can produce at the highest level of efficiency? To what extent can the ***Green Revolution***, the application of hybrid crops and agricultural technology, increase the production of foodstuffs? Such crops as the new "miracle rice" can apparently provide tenfold yields with the same number of hours of worker input. Can new developments in biotechnology produce genetic transformations to expand food availability dramatically through the *creation* of "new" plants and animals by gene splicing? By no means the most minor of considerations is the world political matrix in which this literally life-and-death drama is played out. It comes down, of course, to a matter of geography. Where are the people? Where is the cultivable land? Where is the technology? Where is the food? And how are the people, the technology, and the food brought together?

Those who look to the past experience of the industrialized countries with respect to the de-mographic transition may be misled if they expect the developing economies to move rapidly through the cycle into the slow growth of Stage IV. This is because Stage IV—as well as preceding stages—is dependent on levels of economic growth. Achieving economic growth is infinitely more difficult, if not impossible, when a country sees even a modest gain in economic development countered by rapid population increase. Every increase in food production is nullified by ever more mouths to feed. Thus, even in the most optimistic light, the population of countries in the developing world will undergo continued rapid growth and greatly increase in size before any appreciable downturn in the birthrate can be expected.

At the present time, the earth's cultivable land can be increased. Unfortunately, in the areas of

Rapid population growth in Hong Kong has necessitated the filling in of this bay to create land for expansion.

short food supply, the limits of cultivation have just about been reached. Of course, with technological improvements some new land may be brought into production, but only at a considerable cost and with uncertain results. For example, several years ago the former Soviet Union initiated the Virgin and Idle Lands project to place 100 million additional acres into wheat cultivation. The land was marginal for cultivation, owing to low and unreliable precipitation, and the project has achieved, at best, decidedly mixed results, with some of the land actually abandoned. Another problem, especially in the industrialized world, is that some of the best agricultural land has been and is being taken over by other kinds of activities and uses, as urbanization has already spread widely over the agricultural landscape.

Technology exists to improve crop yields and world food production. The problem is one of technology transfer involving both cost and cultural resistance. Similarly, transportation technology could permit the transfer of large volumes of foodstuffs from one part of the world to another. Again, the problem consists of cost and economic incentive. Can the nation in need of food afford to pay for it? Can a potential agricultural-exporting country gain greater profits by producing nonagricultural products? Could a world fleet of shipping vessels be economically placed into service to transport the foodstuffs? Thus, humans have, at the present time, sufficient cultivable land and sufficient technical know-how in agriculture and transportation to feed adequately all their numbers. At least a third of humanity is inadequately fed because of the geographically unequal distribution of people, cultivable land, agricultural technology, and transportation facilities. Probably the major issue confronting the earth today is whether or not human beings, using their political systems in positive, cooperative ways—rather than in short-sighted, self-serving ones—can overcome these geographic limitations to slow population growth

while speeding up food production. If not, the Malthus theory may prove more descriptive of the future in developing economies than it has in the past for developed countries; for if world population continues to grow at its present rate of 1.5 percent a year for the next 700 years, we will have a "standing room only" world, or one person per square yard! Assuredly, something will have to interpose before then, and that something may well be predicted by Malthus's theory.

SUMMARY

The spatial distribution of human beings is critical to an understanding of economic geography, because people are the producers and consumers of goods and services. World economic power stems from the interplay of technology (taken up in Chapter 3) and people. There is power in numbers. And world political power is very much tied in with "population power" as manifested in complex ways through economic stability and development. Thus, the future of human beings on spaceship Earth depends in large measure on the balance of political powers, as fundamentally derived from world patterns of population distribution as affected by technology and translated into world economic activities. How will humans resolve the problems and conflicts between Third World and industrialized countries and between OPEC (Oil Producing Exporting Countries) and the petroleum-consuming nations?

Further Readings

Bennett, D. Gordon. *World Population Problems* Champaign, Ill.: Park Press, 1984.

Bogue, D. J., *Principles of Demography*. New York: Wiley, 1969.

Brunn, S. D., and J. Williams, eds. *Cities of the World: World Regional Urban Development*. New York: Harper & Row, 1983.

Christopher, A. J. "Partition and Population in South Africa." *Geographical Review* (1982), pp. 127–138.

Clarke, John I., et al., eds., *Population and Disaster*. London: Basil Blackwell, 1989.

Clem, Ralph S. "Regional Patterns of Population Change in the Soviet Union, 1959–1979," *Geographical Review* (1980), pp. 137–156.

Donaldson, Loraine. *Fertility in Transition: The Social Dynamics of Population Change*. London: Basil Blackwell 1991.

Gilbert, A. J., ed. *Modelling for Population and Sustainable Development*. London: Routledge, 1991.

Goode's World Atlas. 17th ed. Chicago: Rand McNally, 1986.

Hart, John Fraser. "Population Change in the Upper Lake States." *Annals of the Association of American Geographers* (1984), pp. 221–243.

Henry, Paul-Marc, ed. *Poverty, Progress and Development*. London: Kegan Paul, 1991.

Lounsbury, John F. "Recent Demographic and Economic Changes and World Crises." *The Journal of Geography* (1975), pp. 411–418.

Malthus, Thomas R., "A Summary View of the Principle of Population" (1830). In George J. Demko, H. M. Rose, and G. A. Schnell, eds. *Population Geography: A Reader*. New York: McGraw-Hill, 1970, pp. 44–71.

McLaren, Angus. *A History of Contraception*. London: Basil Blackwell, 1991.

Meadows, Donella H. et al. *The Limits of Growth: A Report for the Club of Rome's Project on the Predicament of Mankind*. New York: Universe Books, 1972.

Newman, James L., and Gordon E. Matzke. *Population: Patterns, Dynamics, and Prospects*. Englewood Cliffs, N.J.: Prentice-Hall, 1984.

Schnell, George A., and Mark Stephen Monmonier. *The Study of Population: Elements, Patterns, Processes*. Columbus, Ohio: Charles E. Merrill, 1983.

Stolnitz, G. J. "The Demographic Transition: From High to Low Birth Rates and Death Rates." In George J. Demko, H. M. Rose, and G. A. Schnell, eds. *Population Geography: A Reader*. New York: McGraw-Hill, 1970, pp. 71–79.

Trewartha, Glenn T., ed. *The More Developed Realm: A Geography of Its Population*. New York: Pergamon Press, 1978.

United Nations, Demographic Yearbook. New York: United Nations, Department of International Economics and Social Affairs, published annually.

Zelinsky, W. *Prologue to Population Geography*. Englewood Cliffs, N.J.: Prentice-Hall, 1966.

CHAPTER 3

Global Economic Development

———◇———

And whilst so many lustrums of the sun
Rolled on across the sky, men led a life
After the roving habit of wild beasts.
—LUCRETIUS

INTRODUCTION

Enormous economic disparities exist from one area of the earth to another. As the old saying goes, "One-third of the earth doesn't know how the other two-thirds live." The gap is indeed wide between the earnings of, say, the chief executive officer of Exxon Corporation and of the primitive subsistence agriculturalist in the Amazon valley. So, too, is the gap between their entire ways of life. Basically, the differences are the result of living in two starkly contrasting economic systems, set in two fundamentally different cultural settings. To the primitive agriculturalist, alternative economic opportunities are severely limited by the cultural background and by access to technology. Economic decisions, though perhaps sophisticated within the context of the environment, are not dependent on a very high level of technology. Conversely, the Exxon CEO—and indeed the entire economic system of which he is a part—is a fundamental part of a complex and multinational technological society without which Exxon could not exist.

Nature of Technology

We should begin by defining *technology*, one of those everyday words that mean a great many things. In essence, technology, as used here, refers to the application of scientific knowledge and methods to economic activity, resulting in changes in productivity. Advances in many areas of the economy are a consequence of technological improvements. For example, transportation has undergone remarkable changes from the days in which human and animal muscle was the only source of power for moving material and people themselves. Manufacturing as we think of it today is a result of the application of many technological elements to the creation of items that, if they could be made in the past at all, were made in the home. Now huge concentrations of people and machines produce intricate and complicated manufactured items that are so far beyond the capabilities of homebound handicraft as to have virtually driven the latter out of an economic existence. This is also the case in all other sectors of the economy.

In fact, one of the most important features of

technological development is the interrelatedness of the advances. Improvements in one area of the economy feed on and have application to many others. Large-scale coal-mining operations in Wyoming, for example, would have no economic basis were it not for the technology developed to transport the bulky product and to permit power plants to generate electrical power from coal, and were it not for a wide array of industries that have become technologically dependent on electricity. Especially in industrial economies, technologies are highly interdependent, and advances in one economic sector reverberate throughout all other sectors.

Another feature of technology, just alluded to, is its energy resource base. Not only does technology enlarge and alter the energy base (as with nuclear energy), but technological improvements in the economy in general are also directly dependent on the availability and use of energy. It made no sense to invent an electric mousetrap before the use of electricity—as if it does now. Or, more realistically, one would not develop an industrial machine unless there was an energy base on which to operate it. Energy resources, treated in Part 5 of this book, are intricately linked to technology, both as a cause and as a consequence.

Similarly, communications technology, especially in the service sector in advanced economies, produces yearly improvements in data handling and transfer. With the relative and absolute decline in manufacturing in advanced economies, productivity improvement in the growing service sector has become an essential component of these economies. World cities are now closely linked with one another, for once critical barriers of distance have been annihilated. For example, the overnight shipment of letters and packages grew increasingly common during the 1980s in the United States, and during the 1990s overseas deliveries began to skyrocket. In the latter 1980s and into the 1990s, FAX mail (facsimile) became a commonplace convenience. The FAX machine "reads" a letter or document and transmits it over regular telephone lines to another FAX machine anywhere in the world and then reproduces a copy of the original document.

A view of an oil tanker moored in loading bay of an oil refinery, Houston, Texas, demonstrating the transportation of energy.

Many kinds of communications can be sent by FAX both efficiently and inexpensively, for this technology does not require the receiver to answer the phone or to be there physically when the message is received. Other kinds of E-mail (electronic mail) exist and are being refined. Thus, recent communications technology has had far-reaching impacts on our lives and promises to have much greater effects on the global economy than, say, the private automobile around which American society has been based.

Global Distribution of Technology

Although technology is not a single entity, but rather reflects a whole range of scientific knowledge and methods applied to economic activities, it nevertheless is possible to gain some perspective on the geographic distribution of technology around the world. The geographical distribution of technological processes reveals that a great many measures may be used to pin down the somewhat elusive concept of technology. Unfortunately, data are not available for all these measures. Nevertheless, we can gain a good perspective on world technology patterns by examining selected variables. Technology relating directly to economic activity can be broken down into four general types: (1) transportation and communication; (2) manufacturing; (3) agriculture; and (4) urban-service technology. In addition, several kinds of technologies relate indirectly to economic activities, such as medical technology and space technology (with their own economic components).

A variable that gives an excellent insight into a country's level of technology is the energy consumed, for the use of energy is required in each of the four general technology divisions. Similarly, changes over time in the amount of energy consumed may be taken as an indicator of technological growth. When the map of energy consumption is studied, one immediately notices its similarities to the map of the demographic cycle and, as a next step, to a map of levels of economic development (Figure 3.1, see Color Plate V). The developing economies of Africa and southern Asia rank lowest in energy consumed, reflecting the low technological inputs to their economies (Table 3.1). Much of Latin America is also low in per capita energy usage. The more highly developed countries of North America, Europe, and the southern hemisphere, as well as Japan, have large energy appetites to sustain their high level of economic productivity. The United States has the world's highest per capita energy consumption, over 9500 kilograms per person, but per capita energy consumed has actually declined slightly since 1970 as the country moves increasingly into a service economy and away from a manufacturing-based one.

Another measure of economic development that is dependent on technology is the number of passenger vehicles per, say, 1000 population (Figure 3.2, see Color Plate VI). The number varies from a high of 572 passenger vehicles per 1000 people in Australia (the United States is second with 520) to a low of one or less for the People's Republic of China and Bangladesh. Many countries have fewer than 50 passenger vehicles for every 1000 people, mostly in Africa and Asia and also in some countries in Central and South America. Western Europe, one of the world's leading areas in passenger vehicles, has

Table 3.1   Energy Consumption

Region	Per Capita Consumption (kilograms)
Africa	424
North America	6,723
South America	1,016
Asia	731
Europe	4,440
Oceania	5,013
World	1,921

Source: United Nations Energy Statistics Yearbook (New York: United Nations, Department of International Economic and Social Affairs, 1987).

fewer per capita than the United States and Canada and Australia and New Zealand. Russia, though an industrial nation, has relatively few passenger vehicles. As we will see in Chapter 6, this region, as well as the People's Republic of China, relies heavily on rail transportation, with motor truck and automobile transportation considerably less developed.

Elements in Economic Development

Presenting the economic development process in the form of a simple flowchart (Figure 3.3) permits directional arrows to show the cause-and-effect links. Four elements are identified as relating to economic development. The first is population growth and structure, which is intimately tied to the economy's development in that the rate of demographic growth and structure and the makeup of the population may accelerate or slow down the economy's growth. A change in economic growth also affects the population's increase and composition—hence the two-way arrow. Also linked with population by a two-way arrow is culture, or ideology. The effects here, though not often sufficiently emphasized, are profound for economic development. Cultural attributes, including political attitudes, are fundamental to the climate of economic change. Traditional societal attitudes have been recog-

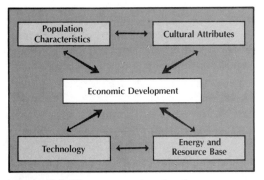

Figure 3.3 The economic development process, though simplified in this diagram, may be viewed in terms of its major components and how they affect one another.

nized as barriers to economic modernization. At the same time, abundant data show that economic development brings with it changed value systems and new ways of life. Again, two-way cause and effect operates.

At the bottom of Figure 3.3, representing something of the foundation on which economic development rests, are technology and the resource base, especially the energy resources. Technology, of course, must be available and applied at the location where the economic activity—hence economic development—occurs. Energy and other resources must also be used at that location. However, the resources themselves need not be produced at that location. In fact, many kinds of resources are imported from other countries or moved considerable distances within a country. As examined more fully in Chapter 6, the highest volume of international trade is between the countries of the developed world, including trade in both resource and finished goods. The industrialized countries also import large volumes of resources from countries in earlier stages of economic development.

We should not forget that governments play an important role in the economic development and well-being of regions. For example, the U.S. Department of Defense (DOD) annually draws up contracts for the military branches, which amounted to $129 billion in 1989. This figure does not include contracts with other U.S. government agencies, such as the National Aeronautics and Space Agency (NASA). The 25 companies with the largest contracts typically account for 50 percent of total DOD expenditures. St. Louis, home of McDonnell Douglas and General Dynamics, the two largest defense contractors, accounted for 12 percent of all Pentagon contract dollars in 1989. The Pentagon's cancellation of a single weapons system can have enormous impact on local and regional areas. Overall, U.S. defense spending accounted for about one-fourth of all government outlays in 1990.

In sum, economic development is a composite of causes and effects. The elements are interlinked in such a complex fashion that neither economic geographers nor economists can agree on any sure-fire formula to generate economic development around the world. Particular combinations of appropriate investments in the four major investment categories (population, culture, technology, and resources) are necessary conditions for economic development to occur. If we do not know exactly what these particular combinations are, at least we know they are highly interrelated and that one ingredient is a necessary but, without the others, insufficient condition to spur growth. By the same logic, an investment in one particular segment of the economy—say, transportation—will not ensure overall development, though some level of investment in that segment clearly is necessary.

WORLD LEVELS OF DEVELOPMENT

Gross national product (GNP) is the total value of goods and services produced by a given country, usually expressed for a one-year period. Frequently, GNP is further refined by dividing it by the total population to get per capita GNP. In order to compare countries around the world, it is necessary to express the values in the currency of a single country, such as United States dollars. GNP is thus a yardstick for measuring the level of economic activity and comparing just how rich or poor nations around the world are (Figure 3.4, see Color Plate VII). GNP varies from a low of $80 per person in Chad to over $23,000 per person in the United Arab Emirates (southeastern Arabian peninsula); the per capita GNP in the United States is $13,160.

Per capita GNP in Africa and South and East Asia is incredibly low by U.S. standards, less then $400 a year. A sizable percentage of the world's people live in the countries placed within the lowest GNP category in Figure 3.4 (see PLATE VII), including the over 2 billion people in the People's Republic of China, India, Bangladesh, and Pakistan. These countries are also among the

most rapidly growing in population, making per capita increments in GNP increasingly difficult. The value of economic activity performed around the world differs greatly, and per capita GNP displays the same basic world regional patterns as energy consumption and a host of other closely related measures.

Regional Growth

Recognizing the interplay of many economic and noneconomic factors implicit in the concept of levels of economic development, W. W. Rostow, an economic historian, formulated a much publicized "model" treating the sequential stages of economic development.[1] The model, a simple verbal description, has been criticized because it permits many exceptions to its generalizations in applications around the world. Being verbally stated and hence imprecise, the model has not led to a consensus of opinion as to what particular stage of development a certain country is in or exactly when it got there. Nevertheless, a review of Rostow's idea can provide some further insight into levels of economic development around the world.

Rostow saw economic development as evolving through several stages over a period of time. Thus, every country presently is at one of these stages, and a close analysis of its economic structure and growth will suggest the likelihood that the country will ascend to the next higher level in a certain period of time. Economic development is like climbing a stepladder one rung at a time. Rostow suggested five stages: (1) traditional society; (2) preconditions for takeoff; (3) takeoff; (4) drive to maturity; and (5) high mass consumption. Although there are tremendous differences among countries in any one stage, certain common elements give meaning to this classification.

The first stage, ***traditional societies***, no doubt

[1]W. W. Rostow, *The Stages of Economic Growth* (New York: Cambridge University Press, 1960).

characterizes a number of countries that have in common agricultural production, lack of a sizable commercial economy, low technological inputs, and an ideological antipathy to, or at least unconcern with, attributes of modernization. The ***preconditions for takeoff*** are met when certain influential elements in society favor economic change and seek modernization for a variety of purposes: national prestige, personal profit, belief in a better way of life. These elements can be organized into political or economic institutions to pursue the goals of economic progress. Absolute and per capita growth increases only slowly, for most of the society remains largely in the previous, traditional stage. The ***takeoff*** stage is marked by the breakdown of resistance to modernization and rapid increases in productivity (GNP, for instance). Growth becomes commonplace, expected, and institutionalized; indeed, political institutions actively encourage economic growth. Whereas the earlier stages typically take longer, this third stage usually lasts 40 to 60 years. These first three stages depict what is regarded as being under the category of developing countries—representing a large segment of the people of the world.

The fourth stage, the ***drive to maturity***, is achieved when technology is so widespread that it is applied everywhere in the economy. Industrial production is highly diversified, and some of the benefits of increased production may be directed into social welfare, investment abroad, or large defense expenditures. The fifth, and final stage, that of ***high mass consumption***, is best exemplified in the United States. Whereas technology had previously been chiefly applied to production, now technological improvement turns to an emphasis on consumption, that is, prepared food, packaging and preserving, styling and luxury items. Investment in production continues, but of overriding concern are educational investment, welfare and security, and leisure-time expenditures. The so-called developed countries of the world fall into the last two stages.

Historically, economic development has evolved in a brief moment in human time to bring about gross disparities in economic production. Since the value of production is recognized as basic, we can expect it to result in great differences in the total way of life among people on this planet. Only after 1760—not that many generations ago—in England and the Low Countries across the North Sea was technology applied to economic production on a large scale. From there the technology of development, principally industrial development, spread to the eastern coast of North America, to other parts of Europe, to the cities of Australia and New Zealand, and so on around the world—now prominently to include Japan. Geographers call this spreading effect ***spatial diffusion***, in this instance with industrial technology diffusing over the

Traditional way of life in an agricultural village in Ghana, West Africa: two women shopping for sandals.

earth. The dispersion of industrial technology today can be noted rather clearly by reference again to Figure 3.4, the level of per capita GNP.

There is another way to look at levels of economic development. We have previously mentioned that in the early stages of development a high percentage of a nation's labor force will be in agriculture. A more complete picture of developmental level emerges when we compare the percentage of the labor force in the three principal economic sectors: agriculture and mining (primary), manufacturing (secondary), and retailing and services (tertiary). Take the United States, for example, (Figure 3.5). In the early stages of development, agricultural employment predominated. But even early on, it was undergoing a relative decline as people turned to manufacturing and to the service sector for employment. Today, nearly 80 percent of the U.S. labor force is in the tertiary and quaternary categories, compared with less than 3 percent in agriculture. The percentage of workers in manufacturing is generally expected to follow a similar decline to that of agriculture over the next 25 years or so because of increasing robotics and the growth of the quaternary sector.

The changes that have occurred in the United States, coinciding with advances in economic development, are typical of the small number of highly developed countries. Most of the other countries are now at the stage in employment breakdown that the Unites States was in at some previous time. India, for instance, has roughly 70 percent of its workforce in agriculture, 20 percent in services, and 10 percent in manufacturing. (Hidden in such data is the fact that the more poorly developed countries have the greatest gap between agricultural and nonagricultural incomes.) Each country proceeds at its own pace in displacing agricultural workers from the land and into manufacturing or service activities, and what has taken the United States 200 years to achieve, most developing countries would like to accomplish overnight.

PROBLEMS OF DEVELOPMENT

The fact that the diffusion of economic development around the world has been geographically so uneven immediately suggests we are not dealing with an automatic, inevitable, or irreversible process—as Rostow's model may have implied. All countries face problems of economic development, including of course countries that are already classified as developed. These countries cannot stand still economically and compete fiercely with one another. Nevertheless, their economic growth problems are much less severe, much less a life-and-death matter, than those of several countries nearer the margins of existence, For these marginal nations, rapid population growth demands even more rapid economic growth to ensure the per capita increases necessary for modernization.

One potential solution to a country's devel-

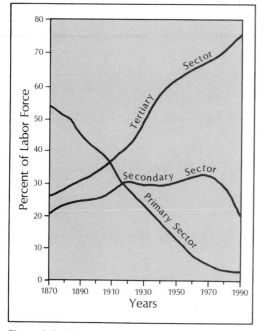

Figure 3.5 The changing percentage of the U.S. labor force in the major economic sectors is a measure of the changes in levels of economic development the country has experienced.

opmental problems, at least at the superficial level, is simply to move people out of agriculture and into manufacturing and service employment. Achieving this reallocation of the labor force, however, is no easy matter. "Natural" market mechanisms, whereby there is growing consumer demand for certain manufactured goods or for particular personal services, are slow and uncertain generators of employment change. Governmental inputs have not proved to be a guarantee to success because construction of a steel mill does not ensure the creation of a market for the steel, especially in the face of less expensive steel produced elsewhere. Since lack of mobility is strongly associated with low levels of development, a number of efforts have been made to spur economic change by ambitious transportation projects. Once again, however, success has been mixed because a superhighway is a waste of a country's scarce resources if there is little or nothing to move on the highway or a lack of vehicles to move it with. Similarly, investment in agricultural technology is not by itself sufficient to bring about desired development, for a rapidly growing population will literally eat up any increases in agricultural productivity. Investment in health and medical facilities will reduce the deathrate, thus increasing the population and making economic growth all the more difficult.

The mechanism that leads to modernization is indeed investment, but a prerequisite to investment is capital accumulation. It is a long process to accumulate sufficient capital to reach Rostow's "takeoff" stage. In the past, many countries, including the United States and Canada, drew heavily on foreign (European) capital for domestic investment just as many countries today look to foreign sources for economic and other types of aid. Amassing sufficient capital for investment over a period of time is one thing; how and where that investment will be made is quite another.

The formerly centrally planned economies of the world—Eastern Europe, Russia, the People's Republic of China—are moving toward a market economy in an effort to spur economic development. These economies are looking toward the most developed countries for capital to invest in the market economy infrastructure. The lack of individual incentives under the planned economy system and the inefficient bureaucracy have proven serious drawbacks to a smoothly functioning economy. Thus, the centrally planned economies are facing different kinds of development problems than those faced by the world's poorest countries in Africa and Asia.

Regional Economic Change

There are two somewhat contrasting theories of regional economic growth. The first, the ***internal growth theory***, related to the Rostow model already described, attributes economic development to changes occurring within a region. The structure of the economy evolves because of internal processes in the region, such as the application of technology to a local resource, or because of a rise, somehow, in purchasing power. The alternative theory, that of the ***export base***, holds that economic growth occurs as a result of the expansion of exports to other regions. Income received from the sale of exports induces economic development. Both theories share elements in common. They differ in that the internal growth theory, though recognizing the existence of exports or interregional trade,

A street scene in Amsterdam, The Netherlands, a great world city.

postulates that trade results from economic changes generated within a region, whereas the export theory views trade as the mechanism that initiates the economic change.

Internal growth theory begins with a self-sufficient subsistence economy in which the provision of food and other necessities is the basis for population distribution. By reducing transportation costs through improvements in the primitive road network or by making technological advances in the means of conveying goods, some elemental and local trade becomes possible (Figure 3.6). As the system of local trade becomes more common and involves a larger number of producers, certain competitive advantages will emerge, as some producers will prove more efficient or their location more advantageous. The more competitive producers will be able to sell their products more widely. Larger sales potential permits the application of new technology whereby the average cost per item may decrease as the number of items produced increases. This concept is known as ***economies of scale***, or per unit savings resulting from enlarged output. Gradually, agricultural trade results in an increased in per capita income, and, with agricultural surplus, local manufacturing and tertiary activities are stimulated. The net outcome is a repeating cycle in which the application of technology to reducing transportation costs and unit production costs brings about increased trade for advantageously located producers.

Taking a closer look, we may begin with the simple illustration of two producers with equal costs of producing and transporting an item (Figure 3.7a). The stem, a, represents the unit production cost of item. The cost, t, refers to transportation costs, which increase gradually away from the point of production. The price, p, is charged to reflect production costs, transportation costs, and normal profit. When both producers have identical cost and price structures, they will split the areal market into two equal parts. Each producer represents a kind of local monopoly; such local monopolies have been commonplace in preindustrial societies.

If a new production technology becomes available to one producer but not to the other, the result is an expanded market area for the former at the expense of the latter (Figure 3.7b). This enlarged market permits greater output, which in turn leads to economies of scale that further strengthen the areal competitive position of the first producer. Similarly, a sudden reduction in transportation costs by opening a new road, for instance, will result in increased market size for the producer with the transportation advantage, assuming equal production costs (Figure 3.7c). The more competitive producer will in this case not only encroach into the second producer's territory but will also confine the latter's area by being more competitive at locations on the opposite side of the second producer. Again, the enlarged areal market allows for economies of scale, reinforcing the competitive position of the lower-cost producer.

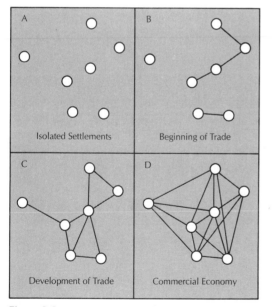

Figure 3.6 The development of commercial economies begins with isolated settlements (a), which gradually begin to develop trade ties (b), until all settlements become involved in some type of exchange (c), leading to the establishment of a mature commercial economy (d).

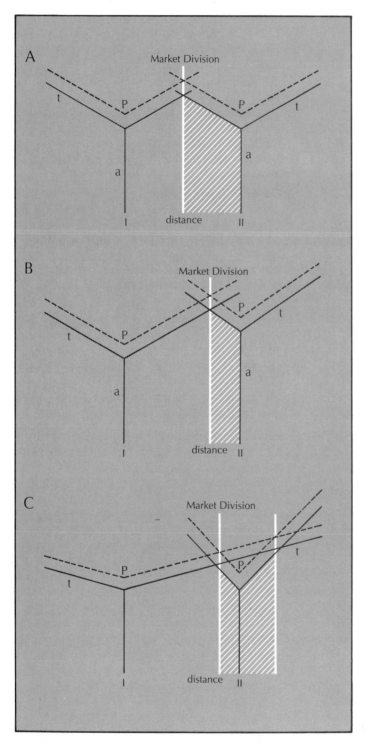

Figure 3.7 The relationship between size of trade centers (I and II) and distance between these trade centers under different assumptions about production costs (*a*) and transportation costs (*t*).

Thus, the internal growth theory holds that a region grows economically through the local application of technology. The economy gradually will move away from almost exclusive trade in agricultural items to trade in manufactured goods. At first, these may be simply processed agricultural products, but eventually a point is reached at which additional growth in per capita income is used not chiefly to purchase agricultural items, but instead to obtain manufactured goods. Even a well-fed person can eat only so much! The region shifts slowly from an agricultural to an industrial base. With industrialization comes increased need for tertiary activities, and this condition is referred to as economic maturity.

The export base theory of regional growth recognizes that many areas have grown economically because of capitalist investment or outside exploitation. Because of a region's natural resource base, foreign capital and technology may be attracted. Income received from the export of the resource is the initial impetus for growth. The region is said to "specialize" in the production of that resource.

This principle, known as ***regional specialization***, deserves a closer look, since it is fundamental to the export base theory as well as to the internal growth theory. For simplicity let us imagine two regions, East and West. At time period one, depicted in Figure 3.8A, both regions are at the subsistence level. Each region consumes only what it is able to produce. Although East is ideally suited climatically for the production of oranges, the region is constrained in orange production by the amount that can be consumed within the region. Similarly, to continue with our illustrative example, West is uniquely able to produce footwear owing to a long cultural tradition; nevertheless, the manufacture of high-quality footwear is limited by the limited market in the West. In Figure 3.8A the volume consumed determines the volume produced, although the volume for different items may differ based on variation in consumer demand.

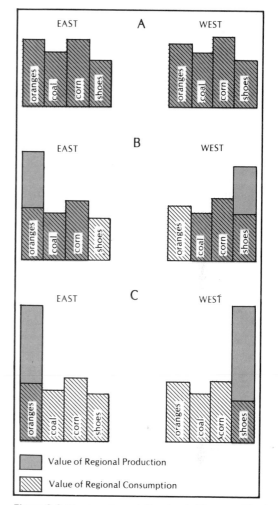

Figure 3.8 Regional specialization is illustrated in simplified form for two regions, East and West, by different assumptions about the value of regional production compared to the value of regional consumption for selected commodities.

Let us suppose that East and West are now linked by new transportation routes resulting from a new form of transportation technology. Given the "inherent" regional production advantages just cited, regional specialization now becomes possible. In Figure 3.8B a simple form of regional specialization is shown to occur. Whereas the economies of the two regions are

Global Communications

At approximately 22,000 miles above the earth, a geosynchronous (stationary) satellite hovers above the equator at 96 degrees West Longitude.[2] A geosynchronous satellite in orbit above the equator revolves at a speed exactly matching that of the earth's rotation so as to remain stationary over the same point on the earth's surface. Since the earth rotates from west to east, an object at the equator will therefore be moving east to west at approximately 1050 miles per hour, the same speed as the earth's rotation.

A transmitting dish in Athens, Georgia, is aimed at the satellite 222 degrees from Polar North, or aimed to the southwest of Athens. The satellite is beaming back signals of the University of Georgia and the University of Florida football game all across America.

Here is a multiple-choice question: Above what point on the earth is the satellite? (A) Brazil (B) Colombia (C) the Atlantic Ocean (D) the Pacific Ocean.

The correct answer is (D) the Pacific Ocean, Why?

A location of 96 degrees West Longitude at the equator places the satellite almost directly south of Dallas, Texas, with all of Latin America except Mexico lying to the east of the satellite's position. Even the famous Galapagos Islands lie slightly east of where the satellite hovers overhead, racing the earth's rotation but never going any faster or slower, as it is geosynchronous, always staying above the same point on the earth.

As we watch the hard-fought football game being shot back to us in Athens, Georgia; Gainesville, Florida; Miami, Florida; and to all other living rooms and dens across the United States and Canada, we also realize that this same satellite is capable of receiving and sending many messages to and from many places in North America and South America—more properly defined geographically as Northwest America and Southeast America. A location of 96 degrees West Longitude is centered on the United States and Canada. The satellite has been placed in an optimum orbital location for serving all the Americas.

[2]How far is 22,000 miles? If you could drive a car completely around the earth at the equator—including over lots of water—you would drive approximately 25,000 miles, the circumference of the earth. So how high is 22,000 miles? It is almost one-tenth the distance to the moon, which is about 240,000 miles. For example, if the distance between New York and Phoenix, Arizona, represented the distance between the earth and the sun, the satellite would be only one-half mile outside New York, with well over 2300 miles separating it from Phoenix, the Sun City.

---

still primarily at the subsistence level, there is surplus production in two items: oranges in the East and footwear in the West. The surplus is, of course, exchanged for the benefit of both regions, for each region is specializing in an item it can produce more inexpensively, even when the cost of transportation is added into the final price.

In reality, there are going to be more than two regions. Figure 3.8C depicts the extreme case of regional specialization in which the two regions, East and West, produce a single item for export, all other goods being imported from other regions. Several regions are linked together in trade relationships in this situation, each region providing what it can produce most efficiently and inexpensively and importing other goods that it could produce, but only at a higher price. Whereas such extreme regional specialization may maximize total production efficiency, it means that each region is at the economic mercy of every other. If, for example, for political reasons one region exports coal to another region, that second region will be placed in a most serious plight if no alternative sources are available. Thus, the extreme case of regional specialization in a single item is very uncommon. It is clear, however, that a region grows economically through income derived from export of items that it can produce easily and that are in demand elsewhere. According to the export base theory, to grow is to expand exports.

Growth Pole Theory

One of the most widely discussed and debated theories of regional growth is the *growth pole theory*, originally put forth by the French economist François Perroux in the early 1950s.[3] This theory is basically one type of the internal growth theory in that its emphasis is on changes within a region that generate economic growth. The growth pole theory has undergone several modifications to give it a more explicitly geographic character. What follows is a synthesis of several writers, notably Albert O. Hirschman, Gunnar Myrdal, and John Friedmann, whose works are cited at the end of this chapter.

Even the most casual observer recognizes that a region does not grow economically at the same rate over all of its area, but rather tends to grow most rapidly at a point or points while lagging or remaining stagnant elsewhere. These rapidly growing points (or poles) are metropolitan areas, which exert dominance over the entire region. The growth pole theory attempts to account for the reasons why growth is geographically unbalanced in this way.

Associated with the growth point is a *key in-*

---

[3]François Perroux, "Note sur la Notion de 'pôle de croissance,'" *Economie Appliquée,* 1955.

dustry noted for its great size and importance and for its interconnections with other industries or activities. As the key industry grows and prospers, so does the local area in which the industry is located; as employment increases, purchasing power rises, and new industries and activities are attracted to the area. The key industry has connections with other industries, called *affected industries*—those with which the key industry does a significant amount of business, whether in purchasing materials or in selling processed goods. An increase in output in the key industry stimulates a whole wave of production increases in the affected industries. Many other activities, from banking and government to retailing and health care, are also affected.

Figure 3.9 shows a hypothetical region and the location of the key industry and the affected industries. It is immediately apparent that there is a concentration of the affected industries near the location of the key industry. This is only natural. The result is that the industries affected by the dominant industry will be most likely to prosper and grow, and that their spatial clustering further reinforces the idea of the growth point or center. Growth feeds upon itself. The remainder of the region is stagnant.

A psychological effect is also operating here. A kind of "gold rush" fever may dominate the thinking of investors and entrepreneurs, leading to further investment and expansion at the growth point. Optimism everywhere prevails at this growth center, resulting in a kind of self-fulfilling prophecy. Similarly, hopelessness may characterize the lagging portion of the region, ensuring continued backwardness even in the face of unrecognized opportunity. Nothing succeeds like success.

The regional disparity in economic growth has both positive and negative elements. First, there are positive elements for the lagging region, resulting from the *trickle-down processes*. These may take the form of purchases in the growth center of goods originating in the lagging region. Second, some investment in the lagging region is bound to occur with capital supplied from the

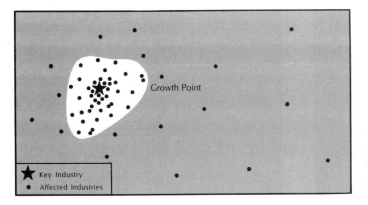

Key Industry
Affected Industries

Figure 3.9 The growth point and the region. The growth point, illustrated by the star, is surrounded by a swarm of affected industries, with the affected industries thinning out away from the growth point.

growth center. Finally, to the extent unemployment exists in the lagging region, the growth center will act to absorb some of the region's labor surplus. In all cases, the advantages so evident in the growth center will partially "spill over" or trickle down to the benefit of the lagging region. Normally, the more remote from the growth center, the less the trickle-down effect will be felt.

At the same time, geographically concentrated growth may have a number of harmful effects on the lagging region. These unfavorable features are the *polarization processes*. Local industries in the lagging region may become depressed by the considerably more competitive industries in the growth center. As already illustrated in the discussion of Figure 3.7, the less efficient high-cost producers in the lagging region will have their market areas severely curtailed, if not eliminated, by the large-scale regional producers at the growth point. Thus, competition is a major polarization effect. In addition, outmigration from the depressed region is likely to drain the region of its most talented personnel as they are attracted to the more progressive and economically attractive growth center. Capital from the lagging region may also be siphoned off to the more favorable investment opportunity at the growth point.

In the long run, the trickle-down effects will normally predominate over the polarization process, but at a given point in time, especially early

in the developmental process, the unfavorable effects in the lagging region may be the most acutely felt. Gradually, the key industry will expand to the point that it spawns other sizable industries, which themselves become secondary key industries linked with their own set of affected industries. In this way the growth center enlarges slowly, and its effects gradually diffuse further into the lagging region. This is growth by *areal accretion* of the growth center itself. A second mechanism of growth, occurring somewhat later in the developmental process, is *leapfrogging*, whereby growth "jumps" from the growth center to an area of secondary key industry located some distance away from the growth center (Figure 3.10). The result is a secondary growth center, with its own area of dominance in which the trickling-down and polarization processes operate on a reduced areal level. Such a process is an example of *hierarchical diffusion*, in which the spread is not even but surges from one area to another in a hierarchical manner, as from city to city. Thus, economic growth eventually diffuses by accretion at the growth center as well as by leapfrogging to an emerging urban center located within the lagging region.

If the argument is developed to its fullest extent and the region is expanded to encompass the world, the result is a division of the world into developed or industrialized countries and underdeveloped or developing nations. In other words,

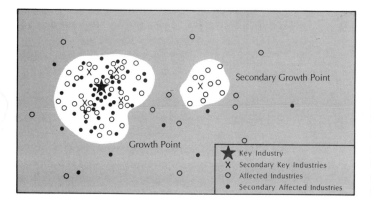

Figure 3.10 At a later stage than in Figure 3.9, the original growth point has spawned a secondary growth point at some distance away. The *X* symbol represents secondary key industries, the filled-in circles show the affected industries, and the open circles are the secondary affected industries.

the concept of growth poles, or points, applies universally at various levels or scales of observation. Japan, for example, illustrates the leap-frogging principle at the world scale. The transmission of economic growth, then, can be seen to occur within a relatively small region of a country (Atlanta versus South Georgia), within a country (the Northeast manufacturing belt of the United States versus the Southwest), or within the entire world (the developed versus the developing countries of the world).

Circular and Cumulative Causation
Allan Pred, following Myrdal, offered further insight into features of regional economic growth.[4] It is readily observed that cities that develop early in a region's evolution are the cities or growth points around which the entire region evolves. Why do large cities grow larger and why do larger cities grow at a faster rate than smaller ones? In addition to the geographic and paralleling economic connections between the key and affected industries, Pred argued that the mere existence of an industry at a location at an early time increases the likelihood that new or enlarged industries will occur at or near that initial location.

[4]Allan R. Pred, *The Spatial Dynamics of Urban-Industrial Growth, 1800–1914* (Cambridge, Mass.: MIT Press, 1966).

The reasoning can be seen by examining Figure 3.11. A local growth point emerges as the result of the location or development of an industry at some place within a region. The new industry enhances the local economy immediately and directly by providing employment, by increasing purchasing power, and perhaps by inducing inmigration. Indirectly, but importantly, the workers attracted to the new industry require supporting retailing and service activities. An additional grocer is needed in the community, half a barber, and three quarters of a doctor's services. In other words, the new industry creates a ***multiplier effect*** whereby additional supporting personnel are attracted to the community to serve the needs of the workers and their families. The service personnel generate the need for still more service workers. The net outcome is an enlarged market for the industry and the opportunity for the industry to expand to fulfill its enlarged market. An excellent example of this process is the automobile industry in southeastern Michigan, especially from 1910 to 1930. A slowdown in auto production typically brings about a deceleration in the local economy, as occurred in Michigan and surrounding states in the late 1970s and early 1980s.

In the early development of a region, its small industries will be significantly tied primarily to the local market. This means that only certain kinds of industries can exist in the region, and

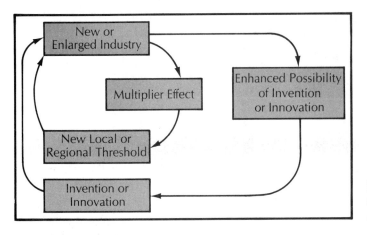

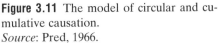

Figure 3.11 The model of circular and cumulative causation.
Source: Pred, 1966.

these will be industries that have a small ***market threshold***. A market threshold refers to the minimum number of people (or minimum aggregate purchasing power) necessary for an industry to exist profitably. A small food-processing factory could then exist on the sales to a small community of, say, 5000 people, but an iron-and-steel mill could not. Once the market threshold of the community reached 10,000 people, a new range of industrial types could come into existence because there would now be a sufficiently large local market to support them. The inner loop in Figure 3.11 begins with the emergence of a new industry, the resulting multiplier effect, the attainment of a new market threshold (at first locally and, subsequently, regionally based), and the creation of a new or enlarged industrial base. The process is both circular, as we have just seen, and cumulative, in the sense that once set into motion it is like a snowball rolling downhill: industry increasingly accumulates at a growth center as the center grows in size. Size by itself is an attraction.

The circular and cumulative process has another loop, this one relating directly to technology. Again we start with the establishment of a new industry at a given level of technology. The possibility of developing new or improved technology with respect to that industry is likely to occur (1) within that industry rather than in some

other industry and (2) in close spatial proximity to that industry. There is then the strong likelihood that invention or innovation will be concentrated near the initial industry location. Most typically, invention or innovation will mean greater production efficiencies, lowered costs, increased sales, and greater profits. All this also means the enlargement of the industry. Technological invention and innovation may likewise lead to the creation of closely related but nevertheless new industries.

The larger the industrial base becomes, the greater are the chances that further technological progress will occur. Large industrial firms have sizable research staffs. Large, modern industrial countries have numerous, highly trained personnel whose research activities tend to uncover new and improved methods of operation. Central to this idea of technological innovation is access to needed information. Typically, the information source for any particular industry is geographically concentrated near the location of the industry.

It has been said that cities are centers of change. This is so because cities have huge information pools, the advanced technology to gain access to their information pools, and the means to transmit that information via transportation and communication facilities. Pred has recognized that regional economic growth is de-

Color Plates

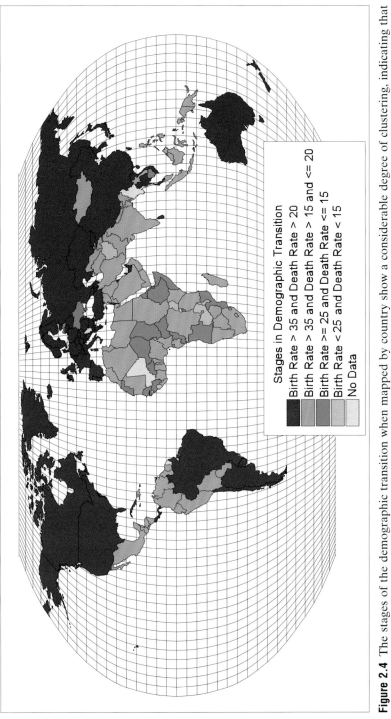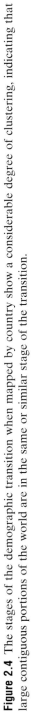

Figure 2.4 The stages of the demographic transition when mapped by country show a considerable degree of clustering, indicating that large contiguous portions of the world are in the same or similar stage of the transition.

Plate I

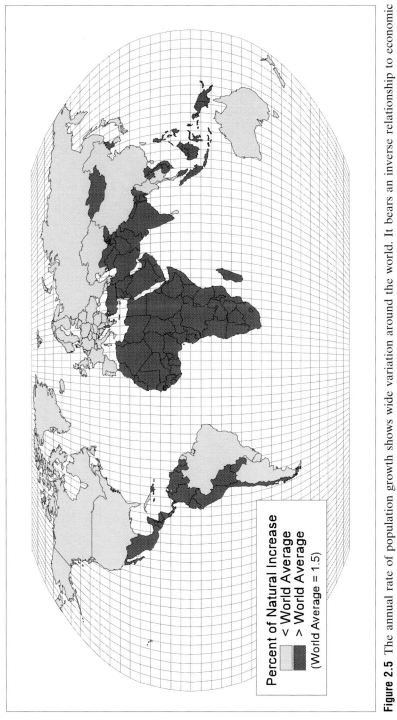

Figure 2.5 The annual rate of population growth shows wide variation around the world. It bears an inverse relationship to economic development, such that where the rate is high the development level is low and vice versa.

Plate II

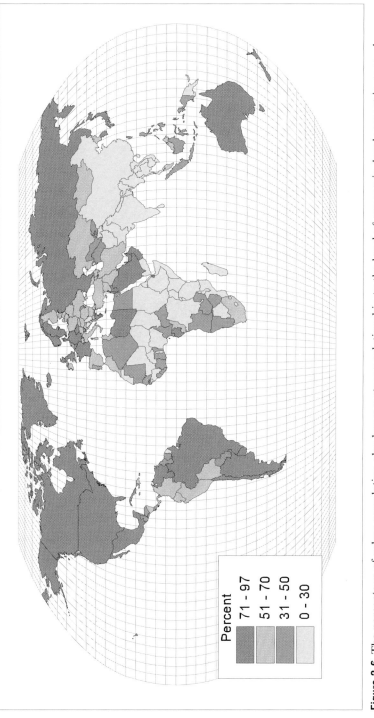

Figure 2.6 The percentage of urban population also bears a strong relationship to the level of economic development in general.

Percent
71 - 97
51 - 70
31 - 50
0 - 30

Plate III

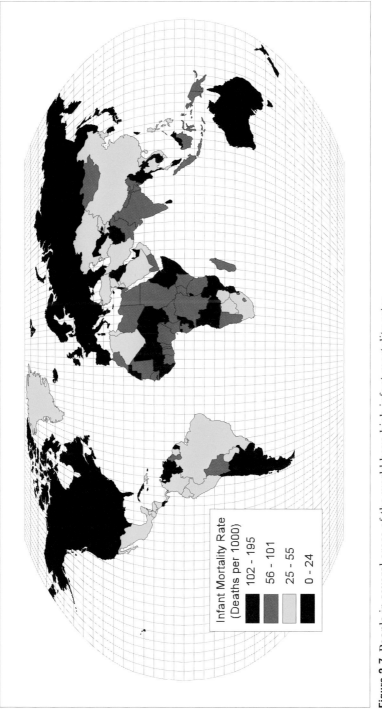

Figure 2.7 People in several areas of the world have high infant mortality rates.

Infant Mortality Rate
(Deaths per 1000)

102 - 195
56 - 101
25 - 55
0 - 24

Plate IV

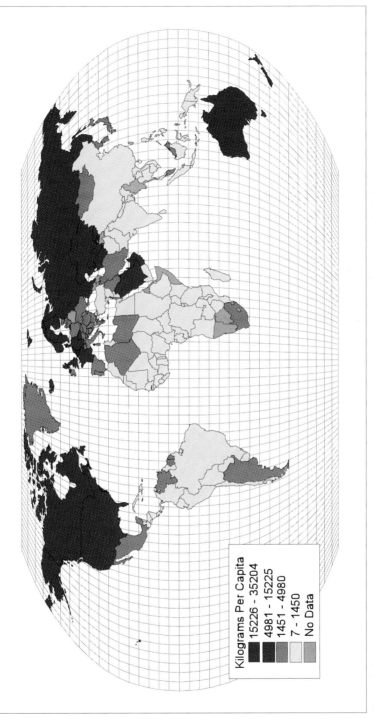

Figure 3.1 Per capita energy consumption is one of the best measures of the level of technological development.

Plate V

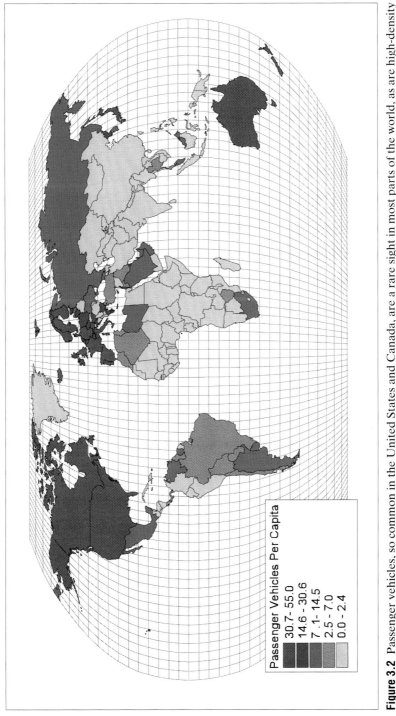

Figure 3.2 Passenger vehicles, so common in the United States and Canada, are a rare sight in most parts of the world, as are high-density and high-quality highways.

Passenger Vehicles Per Capita

30.7 - 55.0
14.6 - 30.6
7.1 - 14.5
2.5 - 7.0
0.0 - 2.4

Plate VI

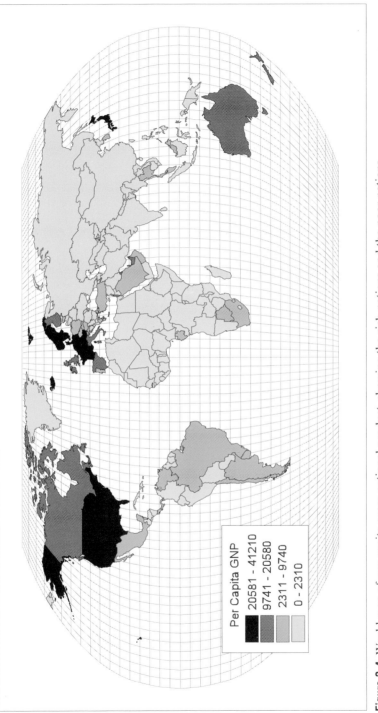

Figure 3.4 World map of per capita gross national product, showing the rich nations and the poor nations.

Plate VII

pendent not just on investment capital, export flows, or rises in per capita income; it also depends very fundamentally on the information base used in making economic decisions and on the role of access to information used in industrial innovation and invention. And information is most unequally spread geographically, being primarily confined in or near the growth center of a region.

This is especially true at a world scale. Although no really good measure of "information supply" is available on a world level, several surrogates may be used as close approximations. The number of telephones per capita is one such measure. There are about 11 telephones on the average for every 100 people on the earth. Over three-quarters of these, however, are in North America and Europe (Table 3.2). South America, by contrast, has approximately 3 percent of the world's telephones. In all of Asia there are fewer than three telephones per 100 people.

Other examples of information availability are the number of books published annually and the number of television sets per 1000 people (Table 3.3). The variation from country to country is incredible. For instance, in Angola, a country with 25 million inhabitants, only 14 books were published in a recent year, in contrast, say, to Den-

Table 3.3 Annual Number of Books Published and Per Capita Televisions for Selected Countries, 1987

Countries	Annual Books Published	Number of Televisions per 1000 People
Angola	14	5
Australia	2,603	472
Bangladesh	1,806	3
Brazil	21,184	188
Chile	1,499	164
Denmark	10,957	386
Ethiopia	227	2
France	37,860	332
Germany	70,210	375
India	12,543	7
Israel	2,214	261
Japan	44,686	585
Mexico	4,897	117
Nigeria	2,213	6
Philippines	804	36
Spain	38,405	322
United Kingdom	52,861	534
United States	NA	813
Former USSR	83,472	321
Zimbabwe	353	14

Source: United Nations Statistical Yearbook, 1987.

mark which has just over 5 million people and publishes nearly 11,000 books in a single year. The disparity in the number of televisions per 1000 people is also unbelievable—from two television sets for every 1000 people in Ethiopia and three in Bangladesh to well over 800 per 1000 people in the United States. Thus, what is commonplace in advanced economies is a rare luxury in the poorest nations of the world. The link between information availability and innovation and invention is unmistakable, as is the link between innovation or technological level and state of economic development.

The Bell-Shaped Development Model
William Alonso, in reviewing economic development models, suggested a bell-shaped model

Table 3.2 World Telephones, 1993

Region	Telephones per 100 Inhabitants	Percent of World's Telephones
Africa	1.1	1.1
North America	53.1	42.5
South America	5.2	2.7
Asia	2.8	15.2
Europe	30.0	32.1
Oceania	34.3	1.7
Former U.S.S.R.	8.0	4.7
World	10.5	100.0

Source: United Nations Statistical Yearbook, Fortieth Issue, 1995.

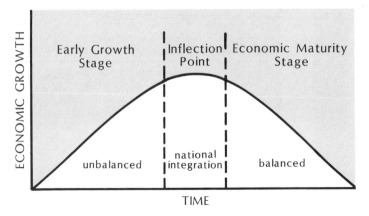

Figure 3.12 Economic growth may be said to follow a bell-shaped curve as a nation's economy becomes more mature. *Source*: Alonso, 1980.

to describe the sequence of change as a nation undergoes the process of economic development.[5] The bell-shaped model looks like the normal curve that describes many statistical distributions (Figure 3.12). Time is plotted on the horizontal axis, and economic development, on the vertical scale. In the *early stages of development* (left-hand side), growth is unbalanced among regions of the country, which will have a rich area and a poor area. Even within a particular region there will be great social inequality as measured by wealth among subgroups of the population, and per capita income among regions may actually become more unequal. Rapid urbanization characterizes an early stage of growth, as one or a few large cities grow most rapidly.

At some point in the economic development process, growth reaches an *inflection point*, and the trends in social and regional inequality and geographic concentration peak and then begin to reverse themselves. Whereas the early stage is characterized by unbalanced growth and inequality, the inflection point implies national integration of the economy. Both capital and labor become geographically more mobile as the national economy becomes more integrated, bring-

ing about more balanced regional growth. Technology and information differ widely across the country, and locational advantages based on distance and accessibility become lessened. Improvements in transportation nationwide give fewer unique advantages to particular locations over others. Urbanization becomes more widespread rather than limited to a few large centers. New development opportunities become available in many locations previously unacceptable before national economic integration. These factors act to restore a greater regional balance during this phase of national economic integration.

The right-hand side of the bell-shaped curve is characterized by *national economic maturity*. The actual pace of economic growth slows, social inequality shows some evidence of reduction, and regional equalization of income increases. Increasingly, the concentration of population in the largest metropolitan areas is reduced as more and more cities join the metropolitan class and as small cities and rural areas grow in population size. The shift from a manufacturing-based to a service-based economy means slower overall growth because of lower economic productivity in the latter. As more women enter the workforce, with consequent reductions in the average number of children, the future workforce is reduced, pointing to possible labor shortages for industrial economies in the future. Manufacturing becomes more capital-intensive or is per-

[5]William Alonso, "Five Bell Shapes in Development," *Papers of the Regional Science Association* 45 (1980), pp. 5–16.

A view of North America looking through the earth from the Indian Ocean, a visual analogue to how the United States and Canada are perceived from a Third World perspective.

formed in low-wage foreign areas. Thus, a number of forces act to bring about a reversal of the trends found in the early, unbalanced growth era.

Some evidence from the United States lends support to Alonso's bell-shaped curve model. For example, over the last three decades there has been a slow but steady shift in the location of major corporate headquarters away from the large metropolitan areas in the Northeast and Midwest to the West and South. The same shift has been observed in new job creation and in population migration to the South and West. These shifts are bringing about increased national integration within the metropolitan system and a more regionally balanced economy. The

South, for instance, which long lagged behind the North economically, has in the last 15 to 20 years been growing at a rapid rate, at least among many metropolitan areas.

The bell-shaped curve model discussed by Alonso is a useful way to view the nature and pace of national economic change. The curve is idealized in the sense that no country will follow the curve exactly, nor will different countries experience the process over the same time periods. Nevertheless, the model is useful to summarize important features of national economic change.

CONCLUDING THOUGHTS AND SUMMARY

An underlying assumption in almost all discussions of economic development is that growth is dependent on manufacturing activities. When industry is attracted, one expects, in the regional context, that growth will be promoted and, in the world scene, modernization will occur. Although rapid growth relies on manufacturing and industrial nations, by definition, have major concentrations of manufacturing, investment solely in manufacturing will not bring desired growth and economic prosperity. Investment, whether by private or public means, must strike some balance among all sectors of the economy. In the past, areas such as South Korea or Taiwan may have been exceptions to this statement because of massive external financial aid. It will require gargantuan investment, wisely made, over a long period of time before much noticeable change is likely to occur in the economies of a great many of the world's poorer countries. The petroleum-producing countries of the Middle East have rather suddenly found themselves able to afford enormous investment in their economies and will, no doubt, greatly accelerate the development process. One of the problems is that most countries lack any concrete and operational regional-economy development policy. With such an overall policy, economic change would be smoother. On the other hand, we must remember that most of the developed world, except in the case of the centrally planned economies, has reached the industrialized stage without any definitive planning strategy.

Geographically, public investment policies have been of two types: (1) dispersal; or (2) concentration. The policy of dispersed public investment has been by far the more common. This policy scatters investment widely over a large region, frequently with an emphasis on many small projects and perhaps with some focus on "backward" or depressed areas. The dispersal policy has been criticized in that it dilutes the impact of investment by expenditures on many marginally efficient operations. It also has proved susceptible to pressures from many scattered locales vying to get a piece of the pie. Such dispersal policies are practiced especially in situations in which the national government seeks and requires support from all parts of the country—and this includes most governments. Sections of greater political clout may gain disproportionate benefits. The result may be a disconnected transportation system or at least one that evolves through fits and starts rather than an integrated and efficient system. On the other side of the argument, however, the dispersed investment policy has the advantage that all sections will be treated more or less fairly. Moreover, in developing economies it often makes more sense to invest in smaller projects for which local managerial and technological competence is available rather than to sink huge sums into a demonstration project or showcase for which foreign expertise needs to be brought in. The smaller projects are usually more in keeping with the planning, engineering, and managerial capabilities of local personnel, and the local area therefore derives primary benefits.

The second policy seeks to concentrate investment into large, sound, "bankable" undertakings to get maximum returns on investment and to spur growth in areas that have already demonstrated the capacity for growth. This policy is more in keeping with the growth pole theory but actually is more descriptive of private expenditures than of public investment. When precipitous and rapid growth occurs at a growth center in a region, however, there is a public demand for investment in projects that will help control the growth or indeed ensure that it continues smoothly. For example, rapid growth at a point may lead to sudden demand for additional housing or for improvements in the transportation system. If private capital is not immediately available in sizable quantities, expenditure of public funds will become necessary to alleviate the growth pains. But as we have already seen, attempts to "catch up" with growth will simply lead in the long run to greater growth.

Investment in technology is a necessary, but by itself insufficient, condition for economic development. Investment in research that may lead to technological breakthroughs is, of course, necessary, but often risky, for technological developments are impossible to predict. Many developing countries are able to "import" technology that has been refined elsewhere. This is achievable at a cost. The result is that the wave of technology spreads around the world sometimes just ahead, but all too often just behind, the wave of the population binge.

Further Readings

Alonso, William. "Five Bell Shaped Curves." *Papers of the Regional Science Association* 45 (1980), pp. 5–16.

Browett, J. G. "On the Role of Geography in Development Geography." *Tijdschrift voor Economische en Sociale Geografie* 73 (1981), pp.155–161.

Cole, J. P. *The Development Gap: A Spatial Analysis of World Poverty and Inequality.* New York: Wiley, 1981.

Davis, Mike. *City of Quartz.* London: Verso, 1990.

Forbes, D. K. *The Geography of Underdevelopment.* Baltimore: Johns Hopkins University Press, 1984.

Friedmann, John. "Cities in Social Transformation." *Comparative Studies in Society and History* 4 (1961), pp. 86–103.

Harvey, David. *The Limits to Capital.* Oxford: Basil Blackwell, 1982.

Hirschman, Albert O. *The Strategy of Economic Development*. New Haven, Conn.: Yale University Press, 1958.

Lim, Gill C. *Regional Planning: Evolution, Crisis and Prospects*. Totowa, N.J.: Allanheld, Osmun Publishers, 1983.

Mabogunje, A. L. *The Development Process: A Spatial Perspective*. London: Hutchinson, 1980.

Miernyk, William H. *Regional Analysis and Regional Policy*. Cambridge, Mass.: Oelgeschlager, Gunn & Hain, 1982.

Myrdal, Gunnar. *Rich Lands and Poor*. New York: Harper Brothers, 1957.

Perroux, F. "Economic Space: Theory and Applications." *Quarterly Journal of Economics* 64 (1950), pp. 89–104.

Pred, Allan R. *The Spatial Dynamics of U.S. Urban-Industrial Growth, 1800–1914*. Cambridge, Mass.: MIT Press, 1966.

Rees, J. "Technological Change and Regional Shifts in American Manufacturing." *The Professional Geographer* 31 (1979), pp. 45–54.

Rees, J., G. Hewings, and H. Stafford, eds. *Industrial Location and Regional Systems*. New York: Bergin, 1981.

Richardson, Harry W. *Regional Growth Theory*, New York: Wiley, 1973.

Rodgers, Allan. *Economic Development in Retrospect*. New York: Wiley, 1979.

Rostow, W. W. *The Stages of Economic Growth*. New York: Cambridge University Press, 1960.

Scott, Allen, J. *Metropolis: From Division of Labor to Urban Form*. Berkeley: University of California Press, 1988.

Thomas, Morgan D. "Growth Pole Theory, Technical Change, and Regional Economic Growth." *Papers of Regional Science Association* 34 (1975), pp. 3–25.

Wolch, Jennifer, and Michael Dear. *The Power of Geography: How Territory Shapes Social Life*. Boston: Unwin Hyman, 1989.

CHAPTER 4

The Interdependent Global Economy

———— ◇ ————

Modern cities are the pillars of the developing global system. It is a poetic illusion to assume that the world is shrinking because communication improves. In reality the world of each of us constantly expands because, as we carry on, we find it necessary to deal with more and more people, in more places, with a greater number and diversity of problems. This is so for individuals and also for cities.

—JEAN GOTTMANN, 1989

INTRODUCTION

The historical trajectory of economic change, as seen from hindsight, has been essentially away from the local toward the global. But it has taken a long time, and the globalization of the economy is far from over. Consider once again the earliest beginnings of human social and economic behavior: the subsistence mode whereby a close group of humans consumed what they produced locally. There was no surplus to trade. During the Agricultural Revolution, some 12,000 years ago, humans began domesticating a variety of animals and plants, and these more efficient agricultural practices allowed the first notable production surpluses.

With surplus production, the opportunity for trade and exchange was born. First, commodities and items were traded for one another, but only over a highly localized area. Gradually, the exchanges began taking place over increasingly greater distances, especially for highly valued items. Eventually, exchanges of commodities gave way to a money system, as particular goods took on an agreed-upon value. All the while the geographic extent of trade became larger and larger.

With the development of relatively large political entities, that is, countries, the scope for extensive trade and transportation again enlarged geographically. The sail ship brought about movement and exchange on a scale previously unimagined, and helped create both economic and political linkages with distant places. Five European powers, Great Britain, France, Spain, Portugal, and the Netherlands, created global empires of colonial rule by exploiting resources, both mineral and agricultural, in far-away places. Later Belgium, Germany, and Italy vied for the remaining places. Later, steam power allowed greater, faster, and more reliable ties among places, both over water and, importantly, over land via the railroad. Only about 200 years ago, the Industrial Revolution—born in England—witnessed the beginnings of the mass production of commodities and thereby the possibilities for extensive exchange. The core was Europe; the periphery was elsewhere.

As Norman Pounds concluded (p. 407)[1]:

[1]Norman J. G. Pounds, *Hearth and Home: A History of National Culture* (Bloomington: Indiana University Press, 1989).

Overall, the periphery was exploited in order to remedy scarcities that had arisen, largely as a result of increasing population and the developing scale of manufacturing, in Europe itself. Industrial raw materials like cotton, wool, and jute, rubber and softwood timber; luxuries like coffee and tea; and necessities like the bread-grains, sugar, and meat were all produced for the European market, and their relative cheapness allowed them to be consumed in relative abundance. In this the Americas assumed a particular importance. The long separation of the New World from the Old meant that some quite different species had evolved in the former from those known in the latter. Some of these were of great food or industrial value and were furthermore capable of translation to Europe.

The significance of this historic expansion in human contact over ever greater distances though immense, is nonetheless dwarfed by recent changes in the global economy. We recall the important precursors to the current instantaneous global communications network: the marathon, the telegraph, the telephone, the airplane. At each of these steps in technology, greater opportunities for human interaction over great distances were achieved. We were marching toward a global economy, and now we are running. Our contemporary satellite communications and our ever-growing global capitalism are bursting barriers of distance at a pace never experienced in previous human history. Let us see what is happening around the world, but first we will start with what *was* happening.

THE HISTORIC ATLANTIC ALLIANCE

With the spread of the Industrial Revolution from the major urban areas in England to cities in Western Europe and North America, the historic North Atlantic Alliance was created. Although colonial powers such as Great Britain obtained many agricultural and industrial resources from economically underdeveloped areas of the

The historic Atlantic alliance, as Europe views North America to the west.

world over which they held political power, the major international trade ties were between the industrializing continents of Europe and North America. The per capita income levels of these countries permitted the purchase of agriculture and especially industrial goods. Complex patterns of supply and demand evolved between the two North Atlantic continents, as consumers became ever more sensitive to subtle differences in style, quality, and price. The interdependence between the North Atlantic nations, essentially beginning with the start of the Industrial Revolution, was to last only two centuries. It was the first major step in the direction of globalization of the human economy.

Was it only by chance that New York became the national economic capital of the United States? Was it not strange that the leading U.S. urban centers of the nineteenth century (New York, Philadelphia, Boston, and Baltimore) were all located on the East Coast and served as major ports? The French geographer, Jean Gottmann, writing in the early 1960s about this urbanized area of the Northeast, referred to the *hinge* role this area played in linking the U.S. economy with that of Western Europe. Similarly, the two largest metropolitan areas in Canada—Toronto and Montreal—are located on water bodies that have direct ties with Western Europe, Lake Ontario, and the St. Lawrence Seaway, respectively. In like manner, the great port cities of Western Europe thrived and established trade ties with other large ports around the globe.

Until 1981 the preponderance of international trade involved the two-way movement of industrial goods across the Atlantic. Secondary flows were from the less developed countries in Latin America, Africa, and Asia to North America and Western Europe. These flows consisted largely of agricultural goods and mineral resources to be processed and consumed by the more advanced economies. In contrast, very little trade occurred among the less developed countries themselves, as they remained largely in a subsistence stage, with a high percentage of the population working in agriculture.

After the Russian Revolution in 1917 and, later, the Soviet Union's political domination of Eastern Europe following World War II, the so-called communist-bloc countries turned inward and were only superficially involved in "international" trade. Trade did take place within the communist countries, but political policy to make each region as self-sufficient as possible limited trade among them—hence the continued dominance of the Atlantic alliance countries in international trade.

THE PACIFIC RIM

Following World War II, Japan rapidly rebuilt its industrial economy with a focus on consumer rather than military production. During the 1950s in the United States, "Made in Japan" meant inexpensive, low-quality products. Honda, now one of the world's largest corporations, started out selling inexpensive motorbikes and motorcycles in the United States. Japan quickly developed into a super economic power, emphasizing high-quality, high-technology production. As noted later in this chaper, it also became the leading world financial center in terms of bank assets.

At the same time that Japan's economy was rapidly expanding, four other Asian economies were transforming themselves from traditional subsistence to dominant commercial systems. These four economies, the so-called Four Tigers of Asia—South Korea, Hong Kong, Taiwan, and Singapore—have developed sophisticated manufacturing for export and have attracted international investment. Other countries in the Pacific region—Indonesia, Malaysia, the People's Republic of China, the Philippines, and Thailand—are attempting to develop economically by following the same export-based strategy. To this list of economies we must add the developed market economies of Australia and New Zealand—as we realize that the Pacific Rim region takes on a formidable global presence.

International Trade

Approximately 70 percent of all international trade involves exchanges among the developed market economies, about 20 percent involves countries classified as developing market economies, and only about 10 percent with the centrally and formally planned economies (Table 4.1). Thus, centrally planned economies have largely remained outside the capitalist world order, but are now generally moving in the direction of freer markets in an attempt to participate in the global economy.

The United States' leading trading partner is

Table 4.1 Percentage of World's Imports and Exports by Major Economic Categories

	Imports	**Exports**
Developed market economies	71.1	70.0
Developing market economies	19.0	20.2
Centrally planned economies	9.9	9.8
World	100.0	100.0

Source: United Nations, *Yearbook of International Trade Statistics 1988* (New York: United Nations, 1990).

Table 4.2 Percentage of United States Exports by Major World Regions

World Regions	Percentage of Exports
Europe	26.5
Canada	22.5
Asia[a]	19.2
Latin America	14.1
Japan	12.0
Australia and New Zealand	2.5
Africa	2.3
Former USSR	0.9
Total	100.0

[a]Excluding Japan.

Source: United Nations, *Yearbook of International Trade Statistics 1988* (New York: United Nations, 1990).

Canada, the destination for over 22 percent of all U.S. exports (Table 4.2; Figure 4.1). Japan, receiving 12 percent of all U.S. exports, is the United States' second leading trade partner. The United States' major trading partners in Europe are Germany, the United Kingdom, France, and Italy, which together account for approximately 15 percent of all U.S. exports as well as imports. All of the countries of Latin America taken together comprise 14 percent of U.S. exports, a figure only slightly larger than that for Japan alone. African countries are the destination for less than 3 percent of U.S. exports, and Russia for less than 1 percent. In all, 64 percent of U.S. exports go to other developed market economies, 33 percent to developing market economies, and less than 3 percent to centrally planned and formerly planned economies.

The United States is, by far, the leading trade partner for Japan, accounting for more than one-third of Japanese exports (Table 4.3; Figure 4.2). All the countries of Asia combined account for a slightly smaller figure. Europe receives over 20 percent of Japanese exports, but all of Africa and Latin America receive just over 5 percent.

The historic Western European alliance with the United States and Canada, which was gradually weakening with the economic rise of Japan

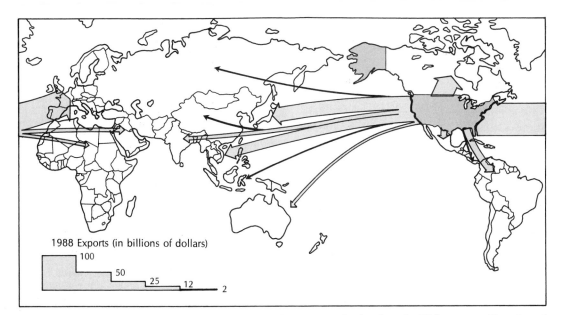

1988 Exports (in billions of dollars)

Figure 4.1 The Pacific Rim countries have surpassed Europe as destinations for U.S. exports. Canada and Japan are the leading importers of U.S. goods.

Table 4.3 Percentage of Japanese Exports by Major World Regions

World Regions	Percentage of Exports
United States and Canada	36.8
Asia	32.4
Europe	21.2
Latin America	3.3
Australia and New Zealand	2.9
Africa	2.2
Former USSR	1.2
Total	100.0

Source: United Nations, *Yearbook of International Trade Statistics 1988* (New York: United Nations, 1990).

and the Four Tigers, was technically broken in 1981, when for the first time total trade (imports and exports) between the United States and Canada and the Pacific Rim countries exceeded trade with Western Europe. In 1988, nearly one-third of U.S. trade was with the Pacific Rim economies compared to just over 23 percent with Western Europe.

U.S. and Canadian trade with the Pacific Rim countries is expected to continue to grow as these economies follow the Japanese export-based experience. Led by Japan, followed by the Four Tigers, plus Australia and New Zealand, the Pacific Rim region promises to occupy a central and growing role in the world economy for decades to come. Although Japan has a population of only about 125 million, the Pacific Rim region has a huge population, including more than 1.4 billion in the People's Republic of China alone. This enormous market will become an even more potent global attraction as investment in human resources leads to increases in personal incomes and purchasing power.

Multinational corporations have been investing heavily in the Pacific Rim, led by U.S. firms and by British and Japanese companies, as well as by other companies headquartered in Canada,

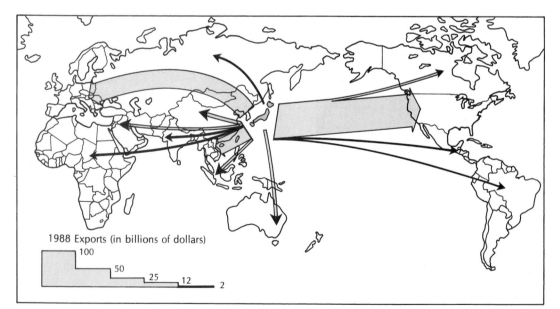

1988 Exports (in billions of dollars)

Figure 4.2 Japanese exports go mainly to the United States (37 percent), Asia (32 percent), and Europe (21 percent).

Western Europe, and Australia. The multinationals have been instrumental in the transfer of technology and capital to this part of the world, in contrast to extremely low levels of foreign investment in Africa, much of Latin America, and South Asia. At the same time that the economies in the Pacific Rim region have been surging, Western Europe, with its stable population and slow-growth economy, has experienced more cautious investments.

Although the growth of the Pacific Rim has important implications for Europe, the United States and Canada are particularly impacted. First, the United States and Canada are themselves part of the Pacific Rim, as the Asians look toward the North American market. One of the most serious difficulties is the large trade deficit the United States has suffered at the hands of the Pacific region, especially Japan. In 1988, for example, the United States imported more than $93 billion from Japan and exported only $37 billion in return. In the same year, the U.S. trade deficit with the Pacific Rim was approximately $80 billion. With respect to the nature of the commodities traded between the United States and the Pacific Rim, the United States is functioning in the traditional role of a Third World country, sending primary commodities and receiving largely industrial goods. A third of U.S. agricultural exports are sent to the Pacific Rim.

CORE AND PERIPHERY RELATIONS

One common way of viewing the world-system is to use the perspective of a core-periphery hierarchy. Such a view of the global economy is based on the role of capitalism. First, the concept of *world-system* implies the innerconnectiveness of all parts of the world economy. Almost all human beings are linked to the world-system through their economic behaviors as consumers and producers. These economic behaviors are organized through complex communication networks that tie together the inhabited continents,

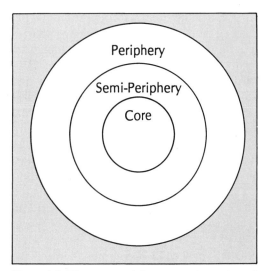

Figure 4.3 The core-periphery concept posits a dominant and economic and political core and a weaker, more remote peripheral region. The semi-periphery occupies an intermediate position.

often mediated by political realities. The world-system is also geographically interlinked via a hierarchy of world cities increasingly based on telecommunications.

The *core-periphery hierarchy* consists of power relations between the dominant core and the weaker, more dependent periphery. Frequently, reference is also made to the semi-periphery, which lies somewhere intermediate between the core and periphery (Figure 4.3). The core-periphery concept describes a *capitalist* world economy consisting of commodity and service production undertaken for profit in a price-setting market. The notion of *hierarchy* implies inequality within the system, in which control and power are exercised in the core region and dependency and subordination are experienced in the more remote periphery.

Immanuel Wallerstein has traced the evolution of capitalism through four historic epochs.[2]

[2]Immanuel Wallerstein, *The Modern World-System I* (New York: Academic Press, 1974).

The first epoch, here termed the *transitional period*, lasted from 1450 to 1640 and was characterized by the slow transition from feudalism in Europe to early agricultural capitalism. Feudalism involved a class structure of lords and peasants, which was replaced by a working class who sold their labor to agrarian capitalists. The center or core of economic power during this epoch shifted from Venice to Genoa and then to Antwerp. The role of Spain and Portugal, in particular, in exploiting resources in Africa and in the New World brought capital accumulation to the European core and established serfdom and slavery in the African and New World periphery.

Wallerstein's second epoch, here termed *colonial capitalism*, lasted from 1640 to 1815 and saw the establishment of Europe as the core region. The Dutch, the dominant power at the start of this epoch, were quickly challenged by the British and the French, in competition for colonial empires, including those of the older Spanish and Portuguese empires. Economic hegemony over the world periphery was reinforced by political control. Thus, core (European) and periphery (colonial areas in the Americas, Africa, and Asia) trade formed the basis of capitalist trade.

The third epoch, here called the period of *British hegemony*, lasted from 1815 to 1917. With Napoleon's defeat in 1815, the British exercised economic, political, and military control over the periphery. The capitalist system spread throughout the world, and for the first time a global world-system appeared. This epoch also saw the rise of a semi-periphery, with powers such as the United States, Belgium, Germany, Italy, Japan, and Russia competing with Britain for control of the periphery and their markets. This epoch ended with World War I.

The fourth epoch, *United States hegemony*, has lasted from the end of World War I to the present. It has been marked by four major forces. The first has been the military superiority of the United States established in World War II and the Korean War but curtailed by domestic polit-

A view of the Tokyo skyline, showing the concentration of advanced services and finance.

ical considerations in Vietnam. Second, the Russian Revolution in 1917 set in motion the forces of anticapitalism and largely blocked the capitalist core regions of North America, Western Europe, and later Japan from expansion into the socialist regions of the world. Third, the Third World periphery became decolonized in South Asia, Africa, and the Middle East, allowing capitalist behavior to continue and expand without the cost of colonialism. Fourth, this transition was increasingly made possible by the rise of huge transnational corporations reaching around the globe, largely independent of any individual country. The disintegration of the socialist economies has opened the door for capitalism to spread into the previously anticapitalist regions, bringing about an even greater world economic integration.

Dependency Theory

One particular issue in the core-periphery debate is known as *dependency theory*, which holds that the dominant core can grow and prosper only by exploiting the dependent periphery. Dependency theory is particularly associated with social scientists writing on Latin America, where many writers applied the theory to explain the region's overall economic plight. It was felt that the uneven economic relationship between the core and the periphery was not a temporary phenomenon but a fundamental and permanent way of holding back the periphery. Thus, understanding low levels of economic development in a particular country can be achieved not by merely studying that single economy but only by viewing that country within the overall world core-periphery structure.

According to traditional economic theory, trade is mutually beneficial for sender and receiver. Dependency theory takes a different view. Competition is high among the many primary producers in the Third World, who are willing to work for extremely low wages on the global level in order to earn a living above the

subsistence level. This severe competition drives down the price of goods being sold to the core region. These price reductions, however, are not passed on to the consumer in the core regions because of imperfect competition among producers who share a common need to keep prices high. As areas of the world became integrated into the global economy via colonialism or external investment and international trade, the economies of these regions were structured into a dependence on the demands of the core and continued to serve the core rather than develop an internal economy.

The Brain Drain

One of the realities of American higher education, despite such shortcomings as inadequate budgets and cramped laboratory space, is that it offers a high-quality product that is much in demand around the world. The United States leads the world in the number of international students in higher education, as well as the number of foreign scholars and researchers. A high percentage of M.A. and Ph.D. candidates in certain fields are foreign students, such as computer science and other mathematically related fields. Many foreign students come from Asia. Most graduate geography programs in the United States have a significant number of foreign students. Canada and the United Kingdom also attract large numbers of foreign students.

At first glance, the education and training of foreign students might seem to be an excellent way to transfer technology to Third World countries, especially in fields such as medicine, engineering, and the sciences in general. What typically happens, however, is very different. Figure 4.4 shows hypothetically the pattern of *brain drain* from Third World countries to the United States and Canada, compared to the much smaller dollar flow in aid to Third World countries. Whereas we can measure the amount of dollar aid to a particular country, it is much more difficult to place a monetary value on human re-

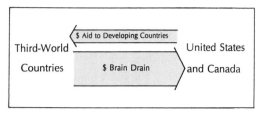

Figure 4.4 Although it is difficult to place a dollar figure on the brain drain, estimates place it much higher than the dollar figure for aid to developing countries.

sources. The purpose of aid to developing countries is to transfer technology to upgrade economic performance and efficiency. Brain drain is known as a *reverse* transfer of technology, where the country's "best and brightest" leave for an education abroad. Instead of returning to their home country for employment, they obtain employment abroad. This practice is believed to deprive the Third World countries of many of their most talented people and to benefit the developed economies by increasing the number of their educated and intellectually productive workers. It has been observed that an extremely high percentage of Japanese graduates return home, where economic opportunities are high. Many other Asian graduates, however, do not return home because of the relative lack of opportunities for high pay, research facilities, and

quality of life in the Third World. Some also consider it a "failure" not to be able to obtain a job in the Americas.

THE ROLE OF MULTINATIONAL CORPORATIONS

Economically large and powerful world corporations operate across political divisions, reaching far beyond the scope of any single country. IBM, headquartered out of New York City, has total annual sales in excess of $60 billion, making it one of the largest U.S. corporations. But is IBM really an American corporation? Over 60 percent of its annual sales are outside the United States. Similarly, over 60 percent of Japanese-based Honda's annual sales are over $25 billion, and more than one-third of its assets are outside Japan. Volvo, out of Sweden, has 80 percent of its $15 billion in annual sales outside Sweden and 30 percent of its assets are held outside the country. These examples highlight the multinational scale of many of the world's largest corporations.

Table 4.4 shows selected comparisons between major multinational corporations and the gross domestic products of countries. (Gross domestic product is the gross national product out of which international exports are subtracted.) For

Table 4.4 Worldwide Sales of Selected Multinational Corporations Compared to GDP of Selected Third World Countries, 1984

Company	Nationality	Industry	Sales ($ billions)	GDP ($ billions)	Country
Exxon	United States	Oil	74	76	Argentina
General Motors	United States	Motor vehicles	64	75	Nigeria
Mobil	United States	Oil	43	42	Thailand
Ford	United States	Motor vehicles	40	33	Philippines
IBM	United States	Office supplies	35	31	Hong Kong
du Pont	United States	Chemicals and energy	28	29	Malaysia
Toyota	Japan	Motor vehicles	18	18	Singapore
Chrysler	United States	Motor vehicles	15	16	Syria

Source: Rhys Jenkins, *Transnational Corporations and Uneven Development* (New York: Methuen, 1987), p. 9.

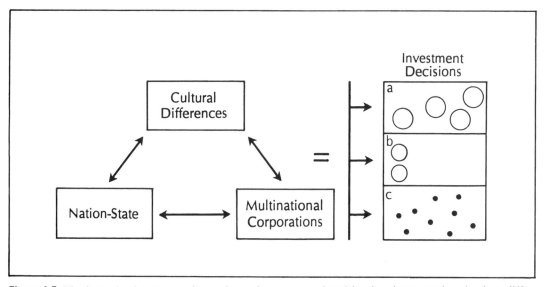

Figure 4.5 The interplay between culture, the nation-state, and multinational corporations leads to different levels of investment and different locations for investment within regions a, b, and c.
Source: After Berry, 1990.

example, Exxon and General Motors have more economic clout than many countries and yet are not confined to any single country. IBM is on an equal footing with the rapidly expanding Hong Kong, and Japan's Toyota is as economically powerful as Singapore, another of the Four Tigers.

This table illustrates some fundamental conflict and implies some cooperation between the political concept of the state or country and the capitalist concept of the world economy. As Brian Berry points out:

In the emerging global economy, the key actors are multinational corporations and nation-states. As they interact, there are different outcomes in different world regions because they play their games on the differentiating checkerboard of culture.[3]

[3]Brian J. L. Berry, "Comparative Geographies of the Global Economy: Cultures, Corporations, and the Nation-State," *Economic Geography* 65, (January 1989), pp. 1–18.

Figure 4.5 attempts to visualize Berry's conception of the new global economy and the role of economic geography in understanding how cultural differences, nation-states, and multinational corporations interact to produce different locational outcomes around the world.

Whereas cultural differences go far back into human antiquity and represent the most fundamental values of human groups, multinational corporations are a modern manifestation of capitalism, which Wallenstein traces back only a few centuries. Culture is learned behavior, such as language, religion, and value system, and is basically centered on the family, however defined. In fact, capitalism itself is part of culture. But capitalism, especially as mediated through powerful multinational corporations, takes on a life of its own, it is more important than any single individual, and it exists for the benefit of the capitalist group.

The national economies are intermediate in their creation between the prehistoric development of culture and the recent evolution of multinational corporations. Sometimes national economies are highly reflective of cultural groups, as in France, Denmark, or Japan. When cultural groups and countries largely coincide, they constitute *nation-states*. In other cases, as in Africa and the Middle East, where colonial powers superimposed boundaries over the region, little attempt has been made to place boundaries around defined cultural groups. These are not nation-states, but rather countries exhibiting cultural diversity (and sometimes local disturbances or civil war), which holds back investment by multinational corporations because of perceived political instability. As examples of outcomes between the forces of culture, the nation-state, and multinational corporations, Figure 4.5 shows three levels of investment decisions: (1) high levels of investment in large cities, (2) high levels of investment in the western area only, and (3) low levels of investment throughout the region.

In discussing the role of multinational corporations in the world economy, the question is invariably raised: Are they a positive or negative force? During the 1960s, there was considerable concern, especially among many European countries, that U.S. multinational corporations would gain control of their economies. The possibility that a corporation headquartered, say, in New York might suddenly shut down a large subsidiary in, say, Belgium raised fears among European nation-states. In the 1970s, less developed countries, especially the petroleum-exporting countries, demanded a greater role in the emerging world economy and began their own investment strategies. Since the beginning of the 1980s, multinational corporations have been seen less as predatory invaders and more as much needed sources of investment. The 1990s has been a period of struggle among many nation-states for the finite share of foreign investment. The issue of the impact of multinational corporations must be answered on a worldwide scale rather than from the point of view of a single country. As the world capitalist system continues to spread, we

realize that it is not limited to political boundaries reflective of the old world order.

The spread of multinational corporations, which view the world for their operational potential, has brought about both intended and unintended changes. Positive effects in the host country include: (1) needed investment capital, (2) job creation, (3) technology transfer, and (4) improved balance of payments.

Negative effects include (1) exploitation of nonrenewable resources, (2) the sudden closing of a subsidiary, with potentially economically devastating impact on the local area, (3) the neutralization of national economic policies by the sheer size and international capacities of the corporations, (4) the modification or destruction of a culture, brought about by a mode of production and consumption foreign to the local culture, and (5) the focus of production on outside needs to the detriment of the local population's essential needs.[4] From the point of view of the multinational corporation, however, there are clear advantages, which, according to Michel Falise (1983, p. 211), are "due to its capacity to use an international field for a broader mobility of [workers], finances, knowledge, and technology." Furthermore, "these advantages are manifested for the corporation in terms of profits and growth rates, of research potentials, investments, and innovations."

A Multinational Example

As an example of a particular multinational corporation, we examine ICI, a British-headquartered enterprise.[5] Originally formed in 1926 by the merger of four companies (two large alkali companies, a chemical firm, and a powerful explosives company), ICI broadened its

---

[4]Summarized from Michel Falise, *Multinational Corporations and Regional Development* (Rome: Herden, 1983, p. 211).
[5]This discussion is based on I. M. Clarke, "The Changing Division of Labour Within ICI," in Michael Taylor and Nigel Thrift, eds., *The Geography of Multinationals* (London: Croom Held, 1982).

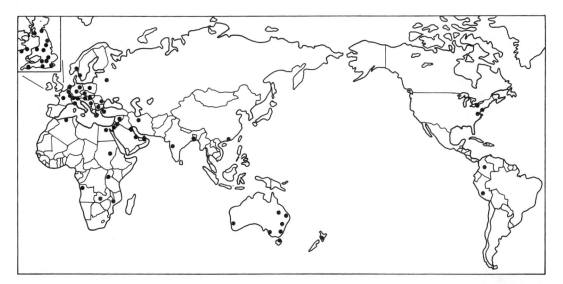

Figure 4.6 The worldwide distribution of ICI's offices (1980), an example of a multinational multilocational corporation.
Source: After Clarke, 1982.

product line to include the following business categories:

    agriculture
    chemicals, general
    chemicals, organic
    fibers
    industrial explosives
    paints
    petrochemicals
    pharmaceuticals
    plastics

Eventually ICI also grew global, with manufacturing plants in more than 40 countries and sales offices in more than 60 countries (Figure 4.6).

This British-based multinational conducts business in all continents except Antarctica. It reflects the historic North Atlantic Alliance (Western Europe and North America) in its geographical distribution of manufacturing sites and office locations, although the Pacific Rim is growing rapidly. In some areas of the world, ICI concentrates its manufacturing geographically, as in the United Kingdom, Western Europe, the east-

ern United States, and South Africa. In other areas, such as the Middle East, office activities dominate without manufacturing, whereas in yet other places such as Australia, Southeast Asia, and West Africa, combined manufacturing and office locations are common. Another glance at Figure 4.6 confirms the truly global reach of this corporation.

THE CHANGING GEOGRAPHY OF GLOBAL FINANCES

With the rise of the Industrial Revolution in Great Britain, it was perhaps inevitable that London, the largest city in the British Isles, would emerge as the financial center of the world. London financed the British Empire and spread capitalism around the globe. It was not until the early twentieth century that it would feel the sting of competition from the upstart New York, which rapidly usurped London's long-standing role as the world's financial center.

In contrast to London's long reign, New York was to be the leading world banking center for

Old meets new: Toronto's tallest building (the CN Tower) blends beautifully with the nineteenth-century Flat Iron Building at center.

only a few decades. John Borchert (1978) and Michael Conzen (1977) have described how New York banking expanded with the westward and southern expansion of settlement in the United States, giving financial backing to small frontier banks scattered across the country.[6] With the economic and political hegemony of the United States after World War I, New York became the undisputed world banking center and Wall Street, a short street in Lower Manhatten, became synonymous with banking and finance the world over.

It is not widely known, however, that as early

[6]Michael P. Conzen, "The Maturing Urban System in the United States, 1840–1910," *Annals of the Association of American Geographers* 67 (1977), pp. 88–108; and John R. Borchert, "Major Control Points in American Economic Geography," *Annals of the Association of American Geographers* 68 (1978), pp. 214–232.

as 1974 Tokyo supplanted New York as the world's leading banking center, at least based on assets held by major banks (Table 4.5; Figure 4.7). New York was nevertheless a close second. London was third, followed closely by Paris and Frankfurt, with San Francisco in sixth place. Of the top 20 metropolitan areas in banking assets, only Tokyo and Osaka were not in Europe or North America. The breakdown was 12 in Europe, six in North America, and two in Japan.

From 1974 to 1980, only relatively minor changes occurred in the banking world (Table 4.6). Indeed, Tokyo more firmly established its first-place rank with $145 billion more in assets than second-ranked Paris banks. Osaka moved ahead of San Francisco.

Table 4.5 The 20 Leading Metropolitan Areas in Bank Assets, 1974

Metropolitan Areas	Assets[a]
1. Tokyo	239.0
2. New York	209.3
3. London	146.9
4. Paris	133.9
5. Frankfurt	112.2
6. San Francisco	83.6
7. Osaka	74.4
8. Milan	59.9
9. Rome	50.8
10. Chicago	46.1
11. Düsseldorf	45.1
12. Montreal	44.6
13. Munich	43.1
14. Los Angeles	37.0
15. Amsterdam	36.6
16. Brussels	35.2
17. Zurich	34.0
18. Toronto	30.1
19. Madrid	27.8
20. Stockholm	26.7

[a]In $ billions.

Source: Compiled by author from *The Banker*, June 1975, pp. 681–723.

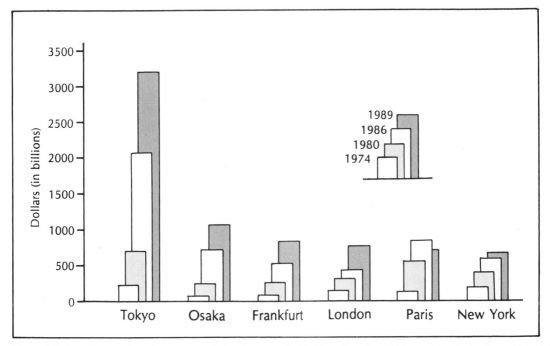

Figure 4.7 Leading world urban centers in bank assets, 1989. Based on the 500 largest banks in the world, including all centers with assets greater than $50 million.
Source: The Banker.

During the 1980s, major changes occurred in world financial circles. The most notable change was the rise of Japanese banking. Assets held by Tokyo banks were comparable to the total assets of banks in Paris, Osaka, and New York combined, or approximately $2.1 trillion (Table 4.7). Osaka moved into third place in bank assets, and Nagoya became fifteenth in the world, while San Francisco was now thirteenth, just ahead of number fourteen, Montreal.

By the end of the 1980s, Tokyo and Osaka were the two leading banking centers of the world, with assets matching those of cities ranked from third through tenth (Table 4.8). Only three North American urban centers were in the top 20—New York, Toronto, and Montreal. San Francisco and Los Angeles had dropped out.

Global Banking Summary

Table 4.9 summarizes bank assets by major world regions from 1974 to 1989. Whereas Europe has seen its bank assets drop from just over 44 percent of the world total in 1974 to just under 40 percent in 1989, the United States and Canada have suffered much greater relative declines. U.S. and Canadian banks held 31 percent of the world banking assets in 1974; they hold less than 15 percent today. Meanwhile, Japan, as well as other Asian countries, have experienced massive increases, from 20 percent of the world total in 1974 to over 40 percent in 1989. In 1980, the world's two largest banks were Citicorp out of New York and Bankamerica out of San Francisco. By 1990, Citicorp had dropped to the eighteenth largest bank in the world, the only U.S. bank in the top 20. In contrast, Japan was head-

Table 4.6 The 20 Leading Metropolitan Areas in Bank Assets, 1980	
Metropolitan Areas	**Assets**[a]
1. Tokyo	718.9
2. Paris	576.2
3. New York	412.3
4. London	326.5
5. Frankfurt	271.8
6. Osaka	249.0
7. San Francisco	147.8
8. Brussels	142.6
9. Munich	137.2
10. Amsterdam	132.0
11. Rome	119.7
12. Düsseldorf	116.7
13. Montreal	102.1
14. Milan	97.8
15. Zurich	90.7
16. Madrid	87.3
17. Chicago	80.4
18. Toronto	70.2
19. Los Angeles	58.7
20. Stockholm	58.6

[a]In $ billions.

Source: Compiled by author from *The Banker*, June 1981, pp. 153–201.

Table 4.7 The 20 Leading Metropolitan Areas in Bank Assets, 1986	
Metropolitan Areas	**Assets**[a]
1. Tokyo	2,123.1
2. Paris	852.5
3. Osaka	722.1
4. New York	617.8
5. Frankfurt	529.9
6. London	467.8
7. Brussels	206.0
8. Rome	195.9
9. Munich	190.0
10. Amsterdam	186.8
11. Zurich	185.0
12. Milan	183.5
13. San Francisco	146.5
14. Montreal	146.0
15. Nagoya	138.5
16. Toronto	132.1
17. Los Angeles	116.5
18. Madrid	114.7
19. Stockholm	110.7
20. Düsseldorf	98.7

[a]In $ billions.

Source: Compiled by author from *The Banker*, July 1987, pp. 113–151.

quarters to 11 of the largest 20 banks, including the six largest banks in the world.

Japanese banking rose during the 1980s primarily because of the booming Japanese economy and the rise of the yen at the expense of the U.S. dollar. In early 1985, the United States became a debtor nation for the first time in decades, joining such Third World countries as Brazil and Mexico. Japan is now the world's largest creditor nation, and during the 1980s it moved aggressively into the U.S. market. For example, the Japanese control approximately one-quarter of California's banking assets. Four of the ten largest California banks are Japanese owned, though two retain their U.S. names. As quoted from perhaps the leading banking journal: "The Japanese moved into California initially to serve trade links and the local Japanese community. But they have grown through acquisition and are now in many cases large state-wide retail banks serving mostly non-Japanese clients."[7]

Interdependent Stock Markets

The many stock markets around the world have become increasingly interlocked. A financial crisis in one market, such as the New York crash of 1987, is almost instantly felt worldwide. In this era of telecommunications, buying and selling takes place with great rapidity, as trading follows the sun around the earth. The Tokyo stock exchange opens for trading, followed a few hours

[7]*The Banker*, July 1990, p. 85.

Table 4.8 The 20 Leading Metropolitan Areas in Bank Assets, 1989

Metropolitan Areas	Assets[a]
1. Tokyo	3,269.2
2. Osaka	1,074.4
3. Frankfurt	807.3
4. London	787.3
5. Paris	720.1
6. New York	694.4
7. Brussels	325.9
8. Rome	307.2
9. Milan	291.8
10. Munich	291.0
11. Zurick	241.5
12. Nagoya	240.1
13. Stockholm	218.5
14. Seoul	213.0
15. Toronto	204.1
16. Kobe	202.4
17. Amsterdam	198.1
18. Tehran	185.6
19. Madrid	185.5
20. Montreal	180.4

Source: Compiled by the author from *The Banker*, July 1990, pp. 100–153.

Table 4.9 Percentage Change in Bank Assets by World Regions, 1974–89

World Regions	1974[a]	1986[b]	1989[b]
Canada	4.06	2.30	2.28
United States	26.90	15.81	12.17
Middle East	1.04	3.04	2.51
Japan	19.50	31.60	35.00
Other Asia	0.91	4.13	5.52
European	44.26	40.22	39.39
Latin America	1.89	1.52	1.18
Africa	0.18	0.30	0.35
Australia	1.26	1.08	1.60
Total	100.0	100.0	100.0

[a]Based on 300 largest banks.
[b]Based on 500 largest banks.

Source: Computed by author from *The Banker*, June 1975, p. 676; July 1987, pp. 81–109; and July 1990, pp. 100–153.

later by the London stock exchange, followed a few hours later by the New York stock exchange. Good or bad financial news follows this sweep of the sun, including industry rumors, anticipated acquisitions, political uncertainties, as well as scandals. Some experts suggest it is only a matter of time until 24-hour worldwide trading will take place.

Not only are we talking about the huge stock exchanges in New York, London, and Tokyo, as well as elsewhere in the developed world, but we are also noting the numerous smaller exchanges in developing countries. Stock exchanges operate in countries such as Brazil, Chile, Greece, Jordan, India, Mexico, and Thailand—to name only a few—often with very different rules and procedures. In some stock exchanges, for example, insider trading is not considered illegal, though it is generally discouraged. However, as

the financial ties around the world grow ever stronger, it is becoming increasingly necessary to establish a global system for financial regulation and to bring together the forces of nation-states, multinational corporations, and culture.

Foreign Direct Investment

Foreign direct investment refers to investment by a foreign-owned company in a particular domestic market. Through this process multinations spread their worldwide wings. The U.S. Department of Commerce, which compiles data on foreign investments in the United States, considers any foreign investment of 10 percent or more to be a foreign direct investment. The magnitude and nature of foreign direct investment has indeed changed considerably since the end of World War II.

As already indicated, after World War II the United States was seen as posing a possible danger to the European economies. Although the U.S. government-sponsored Marshall Plan was a welcome success, foreign direct investment by the United States was at first viewed as uncertain

An aerial view of Rio de Janeiro, perched on the Atlantic Ocean on the Bay of Guanabara, with Sugarloaf Mountain in Center background.

in its effects. Such investment, in fact, was a great boon to the rebirth of the Western European economies. It was not long thereafter until foreign investments by European firms in the United States became commonplace. Large investment ties have long been a commonplace and perhaps a source of controversy for Canada and the United States.

Only in the 1980s did Japanese foreign investment spread worldwide. During the period 1986–88, Japan became the single largest investor in the United Sates, ahead of the United Kingdom and Canada, which along with other Western European countries had been the leading investors in previous years. During the 1980s, the United States was the leading country in attracting foreign investment.

The new global economy, with its reliance on telecommunications, enables multinationals to operate geographically in a way that was impossible only a few years ago. Most corporations maintain centralized management functions and research and development activities (Figure 4.8). In contrast, their production tends to be decentralized, especially routine production. Although they serve a global market and thus operate on

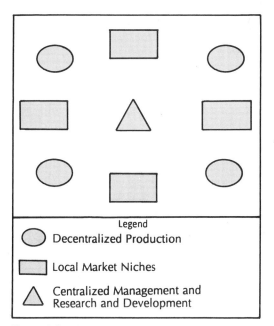

Figure 4.8 The spatial organization of a multinational firm.

a gigantic scale, sales are directed to local market segments in which local experts act in a decentralized way with overall coordination from the central headquarters, because they know the local culture.

What are the advantages of foreign direct investment? In a nutshell, it enables a country to remain globally competitive. This competition involves minimizing uncertainty and risk by spreading investment more widely, gaining access to a particular labor force, either high skilled or low skilled, depending on strategy, and taking advantage of scale economies by penetrating large markets. Foreign investment is attracted to areas that are perceived as politically stable, such as the United States rather than, for example, Israel. Foreign firms may seek out investment in order to gain access to technology and expertise that is not otherwise available. But probably the single most important reason for foreign investment in the United States is to serve the large American market.

Much of the foreign direct investment in the United States during the 1970s was in manufacturing. Initial investment was largely in New York and other large port cities, in contrast with the overall spatial pattern of manufacturing in the country in the traditional manufacturing belt and selected centers in the West and South. More recent investment in the United States has been in the service sector, including banking and other financial services and real estate. As more joint venture operations are carried out, the notion of foreign investment begins to blur, and we realize that we now inevitably live in an interdependent global economy.

GLOBAL COMMUNICATIONS AND WORLD CITIES

A handful of huge capitalist cities in North America, Europe, and Japan exert an enormous influence on the world economy. These centers function as control points, with administrative and decision-making authority, and they send out economic impulses to a much larger set of subordinate centers. Some of these centers are extremely large cities, such as Mexico City, but most of the subordinate ones are small in population size.

Seventeen world cities have populations of over 10 million people (Table 4.10). The Tokyo–Yokohama metropolitan region has a population of about 27 million people, making it the world's largest, ahead of Mexico City's 25 million people. New York ranks fifth in the world with approximately 15 million people. Osaka–Kobe–Kyoto, Japan, ranks sixth at 14 million. Of the ten largest cities in the world, seven are in developing areas and growing at a rapid pace. Despite the size of these cities, they do not function as true economic control points in the world economy but rather as centers of regional or national importance. Thus, many intermediate-size centers are of far greater importance in the world economic order: London, Los Angeles, Paris,

Table 4.10 Estimated Population Size of World's Largest Cities, 1992

City	Population Size
Tokyo–Yokohama, Japan	27,000,000
Mexico City, Mexico	25,000,000
São Paulo, Brazil	22,000,000
Seoul, South Korea	19,000,000
New York, United States	15,000,000
Osaka–Kobe–Kyoto, Japan	14,000,000
Bombay, India	14,000,000
Calcutta, India	13,000,000
Buenos Aires, Argentina	13,000,000
Rio de Janeiro, Brazil	13,000,000

Source: Information Please Almanac, 1992.

Rome, Toronto, Chicago, Sydney, and Hong Kong.

SUMMARY

The economic history of human activities has gradually moved away from an almost total focus on the local to an increasingly greater concern with international ties. Nevertheless, local, regional, and national ties remain strong, especially for those in developing economies. It is at the very highest levels of the corporate system that we see the multinational, multilocational focus. Here global economic strategy may, in fact, be in conflict with regional or even national interests. Globally organized financial interests seek out international rather than regional or national economic advantages. The economy of the world, which was so long organized around national political boundaries, is now in conflict with giant multinational firms that may have more financial clout than many of the countries in which they operate.

Further Readings

Castells, Manuel. *The Informational City: Information Technology, Economic Restructuring, and the Urban-Regional Process.* Oxford: Basil Blackwell, 1989.

Chase-Dunn, Christopher. *Global Formation: Structures of the World-Economy.* Oxford: Basil Blackwell, 1989.

Juttner, Johannes D. *International Finance and Global Financial Markets.* Melbourne, Australia: Cheshire Pty Limited, 1989.

Lamont, Douglas. *Winning Worldwide: Strategies for Dominating Global Markets.* Homewood, Ill.: Business One Irwin, 1991.

Marton, Katherin. *Multinationals, Technology, and Industrialization.* Lexington, Mass.: Lexington Books, 1986.

Mueller, Dennis C. *The Modern Corporation.* Brighton: Harvester Press, 1986.

Peet, Richard. *Global Capitalism: Theories of Societal Development.* New York: Routledge, 1991.

Pounds, Norman J. G. *Hearth and Home: A History of Material Culture.* Bloomington: Indiana University Press, 1989.

Roscow, Jerome M., ed. *The Global Marketplace.* New York: Facts on File, 1988.

Rubner, Alex. *The Might of the Multinationals: The Rise and Fall of the Corporate Legend.* Westport, Conn.: Praeger, 1990.

Shachar, Arie, and Sture Oberg, eds. *The World Economy and the Spatial Organization of Power.* Aldershot: Avebury, 1990.

Sheppard, Eric, and Trevor J. Barnes. *The Capitalist Space Economy.* Boston: Unwin Hyman, 1990.

Sijben, Jac. J., ed. *Financing the World Economy in the Nineties.* Boston: Kluwer Academic Publishers, 1989.

Sklair, Leslie. *Sociology of the Global System.* New York: Harvester-Wheatsheaf, 1991.

Taylor, Michael, and Nigel Thrift, ed. *The Geography of Multinationals.* London, Croom Held, 1982.

Webster, Allan, and John H. Dunning, eds. *Structural Changes in the World Economy.* New York: Routledge, 1990.

PART TWO

How Places Interact, Locally and Globally

CHAPTER 5

Principles of Spatial Interaction

—◇—

Injurious distance should not stop my way;
For nimble thought can jump both sea and land.
—WILLIAM SHAKESPEARE

INTRODUCTION

The economic geographer seeks to understand the interdependence between the transportation geography of an area and the economic activities located there. This understanding is normally most satisfying when it is explained in the context of interaction principles and theory.

Movement of goods and people is essential to any economic system whether primitive or highly developed. Primitive economies are involved in small-scale, local transfers of goods: fish from stream to table or grain from nearby field to village. Modern industrial economies engage in large-scale, international movement of commodities of many types. Normally, the more economically advanced a country is, the wider the geographic range of its industrial inputs, the more extensive its transportation ties, and the more completely developed its transportation system. Developed countries are highly dependent on distant sources to maintain economic productivity, and the international movement of goods has become widespread and spatially complex. For this reason, transportation is also essential to world economic and political power.

Transportation refers to the movement of commodities, people, and ideas from one place to another. Although the transfer of ideas and information is sometimes reserved for the word *communications*, certain common principles operate in the transfer of commodities, people, and ideas. Our immediate concern is with the geographic aspects of transportation, but most of the principles enunciated here also apply to the movement of ideas. These **spatial interaction** principles involve the nature and function of connections among places on the earth. These connections may be viewed on the one hand simply as the geographic layout of **routes**, such as seen on a map of airline routes or on a street map of a city. On the other hand, the connections may also be represented by information on the volume of movement, or **flow**, among places, such as the number of tons of coal or the number of telephone calls moving among different locations. The point is that places—or rather, people and activities at those locations—interact over space with one another. An examination of the economic components of spatial interaction reveals several common elements or principles that repeat themselves in one case after another. Knowledge of these principles of spatial inter-

---

76

action is important and may have practical applications to business and industry.

Transportation is necessary because not all economic activity occurs at one point; if it somehow did, there would, of course, be no need for transportation. The fact that activity is dispersed over a region, be that region a metropolis, a subnational area, a country, or even the entire world, means that some type of connection or spatial interaction will exist. The geographic pattern of this spatial interaction may take many forms. The basic question, then, is, which places are connected with which others, to what level of intensity, and why?

Coal exists in the ground in West Virginia; it is needed, for example, in Pittsburgh. Because of supply and demand, coal is transported between these two points. It is not always this simple, however. Movement always involves a cost. Someone must need a commodity enough that he or she is willing to pay for it plus its transport. If the item being moved is considered valuable, especially with reference to its weight, it is said to bear more easily a high transport cost because the transport cost, though high, constitutes a small percentage of the total cost of the item.

Alternative sources of supply necessitate decisions about which source is "best," in costs, convenience, or speed of delivery. Many considerations, of which cost is but one, enter into the complexity of decisions that result in patterns of spatial interaction.

THE INTERACTION MATRIX

Figures 5.1*a* and *b* illustrate, in abstract form, some hypothetical patterns of spatial interaction by use of the *interaction matrix* and its geographic counterpart, the map. The map actually contains more information in that precise locations for each point, A through E, are shown. The map demonstrates direct connections between points (representing cities, factories, or households, for example) by lines. The interaction matrix shows the same direct connections by the inclusion of the number 1 (unity) in the respective cell, with zeros depicting a lack of direct connection. Both the rows and columns of the matrix refer to the points or nodes. No distinction is made between origins and destinations; consequently, the matrix is symmetrical (the

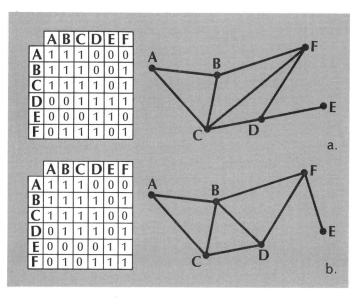

a.

b.

Figure 5.1 The concept of connectivity is illustrated first by the table at the upper left showing whether a direct connection exists between locations A to F. Second, at the upper right a mapped version of the table is given. Another example is shown in the lower portion of the figure. Thus, connectivity may be seen in either map or table form.

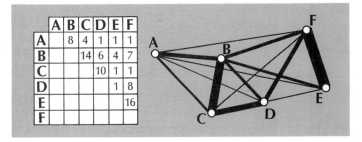

	A	B	C	D	E	F
A		8	4	1	1	1
B			14	6	4	7
C				10	1	1
D					1	8
E						16
F						

Figure 5.2 Similar to Figure 5.1, here we illustrate flows in networks, that is, volume or frequency of movement, by magnitude of movement in the table on the left and by variable-width flow lines on the map on the right, with the wider lines representing the greater movement volumes.

same elements above and below the diagonal). Unities are in the diagonal, as each place is considered to be connected with itself. In Figure 5.1*a* the simple network configuration is placed in matrix form. By summing the columns, one can see that node C has the largest number of direct connections in the network. Figure 5.1*b* shows a somewhat different network configuration; here, node B has the largest number of direct links. The basic questions that spatial interaction principles seek to answer are, What is the geographic structure of the network, and Why does it have its particular configuration? The type of interaction matrix depicted in Figures 5.1*a* and *b* is described as a **connectivity matrix,** and it is appropriate when considering direct links on a network.

A second type of interaction matrix is the **flow matrix,** which contains data on the volume of movement among places: tons of coal, bushels of wheat, number of trucks. Figure 5.2 gives an example of the flow matrix as well as a flow map, on which the volume of flow is indicated by the width of the lines. The question that arises when an economic geographer examines such data is, Why does this pattern exist on the economic landscape? The question of the flow pattern, in fact, has three parts: (1) What is the volume originated at each node (sum of a row or origin)? (2) What is the volume terminated at each destination (sum of a column)? (3) What is the allocation of flow volume from origins to destinations (the individual cell totals in the matrix)? These questions have to do with describing the geographic pattern or configuration on the landscape. The counterpart to each of these three

questions is, Why do these three patterns exist? The answers lie in the characteristics of the economic system.

THE BASES FOR SPATIAL INTERACTION

The geographer Edward L. Ullman was the first to organize (mid-1950s) the concept of spatial interaction around general principles.[1] He recognized three bases for interaction over the earth's surface, and we will emphasize these three: **complementarity, transferability,** and **intervening opportunity.** The first concept, borrowed from the Swedish economist Bertil Ohlin, holds that areas are complementary to one another when the first area has a surplus of an item demanded by the second area.[2] The mere existence of a resource in an area, for example, is not a sufficient condition for trade to occur; that resource must be needed elsewhere. The rich petroleum of the Middle East lay untapped for millennia until demand arose following particular technological developments. Complementarity arises from regional variation in human and natural resources. Japan's rapid economic growth, as an example, has been largely related to human rather than to material resources. Finally, complementarity may arise from regional variation in size of enterprise, in which economies of scale affect the pattern of flow. Figure 5.3, for example, demonstrates that a region may be served in two

[1]Edward L. Ullman, *American Commodity Flow* (Seattle: University of Washington Press, 1957).
[2]Bertil Ohlin, *Interregional and International Trade* (Cambridge, Mass.: Harvard University Press, 1933).

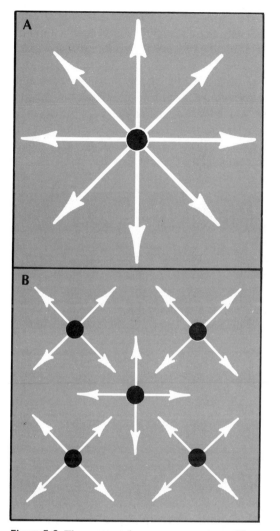

Figure 5.3 Flows may take on many patterns. Here are two quite different examples, with the illustration above (*a*) showing flows from one node or center serving the entire region and below (*b*) from several nodes combining to serve a region of the same size.

ways. For region *A*, one large origin point (a mine, a factory, or a shopping mall) serves the entire region, reflecting one pattern of flow. In region *B*, several smaller origin points combine to serve the same total area, but with a quite different flow–configuration.

Another way of looking at complementarity is through the concept of ***place utility.*** A mineral

resource has a certain value or utility as a result of its being mined and smelted. The activity of mining and smelting gives the resource what is called ***form utility,*** which increases its usefulness. Similarly, the act of transporting the resource to a point of demand gives it place utility, or greater value. Without transportation the resource has only very local and limited utility; the availability of the resource as a result of its movement adds the place utility. The demand for movement, at least in the economic sense, is not for the pleasure of the movement itself, but arises out of demand for getting something from one place to another—that is, demand for the product. Transportation is a means of overcoming the barrier of distance. It is an attempt to bring separate locations of economic activity closer together. Transportation adds utility to economic goods by placing them at locations where they are demanded, or "consumed."

The second of Ullman's concepts, transferability, refers to the ease with which an item may be transferred between two places. The basic impediment to the transferability of an economic good is the distance between two points, manifested in time and cost of movement. Although complementarity may exist between two points, transferability problems may be so great that no interaction will take place. In general, it is recognized that for nearly all kinds of movement, the interaction between places is inversely dependent on the distance between the places. Thus, places located near to each other will tend to have a high degree of interaction, and places remote from each other will likely have little interaction. Although shipping time and cost are the major constraints, political barriers may reduce or eliminate trade. The quality of the transport route, the degree of congestion, the ruggedness of the terrain, and the level of technology are other factors that may retard interaction. Places are not equally linked with one another for a number of fairly obvious reasons.

The operation of the transferability principle on the economic landscape leads, in a wide variety of circumstances, to the observed phenom-

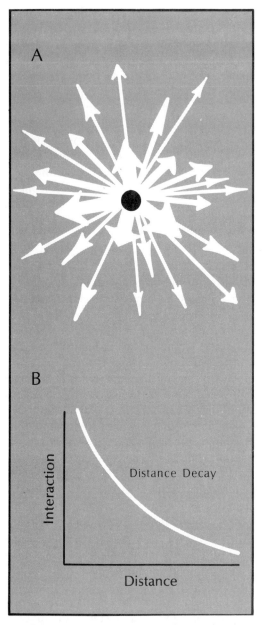

Figure 5.4 One of the most fundamental concepts of spatial interaction is distance decay, that is, the tendency for trips or flows to decline (decay) with increasing distance between the origin and destination.

enon of ***distance decay,*** or the decrease in interaction with increasing distance. Take the number of telephone calls made from a particular apartment complex over a period of time. When these calls are mapped by the distance between caller and receiver, a distance decay function will be observed (Figure 5.4*a*). The greater the distance, the fewer the calls. Distance decay rates may be represented, in more generalized form, on a two-dimensional diagram in which the intensity of the interaction increases on the vertical axis and distance increases on the other axis (Figure 5.4*b*). The line depicting distance decay shows a high degree of interaction at short distances and a gradual tapering off as the spread between "origin" and "destination" enlarges.

Interaction drops off until at some point it is no longer economically significant, though it may still exist. If we draw a line on the map to include the area comprising, say, 95 percent of the interaction, we have delimited a nodal region (see Chapter 1). The particular kind of nodal region is the *umland* (from the German, "land around"). This term is used with reference to the economic area served by a town or city (Figure 5.5). The *umland* of a town or city is then based

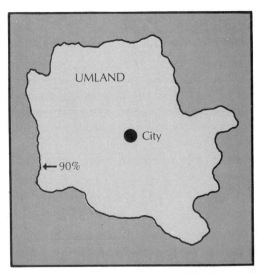

Figure 5.5 The city and its *umland* (land around).

Commuting Field Change:

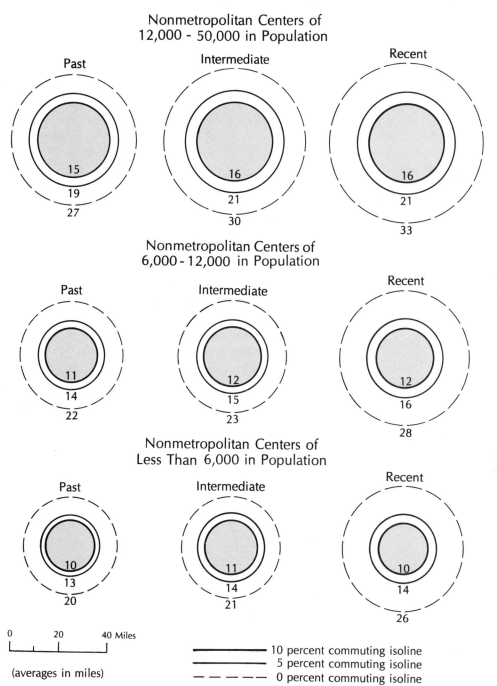

Nonmetropolitan Centers of 12,000 - 50,000 in Population

Past
15
19
27

Intermediate
16
21
30

Recent
16
21
33

Nonmetropolitan Centers of 6,000 - 12,000 in Population

Past
11
14
22

Intermediate
12
15
23

Recent
12
16
28

Nonmetropolitan Centers of Less Than 6,000 in Population

Past
10
13
20

Intermediate
11
14
21

Recent
10
14
26

0   20   40 Miles

(averages in miles)

———————— 10 percent commuting isoline
———————— 5 percent commuting isoline
– – – – – 0 percent commuting isoline

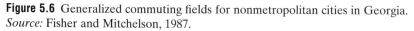

Figure 5.6 Generalized commuting fields for nonmetropolitan cities in Georgia.
Source: Fisher and Mitchelson, 1987.

on the distance at which the movement of people and goods to and from that center drops below the threshold of economic significance, here judged to be 95 percent of all movement. The principle of transferability and its manifestation, distance decay, operate as a basic constraint on the economic system.

As an example of distance decay, Figure 5.6 shows commuting fields for major metropolitan areas in Georgia. These commuting fields have expanded over time, as distance decay has become slightly less important with improvements in highways and automobiles. Large metropolitan areas also have larger commuting fields than smaller centers. Commuting by air, which has been on the increase, may considerably extend the land-based journey to work and, up to a point, defy the distance-decay concept.

The last of Ullman's interaction concepts is intervening opportunity, noted previously by Samuel A. Stouffer in the context of migration theory. Stouffer found[3]

> *no necessary relationship between distance and mobility, but the number of persons going a given distance is directly proportional to the number of opportunities at that distance and inversely proportional to the number of intervening opportunities between origin and destination.*

For example, in Figure 5.7a the degree of interaction for an economic good between nodes X and Y is based, let us suppose, simply on their complementarity and the transferability of that good. However, in a 5.7b, an intervening opportunity, node Z, is introduced. Node Z intervenes locationally between nodes X and Y and in effect restricts the volume of flow from X, since Z is located closer to Y. It has been suggested, for example, that the migration of blacks from the U.S. South to Boston is less than "expected"

[3]Samuel A. Stouffer, "Intervening Opportunities: A Theory Relating Mobility and Distances," *American Sociological Review* 5 (1940), pp. 845–867.

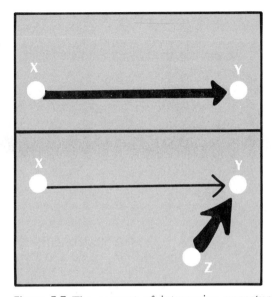

Figure 5.7 The concept of intervening opportunity holds that the "expected" distance decay (*a*) between two locations may be modified by a third location that (*b*) intervenes between the first two, as with location Z above.

from the size of the city and the distance from the South because of the several large metropolitan areas lying just to the south of Boston and acting as intervening oportunities to absorb the migrants (New York, Philadelphia, Baltimore, and Washington, D.C.). All three of these concepts—complementarity, transferability, and intervening opportunity—act simultaneously to determine spatial interaction.

Whereas Ullman's three bases for spatial interaction have been widely accepted and employed to study human migration and commodity movement, recent research by Wheeler and Mitchelson suggests that these concepts are less useful to the study of modern information exchange. They propose a threefold basis for information flows: (1) *information genesis*, (2) *hierarchy of control*, and (3) *distance independence*. Information genesis argues that, unlike complementarity which is a supply and demand concept, information flows are based primarily on supply

Traveling in the Global Economy

In the year 2005, if plans for building Concorde II go as some expect, it will be possible to board this second-generation aircraft in New York and arrive in Toyko in just over six hours, almost enough time to get a good night's sleep. Flying at Mach 2.4 (2.4 times the speed of sound, or approximately 1850 miles per hour) and having a range of over 7000 miles, Concorde II could easily span the vast Pacific Ocean, giving new meaning for the United States to the term *Pacific Rim countries*. A current New York to Toyko flight by commercial aircraft takes at least 14 jet-lagged hours, about the same number of hours it now takes to fly from Paris to Toyko, and a typically large jet flies at about 550 miles per hour.

Only 16 Concordes have been built, produced and flown by Air France and British Airways. Beginning service in 1976, the Concorde has daily flights between Europe and New York. The aircraft makes the North Atlantic puddle jump in just over three hours, compared to about eight hours for regular commercial jets.

Concorde II opens up another intriguing possibility. Cities in Western Europe would also be approximately six hours from Japan, giving yet more meaning to the term *Pacific Rim countries* and lending a different perspective to the "global economy." At the same time, Concorde II could return Europe to the center of the world economy, enabling it to compete effectively with the United States and Canada for Pacific world business and having ever closer puddle ties with the traditional trading partners of the North Atlantic.

A sizable proportion of the U.S. population lives within a two-hour flight from New York—indeed, from a large number of eastern U.S. cities. Such quick flights make it possible for a businessperson to fly out of New York, conduct a day's business, and fly home the same day. The Concorde II may extend this range to a day's flight to Europe and back. (As my grandfather used to say, upon returning from a three-mile trip via horse and buggy into town, "Well, we made it back home in the same day.")

rather than demand.[4] That is, in many cases information is sent out from a source of supply that is not demanded at the destination but is merely received. This situation is particularly true of large corporate headquarters that act as control points for U.S. and Canadian and, indeed, the global economy. The genesis or origin of information controls where the information is being

sent and the nature of that information, independent of any demand at the destination.

The concept of hierarchy of control suggests that information flows are largely conditioned by the size of the sending and receiving metropolitan area. The notion of a hierarchy may be likened to stairsteps, with city size ranging from the top step (largest size) successively down to the lowest step (floor). The hierarchy of control concept says that the largest center—say New York—will be the leading sender of information within the hierarchy of all centers such as Los Angeles and Chicago. While New York in our

[4]James O. Wheeler and Ronald L. Mitchelson, "Information Flows Among Major U.S. Metropolitan Areas," *Annals of the Association of American Geographers*, Vol. 79, 1989, pp. 523–543.

example would dominate the United States and Canada, other large centers such as Los Angeles, Chicago, and Toronto would dominate extensive surrounding regions as leading senders of information. Merely a few of the largest centers would comprise the great majority of total information to the largest centers but the smaller centers exchange little information among themselves. The largest centers are dominant because they contain corporations, institutions, and agencies generating the greatest volume of highly specialized, technical, expert, and perishable information.

The third concept, distance independence, argues that, unlike migration and commodity flows, distance will play a relatively minor role in the flow of information over space. Indeed, the two leading flows of information in the United States and Canada are between New York and Los Angeles and Los Angeles and New York. At the top of the hierarchy, distance plays an almost insignificant role. It is only the smallest centers that show distance sensitivity, focusing largely on regional and local centers.

Thus, the flow of information seems to operate on quite different principles from those explaining migration and commodity movements. As the North American and global economics become more dependent on communications in our day-to-day affairs, a changing economic geography is rapidly emerging. In the United States and Canada, for example, we have seen a shift from manufacturing to services. Manufacturing, which pulled migration from areas of low economic opportunity, such as whites from Appalachia or blacks from the rural low-land South to industrial plants in the North, as well as complex patterns of commodity flows, followed Ullman's bases for spatial interaction. Then, manufacturing took place at strategic locations for the movement of goods from material sites and to market areas. A concentrated industrial region was established in the Northeastern United States and along the Windsor–Montreal corridor in Canada. But with growing reliance on services and the communications technology they required, a different set of variables came into play. Advantageous locations were now large centers, many of which were in the fast-growth South and West and away from the older industrial centers. Thus, the greater reliance on information flows rather then on the movement of products has led to a new economic system, both locally and globally.

TRANSPORTATION NETWORKS

Transportation routes and their resulting networks are laid out primarily to serve economic needs, though occasional examples of routes developed for military, political, or religious reasons may be noted in various areas around the world. The geographic distribution of the transportation networks constitutes a pattern of spatial interaction as it reflects the unequal level of connections among places. On the one hand, we have said that the economic system functions as a result of the transportation system of routes; at the same time, the transportation networks function as the result of economic activity. The two-way cause and effect between the economic system and the transportation system stems from the considerable overlap between the two systems. They are interdependent. In examining transportation networks as they relate to economic activity, we will start with the principles of route location and network evolution and then turn to a discussion of network structure.

Route and Network Location

A route is a single link between two points, whereas a network comprises two or more routes. In the decision to locate transportation facilities, a single route is usually selected rather than the entire network at once. In the historical context especially, networks evolved by the addition of new routes or links. Route location typically has involved local decision making; network planning for a large region necessarily implies a central decision-making process, but

An interstate exchange, a large consumer of land.

even here the specific route-location decision is often made locally within the confines of the overall network layout.

With a change in economic activity, there is enhanced potential for increased population within the area influenced by the route. People are attracted to the area through migration. This migration and the ensuing population change generate the need for further economic development and change to serve the expanded population (see the discussion of circular and cumulative causation on pp. 000–000). Expanded economic productivity creates a greater demand for transportation as more commodities require movement into and out of the area. Similarly, the population growth itself necessitates greater demand for personal mobility. The conclusion we are forced to recognize from this discussion is that the development or expansion of a transport link in a network leads, over a period of time, to a growth in the demand for a new or improved transport link. This is *induced demand* (see p. 101), and it results from a superior route's being added or expanded, attendant congestion on the route as its advantages become recognized, and the further need for route improvement.

Will such a new link be established? This decision will be influenced by positive, negative, and uncertainty features. The principal positive impetus to network growth is simply the increase in transport demand. Recognition of the advantages of interaction between points is normally a strong influence on the decision to construct or improve a route. Will the route be economically profitable to the user? Will substantial advantages accrue to the affected area? If the answer to these questions is clearly yes, the network normally will be expanded. Negative effects on the decision involve the role of barriers, be they economic, physical, political, cultural, or social or varying combinations of these. The cost of construction may be too high at a given level of technology: There are no railroads crossing the Atlantic Ocean to connect New York with London; in like manner, no railroad reaches across the Himalayas. In other words, the positive forces must outweigh the negative.

A separate influence on the route–location decision is the level of uncertainty associated with the consequences of the decision. If the economic advantages of a particular decision are 90 percent certain but calamitous political or military consequences are at the same time 50 percent certain, it is too risky, most of us would agree, to decide to begin construction. By the very nature of uncertainty, however, no precise percentages can be attached to a future outcome. And yet, subjective judgments must be made. In sum, when economic advantages are realized by route extension, when the cost of overcoming barrier effects is not too great, and when uncertainty of the consequences is low, it is likely that a decision will be reached to expand the network.

Network expansion has a reciprocal relationship with political-military decisions. Expansion of a transport network may be wholly or partly for military-strategic reasons. On the other hand, the existence of a network across political boundaries may lead to either an intensification or a resolution of latent hostilities, as the network enhances the opportunity for contact but does not control the nature of the political interaction.

An excellent example of how political boundaries affect transportation development is shown

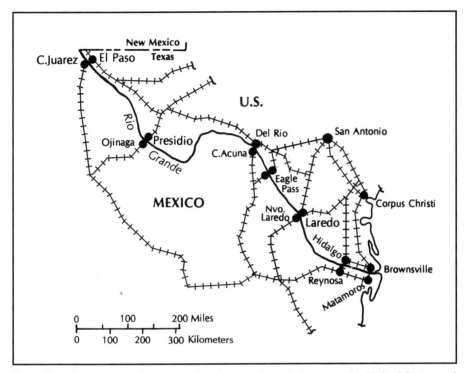

Figure 5.8 The Rio Grande acts as a barrier to rail traffic between the United States and Mexico.

in Figure 5.8. The U.S. and Mexican border along the Rio Grande River exerts a powerful barrier to rail links between the two countries, as does the U.S.-Canadian border even in the case of the 49th parallel from Vancouver to southeast of Winnepeg where there is no river boundary.

In summary, these are the essential inputs to the process of network growth, along with the connecting chain of impacts. The specific way in which a network changes will depend on the particular characteristics and areal arrangements of demographic, economic, and social conditions. An understanding of these characteristics and how they interrelate in terms of the process of network growth leads to an explanation of the spatial arrangement of the network and how that configuration changes over time. In order to illustrate, in normative fashion, how network con-

figuration changes over time with economic growth, we now turn to a discussion of Taaffe's classic four-stage sequence of transport development.

Taaffe's Network Model. Based primarily on observations of network change in West Africa, Edward Taaffe, Richard Morrill, and Peter Gould presented an ideal-typical sequence of transportation develment that applies, at various levels of generalization, to many areas around the world (Figure 5.9)[5] Theirs is a descriptive model, highly generalized and, therefore, imprecise

[5]Edward J. Taaffe, Richard L. Morrill, and Peter R. Gould, "Transport Expansion in Underdeveloped Countries: A Comparative Analysis," *Geographical Review* 53 (1963), pp. 503–529.

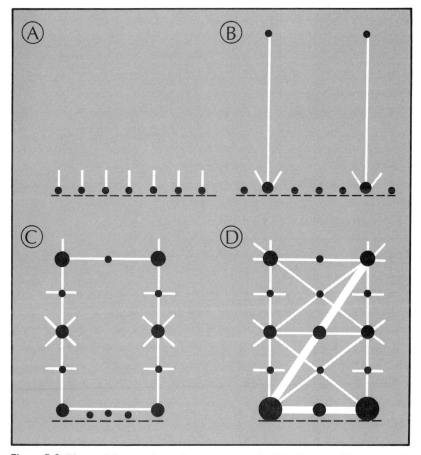

Figure 5.9 The well-known four-phase sequence by Taaffe, Morrill, and Gould of transport development, showing the ideal-typical spatial changes in the network. Note the relationships between size of centers and the importance of the routes. (Courtesy of the American Geographical Society.)

when it comes to detailed application to any particular area. The model applies especially well to "colonial" situations as it assumes that development occurs first along a coast and later spreads into the interior. In the colonial experience, the stimulus for growth comes from outside the region, transforming in a series of stages the form and function of the transportation network. In the example of the United States, however, the Taaffe model also describes the spatial development of transport expansion, even though the

stimulus for the westward expansion from the Northeast coastal area was agricultural production in the interior and markets in the Northeast. The Taaffe model is ideal-typical in the sense that it describes the typical sequence of network change in an idealized fashion. The model recognizes that in many parts of the world the development of transport networks has evolved through a somewhat similar set of stages, spurred by a roughly similar series of processes.

The first phase is that of *local ports* lacking

lateral connection by land and each having areally restricted transport ties with the interior. The area served by the ports, for both imports and exports, is referred to as the **port hinterland** in this work. At this stage, little actually moves in or out of the ports, the lack of transport routes to the interior severely limiting the extent of the hinterlands. Some lateral movement between ports may occur by sea, but again this will be restricted to local trade. Each port settlement is approximately of equal size, for all lack strong ties to the interior. If agriculture is the principal economic activity, as is typical of developing regions, each port will serve a hinterland of about the same size and level of productivity. A high degree of economic self-sufficiency will predominate.

Phase Two occurs with the development of **penetration lines** into the interior, along with the evolution of feeder routes focusing on selected ports. The penetration of lines far into the interior most usually is to tap a natural resource, such as a mineral for export. Normally, a settlement will emerge, if it did not previously exist, at the terminus of the line. This settlement will act as a collection or distribution center for a small *umland*. The feeder routes serving the enlarged ports will, of course, mean enlarged hinterlands for those ports better supplied by transportation. Many, if not most, of the scattered ports of the earlier phase will have ceased their local-port functions though they may continue to exist as settlements. The ports with transport advantages (i.e., locational advantages on the emerging transport network) are able to overshadow the other centers so completely that the poorly located centers cannot compete economically.

The third phase in the Taaffe sequence is **network interconnection**. Hinterlands that had heretofore been areally discrete may now overlap as commodities that could logically be shipped only to one port or another may now involve a choice among certain parts of the interior of which port to ship to. Concomitant with interconnection of the network is the burgeoning of inland centers, along with the continued growth of the major ports. Feeder lines jut out from these centers to serve their enlarging *umlands*. Expansion of the centers at the terminus of the penetrator lines may proceed remarkably fast, as these centers find themselves located at strategic points on the evolving transport network. Frequently, the most rapidly growing cities tend to be located at some distance from one another because they are in competition to serve areas around them. We note a close correlation between the importance of a center and the position it has on the network, especially considering the feeder lines.

The final phase occurs when **high-priority linkages** emerge on a network that has a high degree of connectivity. In Figure 5.9, high-priority links occur between the two port cities and between one port and one interior city. The largest urban centers are served by the best routes and originate and terminate the greatest amount of freight, as well as the largest number of passengers. New interior centers spring up at strategic, central locations on the network. Hinterlands, as well as *umlands*, overlap in large degrees. The transport network may be described as complex and interconnected. Both route den-

A train carrying double-stacked containerized freight passes through Amsterdam, New York. The stacked containers were removed directly from ships and put on this freight train.

sity (the number of miles of routes per unit of area) and traffic density (volume of traffic per unit of area) are high. This final phase of transport development occurs only when a region has achieved a high level of economic development. A good example of a high-priority linkage is the route, or rather routes, between New York City and Washington, D.C. Often a final phase, not mentioned in the Taaffe model, is the abandonment or thinning out of lower-priority links, as with Amtrak in the United States.

One feature of Taaffe's four-phase sequence deserves emphasis: the relationship between the size and importance of a city and the position that city occupies on the transport network. The reason large cities possess the most advantageous locations on the transport network is somewhat like the chicken and egg argument. Did the large cities create the transport facilities, or did transportation make the cities important? The answer, of course, is that both hypotheses are correct. Economic activities are attracted to locations with transport advantages; transport developments and improvements are attracted to areas with high levels of economic activities.

Locating a Single Route.   The decision making involved in selecting a single route forms the basis for network evolution, and a more detailed look at how these decisions are made is important in understanding relationships between the geography of transport networks and the geography of economic activities. Even in the simplest circumstances, a large order of complexity confronts the decision maker in selecting a single route. Consider two points, X and Y, to be connected by a transport route (Figure 5.10). These points may be cities and the route, a highway. The *minimization principle*, sometimes called the least-effort principle illustrated in Figure 5.10, is a fundamental—though by no means the only—influence on route location. The basis for this principle is the minimization of the cost of constructing the route by selecting the shortest distance between the cities. Such a route also

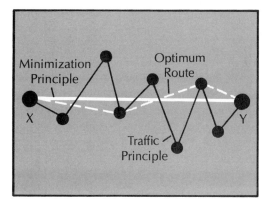

Figure 5.10 One important principle of route and network development is the minimization or least-effort principle.

minimizes the travel time between points. In this example, both construction costs and travel or operating costs (user costs) will be at their lowest level. However, because of barrier effects of one type or another, it is quite possible that the route with lowest construction cost may not be the straight-line route or the route of least distance. Lengthening the route may actually reduce the total construction costs by avoiding construction through a high-cost barrier, such as a lake, mountain, or congested urban area.

The principle of *route refraction* follows this lowest-cost approach. Refraction, or bending of the route, occurs when two transport rates are charged in two different areas through which the route passes or when construction costs differ between two sections of the route. (Actually, our number is not limited to two, as Christian Werner has noted: when there are two costs, there is one bend in the route; when there are three costs there are two breaks; and so on.)[6] Route refraction may be likened to the path taken by a ray of light passing through different media. Light follows an optimal path, given the density of the media through which it passes, and hence follows

[6]Christian Werner "Networks of Minimum Length," *Canadian Geographer* 13 (1969), pp. 47–69.

the minimization principle. Whereas deviations in the light's path result from passing through different media, deviations in the transport route stem from different costs in the areas through which the route goes. In all cases the alignment of least resistance is followed.

Again take two points, X and Y (Figure 5.11). A commodity is to be shipped as cheaply as possible between these points. However, point X is located inland, and point Y is the coast of an island and, therefore, separated from X by a water body. The transport rate for the distance between Y and Z will be lower than for the distance between Z and X because ocean freight rates are cheaper than rates over land. It then makes sense to ship the commodity as far as possible at the cheaper ocean rate and to minimize the distance for the high-cost charge. The result is a refraction in the lowest-cost route. The higher the cost of the land rate relative to the ocean rate, the greater will be the bending of the route. The route refraction principle also holds in the case of bridge construction: the higher the cost of constructing the bridge, the greater will the bridge deviate from the main direction of the route in order that the bridge crossing will be as short as possible. Consider a student without an umbrella, caught in an unexpected downpour, rushing to avoid being late for an economic geography class. Will he or she take the shortest path to class, which is mainly in the rain? Or will the student refract the route (i.e., change course) by maximizing the length of the trip that provides shelter from the thunderstorm?

The ratio of water to land costs not only determines the lowest-cost route, but also point Z. If all the commodities in the region moved between X and Y and if all points along the coast were equally suitable as harbors, the optimum port location would be Z. This port would act as a **break-of-bulk point**, that is, a location at which there is a transfer of commodities from one carrier to another. Port functions, as we have seen, are associated with growing population clusters and concentrations of economic activities. If along this coast there were evenly scattered, small port settlements, but if the great majority of commodity flow was between points X and Y, the port that would occupy the best geographic position to take advantage of the rate structure would be point Z, which would also be the fastest-growing in population. The economic ac-

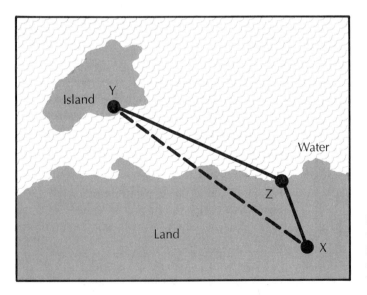

Figure 5.11 The principle of route refraction (bending of routes) follows the minimization principle, here illustrated by the different transport costs between land and water.

tivities already located there would have an excellent chance of prospering, and entrepreneurs within this region would be attracted to location Z.

The concept of network density (see pp. 124–125) relates to traffic-serving functions. Network density may be defined as the number of miles of route divided by the area (in square miles). Thus, a high value represents an area with lots of routes per unit area; a low network density means few routes. As an example, one may contrast the low density of the highway network in an area of western Nevada (near Reno) with the much higher density of an equal-size area in southwestern Michigan near Kalamazoo (Figure 5.12). It is clear that the higher-density highway network serves the area better than the low-density one, is capable of moving greater volumes of traffic, and has higher overall accessibility to places within the mapped area. There is also an apparent difference in the intensity of economic activity, again demonstrating the relationship between transportation and economic activity.

A route may be lengthened for reasons other than to maintain lowest construction costs or lowest user costs. These reasons have to do with the *traffic-serving functions* of the route. For example, a bus passenger route between X and Y may be able to generate more traffic if it included other nearby nodes on its stops. How many nodes should be included, how far off the minimum path line are they located, and what will be their traffic-generating capacity? One extreme solution is illustrated in Figure 5.11, in which the addition of several nodes creates such a high degree of circuity and slowness of movement as to detract from traffic volumes. The added inputs of route length up to some point result in increased traffic volume and, therefore, user benefits; beyond that point the famous law of diminishing returns sets in. The optimum route, following the traffic-serving principle of route location, is stretched out as much as possible up to the point where an added mile reduces the overall traffic

flow in the system. Obviously, some balance must be reached between these two extreme pulls on route location, which under minimization reduces the length and under the traffic principle seeks to extend it. The solution is usually an arbitrary one in which an approximate balance between the two principles is achieved. In this regard, it is interesting to note the routes chosen between New York City and Buffalo by the New York Central Railroad versus the Erie Railroad. The New York Central's route was more circuitous, but it went through the population centers of Albany, Syracuse, and Rochester, as well as several smaller centers. The Erie Railroad had the advantage of a more direct route between New York City and Buffalo but had the disadvantage of serving fewer markets along the route.

In reality, many route locations are chosen by *cost-benefit analysis*. Several alternative routes between points X and Y are proposed. Estimates are made: usually rather accurately on the cost of construction and somewhat less accurately on the operating costs. Operating costs depend on the estimates of traffic volume, which may in turn depend on estimates of future demographic and economic changes. All of the costs, including, in recent years, environmental and social costs, are added up. Anticipated benefits are also calculated, and here is where the greatest criticism of the cost-benefit method has been focused. Just as certain elements of the operating costs depend on traffic totals, so too do the estimates of benefits. There are not only user benefits but also advantages to nonusers. The problem is that these benefits are hard to quantify, especially at the level of dollars and cents. Guesstimates can be made for several aspects of economic activities, but the many social and environmental impacts of the route are almost impossible to translate into monetary meaning. Certain decisions, for example, may lead to an increased accident rate. What amount of money will we assign to the loss of a human life? Although many improvements have been made over the years in

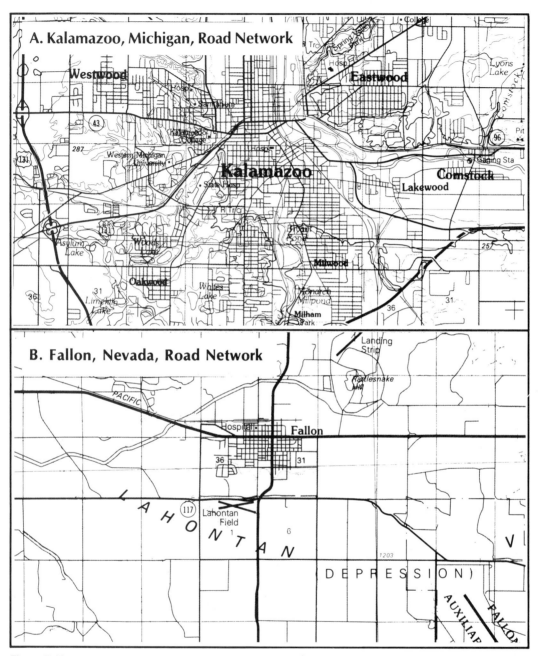

Figure 5.12 Contrast the density of the highway network in an area of southwestern Michigan with an area in western Nevada.

cost-benefit analysis as applied to route location, much subjectivity lies underneath the dollar totals representing costs and benefits.

One other influence on route location must be emphasized—political influence. In the days of railroad construction in the United States, one community after another sought to induce the rail companies, sometimes through financial incentive, to build through that particular community, recognizing that with the railroad, industries would prosper and business generally would be good. Highways today are heavily dependent on public funds. Public regulation, in one form or another, is accepted in all forms of transportation, though deregulation has been the trend in the last several years. Railroads in almost every country except the United States are nationalized; Many rail lines have been built primarily for political or military reasons; for reasons of national pride and to lay effective claim to territory, as in northern Canada or Siberia in the former Soviet Union; or because a senator from, say, Montana wants two lines to serve him (Amtrak).

Network Structure and Economic Activities

Every transportation network has an areal arrangement or layout, known as its spatial pattern.

Such a pattern may also be referred to as a *spatial structure*. By studying a network's structure or pattern of routes, one can gain much insight into the economic geography of the area the network serves. Although perhaps no two transport networks are exactly alike in spatial arrangement, there are similarities in structure that reflect the function the networks serve. Three basic measures of a network's spatial structure are important in the location of economic activity; accessibility, connectivity, and circuity.

Transport networks differ in their *accessibility*, or the ease of movement among the nodes or points on the network. Generally, a major impediment to accessibility is the distance between nodes on a network. In the simplest indexes of accessibility, therefore, only distance is used. Consider the road and rail networks in Tables 5.1 and 5.2. Which has the lower overall accessibility? In this example, both networks consist of nine nodes. The solution is to measure the route distance from each node to every other node using the shortest distance. A symmetrical interaction matrix is formed for each network, the number in each cell corresponding to the least route mileage between the respective nodes. Each column in the matrix is summed; each column sum is divided by the number of nodes to give the accessibility index for the node identified

Table 5.1 Highway Networks										
	1	2	3	4	5	6	7	8	9	
1	—	31	24	34	51	66	58	57	36	
2	31	—	16	26	24	49	51	59	38	
3	24	16	—	10	27	42	35	43	22	
4	34	26	10	—	17	32	25	33	12	
5	51	24	27	17	—	25	42	50	29	
6	66	49	42	32	25	—	57	65	44	
7	58	51	35	25	42	57	—	58	37	
8	57	59	43	33	50	65	58	—	21	
9	36	38	22	12	29	44	37	21	—	
Sums	357	294	219	189	265	380	363	386	239	2,692
Accessibility index	39.7	32.7	24.3	21.0	29.4	42.2	40.3	42.9	26.6	33.2

Table 5.2 Railway Networks

	1	2	3	4	5	6	7	8	9	
1	—	43	26	35	43	66	55	67	50	
2	43	—	17	26	34	57	46	58	41	
3	26	17	—	9	17	40	29	41	24	
4	35	26	9	—	26	40	20	32	15	
5	43	34	17	26	—	23	43	55	41	
6	66	57	40	40	23	—	20	35	55	
7	55	46	29	20	43	20	—	12	35	
8	67	58	41	32	55	35	12	—	50	
9	50	41	24	15	41	55	35	50	—	
Sums	385	322	203	203	282	336	260	350	311	2,652
Accessibility index	42.8	35.8	22.6	22.6	31.3	37.3	28.9	38.9	34.6	32.7

at the top of the column. The individual indexes are then summed and divided by the number of nodes to give the overall accessibility index of the network. The accessibility measure for a network is, therefore, simply the average accessibility of the nodes on the network. In our example, the railway network, with an accessibility average of 32.7, is slightly more accessible than the highway network, with an index of 33.2 Using the same methods, we might wish to compare the highway networks in two different regions or compare changes in network accessibility for a single network over different time periods.

Since accessibility has also been calculated for the individual nodes by summing each column, it is useful to examine which nodes are the most accessible. Usually, the more centrally located a node is on a network, the more accessible is the node to other nodes. Hence, we expect accessibility, centrality, and economic growth to be geographically correlated. Returning to our example, we find a somewhat different ordering of accessibility indexes by node for the two networks, but centrality and accessibility are nonetheless related in both cases. An economic activity that happens to be located at node 3 or node 4 will derive natural locational benefits. Any economic activity wishing to select a location at

some node on the networks will likely choose node 3 or node 4, especially if accessibility is important for that activity. It is at these nodes, therefore, that economic growth will be most likely to occur.

There are several ways of measuring ***connectivity***, or the degree to which nodes on the network are connected. The easiest is to count, for each node, the total number of direct connections with other nodes. In this way, nodes can be compared, and by taking an average for an entire network, an overall index of connectivity can be derived for comparison with other networks. An only slightly more arduous method takes into account the minimum and maximum levels of connectivity possible for a given network. Letting the symbol N stand for the number of nodes, the maximum possible connectivity, or number of direct links, for any network is $N(N-1)/2$. The minimum will always be $N-1$. By counting the actual number of links, L, the ratio of actual connectivity can be found by dividing L into the maximum number of links. By setting the maximum connectivity figure at 100 percent and the minimum figure at zero, the degree of connectivity calculated for an actual network can be interpreted, for example, as being 70 percent as connected as possible. On a percentage basis, then, comparison may be easily made among quite different networks.[7]

Given the same number of nodes, the connectivity percentage normally increases with economic growth. The index is, therefore, an indirect measure of the level of economic activity in the area served by the network. To the close associations we have already mentioned among accessibility, centrality, and economic growth, we must now add connectivity. However, a shortcoming of the connectivity indexes described here is that they take into account only direct links. Other procedures, too complicated to launch into here, are available to overcome this problem.

Networks also differ in degree of *circuity*. A network will have some circuity unless all routes proceed in a straight line between nodes. High levels of circuity in a network make for inefficient movement, adding unnecessary time and cost to commodity shipment. Circuity is simply the difference between the *desire line distance*, represented by a straight line between nodes, and the actual route distance. A circuity index may be calculated for each node on a network by finding the total circuity involved in going from that node to all other nodes on the network. The circuity index for a network is the average

circuity for all nodes. This index is an indication of the geographic efficiency of the network and of the nodes. Economic activity, everything else being equal, will shy away from locations with high circuity values. Networks with high circuity figures are usually in early stages of evolution (low levels of connectivity) or are in regions of severe construction barriers.

Throughout the world, there is a close association between networks and economic development. Transportation networks are integrated parts of economic systems. Any change in the network's spatial structure has an impact on the economic system as there is an adjustment in the accessibility, connectivity, and circuity of nodes. Similarly, a change in the economic system, such as rapid growth in part of a region, affects the network because more commodities may need to be moved over it, or expansion or improvement of the network may be necessary. Geographers continue to gain a better understanding of the complex interdependencies between transport networks and the economic systems they serve by examining network impact on economic activities.

Figure 5.13 shows interstates in Florida. Imagine a manufacturer wishing to locate a plant in Florida to serve the state market. Let us suppose that a major cost in serving this market is the transport charge to deliver the product to the market. Mobile home manufacturing would be an excellent example, where the cost of moving a mobile home is well over $2 per mile, a cost that is added to the purchase price. Where to locate?

The question, then, is to find the point of greatest accessibility. If we limit our search to just those metropolitan areas shown in Figure 5.13, it is simply a matter of finding the road mileage from each center to all of the other centers. As noted above, we sum the distances from each node to all other nodes and divide, in this case by the 10 centers. We will find the average interstate highway distance for each center. Look at

---

[7]In a nine-node example, the maximum number of possible connections is $9(9 - 1)/2$, or 36. The minimum is $N-1$, or 8. Let us suppose that the actual is 11 for the highway and 9 for rail. To calculate the actual percentage of connectivity, one must first determine the ratios for maximum and minimum connectivity. The maximum ratio is equal to one ($36/36 = 1.0$) or 100 percent. The minimum connectivity ratio is equal to the minimum number of links $(N - 1)$ divided into the maximum links $[N (N - 1)/2] = 4.5$ The actual connectivity ratio is 3.27 for highway ($36/11 = 3.27$) and 4.0 for rail ($36/9 = 4.0$). The percentage of maximum connectivity is found by subtracting the quotient of the division of the actual ratio (3.27 and 4.0) by the minimum ratio (4.5) from 1. Thus, in our example the rail network is only 11 percent as connected as possible, and the highway linkages are only 27 percent complete: $1 - (3.27/4.5) = 0.27$, or 27 percent, and $1 - (4.0/4.5) = 0.11$, or 11 percent.

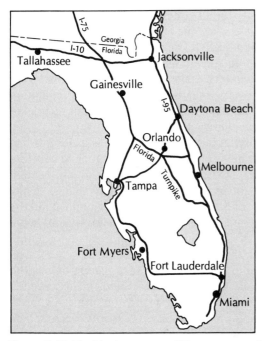

Figure 5.13 Florida interstates. What center enjoys maximum accessibility on the interstate system?

Figure 5.13 again. Can you guess the center of greatest accessibility for the manufacturer? Is it Miami or Tallahassee? No, it is Orlando. Melbourne and Daytona Beach would also have been good answers.

FLOWS ON NETWORKS

Having examined transport routes and networks, we now turn to how and why flows occur on networks; that is, why is the volume of movement between any two places greater or lesser than the volume between any other two places? To begin, we go back to Ullman's bases for spatial interaction. Complementarity implies the existence of a surplus or supply at one location and a demand or a need for that same good at another place. One may argue therefore that the larger the two places are in population size, the greater the chances that complementarity will occur. Population size is, indeed, one factor that explains the

volume of flows on a network. Ullman's second concept of transferability relates to the role of distance (or the cost of overcoming distance) in the level of interaction. The greater the cost–distance separation between two places, the lower the level of interaction.

The Gravity Model

The gravity model is a highly simplified but powerful concept that puts together the notions of population size and distance. Over the years it has been one of the most widely used models in economic geography. The model was developed in the early 1940s based on Sir Isaac Newton's much earlier formulation for how gravity operates. It was then applied to human activities.

The gravity model, when used in economic geography, takes on the following general form

$$I_{ij} = k \frac{P_i \cdot P_j}{D_{ij}^b}$$

where I is the volume of flow between place i and place j, P_i is the population size of place i, P_j is the population size of place j, and D_{ij} is the distance between places i and j. As the model is calculated, k is a constant term and therefore need not concern us here, and b is a parameter (exponent) to be calculated and tells us how important distance is in curtailing the flow volume. Frequently, population parameters (not shown in the formula) are also calculated to gauge the importance of population in the volume of flows.

In economic geography, for example, the gravity model might be applied to the number of commuters in a rural region, where data inputs would simply be the population size of each center and the highway distance or driving time among centers. The model can be calculated between any two centers or for an entire group of centers. Similarly, the number of commuters among traffic zones in a metropolitan area can be computed by knowing the population size of the zones and the travel times from one zone to all others. Thus, the model has many applied and practical uses.

The gravity model is not a single model but rather a whole family of models with many variants. One of the most insightful modifications of the classic gravity model was published in a series of papers and a monograph by Fotheringham.[8] He pointed out that the distance parameter (b) could be misleading depending on the distribution of destinations for a flow origin. First, a high value of b, say of 3.0, would indicate that distance played an extremely strong role in the pattern of flows, compared to, say, a b-value of 1.0. In the example of b = 3.0, the majority of flows would be a short distance, and in the latter ($b=1.0$) there would be many flows over long distances. Fotheringham pointed out that, if the destinations were either bunched together geographically or spread widely apart, the value of b might be affected. He devised a "competing destinations" model, which in certain ways is similar to Ullman's intervening opportunities concept, to measure the effect of the distribution of destinations, if any, on the distance parameter. We will not go into the details of Fotheringham's modification of the gravity model except to note that he added an important concept to calibrating the effect of the spatial distribution of the destinations.

For example, if Fotheringham's term took on a negative value, then so-called competitive effects were said to occur, meaning that isolated destinations were receiving more flows than would be expected based on their distance and population size. Conversely, if the term were positive, then clustered destinations would receive more flows than expected, termed an *agglomerative effect*. Of course, if the term has a zero value, then no effect either way will occur. Thus, a competitive effect might be likened to a bank locating its own branch banks away from

one another in order to serve a wide market and avoid competing with itself. An agglomerative effect might be compared to stores clustering together in a shopping mall, each hoping to get a greater share of the action than if each store were isolated from one another.

TRANSPORT IMPACT ON ECONOMIC ACTIVITIES

The modes of transportation that have had the greatest impact on economic activity around the world are rail and road. Since World War II, air travel has also become important, principally for passengers rather than for commodity movement. Transport of commodities by water, pipeline, and air restricts the impact on economic activity to the area surrounding the origin or terminus of the route. River cities, especially in the days before the railroad, were important nodes for the riverboats; New Orleans and St. Louis were proud cities when Chicago was a swamp. Today air terminals are increasingly becoming a location around which more and different kinds of urban activities, from hotels to manufacturing, are concentrating. Rail impact, particularly in the latter half of the nineteenth century, was quite significant in the cities served, but entire agricultural regions and industrial dis-

Motor trucks lined up at a loading dock of a large warehouse.

---

[8]See A. Stewart Fotheringham and M. E. O'Kelly, *Spatial Interaction Models: Formulations and Applications* (Boston: Klurver Academic Publishing, 1989).

Atlanta: A Regional Transportation Hub

Atlanta is the Southeast's largest city and serves as a transportation hub for a broad region. The city has consolidated its position over several decades as the region's preeminent transportation center, serving a significant portion of the United States and its people. Atlanta's

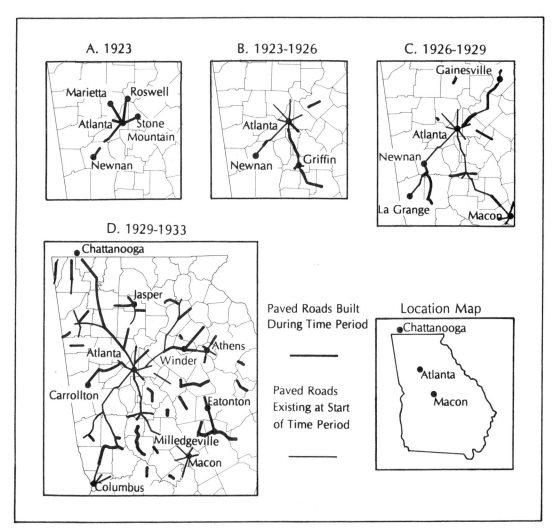

Figure 5.14 The spread of paved roads out of Atlanta and the growing connectivity of the highway system, 1923–1933.
Source: From James A. Liesindahl, "Expansion of the Paved Road in the State Highway System of Georgia, 1923–1962," M.A. thesis, University of Georgia, 1964.

economic dominance, translated through its transportation services, has day-to-day implications for the people who live within the Southeast. Since this economic dominance was achieved in large measure as a result of economic and political decisions made possible by transportation investments and advantages, it is useful to examine the relationships between Atlanta's size and significance and its transportation role (Fig. 5.14).

Historically, Atlanta was stimulated in its early growth by the railway. Despite Atlanta's function as a major rail center, the city remained for a long time rather small by the standards of cities in the industrialized East. At the start of the Civil War, for example, Atlanta was estimated to have only about 15,000 people. It was not until 1900 that Atlanta, with its location on an increasingly accessible railway network, overtook Savannah, which relied on ocean transportation but which was not able to compete effectively with the ports of the industrialized East. At the turn of the century, Atlanta had not yet reached 100,000 people. In 1985, Atlanta became the fourteenth largest metropolitan area in the United States, with 2.4 million people. Atlanta in 1997 ranked twelfth with over 3.4 million people.

Having gradually emerged over nearly a century as a center of importance because of rail shipping advantages, Atlanta developed during the 1930s into the major air-passenger center within the Southeast. Whereas Atlanta and Birmingham, Alabama, were virtually equal in population size in 1930, Atlanta thereafter rapidly outdistanced its Alabama counterpart by establishing itself as the region's major air-transport center and as headquarters for Delta Airlines. As a result, the Atlanta metropolitan area grew unbelievably, reaching a million people during the 1950s.

Atlanta's most recent role as a transportation center came with the construction of freeways in the 1960s (Fig. 5.15). The reach of the freeways was a great boon to the trucking industry, and Atlanta is now recognized as the leading motor-truck distribution center for the Southeast. Atlanta has over 80 truck terminals; 180 regulated motor carriers are based in the metro area. The Atlanta Chamber of Commerce is quick to point out that more than 50 million people live within 500 miles of the city. The attraction of the trucking industry to Atlanta is, of course, associated with the growth of industrial parks, suburban offices, and warehousing facilities located near the freeways. The extent of the second-morning freight delivery area from Atlanta stretches as far as Miami, New York City, Detroit, and Chicago.

It is likely that Atlanta will maintain, if not further consolidate, its position as a distribution center, at least up to some point. However, the many decades of gradual improvement in transportation systems, whether rail, air, or truck, are probably over. Accessibility to distant places will probably not continue to increase as much in the immediate future, barring an unforeseen breakthrough in transportation technology. Existing transportation systems have pretty much reached their limits of growth, and in some cases, namely, the railroad, have long been cutting back. To be sure, additional residential streets will be constructed, but not many new intercity routes to improve a city's overall accessibility will be built. The cost of energy for transportation will further stabilize the accessibility equation.

The metropolitan areas of the Northeast, with their stabilized or declining populations, have some time since reached their points of maximum accessibility to their surrounding hinterlands. Because of transportation congestion and other associated forms of congestion, they are suffering either absolute or relative decline, compared with the metropolitan centers of the so-called Sunbelt, including Atlanta.

The growth of metropolitan Atlanta, encouraged by its regional transportation role, is

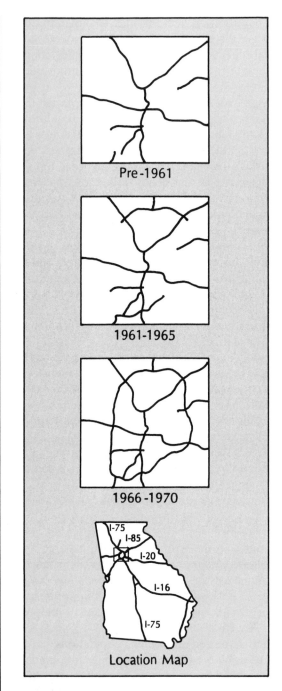

Pre-1961

1961-1965

1966-1970

Location Map

Figure 5.15 The growth of Atlanta's freeway system, completed earlier than in most other metropolitan areas.

spreading ever wider into the surrounding area. Growth corridors, such as the Atlanta–Chattanooga corridor along Route I-75, can be readily identified from population and economic-growth statistics. The Atlanta–Chattanooga corridor is sure to continue to grow, bringing with it both an increased market for Altanta's distribution functions and increased congestion. The 20-county Atlanta metropolitan area nearly joins the surrounding metropolitan areas of Chattanooga, Tennessee; Birmingham, Alabama; Greenville-Spartanburg, South Carolina; and Macon and Augusta, Georgia. Phenomenal growth in office building has been occurring in areas of north Atlanta along Route I-285, a 64-mile perimeter highway encircling Atlanta. Here to the north at major interchanges "suburban downtowns" have sprung up with 20- and 30-story office complexes. Recently constructed residential homes are being bulldozed to make room for more high-rise structures, fundamentally changing the spatial structure of the metropolitan area.

What the long-term trends and implications are, is difficult to know. One possibility, which is far in the future and dependent on rapidly changing technology in the electronics industry, is the substitution of telecommunications for transportation. Already we know the advantages in cost and time of transmitting information by electronic signals instead of by physical transfer. Telecommunications is practiced only on a quite limited scale at present, the most familiar use, of course, being the telephone. There are still rather massive cost barriers to the widespread use of telecommunications as a substitute for transportation. If and when this comes, it is likely that telecommunications will be utilized especially by the information-processing businesses. If costs can be significantly lowered, Atlanta, with its important distribution and information-processing functions, may achieve a fourth major breakthrough in developing and sustaining its regional transportation advantages as a future communications center superimposed on its historical rail system, its air traffic connections, and its motor freight distribution.

tricts were also affected. The modern highway has had the greatest overall impact in most countries around the world, including the vast majority of the developing nations, and it will be in this specific context that we will discuss principles of transport impact.

Three phases of economic growth are linked to new highway development. In the *substitution phase* the new highway serves the existing population by substituting the new transport route for older forms. For example, a shipper will now utilize the new highway facility instead of the existing railroad. The substitution phase begins immediately on the opening of the new route, although some users will be slower than others to make the switch, and some may not change at all. The *transition phase* follows. Here population follows after the highway, creating higher population densities and land values near the route. The result is an increase in use of the highway stemming from *induced demand*. In this sense, the mere existence of a highway creates part of the demand for its use. Perhaps the best example of induced demand is the U.S. interstate system; the interstates were designed in the 1950s to carry the traffic of 1976. But because induced demand in urban areas was not sufficiently taken into account in these projections, the interstates in metropolitan areas became overloaded almost as soon as the ceremonial ribbons were cut. The last stage is the *developmental phase*. At this point the highway begins to determine the location of economic activity and of land-use change. Further demand for the highway services is created. In this stage, the transportation route is fully interdependent with the economic system.

The impact of a transportation route on the economy will vary from place to place along the route. What are the transportation-induced changes in economic activity at specific locations? These changes include alterations in the patterns of retail sales, manufacturing location, residential land use, agriculture, and land values—components that are themselves interrelated. The changes may be of a positive or a negative kind. Positive economic changes may entail environmental costs. Transportation-induced shifts in production and consumption patterns will mean positive changes at some locations and negative changes at others. Ultimately, some people will be helped, and some will be hurt economically by transportation change.

One of the most widely observed features of transport impact, especially for highways, is the increase in land values near the route. Land values rise sharply in locations where routes cross, such as freeway interchanges. The highest values are achieved nearest the route, and land values gradually decline away from the route. The reason for this spatial variation in land value is the premium placed on accessibility in economic systems. One is willing to pay a higher price for accessibility or rather for the benefits accessibility will bring. Figure 5.16a illustrates an idealized decline in land values away from a two-lane road leading into an urban area. In Figure 5.16b, the road has been four-laned, bringing about a steep jump in land values along the road and extending the road's sphere of influence over a greater distance. Whereas in the earlier situation residential land-use predominated, with the widening of the road, land values have risen so high that residential land use is outbid for the use of the most accessible land. Commercial and industrial use will be found adjacent to the highway, and residential subdivisions will locate at some distance away from the highway, the latter being less dependent on accessibility. More will be said about spatial competition for land in later chapters.

Other generalizations regarding transporta-

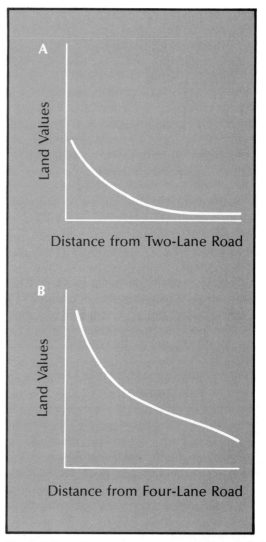

Figure 5.16 Often, land values are significantly influenced by accessibility, with the most accessible locations being the most sought-after and hence the most valued.

tion-induced changes should be noted. One tendency, when any substantial alteration is made in an existing transport system, is for economic activities to become more centralized or concentrated areally. Small hamlets lose their mom-

and-pop grocery stores to large, centralized shopping centers. Small, scattered manufacturers operating at high unit costs are forced out of business by large producers taking advantage of the economies of scale that grow out of a more accessible location on the new or improved transport route. The repetition of these examples throughout the U.S. economy has resulted in a high degree of centralization of economic activity in large metropolitan areas. In fact, the entire metropolitanization process, which has brought about such dramatic change away from the agrarian past, has been possible largely because of transport improvements.

At the same time, transport improvements induce decentralizing tendencies. The fact that cities in industrial societies have long since spilled out of their areally restricted political boundaries testifies to the centrifugal forces unleashed by transportation. Suburbanization is one manifestation of this deconcentration process. More rapid speed of movement means that places located far apart may function as if they are close together. Faster travel allows one to reside in the suburbs and yet quickly reach his or her workplace located downtown or, more frequently today, in a suburb across the metropolis. Thus, the small hamlets near metropolitan areas may lose their economic functions, but they often gain in residential importance. The concentration tendencies are prevented from reaching intolerable excesses by the greater locational flexibility of decentralization.

Donald Janelle uses the term *time–space convergence* to describe the process by which nodes become functionally closer over time with transport improvements.[9] Figure 5.17 shows an idealized example, following Janelle, of how two points, *X* and *Y*, which may represent two cities, have been converging in time–space between

[9]Donald G. Janelle, "Spatial Reorganization: A Model and Concept," *Annals of the Association of American Geographers* (1969), pp. 348–364.

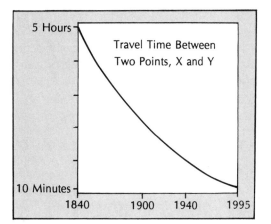

Figure 5.17 With improvements in transport technology, cities converge over time, as shown here for two hypothetical cities, X and Y.
Source: after Janelle, 1969.

1840 and 1995. With poor transportation technology, the two points were nearly five hours of travel time apart. Now they are only a few minutes away by air. The savings in minutes of travel time are equivalent to relocating the cities closer together on the earth's surface. The old saw that we live on a shrinking globe turns out to be truer than we may have realized as we can calculate between any two years the speed, in miles per year, that two cities have been moving closer together.

SUMMARY

Among the most important characteristics of a place are its transportation linkages with other places. A node's location on a transportation network reflects its *relative location* and expresses economic potential as well as problems at that node. The technological phenomena collectively referred to as transportation manifests our ability to overcome distance between places. It is both necessary and advantageous to carry out economic activity at myriad locations on the earth; it follows that transportation is not only necessary, but that it also allows higher degrees of efficiencies and a better geographic allocation of the earth's human and physical resources. In Chapter 6, we will treat actual patterns of transportation on the landscape and how these structures serve the economic system.

Further Readings

Abler, Ronald, J. S. Adams, and P. Gould. *Spatial Organization.* Englewood Cliffs, N.J.: Prentice-Hall, 1971.

Akaha, Tsuneo, ed. *International Handbook of Transportation Policy.* New York: Greenwood Press, 1990.

Daniels, P. W., and A. M. Warnes. *Movement in Cities: Spatial Perspectives in Urban Transport and Travel.* London: Methuen & Co., 1980.

Eliot Hurst, M. E., ed. *Transportation Geography: Comments and Readings.* New York: McGraw-Hill, 1974.

Fotheringham, A. Stewart, and M. E. O'Kelly. *Spatial Interaction Models: Formulations and Applications* Boston: Kluwer Academic Publishers, 1989.

Gauthier, Howard L. "Transportation and the Growth of the São Paulo Economy." *Journal of Regional Science* 8 (1968), pp. 77–94.

Haggett, Peter, and Richard J. Chorley. *Network Analysis in Geography.* New York: St. Martin's Press, 1969.

Hay, Alan. *Transport for the Space Economy: A Geographical Study.* Seattle: University of Washington Press, 1973.

Haynes, Kingsley E., and A. Stewart Fotheringham. *Gravity and Spatial Interaction Modeling.* Beverly Hill: Sage Publications, 1984.

Hoyle, B. S. *Transport and Development.* New York: Harper & Row/Barnes & Noble Import Division, 1973.

Lowe, John C., and S. Moryadas. *The Geography of Movement* Boston: Houghton Mifflin, 1975.

Olsson, G. *Distance and Human Interaction.* Philadelphia: Regional Science Research Institute, 1964.

O'Sullivan, P. *Transport Policy: Geographic, Economic and Planning Aspects.* London: Batsford Academic and Educational, 1980.

Stutz, Frederick P. *Social Aspects of Interaction and Transportation.* Washington, D.C.: AAG Resource Paper, No. 76-2, 1977.

Taaffe, Edward, Howard L. Gauthier, Jr., and Morton E. O'Kelly. *Geography of Transportation.* Englewood Cliffs, N.J.: Prentice-Hall, 1996.

Taaffe, Edward, Richard L. Morrill, and Peter R. Gould. "Transport Expansion in Underdeveloped Countries: A Comparative Analysis." *Geographical Review* 53 (1963), pp. 503–529.

Ullman, Edward L. "Geography as Spatial Interaction." In M. E. Eliot Hurst, ed., *Transportation Geography: Comments and Readings.* New York: McGraw-Hill, 1974, pp. 29–40.

CHAPTER 6

The Role of Transportation in Economic Geography

⸻◇⸻

Sweetest melodies
Are those that are by distance made more sweet.
—WILLIAM WORDSWORTH

TRANSPORT ERAS

The human ability to overcome distance has always been closely tied to the available level of technology. It is easy to forget that the rather widespread mobility seen today in industrial countries is all quite recent. The automobile dates back only about a century; the railroad, a century and a half; and the airplane, in terms of its significant utilization, scarcely two generations. The oldest form of transport relied on muscle power, first human and then animal. Utilizing the power of the wind, sailing vessels greatly enlarged the scope of human movement and permitted for the first time contact and trade between people over great distances. The range of economic alternatives changed with each advance in transport technology, from muscle to sail to steam to petroleum power, with other alternatives along the way and future alternatives now on the horizon.

Whereas many industrial nations progressed through a similar sequence of transport evolution, the developing countries today find themselves in the enviable position of being able to "skip" transport eras, not being restrained by the development of transport technology. Concomi-

tant restrictions, however, may be equally, if not more, difficult than those faced by the industrial nations in the past. The transport problems in developing countries reflect both little capital for investment—and that often imported—and a scarcity of technological and managerial know-how, which must also be imported. An overriding problem in these countries is how to integrate transportation with economic development.

The transportation history of the United States can be summarized, from a geographic point of view, following Edward J. Taaffe, into four eras: the local, the trans-Appalachian, the railroad, and the competition eras.[1] The first three eras saw a progressive lowering of transport costs relative to other costs; the last era, since World War I, has been one of a relative rise in transport costs despite increased intermodal and interregional competition.

The ***local era*** of U.S. transport evolution ran from the beginning of settlement until the open-

[1]Edward J. Taaffe, "The Transportation Network and the Changing American Landscape," in Saul B. Cohen, ed., *Problems and Trends in American Geography* (New York: Basic Books, 1967), pp. 15–25.

ing of the Erie Canal in 1825. Short-distance hauls predominated. Long shipments were almost impossible at worst and incredibly expensive at best. Roads were scarce and quality was low. Regional specialization was severely restricted by the generally poor quality of transportation. The railroad did not yet exist, and the only decent roads were wooden planks and turnpikes. The plank or post roads were simply tree trunks and large limbs placed next to one another, creating a jarring, bumpy locomotion. The Northeast supplied its own agricultural produce despite inferior soils and a short growing season, especially in New England. West of the Appalachians, on rich agricultural land, farming was still largely limited to items for local consumption because the cost of transporting grain, livestock, and other commodities to the East Coast was prohibitive. Economies were locally focused, and items moved in small bulk over only short distances.

In the second quarter of the nineteenth century, the *trans-Appalachian* routes became the dominant feature of U.S. transport. The trans-Appalachian routes included the Erie Canal and several other interregional canals; the National Road from Baltimore, Maryland, to Wheeling, West Virginia (opened in 1818); and rail lines penetrating across the Appalachians into the interior by the mid-nineteenth century. The nation's largest cities of the time—Baltimore, Philadelphia, New York, and Boston—were each vying for primacy. New York, of course, won out. Not only did New York occupy the most accessible location with respect to the U.S. population distribution at that time, but the Erie Canal, passing through the Appalachians via the Mohawk valley in upstate New York and connecting with the Hudson River, gave New York City undisputedly superior access to the fertile agricultural interior. The Mohawk–Hudson route was also traversed later by the New York Central Railroad to provide ties to Chicago, suddenly emerging as the major city of the agricultural Midwest.

New England's agriculture, always tenuous, declined, being unable to compete with the better yields in the Midwest. Coastal New England and the mid-Atlantic states (an area later to become known as Megalopolis) began specializing in industrial products, especially high-value items, and trading these products to the Midwest for agricultural goods. Grain production in the Midwest, which had formerly been limited to areas near canals or rivers, spread widely as settlement of the interior rapidly advanced. In the 30 years from 1804, the highway network expanded rapidly into the interior. During the period from 1825 to the Civil War, the trans-Appalachian era was prominent in shaping the economic growth of the country. On the eve of the Civil War, in 1860, rail connections between the North and the South were strikingly few, and rail gauges (distance between rails) were in most cases different in the two areas (Figure 6.1).

Although the first railway was placed into service in the United States in 1830, rail development proceeded rather slowly for the next 20 years. From 1850 to the Civil War, an initial construction spurt occurred, only to be interrupted by the war. It was after the war that the real *era of railroad dominance* began. Railway mileage jumped from 52,000 miles in 1870 to 252,000 in 1920, the peak in miles of track. (It has dropped, as of 1990 to approximately 150,000 miles.) The railroad was the principal mover of both people and goods over both long and short distances. The canals became almost totally abandoned in the face of rail competition, and the road system remained poorly developed. At this time, the railroad was not only the cheapest but also the fastest form of transportation.

During the railway era, which lasted through World War I, the American economy greatly expanded its productivity, providing a foundation for the world's foremost political power. The north-south orientation of transportation during the local era, albeit weak, was realigned to east-west during the trans-Appalachian era and became firmly entrenched in the east-west direc-

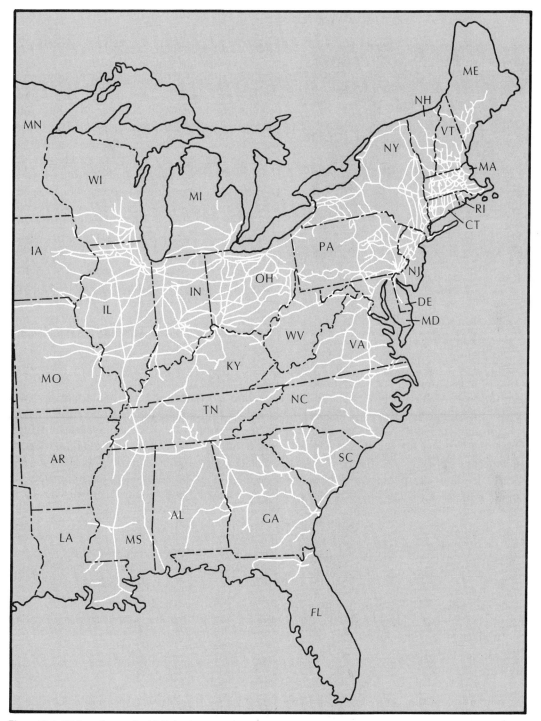

Figure 6.1 U.S. railways in 1860 had a very uneven spatial distribution. Most noticeable is the relative lack of connections between the North and the South, on the eve of the Civil War. Also notable is the dense pattern in coastal New England and the general east-west orientation of the rail lines.

Norfolk Southern coal unit trains, Big Rock, Virginia.

tion during the railroad period. Before the coming of the railroad, the largest U.S. cities were located on the coast or along such major rivers as the Mississippi and the Ohio. The railroad opened up the Midwest and spurred the growth of manufacturing cities on the Great Lakes. Chicago, lying near the southern extremity of Lake Michigan, "captured" the rail lines that might otherwise have crossed the lake farther to the north to become the rail capital of the country and the second leading metropolis after New York in population size until the highway elevated Los Angeles to the second position. The railroad, more than anything else, was the "creator" of the American urban pattern, connecting the already large port cities with the rapidly emerging cities of the interior. Port centers were thus assured of their continued dominance. *Gateway cities* also became recognized, acting as a gate through which goods and people passed between the Western farm lands and the growing industrial sections of the Midwest. St. Louis and Kansas City were examples.

Other forms of transportation gradually became more competitive during the second quarter of the twentieth century. The road network, which had so long lagged because of the lack of efficient motive power to propel vehicles, spread rapidly and seemingly everywhere after World War I. At this time the intercity trucking industry began, and almost immediately it became competitive. Pipeline transport, though used as early as 1865, came into its own about this same time for the transport of petroleum and petroleum products needed for motor vehicles. Commercial air transport began in 1926, and modern diesel towboats, put into service in 1920, placed water transport in a competitive position once again. Although the railroads declined slightly in relative importance between the two world wars, it was not until after World War II that the ***competitive era*** blossomed.

After World War II, the railroad's relative share of U.S. intercity freight traffic plummeted from nearly 70 percent of all commercial traffic in 1944 to approximately 37 percent today (Table 6.1). Other modes gained significantly during this same period. The truck has gained a significantly greater share over the past 10 years. Still, these data give undue emphasis to the railroad's importance as they are based on ton-miles (obtained by multiplying the number of tons loaded by the number of miles they are carried). Because railroads carry more bulk commodities, especially compared to the motor truck, ton-mile data do not adequately reflect the importance of truck transportation. Today, U.S. railroads carry about one trillion ton-miles of intercity freight compared to 800 billion ton-miles for truck.

Table 6.1 Percent of U.S. Intercity Ton-Miles by Mode

Year	Rail	Truck	Water	Oil Pipeline	Air
1944	68.6	5.4	13.8	12.2	—
1950	56.2	16.3	15.4	12.1	—
1960	44.1	21.7	16.8	17.4	0.1
1972	38.9	22.1	16.1	22.7	0.2
1978	36.0	23.8	16.0	24.0	0.2
1983	35.9	23.6	15.3	24.9	0.2
1992	37.0	27.3	15.8	19.3	0.4

Source: Association of American Railroads, 1993.

About one-third of the truck ton-miles are moved by commercial interstate carriers; the rest, by intrastate and private truck transportation. Private trucking has been growing especially rapidly. Because trucks tend to transport high-value manufactured products on which there is high revenue, whereas the railroad hauls primarily products of mines, on which revenue is lower, data on revenue, as opposed to ton-miles, clearly show the truck to be the most important mode of transportation in the United States. Despite the larger ton-mile figure for rail, the average freight revenue per ton-mile is relatively low—just over 3 cents (Table 6.2). In contrast, it averages about 14 cents per ton-mile for truck, which hauls higher-value commodities. Although air cargo accounts for less than 1 percent of all intercity freight ton-miles in the United States, the average revenue per ton-mile for air cargo is by far the highest of any mode, nearly 50 cents per ton-mile, because of the extremely high value of the items transported. Piggybacking (hauling a truck trailer on a railcar), which has been growing rapidly in recent years, results in advantages to both truck and rail transport.

Contrasting the data in Tables 6.3 and 6.4 gives us some insight into other differences among transport modes. Based on volume (tons) moved, the rail exceeds trucks and pipelines combined. By volume, the motor truck appears relatively unimportant, ranking behind rail, water, and pipeline. In reality, of course, we know that the last three modes haul mainly bulky, low-value items. Table 6.4 shows, based on earnings, that the truck is over six times more profitable

Table 6.3 Percentage of U.S. Intercity Freight Volume	
Rail	37.4
Trucks	25.2
Water	16.0
Oil pipeline	20.0
Air	0.3

Source: Statistical Abstract of the United States.

than the rail, with only air cargo a distant second. Airplanes carry almost exclusively low-weight, high-value goods.

Another way in which to view intermodal relationships is through a comparison of outlays or expenditures (Table 6.5) Over three-quarters of total transport outlays for the movement of freight in the United States goes for motor-truck operations. Lagging far behind at 11 percent of all freight transportation expenditures is rail, and lagging even further behind are water shipment and oil pipeline flows.

For passenger movement, which constitutes 62 percent of total transport outlays in the United States (freight and passengers), 83 percent involves private transportation. The remaining traffic, 17 percent, represents for-hire passenger movement. The private automobile alone accounts for 81.1 percent of all expenditures for U.S. passenger movement. Of the intercity for-hire traffic, the airlines account for 91 percent of the travel expenditure, far outclipping rail and bus outlays. Over 80 percent of all U.S. intercity passenger traffic is by private auto and over 17

Table 6.2 Average Freight Revenue per Ton-Mile for the United States (in cents)	
Air	46.8
Rail	3.2
Motor truck	14.1
Oil pipeline	1.3
Water	0.9

Source: U.S. Statistical Yearbook.

Table 6.4 Percentage of U.S. Total Earnings by Transport Mode	
Rail	9.2
Trucks	57.5
Water	6.6
Oil pipeline	0.6
Air	26.0

Source: Statistical Abstract of the United States.

Table 6.5 Freight and Passenger Outlays by Transport Mode for the United States, 1991

Transport Mode	In Billions of Dollars	Percentage of All Modes by Freight and Passengers
Freight Mode		
Rail	29.9	8.4
Motor truck	278.0	79.0
Oil pipeline	8.1	2.7
Water	20.6	5.8
Air	14.9	4.1
Total	351.5	100.0
Passenger Mode		
Private transportation	510.9	83.1
Automobile	500.4	81.1
Air	10.5	1.7
For-Hire	104.2	16.9
Local	35.8	5.8
Intercity	52.8	8.6
Air	48.9	7.9
Rail	1.8	0.1
Bus	2.1	0.1
Total	615.1	100.0

Source: U.S. Statistical Abstract.

percent is by air, leaving only about 1 percent by bus and rail.

The result of the accumulation of transport facilities in the United States is a massive transport system consisting of several different modes of transportation and highly integrated and high-density networks (Table 6.6). Far and away the

Table 6.6 Intercity Mileage within the Continental United States

Rail	150,000
Oil pipeline	235,000
Gas pipeline	1,030,000
Inland waterways	25,500
Airways	340,000
Highway	3,889,000
Primary federal aid	305,000
Secondary federal aid	400,000
Other	3,184,000

Source: U.S. Statistical Abstract.

most complete of these systems is the intercity highway, constituting 3.9 million total miles. (An additional 750,000 miles of highway are in urban areas.) Approximately 850,000 of the intercity miles are made up of federal-aid primary and secondary highways, including the 45,000 of limited access interstates. Miles of rail lines, which have been decreasing over the past 70 years, are now only 150,000, much in contrast to the gigantic highway network that continues to enlarge. We may forget that there exist in the United States over one million miles of natural gas pipeline, as well as approximately 235,000 miles of oil pipeline.

The shift to truck transportation in the United States has brought locational readjustments in economic activity. The nation's freight bills have increased, with the greater reliance on the truck as the average ton-mile cost of the motor truck is higher than for rail. With this rise in transport cost, economic activity has tended to locate at or near market locations (near population clusters). As population has spread to the West and South, industry also has tended to disperse from the Northeast, especially industries with high freight costs. The widening gap between the freight rates charged on raw materials and on finished products (the latter rising more rapidly) has also encouraged market locations, as firms seek to avoid paying the high cost of shipping manufactured goods over long distances.

TRANSPORT RATES

Transport rates are the prices charged for moving goods. They have geographic expressions in that they may be mapped. Moreover, rate making, or the setting of rates, usually incorporates geographic variables, such as distance. Just as the layout of a network may affect the nature and intensity of movement over the system, so too does the structure of freight rates greatly affect the pattern of commodity flow in an economic system. The making of rates is extremely complicated, if only because over 2 million commodities are shipped in the United States among several thousand origins and destinations. A number of possible routes are usually available for a shipment, and a combination of alternative carriers may be used. Historically, rates have largely been set on a piecemeal basis; and although rates have historically been regulated by the Interstate Commerce Commission (except for air cargo and private transportation), it is difficult to sift through rate publications and discern the guiding principles behind their establishment. More recently, with the deregulation of truck, rail, and air transportation, a gaggle of rates exists, some for only a short time interval. In some instances, these rates take into account competition more than they reflect distance or cost.

Two categories of rates are the ***commodity rate*** and the ***class rate***. The class rate refers to rates established for classes, or groups, of commodities; all commodities in that class take the same rate. The class rate greatly simplifies rate making, but it may at the same time encompass a range of commodities with somewhat different handling and movement costs. For this reason, commodity rates may be established for specific commodities. Generally, commodity rates are lower than class rates for the same item. Whereas all commodities may be classified within the class-rates system, not all commodities are included in the commodity rates. Geographically, class rates vary with distance in a more regular and consistent manner than commodity rates.

Rates may be set on the basis of the cost involved in shipping a commodity, called ***cost-of-service rate making***, or on the level of demand for the transport service, known as ***value-of-service rate making***, or on some combination of these two. Cost of service may depend on whether refrigeration is required, whether the item is fragile or otherwise requires special handling, whether the item is bulky in relation to its weight (cubage or how much room it takes up), whether the shipments are on a steady basis in

high volume, and, or particular interest, whether the commodity is to be shipped a long or short distance. Value-of-service pricing depends on charging higher rates to customers with relatively ***inelastic demand***, that is, customers who cannot do without a commodity and who are, therefore, relatively indifferent as to the price of the item. Any good with an inelastic demand will continue to be purchased with little change in volume even if its price changes considerably. Value-of-service pricing also recognizes that the value of a commodity is an indication of commodity's ability that to bear a high transport cost, and it is a general rule that the more expensive an item, the higher will be the charge for moving it. The rate charged is meant to reflect the value of service in transporting the item rather than unreasonable or discriminatory charges.

Geographic Aspects of Freight Rates

Distance is a basic factor underlying cost of service. Transportation costs increase with length of haul, save for certain important exceptions. One exception is the ***tapering principle*** of freight rates (Figure 6.2). Instead of rates increasing as

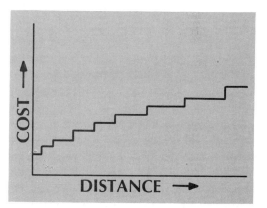

Figure 6.2 An illustration of the tapering and stepwise rate principles of transportation. The tapering effect holds that it does not cost twice as much to ship a commodity twice as far, and the stepwise principle indicates that rates are "stepped" like a stairway into distance zones.

a direct function of distance, they taper off with increased distance or increase in a decreasing manner. For example, if a rate is $1.00 to ship something 100 miles, the rate to ship it 200 miles will be less than $2.00, say $1.80. The longer the shipment, the greater the taper, thus encouraging longer hauls. Tapering rates are justified both because the actual cost of movement is less for longer hauls and because **terminal costs** can be spread out further to produce a lower ton-mile cost. Also illustrated in Figure 6.2 is the **stepwise principle**. Rates are calculated by zones, or steps, rather than on a continuous-distance basis, for reasons of simplification. Rates are identical within a given distance zone no matter where the shipment is terminated within that zone. Such an arrangement is similar to parcel post zones and telephone area code districts. If the shipment goes just beyond that zone, the next higher rate will apply. Stepwise rates are devised to avoid the burden of an overwhelming number of rate calculations for every possible point along the way.

Related in rationale to the stepwise principle is the **grouping principle**. The operation of this principle also reflects a significant exception to the idea that rates increase proportionately with length of haul. For classes or categories of commodities, rates are quoted from one area to an-other, rather than among all possible points. Normally, a major city or shipping point is taken as the center or control point for the determination of rates. Several proximate shipping points will also be included in that group; all points in that group or area have the same rates to any other group of shipping points. A state, for example, may be divided into several areas or groups of shipping points. The value of this system is, of course, to simplify the publication and quotation of rates. A short-distance shipment that crosses a group boundary suffers a high payment in terms of the actual costs involved, whereas a shipment that crosses a single group boundary but that is sent from the extremity of one region to the farthest point in the other will benefit by a rate lower than distance alone would suggest. Taxicab fare zones are an example.

From any given shipping point, rates increase unevenly in different directions. For example, the carload rate for wheat over the 500 miles from Kansas City to Chicago may be $7.86 per ton. The same shipment from Kansas City to Minneapolis, also 500 miles, is $8.38 per ton and to Dallas from Kansas City, again 500 miles away, is $10.13. There are numerous reasons for rates to vary with direction, such as different shipping volumes, differences in operating conditions, empty-car movement involving back-hauls, and differences in competition. For these same reasons, there are even many cases in which the rate is not the same in both directions. For rail shipments the **short line principle** provides that the rate must be based on the mileage of the shortest route over which the traffic can be transported without transfer of the cargo. In the absence of several routes radiating outward from the shipping point, it is to be expected that rates determined on this principle will vary by route direction.

Most of the principles of rate structure were first applied to the railroad and later substantially adopted by truck transportation. Yet the costs of rail and truck transportation differ considerably. Joel Dean has suggested five factors important

The MARTA rapid rail passenger system in Atlanta operates 46 miles of track and carries an average of 240,000 riders on a weekday.

in determining the optimum trucking costs per ton-mile for any given traffic.[2]

1. Mileage utilization of equipment and empty-return ratio.
2. State highway weight limits.
3. Length of haul (road mileage).
4. Degree of metropolitan concentration and other terminal characteristics.
5. Type of equipment required.

Trucks thus have economic incentives to reduce costs by quick delivery, to travel heavily loaded, to handle loading and unloading quickly and inexpensively, to utilize equipment fully, and to extend their hauls greater distances to compete with rail shipments. For these reasons, trucks have become a dominant mode of commodity movement in the United States.

Modal Comparison of Rates and Services

Two factors influence the rate difference for alternative transport modes: **terminal costs** and **line haul** (or "over-the-road") **costs.** Terminal costs are those associated with loading and unloading the commodities and the accompanying paperwork. These costs, of course, vary with the type of commodity being moved, but it is also possible to generalize about the level of terminal costs by mode of transportation (Figure 6.3). Comparing water, truck, and rail, terminal costs for water transport obviously are highest because of the expense of developing and maintaining a harbor and the cost of labor and equipment for the loading and unloading operations. Equally unsurprising is that the cost of loading a truck is not very great and involves much less costly equipment than the other modes. This leaves rail terminal costs somewhere between water and truck.

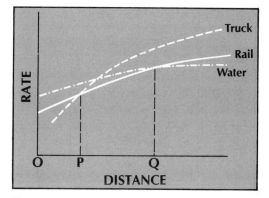

Figure 6.3 Different transport modes have different transport charges that vary with distance: least expensive are the motor truck for short distances, the rail for intermediate-to-long distances, and water movement for the longest hauls.

Line-haul costs refer to the expense entailed in the actual movement of goods once they have been loaded. These costs, in contrast to terminal costs, vary with distance; but, because of the tapering effect already discussed, they are not linearly related to mileage. Water movement is invariably the least expensive, whereas over-the-road operating costs are highest for trucks. Once again, rail transport falls in between. Looking at the distances at which each of the three modes are most competitive, we see that truck transportation, owing to low terminal costs, is the lowest cost mode at short distances, from O, the shipping point, up to distance P. This distance extends roughly up to 300 miles.[3] At an intermediate distance, from P to Q, rail offers the lowest costs, the competitive distance varying from about 300 miles up to 2000 or more, depending on the availability of water transport. Beyond distance Q, water is the most economical form of transport, and it is, of course, the dominant mode in world trade.

The freight rate is only one factor a shipper

---

[2]Joel Dean. "Competitive Pricing in Railroad Freight Rates," in Martin T. Farris and Paul T. McElhiney, eds., *Modern Transportation* (Boston: Houghton Mifflin, 1973), pp. 333–345.

[3]It is interesting to note at this point that Ford Motor Company ships automobiles up to 300 miles by truck from Detroit: beyond that distance, the automobiles are shipped by rail (85 percent of all shipments).

must consider in choosing among alternative transport modes. Another, at least equally important, is service. Transportation service implies a great many things, including speed of delivery, scheduling convenience, avoidance of damage, and reliability. Figure 6.4 illustrates how four modes, with air cargo now added, stack up, on the average, with respect to speed of service, which is probably the most important service consideration. Loading time is indicated where the respective lines meet the vertical axis; the lines themselves show total delivery time as it increase over distance. Loading time is highest for ocean shipping, followed by rail, air, and truck, in that order. Movement time, as opposed to loading time, naturally favors air by a sizable margin. Water and rail, again in that order, are slow in moving freight, whereas truck service is, by contrast, fast. The average distance a railroad boxcar moves in the United States is 70 miles per day. Total delivery time favors the truck at short distances, beyond which air transport has the distinct advantage. The ton-mile cost of air cargo, however, is still outlandish compared with all other modes. Consequently, little freight (on a ton-mile basis) moves by air (about 0.4 percent of all U.S. intercity freight).

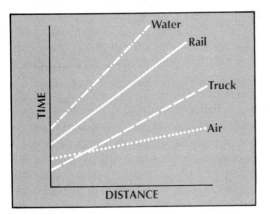

Figure 6.4 The quality of freight service, here measured by transport time, also varies by transport mode, with truck being the fastest for short distances, followed by air cargo. Rail and water transport are the slowest means of conveying goods.

All in all, the mode possessing the greatest advantages, considering both cost and service, is the motor truck. Air shipments occur primarily as emergency services, when an auto assembly plant is running short of fenders, for example, and is willing to pay the high air-transport cost to avoid the significantly higher cost of shutting down the assembly line for lack of parts. High-value goods per unit of weight may be sent air freight when speed of delivery is of overriding importance. Cut flowers, for example, are being flown in daily from the Netherlands and Colombia to metropolitan areas in the United States. Rail and water transport compete for long-distance movement of bulky items (low in value per unit of weight) for which speed of delivery is not particularly crucial. The railroad's advantage over water movement is in its more articulated network, which serves more areas and in its somewhat greater speed of delivery. Pipeline transport, closely associated both functionally and financially with the petroleum industry, is discussed in Chapter 12.

Multimodal Freight Transport

From the above classical comparison of modal differences, we now turn to the topic of multimodal transport of freight, which increasingly characterizes modern transportation.[4] Multimodal transport is simply the utilization of two or more modes of transportation to move commodities between an origin and a destination. The purpose of using more than one mode is to increase speed and efficiency and to reduce cost.

The key to multimodal transport is *containerization*—the use of container units for shipping a great variety of goods. This innovation has resulted in a revolution in the handling of commodities. The containers are portable by different transport modes and are, of course, reusable.

[4]This discussion is based on B. S. Hoyle and R. D. Knowles, eds., *Modern Transport Geography*. New York: Belhaven Press, 1992.

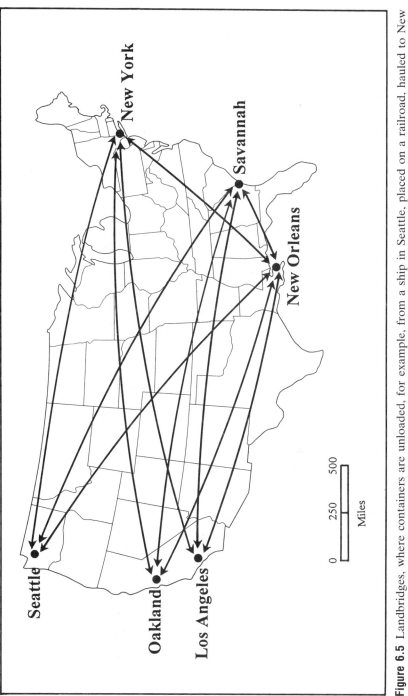

Figure 6.5 Landbridges, where containers are unloaded, for example, from a ship in Seattle, placed on a railroad, hauled to New Jersey, where the container is unloaded onto an oceangoing vessel for shipment to a European port. *Source:* after Hayuth, 1982.

Containerization has grown rapidly since the mid-1960s, when container trade developed between ports on the U.S. East Coast and Europe. With the global growth in trade, containerization has become commonplace. The container not only facilitates ocean movement, including loading and unloading, but also can be placed on trains or even airplanes for easy handling and movement. Trains loaded at a port with double-stack containers (one atop another) enjoy tremendous economies of scale in shipping cargo to inland locations or from one U.S. coast to the other, where the containers may be reloaded onto an oceangoing ship (Figure 6.5). In this way, the United States serves as a kind of land bridge to overseas destinations.

Multimodal transportation has led to a "total-systems" approach to transportation. The evolution of large multimodal transport companies in the late 1980 and 1990s provides total transport services to customers, who have to deal only with one company and receive only one bill of lading showing a single rate for the cargo shipment. The shipper is spared dealing with several separate companies and coordinating pickups and deliveries. For example, CSX started as a railway company and acquired Sea-Land in 1987 (a large container line). Today CSX is a total-systems transport company. Deregulation in the late 1970s and early 1980s permitted the evolution of multimodal transport.

Airplane construction at Boeing's manufacturing facility in Seattle.

Transport Rates and Economic Location

To illustrate locational choice as affected by transport rates, let us take an exceedingly simple example. A producer of some manufactured item requires a material available from a single source and sells to a single market. Where will the producer locate the processing operations? Transport costs will consist of two parts: the cost of *assembly* and the cost of *distribution*. We will assume (1) that the producer wishes to locate at that point where the transport costs (sum of the assembly and distribution costs) are at a minimum and (2) that production costs will not vary with location. Production costs include all costs involved in processing, such as labor, taxes, fuel,

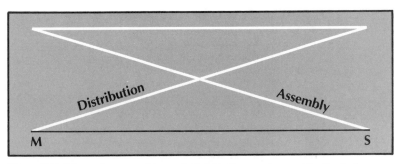

Figure 6.6 When the assembly and distribution costs are identical, the producer may locate at any point between the market (M) and the supply point (S).

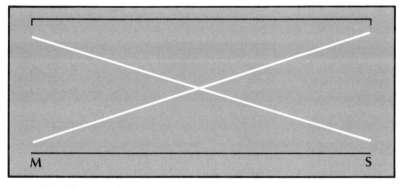

Figure 6.7 When terminal costs at the market and the supply point are taken into account, the lowest-cost locations for the producer become the market (M) or the supply point (S).

cost of material, and plant maintenance. We are separating transport costs from production costs.

If no terminal costs were associated with assembling the material or distributing the finished product, if transport costs were linear (no taper), and if assembly and distribution costs were equal, the producer would be indifferent as to where to locate because the costs would be identical at all locations. Figure 6.6 shows that the sum of the assembly and distribution costs is constant from the material source, *S*, to the market, *M*. A location at *S* would entail no assembly cost, but would result in a high cost of distribution. Conversely, location at the market would mean a high assembly cost but no distribution charge.

In Figure 6.7 we include, more realistically, terminal costs. The result is to place the lowest-cost locations at the material source and the market. The firm has the choice of saving the terminal cost on assembly by locating at the material source or the cost on distribution by a market location.

The tapering and stepwise principles are included in Figure 6.8. By glancing at the total transport cost line at the top, we immediately see this cost is highest at locations between the market and the material site, where cost is lowest. On closer inspection, we see it is the tapering effect that causes the total transport cost to rise to such high levels at *intermediate locations*. We may, therefore, state as a general rule that most firms seldom prefer intermediate locations and

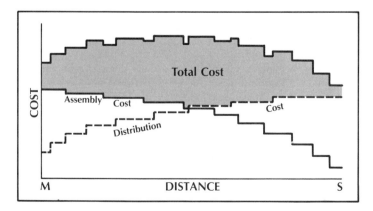

Figure 6.8 When the tapering and stepwise effects are added to the assembly and distribution costs, including the terminal costs, the least-cost location for the producer becomes the supply point (S).

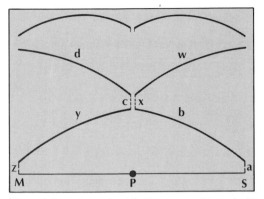

Figure 6.9 The break-of-bulk concept, illustrated here, allows an intermediate location (the break-of-bulk point) to become the lowest-cost location for the producer.

we will note some exceptions later. By a location at the market or material source, one gains the savings from the tapering rate; at an intermediate location, one pays two separate rates (one for the material and one for the product) and cannot take any significant advantages of the tapering effect. We have here a partial explanation for the clustering of economic activity as opposed to its dispersal.

Continuing with our one-material and one-market example, we find that when a break-of-bulk, or transshipment, occurs, the intermediate location becomes the preferred location (Figure 6.9). Petroleum is brought by the tanker to a European port, such as Rotterdam. There it must be unloaded and sent to the interior, where it will be marketed. Because a change of mode is necessary, it may prove economical for processing to occur at the break-of-bulk point, *P*. In Rotterdam a large petrochemical industry has developed. With the market at *M* and the material site at *S*, the costs for assembly will be *a*, *b*, *c*, and *d*, where *a* is the terminal cost for loading the tanker, *b* is the movement cost to reach the port, *c* is the cost at the port of transferring the petroleum from tanker to rail cars, and *d* is the rail charge to the market. For distribution costs (*w*, *x*, *y*, and *z*), *y* and *w* are the line-haul costs, and

x and *z* are the handling costs. In this example, with equal assembly and distribution costs, there are three least-cost locations: the market, the material source, and the intermediate port. Which of these would be selected by an entrepreneur would no doubt depend on other kinds of locational factors.

Let us turn next to an example involving more than two raw-material sites. We will use the word *isotim* to refer to lines on a map connecting points of equal transport cost. Figure 6.10 shows a hypothetical pattern of isotims. If a firm is located at the market, *M*, there will be no cost of distributing the processed good. The only transport costs will be the assembly costs from *S*. By examining the isotims for assembling the material, we see they increase irregularly away from the source location, reaching the level of 30 cents per hundredweight at the market. The distribution costs also increase away from the market location, and in this example they rise more rapidly than those for assembly. Thus, an individual locating at *S* would have no assembly costs, but the distribution costs would be 40 cents per hundredweight. A location at point *I*, an intermediate location, would incur a 20-cent charge to assemble a unit of materials and another 20-cent cost to distribute the product to market, for a

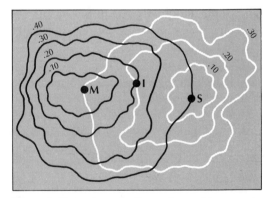

Figure 6.10 Isotims are lines of equal transport cost; that is, they connect all points having the same transport cost. In this example, the lowest-cost location is the market (M).

total of 40 cents. It is obvious in this example that the lowest-cost transport location is at *M*, the market.

The illustrations of the effect of freight rates on the location of economic activity, though elementary, point up some of the basic considerations entrepreneurs and locational analysts confront. The pricing of transportation can have a strong influence on the location a firm selects and on the success the firm enjoys at that location. Because freight rates are part of the cost of making a good available, these rates are passed on, in one way or another, to the buyer. A uniform increase in rates will normally raise the price of the good, whereas selective increases on different commodities or on different routes may or may not, depending on the competitive situation. When rates are upped on some routes but not on others, the advantages and disadvantages are unevenly spread, and some productive readjustments may result at these locations. Because freight rates enter into the price of the good at the market, we turn our attention to geographic pricing systems.

Freight Rates and Pricing

The most common pricing system is the ***uniform delivered price***, also known as net mill pricing and as ***c.i.f.*** ("cost, insurance, and freight"). Although the actual costs of delivery at every point do not coincide with the price, the price is established to absorb the freight rate and to average into the price the rate among all customers (Figure 6.11). The advantage of uniform pricing is its simplicity: One price is charged to everyone, regardless of location. The locational effect of this pricing policy is to reduce or eliminate a processor's dependence on a location near a material source. A second effect is that the market for the product can be expanded beyond the range that would correspond to actual costs. Thus, the nearby buyer in effect subsidizes the distant buyer because the former pays a price above the cost and the latter buys below the cost figure. As an example, Crest toothpaste is produced in Cin-

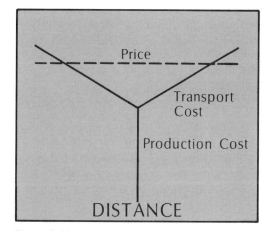

Figure 6.11 The uniform delivered price is the commonly used pricing plan whereby the same price is charged throughout an area, even though the actual cost of providing the product varies with distance.

cinnati and sells nationally, let us say, at $1.29. Its actual cost at Cincinnati is only $1.10, whereas its cost in Maine, including transportation costs, is $1.35 and in Hawaii, $1.45. Because of bookkeeping ease and the advantages of regional or national advertising, the uniform pricing system has become increasingly common.

A second pricing system is the ***f.o.b.*** ("free on board") alternative. Under this system, the price of a good is established at the factory site and the buyer pays the transport costs depending on the buyer's distance from the plant (Figure 6.12). Under f.o.b. pricing, the customer wishes to be as close to the producer as possible in order to minimize the transport cost. Location with respect to material sources then becomes a critical factor. It is interesting to note that much of the location-theory literature has assumed an f.o.b. pricing system despite the apparently growing importance of the uniform pricing policy. In contrast, Federal Express Corporation, which had long used the c.i.f. pricing system—one price to anywhere in the United States—switched in 1997 to the f.o.b. system, pay by distance shipped.

A last type of pricing system, the ***basing-point system***, has been used in certain industries, most

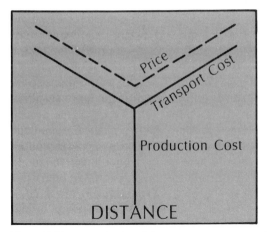

Figure 6.12 In the f.o.b. pricing, transport costs are incorporated into the final price of the item, and thus prices vary geographically (factory price plus the cost of transport).

notably the iron and steel industry in the United States. A basing point is established at whatever location a price is set. All production, whether originating at the basing point or elsewhere, takes the price at the basing point plus the freight from the basing point to the buyer. For example, if a customer for steel is located in Minneapolis and the steel is purchased from a steel mill in Gary, Indiana, the price paid will be the factory price as set at the basing point, Pittsburgh, plus the freight *as if the steel had been shipped from Pittsburgh*. Farmers living at the edge of Birmingham, Alabama, in the shadow of the huge Sloss blast furnace, purchased wire fence to keep their livestock from wandering freely. The wire was made and purchased in Birmingham; the farmers paid a price as though it had been shipped from Pittsburgh. The United States iron and steel industry used this basing-point system, known as the **Pittsburgh Plus**, until the mid-1920s, when a multiple basing-point arrangement was substituted. That system was finally declared illegal in the late 1940s by the U.S. Supreme Court and had to be abandoned. The locational

effect of a basing-point system is to encourage geographic concentration of an industry near the basing point, as buyers will prefer to locate in or near Pittsburgh, for example, rather than in Minneapolis. Basing-point pricing also tends to squash outlying competition, such as in Birmingham, Alabama, in iron and steel production.

Physical Distribution Costs

Many elements in the cost of transportation are substitutable, or partially so, with transportation. To be concerned only with minimizing the cost of transportation may mean raising other kinds of costs such that total costs are actually increased as a consequence of decreasing transport costs. *Physical distribution costs* are those involved in the functions of transportation, warehousing, packaging, inventory control, and materials handling. A firm seeks to minimize its total physical distribution costs rather than single-cost elements. For example, by using a higher cost mode with guaranteed daily delivery, a firm may reduce overall costs by eliminating much of the inventory control. Higher packaging costs may permit lower insurance rates and a lower cost transport mode.

Consider the following case of an actual manufacturing plant located in Peoria, Illinois.[5] The firm's location was primarily determined by its access to raw materials, despite the fact that almost its entire market was located between Portland, Maine, and Richmond, Virginia. A large warehouse owned by the firm was located in Philadelphia, a central location from which to supply the several wholesalers along the East Coast. The plant's output moved by rail, about 10 carloads per day, from Peoria to Philadelphia. The wholesalers received the shipments from the

[5]George W. Wilson, John C. Spychalski, and George M. Smerk, *Physical Distribution Management* (Bloomington, Ind.: Bureau of Business Research, 1963).

"Big" Truck Routes: The Case of Georgia

The Surface Transportation Assistance Act (STAA) of 1982 allowed the use of 102-inch truck width and 48-foot trailers and twin trailers (28-foot units) along with a standard 80,000-pound weight limit, and it directed the secretary of transportation to designate a national highway network on which this equipment could operate. The purpose of STAA was to increase trucking productivity, but only a limited network permitting the use of this equipment has thus far been approved. The result is that several constituencies have become involved in the selection of the "big" truck routes, transforming what one might have viewed as an economic efficiency issue into a full-blown political battle. On the one hand, there is the Federal Highway Administration, which has designated the interstate system as approved for the "big" trucks; on the other hand, there are the various state departments of transportation, which are in the process of deciding with noninterstate routes should be approved. On the private side is the American Trucking Association, along with its state affiliates, and many of the major trucking firms. Finally, private shippers, such as manufacturing firms, have an interest in the routes selected. If you add to this the much-debated issue of safety on the highways and the need for widening and upgrading the roadway, the result is to place the "big" truck issue squarely in the public spotlight because of the potential for increased taxation to pay for these improvements. In question, then, is a classic geographic issue: Since the routes selected will give locational advantages to some while denying these advantages to others, what areas will benefit and which will be harmed?

Background

Shortly after the secretary of transportation in February 1983 announced that, in addition to operating on the interstate highways, "big" trucks could operate on certain other federal-aid highways that were divided highways with four or more lanes and full control of access and that the Georgia Department of Transportation (GDOT) would be allowed to designate additional highway routes for the big trucks, the Georgia DOT initially designated 1168 miles of interstate and 140 miles of noninterstate routes. In April 1983, the Federal Highway Administration designated an additional 2866 miles of primarily two-lane highways in Georgia for "big" truck use, resulting in a suit before the United States District Court. A temporary restraining order was issued enjoining the federal officials from requiring the opening of nearly 3000 miles of highway to the "big" trucks. State and federal negotiations are continuing. At present, 1180 interstate miles and 513 noninterstate miles have been approved for the operation of the "big" trucks in Georgia (Figure 6.13).

It is estimated that the cost of upgrading the noninterstate routes (513 miles) to more acceptable safety levels would be approximately $40 million (GDOT). The currently approved 1693 miles for the "big" trucks will connect all Georgia cities of 15,000 people and above. A second, long-range plan would add some 600 miles to the present routes at an additional estimated cost of approximately $150 million. This future plan would connect all Georgia cities of 10,000 population and above.

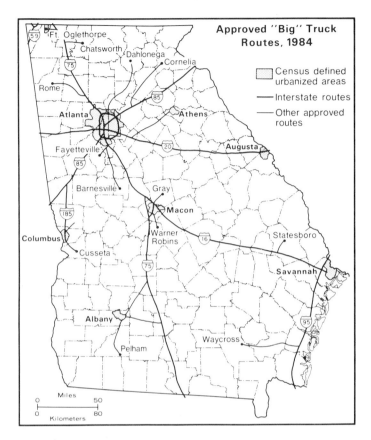

Figure 6.13 Approved "big" truck routes in Georgia.

Safety

Major opposition to the additional "big" truck routes by the Georgia Department of Transportation centers on the safety issue. Two studies have been carried out on the hazards associated with allowing these larger trucks to use two-lane roads. The hazard is real: A tractor and a pair of 28-foot trailers "stretch five times the length of a Honda hatchback and weigh 44 times as much, fully loaded" (June 4, 1984, *U.S. News & World Report*). On the other hand, Bennett Whitlock, president of the American Trucking Association, said that "the safety issue is a bugaboo that is depriving us of the most flexible, safe, and efficient piece of equipment that we have" and that the increased use of twin trailers will actually reduce the number of trucks on the highways. Georgia DOT studies conclude that "the fatality rate for large trucks on the state highway system in Georgia is more than triple that of all classes of vehicles. The approval of the use of larger trucks and the granting of more liberal access of large trucks to two-lane roads make it likely that losses from large truck crashes will increase." In addition to the safety issues are the "increased damage to pavements due to heavier wheel loads and the delays and inconvenience to automobile drivers attempting to pass the larger trucks."

Benefits of "Big" Truck Routes

Little is known precisely about the benefits of the larger trucks in terms of economic development. That there are operating cost benefits seems clear, and several trucking firms have purchased twin-trailer fleets. Other firms are proceeding more cautiously. One study, based on a 200-mile trip length, estimates the savings at nearly 20 cents per vehicle mile, with a 17 percent increase in cubage. Other studies place the cost savings even higher. In any case, not all shippers or commodities would accrue equal benefits. In the shipping of lightweight commodities, the added cubage would be of clear benefit. With heavy commodities, the weight limit might be achieved before the cubage maximum could be reached. "General commodity common carriers could more readily realize the operating efficiencies of the tractor-twin-trailer because of the larger number of terminals and break-bulk operations. Predominantly truck-load shippers may be less likely to use and benefit from the twin-trailers configuration."[6]

Although some authorities have suggested that economic development benefits will result from the greater use of larger trucks, it is likely that any benefits will be modest. If the route network is significantly enlarged, as the American Trucking Association wishes, the benefits will be diffused widely. With a more constricted route network, however, particular areas will see greater benefit, and other locations will not.

[6]Paul H. Wright, "Truck Routing Criteria Study," unpublished report, Atlanta, Georgia, Department of Transportation, January 11, 1984, p. 14.

warehouse by truck. The rail rate was 127 cents per hundredweight, whereas the rate by truck was 183 cents per hundredweight. Rail deliveries were fourth-morning at best and often took up to six days, requiring a minimum of six days' inventory at the Philadelphia warehouse. Truck deliveries from Peoria to Philadelphia were second-morning. Because of the substantially lower rail rate, the firm relied exclusively on the rail carrier.

Because the Philadelphia warehouse was in the path of a proposed urban freeway, a new warehouse location was sought nearby. Before it could be found, however, a new marketing manager raised the question of eliminating the warehousing function altogether, given the considerable expense of maintaining such a facility. After careful study, it was discovered to be cheaper to bypass the warehouse entirely and ship by the more costly truck alternative, providing direct plant-to-wholesaler service. In addition, a certain packing protection had to be provided for the rail movements. The point of all this is that the firm in fact did not know what its physical distribution costs were because those responsible for the various components of the costs were scattered through the firm's organizational chart. The geography of the firm—that is, the location of its various facilities—is tied together by its physical distribution costs, and the optimal cost stems from substitution alternatives among the physical distribution costs of transportation, warehousing, packaging, inventory control, and materials handling.

WORLD TRANSPORTATION PATTERNS

Three general patterns of transportation stand out on the earth as a whole. First are the large

Gridlock during rush hour on the Bay Bridge, Oakland, California, as vehicle demand for transportation even here exceeds freeway supply or capacity.

areas that greatly lack transportation facilities and that move only a small portion of the total goods and people transported. These are, of course, the developing nations, which stand in marked contrast to the second world transportation pattern: the industrialized economies, characterized by high levels of mobility, dense transport networks, and quickness and ease of movement. To these two patterns must be added Russia, and other countries of the former Soviet Union, a third transportation pattern that is distinct because of its overwhelming reliance on the railroad to move bulk material long distances. There are, however, certain nations that fit this

threefold classification only poorly. The system in India, for example, because of the rail construction during British colonialism, resembles, in terms of the importance of the railroad features, the Russian transport system, but in most other ways typifies that of a developing economy.

The transport characteristics of a country may be analyzed in terms of *route density* and *traffic density* (see Chapter 5). The concept of density connotes how closely packed these transport features are within an area. (To compute route density, divide the number of route miles by the area; to find traffic density, divide a measure of traffic volume, such as ton-miles, by the number of miles of route.)

Route Densities

Only two sizable areas of the earth have truly high railroad route densities: the eastern half of the United States and southern Canada (extending into the wheat-growing areas of the prairie provinces); and Western Europe. Several other, smaller areas also have a high railroad-route density, such as the Pampas of Argentina, focused on Buenos Aires; southeastern Brazil, focused on São Paulo and Rio de Janeiro; Japan; India, especially in the Ganges valley; portions of South Africa; and southwestern and southeastern Australia. Vast areas on all the continents lack rail networks. Russia, despite being the leading railroad nation on the earth, does not have a particularly dense network of tracks compared to Western Europe and eastern North America. The densest portion of the Russian railway system is in the European west, an area in which the rail system had largely been completed by 1917, when the Soviets took over, though much of it was destroyed during World War II and had to be rebuilt.

Areas of high railroad-route densities are also likely to be areas of high route density for highways. Highway mileage, however, is several times greater than that of rail mileage. In the United States, for example, there are just over 150,000 miles of railway, compared with over 4 million miles of roads and streets. Only about 600,000 miles, however, make up the basic intercity highway linkages, the remainder consisting of rural roads and city streets. Over 40,000 of these are limited-access interstate expressways.

Traffic Densities

The highest traffic densities in the world occur on the Russian rail network. In 1976, for example, Soviet railways hauled over 2000 billion ton-miles, the highest figure in the world. Yet the Russian rail system consists of only 60,000 miles of track. The reason behind these unusually high traffic densities goes back to the old Soviet transportation policy of developing and utilizing a skeletal railway network to move bulky commodities over the long distances in the largest country in the world. The rail system operates at a high technological level, nearly 30 percent of the rail system being electrified, for instance. Russia's railways operate long, heavily loaded trains at frequent intervals.

The Russian road network is only one-quarter as large as that of the United States, just over 1 million miles, most of it in inferior condition. The policy of the former Soviet Union did not emphasize road construction and improvement as much as rail development. Consequently, the amount of freight carried by motor truck in Russia today is surprisingly low, less than 2 percent of its intercity freight traffic. Russian pipelines

move approximately 26 percent of Russian freight, and 16 percent is moved by inland waterways and sea, leaving over 56 percent of total freight to the rail system.

The United States, the second leading railroad nation on the earth in total freight moved, has nearly three times the rail mileage of Russia. Traffic densities are obviously much lower. U.S. rail mileage has actually been decreasing from its peak in 1920 of about 250,000 miles to just over 150,000 today. The U.S. rail system, as previously noted, is unique in the world in being privately operated, except for Amtrak, a passenger service. The extensive mileage is largely a result of competing lines' providing "duplicate" service between the same points. The retrenchment in the system over the past 75 years has, of course, stemmed from other modes gaining competitive advantages, leading to rail abandonment and company mergers. The most heralded was the short-lived merger of the New York Central and the Pennsylvania Railroad to form the Penn Central in 1968, creating the largest rail company in the United States (over 20,000 miles). The Penn Central, until its demise and incorporation into CONRAIL in 1976, served the most densely populated and highly industrialized part of the country.

The Western European countries, in general, have relatively short, frequent, and lightly loaded trains. Because of the high route density of European railways, traffic densities are low compared with those of Russia and moderately low compared with those of the northeastern United States. (They are, of course, quite high compared with those of developing countries around the world.) Take France as an example: the French National Railway system, including main lines, secondary lines, and "freight lines," totals about 24,000 miles. The freight density is just under 2.0 million ton-miles per mile of track, taking the system as a whole. This figure compares to 3.7 ton-miles for the United States and to a whopping 21.0 ton-miles for Russia. In France, the railway carries about 45 percent of intercity

A view of a Federal Express sorting facility.

ton-miles, compared with 36 percent by road and about 9 percent each by waterway and pipeline.

Because data on road mileage may be misleading owing to the considerable variation in road conditions around the world, we may see the number of motor vehicles in use as one measure of the importance of highways (Table 6.7). Nearly half the motor vehicles in the world are in North America. A third are in Europe, and just over 10 percent are in Asia—excluding China, for which data are not available. (If we consider commercial vehicles only, Asia is slightly ahead of Europe.) Africa, South America, and Oceania collectively have less than 10 percent of the world's motor vehicles.

The railway is the clearly dominant mode for moving the world's freight, accounting for about 60 percent of the total intercity ton-miles of domestic trade. Inland waterways, trucks, and pipelines divide the remaining 40 percent rather evenly. River and canal traffic is most significant in Western Europe and in the Far East. Pipeline ton-miles make up a sizable proportion of traffic in the Middle East and to a lesser extent in Latin America (primarily in Venezuela). Highway traffic is found everywhere but is nowhere dominant, reaching its greatest relative and absolute development in North America.

International Trade

The basic principles of spatial interaction may be used to understand world patterns of international trade, with appropriate political modifications. Whereas almost all goods produced require some form of transportation, it is estimated that only about 12 percent of the world's seaborne trade on a *ton-mile basis* consists of petroleum and petroleum products, with the flow patterns extending principally from the Middle East to the industrial countries. A secondary pattern of these flows is from Venezuela to the East Coast of the United States.

Based on **value of merchandise**, however, a quite different pattern of trade flow occurs. The primary movement is between Western Europe and the United States and Canada, with secondary flows among other industrialized nations of the world. The petroleum flows are still significant when trade is measured on a value basis, but not nearly so important as on a volume scale. Japan stands out both as an importer of resources—thus important on a tonnage basis—and as an exporter of manufactured goods—outstanding on a value measurement. Together, the United States, Canada, and the Western European countries account for over half of all international trade by value. The countries of the world classified as developed, taken as a group, account for about two-thirds of all imports and exports by value; developing countries send and receive about one-fifth of all international trade; and the former communist countries account for the other 12 percent.

International trade flows may be summarized into three patterns: (1) flows among the industrialized countries, most of which involve manufactured goods; (2) flows between the lesser-developed countries and the developed countries, involving exports of raw materials (agricultural products, ores, and fuels) from the former in exchange for modest imports of manufactured items from the developed nations; and (3) flows from one former communist country to another, excluding the People's Republic of China, but including a little trade with noncommunist areas. These latter flows have become less significant with the breakup of the Soviet Union in 1991 and with the independence of Eastern European countries.

Table 6.7 Motor Vehicles in Use (in percent).

North America	39.8
Latin America	6.3
Europe	36.1
Africa	2.4
Asia	13.6
Oceania	1.8
World	100.0

In general, the level of international trade seems to be closely related to the level of economic development. The industrialized nations dominate the map of world trade, both as exporters and importers (see Chapter 4).

International trade occurs, as with all types of transportation, because of unequal spatial distributions of land, capital, and labor. Although capital is rather mobile, labor and especially land are not. Particular countries develop a comparative advantage in the production of a commodity or product. The *law of comparative advantage* states that a country will benefit by exporting a good that it produces at a lower relative cost than other countries and, conversely, that a country will benefit by importing a good that it might produce at a higher relative cost. As an example, because of its agricultural advantages country A produces wheat at a lower relative cost than country B. However, country B is able to produce apparel at a lower relative cost than country A owing to lower labor costs. Following the law of comparative advantage, country A should export wheat to country B, and country B should export apparel to country A. Needless to say, with many commodities and countries, the law of comparative advantage becomes highly complex to measure.

Often barriers to trade are established, such as *tariffs* and *quotas*. These are governmentally induced. A tariff is a tax or duty levied on particular merchandise entering or leaving a country. The tariff may be used to generate revenue or to protect domestic producers of the same category of merchandise. For example, a tariff may be set on apparel imports to raise the price of, say, imported shirts to allow higher-cost domestic shirts to remain competitive. A quota limits the number of items a country allows to be imported in a given period of time. Quotas are also a way to protect domestic producers. A country may limit the number of Japanese automobiles imported, for example, so that the domestic auto manufacturers may retool their plants and become competitive.

SUMMARY

The characteristics of the transportation system are fundamental to the functioning of the economic system. The transportation system connects the various components of the space economy. In this sense, transportation influences the broader features of economic activity. At the same time, however, economic activity exerts an influence on the location and quality of transportation. It is a two-way street. Said another way: transportation and economic activity are interdependent.

In Chapter 1, we pointed out that transportation cuts across all the economic sectors and links them as a highway network links cities. It follows that transportation is an important economic activity in its own right. Indeed, in the United States it is estimated that one of every five dollars spent goes for transportation; that is, about 20 percent of GNP is for transportation. Over 13 percent of the U.S. labor force is employed in the transportation field—more than 11 million people.

Because of the intricate ties between transportation and all types of economic activity and the importance of transportation itself as an economic activity, we have begun our analysis of economic systems by looking at transportation. Having considered these vital linkages, we now turn to an examination of economic nodes, or concentrations of economic activities—more commonly known as cities or metropolises.

Further Readings

Abler, R., J. Adams, and P. Gould. *Spatial Organization: The Geographer's View of the World*. Englewood Cliffs, N.J.: Prentice-Hall, 1971.

Altschiller, Donald, ed. *Transportation in America* (New York: H. W. Wilson, 1982).

Black, W., "Interregional Commodity Flow: Some Experiments with the Gravity Model," *Journal of Regional Science* 12 (1972), pp. 107–118.

Gray, George E., and Lester A. Hoel, eds. *Public*

Transportation: Planning, Operations and Management (Englewood Cliffs, N.J.: Prentice-Hall, 1979).

Hanson, Susan, ed. *The Geography of Urban Transportation.* New York: Guilford Press, 1995.

Hay, Alan, "Transport Geography," *Progress in Human Geography* (1980), pp. 271–275.

Hayuth, Y. *Intermodality Concept and Practice: Structural changes in the Ocean Industry.* London: Lloyds of London Press, 1987.

Hoover, E. M., *The Location of Economic Activity* (New York: McGraw-Hill, 1948).

Hoyle, B. S., and R. D. Knowles, eds. *Modern Transport Geography* New York. Belhaven Press, 1992.

Kagan, R. A. *Patterns of Port Development.* Brimley: Institute of Transport Studies 1990.

Locklin, D. P., *The Economics of Location*, 7 ed. (Homewood, Ill.: Richard D. Irwin, 1972).

Mitsubashi, S., *The Spatial Structure of Japanese Commodity Flows* (Chicago: Department of Geography, University of Chicago, Research Paper No. 187, 1978).

Pederson, E. O., *Transportation in Cities* (New York: Pergamon Press, 1980).

Ralston, Bruce, and Gerald M. Barber, "A Theoretical Model of Road Development Dynamics," *Annals of the Association of American Geographers 72*: (June, 1982), pp. 201–210.

Sampson, R. J., and M. T. Farris, *Domestic Transportation: Practice, Theory and Policy* (Boston: Houghton Mifflin, 1966).

Taaffe, Edward J., "The Transportation Network and the Changing American Landscape," in Saul B. Cohen, ed., *Problems and Trends in American Geography* (New York: Basic Books, 1967), pp. 15–25.

———, Howard Gauthier, J., and Morton E. O'Kelly, *Geography of Transportation* (Englewood Cliffs, N.J.: Prentice-Hall, 1996).

Thoman, R. S. and E. C. Conkling, *Geography of International Trade* (Englewood Cliffs, N.J.: Prentice-Hall, 1967).

Ullman, Edward L., *American Commodity Flow* (Seattle: University of Washington Press, 1957).

PART THREE

*Economic Activity
and the
City*

CHAPTER 7

The City as an Economic Node

⸻◇⸻

We will now discuss in a little more detail the struggle for existence.
—CHARLES DARWIN

INTRODUCTION

Cities are large, high-density concentrations of people and their activities. Although primary activities such as mining may provide an initial impetus for settlement and town growth, almost no primary activities of any consequence are performed in cities. Manufacturing (a secondary activity) is quite strongly associated with locations in metropolitan areas, though much less strongly today. Manufacturing acted in the past as a catalytic activity *around* which urban growth *depended,* and industrial centers such as Pittsburgh and Detroit blossomed almost overnight. The processing of goods continues to be a basic source of employment for urban dwellers, as will be seen in Chapter 10. In addition to the important role of manufacturing, tertiary activity (the provision of retail goods and services) is everywhere recognized as an urban function and, therefore, a city-forming activity. In fact, the wide range of tertiary jobs, invariably located where people are, is more significant in total numbers than secondary employment in our metropolitan areas. The most rapidly growing component of the tertiary sector in recent years is the advanced service industries, which

deal to a large extent with the processing of information.

Cities exist because of the advantages of locating economic activities close to people, one type of economic activity close to another type, and one person close to another person. Manufacturing and tertiary activities necessitate large numbers of people in fairly close proximity. Certain activities, especially tertiary services, take place when one person interacts face to face with another person, as with doctor–patient, teacher–student, or many kinds of salesperson–buyer relationships. It is for mutual convenience that people cluster like clumps of grass in a desert at locations of recognized advantage and centrality.

We can look at cities as containing a gigantic pool of information. The information may relate to medical, educational, manufactural, governmental, and many kinds of business and financial matters. By locating in a city all of this information (i.e., people knowledgeable in these matters), any single individual has access to an overwhelming mountain of information. In fact, the problem may be how to gain access to that one bit of information that an individual desires. Metropolitan areas continue to grow because

The famous 110-story Twin Towers, as seen from the Hudson River west of Manhattan.

this information has an economic cost—a charge for obtaining it. A sizable proportion of the urban labor force deals with the handling and exchange of information, in whole or in part. Because, on the average, large metropolises have more information, both in quality and quantity, they tend to have more viable economic bases than smaller centers.

URBAN ECONOMIC FUNCTIONS

Urban economic geographers refer to cities by their dominant type of economic function. Thus, there are commercial cities, manufacturing centers, transportation cities, financial capitals, and even some mining cities. The problem with this approach to classification is that a metropolis has all of these functions, and to regard a city as, say, primarily a manufacturing center, is to overlook its importance in many other economic areas. The fact is that cities are usually more similar in economic functions than they are different, and many of the characteristics that differ from city to city are actually a result of population-size differences among the cities. Historical factors may also help explain differences among cities. Cities are not really that specialized in performing economic functions; they are mainly unspecialized or diversified. The larger the city, the greater the diversity normally is.

There is a long list of urban economic func-

tions. As already mentioned, the most important activities fall into the tertiary category. Tertiary functions in urban areas include retail trade; wholesale trade; finance, insurance, and real estate; business and repair services; personal services, including entertainment; professional services, comprising medical, other health, and educational services; public administration; and utilities and sanitary services. Secondary functions, in addition to a wide range of manufacturing activities, include construction industries. Transportation and communication services constitute yet another category of urban economic functions, though they are often included under the tertiary category. All urban areas have all these activities to one degree or another.

For the United States, we have seen a long-term shift in metropolitan economies. Let's take total employment and divide it into jobs involving producing goods (manufacturing, mining, and construction) and producing services (all other jobs). Jobs in the goods-producing sector have dropped dramatically, from over 40 percent in 1940 to just over 21 percent today (Table 7.1). At the same time, service-producing jobs have risen from 59 percent in 1940 to nearly 79 percent today. The absolute number of manufacturing jobs has decreased, despite the overall growth in metropolitan economies. Manufacturing jobs reached their peak in 1979 (21 million jobs) and now account for only 18 million workers. Service jobs, in marked contrast, have grown from 65

Corporate headquarters of Wal-Mart in Bentonville, Arkansas. Sam Walton, its founder, defied all traditional logic by locating his headquarters in a small town but also locating his first set of retail stores in small towns not otherwise served by retailers.

million jobs in 1980 to over 85 million today, a 30-percent jump.

Almost all of this growth in services occurred in metropolitan areas, especially the very largest centers. Most of these service jobs have been created in suburban areas. The fastest-growing service industries are computer, data-processing, and telecommunications equipment; engineering, architectural, and surveying services; and management, consulting, public relations, and finance. Note that all these fastest-growing categories deal with specialized information processing.

Table 7.1 Percentage of the U.S. Labor Force by Industry Sectors

Years	Manufacturing	Goods Producing	Service Producing
1940	33.9	40.9	59.1
1950	33.7	40.9	59.1
1960	30.9	37.7	63.3
1970	27.3	33.3	66.7
1980	22.4	28.4	71.6
1992	16.6	21.3	78.7

A basic question for the economic geographer is why such a broad spectrum of activities is attracted to one metropolis after another. As indicated, an overriding reason has to do with the higher levels of productivity that can be achieved by clustering rather than dispersing activities. This higher level of production efficiency translates, at a practical scale, into higher levels of personal income; metropolitan areas have invariably had higher median family incomes than rural areas. (Recent growth in nonmetropolitan areas has begun to blur this relationship, however.) The two general reasons for the greater levels of urban production efficiencies are discussed under the headings of "agglomeration economies" and "communication economies."

Agglomeration Economies

Agglomeration refers to the geographic concentration of activities. Economies means savings. As a result of agglomeration, savings are often possible through reductions in the *average costs* of production or service provision. There are several ways in which this process works. *Economies of scale* (mentioned in Chapter 3) are cost savings internal to a producing unit (e.g., a factory) made possible when the level or scale of operations is large. For example, Figure 7.1 compares the average costs to manufacture a unit of produce (a good or service) with the scale of production for two different types of economic activities, types A and B. Generally speaking, the average cost per unit of output decreases as the level of output increases. For this reason, economic establishments tend to enlarge with growth in the economy. If market demand for the output grows, often an additional market may be reached because of lower unit costs that can be passed on to the consumer in the form of lower, more competitive prices. However, as Figure 7.1 indicates, not all establishments are equally able to achieve scale economies.

Activity type A has little incentive to enlarge its scale of output beyond a particular size, *O-P*,

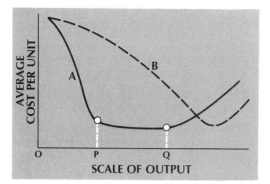

Figure 7.1 The average cost of producing a unit of a manufactured good varies with the scale of output. For different kinds of manufacturing, however, this relationship varies. In this example, manufacturing type A is able to reduce the average cost rapidly with small increases in output, but type B must increase output considerably before being able to enjoy the full benefits of scale economies.

because such enlargement would not bring about significant additional reductions in average costs. Type A activities, such as a grocery store, tend to remain of a given size range, as ***diseconomies*** (increases in average cost) become associated with levels of output beyond threshold Q. If type A activities are consumer or service dependent, as in the case of the grocery store, they will seek out locations in population centers (i.e., urban areas). They will, however, spread themselves out more or less evenly with respect to the population or, rather, the purchasing power. If type A activities, on the other hand, represent a type of manufacturing industry that is not tied strongly to a local market or to any other particular locational criteria, the location of this type of industry will be "footloose," or indifferent as to a rural or an urban setting. The men's apparel industry of the rural Southern Piedmont is an excellent example of an industry that is widely scattered in rural and small-town locations because of its attraction to inexpensive rural labor. The large amount of handwork still required gives little advantage to the development of larger plants.

Type B activities continue to improve their average costs until the scale of output is quite high. Automobile production is one illustration. Smaller firms cannot compete and are squeezed out of their portion of the market. Because type B activities are economically efficient only at a large scale, they almost invariably are forced to locate in a large metropolitan area that has the quantity and quality of labor force to sustain their desired level of production. Activities uniquely able to take advantage of scale economies possess some or all of the following characteristics: a high degree of labor specialization (production-line operations), a considerable use of specialized machinery and equipment (automation), large advertising expenditures, a sizable research budget, and the purchase of large volumes of materials. Mass production results. Beyond some point, however, diseconomies may prevail as size becomes too large for efficiency to be maintained. These diseconomies are known as *diminishing returns*. To take a simple example, the addition of one more worker to a confined working space in a factory may result in everyone being in everyone else's way (bumping elbows) and lead to a less efficient and more costly operation. In sum: type B activities are urban in location; type A may be both urban and rural, but the urban dominance is especially notable for population-dependent and information-dependent economic activities.

Whereas scale economies are internal to the establishment, certain savings from agglomeration are external, or beyond the control of a single firm: ***localization economies,*** for example. These are savings a firm enjoys because it locates near other firms in the same or a closely related activity. Manufacturing firms may benefit from sharing a skilled labor pool, machinery repair equipment, or research findings. Specialized suppliers of materials may serve several firms in the same industry, allowing the suppliers to pass along to each firm savings from scale operations. Once again, the average cost of unit production decreases as like industry expands in localized area, most typically a single metropolis or a group of proximate cities. In retailing, competing stores will often locate near one another, as in a shopping center, where the provision of parking space is shared by several stores and the benefits of the "image" of the commercial cluster are shared by all. A basic localization economy in the case of shopping centers exists for the customer as well as for the establishment. Sales at each store increase because consumers are attracted by the travel-time convenience made possible by multiple-stop shopping at these centers; because of comparison buying, especially for ***shopping goods*** such as shoes (as opposed to ***convenience goods*** such as food and drugs), firms offering the same or similar goods will be attracted to similar locations.

A good example of localization economies is found in carpet manufacturing in Georgia. Over 70 percent of the total U.S. domestic value of tufted production (census terminology for "carpet manufacturing") is produced within 50 miles of the small city of Dalton, Georgia (25,000 population), located 30 miles south of Chattanooga, Tennessee. An explanation of this unusually high degree of spatial clustering lies in the similar concentration of related industries that provide needed goods and services to the local carpet mills or utilize byproducts of the mills. Major suppliers of goods and services to the Dalton, Georgia, area carpet mills are highly concentrated near Dalton. The carpet industry is highly localized because of the necessity of ready access to suppliers, and a new firm entering the carpet

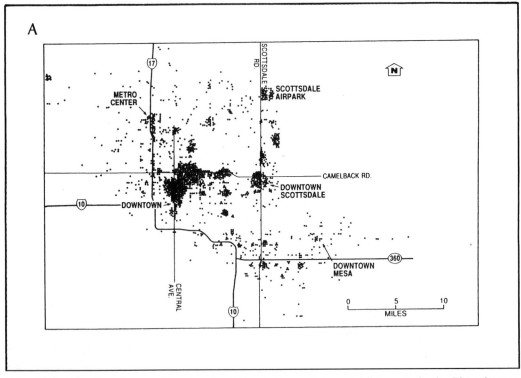

Figure 7.2a Location of management and public relations service establishments in the Phoenix metropolitan area.
Source: Ó hUallacháin and Reid, 1992.

business is attracted to an area in which suppliers are already available.

In a study of carpet manufacturing, locational factors that were found to be of significantly greater importance to the carpet mills clustered around Dalton compared to mills in the rest of the country included (1) good service from suppliers of raw material, (2) access to skilled labor, (3) proximity to suppliers of raw material, (4) location near other plants, (5) access to machinery manufacturing, (6) proximity to suppliers of auxiliary material, and (7) proximity to center of the textile industry.[1]

[1]See Billie J. Walters and James O. Wheeler, "Localization Economies in the American Carpet Industry," *Geographical Review* 74 (April 1984), pp. 183–191.

Urbanization economies are a second kind of savings made possible by agglomeration external to a firm. The average costs of a firm are lowered when location is sought near other firms representing many different kinds of economic activity. Such locations are urban areas. Firms in urban areas share many kinds of costs that they would have to provide internally if they located in a rural setting—fire and police protection, for example. All establishments in an urban area take advantage of the transportation services provided by that city: the varied labor market; the municipal services, such as water and sewage; banking and commercial services. By sharing the costs of these very expensive and rather specialized urban services, all establishments derive lowered average costs over what would result if

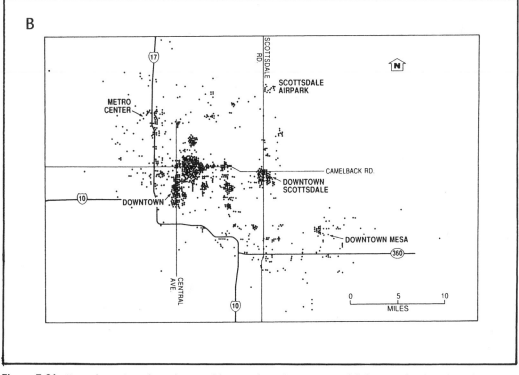

Figure 7.2b. Location of engineering, architectural, and survey establishments in the Phoenix metropolitan area.
Source: Ó hUalláchain and Reid, 1992.

each establishment independently had to provide these services.

Other examples of urbanization economies are seen in the agglomeration of (1) management and public relations service establishments and (2) engineering, architectural, and surveying service establishments in Phoenix, Arizona (Figure 7.2). These firms are generally quite concentrated (with some notable exceptions) to serve their respective specialized clientele. Even though the land and office costs are high in the downtown, a central location is desired to be near firms in other economic sectors. Thus, shared information costs are more important than land costs for these firms, which therefore concentrate in urban areas rather than in rural settings.

It follows that scale economies, localization economies, and urbanization economies will be more pronounced the larger the metropolitan complex. For these reasons, size attracts size. This means that urbanization economies will be greater than in smaller urban areas, all other things being equal. In addition, localization economies are more likely to occur for more industries in larger metropolises. A point may be reached, however, when further increases in size are met by urbanization and localization diseconomies. A cluster of economic activities may grow too large for efficient operation as old rail and water terminals, which originally attracted the growth at the cluster, become so congested and costly as to discourage utilization. No one knows what the optimum size is or even if we have reached it yet.

Communication Economies

Whereas we readily think of cities as nodes into and out of which commodities of all types flow, we do not as often realize that cities also act as nodal points for the collection, sorting, and dissemination of information. We can usually see

the transportation facilities (except for pipelines buried underground), but communication routes are less visible and also less widely understood. Furthermore, we can measure the movement volume of commodities by tonnage or value of shipment; there are no corresponding measurement units for information, especially as regards dollar value. And yet from an economic point of view, communication has a cost and plays a basic, undeniable role in the functioning of the metropolis. For every commodity that moves, for example, there has to be written or oral authorization, as well as a financial transfer. For locational decisions themselves, there will typically be examination of alternatives, involving the amassing of diverse bits of information, and decisions of an individual or, more frequently, a group.

Certain kinds of information may be accumulated slowly and carefully, as with a research team developing a new product. Other types of day-to-day communication may be dispatched via the postal service, such as orders for products and other routine business matters. The use of computers and fax communications also speeds the processing of large amounts of data. More immediate issues may be resolved by use of the telephone for both local and long-distance conversations. Certain issues and decisions are most easily resolved by face-to-face communication, where the parties sit down with one another to hammer out decisions. In all these examples, cities provide unmistakable communication advantages, and these advantages reflect dollar savings even if they cannot be measured precisely.

Urban areas provide settings for the accumulation of information, both in the form of centrally located record storage for a firm's headquarters and also in the sense of concentrating many technical and managerial experts in close proximity. The largest metropolitan areas are the headquarters of the largest corporations; and the decisions made in these centers, on the basis of information often assembled from afar, influence economic activity and the well-being of people throughout the region, country, or countries served by the corporation (see Chapter 11 for discussion of changing trends in headquarters location). To the list of city functions, we must then add that of *managerial function,* a direct result of urban communication advantages, expressed through personnel proximity. In addition, the city acts as a *switchboard* that assembles, transfers, and disseminates information that allows the economic activities in the city to be carried out more cheaply and efficiently than in a non-urban environment.

One example of the communication of specialized information is law firms serving corporate, government, institutional, and private clients. Where do such firms locate to carry out their particular types of information-based functions? The answer is large cities (Table 7.2). New York has nearly doubled the number of legal employees found in second-place Washington, D.C. Most of Washington's legal employees are, in fact, in branch law offices headquartered elsewhere, especially in New York. Thus, legal services seek to locate with proximity to clients (whether they be civil and corporate, divorce, criminal defense, taxes, patents, bankruptcy, antitrust, securities, mergers, labor, medical, or environmental law).

Another example of information flows is the number of Federal Express boxes, packages, and letters sent among U.S. metropolitan areas. Figure 7.3 shows Atlanta's exports of Federal Express information (packages) to major metropolitan areas in the United States, especially within the Southeast. New York is the leading destination for Atlanta's information, followed by Los Angeles, Washington, D.C., Miami, Chicago, Charlotte, and Dallas. Obviously, big cities are strongly linked to other big cities. Whereas small centers are also strongly linked large centers, small centers are weakly linked among themselves. Small centers are more strongly

Table 7.2 Employees of 500 Largest Law Firms in Large U.S. Cities, 1990

City	Total Legal Employment
New York	13,964
Washington, D.C.	7,571
Chicago	6,075
Los Angeles	5,258
Philadelphia	3,091
Boston	2,998
San Francisco	2,964
Dallas	2,383
Atlanta	1,620

Source: Warf and Wije, 1991, *Growth and Change,* p. 161.

linked when they are close together but not when separated by a great distance.

The largest flow of information occurs between New York and Los Angeles, the two largest metropolitan centers. Knoxville's leading export destination is New York. Austin, Texas, has its strongest ties with Dallas, and Grand Rapids, Michigan, hardly speaks with Salt Lake City. Big centers dominate information flows no matter how far apart they are. Small centers are sensitive to distance and thus have regional rather than national information exports.

There is a serious danger, however, that the very advantages of the city for amassing information may result in *communication overload.* Just as traffic may build up on an urban freeway until the system is clogged and traffic is forced to halt, so, too, may communication systems reach their capacity, resulting in lost information, misinformation, or the wrong information. In terms of locational implications, communication overload may result in an establishment's selecting a wrong location in the short run, the long run, or both. Probably even more frequently, however, poor locational decisions result from too little information rather than from too much poorly digested or inaccurate information.

Pred suggested a useful way to relate the quan-

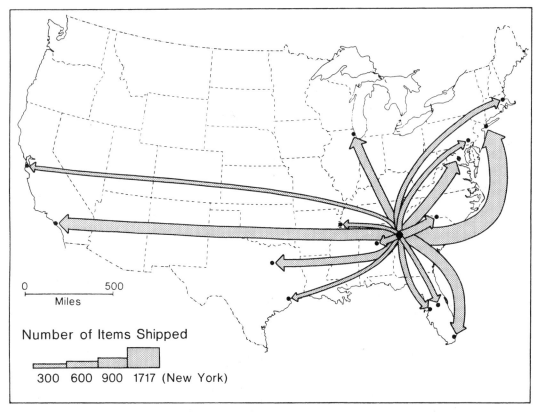

Figure 7.3 Atlanta's export of information to selected centers.
Source: Wheeler and Mitchelson, 1989.

tity and quality of information to the locational decision.[2] He set up a ***behavioral matrix*** with the quantity and quality of information along one axis and a measure of the ability to use information (managerial abilities) and decision making along the other (Figure 7.4). The information scale ranged from perfect knowledge (what economists attribute to their hypothetical being called economic man) to no knowledge. The ability scale also ranged from the optimal solution at one end to random decision making at the other. In the context of our discussion there is a higher probability that decisions falling into the lower

right-hand quadrant of the matrix will be made in an urban communication node than in the nonurban setting lacking a full communication base. The upper left-hand quadrant reflects decisions made with only a small amount of low-quality information by decision makers of low ability. Such decisions will usually prove to be economically foolish, and the establishment so located typically will fail financially. Although a great many significant locational factors are not taken into account by the behavioral matrix, the concept is useful in understanding how information forms the basis of locational decisions in metropolitan areas. In summary, large urban areas provide the communication base for decisions whether to locate or to operate the economic establishment by advantageous

[2]Alan R. Pred, *Behavior and Location: Foundations for a Geographic and Dynamic Location Theory, Part 1* (Lund: Lund Studies in Geography, 1967).

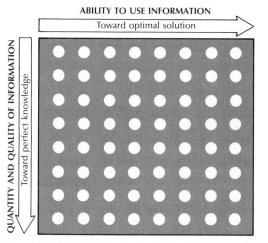

Figure 7.4 Pred's behavioral matrix, illustrating the relationship between the quantity and quality of information used in making a locational decision and the ability to use that information. The optimal locational decision will be represented by a point in the lower right-hand corner of the matrix, and the worst decision by a point in the upper left-hand side.
Source: Pred, 1967.

communication economies and by a geographic clustering of high-quality decision makers.

THE URBAN ECONOMIC BASE

In Chapter 3 we noted the importance of the specialization of labor in regional economic growth. We referred to this phenomenon as regional specialization. One form of regional specialization is the urban region, which specializes in certain kinds of economic activities to serve a wide area. All cities specialize in the sense that they provide economic goods and services for other areas. Specialization does not mean that the economic activity is found in only one place; rather, the term denotes that all cities, in order to be economically viable, must sell some portion of their goods and services beyond the city in which they are produced. Any activity is city-serving or reflects urban regional specialization to the extent that it serves the territory beyond the city and, therefore, brings money into the city.

Basic and Nonbasic Activity

The concept of basic and nonbasic activities lies at the core of understanding the city as an economic node. The distinction is probably more meaningful conceptually than it has proved to be empirically because of the several problems in defining the concepts in terms of data for actual cities. It is, therefore, at the conceptual level that we will consider the basic–nonbasic concept.

All economic activity in an urban area can be divided into basic and nonbasic parts. ***Basic activity*** produces goods and services in the urban area but sells them beyond the city. The export of these goods and services brings income into the city and provides the base for urban viability and growth. The more a city can produce for export, the more income it can attract. ***Nonbasic activity*** refers to the provision of goods and services for the city itself. Because there is no export involved, no income is attracted from outside, but only exchanged within the urban unit. Activities obviously vary considerably in their dependence on the local market.

Corporate decision making at a headquarters location acts as an information service export. Thus, an important basic, income-generating activity in the New York metropolitan area is the many headquarter locations of the largest U.S. corporations.

To measure the importance of a city's economic base, one may calculate a simple ratio between the total basic activity and the total nonbasic activity: B/NB, where B is total basic activity and NB is total nonbasic activity. Frequently, employment activity will be the actual measurement used. Because total employment activity, TA, equals the sum of B and NB, the basic–nonbasic ratio will express the projected increase in total employment activity for any increase in basic employment activity. We know that $TA - B + NB$. If, for a given city, total employment is 60,000 ($TA = 60,000$), and if employment in basic activities accounts for 20,000, leaving 40,000 in the nonbasic category, then: $60,000 = 20,000 + 40,000:3 = 1 + 2$. This expression tells us that for every person working in an export (basic) activity, there will be two people employed to serve the urban population. We are assuming, for purposes of illustration, that one may divide workers into either the basic or the nonbasic category, whereas in reality a given worker may perform both kinds of activities, as with a barber cutting the hair of an out-of-town visitor (basic activity) versus clipping a resident of that center (nonbasic).

We have thus calculated a measure of the urban multiplier effect mentioned in Chapter 3. If a new firm employing 1000 people locates in the city and produces entirely for export, the estimated projection in total employment will be 3000 for $1 \times 1000 = 1000$ and $2 \times 1000 = 2000$ for a total employment change of 3000. In other words, the new firm will create not only 1000 jobs but will also generate the need for 2000 additional jobs to serve the firm's workers and their families. Knowing the increase in basic employment allows a prediction of the likely increase in total employment within the urban economy. Needless to say, such estimates are invaluable for planning future urban growth and development. Thus, the basic economic structure of a city is not the same as that reflected in total employment data, for much of the total consists of nonbasic workers.

The basic–nonbasic ratio varies with city size: the larger the city, the greater the nonbasic proportion of total employment. In other words, 100 basic jobs will create a larger number of nonbasic jobs in New York than in Tallahassee, Florida. The basic–nonbasic ratio for New York might be 100:225; for Cincinnati, 100:175; for Tallahassee, 100:90; and for Sullivan, Wisconsin (population 434), located halfway between Milwaukee and Madison, 100:35.

There are several advantages to viewing urban economic activities through the basic–nonbasic concept. First, it enables one to classify cities in terms of those activities that are most important to its economic viability. If a city produces a large number of, say, ball bearings for export through-

out the region or country, that manufacturing activity is certainly of greater importance to the economic growth and well-being of the city than barber shops, even though the latter may represent a necessary economic activity. The point is that if an export or basic activity expands or cuts back production because of market fluctuations, there will be economic repercussions throughout the city, for even the barbers will be affected by an expanded or reduced purchasing base. Barbering is a service activity that typically follows rather than leads economic activities in which a city specializes.

A second and related value of the basic–nonbasic concept is its usefulness to urban and regional planners. By knowing which economic activities are basic to an urban area, planners are able to gauge the dimensions of urban change brought about by anticipated or predicted changes in the basic activities. This idea holds not only for kinds of activities but also for specific firms, establishments, and plants. Thus, if basic firms located in the eastern part of the urban area are projected to grow, it may be expected that this part of the city in general is more likely to undergo expansion in residential, commercial, recreational, and institutional activities. The basic–nonbasic ratio will give some estimate of just how much additional growth is likely to take place, allowing the planner to guide and coordinate this growth by recognizing the interrelated nature of the growth.

A third advantage of the basic–nonbasic concept is that it emphasizes the geographic ties of a city with its region. If one maps the shipment of commodities produced in a city to the locations that purchase these commodities, a fairly clear understanding of the city's regional position and pattern of spatial interaction emerges. When such mapping is repeated for several cities, comparative evaluations are possible regarding the spatial functional organization of cities. In Figure 7.5, in which the import functions of ports is regarded as a basic activity in that it generates revenue from outside the city, one sees that the

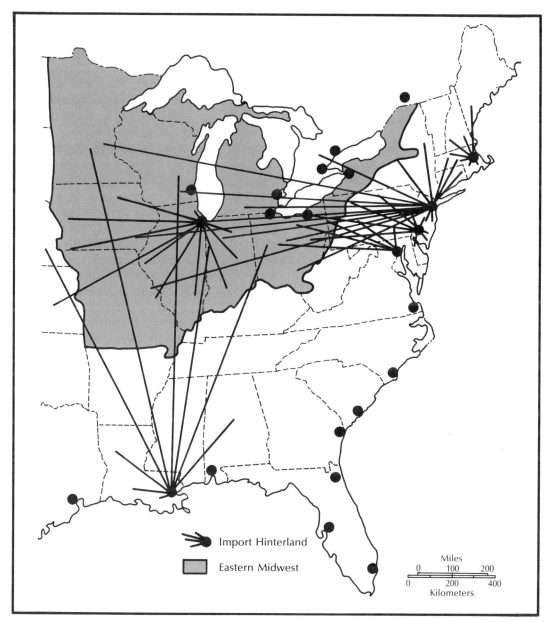

Figure 7.5 Generalized import hinterlands of selected U.S. ports.
Source: Kenyon, 1970, p. 12.

Import Hinterland

Eastern Midwest

Miles
0   100   200

0   200   400
Kilometers

pattern of inflows of commodities to ports is highly variable. There is considerable overlap among the largest port cities mapped, such as New York, Philadelphia, Baltimore, Chicago, and New Orleans. Boston, in contrast, shows little overlap, serving the local regional market of New England. By mapping and analyzing the flows of commodities associated with a city's basic activities, an understanding of the city's spatial linkages emerges, which, in turn are related to economic importance, composition, and future prospects for that city.

Minimum Requirements

There are various ways to determine the number of people employed in the basic and nonbasic categories. One approach, suggested by Edward L. Ullman and Michael Dacey, is based on the theoretical minimum proportion of a city's employment engaged in nonbasic or cityserving activities.[3] If one takes a large number of cities of approximately the same population size and examines the proportion of workers in a particular industry for each of the cities, there will be one city that has the lowest proportion. Ullman and Dacey argued that this lowest proportion represents the minimum requirements for that industry of a city in a given population-size range. By examining these minimum requirements for 14 industries in 6 size-categories of U.S. cities, they found that minimum requirements increased with city size. Any proportion employed above the minimum for a particular city size can then be attributed to basic activity. By knowing total employment in a city, one may calculate the number of workers in the basic and nonbasic categories for each industry.

There are two fundamental shortcomings of

the minimum-requirements approach, however. One is that the resulting basic and nonbasic employment totals are directly dependent on the minimum proportion found for that industry among that particular city size group. Had a larger or smaller number of cities been included within the size group, it is quite possible that a different minimum proportion might have been observed. Thus, minimum requirements among small Texas cities may differ from those of small cities in Montana, which may differ from values of small cities in the United States as a whole. A second problem with the minimum-requirements approach is that it seeks to determine basic versus nonbasic city structure indirectly. As indicated earlier, basic activity refers to the export of goods and services, which results in the inflow of money to the city. Nonbasic activity represents an exchange of money within the urban area. The minimum-requirements approach does not directly measure money inflow, which generates economic growth and sustains economic viability but, rather, indirectly attempts to determine money flow through a labor-force breakdown into the basic and nonbasic groups. Nevertheless, because no detailed data exist on intraurban and interurban money flows, the minimum-requirements approach has proved the only practical method for estimating a city's economic exports.

A final shortcoming of the basic–nonbasic concept, which is not limited to the minimum-requirements technique, is the delimitation of the area being studied. If one selects a small industrial section of the city, virtually all employment in this section presumably is engaged in activity that brings money into (rather than circulates it within) that section. All workers are basic. An example of the problem of delimiting major employment centers is seen in Figure 7.6, which shows the highly fragmented major employment centers in the Dallas–Fort Worth metropolex. Most of the highest density employment centers are found in northern Dallas and in

[3]Edward L. Ullman and Michael Dacey, "The Minimum Requirements Approach to the Urban Economic Base," *Proceedings of the IGU Symposium in Urban Geography* (Lund: Lund Studies in Geography, 1962), pp. 121–143.

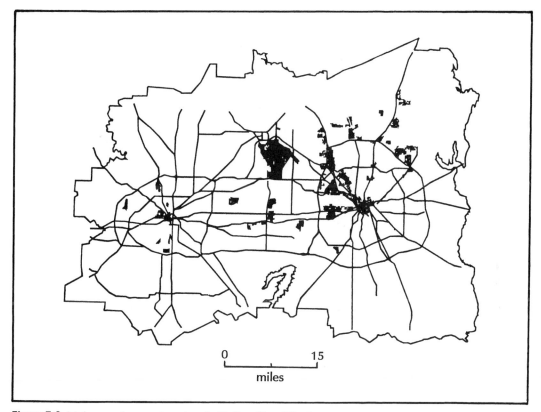

Figure 7.6 Major employment centers in Dallas–Fort Worth.
Source: Waddell and Shukla, 1993.

and around the Dallas–Fort Worth airport, located just to the north and between these two cities.

Going to the opposite extreme, one may envision the entire world. Lacking trade ties in outer space, all economic activity in the world must be regarded as nonbasic, involving exchange within. Clearly, the scale at which one is determining the basic–nonbasic ratio is fundamental. Although the examples just given are extreme, the same problem in a very practical sense is encountered when one examines an urban area. Where are the "proper" boundaries? Given the very considerable extent and nature of urban sprawl, so pronounced in U.S. cities, and the development of "continuous" cities through coalescence over time, it is almost impossible to select "correct" boundaries for the analysis of basic–nonbasic activities. Thus, the basic–nonbasic theme is most useful at the present time as a conceptual device for understanding cities as economic nodes rather than for empirical application.

URBAN ECONOMIC STRUCTURE

We have seen that cities perform economic functions as commercial, service manufacturing, and transportation centers. Some of these economic functions are more basic than others in generating economic viability and growth from money inflow. The economic composition of a city—a result of that city's basic and nonbasic economic functions—may be regarded as comprising its *economic structure*. This economic structure is expressed in the location and distribution of activities within the metropolitan area. What is the internal spatial structure of the city?

Classic Spatial Structure

Metropolitan areas not only reflect similarities in economic structure but also express certain common patterns of location of economic activities within the metropolis. These spatial patterns, repeated with minor variations in city after city, have long been observed by urban scholars and laypersons alike. Just as particular kinds of economic activity are city-generating, certain kinds of activities exercise strong influences on the geographic layout of the metropolitan area. In fact, all economic activities compete for urban space; some are more successful than others. Because certain kinds of economic activities are generally more competitive than others, these activities are typically found in similar kinds of urban locations. The role of inertia is commonly observed in these spatial patterns, for the land-use decisions that led to these patterns largely were made in the past. Just as each land-use decision one might make today is constrained by the existing land use as based on past decisions, so, too, were the land-use decisions of the past limited by the spatial patterns of land use at that time.

Classically, three types of urban spatial structure have been proposed: the *concentric zone*, the *sector*, and the *multiple-nuclei city* (Figure 7.7). All three concepts of city structure offer generalizations about the geographic layout of the city. Because these are generalized constructs, it should not be expected that any metropolitan area will fit neatly into any of these three schemes. Rather, certain elements of, say, the concentric zone concept may be observed for a particular city. As we are about to see, these classic concepts of urban structure are not pre-

cise mathematical statements but instead highly generalized verbal descriptions. Therefore, if one expects these concepts to apply directly and fully to a given city, he or she will be disappointed, no matter which city he or she observes. If, on the other hand, one examines any given city, elements of each of the three concepts of urban spatial structure may be observed at some level of generalization. For this last reason, we will review the classic patterns of urban spatial structure.

Concentric Zone. The concentric zone view, developed by Ernest W. Burgess and Robert E. Park in 1925,[4] emphasizes the pattern of city growth, especially residential growth. They saw the urban area as comprising five concentric zones (Figure 7.7a) Zone one is the *central business district* (CBD), the focus of transportation routes and the foremost location of commercial, social, and business activities. Retailing ranges from huge department stores to small, specialized shops. Here is the city's financial and organization hub, with large banks, office buildings, governmental centers, hotels, and corporate headquarters. The social life of the city also focuses on the CBD, with theaters, museums, restaurants, and nightspots. The wholesaling district encircles the CBD as a part of zone one.

The *zone in transition*, the second zone, surrounds the CBD. Here is an area undergoing change, with many homes poorly kept up. Apartments and rooming houses are found, with large houses subdivided among several families. Often this transition zone is referred to as a slum or, if inhabited by blacks, a ghetto. Population density is often high; poverty common; and crime, a serious problem. Prior to the inmigration to blacks, the zone in transition was often inhabited by recent European immigrants. Also intermixed in

---

[4]Ernest W. Burgess, "The Growth of the City," in *The City,* Robert E. Park, et al., eds. (Chicago: University of Chicago Press, 1925), pp. 47–62.

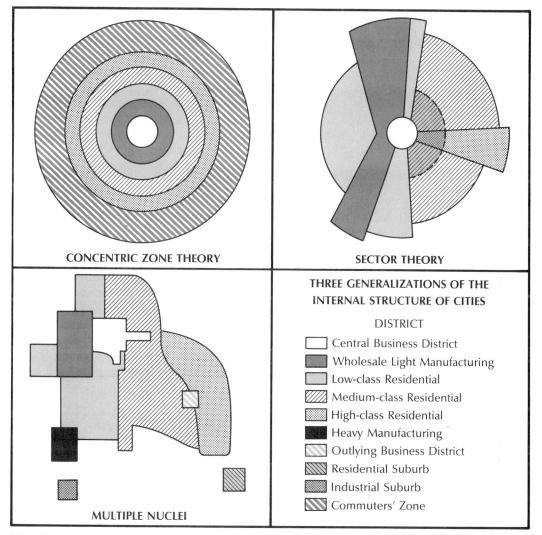

Figure 7.7 The classic models of the internal structure of cities, the concentric zone model of Burgess, the sector model of Hoyt, and the multiple nuclei of Harris and Ullman.
Source: Harris and Ullman, 1945.

this inner-city zone are various business and manufacturing activities.

Zone three, the area of ***independent workingmen's homes***, is comprised primarily of industrial workers living largely in single-family dwellings. In many cases, these households have migrated, or "escaped" from the zone in transition. The ***zone of better residents***, the fourth concentric

area, is composed of high-income families. Here are rather exclusive residential districts and subdivisions, as well as high-class apartment buildings. Population densities are lower, with single-family homes more widely spaced. The outermost concentric ring is the ***commuters' zone***, often lying well beyond the central-city limits and including residential suburbs and exurbs, as well as several older satellite settlements. The commuters' zone socially and economically is highly fragmented, being largely concentrated along important transportation routes. Thus, zones three, four, and five are almost entirely made up of residential land use, a structural pattern no longer observed in the late twentieth-century American metropolis.

Sectors. Proposed by Homer Hoyt in 1939, the sector concept holds that urban development takes place largely along major radical transportation routes, with areas or sectors of similar land use producing a star-shaped city (Figure 7.7b).[5] Many cities take on something of a star-shaped form as fingers of development stretch out along major highways (or rail and trolley lines before World War I). Very simply, cities grow faster in some directions than others, and, because of the importance of access, those areas best served by transportation naturally are favored for growth. Basic to the sector concept is that land use in particular sector will be similar. Land-use types that initially might be found near the center of the city radiate outward as the city enlarges. For example, a high-income residential area, originally concentrated near the city center on the east side, would expand eastward, excluding through zoning and other regulations the encroachment of lower-value homes. Likewise, an industrial area—and perhaps associated lower-income residences—might migrate outward over time within a particular city sector. The end result of this process of axial development is a sectoral pattern of urban land use.

Multiple Nuclei. A characteristic of many cities—and especially a feature of modern urbanization—is the development of several types of land use around a number of distinct nuclei (Figure 7.7c). Set forth by Chauncy D. Harris and Edward L. Ullman in the 1940s, based on earlier work by R. D. McKenzie, the multiple-nuclei concept views the city as a mosaic of land uses.[6] Although in many cities the central business district formed the initial nucleus, cities have increasingly spread outward and have developed many separate nuclei.

There are four basic reasons for the land-use differentiation by major nuclei. Many kinds of economic activities require specialized facilities or certain kinds of locations. Central-business-district activities are clearly attracted to points of high centrality and are so located because of accessibility advantages. Manufacturing may require large tracts of land that provide rail, water, or highway access. Second, several kinds of urban economic activities cluster together for mutual benefit, a localized manifestation of agglomeration economies. For instance, office buildings often group together because of face-to-face communications needs, as noted earlier (p. 136). A third reason for the evolution of distinct land-use nuclei is that some activities are mutually detrimental. Well-known examples are the conflict in land use between high-income residential neighborhoods and industrial districts. A final reason relates to the fact that not all activities are equally able to afford the high costs (such as rent) associated with the most desirable locations, some activities being relegated to less advantageous sites. As seen in Figure 7.7c, land uses that typically may be distinguished through the multiple-nuclei concept are the central business district, a "heavy" industrial zone, a "light" manufacturing district, outlying retail clusters, and various socioeconomic classes of residential

[5]Homer Hoyt, *The Structure and Growth of Residential Neighborhoods in American Cities* (Washington, D.C.: Government Printing Office, 1939).

[6]Chauncy D. Harris and Edward L. Ullman, "The Nature of Cities," *Annals of the American Academy of Political and Social Science 242* (1945), pp. 7–17. See also R. D. McKenzie, "The Ecological Approach to the Study of the Human Community," in Robert E. Park, Ernest W. Burgess, and Roderick D. McKenzie, eds., *The City* (Chicago: University of Chicago Press, 1925), pp. 63–79; and R. D. McKenzie, "Spatial Distance and Community Organization Patterns," *Social Forces 5* (June 1927), pp. 623–638.

A view of downtown Mumbai (Bombay), India.

neighborhoods. As has been widely noted, a basic feature of urban economic geography is that the rich and the poor concentrate residentially in different parts of the city.

The Restructured Metropolis

Obviously, many forces are at work influencing the city as an economic node. Many of these forces are *centripetal;* that is, they mold the economic structure toward a single economic node, classically focused on the central business district, which was the dominant center of urban organization. At the same time, *centrifugal* factors have had deconcentrating and fragmenting influences, emphasizing a multinodal economic organization. Whereas the concentric zone concept places greatest emphasis on the centripetal forces, the sector concept—and even more so the multiple-nuclei viewpoint—stresses centrifugal factors. In many ways, these centrifugal factors have gained ascendancy in recent decades in the industrial city for both economic and noneconomic reasons.

As a result, the city, as described by these three classic concepts, has been evolving into a rather fundamentally restructured form, which for want of a better term we will call the ***suburban downtown***. The United States has been experiencing a transformation of economic activity and power from a focus on the downtown of the inner city to diffused suburban locations that in the aggregate are economically dominating the older inner city. The suburban city has become the essence of the contemporary American city in terms of economic viability and spatial organization, as seen in Chapter 9.

In addition to the three classical concepts of urban spatial structure, there is the contemporary model of Erickson.[7] Erickson's model of the spatial and structural evolution of the suburban space economy may be seen as an extension of the three classical models. The concentric zone, sector, and multiple nuclei concepts attempted to describe the city prior to the rapid and extensive suburbanization, which has become pervasive since 1960. Erickson's model focuses specifically on the suburbs. The Erickson model involves

[7]Rodney A. Erickson, "The Evolution of the Suburban Space Economy," *Urban Geography* 4 (April-June 1983), pp. 95–121.

The skyline of San Francisco.

three phases, each associated with a particular period of time. Like the Taaffe model (see Chapter 5), it is an ideal-typical model of spatial change. No metropolitan area will follow the exact geometric structure of the model, but rather virtually all metropolitan areas will follow the basic principles identified in the three phases.

The first phase, extending for American cities from about 1920 to 1940, is characterized by *spillover and specialization*. The city literally grows out of its boundaries as specialized employment begins to locate in suburban areas. The employment, specialized in one or a few economic sectors, develops in the inner suburbs, the early ring of suburbs surrounding the corporate city boundary.

Phase two, *dispersal and diversification,* occurs in the 1940s and 1950s. Now employment grows rapidly throughout the suburbs, including the outer suburbs, the ring of suburbs farthest from the city. As employment becomes geographically dispersed, the employment structure becomes more diversified. Instead of the situation in phase one, in which suburban employ-

ment might constitute one particular manufacturing plant, in phase two other kinds of employment, such as retailing, wholesaling, and service, move into the suburbs.

Finally, phase three, post–1960, is characterized by *infilling and multinucleation*. Infilling occurs particularly in the inner suburbs as land passed over in the suburban leapfrogging process now becomes occupied. Major suburban nucleations emerge, often around shopping centers. The shopping malls, usually located at exchanges of one or more interstate highways, attract office buildings and apartment and condominium development. Soon a suburban downtown has been built, with employment concentrating in the nucleations.

THE METROPOLITAN HIERARCHY

We may think of a group of metropolitan areas as constituting a system of cities. This system forms a hierarchy, with one metropolitan area at the top and many at the lower end of the hierarchy. New York is at the apex of the U.S. hierarchy, as Toronto is for Canada, whereas Goodland, Kansas, or Medicine Hat, Saskatchewan, are near the bottom of the hierarchies. The significance of the metropolitan hierarchy to the economic geographer is that nodes that are high up the hierarchy have disproportionately greater influence than smaller centers. In terms of managerial functions, the biggest metropolitan areas act as headquarters for the largest corporations. Decisions made in these cities affect the economic landscape all across the country—and indeed the world. External control is a major fact of life in the contemporary economy.

An example of the metropolitan hierarchy may be seen in corporate spatial linkages. If we take the major corporations headquartered in New York City and map the location of their subsidiaries, we see New York firms (at the top of the hierarchy) owning subsidiaries all across the United States (Figure 7.8). The leading metropolitan areas with New York-owned subsidiaries are the largest metropolitan areas in the United States. Figure 7.8 shows the complex ownership web among metropolitan areas and hence the high degree of independence among U.S. metropolitan economies.

The metropolitan hierarchy also acts to channel diffusion of clothing styles and other societal trends. Many innovations begin at the upper end of the hierarchy and spread downward through the metropolitan system. Topless bars, for example, began in the 1960s in San Francisco, jumped to Los Angeles, and then jumped to New York, from where they gradually diffused down the urban hierarchy.

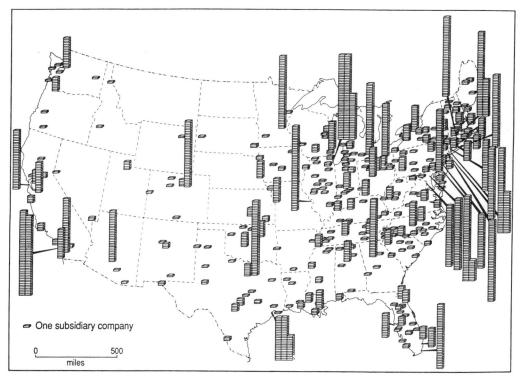

➥ One subsidiary company

0 — 500
miles

Figure 7.8 The location of subsidiaries of parent firms with headquarters in New York City.
Source: Wheeler, 1990.

THE NEW SERVICE ECONOMY

Whereas city growth from the beginning of census taking in the United States in 1790 was dependent on the location of manufacturing, since at least the mid-1970s it has been the service economy that has powered metropolitan growth. Cities that had favorable transportation advantages as ocean ports (New York), on major rivers (St. Louis), or rail centers (Chicago) came to dominate the urban hierarchy. In contrast, the new service economy is dependent on communications technology, which is concentrated in the largest metropolitan ares. Somewhat ironically, these large centers which became large because of manufacturing advantages are the very centers in which the new advanced service economy is located.

One measure of the new service economy is the number of square feet of occupied office space, shown in Figure 7.9 by metropolitan area. A clear urban hierarchy is evident, with New York by far the leading service center in the United States, followed by Los Angeles and Chicago. Other notable centers include San Francisco, Boston, Philadelphia, Washington, D.C., and Dallas–Fort Worth. At the next level of the hierarchy are Detroit, Minneapolis, Atlanta, and Miami–Ft. Lauderdale. Thus, the new advanced service economy, highly dependent on telecommunication, follows the metropolitan hierarchy.

SUMMARY

Although it seems paradoxical to end a chapter titled "The City as an Economic Node" with an

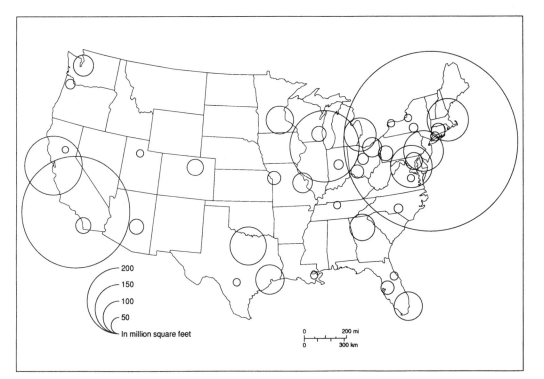

Figure 7.9 Primary occupied office space in major U.S. metropolitan areas, 1990 (> 19 million sq. ft.)
Source: Sui and Wheeler, 1993.

emphasis on the lack of nodality—or more properly, the multinodality—of the contemporary American city, such have been the transformations in urbanization processes during the last decades. The metropolitan area, taken as a diffused whole, does indeed act as the organizational focus for the regional and national economy. In the past, economic activities were geographically concentrated in the central business district, and the nodality and importance of any city could be more easily recognized and appreciated, if only by glancing at the height and extent of the buildings in the central business district. The classic city, with its various features of internal spatial economic structure, has undergone a gradual, continuing, but dramatic restructuring, maintaining and strengthening its traditional urban functions, as well as its advantages of agglomeration communication economies. Having examined the city as an economic node, we will describe in Chapter 8 the tertiary activities within and among cities from the viewpoint of central place theory.

Further Readings

Bakis, Henry, Ronald Abler, and Edward M. Roche, eds., *Corporate Networks, International Telecommunications and Interdependence: Perspectives from Geography and Information Systems*. London: Belhaven Press, 1993.

Brunn, Stanley D., and James O. Wheeler, eds., *The American Metropolitan System: Present and Future* Silver Spring, Md.: V. H. Winston & Sons, 1980.

Burgess, E. W., "The Growth of the City: An Introduction to a Research Project," in Robert E. Park, Ernest W. Burgess, and Roderick D. McKenzie, eds., *The City*. Chicago: University of Chicago Press, pp. 47–62, 1925.

Gappert, Gary, and Richard V. Knight, eds., *Cities in the 21st Century* Beverly Hills: Sage Publications, 1982.

Gottmann, Jean, *Megalopolis: The Urbanized Northeastern Seaboard of the United States*. Cambridge, Mass.: MIT Press, 1961.

Gottmann, Jean and Robert A. Harper, eds., *Since Megalopolis: The Urban Writings of Jean Gottmann*. Baltimore: Johns Hopkins University Press, 1990.

Harris, C. D., and E. L. Ullman, "The Nature of Cities," *Annals of the Association of American Academy of Political and Social Science* 242 (1945), pp. 7–17.

Hart, John Fraser, ed., *Our Changing Cities*. Baltimore: Johns Hopkins University Press, 1991.

Hartshorn, Truman A., *Interpreting the City: An Urban Geography*. New York: Wiley, 1992.

Hepworth, Mark, *Geography of the Information Economy*. New York: Guilford Press, 1990.

Hoyt, H., *The Structure and Growth of Residential Neighborhoods in American Cities*. Washington, D.C.: U.S. Government Printing Office 1939.

Isard, Walter, *Introduction to Regional Science*. Englewood Cliffs, N.J.: Prentice-Hall, 1975.

Knox, Paul, ed., *The Restless Urban Landscape*. Englewood Cliffs, N.J.: Prentice-Hall, 1993.

Mattila, J. M., and W. R. Thompson, "The Measurement of the Economic Base of the Metropolitan Area," *Land Economics*, Vol. 31 (1955), pp. 215–228.

Mills, Edwin S. and John F. McDonald, eds., *Sources of Metropolitan Growth*. New Brunswick: Rutgers, Center for Urban Policy Research, 1992.

Noyelle, Thierry J., and Thomas M. Stanback, Jr., *The Economic Transformation of American Cities*. Totowa, N.J.: Roman & Allanheld, 1984.

Ó hUallacháin, Breandán and Neil Reid, "The Intrametropolitan Location of Services in the United States," *Urban Geography*, Vol. 13, July–August, 1992, pp. 334–354.

Pred, Allan, *City-Systems in Advanced Economies*. New York: Wiley, 1977.

Stanback, Thomas M., Jr., et al., *Services: The New Economy*. Totowa, N.J.: Allanheld, Osmun, 1981.

———, and Thierry J. Noyelle, *Cities in Transition*. Totowa, N.J.: Allanheld, Osmun, 1982.

Sui, Daniel Z. and James O. Wheeler, "The Location of Office Space in the Metropolitan Service Economy of the United States," *Professional Geographer*, Vol. 45, February, 1993, pp. 33–43.

Ullman, Edward L. and Michael F. Dacey, "The Minimum Requirements Approach to the Urban Economic Base," *Papers and Proceedings of the Regional Science Association*, Vol. 6 (1960), pp. 175–194.

Waddell, Paul and Vibhooti Shukla, "Manufacturing Location in a Polycentric Urban Area: A Study in the Composition and Attractiveness of Employment Subcenters," *Urban Geography*, Vol. 14, May–June, 1993, pp. 277–296.

Wheeler, James O., "Corporate Role of New York City in the Metropolitan Hierarchy," *Geographical Review*, Vol. 80, October 1990, pp. 371–381.

Wheeler, James O. and Ronald L. Mitchelson, "Atlanta's Role as an Information Center: Intermetropolitan Spatial Links," *Professional Geographer*, Vol. 41, May, 1989, pp. 162–172.

CHAPTER 8

The Location of Tertiary Activities

———— ◇ ————

Happiness depends on what we have in our heads rather than on what we have in our pockets.

—WILL DURANT

INTRODUCTION

Commercial activities are not only a dominant urban function in all cities, but are also the single most important economic function in many cities. As noted in Chapter 7, cities exist economically to serve other areas. Retail and service activities not only provide for the needs of residents in the city, but also serve people from the surrounding region or *umland*. In cities lacking an important manufacturing base, the location and growth of the city are dependent on the various commercial functions. From the earlier comments on a city's economic base, it is clear that a city whose retail and service function serves large numbers of people outside the city will have a sizable money inflow and be an economically viable center. In fact, there are a great many relationships that may be pointed out regarding a center's location, size, and retail and services characteristics. These relationships have become formalized in a set of location principles that comprise **central-place theory**. In this chapter we will review classical central-place theory and examine the modifications of this classic location theory.

CLASSICAL CENTRAL-PLACE THEORY

In 1933, Walter Christaller wrote *Central Places in Southern Germany*, a pioneering work in theoretical economic geography.[1] Christaller's classic statement sought to explain the size, number, and distribution and spacing of a set of towns known as central places. These urban places, in contrast to dispersed places, were termed central because they located centrally to their trade area. Christaller argued that there was an overall ordering theory that explained the distribution of towns. The distribution of central places is dependent on the success of a center serving a complementary region or *umland*. Central places are viewed as settlements that function entirely as market centers for their surrounding areas. These views of Christaller and his formalized theory as extended later by August Lösch have had an enormous impact on research developments in urban economic geography. Central-

[1]Walter Christaller, *Die Zentralen Örte in Süddeutschland* (Jena: Gustav Fischer Verlag, 1933). C. W. Baskin, trans., *Central Places in Southern Germany* (Englewood Cliffs, N.J.: Prentice-Hall, 1966).

place theory, then, seeks to explain the size, number, and distribution of towns on the basis of tertiary activities, but does not directly take into account the important role of manufacturing in the growth and development of cities.

"The crystallization of mass around a nucleus is ... an elementary form of order of things which belong together—a centralistic order."[2] This same principle of centrality is found in various forms of human organization; and function and form often bear certain logical relationships, as with the size of buildings and their purpose. The chief characteristic of a town is to be the center of a region. Larger towns serve larger regions because a larger place is more centrally located and more accessible to its region. Thus, the importance of a town is directly related to its *centrality*, which may be defined as the relative importance of a place with regard to the region surrounding it. Importance and town size, however, are not necessarily related. If the importance of a central place is I, of which I_p represents the importance attributed to the town's population, then $I - I_p$ is the importance of the central place that reflects the importance of the surrounding region. $I - I_p$, then, is a measure of a town's centrality.

Central places vary in their geographical importance (see Figure 8.1). These places may be ranked or ordered. Higher-order places geographically dominate lower-order places because higher-order places have a larger number of *central functions*. Central functions are the goods and services provided at a central place because it is central.

Goods and services may be ranked into orders. Convenience goods and services that are in everyday use, as with convenience stores, are found scattered more or less evenly according to population distribution and are, therefore, designated as lower-order goods. Goods and services that are in frequent—but not everyday or every-week—use are of medium order, as with

[2]Ibid., p. 14.

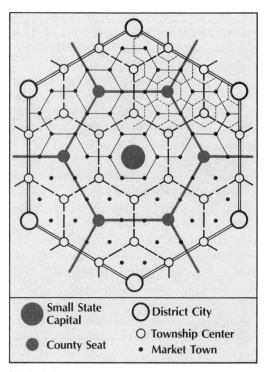

Small State Capital   **District City**

County Seat   **Township Center**   **Market Town**

Figure 8.1 Christaller's five levels of urban centers are geometrically located and have hexagonal trade areas. The larger the center, the farther apart it is from a center of the same size.

drugs or banking. Higher-order goods might be furniture, purchased on a more occasional basis, or a lawyer's services. Thus, from a retail firm or service establishment point of view, there are certain orders of central places in which to locate; and the higher order of the good or service, the higher the order of the central place that will economically support that good or service.

Range of a Good

Consumer travel is closely related to the locations of the central places. The *range of a good* is the farthest distance the consumer is willing to travel for a particular good offered at a central place. Naturally, the distance one is willing to travel for groceries or a low-order good is not too great. If a good is offered at a distance too great for the rural or dispersed population, that population simply will not be willing or able to travel that far to make a purchase. Because goods and services are of different orders, it follows that the range of a good varies with its order, such that the higher the order the greater the distance the consumer is willing to travel. Lower-order goods are found in every central place, whether large or small. But the higher-order goods are found only in the higher-order places to which consumers are willing to travel greater distances. From this discussion it is clear that there are relationships between the kinds of functions found in a central place, the size of the central place, and the location of the central place vis-à-vis other central places.

Some of these relationships need further elaboration. First of all, because the order of a good or service is related to the accessible consumer population (or even more correctly, to their purchasing power), the size of the central place itself exerts a major influence on the order of goods and services it offers. Much is consumed by the local populace. Because of the dominance of the local purchasing power, higher-order goods and services are economically attracted to locate in larger places. In turn, the availability of these goods and services draws consumers from a wide area surrounding the central place, further en-

hancing that place's centrality and economic importance (Figure 8.2).

The range of a good may take on a lower limit when there is competition. Consider first a linear-market situation. If the range of a good, G, is distance D, and the good is offered at only locations X and Y, as in Figure 8.2, there will be locations that will not be economically accessible to the good, such as the locations between O and P. The dispersed rural population between O and P will either do without the goods, substitute another, or, following central-place theory, generate an independent central place at a location between X and Y. Because of spatial competition, the range of a good takes on a minimum distance.

Each order of good also takes on a range corresponding to the maximum distance one is willing to travel for that good or service. Hence, every good has a characteristic range. The role of competition is vital in determining which centers will support a particular level of good or service. It is evident that low-order centers cannot support goods or services dependent on a population or purchasing power in excess of that found in the center and its complementary region. On the other hand, high-order centers are able to support lower-order functions—and a great many of them—because of their large pur-

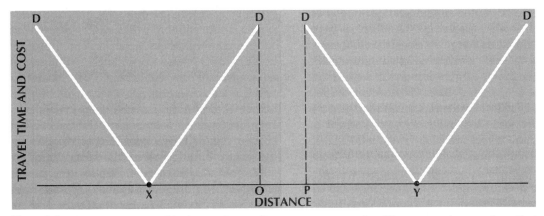

Figure 8.2 The range of a good is the maximum distance a consumer is willing to travel to purchase that good from a given central place.

chasing power. At the same time and for the same reasons, these high-order centers are able to support goods and services in less common demand, such as jewelry stores or more exquisite restaurants. In other words, it takes a larger population to support a high-order good or service. Although this larger population is, in part, derived from the larger population of the central place, it is also in the other part derived from the larger surrounding, dispersed rural population. Therefore, the range of a good or service is related to the size of the population required to support that good or service at a minimum level and to the economic importance of the center.

Threshold

If we examine tertiary activity from the point of view of the establishment, it is clear that each establishment must enjoy a minimum level of sales in order to operate at a profit. This minimum sales level is called its *threshold*. From what has already been said, we know that threshold size varies directly with level of centrality required by an establishment. Establishments whose goods and services necessitate a very high level of sales to achieve profit must locate in places of very high centrality. By contrast, establishments whose lower-order goods and services are *ubiquitous*—that is, found in every center—obviously do not need a high level of centrality to realize a profit. Because of the threshold concept, one may buy a loaf of bread in every central place but an oboe only in the largest places.

Central-Place System

Central places constitute a system, or a set of interrelated principles, that has a spatial expression on the landscape. By assuming a uniformly distributed rural population and equal access in all directions, Christaller was able to demonstrate theoretically that a particular geometric arrangement of central places would exist. Based on the concepts of range of a good and of threshold, a system of central places would emerge that would serve the dispersed rural population of the entire area from a minimum number of central places. Central-place theory, following Christaller, is based on the **marketing principle**, which is based, in turn, on the assumption of equal access (Figure 8.3*a*). However, the **transportation principle** holds that it is optimal to locate as many central places as possible along major traffic arterials between towns (Figure 8.3*b*). Third, the **administrative principle** is based on the separation of political areal units or complementary regions (Figure 8.3*c*). These three principles thus determine three theoretical systems of central places. These three principles operate simultaneously, one predominating in one place or time and a second at another time or place.

Central-Place Hierarchy

The central-place system has a hierarchical geographical arrangement, with smaller centers linked to larger ones. This spatial organization or marketing is manifested in the population size of centers, their location or spacing, the nesting of trade areas, and the composition of tertiary activities of the center. Several relationships may be summarized.

1. The larger the central place, the greater the variety of central functions.
2. The larger the central place, the greater the distance to a place of comparable size. Places at the upper end of the hierarchy are widely spaced, whereas smaller centers are much more closely packed together.
3. Places at the same level in the hierarchy offer the same mix of tertiary goods and services. They also offer the same set of functions found in lower-order centers.
4. The higher the level in the hierarchy, the fewer the number of central places at that level. There are, then, numerous lower-order places, several intermediate-order places, and only a few higher-order central places.

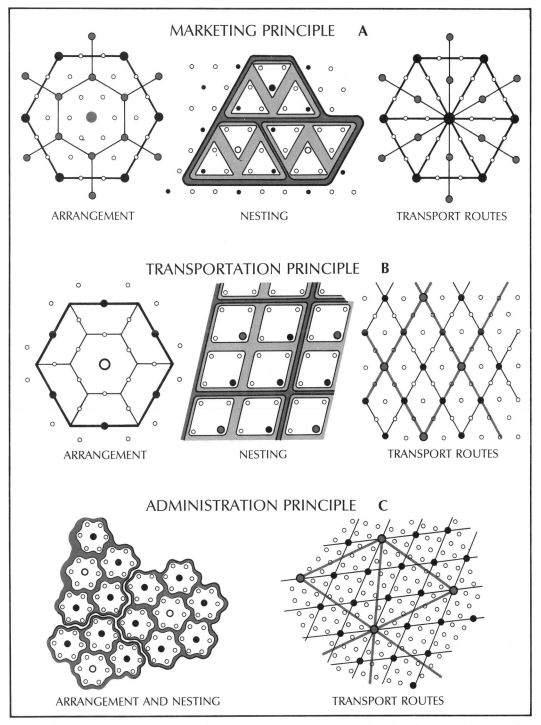

Figure 8.3 Christaller's marketing, administrative, and transportation principles of central places, showing the effects of marketing, political, and transport considerations on the location of the central-place system. *Source*: Berry and Pred, 1961.

Christaller's Hexagonal Trade Areas

In setting forth and integrating his theory of central places, Christaller began with two basic assumptions. The first was the ***isotropic plain***. This plain has no natural physical features; movement is equally possible in all directions; and the population is uniformly distributed. The second was the ***rationality*** assumption: Consumers behave strictly on economic motivation and will travel to the nearest place offering the desired good or service; ***distance minimization*** is their guiding principle.

It might be assumed that the trade areas for each central place would be circular, given the above assumptions (Figure 8.4*a*). However, circular trade areas would result in some areas being unserved by any central place. When the centers are moved closer together, as in Figure 8.4*b*, all areas are served. Because there can be no

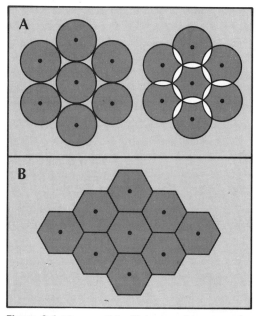

Figure 8.4 The spatial efficiency of hexagonal trade areas is illustrated in the lower portion of the diagram. Above at left, gaps are left when circles are used; that is, there would be areas unserved by any market. Above at right, the circles have been forced together to cover the entire area, but the result is clearly a less efficient form than the hexagons.

overlap of trade areas under the distance minimization principle, the result is a hexagonal trade-area pattern as circles are "packed" together. Each center is surrounded by six other centers of the same level in the hierarchy. Within each trade area is a sales volume (based on uniform population) that meets the threshold criterion. This hexagonal arrangement is the most efficient geometric pattern, as compared with a square, a triangle, or any other shape.

Lösch and the Uniform Plain. Christaller began his central-place theory by locating the highest-order center and then distributing centers of successively lower orders until the landscape was packed with places beyond which thresholds for goods or services could not be reached. August Lösch, in *The Economics of Location* (published in German in 1939 but not translated into English until 1954), began his considerable contribution to classical central-place theory by starting with the lowest-order center and building toward the higher orders.[3] Specifically, Lösch extended and refined Christaller's theory and demonstrated the economic rationale underlying the theory. Lösch's contribution to location theory included an attempt to integrate central-place theory with industrial and agricultural location theory.

Lösch, like Christaller, began with certain assumptions and also assumed an isotropic or homogeneous plain. On this plain was a dispersed pattern of self-sufficient farms. Furthermore, the farmers had similar tastes and economic needs (or in the language of economics, the same demand curve). The economic raw materials were equally, uniformly, and adequately distributed over this plain. The fundamental question Lösch addressed was, How could spatial economic differences develop on this homogeneous plain?

Commercial activity can begin only if individual farmers are able to produce a surplus to be

[3]August Lösch, *The Economics of Location* (New Haven, Conn.: Yale University Press, 1954), William H. Woglom and Wolfgang F. Stolper, trans. (originally published in 1939).

sold to others. Commercial activity is handi-capped by the cost of transportation on any sur-plus produced, but at the same time it is assisted by the advantages of economics of scale. Let us suppose, using Lösch's example, that one of the farmers wishes to produce beer over and above his own needs. How large will his market be? Large-volume production will mean that his per unit cost will be lower than that of the surround-ing farmers. Nevertheless, the cost of transport-ing the beer to other farmers at some point will negate any per unit savings. The farmer's market area for his beer sales will then be limited by transportation cost (Figure 8.5).

There is a relationship between the quantity of beer that will be purchased by a farmer and the price he will have to pay. We know from simple economic theory that consumption declines at some rate with increases in price, depending on the elasticity of demand for a good. Figure 8.6 depicts a relationship between price and quan-tity. The price of beer at the center of production is represented by OP. The demand for beer at the center of production is then PQ, which rep-

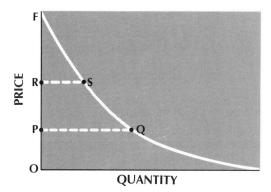

Figure 8.6 The relationship between the price of beer and the quantity produced.

resents the quantity consumed at market price. If the beer is shipped to location R, the price at R is OR, and the freight cost to R is PR. Because the price has increased owing to the freight cost, the quantity demanded at R is RS, considerably less than at the production center. PF is the freight from P to F. At F, no more beer will be sold, since PF is the maximum shipping distance for beer, as already shown in Figure 8.5.

If we take the demand curve in Figure 8.6 and turn it on its side, so that PQ takes on a vertical instead of a horizontal dimension, we have cre-ated a ***demand cone*** (Figure 8.7). In other words, by turning the demand curve on its side and by rotating it through 360 degrees, we form a cone that represents geographically the quantity con-sumed at any location away from the center of production. Beer sales would be equal to the vol-ume of the cone that would result from rotating the triangle PQF on PQ as an axis.

We may imagine a whole series of demand cones for beer superimposed on Lösch's uniform plain. How would these demand cones—that is to say, market areas—best be arranged? As in Christaller, the most efficient arrangement of trade areas is reached when the areas are hex-agonal in shape. Thus, Lösch demonstrated how a uniform plain may come to develop com-mercial functions. Furthermore, because the con-sumer tastes are similar and all farmers operate on the basis of economic rationality, the entire

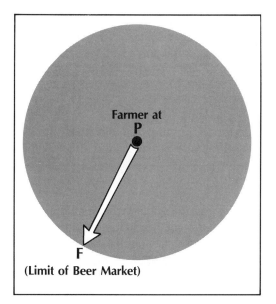

Figure 8.5 The market for beer is limited by distance (transport costs) away from the producer (farmer at P).

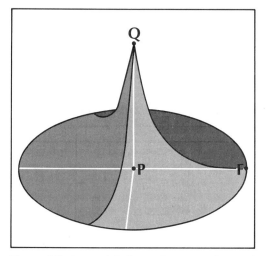

Figure 8.7 A spatial demand cone, with a three-dimensional view. Demand declines from level Q at location P to point F.

landscape will be served by a uniformly distributed pattern of beer-producing farmers.

Beer is only a single good, and the central-place landscape provides multiple goods and services. Lösch argued that the agglomeration of economic activities should be at a maximum. He, therefore, selected an arbitrary central place at the starting point (initial beer producer). Every additional order of good or service introduced is assigned to the initially selected central place, and each of these additional orders is associated with an increasingly larger hexagonal market arrangement. The result is a pattern of central places, which—unlike in Christaller—was generated from lower to higher order. Lösch began with the most ubiquitous good; Christaller started with the good with the highest threshold.

APPLICATIONS OF CENTRAL-PLACE THEORY

Three examples of applications of central-place theory illustrate how an abstract theory can have practical applications. First, we look at *Rushton's indifference curve* which focuses on the behavior of rural consumers living outside towns in Iowa. By extension, we examine the *DeTemple Model*

of the spread or diffusion of a feed-crop storage system. We then focus on the *Wyckoff Model* of how a frontier center becomes historically integrated into the U.S. national system of central places.

According to Christaller, a consumer will shop for a good at the nearest center offering that good. Thus, the decision of where to shop is made entirely on the basis of distance. Rushton, however, found that Christaller's assumption of distance minimization did not fit actual consumer travel behavior.[4] Again, according to Christaller, a consumer will be indifferent in his/her choice between two central places if they are located exactly the same distance from the consumer. For example, suppose that two towns, one with a population of 1000 and the other with a population of 10,000, are both located exactly four miles from a consumer. Christaller's model says the consumer will be indifferent in the choice of which center to choose. Therefore, the vertical lines in Figure 8.8*a* indicate that the population size of a center will exert no influence—only distance with a vertical *indifference curve* will be important. (Similarly, if the lines were horizontal, only town size would enter the consumer's decision, not distance.) Rushton, however, demonstrated that actual and realistic consumer behavior would be represented by curved lines or a curvilinear indifference curve. Rushton's contribution was to add an element of reality to shopping behavior by showing that *both* distance and town size matter in the choice of where to travel. In Figure 8.8*b*, the consumer is indifferent, for example, between going eight miles to a place of 1000 population size and traveling 20 miles to a place of 9000, for instance. Thus, a person is normally willing to travel farther to a larger place than to a smaller place, because multipurpose trips (having more than one retail stop) are, of course, more feasible in a larger central place.

[4]Gerald Rushton, "Analysis of Spatial Behavior by Revealed Space Preferences," *Annals of the Association of American Geographers*, 59 (1969), pp 391–400.

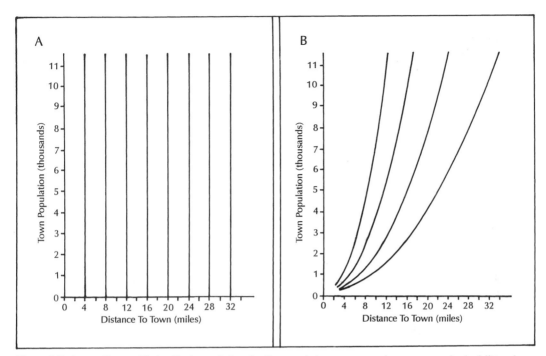

Figure 8.8 According to Christaller's model, only distance is important to the consumer in deciding where to shop. (Figure 8.8 *a*). However, in Rushton's indifference approach, town size is also important along with distance (Figure 8.8 *b*).
Source: Rushton, 1969.

The DeTemple Model takes central-place concepts and applies them uniquely to a *diffusion of innovations* approach. This approach shows how an idea or a behavior spreads geographically over an area. In our age of mass communications, an idea or style may be instanteously transmitted over a wide area. In other cases, the spread or diffusion may be much slower.

DeTemple studied the Harvestore system, which "is a unique feed-crop storage system that has a number of advantages over ordinary farm silos" (p. 27).[5] His study area was northeast Iowa, an agricultural area with cold winters and hence the need to winter-feed livestock. The blue Harvestore silo has many advantages over tra-

ditional systems of feed storage. For example, it is loaded automatically from the bottom, it is impervious to air and thus preserves feed crops better, and it has many other operating and cost advantages. Since the setup costs are relatively high, especially considering the fact that the farmer who might purchase a Harvestore system already has a traditional silo, the farmer must be personally convinced that the system has sufficient advantages. And there is no better way to be convinced than to have a fellow farmer rather than a traveling salesperson explain the advantages.

Without going into the precise qualitative computer modeling of the DeTemple approach, suffice it to explain how he predicted the Harvestore system would spread and how well his model matched the actual spread of this new farm technology. The DeTemple Model is de-

[5]David J. DeTemple, *A Space Preference Approach to the Diffusion of Innovations* (Bloomington, IN: Department of Geography, Indiana University, 1971).

ceptively simple and, with one exception, remarkably accurate. He used Rushton's indifference curve. Here is what he argued.

Farmers will adopt the idea of buying the Harvestore silo when told about it by another farmer. Just because farmer A is told of its advantages does not necessarily mean adoption. Some will, and some will not. Whether a given farmer adopts or does not adopt is partly a random process. Whether farmer A hears about the silo's advantage will depend on the probability of meeting up with a farmer who has the silo and can boast of its superiority. This probability of meeting depends on (1) the size of the town in which the farmers happen to meet and (2) the distance to a central place. DeTemple estab-

lished probabilities based on population and distance.

DeTemple used this procedure to model the diffusion of the silos from 1950 year by year to 1967. Figure 8.9*a* shows the actual distribution of farmers with the Harvestore system in 1967, whereas Figure 8.9*b* shows the simulated or computer-modeled distribution for that year. The patterns show some interesting similarities and one fatal flaw, the *edge effect*. As the model takes into consideration only central places within the study area, the probabilities of meeting in centers in adjacent areas are not included.

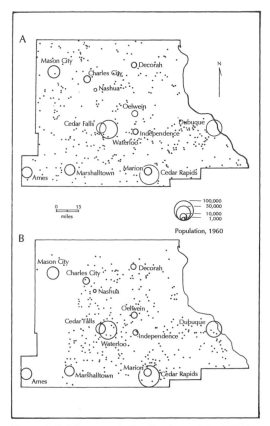

Figure 8.9 The actual distribution of the Harvestore system in northeast Iowa, (Figure 8.9 *a*) and (Figure 8.9*b*) the simulated distribution based on population size and distance.
Source: DeTemple, 1971.

The Harvestore silo system expertly preserves feed crops for winter livestock consumption. The blue silos, one big and one small, are on a dairy farm near Muncie, Indiana.

This leads to the paucity of adopters around the edge of the study area, the edge effect. Even so, it is remarkable how a probability model, based only on population size and distance to a central place, could show a pattern not unlike that in reality. Since it is a model based on probabilities, different computer runs will result in slightly different distributions. Could we then argue that the actual pattern (Figure 8.9*a*) is just the probability pattern that actually came true, as many other similar patterns could just as likely have occurred?

Wyckoff, drawing on and extending a model of frontier urban growth developed by David Meyer, shows how an urban place becomes integrated into the national urban system.[6] The model examines interregional linkages between the frontier center and the larger set of urban places. It is a three-stage historical model, based on an empirical analysis of Denver, Colorado, between 1859 and 1879 (Figure 8.10). Let Wyckoff explain his own model:[6]

At t_1, the recently established frontier center (G) has strong links to a pair of nearby gateway centers (E and F) that are supplying the new frontier town with necessary transportation connections and with a considerable flow of unspecialized goods. There are also secondary connections with two large metropolitan centers (A and B), but a poor transport infrastructure makes many direct linkages prohibitive.... Centers E and F are engaged in active competition for business in frontier center G.... In the case of Denver, this phase is analogous to the initial 1859 period when links to the competing Missouri Valley trade center dominate the pattern.

By t_2, considerable change characterizes the sizes (and perhaps economic bases) of centers A through G, and significant changes in the

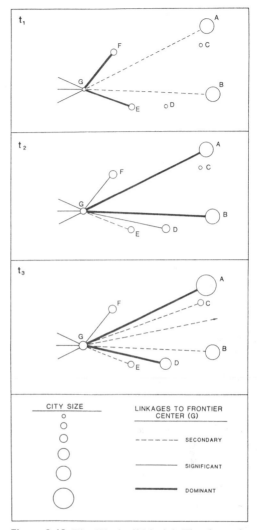

Figure 8.10 The Wyckoff Model. The dynamic geography of linkages between a frontier center and the national urban system.
Source: Wyckoff, 1988.

linkages between the frontier center (G) and the rest of the national urban system are evident. Center G's growth has created new demands for goods and services. Some of these demands are satisfied by new entrepreneurs locating in Center G itself, thus reducing its dependence on Centers E and F (especially for less specialized

[6]William Wyckoff. "Revising the Meyer Model: Denver and the National Urban System, 1859-1879," *Urban Geography*, Vol. 9, 1988, quote pages 13-16.

goods and services). Center F does manage to hold on to significant linkages, however, because it succeeds in providing some more specialized goods and services in demand at G (but not available in E). Many of G's demands for new linkages are satisfied through closer ties with national centers and A and B. Improved transportation connections and the continued growth and increasing diversity of centers A and B make such long-distance linkages possible. The rapid growth of Center D, perhaps propelled by aggressive entrepreneurs, favorable transport links, and abundant local resources, also provides a new opportunity for increased linkages to frontier center G. . . . The metropolitan centers A and B are assuming increasing importance. They continue to grow, a function of important economies of scale and new innovations. Center G also grows . . . and its changing economic base is creating a changing geography of linkages. In addition, the rapid emergence of Center D is a reminder that selective growth in the national urban system as well as the changes occurring in Center G are to have an influence on Center G's pattern of linkages. . . . In the context of the Colorado frontier, the steady growth in the importance of New York and Chicago is the sum expression of these several interrelated processes operating in the 1860s and 1870s. As Denver grows, interregional rail links are established, and the national urban system continues to mature.

Finally, t_3 suggests the continued dynamic influence of selective growth in the national urban system. Center A emerges to become the single dominant national-level metropolis and thereby continues to capture many direct links with Center G. Center B, growing more slowly, loses out in relative importance to both Centers A and D. Center D manages to forge even closer connections with Center G as good transport links and economic complementarity provide more opportunities for interaction. The rise of Kansas City by 1979 provides an example in the

Colorado study. . . . The increasing complexity of frontier center G's economic base is suggested by new secondary ties with Center C, a distant, small town nominally in the trade hinterland of Center A. . . . These linkages will not likely dominate the geography of Center G'S interdependencies, but to ignore them no doubt reduces the conceptual power of the model to explain changes within the system.

MODIFICATIONS OF CLASSICAL THEORY

Christaller and Lösch began the attempts to test and verify empirically the concepts of central-place theory. They both recognized that the value of the theory was to improve the understanding of reality rather than to find perfect hexagonal trade areas on the landscape. In this sense, Lösch went on to note that theory is more interesting than sorry reality! Nowhere on earth will there be found the exact patterns described by Christaller and Lösch. Nearly everywhere, however, there are tendencies toward such a pattern, some more clearly evident than others. The essential reason the theoretical patterns are nowhere perfectly reproduced in reality is that the normative assumptions underlying the theory do not always operate in the real world. Most of the modifications of the classical theory have to do with relaxing original assumptions in light of empirical evidence. Three general modifications of central-place theory are summarized in the following sections. The first deals with the role of spatial competition and travel behavior; the last two treat applications of the theory to intraurban retail location and to different cultural areas of the world.

Spatial Competition

One of the most rigid and limiting assumptions of classical central-place theory is related to the nonoverlapping trade areas. Consumers were assumed to travel to the nearest center offering the

A surplus store with a going-out-of-business sale in Catskill, New York.

desired good or service, and consumers were deemed to be perfectly sensitive to extremely small fluctuations in the prices of goods. Even casual observation of marketing patterns in the real world suggests a much more highly complex delineation of trade areas. Therefore, the regular hexagonal market patterns are simply not found on any landscape of the world.

Most consumers are indifferent to small variations in price, travel, distance, and even quality. When these differences become large, however, most consumers will recognize the differences and react accordingly. Following this reasoning, a much more realistic model has been put forth by Nicos E. Devletoglou, although it is far less elegant and encompassing than that of central-place theory.[7] Like Christaller and Lösch, Devletoglou assumed an isotropic plain, equal accessibility in all directions, an evenly spread rural population, and identical consumer tastes. If two locations, A and B, are selling identical goods at the same price, which will the consumer prefer? Given Devletoglou's assumptions, the consumer must decide simply on the basis of distance.

In Figure 8.11a, the two places offering a good are located a great distance apart. A consumer

located near A, therefore, will almost invariably travel to A to make a purchase. On the other hand, a consumer located about halfway between A and B is largely indifferent as to which retail location he or she will patronize. In fact, the more similar the distance between the two locations, the greater the likelihood of consumer indifference. Thus, an *indifference zone* exists between A and B in which the consumer has little preference as to which location he will choose. When the distance between A and B is large, the indifference zone is relatively small; and when A and B are located nearby, the zone of indifference covers a broad area (Figure 8.11b). The indifference zone is separated from the normal trade areas of A and B by a *line of minimum sensible distance*, that is, a line beyond which the consumer finds the difference in distance incon-

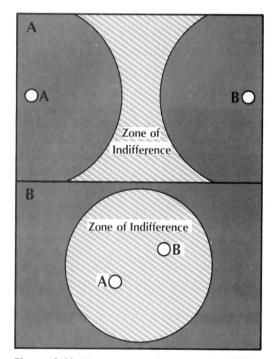

Figure 8.11 The consumer's zone of indifference changes depending on how close the two competitors, A and B, are located from one another.

---

[7]Nicos E. Devletoglou, "A Dissenting View of Duopoly and Spatial Competition," *Economics* 32 (1965), pp. 14–160.

sequential. The concept of the indifference zone, allowing for overlap of market areas, is therefore much more attuned to actual consumer behavior than the rigid concept of economic man assumed by classical central-place theory.

Empirical mapping of trade areas reveals considerable overlap, especially pronounced in high-density urban areas. It is obvious that distance does play a major role in the consumer's choice of shopping destination, but it is certainly not the only factor. It may be more meaningful to think in terms of the probability of a consumer at a given location traveling a particular distance to make a purchase. The probability is very high when the distance is quite short, and the likelihood of interaction decreases in some manner as distance increases.

The decision-making process used by the consumer is, therefore, not so simple that it incorporates only distance and is not so sensitive that it recognizes distance down to the half-inch. Rather a great many other factors are significant. Louis P. Bucklin, in a study of shopping patterns in Oakland, California, found that such variables as income and race of shopper exerted an influence as to which center was visited because certain centers cater to a particular income bracket more than others or to a particular racial or ethnic group.[8] In addition, the variety of products offered at a center affects its attractiveness, greater variety, of course, having a pull over a greater distance. The role of advertising, especially the media circulation of the advertising, plays an important part. Other factors relating to levels of consumer information about shopping center alternatives include recommendations by others and personal past experience and preferences. Free parking in shopping centers may play an important role in shopping decisions. Furthermore, these are all dynamic factors that change at different rates in their importance in the minds of the consumers. Empirical research has also established that for most personal travel, such as for shopping, there will be a *frictionless zone*, that is, a zone in which one is indifferent to the differences in distance among alternative destinations. For all of these reasons, trade areas overlap considerably, and a major extension and modification of classical central-place theory has been toward a more realistic interpretation of the decision-making process consumers.

Intraurban Retail Location

Central-place theory was originally envisoned and applied, as we have seen, in the context of a system of centers. One significant direction in which the theory has been extended is in the application to retail location within urban areas. Just as there is a hierarchy of market centers serving rural areas, there is also a hierarchy of

Toronto's Eaton Centre, part of the largest retail underground complex in North America.

[8]Louis P. Bucklin, *Shopping Patterns in an Urban Area* (Berkeley: University of California, Institute of Business and Economic Research, 1967).

intraurban retail shopping centers providing goods and services for the growing metropolitan area. As might be expected, the retail structure is infinitely more complex within the urban area, because it is here that the isotropic plain assumptions are most readily violated. Population density may vary somewhat over a rural landscape, for example, but the variation is frequently not sufficient to create dramatic deviations in the spatial distribution of central places, à la Christaller and Lösch. Within metropolitan areas, however, population densities differ greatly; income per capita, demographic structure, and racial or ethnic composition are unusually complex. It is no wonder that the application of central-place theory to metropolitan areas was slow to be recognized.

It must be remembered, of course, that a basic feature of central-place theory is the fact that we are dealing with a *system* of centers. It matters little whether these centers constitute a rural or an urban system. The fact that they are a system—that is, a group of *interrelated* locations—is paramount. Spatial competition is the integrating concept that describes this system, as based on a rural population requiring goods and services available only at specified locations. But as outlined in Chapter 7, the metropolitan area itself constitutes a kind of economic system, and the retail system of the metropolitan area evokes more than a few parallels with the system of rural market centers even though the retail density is much greater within the metropolitan area. The essential point is that rural population normally spreads fairly evenly over the landscape, for agriculture is a space-consuming activity whereas urban population, being sensitive to accessibility constraints, is more likely to cluster and, therefore, to produce a more bunched and complex locational pattern of retail establishments.

The location of stores of various retail chains follows certain elements of central-place theory within metropolitan areas. First, the chains in a particular retail category, say, fast-food stores,

wish to compete among themselves, accounting for Burger King and Wendy's locating next to or across the street from one another. Second, the chain itself wishes to avoid competing among its own stores and thereby seeks out a dispersed pattern of store locations.

Figure 8.12 shows drugstore locations in downtown Toronto. Those drugstores that have gone out of business were generally small independent neighborhood stores.[9] The 28 new stores opened between 1974 and 1985 tended to be larger chain drugstores. Over twice as many new, larger stores were opened than smaller stores were closed, suggesting the actual growth in consumer demand, as the target market of older people has increased. There has also been a spatial shift away from locations nearer Lake Ontario to Danforth Street with its subway.

The metropolitan area is not only nonisotropic but also more highly changeable than the relatively stable rural market system of central places. Most strikingly, these changes have been seen in the altered character of the central business district (CBD) of virtually all industrialized cities. Once the pulse of commercial as well as industrial life, the CBD was the organizational node of the entire urban area. Here was the point of maximum accessibility, just as the higher-order center in the rural center-place system was the point of maximum centrality. Other retail locations within the urban area responded to and owed their existence to the strength or weakness of the CBD. Spatial competition among retail centers was intense. A center could not expand too greatly because of the greater influence of the CBD. At the same time, a retail cluster could not locate too far away from the CBD, or else its inaccessibility would be a serious deterrent to a sufficient sales volume to meet costs and achieve a reasonable profit. A highly centralized cen-

---

[9]Ken Jones and Jim Simmons, *Location, Location, Location: Analyzing the Retail Environment* (Methuen: New York, 1987).

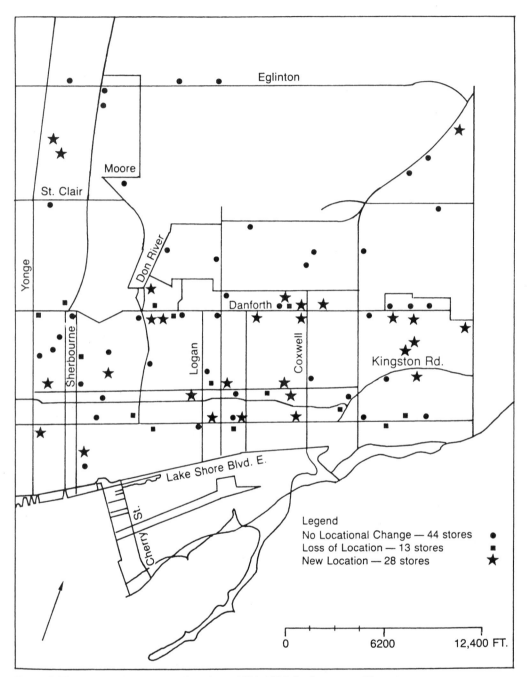

Figure 8.12 Changes in drugstore locations, 1974–1985, in downtown Toronto.
Source: Jones and Simmons, 1987.

tral-place system thus characterized the traditional urban area.

With improved transportation technology—notably the private automobile—population expanded ever more widely into suburban and rural areas, which then required their own retail services. Initially, only the lower-order goods and services were likely to be found in the suburban environment as retailers were at first reluctant to adapt to these changes. As the outlying population grew, however, higher-and-higher-order establishments—concentrated at major retail centers—now began to compete effectively with the CBD. Because the population migrating to suburban locations had a higher socioeconomic level, greater purchasing power also gave added impetus to suburban retail and service locations once the break with the past was accomplished in the 1960s.

In the United States by the early 1950s, there were indications that suburban shopping centers would not only effectively compete with the CBD, but that they might seriously reduce the role of the CBD as the organizational node of the urban area. These indications now, of course, are reality as the CBD in almost every major urban area has undergone both relative and absolute decline. At present in major metropolitan

Center, Georgia, a tiny central place in the center of nowhere. A patron exiting a low-order central function.

areas, large, integrated shopping centers in suburban areas have in great measure eliminated the need for consumer trips to downtown locations as the full array of goods and services are available in suburban areas. The CBD as a major retail center is dead in almost all American cities.

The basic concepts of central-place theory continue to describe the retail structure of metropolitan areas. The geometric pattern, however, bears little, if any, resemblance to that detailed for the dispersed rural farm population. If the metropolitan population were to be spread evenly over the landscape via a map transformation, the similarity of the metropolitan retail pattern to that of classical central-place theory would be more clearly evident, though still imperfect. A great deal of added insight has been lent to the distribution of retail location within metropolitan areas by the theoretical concepts of central-place theory. It is the modification of the rigid geometric interpretation of the theory that is of particular interest, however, and it is within the urban area that these deviations have been most obvious.

Central Places Around the World

Because of differing cultural and economic systems around the world, it is not surprising that marketing patterns may take on different geometric and functional forms. After all, modern technological society differs very substantially from traditional societies. Attitudes toward life—including economic life—may be vastly different. As the geometrical arrangement of marketing systems is a manifestation of human decisions and as these decisions are, in turn, based on attitudes and beliefs, the geographic expression of the economic landscape may well be expected to vary dramatically between modern technological and traditional society. A rather sizable research literature has been developed to answer the question of just how closely central-place theory describes the marketing patterns around the world.

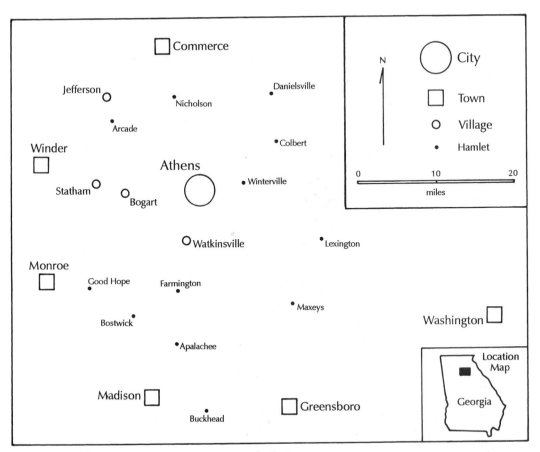

Figure 8.13 Central places on the Middle Georgia Piedmont.

Variations in Industrial Societies. Even within an industrial society, one should not expect exactly the same geometrical and hierarchical pattern to be repeated everywhere for there are important differences within a given industrial economic system. Take the United States as an example. Even a quick glance at the pattern of urban centers in Iowa suggests a hierarchical system, and the distribution of centers indicates that important elements of central-place theory must be operating. The precise hexagonal trade-area features obviously do not exist, and yet certain patterns of regularity may be observed in the size and spacing of centers. It is evident that the highway and railway systems exert an influence on the distribution of centers, creating deviations from the equal-spacing principles of central-place theory. Nevertheless, centers are reasonably equally spaced from one another, with smaller centers more closely spaced than larger ones.

Contrast the Georgia Piedmont central-place pattern with the distribution of centers in the Chicago region (Figures 8.13 and 8.14). In Chicago, the clustering of centers along Lake Michigan is especially evident in contrast to the dispersed hierarchical pattern spread over a portion of the Georgia Piedmont. A closer look shows a denser pattern of settlements to the west than to the east, because of the influence of Atlanta 65

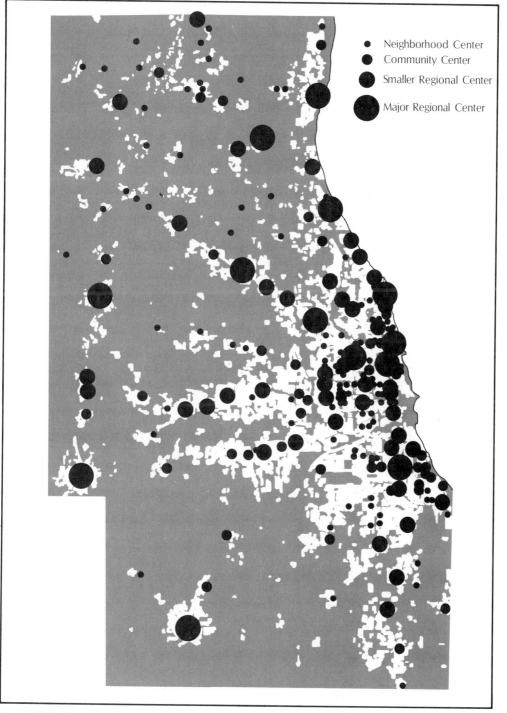

Figure 8.14 Central places in Chicago. *Source*: Berry, 1967.

miles west of Athens. Another contrast between the two figures is the overall density of commercial establishments in the two population and economic environments. In the Chicago example, the commercial centers, especially in downtown Chicago, are jammed together, making neat geometrical arrangements almost impossible to recognize. On the gently rolling Georgia Piedmont, on the other hand, the map is portrayed quite differently, with the urban places being mapped simply as city (Athens) towns, villages, and hamlets. In accordance with central-place theory, these categories are based on both population size and commercial functions. Such terminology is most inappropriate for a metropolis as Chicago, where major regional center, community center, and neighborhood center capture the essence of the urbanized central-place pattern.

Looking again at the two maps, we can note some features in common despite the diverse human and environmental settings. After all, there is an order to the locational arrangement of the centers. Athens is the dominant central place in Figure 8.13, so that no other center of any magnitude has historically been able to grow up in Athens' shadow. In fact, the centers closest to Athens tend to be quite small. Whereas Athens is a metropolitan area (with a city–county population of 88,000), the second largest central place on the map is Monroe (8854 people), representing the town category. Villages such as Boswick have about 1000 people, and hamlets such as Good Hope have fewer than 500 persons.

Another common relationship between the two maps is the way in which the centers are located with respect to the transport patterns. In both cases, it is evident that transportation channels the growth and development of centers, as well as their size and spacing. Although central places on the Georgia Piedmont do not fit the precise central-place pattern as seen in Figure 8.13, there are six towns roughly equally spaced around Athens. There are also a large number of hamlets, as expected by central-place theory. On each map we see, albeit imperfectly, the role

of spatial competition, with smaller centers hemmed in by the larger centers. If we generalize this spatial competition concept over the arrangement of centers on both maps, it is evident that, despite vast differences in population densities, several significant similar features appear to operate within these two contrasting economic settings within a similar cultural environment. But what of markedly disparate cultural systems?

Variations in Developing Economies. One interesting and important variation in the central-place system is the *periodic market*, very common in many traditional societies. Periodic markets derive their name from the fact that the markets move periodically from one place to another to serve the low-mobility and low-density consumers better. Market or sales volume does not justify establishing permanent markets, as is customary in the retail structure of industrialized economies.

These periodic markets follow central-place principles of spacing in that the itinerant merchant, peddler, or artisan appears in specific places on particular days. The system favors the

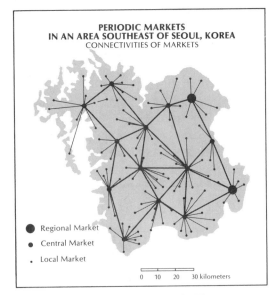

Figure 8.15 Market connectivity in Korea.

A 24-hour fruit stand in Chinatown, Manhattan Island, tempting the heavy pedestrian traffic on Broadway but closely watched by its proprietor for would-be snitchers.

consumer who has to travel only relatively short distances on specified days to obtain goods and services. The market locations are chosen to gain access to as many people as possible each day, and, therefore, the periodic market locations tend to be rather evenly spaced from one another. Periodic markets are characteristic of areas with low levels of personal mobility—primarily nonmotorized. G. William Skinner, who has studied the periodic marketing system of rural China, found three levels of markets: standard, intermediate, and central.[10] The central market is the highest order and may have some permanent shops and businesses. Standard markets are the lowest-order central places and act as local collection and distribution points.

Figure 8.15 shows three levels of markets in western Korea: local, central, and regional.[11] In 1925 the markets were isolated from one another, but they have now become integrated or connected in particular ways. In 1925 all markets were periodic, with sellers traveling on a five-day schedule to different markets. Now there are 20 permanent markets (in the larger centers) coexisting with the periodic market system. The pe-

riodic markets follow the central-place hierarchy, with more merchants appearing on given days at the larger or regional markets than at central markets and with the fewest merchants offering goods periodically at local markets.

SUMMARY

Tertiary economic activity has become the single largest employer of the economic sectors (ahead of primary and secondary) in the industrialized countries of the world. Retailing and services are strongly people-dependent; that is, the spatial distribution of retailing and services closely follows where people are located. Whereas many kinds of economic activities are production-oriented, the tertiary sector is consumption-oriented. In urbanized societies, tertiary activities are quite naturally located predominantly in urban areas.

At the level of the metropolitan area, tertiary activities may be classified locationally, following Berry, into (1) *ribbon development*, (2) *specialized functional area*, and (3) a *hierarchy of business centers*, both planned and unplanned.[12] Ribbon developments are primarily oriented to highway traffic, including not only such activities as service stations but also fast-food outlets and various convenience shops. The spatial structure of ribbon developments, strung out along major urban arteries or at street-corner locations, is closely related to the function of the goods and services provided. Specialized functional areas include such activities as medical centers, automobile rows, and various kinds of office parks. These functional areas exist because of advantages in comparative shopping, advertising economies, or the provision of specialized services. Superimposed over the ribbon developments and the specialized functional areas is a hierarchy of business centers, following the principles of

[10]G. William Skinner, "Marketing and Social Structure in Rural China," *Journal of Asian Studies* 24 (1964), pp. 3–43.

[11]Siyoung Park, "Rural Development in Korea: The Role of Periodic Markets," *Economic Geography* 57 (1981), pp. 113–126.

[12]Brian J. L. Berry, *Commercial Structure and Commercial Blight* (Chicago: Department of Geography Research Paper No. 85, University of Chicago, 1963).

central-place theory. In addition to the CBD are *major regional centers, smaller shopping-goods centers, community centers*, and finally, *neighborhood centers.* Each of these levels in the hierarchy may be planned or unplanned, though most of the planned centers are to be found in suburban and outlying areas and date from the late 1940s. Again, a relationship exists among the size, location, and function of these levels in the hierarchy.

It is difficult to speculate on the geographic arrangement of tertiary activities in the metropolitan area of the future. It is certain, however, that the computer will play an increasing role. Computerized shopping from the home is becoming common, at least for certain items. Even now, a significant amount of television advertising time is devoted to showing a product and how it works, where it may be obtained, and even the telephone number through which it may be ordered. One may dial a grocery channel or a pharmacy channel and select to view a variety of products. Purchase could be made directly, with the retailer processing the order and billing the customer on a monthly basis or directly deducting the amount from the customer's bank account. Despite the efficiency advantages of such procedures, many shoppers may prefer to shop "hands-on," especially for major items such as furniture, but also for such everyday items like fresh produce. Even if computerized shopping becomes frequent in the future for the purchase of certain kinds of retail goods, the services (doctors, dentists, lawyers, and even teachers) are going to continue to involve travel for face-to-face visits. Routine information may be handled by telephone, but more complex social and economic interactions will require personal contact. Thus, the location of tertiary activities will continue to occupy an important role in the economic geography of metropolitan areas.

Many services are rendered in public facilities, such as municipal hospitals, governmental buildings, and even parks. As a metropolitan area grows and the need for public services increases, conflict will quite naturally arise among groups trying to decide where particular public facilities should be located. These are political decisions. It is recognized that the location of a large public facility at a given site will affect land values and land use in the area around the facility. Often a public facility, such as a drug treatment center, is perceived as producing negative change in the surrounding area. A wide range of public facilities are currently located within our metropolitan areas and will continue to be so located in the future. These facilities are locationally sprinkled throughout our urbanized areas and form a part of the social and economic geography of our metropolitan regions.

Having examined cities as economic nodes in Chapter 7 and discussed, both in theory and reality, the location of tertiary activities among and within metropolitan areas, we will turn in Chapter 9 to a look at how the economic geography is changing in contemporary metropolitan areas.

Further Readings

Bell, Thomas L., Stanley R. Lieber, and Gerard Rushton. "Clustering of Central Places." *Annals of the Association of American Geographers* 64 (1974), pp. 214–225.

Berry, Brian J. L. *Commercial Structure and Commercial Blight* Chicago: Department of Geography, Research Paper No. 85, University of Chicago, 1963.

Berry, Brian J. L., H. G. Barnum, and R. J. Tennant. "Retail Location and Consumer Behavior." *Regional Science Association, Papers and Proceedings* 9 (1962). pp. 56–106.

Berry, Brian J. L., Edgar C. Conkling, and D. Michael Ray. *Economic Geography*. Englewood Cliffs, N.J.: Prentice-Hall, 1987.

Berry, Brian J. L., and William L. Garrison. "A Note on Central Place Theory and the Range of Good." *Economic Geography* 34 (1958), pp. 304–311.

Berry, Brian J. L., and John B. Parr, *Market Centers and Retail Location: Theory and Applications.* Englewood Cliffs, N.J.: Prentice-Hall, 1988.

Berry, Brian, J. L., and A. Pred. *Central Place Studies: A Bibliography of Theory and Application.* University of Pennsylvania, Regional Science Research Institute, Bibliography Series 1, 1961.

Bucklin, Louis P. *Shopping Patterns in an Urban Area*. Berkeley: University of California, Institute of Business and Economic Research, 1967.

Christaller, W. *Die Zentralen Örte in Süddeutschland*. Jena: Gustav Fischer Verlag, 1933. C. W. Baskin, trans. *Central Places in Southern Germany*. Englewood Cliffs, N.J.: Prentice-Hall, 1966.

Colwell, Peter F., and Truman A. Hartshorn. "Measuring the Impact of Inner City Markets on CBD Retail Trade." *Urban Geography* 1 (1980), pp. 130–140.

Davies, R. L., and D. S. Rogers, eds. *Store Location and Store Assessment Research*. New York: Wiley, 1984.

DeTemple, David J. *A Space Preference Approach to the Diffusion of Innovations: The Spread of Harvestore Systems Through Northeast Iowa*. Bloomington, Ind.: Department of Geography, Geographic Monograph Series, Vol. 3, Indiana University, 1971.

Getis, Arthur. "The Determination of the Location of Retail Activities with the Use of a Map Transformation." *Economic Geography* 39 (1963), pp. 1–22.

Hartshorn, T. A., *Interpreting the City: An Urban Geography*. New York: Wiley, 1992.

Jones, Ken, and Jim Simmons. *Location, Location, Location: Analyzing the Retail Environment*. New York: Methuen, 1987.

Lösch, August. *The Economics of Location*. New Haven, Conn.: Yale University Press, 1954, William H. Woglom and Wolfgang F. Stolper, trans. (originally published in 1939).

Park, Siyoung. "Rural Development in Korea: The Role of Periodic Markets." *Economic Geography* 57 (1981), pp. 113–126.

Robertson, Kent A. "Downtown Retail Activity in Large American Cities, 1954–1977." *Geographical Review* 73 (1983), pp. 314–323.

Rushton, Gerald. "Analysis of Spatial Behavior by Revealed Space Preferences." *Annals of the Association of American Geographers* 59 (June 1969), pp. 391–400.

Rusk, David. *Cities Without Suburbs*. Washington, D.C.: Woodrow Wilson Center Press, 1993.

Schmenner, Roger W. *Making Business Location Decisions*. Englewood Cliffs, N.J.: Prentice-Hall, 1982.

Skinner, G. William. "Marketing and Social Structure in Rural China." *Journal of Asian Studies* 24 (1964), pp. 3–43.

Wyckoff, William. "Revising the Meyer Model: Denver and the National Urban System, 1859–1879." *Urban Geography* 9 (1988), pp. 1–18.

CHAPTER 9

The Changing Economic Geography of the Restructured Metropolis

———— ◇ ————

[New suburban cities] *are springing up on the edges of old urban fabrics where nothing existed 10 years ago but residential suburbs and cow pastures. These new communities represent . . . the biggest change in 100 years in how Americans live and work.*

—JOEL GARREAU

After discussing in Chapter 8 how cities are linked together within far-reaching intermetropolitan systems, we now turn from the macrourban to the intraurban scale to focus on the changing internal spatial organization of the metropolitan complexes that form the major nodes in the national city-system. As pointed out at the end of Chapter 7, the single-core/periphery model of urban structure is no longer a valid representation of the multinodal metropolitan reality of the 1990s. This chapter explores the economic geography of the transformed metropolis by seeking to answer several key questions: What is the evolutionary context of today's dispersed, multinodal metropolitan city? What are the dimensions of recent data trends with respect to the economic geography of urban areas? Why has the continuing tilt toward the suburbanization of economic activities been so pronounced since the 1960s? Why are noneconomic location factors becoming increasingly important for understanding the distribution of employment within the metropolis? What are the impacts of these economic spatial changes on the urban labor force as expressed in the shifting locational relationship between residence and workplace?

SPATIAL EVOLUTION OF THE AMERICAN METROPOLIS

The historical geography of metropolitan form is efficiently summarized in the schematic diagram shown in Figure 9.1, which describes four major stages of urban expansion in response to new movement technologies. Spatial development at this scale, too, is largely shaped by the same kind of transportation processes that influenced the organization of economic space at the regional and national levels (pp. 93–94). An overview of each stage of intrametropolitan growth follows.[1]

Prior to the arrival of the electric trolley, just

———

[1]Lengthier accounts of the evolution of metropolitan form are found in Joel A. Tarr, "From City to Suburb: The 'Moral' Influence of Transportation Technology," in Alexander B. Callow, Jr., ed., *American Urban History: An Interpretive Reader with Commentaries*, 2nd rev. ed. (New York: Oxford University Press, 1973), pp. 202–212; James E. Vance, Jr., *The Continuing City: Urban Morphology in Western Civilization* (Baltimore: Johns Hopkins University Press, 1990); and Peter O. Muller, "Transportation and Urban Form: Stages in the Spatial Evolution of the American Metropolis," in Susan Hanson, ed., *The Geography of Urban Transportation* (New York: Guilford Press, 2 rev. ed., 1995), pp. 26–52.

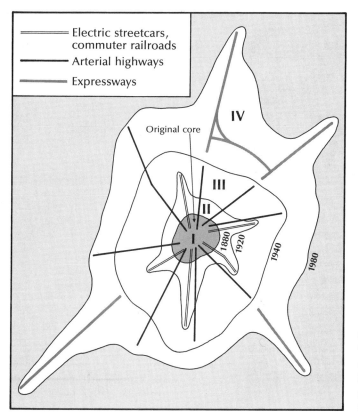

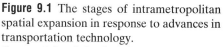

Figure 9.1 The stages of intrametropolitan spatial expansion in response to advances in transportation technology.
Source: After John S. Adams, "Residential Structure of Midwestern Cities," *Annals of the Association of American Geographers*, 60 (1970), p. 56.

before 1890, the American city was both highly compact and badly overcrowded because urban transportation was virtually nonexistent (Stage I in Figure 9.1). Even though full industrialization after the Civil War had attracted thousands of new migrants annually, most city residents could still get about only on foot. Little had changed since the city's origin in the preindustrial colonial period, when homes, shops, and workplaces were required to cluster tightly within easy walking distance. By the late nineteenth century, the rapid growth of industrial cities was exacerbating problems of extremely high residential densities, especially as the ethnic diversity of the urban population intensified without sufficient space for disparate social groups to stake out their own neighborhood turfs. Efforts to relieve these pressures by developing fast and cheap transit to en-

able the city's physical expansion were not initially successful. Stagecoaches, steam engines, and cable-car systems all failed. Although the lightweight street railway was a useful innovation after 1850, its horse-drawn trolley cars were only minimally faster than pedestrians.

All that changed dramatically after 1888 with the invention of the electric traction motor. Electricity could now power streetcars, whose much higher speeds (15–20 m.p.h., including stops) quickly permitted the significant urban expansion exhibited in Stage II of Figure 9.1. Light-rail traction lines quickly penetrated deep into the surrounding countryside and spawned elongated corridors of residential development. This phenomenon was repeated in older railroad corridors whose newly electrified commuter trains were far more efficient than their steam-powered

An aerial view of Country Club Plaza in outer Kansas City, the nation's first modern shopping center, opened in 1922 by developer Jesse Clyde Nichols.

predecessors. The detached housing tracts of these "streetcar suburbs" were highly popular and soon became the bastions of the new middle class launched by the burgeoning industrial economy, with upwardly mobile families constantly seeking to improve their social circumstances and residential environment. The electric trolley also achieved a transit breakthrough inside the central city. Its speed and low fares now gave everyone the opportunity to ride, and the city's less affluent socioeconomic groups were finally able to congregate in uniform neighborhood communities defined by ethnicity and income level. Improved local transportation also prompted large manufacturers to decentralize after the turn of the century, favoring waterways or intercity rail corridors and spawning

numerous industrial satellite suburbs.[2] The decidedly star-shaped urban area that had emerged by World War I, near the close of the electric streetcar era, was already well along in making the transition from simple city to complex metropolis.

That passage was swiftly completed in the 1920s, as the trolley yielded to the next and most influential urban transport revolutionizer—the automobile. America's fascination with cars was instantaneous, and by 1920 the rapidly expanding middle class could easily afford them. As auto ownership levels skyrocketed, governments re-

[2]See Graham R. Taylor, *Satellite Cities: A Study of Industrial Suburbs* (New York: Arno Press, 1970, reprint of 1915 edition).

sponded by building arterial highways into the metropolitan fringes, which again transformed the urban complex into a circular-shaped nodal region, but with a development radius now exceeding 20 miles (Stage III in Figure 9.1). Although intended to serve as recreational roadways for weekend city drivers, these highways soon became the umbilical cords linking downtown to the new, outlying housing tracts that developers were selling like hotcakes to motorists who obviously liked what they saw in the now readily accessible suburban landscape. Producers, however, were reluctant to abandon the railroad corridors that cut across the suburban ring, because the motor truck was still decades away from becoming an effective short-distance hauler of goods. Only lower-order functions, such as small retail outlets, followed people into suburbia during the interwar era. Large department stores chose to remain downtown because, in most cities, traffic congestion had not yet made

travel to the CBD (central business district) unbearable. But a few bold chains followed pioneering Sears & Roebuck to outlying highway sites, and the prototype suburban shopping center, Country Club Plaza, was successfully opened at the edge of Kansas City as early as 1922 (see photo).

The full flowering of the automobile age occurred in the post–World War II period, when high-speed expressways ultimately expanded the now all but frictionless urban region into the outermost suburbs by 1970 (Stage IV in Figure 9.1). (The suburban frontier, of course, has continued to push outward during the past three decades.) Federal government policies had much to do with creating this new metropolitan reality. The 1956 Interstate Highway Act underwrote much of the construction of the new freeway network, and Federal Housing Administration and Veterans Administration mortgage-guarantee policies favored new suburban houses rather than

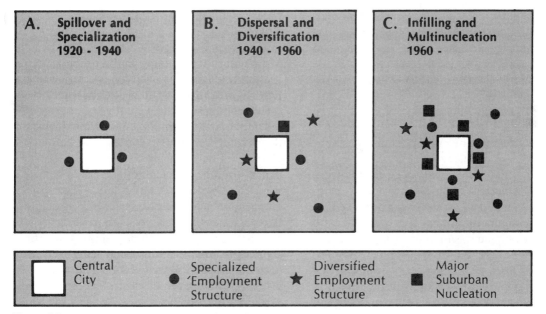

Figure 9.2 A generalized view of the suburbanization of economic activity since 1920.
Source: After Rodney A. Erickson. "The Evolution of the Suburban Space Economy," *Urban Geography* 4 (1983), p. 96.

the recycling of older multiple dwellings in central-city neighborhoods. Thus the nation's huge pent-up housing demands, stifled by more than a decade of economic depression and war, were unleashed with a vengeance along the city's edges after 1945, until by 1970 more people lived in suburbia than in either the central cities or nonmetropolitan America.

The massive postwar population growth of the suburbs is a familiar phenomenon. What is less well known, and ultimately of greater importance to the future of metropolitan America, is the massive suburbanization of economic activities that began in the 1960s. Even that deconcentration of production, however, was preceded by a steady centrifugal drift that Rodney Erickson captured in his evolutionary model of the suburban space-economy (Figure 9.2). The evidence that accumulated in the 1970s and 1980s showed that the suburbanization trend was so strong that by the late 1990s the intrametropolitan economy would turn inside out. The rest of this chapter focuses on this still continuing economic-geographic revolution, which, as the opening epigraph of this chapter underscores, embodies the twentieth century's single biggest change in urban spatial organization.

CURRENT METROPOLITAN TRENDS

The suburban rings of metropolitan areas continue to be the mainstay of national growth in the United States. In 1990, the suburbs were home to 48.5 percent of the U.S. population, with the remainder roughly split between the central cities and nonmetropolitan areas; by the late 1990s, it is estimated, suburban America's share of the national population had climbed past the 50 percent mark. Although traditionally strong in the heavily urbanized Manufacturing Belt and the West Coast states, since 1970 the suburbanization trend has been particularly pronounced in the newer metropolises of the Sunbelt. Among the suburbs that have grown the fastest since 1980 are those surrounding Phoenix, San Diego,

Orlando, Dallas-Fort Worth, Los Angeles, and Tampa. With the nation's 400-odd central cities remaining about the same in total size between 1970 and 1995, the intraurban distribution of population continued to favor suburbia, which increased its share within all metropolitan areas from 56 percent in 1970 to more than 65 percent in the mid-1990s. Moreover, those migrating out of the cities were largely in higher-income groups, as numerous studies have documented.[3]

Although residential suburbanization strongly persisted, the most dynamic trend of the late twentieth century has been the increasing ability of metropolitan activities to follow and spatially realign themselves to that population deconcentration. *County Business Patterns*, an annual economic census series, provides detailed coverage for major metropolises whose central cities are also counties. Eight of these metropolitan areas are sufficient to represent the broad regions of the United States, and their economic-sector breakdowns shown in Table 9.1 clearly reveal widespread and rapid suburbanization in all employment categories between 1976 and 1994.

The **Northeast**, as indicated by the data for New York, Philadelphia, Baltimore, and Washington, D.C., has experienced the suburbanization of a critical mass of jobs as each employment category (with only a single exception among all the individual metropolitan sectors) surpassed the pivotal 50 percent mark. Even New York City's national business community, which still hangs together, is undergoing considerable erosion (the discussion of the suburbanization of corporate headquarters later in this chapter will demonstrate the new locational forces whose emergence is clearly threatening Manhattan's continued commercial dominance). And with each employment sector at least two-thirds suburbanized, those forces have already turned Washington's booming business economy inside

---

[3]See, for example, William H. Frey, "Metropolitan America: Beyond the Transition," *Population Bulletin* 45 (July 1990), 51 pp.

Table 9.1 Suburban Percentage of Metropolitan Employment, by Sector, 1976–1994

	1976	1982	1988	1994
New York				
Total employment	50.8	53.7	57.5	58.4
Manufacturing	60.4	64.4	69.6	70.9
Wholesale trade	51.5	56.6	64.1	66.6
Retail trade	60.7	64.0	66.7	67.3
F.I.R.E.[a]	30.0	32.1	38.2	41.6
Services	44.4	47.0	50.3	52.8
Business services	40.6	45.2	51.1	56.7
Health services	52.2	53.4	54.3	54.7
Philadelphia				
Total employment	57.6	63.2	68.3	69.8
Manufacturing	63.5	70.3	75.0	78.6
Wholesale trade	55.2	67.6	73.6	79.0
Retail trade	65.6	70.4	73.0	75.8
F.I.R.E.	46.0	51.1	59.2	59.6
Services	49.4	55.3	61.6	63.8
Business services	44.2	66.1	74.0	83.2
Health services	51.0	56.0	57.4	62.1
Baltimore				
Total employment	50.8	58.8	64.4	66.9
Manufacturing	54.3	62.2	66.6	66.8
Wholesale trade	40.6	57.4	65.3	72.2
Retail trade	62.9	70.9	76.7	80.8
F.I.R.E.	36.0	45.1	51.8	58.7
Services	45.2	53.8	56.3	59.4
Business services	48.2	62.9	62.6	71.4
Health services	40.1	46.6	47.3	52.8
Washington				
Total employment	63.3	69.1	73.9	74.4
Manufacturing	69.5	74.4	81.4	82.4
Wholesale trade	69.2	81.4	87.6	91.6
Retail trade	74.2	79.8	83.1	84.3
F.I.R.E.	55.1	60.7	68.4	72.7
Services	52.3	59.8	64.2	65.9
Business services	66.2	74.8	78.2	85.4
Health services	61.4	64.0	64.7	67.7
St. Louis				
Total employment	63.0	69.4	71.9	75.1
Manufacturing	62.8	67.9	71.5	76.7
Wholesale trade	55.5	65.4	67.4	68.4
Retail trade	74.5	80.0	82.4	83.6
F.I.R.E.	52.2	63.9	69.0	70.1
Services	60.2	71.8	71.9	71.9
Business services	55.5	64.8	68.2	69.0
Health services	58.8	67.4	68.8	69.8
New Orleans				
Total employment	39.7	47.3	51.2	54.0
Manufacturing	47.3	51.5	56.9	63.3
Wholesale trade	42.7	58.6	66.0	69.1

Table 9.1 Suburban Percentage of Metropolitan Employment, by Sector, 1976–1994 (continued)

	1976	1982	1988	1994
Retail trade	48.0	55.3	59.7	60.6
F.I.R.E.	28.9	36.7	45.1	49.8
Services	28.4	38.3	43.6	46.5
Business services	29.2	47.2	52.0	54.5
Health services	32.8	39.1	49.5	51.7
Denver				
Total employment	46.2	52.7	58.4	62.0
Manufacturing	49.7	68.8	72.0	75.2
Wholesale trade	31.2	40.3	50.4	57.3
Retail trade	57.4	64.6	69.2	72.6
F.I.R.E.	33.7	42.3	51.6	55.8
Services	42.6	45.9	52.5	56.1
Business services	39.0	44.5	53.9	61.1
Health services	42.1	43.6	47.9	50.1
San Francisco				
Total employment	59.0	64.0	68.1	70.5
Manufacturing	76.3	75.7	76.8	80.8
Wholesale trade	65.6	72.2	75.5	80.7
Retail trade	72.1	74.4	75.3	75.8
F.I.R.E.	37.2	43.0	53.0	58.6
Services	54.1	60.2	62.6	65.1
Business services	50.5	58.4	64.5	69.8
Health services	61.1	70.0	72.3	73.4

ªFinance, insurance, and real estate activities.

Source: U.S. Bureau of the Census, *County Business Patterns.*

out: the capital's circumferential Beltway corridor in suburban Virginia and Maryland has clearly become the essence of that metropolitan city.

At the other end of the Manufacturing Belt, in the *Midwest*, suburban St. Louis exhibits an identical trend as the central-city economy has all but unraveled since the mid-1970s. At the same time, New Orleans demonstrates that the *South* is quickly catching up to the restructured metropolitan patterns of the North. Long prevented from expanding by unbridged water barriers and poorly drained floodlands, the Crescent City overcame those technological obstacles in the 1970s and 1980s to launch a prodigious suburbanization boom that included the development of major new activity centers.

The *Western Sunbelt* is also experiencing the same economic-geographic trends, the data revealing that suburban Denver has now captured a majority of employers in every one of that metropolitan region's productive sectors. Paradoxically, this deconcentration is being accelerated by the search for amenities at an urban center supposedly endowed with so many. In fact, rapid development has so polluted Denver's air with a recurrent Los Angeles-type smog that a secondary exodus to the nearby Rocky Mountain foothills is all but complete. San Francisco, of course, typifies the spread cities of *California*, which have long exhibited strong suburban economies. The most recent trend further reinforces that intrametropolitan dominance by the outer ring.

Tyson's Corner in Vienna, Virginia, is the crown jewel of the Capital Beltway corridor that rings Washington, D.C., and its inner suburbs. Its location, at the intersection of the Beltway and the radial Dulles Airport Toll Road, gives "Tyson's" outstanding regionwide accessibility and enabled it to grow from a semirural crossroads in 1960 to become one of the nation's three largest suburban activity centers by 1990.

THE CAUSES OF ACTIVITY SUBURBANIZATION

As we noted earlier, urban manufacturing and even retailing began to decentralize well before World War II (see Figure 9.2). This early suburban trend was initiated and sustained by both central-city *centrifugal* forces—congestion, high land values, high taxes—and such outlying *centripetal* influences as more abundant space, cheap land, and low tax rates. The leisurely outward drift persisted into the early postwar era but did not accelerate markedly despite the huge suburban population increases of the late 1940s and 1950s. Only toward the middle of the 1960s, with the completion of the metropolitan freeway network and its immediate impact on greatly reduc-

ing the costs of intraurban trucking, did activity deconcentration suddenly surge from a steady trickle into a tidal wave. Designed, ironically, to accentuate the central city's accessibility within the metropolitan area, the new expressways accomplished exactly the opposite. It quickly became obvious to producers that any location on this high-speed freeway system was now equally accessible to the rest of the metropolis, and that heretofore inefficient truck movements could now be eliminated by rerouting them around the chronic traffic congestion of the older core city. These time savings were translated into cost economies, and by the 1970s a new economic-geographic reality could be recognized: the differential in location costs between central city and much of suburbia had virtually been eliminated.

Thus producers were no longer bound to locations in the central city. Many chose to remain—at least initially. Many more did not, taking advantage of their new geographic freedom to vote with their feet (or rubber tires) and shift operations to suburban sites. Locational decision-making today, therefore, is increasingly shaped by **noneconomic** considerations within an all-but-frictionless metropolis. These changes are having an understandably disastrous impact on the central city's industrial economy because as the spatial pull of old rail and water terminals was eliminated, so were downtown's urbanization economies that until recently made large cities the nation's most important manufacturing nodes. Perhaps hardest hit were the old industrial cities of the Manufacturing Belt, where aged physical plants forced entrepreneurs to consider rebuilding at exactly the time when much more attractive suburban locations suddenly became feasible alternatives.

The suddenness of the post–1965 industrial exodus from the big cities has surprised many, but, as Berry and Cohen have made plain, the central city has always possessed major disadvantages as a manufacturing center:

The concentrated industrial [city] only developed because proximity meant lower transportation and communication costs for those interdependent specialists who had to interact with each other frequently or intensively and could only do so on a face-to-face basis. But shortened distances also meant higher densities and costs of congestion, high rent, loss of privacy, and the like. As soon as technological change permitted, the metropolis was transformed to minimize these negative externalities.[4]

An abandoned factory in the inner city of North Philadelphia. This once overindustrialized city, burdened by a rapidly deteriorating physical plant, has seen its manufacturing employment plummet over the past quarter-century.

Even more significantly, Thompson pointed out the underlying weak attachment Americans have always had to their central cities, which made breaking that bond so easy:

We did not, for the most part, build great cities in this country; manufacturing firms agglomerated in tight industrial complexes and formed labor pools of half a million workers. That is not the same thing as building great cities. We sort of woke up one day and there was Cleveland. There was Detroit, with four and a half million people [sic], the biggest factory town on earth.[5]

With the disappearance of the geographic conditions that created the central city in recent years, manufacturing has been joined by the suburbanization of the rest of the metropolitan economy as we have noted. We now turn our attention to the forces that are shaping the new economic geography of the outer suburban city.

[4]Brian J. L. Berry and Yehoshua S. Cohen, "Decentralization of Commerce and Industry: The Restructuring of Metropolitan America," in Louis H. Masotti and Jeffrey K. Hadden, eds., *The Urbanization of the Suburbs* (Beverly Hills, Calif.: Sage Publications, 1973), p. 454.

[5]Wilbur R. Thompson, "Economic Processes and Employment Problems in Declining Metropolitan Areas," in George Sternlieb and James W. Hughes, eds., *Post-Industrial America: Metropolitan Decline and Inter-Regional Job Shifts* (New Brunswick, N.J.: Rutgers University, Center for Urban Policy Research, 1975), p. 189.

THE STRUCTURE OF TODAY'S SUBURBAN SPACE-ECONOMY

As we have already observed, noneconomic forces are becoming dominant in shaping the distribution of activities inside the contemporary metropolis. Thus, with any location near the metropolitan expressway network now endowed with a superior *situation* vis-à-vis the entire urban region, more and more location decisions are being governed by *site* factors. This usually means that companies today behave very much like individuals when seeking new residential locations: increasingly, they opt for amenity-rich sites with pleasing living conditions that most enhance their image and status—which, of course, tends to heavily favor booming new suburbs.

In today's parlance, "amenities" are frequently grouped under the more general term *quality of life variables*, which for a firm usually means a location in a glamorously perceived community that possesses an attractive local environment where work may be carried out in a pleasant, stress-free atmosphere. Large office companies are especially conscious of this geographic commodity. Most believe such locations are essential for recruiting young managerial tal-

Research facilities and electronics plants crowd cheek-by-jowl in Silicon Valley, one of the world's leading high-technology complexes that sprang up during the 1970s near Stanford University, between Palo Alto and San Jose, along the southern end of California's San Francisco Bay.

ent, and nearly all the major corporations that have moved their headquarters out of New York City since 1965—a trend to be examined later in this chapter—cite quality of life as crucial in the decision to suburbanize. Given the nation's overwhelming preference for commuting to work by automobile, *convenience of access* also tends to greatly favor suburban locations (although traffic congestion has become a serious problem in suburbs that have experienced recent employment growth). Critics sometimes argue that suburbanizing an office greatly disadvantages workers who live in other metropolitan sectors. Yet Hartshorn's analysis of commuting to workplaces clustered near Atlanta's airport showed no biases that favor local suburban areas, because the circumferential Perimeter freeway (I-285) facilitates work trips that originate in every outlying sector.[6]

A third noneconomic force that integrates the others is the *geographic prestige* of a company's location. Since 1980, many suburban nodes—among them Orange County's Costa Mesa and Irvine near Los Angeles, Houston's Galleria/City Post Oak, and the corporate-row "Platinum Miles" of Fairfield and Westchester counties outside New York City—have acquired some of the nation's most glamorous images. In fact, entire industries are now affiliated with high-amenity suburbs, such as microprocessor electronics/computers in Silicon Valley on the southern outskirts of the San Francisco Bay Area metropolis (as well as similar locations near Boston, Dallas, San Diego, and Raleigh, North Carolina).

Geographic prestige has much to do with the recent emergence of major suburban activity centers. Originating in the 1960s as new regional shopping centers, these places swiftly acquired glamorous business-location images that lured light industry, office companies, and myriad other high-order economic and cultural functions. By the mid-1970s, this gravitation of activ-

[6]Truman A. Hartshorn, "Getting Around Atlanta: New Approaches," *Atlanta Economic Review* 28 (January–February 1978), pp. 43–51.

ities toward regional centers had become so pronounced that many became full-fledged *suburban downtowns*, mixed nonresidential land-use concentrations that offered their surrounding populations the entire array of metropolitan goods and services (a phenomenon discussed previously on pp. 147–148).

King of Prussia, Pennsylvania, a massive suburban downtown 20 miles northwest of central Philadelphia, is a classic example of this newest American urban activity node (Figure 9.3). Located close to historic Valley Forge and Philadelphia's elegant Main Line suburbs, the nuclear shopping mall achieved an instantly prestigious image following its opening in 1965. The area's

attractive setting amid the Piedmont foothills and the striking architecture of much of its recently built physical plant combine to greatly enhance local quality-of-life variables. Moreover, in terms of accessibility, King of Prussia lies at the junction of the region's main radial and circumferential expressways.

At least a half-dozen additional suburban downtowns have arisen in other outlying Philadelphia sectors since 1970, as that outer city captures more and more of the central city's leading functions (see Table 9.1). Collectively, they now constitute a multinodal metropolis whose normative spatial structure is diagrammed in Figure 9.4. This "pepperoni pizza" model may be placed

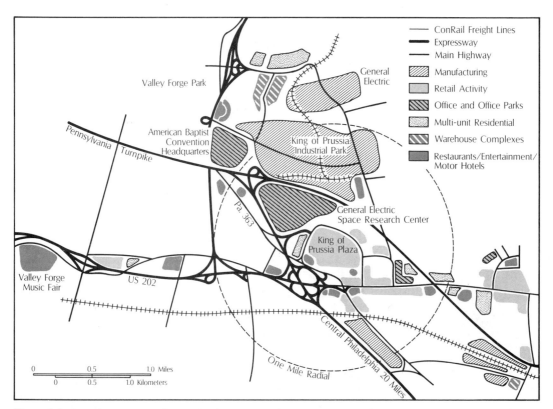

Figure 9.3 America's newest form of urban economic concentration: *the suburban downtown*, as exemplified by King of Prussia, Pennsylvania, near Philadelphia. *Source*: After Peter O. Muller, *The Outer City* (Washington: Association of American Geographers, Resource Papers for College Geography 76–2, 1976), p. 41.

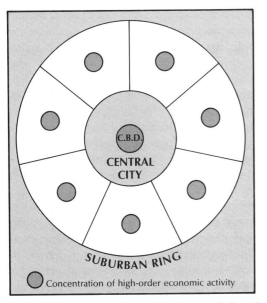

Figure 9.4 The general spatial characteristics of the contemporary multinodal American metropolis.

alongside the three classical generalizations of urban form (see pp. 144–146) to help us accommodate our structural conceptualizations to the intrametropolitan reality of the dawning twenty-first century.

Another important trend in the restructuring of metropolitan economic geography that strongly reinforces activity deconcentration is the shift to a postindustrial national economy. The proportion of the U.S. labor force holding manufacturing jobs has steadily declined since midcentury, and by 1990 more than three-quarters of all workers were employed in the white-collar tertiary, quaternary, and quinary economic sectors. (Tertiary activities involve the production of *services* of all kinds; the quaternary sector includes the production, processing, and consumption of *information*; and quinary activities involve high-level decision making or *control functions* that manipulate the vast resources of private businesses and governments.) Since these three sectors deal almost exclusively with the assemblage and movement of intangible commod-

ities, communication via telephone and computer network may increasingly be substituted for the transportation of people and goods. This, of course, promotes geographic footlooseness and intensifies the association between economic activities and high-amenity, high-status metropolitan locations.

Because tertiary, quaternary, and quinary functions are almost always performed in offices, it is hardly surprising that the suburban office industry has enjoyed phenomenal growth since 1970. Most of these firms tend to cluster in or near suburban downtowns in ultramodern office parks that offer their own amenities at the microscale. Manners calculated that as much as 90 percent of an office's expense involves labor, a factor of production that has decidedly suburbanized over the past three decades.[7] The central-city downtown's loss of its metropolitanwide centrality advantage has also freed a growing number of business activities from locating in

View of a new suburban office complex in Burlington, Massachusetts. The expressway in the foreground is Route 128, one of the nation's earliest circumferential freeways, that was built to bypass nearby Boston in the 1950s. Today, this state-of-the-art superhighway bills itself as the spine of "America's Technology Region," and is enjoying a major comeback in the wake of a decade-long recession that ended in 1997.

[7]Gerald Manners, "The Office in Metropolis: An Opportunity for Shaping Metropolitan America," *Economic Geography* 50 (April 1974), p. 98.

A Close-up of Two Corporate Moves From New York City to the Suburbs

The Simmons Mattress Company left New York City in 1975 for a location in the Sunbelt, having chosen a new headquarters site in Norcross, Georgia, in Atlanta's northeastern suburbs. Meyer has identified the factors that shaped the relocation decision.[8] The first was the initial realization in 1971 that the company was no longer required to remain in Manhattan because telecommunications and jet travel made several other places just as accessible to the national business scene and that nearby bankers, lawyers, and advertising agencies would keep up with Simmons if it left the city. Second, like many other large corporations in the 1950s and 1960s, Simmons had diversified by acquiring many smaller companies, and the need to consolidate all at a single location was becoming critical. And third, the growing inconvenience of commuting to Manhattan for the largely suburban-dwelling head-office staff was beginning to affect the efficiency of daily operations. Once the company decided to leave, its executives quickly chose metropolitan Atlanta because of its good image and proximity to furniture manufacturers. The final search space was immediately narrowed to the northeastern suburban sector because its superior expressways facilitated both long-distance highway and local airport con-

Union Carbide Corporation's former headquarters in New York City (a) and its newer home since 1981 near Danbury, Connecticut (b), 40 miles northeast of midtown Manhattan.

[8]Herbert E. Meyer, "Simmons Co. Likes It Down South," *Fortune*, May 1976, pp. 255–258, 262, 266.

nections. (Atlanta's rising prominence as an international jet-travel node also made its airport particularly attractive to foreign clients.) The Norcross site itself was selected because of its outstanding amenities—70 wooded acres along the bank of the scenic Chattahoochee River. Simmons was fully satisfied with the whole experience, citing as the most important benefit the significantly higher productivity of its staff amid the superior quality of life of its convenient, high-amenity suburban location.

Union Carbide's 1981 headquarters move from its famous Park Avenue skyscraper to an ultramodern business campus in suburban Danbury, Connecticut, was a similar experience except that the relocation was confined to the outer ring of the same (Greater New York) metropolis. Carbide's move was also a much larger undertaking (the corporation ranked thirty-fifth on the Fortune-500 list), and its move involved the transfer of 3500 head-office employees versus only 45 for Simmons. Because of its prominence in the local business community and the timing of the company's relocation announcement in 1976 at the height of the city's financial crisis, the decision raised an enormous outcry in New York. Public officials and the local news media launched a loud and sustained protest, and Maestro Leonard Bernstein even threatened to organize the picketing of the Union Carbide Building by the New York Philharmonic Orchestra! Union Carbide stuck to its guns and rode out the storm, which only abated weeks later when New York's Episcopal bishop wildly overreacted by delivering an Easter sermon that crudely condemned exiting companies for running away from the city's multiplying problems. This emotional affair underscores what is at stake as big central cities face irreversible economic decline. In New York's case, the loss of prestige as its corporate leadership position erodes shows that psychological factors also play an important role in the health of a local economy. Since Carbide's public relations disaster, companies have departed much more quietly. Despite an economic revival in the 1980s—which ended in a sharp downturn in the early 1990s—the corporate exodus continues, led by the top Fortune-500 company, Exxon (which has relocated to a suburban downtown just outside Dallas).

that central business district. Although face-to-face interaction is still traditional for certain commercial transactions, suburban locations are at no particular disadvantage: executives can easily attend CBD business lunches by confining their driving on radial expressways to the lighter traffic of the late morning and early afternoon off-peak hours.

The suburbanization of highest-order office facilities is best seen in the headquarters movements of the nation's largest industrial corporations. *Fortune*'s 1965 listing of the 500 biggest companies showed only 47 with suburban head offices; by 1969 that total had reached 56, and a trend was being established. The pace of de-

concentration accelerated markedly during the 1970s, and by 1975, 135 of the Fortune-500 were headquartered in suburbia. By 1980 that total had swelled to 178, and in 1994 it reached 233. No metropolis has felt the impact of this relocation trend as strongly as New York. Manhattan's 1968 total of 138 headquarters was cut to 29 a quarter-century later, and for the 1000 largest Fortune companies, New York City as long ago as 1978 fell behind its outer suburban city.[9] The

[9]Peter O. Muller, "The Suburbanization of Corporate Headquarters: What Are the Trends and Consequences?," *Vital Issues*, Washington, Conn.: Center for Information on America, April 1978.

pair of case studies outlined in the box focus on the motivations underlying the relocation of these head offices to the suburbs.

THE IMPACT OF EMPLOYMENT DECONCENTRATION ON COMMUTING PATTERNS

The evolution of a frictionless, freeway-dominated metropolis has also meant that people are becoming far more footloose with respect to their residential location. In the past, one's home was almost always located as close to one's workplace as feasible; at the metropolitan scale, work–journey flows were overwhelmingly directed toward the central-city CBD where most regional employment was concentrated. Today, however, the opposite is true: distance *accretion* has replaced distance decay in the spatial patterning of work trips, and the multinodal transformation of the geography of intraurban employment has redirected aggregate work–journey flows so that suburb-to-suburb commuting now dominates, with reverse (central city-to-suburb) commuting steadily catching up to the residue of suburb-to-city travel.

The eroding spatial affinity between home and workplace since the 1950s can be seen in the following sequential examination of commuting distance relationships. Figure 9.5 shows the normative pattern: employees are evenly distributed outward from a workplace until a reasonable commuting distance is reached, beyond which travel declines sharply. Getis defined this limit that circumscribes a frictionless commuting zone as the **critical isochrone** and graphed its theoretical curve (Figure 9.6).[10] When fitted to an empirical case in Figure 9.7, which is based on data mapped by Alexander in the 1950s,[11] Getis's

[10]Arthur Getis, "Residential Location and the Journey from Work," *Proceedings of the Association of American Geographers* 1 (1969), pp. 55–59.

[11]John W. Alexander, *Economic Geography* (Englewood Cliffs, N.J.: Prentice-Hall, 1963), p. 568.

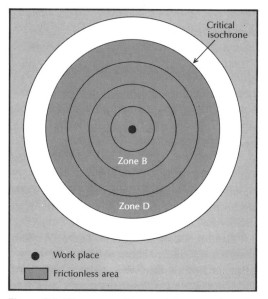

Figure 9.5 The normative spatial patterning of work trips.
Source: After Arthur Getis, "Residential Location and the Journey From Work," *Proceedings of the Association of American Geographers*, 1 (1969), p. 57.

model expectedly shows a strong distance–decay effect characterized by a critical isochrone of just over two miles.

Because urban freeways diffused rapidly after 1960, we anticipate that the frictionless commut-

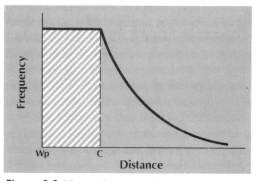

Figure 9.6 Normative graphic relationship of commuting distances, showing the influence of the *critical isochrone*.
Source: After Getis, 1969, p. 57.

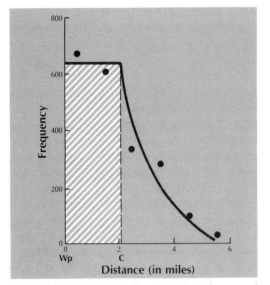

Figure 9.7 Commuting distances of workers employed at Oscar Mayer factory in Madison, Wisconsin, 1950s. *Source*: After Getis, 1969, p. 57; data from Alexander, 1963, p. 568.

ing zone will also begin expanding as the same travel times now encompass greater distances. This is certainly the case in Figure 9.8, which employs data gathered a few years later by Taaffe

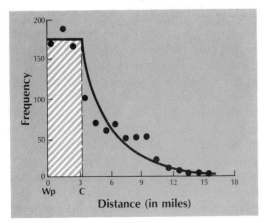

Figure 9.8 Commuting distances of workers employed at a West Chicago workplace, early 1960s. *Source*: After Getis, 1969, p. 57; data from Taaffe et al., 1963, p. 55.

et al.,[12] and reveals a critical isochrone located almost four miles from the place of work. By the mid-1960s, Wolforth's commuting data (Figure 9.9) show not only a widened frictionless zone but also a tendency for a distance–accretion pattern to develop before the critical isochrone is reached.[13] Figure 9.10 carries the sequence into 1973, using data compiled by Herman and Lam,[14] again establishing an accretion pattern and a frictionless zone now widened to nearly 12 miles. By the end of the 1970s (Figure 9.11), the frictionless area in some cases extended up to 20 miles. The most recent data set for 1991 (Figure 9.12) closely resembles the graphic pattern of the 1979 case study (Figure 9.11), suggesting that during

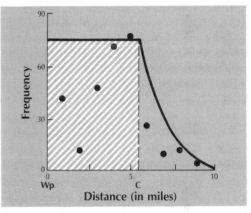

Figure 9.9 Commuting distances of workers employed at MacMillan, Bloedel and Powell River's head office, Vancouver, Canada, 1965. *Source*: After Arthur Getis, *The Journey from Work and the Critical Isochrone* (New Brunswick, N.J.: Rutgers University, Department of Geography, Discussion Paper No. 2, September 1970), p. 9.

[12]Edward J. Taaffe, Barry J. Garner, and Maurice H. Yeates, *The Peripheral Journey to Work* (Evanston, Ill.: Northwestern University Press, 1963), p. 55.

[13]J. R. Wolforth, *Residential Location and the Place of Work* (Vancouver: University of British Columbia Geographical Series No. 4, Tantalus Research, Ltd., 1965).

[14]Robert Herman and Tenny Lam, "Carpools at Large Suburban Technical Centers," *Transportation Engineering Journal* 101 (May 1975), pp. 311–319.

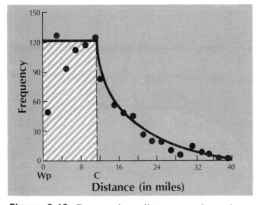

Figure 9.10 Commuting distances of workers employed at G. M. Labs research facility, Warren, Michigan, 1973.
Data source: Robert Herman and Tenny Lam, "Carpools at Large Suburban Technical Center," *Transportation Engineering Journal*, 101 (May 1975), p. 315.

the 1980s an upper commuting distance limit may have been reached.

These lengthening commuting distances clearly show that proximity to one's place of employment is no longer an important determinant of residential location. Far from serving as a constraint, the workplace now provides a locus of opportunity for an individual to reside in the highest-status neighborhood possible, virtually anywhere in the metropolis. Earlier we saw that

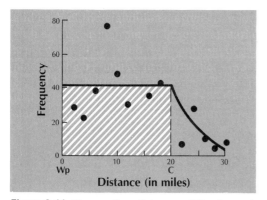

Figure 9.11 Commuting distances of faculty and staff employed at the Ambler Campus of Temple University, Ambler, Pennsylvania, 1979.
Data source: 1978–1979 Ambler Campus Directory.

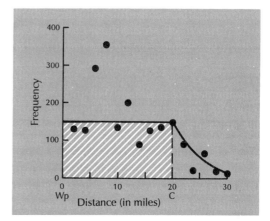

Figure 9.12 Commuting distances of faculty and staff employed at the main campus of the University of Miami in Coral Gables, Florida, 1991.
Data source: University of Miami, Office of Planning and Institutional Research; courtesy Mary M. Sapp, Director.

the linkage between upward social and spatial mobility was already forged when the middle class emerged in the late-nineteenth-century streetcar suburbs. The tendency for people to form homogeneous social districts—voluntary congregations of families possessing the same incomes, occupational status, lifestyles, values, and aspirations—was greatly enhanced by the automobile. These uniform communities could now spread out at much lower densities, increasing their scale and ability to isolate themselves spatially from other residential congregations. The arrival of freeways finally gave people access to the entire metropolitan social mosaic. And mobility within that increasingly specialized residential mosaic was made easier than ever after 1970, as builders increasingly offered entire lifestyles in the form of "total living packages," and realtors formed metropolitanwide and even nationwide computerized information networks to meet the ever more specific housing needs of people who knew exactly what they were looking for in the residential environment.

For those unable by virtue of income or race to gain entry to the specialized social mosaic of contemporary suburbia, the recent deconcentration of employment has created serious work-access problems. The steady outmigration from the central cities of manufacturing and the non-specialized service jobs most compatible with the modest skills possessed by lower-income and minority city residents created a worsening geographic mismatch of people and employment. Exclusionary suburban barriers involving lot size and building standards maintained through local zoning ordinances, in effect, have set housing prices and rentals that can be afforded only by those whose incomes are at least equal to the prevailing community level. Dual housing markets widely continue to segregate populations by race, and the post–1970 suburbanization of middle-income blacks is overwhelmingly steered into already nonwhite areas or, in the urbanizing Sunbelt, to new minority enclaves.[15] Besides the obvious commuting hardships for a population whose auto ownership level is well below the metropolitan average, the central city's resident labor force is becoming cut off from job information flows that are increasingly restricted to suburban highway-oriented employment centers.

SUMMARY

This chapter concluded our survey of cities as economic nodes by focusing on the internal spatial organization of the contemporary restructured metropolis. We observed that conventional center-periphery models no longer fit today's urban reality as activities increasingly suburbanize and a restructured, multinodal metropolitan form rapidly matures. We also saw that this new economic geography is heavily influenced by noneconomic locational forces within the now all-but-frictionless metropolis. A number of problems, however, accompany this intraurban

spatial transformation. The declining accessibility of underprivileged central-city residents to metropolitan employment opportunities is perhaps the most pressing dilemma, although several researchers[16] conclude that a solution is much more a matter of upgrading education and job skills than improving transportation between the inner city and suburban employment nodes.

Another issue of considerable importance is the energy efficiency of the changing metropolis as the nation's fuel supply faces an uncertain future. Although American economic health is not immediately threatened as energy problems refuse to disappear—a topic investigated in Chapter 12—current wastefulness must be replaced by conservation to get us through the decades just ahead. Whereas critics have castigated dispersed suburban living as an energy-wasting settlement pattern, the emergence of the multinodal metropolis is an encouraging step because the provision of high-order urban goods and services is increasingly available locally at several outlying sites rather than at only a single center to which every metropolitan resident must travel. The truth is that we still do not have an accurate measure of the energy efficiency of contemporary suburbia, but the evidence to date indicates that it is much higher than many observers suspect. Certainly, we would not plan spread-out urban settlements if we were starting to build from scratch today. But the automobile is a fact of life, a critical mass of leading economic activities has irreversibly suburbanized, and the polycentric freeway city has become the urban morphology of the foreseeable future.

The key to continued success lies not in a return to the concentrated industrial city—a political and social impossibility anyway—but in a better planned and more efficiently utilized multinodal metropolis in which both the central-city

---

[15]Larry Ford and Ernst Griffin, "The Ghettoization of Paradise," *Geographical Review* 69 (April 1979), pp. 140–158.

[16]See, for example, Sanford H. Bederman and John S. Adams, "Job Accessibility and Underemployment," *Annals of the Association of American Geographers* 64 (December 1974), pp. 378–386.

and outer-city components can harmoniously operate to advance the economic prospects of the whole.

Further Readings

Adams, John S. "Residential Structure of Midwestern Cities." *Annals of the Association of American Geographers* 60 (March 1970), pp. 37–62.

Alexander, John W. *Economic Geography*. Englewood Cliffs, N.J.: Prentice-Hall, 1963.

Baerwald, Thomas J. "The Emergence of a New 'Downtown.'" *Geographical Review* 68 (July 1978), pp. 308–318.

Berry, Brian J. L., and Yehoshua S. Cohen. "Decentralization of Commerce and Industry: The Restructuring of Metropolitan America." In Louis H. Masotti and Jeffrey K. Hadden, eds., *The Urbanization of the Suburbs*. Beverly Hills, Calif.: Sage, 1973, pp. 431–455.

Breckenfeld, Gurney. "'Downtown' Has Fled to the Suburbs." *Fortune*, October 1972, pp. 80–87, 156, 158, 162.

Brunn, Stanley D., and James O. Wheeler, eds. *The American Metropolitan System: Present and Future*. New York: Halsted Press/V. H. Winston, 1980.

Cervero, Robert. *America's Suburban Centers: The Land Use-Transportation Link*. Winchester, Mass.: Unwin Hyman, 1989.

Cervero, Robert. *Suburban Gridlock*. New Brunswick, N.J.: Rutgers University, Center for Urban Policy Research, 1986.

Christian, Charles M., and Robert A. Harper, eds. *Modern Metropolitan Systems*. Columbus, Ohio: Charles E. Merrill, 1982.

Clark, David. *Post-Industrial America: A Geographical Perspective*. London and New York: Methuen, 1985.

Erickson, Rodney A. "The Evolution of the Suburban Space Economy." *Urban Geography* 4 (1983), pp. 95–121.

Fishman, Robert. "Megalopolis Unbound." *Wilson Quarterly*, Winter 1990.

Garreau, Joel. *Edge City: Life on the New Frontier*. New York: Doubleday, 1991.

Hartshorn, Truman A. *Interpreting the City: An Urban Geography*. 2nd rev. ed. New York: Wiley, 1992.

Hartshorn, Truman A., and Peter O. Muller. "Suburban Downtowns and the Transformation of Metropolitan Atlanta's Business Landscape." *Urban Geography* 10 (July–August 1989), pp. 375–395.

Hartshorn, Truman A., and Peter O. Muller, "The Suburban Downtown and Urban Economic Development Today." In Edwin S. Mills and John F. McDonald, eds., *Sources of Metropolitan Growth*. New Brunswick, N.J.: Rutgers University, Center for Urban Policy Research, 1992, pp. 147–158.

Herman, Robert, and Tenny Lam, "Carpools at Large Suburban Technical Centers," *Transportation Engineering Journal* Vol. 101, May 1975, pp. 311–319.

Hughes, James W., ed. *Suburbanization Dynamics and the Future of the City*. New Brunswick, N.J.: Rutgers University, Center for Urban Policy Research, 1974.

Jackson, Kenneth T. *Crabgrass Frontier: The Suburbanization of the United States*. New York: Oxford University Press, 1985.

Leinberger, Christopher B., and Charles Lockwood. "How Business Is Reshaping America: Commercial Expansion from City to Suburb Is Changing the Way We Live and Work." *Atlantic Monthly*, October 1986, pp. 43–52.

Manners, Gerald. "The Office in Metropolis: An Opportunity for Shaping Metropolitan America." *Economic Geography* 50 (April 1974), pp. 93–110.

Muller, Peter O. *Contemporary Suburban America*. Englewood Cliffs, N.J.: Prentice-Hall, 1981.

Muller, Peter O. "The Suburban Transformation of the Globalizing American City." *The Annals of the American Academy of Political and Social Science* Vol. 551, May 1997, pp. 44–58.

Muller, Peter O. "Transportation and Urban Form: Stages in the Spatial Evolution of the American Metropolis." In Susan Hanson, ed., *The Geography of Urban Transportation*. 2nd rev. ed. New York: Guilford Press, 1995, pp. 26–52.

Quante, Wolfgang. *The Exodus of Corporate Headquarters from New York City*. New York: Praeger, 1976.

Roberts, Sam. *Who We Are: A Portrait of America Based on the Latest Census*. New York: Times Books, 1993.

Saxenian, AnnaLee. "The Genesis of Silicon Valley." In Peter Hall and Ann Markusen, eds., *Silicon Landscapes*. Winchester, Mass.: Allen & Unwin, 1985, pp. 20–34.

Schaeffer, K. H., and Elliot Sclar. *Access for All: Transportation and Urban Growth*. Baltimore: Penguin Books, 1975.

Stanback, Thomas M., Jr. *The New Suburbanization: Challenge to the Central City*. Boulder, Colo.: Westview Press, 1991.

Taaffe, Edward J., Barry J. Garner, and Maurice H. Yeates, *The Peripheral Journey to Work*. Evanston, Ill: Northwestern University Press, 1963.

Taylor, Graham R., *Satellite Cities: A Study of Industrial Suburbs*. New York: Arno Press, 1970, reprint of 1915 edition.

U.S. Congress, Office of Technology Assessment. *The Technological Reshaping of Metropolitan America* (OTA-ETI-643). Washington, D.C.: U.S. Government Printing Office, September 1995.

Vance, James E., Jr. "The American City: Workshop for a National Culture." In John S. Adams, ed., *Contemporary Metropolitan America: Volume 1, Cities of the Nation's Historic Metropolitan Core*. Cambridge, Mass.: Ballinger, 1976, pp. 1–49.

Vance, James E., Jr. *The Continuing City: Urban Morphology in Western Civilization*. Baltimore: Johns Hopkins University Press, 1990.

Wolforth, J. R. *Residential Location and the Place of Work*. Vancouver: University of British Columbia Geographical Series No. 4, Tantalus Research, Ltd., 1965.

PART FOUR

Manufacturing Location

CHAPTER 10

Manufacturing:
Where Plants Locate and Why

———◇———

It is a capital mistake to theorise before one has data.
—SIR ARTHUR CONAN DOYLE

INTRODUCTION

One of the most important economic activities is the manufacturing process, in which economic value is added to material, labor, and other production inputs. Material is transformed into a more useful form by changing its shape, function, or composition. Materials are brought together at a manufacturing plant, where they are changed in some way—normally through the application of energy and labor input—and then the "finished" product or products are shipped on to the market. What constitutes a finished product for one plant may be one of several materials assembled for manufacturing at another plant.

We study manufacturing location in order to understand why plants locate where they do. A different choice of location will involve a different mix of costs, as well as different access to the market. Any one location will have a particular set of costs and generate a given level of revenues. Insofar as there is a *spatial pattern* to these costs and revenues, a clustering of manufacturing plants may occur on the economic landscape. Thus, virtually all manufacturers consider certain

basic locational factors or influences in the plant location decision. Not all manufacturers, of course, choose the same plant site because their production (costs) and market needs differ and because manufacturers may simply attach a different perception to the relative importance of these locational influences. Not all decisions are made with full knowledge of the consequences for profit or other kinds of satisfaction, in the short run as well as in the long run.

GENERAL LOCATIONAL FACTORS

Why does a manufacturing plant locate at a particular place? The answer is seldom simply because of one locational factor. Much more typically, the place selected has multiple advantages and few, if any, serious disadvantages. To be sure, there may be one or a small number of primary attracting factors, but a listing of all the advantages of any particular location may be considerable. The difficulty is that many places may have locational advantages for a given manufacturing establishment. How does one sort out all these places and all their advantages and disadvantages and then decide on an appropriate lo-cation? The answer, as explored in this chapter, is by no means easily found, because of the extreme complexities involved in location decisions.

The locational problem is further complicated by changes that occur over time. A location chosen, for example, because of low labor cost may be attractive to many manufacturers, and as a result the competition for low-cost labor brings about an increase in the wage rate. Or a location selected because of high market demand may suffer a serious disadvantage when competitive manufacturers begin to carve up that market. So locational advantages change, often in rather unpredictable ways. Yet investment in a plant and facilities may run into many millions of dollars. Obviously, under most circumstances the plant cannot pick up and move every time locational influences shift. Plant location decisions are, therefore, made on the basis of present uncertainties and with an eye, insofar as possible, on the future.

Corporate location decisions are not merely mundane exercises in site selection, but involve many considerations such as planning new capacity in response to anticipated changes in production cost and market conditions. Bruce Wardrep (1985, p. 8) notes that corporate location decisions usually entail production life-cycle considerations and must therefore be viewed as part of a broader corporate strategy framework that includes (1) a recognition of future production capacity shortfalls (or surplus); (2) options and contingency plans for remedying shortfalls; (3) an organizational structure and process for determining where a new production site should be located (if and when needed); and (4) actual site selection. The organizational structure within which these decisions are approached may be centralized (corporate staff-led or division controlled), depending on the nature of the production process, the importance of various location factors, and capital intensity of the manufacturing firm or process in question.

The Influence of the Market

For a growing number of industries, in the developed world at least, the market has become increasingly important in the locational choice. Historically, manufacturing in the United States was concentrated in the so-called American Manufacturing Belt, and area extending roughly from Boston to Washington, thence to St. Louis, to Minneapolis, and back to Boston. This area has traditionally contained the great bulk of the U.S. population and has provided a large market for all variety of manufactured products. As discussed later, manufacturing has spread increasingly away from this northeastern quarter of the United States into the West and South. Much of this manufacturing spread has been the result of a shift in the markets to California, Florida, Texas, and other areas outside of the Northeast. More than half of such shifts have resulted from the deaths of plants in the Manufacturing Belt and the births of plants in the West and South, not from the relocation of plants from one part of the country to another.

As illustrated in an earlier chapter, industry locates near markets, in part because it normally costs more to transport a manufactured product than a nonmanufactured material. Furthermore, there is often a weight gain in the manufacturing process. A location near the market avoids the transport charge on materials added during manufacturing. For example, Figure 10.1 shows the distribution of Coca-Cola bottling plants in Georgia. The distribution is spread out in order to serve a generally dispersed market. Because water, found everywhere, is the principal ingredient (by weight) in Coca-Cola, it makes sense to locate the bottling plants as close as possible to the consuming areas in order to avoid shipping large quantities of water long distances. Two basic reasons for market location are therefore (1) the higher freight rate on the finished product and (2) a weight gain in the manufacturing process.

Another reason involves perishability and communication cost and convenience. A daily

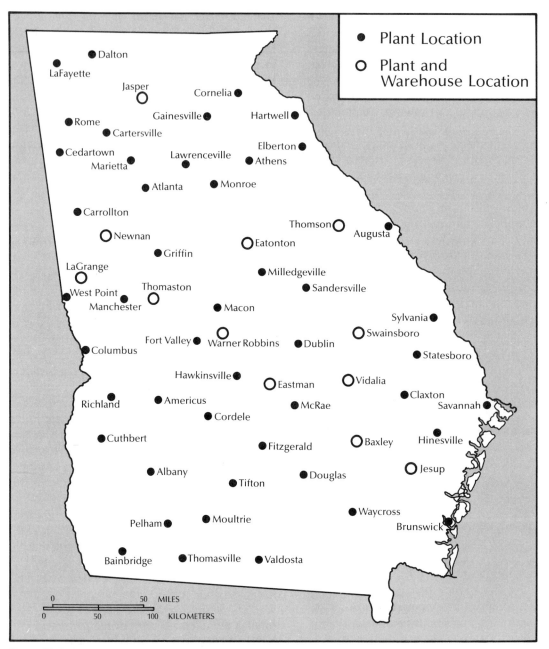

Figure 10.1 The distribution of Coca-Cola bottling plants and warehouses in Georgia, showing a remarkably regular spatial arrangement.

newspaper may be viewed as a product of a specialized kind of manufacturing process. The product is highly perishable, both in time and in space. Who wants to read yesterday's news? Furthermore, most newspapers contain a large amount of information about the local area or region but only the most pertinent or sensational national or international news. Because of their "perishability," newspapers are manufactured in their primary market area, where they can be quickly placed in the hands of the consumer/reader. A local newspaper should be contrasted with *Time* magazine, which gives weekly news. Numerous studies have delineated the market area of newspapers and the decline in readership with distance from the manufacturing locale.

One type of manufacturing that is highly sensitive to communication costs and convenience is the women's apparel industry, especially that segment representing the production of stylish clothes. For years Paris has dominated women's fashions. In the United States, New York, with its famous garment district in midtown Manhattan, and Los Angeles stand out. Because design, fabric, color, trim, and other features of style are highly individualized, large amounts of information transfer from designers to manufacturers are required. Styles change quite rapidly, and women's apparel manufacturers especially must be able to adjust to these changes immediately. Traditionally, therefore, the most stylistic apparel manufacturing has been located in those large metropolitan areas where new styles have been set. Mass-produced clothing, on the other hand, has sought out low-cost labor locations, often in the rural South and increasingly in Third World nations where labor cost is low.

Market-oriented locations are not always the lowest-cost processing points. In fact, location in a large metropolitan area may mean rather high wage rates, high land costs, high taxation, and considerable transport congestion. The market advantage outweighs these higher cost disadvantages. After all, a firm is basically interested in maximizing its profits. Profits may be increased

by minimizing production costs, maximizing sales revenue, or, ideally, both. A market location implies a desire to improve sales, and if the sales revenue is high enough, a somewhat higher production cost can easily be accommodated.

Figure 10.2 illustrates why a market location may be advantageous despite high production costs. The vertical axis displays both revenues and costs; the horizontal axis shows distance away from the center of the market. Figure 10.2*a* (top) demonstrates a market-oriented industry. Although total production costs are highest at the center of the market and decline with distance, the revenue curve has a steeper decline with distance. Thus, the profit level is highest at the center of the market. By contrast, the type of industry depicted in Figure 10.2*b* (bottom) is

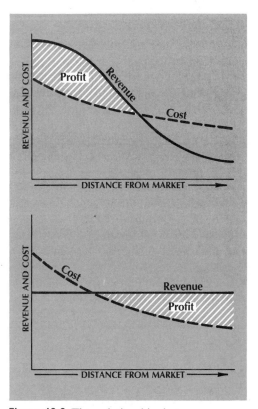

Figure 10.2 The relationship between revenue and cost with distance from the market.

not market-oriented, and the revenue curve, unlike the cost curve, does not change with distance. In this case, the industry cannot operate economically near the market center because of the higher production cost. Instead, the area of highest profit occurs at some distance from the market. This second type of industry is highly sensitive to production costs and seeks to locate so as to minimize these costs. The former industry type is sensitive to high-revenue locations. For either the minimum-cost or maximum-revenue manufacturing case, the choice of location will be determined by where profits can be maximized.

Production Costs

It is possible to substitute among the several elements of production costs. We may, for instance, substitute more capital for less labor, or vice versa. Or we may use more energy or fuel and thereby reduce the cost of waste disposal. The higher cost of a better grade of material may allow savings on the energy bill to process this material. Just as various locations have different production cost levels, so too do these locations permit different alternatives for substitution among the production elements. If both labor and capital costs are high at a location, it is obvious that the substitution of one high cost for another has no real advantage. Recent developments in manufacturing in industrial nations have seen massive substitution of capital for labor, leading to increased automation and robotics. The increasing use of computer technology in the workplace (computer-assisted manufacturing) has reinforced this trend.

Labor Cost.   For many kinds of manufacturing, labor is a major cost item. Manufacturing processes that require highly specialized and skilled labor must pay high wages. Any kind of processing involving individualistic decisions and skills, such as wine tasting, cannot easily be automated, and labor is then a significant cost item. Even if

the job does not require extensive training or skills, as is the case with sewing a wide variety of garments in apparel manufacturing, the cost of labor is typically very high. For this reason, industries that are labor-intensive but require unskilled workers always tend to locate in low-wage areas. Largely for this reason, the cotton textile industry moved out of the high-wage New England area in the 1920s and into the rural Piedmont area in the South. Now the southern textile mills are feeling the competitive pinch from foreign producers, where wage rates are extremely low vis-à-vis the United States. For the same reason, much of the clothing Americans wear is manufactured in overseas locations such as Hong Kong, Taiwan, South Korea, India, and China.

Labor Availability.   The cost of labor is not the only important factor in manufacturing location. The availability of labor is also critical, especially skilled labor. A particular manufacturer wishing to locate a plant within a given area, everything else being equal, will wish to minimize the labor costs. But labor must be available. One option, which is not an attractive alternative, is to locate in an area with a tight job market and, by paying higher wages, attract the necessary labor from other manufacturing plants where wages are lower. Not only is this option unattractive to the newly locating plant, but certainly the existing industry in the area will not welcome it. In fact, the chambers of commerce in many communities with rather low wage rates do not seek out or encourage the location of industries that pay high wages relative to the community rate. A more realistic option for a manufacturing plant is to locate in an area of surplus labor. Not only will there be ample labor, but it is also quite likely that the wage rate will be somewhat depressed, and people will, therefore, be willing to work for lower wages.

Labor productivity is another consideration vital to the locational choice. "Productivity" means the amount and quality of the product manufactured in a given period of time. If a labor

NAFTA

The North American Free Trade Agreement or NAFTA—a free trade accord involving the U.S., Canada, and Mexico—was enacted on January 1, 1994. The NAFTA continues to bring about the gradual elimination of tariffs and non-tariff trade barriers and facilitates cross-border movements of most industrial and agricultural goods and services produced in the tri-nation complex. Moreover, NAFTA will promote the free flow of goods and investment dollars across international borders and lead to intensified competition among producers operating within the free-trade zone. The NAFTA has served to create the world's largest free trading zone with a combined total Gross Domestic Product that exceeds $8 trillion dollars (87% of which is accounted for by the U.S.) and a market, although somewhat geographically dispersed, of over 370 million prospective consumers. The agreement makes North America increasingly competitive in the global economy and offers tremendous potential for the tri-nation complex to realize further export-led growth. U.S. industries stand to benefit greatly from the growth and vitalization of the Mexican economy. Roughly 70% of Mexico's imports currently come from suppliers in the United States. Not surprising, Mexico and Canada accounted for half of the U.S. export gain in 1994. The true export-related benefits of the NAFTA are still to be realized by the U.S. economy. As the Mexican economy matures, wages and income rise, the value of the peso stabilizes, and Mexico's demand for high-valued manufactured goods produced in the U.S. increases, it will bring about a likely reversal of the relatively small bilateral trade deficits observed in 1995 and 1996. Critics of the NAFTA argue that free trade between the U.S. and Mexico will ultimately translate into the loss of American jobs as industries move in search of cheap labor. While some labor-intensive industries and sectors are likely to experience employment losses, the majority of industries and sectors are likely to remain unaffected.

Downsizing trends of corporations and the use of other cost-cutting measures including relocation and decentralization of the production process—moving portions of the production process across national borders—have been observed prior to the NAFTA. The U.S. and Mexico had already established border production and free-trade zones long before the signing of the NAFTA, as foreign-owned-and-operated assembly plants have existed for some time along the U.S.-Mexican border. Multinational corporations have long been aware of Mexico's wage production cost advantage, not to mention the absence of strict environmental regulations. Mexican assembly plants—"maquiladora"—found throughout the border region produce goods almost exclusively for the U.S. market. Many U.S. firms have relocated to over-the-border locations to take advantage of a cheap and abundant labor force and the lack of import tariffs and restrictions on commodities produced there and brought back into the U.S.

Production in the maquiladoras is primarily driven by external forces (in particular by demand in the U.S.). Note, however, that the lack of domestic (Mexican-made) inputs in the maquilas and absence of a regional internalized supply network has severely limited the expansion of these production facilities. Opponents of the NAFTA, nonetheless, continue to argue that the elimination of trade barriers between the U.S. and Mexico will accelerate the movement of U.S. firms southward. They contend that this movement will result in a substantial loss of revenue and American jobs as cheap imported products allow companies based in Mexico to capture an increasing share of the U.S. market. These arguments are not compelling, however, given that Mexico is somewhat far removed, in terms of its location, from the major U.S. markets along the Eastern Seaboard. In many cases, the added transportation cost premium may negate the wage advantage. Moreover, the net benefits of firm relocation are not entirely clear from a productivity standpoint. U.S. labor offers a significant productivity advantage over a wide range of skill levels when comparison to labor in the underdeveloped world.

While the NAFTA may lead to job and revenue losses for industries vulnerable to the globalization process; especially small and rural producers and low-technology sectors. Regional variations in the impact of the NAFTA on various economic sectors will unavoidably translate into an uneven distribution of both costs and benefits over space. It is uncertain just how severe the losses will be in any particular region or sector as the North American production network adjusts to changes brought about by the agreement. Nonetheless, trade liberalization under the NAFTA is not likely to cause a mass exodus of high-value-added jobs from the U.S. to Mexico; although production shifts are expected in some low-skilled and/or labor-intensive industries. These shifts, however, will help raise wages of labor and increase purchasing power of consumers in the Mexican economy, creating new opportunities for U.S. companies to market goods and services. In short, industrialization and a higher standard of living in Mexico will ultimately increase the demand for U.S. products; creating further trade, economic growth, jobs, as well as increased investment possibilities in North America. The big winners here are the transportation, communication, and financial service sectors.

---

force is available at a low wage rate and the workers' productivity level is low, it may well be more economical to select a location that has higher productivity and higher wages. In other words, one saves little in wages that buy little in productivity.

Energy. Energy costs, though fluctuating unpredictably over the past few decades, are likely to continue to increase. As a result, they will become a greater consideration in the industrial location decision. Certain kinds of manufacturing are more energy-dependent than others, however. The aluminum industry is probably the best example of industry that has located near large quantities of relatively inexpensive electricity. The manufacturing process, through electrolysis, breaks down aluminum oxide into pure aluminum and carbon dioxide. Historically, the industry has undergone profound locational shifts in response to changes in the location of inexpensive electricity. Before the turn of the century, the first aluminum manufacturing plant located at Niagara Falls to utilize the site's hydroelectric power. Several years later, two additional plants located in the southern Appalachians, also near hydroelectric power sources. During World War II, aluminum suddenly was in short supply, and four plants were developed in the Pacific Northwest to utilize cheap hydroelectricity. More recently still, aluminum manufacturing has spread into the Ohio River valley, where the power source is coal-generated electricity. In addition, natural gas has served as a power source for plants recently locating on the Gulf coast.

Most industries are affected in some way in their energy needs. The degree to which energy costs and availability vary geographically shapes the locational sensitivity of manufacturers to energy. A detailed analysis of the role of energy in economic geography is taken up in Chapter 12.

Materials.   One major cost for many kinds of manufacturing is the purchase of materials. These are fewer and fewer *raw* materials, in the sense that they arrive at the plant directly from the farm or mine, but rather materials that have likely been processed in some way by previous manufacturing at a different location. As noted earlier, what one plant ships out as a finished product may be considered a material input at a second manufacturing plant. The greater a manufacturing region's industrial maturity, the greater the proportion of materials that have previously undergone manufacturing. It follows, then, that material costs will be especially significant in a region or country and at an advanced stage of economic development.

Having said this, let us nevertheless first examine the effect of a raw material on manufacturing location. Assume that a plant's location is fixed, but that there are many alternative sources of a particular raw material. Which source or sources will be used? One consideration will be the distance of the material site from the manufacturing plant, as discussed earlier. The transport cost, however, may be only a small part of the total cost of the material. One other kind of cost is the extractive cost of working the material deposit—say, iron ore. At deposits where one has to dig deeper or where, for whatever reason, the technology of extraction is more costly, the total charge for the materials will naturally be greater. It is easy to imagine a situation in which a manufacturing plant prefers a more distant site because of that site's lower cost. One other consideration is important: Not all deposits will be of equal quality, and, everything else being equal, the higher-quality deposits will be preferred. It is quite common for a manufacturing plant to have a pattern of raw-materials ties that

are not closely related to distance or transportation costs. This situation occurs when there is spatial variation in the cost of extracting the material and in the quality or grade of the material. A geographic pattern of raw-material ties illustrates the role of extractive costs and quality of deposit.

Let us now assume, alternatively, that the manufacturing plant's location is not specified, even though we have information on the location of each resource site and on the extractive cost associated with the deposit at each site. Where should the manufacturing plant locate? If material cost is the only relevant locational consideration (not a realistic likelihood), the plant location may quite easily be determined as adjacent to the lowest total-cost deposit. An extractive cost per unit of output may be established for each location. Second, the quality of the deposit may be translated into cost terms, for lower-quality deposits will normally cost more to refine or otherwise process or will involve a larger number of units to be shipped. The preferred location will be as close as possible to the site with the lowest combined extractive and quality costs. The problem becomes more difficult, but mathematically solvable, when the manufacturing plant requires more than one raw-material site to meet its processing needs.

The role of suppliers of materials for a manufacturing plant is important, especially for plants that are purchasing several different kinds of materials that have been previously processed. Many times, suppliers will develop near a manufacturing plant or, more commonly, an industrial concentration. At other times, manufacturing plants will locate because of the services of suppliers in a particular area. Suppliers who understand the material requirements of a manufacturing plant and who provide reliable, timely, and convenient services play a vital role. In fact, these service features may be more critical than the actual cost of materials because most manufacturing operations require a consistent flow of material inputs.

Other Factors. A long list of other factors influence the locational decisions of manufacturing plants. For certain plants, these other, or minor, factors may be the major reason for location. These factors include access and cost of capital, tax advantages, community development, local amenities, and personal considerations. A plant may locate for executive convenience (nearness to golf course or better schools) or because of proximity to corporate headquarters. Many manufacturing establishments locate in the hometown of the founder and remain there because of personal ties and friendships, even if more profitable locations are recognized.

Although it may surprise one who imagines that industrial locations are invariably scientifically selected on a strictly profit basis, empirical research has demonstrated that personal factors and local amenities influence the location decision of many manufacturers.

Agglomeration Economies

The term *agglomeration* implies a concentration or clustering of activities in one place. Economies mean savings. *Agglomeration economies*, then, are those savings that result from concentrating economic activities in one place or adjacent to one another. Hugh Nourse has identified four kinds of agglomeration economies that result in profitability to an industrial firm: transfer economies, internal economies of scale, external economies of scale, and urbanization economies.[1] Each of these concepts is important to understanding the location of manufacturing activity.

Transfer economies are the transportation savings that a plant gains by locating close to other plants. Manufacturing tends to locate in nodes on a transportation network. Typically, the larger the node, the greater its transportation advantages, as discussed earlier. Plants may locate near one another to benefit from successive stages of production. The same advantages that lead shopping centers to concentrate commercial activities to attract customers who save travel time and cost by going to one place rather than to many dispersed locations operate through transfer savings for manufacturing firms. When material sources and markets are dispersed for a manufacturing plant, a location at a strategic node on the transport network means a saving in transport costs.

Internal economies of scale are the savings a particular plant enjoys from increasing its scale of operation or size. Size may be measured in number of employees, amount of payroll, value added, or volume of output. As the size of the

The old Sloss steel mill in Birmingham, Alabama, was the first steel mill in the area. Since its closing in 1971, it has become a tourist attraction where elderly former steel workers guide tours and tell tales of the glory days gone by.

[1]Hugh O. Nourse, *Regional Economics* (New York: McGraw-Hill, 1968).

plant increases, the average production cost of the items manufactured normally decreases. Purchases may be made in larger quantities, labor and machines may be used more efficiently, and distribution in bulk may result in lower average per-unit costs. Clearly, if internal-scale economies were the only operative factor, all industries would be represented by a single plant of gigantic size supplying the entire market at such a low price per item that no other manufacturer could economically enter that market. At some point, of course, the average cost of production per unit may begin to rise as inefficiencies and diseconomies are encountered.

Not all types of manufacturing activities benefit equally from increasing the size of the operation. Take the examples of the automobile industry and a soft-drink bottler, the first of which is able to benefit enormously from scale increases and the second to derive only minimal cost savings. The average cost curve for the auto manufacturer drops slowly with increases in plant size and continues to drop until the size of plant is extremely large. At some point, at least in theory, the plant size will be optimal. In contrast, a soft-drink bottler, largely for market reasons as noted earlier in this chapter, cannot benefit nearly as much by increasing plant size. If the bottling operation is extremely small, scale economies may dictate that the size be increased. But the optimal size is quickly reached; further increases in scale bring no further savings. The result of such differential scale economies for various types of manufacturing is reflected in the spatial pattern of economic activity. Manufacturing that is able to utilize scale economies tends to have a small number of extremely large plants serving a wide market and drawing on distant resources. Plants in which scale economies are of little advantage are more numerous and more spread over the landscape.

A third agglomeration advantage is *external economies of scale* or *localization economies.* These cost reductions come about from a spatial concentration of plants in the same industry. The scale economies are external to a particular plant but internal to the specialized machinery replacement for its manufacturing operation. The individual plant may produce the machinery itself at a high average cost. If, however, several plants with the same specialized machinery needs were located close by, a separate manufacturing firm could produce the machinery at lower average costs and pass on these savings to plants in that industry. An example of manufacturing with external economies of scale to the plants but internal to the industry is carpet manufacturing, and industry that is highly concentrated in the small community of Dalton, Georgia. Once the industry got started, the external economies were so important that the industry grew almost entirely in one locale.[2]

Urbanization economies occur when the average cost of production units is lowered as many industries develop in one place, such as a large urban area. The economies of scale are external to manufacturing plants in many industries. Thus, several industries share the burden of certain costs, and this results in a reduction of average costs to all. A large urban area has a large, flexible labor pool; well-developed commercial and financial services; and public services, such as fire and police protection. These are examples of savings possible in urban areas. Moreover, savings will likely increase with the size of the population. Urbanization economies probably increase rapidly as one goes from 1000 to 10,000 to 100,000 people, and then increase more gradually as population size continues to increase. The actual savings will depend on the level of technology. It is also possible that population centers may grow so large that diseconomies set in.

In short, agents involved in production tend to agglomerate or cluster in space for two basic reasons: (1) certain locations on the economic land-

[2]John R. McGregor and Robert H. Maxey, "The Dalton, Georgia, Tufted Textile Concentration," *Southeastern Geographer* 14 (1974), pp. 133–144.

scape offer a comparative advantage that facilitates fulfillment of a producer's goal (e.g., clusters of firms at raw material sites, terminals, transhipment points, or locations with production cost advantages from, say, cheap and abundant labor); and (2) the agglomeration process itself is one that creates cost reductions by minimizing transport costs and maximizing access to suppliers (something that is particularly important among linked or interdependent firms).[3] As noted earlier, cost reduction may come about through transfer, scale, localization, or urbanization economies.

Environmental Factors

Classical locational concepts, as we will see later in this chapter, did not directly take into account environmental factors in manufacturing location. Although terrain in some cases was recognized as a factor, it was incorporated only as it influenced transportation costs. Over the last several years, however, environmental factors have been taken directly into account in the location decision either through the perception of the businessperson or through policy requirements at the federal, state, or local level. Environmental regulation clearly will have a major and continuing effect on the location of manufacturing.

A quarter-century ago, Pittsburgh's smokestack industries gave the city a negative image because of the dirty air and grime they produced. Now the air in Pittsburgh is among the cleanest of any U.S. city because of a major effort to reduce air pollution. Pittsburgh today is regarded as one of the more desirable metropolitan areas in which to reside. Although it has lost a large number of manufacturing jobs over the past couple of decades, especially in iron and steel mills, the metropolitan area is expanding in service employment, particularly in the producer services.

The 1969 National Environmental Policies Act requires that environmental impact statements be written before major projects, such as large manufacturing plants, can be constructed; that adverse environmental effects be identified; and that alternatives to the proposed action be specified. The principal concerns are with air, water, noise, solid wastes, and land use. Although the regulations are relatively recent and continue to evolve, it is clear that their impact is going to be felt significantly in the location of manufacturing activity in the United States. Howard Stafford has suggested four types of impact of environmental regulations on manufacturing: same site versus new site, regional development, changes in the location decision process, and increased awareness of space.[4]

Under most circumstances manufacturing plants have tended to expand production at the same site rather than to seek out a completely new location because on-site expansion normally involves less risk and uncertainty. The new environmental regulations should reinforce this tendency because of economies of scale to waste disposal and because expansion only incrementally changes the character of the existing location, whether through changes in land use or in air pollution. Moreover, the location of a new facility would probably result in longer delays than expansion on-site. In a small number of instances, however, expansion may be virtually ruled out. For example, in certain regions of the United States with already serious air-quality problems, any significant deterioration in air quality would preclude expansion. Overall, expansion in place will probably accelerate for most industries in contrast to relocation.

The regional impact of environmental controls is difficult to assess, but the greatest restrictions to growth will likely be felt either in areas that are already highly developed or in places that

---

[3]Gordon F. Mulligan, "Agglomeration and Central Place Theory: A Review of the Literature," *International Regional Science Review* 9 (1984), pp. 1–42.

[4]Howard A. Stafford, "Environmental Regulations and the Location of the U.S. Manufacturing Speculations," *Geoforum* 8 (1977), pp. 243–248.

View of an industrial complex with adjacent rail lines: An oil refinery, Gallup, New Mexico.

now have limited development. According to Stafford, areas that are currently experiencing rapid growth are likely to remain as industrial "targets." Thus, states in the northeastern quarter of the United States, where industrial growth has already slowed or declined, are likely to exclude industries that have negative environmental impact. States with relatively little industrial development, as in parts of the West (Colorado or Oregon), may wish to protect their relatively unspoiled environment by excluding "dirty" industrial growth. States of the Southeast and South-Central United States will probably be sought out by many manufacturers, reinforcing existing shifts in U.S. industrial location.

Environmental factors are now rather generally recognized as important in the location decision process. In questionnaires sent to manufacturers as late as the middle 1960s, environmental reasons for location were not recognized as very significant. At present, by contrast, manufacturers place various environmental considerations very high on the list of most important factors. Such items as waste disposal, water quality controls, and air pollution standards are now basic influences on location decision. Because many large-scale developments are being challenged through the courts, "the developer is faced with considerable delay and cost as he researches and presents his case, listens to counter-

arguments, and awaits the judgment. Win or lose, the manufacturer must contend with greater uncertainty, increased site selection costs, and a longer time frame."[5]

A final consequence of the greater environmental concern is the enhanced awareness of spatial factors. Although industrial location decisions obviously have always been based on spatial considerations, the focus is now more explicit for an increasing number of manufacturers. Firms are literally being forced to undertake systematic evaluation of alternative sites for environmental purposes, and such evaluations force all other relevant factors to be incorporated into the location decision. This increased awareness of space should ideally result in a better pattern of location in the long run for American manufacturing.

Location Search and Site Evaluation

Many site-specific location factors are quantifiable; others are not. The quantifiability of a location factor depends on the existence of a physical or an analytical process that permits usable numbers to be generated in the site evaluation process. Table 10.1 lists a number of location factors that are typically quantified by location analysts. Quantified factors are commonly used in *cost-benefit assessment* (CBA), a technique commonly employed to test whether or not a site location decision will generate benefits to the corporation or firm which outweigh the costs. The CBA is also useful in determining the best location when two or more prospective sites are being evaluated.

The table lists some quantifiable site-specific location factors. Once a potential site or group of sites are identified, the costs and benefits associated with the various factors listed in the table may be calculated or projected. Note, however, that the evaluation of a single production site or a comparative assessment of two or

[5]Ibid., p. 246.

Table 10.1 Site-Specific Quantifiable
Location Factors

Site and preparation costs (including land)
Construction and/or renovation cost
Cost of equipment and infrastructure
Startup and training costs
Labor and fringe benefit costs
Working capital requirements (e.g., inventories)
Freight and transshipment expenses
Property and business taxes
Workman's compensation premiums
Unemployment compensation premiums
Facility relocation expenses
Facility expansion or downsizing expenses
Product sales and revenue forecast in relation to
    product cycle, spatial competition, market
    characteristics and conditions, etc.

Source: Wardrep (1985, p. 10), with modifications.

more potential sites is an afterthought to the location search process. Before a location search is
initiated, a checklist of all factors that may have
direct bearing on the location decision must be
compiled and examined. Table 10.2 offers a useful summary of the more important factors that
influence the initial location search prior to site
selection. Problems in the location search process may arise from the fact that many of the
major factors in the location search process are
nonquantifiable or only partially quantifiable.
While it is easy to identify some of the prominent
factors that may influence a location search, and
ultimately site selection, the final determination
of the feasibility of a proposed site must be examined in terms of (1) how the proposed site fits
into the existing or restructuring corporate production network; (2) its competitive position in
the industry as defined by its potential to vie for,
expand, or increase market share or compete
with spatial rivals; (3) its immediate and nonim-
mediate impact on the area in which it locates;
and (4) the anticipated response or actions taken
by competitors or other affected parties within
the site's sphere of influence.

One must also differentiate between whether
the decision to locate is part of a competitive

or an acquisition strategy. In reference to geographic area, Watts has noted that the firm has
an almost limitless number of potential locations
in which to consider a branch plant that does not
entail the acquisition of an existing production
facility. Yet, the choice-set of locations is highly
constrained if the location decision is limited to
the acquisition of a particular type of facility or
the buyout of a competitor at a previously owned
site that is thought to best suit the needs of the
firm (while allowing it to capture a greater share
of the regional market in the same industry).[6]

*The characteristics of the firms may be more
important than the features of the areas in
which their plants are located and the "location" of acquired firms is very much circum-
scribed by the location of potential acquisition
candidates. . . . Proximity to head office and access to markets and/or supplies appear to be
"location factors" which can influence the acquisition decision. (Watts, 1987, pp. 173–174)*

Location decisions may also be influenced by
how the locating agents view the company's
growth potential, as part of its strategies to compete and expand market share. This may involve
a good deal of speculation on the health and vi-
tality of the industry itself and its geographic
markets. As Bruce Wardrep (1985) notes:

*the economics of a particular industry, or the
extent and degree of competition in a given industry, or the problems associated with supply
and distribution costs, or a number of other influences (labor costs, labor unionization, proximity to markets and competitors, proximity to
suppliers and resources, proximity to other
company facilities, quality of life considerations) can become a controlling influence on
the location search process. In some cases the
location search focus is particular to the company and how it views its competitive position*

[6]H. D. Watts, *Industrial Geography* (New York: Wiley, 1987),
pp. 168–177.

Table 10.2 Major Factors in Location Searches

Access to Markets/Distribution Centers
***Ability to compete and penetrate local and
  regional markets
  **Cost of serving local and regional markets
   *Demographics
   *Relative location to local and regional markets
***Trends in sales by geographic area

Access to Supplies/Resources/Personnel/Materials
  **Agglomeration, urbanization, and network
    economies
  **Cost of transporting supplies (acquisition costs)
  **Movement of materials and people between
    facilities
***Trends in supplier by area

Community/Government Aspects
  Ambiance and quality of life
  **Business climate
   *Cost of living
  Cooperation with established local industry
  Community pride (appearance, activity, citizen
    views)
   *Housing availability and price
  Political stability of locality and region
  **Quality of schools, cultural and recreation
    programs and facilities
  **Quality of colleges and graduate programs

Competitive Considerations
   *Existing trade barriers and laws
  Expectations regarding reactions of competitors
    to new site
  **Internalized economies of scale in relation to the
    size or scale of the operation
  **Localization economies
   *Type and location of existing competitors
  Type and location of future competitors

Environmental Considerations
  ††Existing laws, rules of conduct, and government
    regulations pertaining to the environment
  **Cost of compliance (out-of-pocket expenses for
    pollution control equipment, production process
    changes, etc.)
  Imposition of cost associated with future
    regulations

Labor
  Ability to attract and retain skilled labor
    component
***Changing labor market conditions
  **Extent and militancy of labor unions in area
  **Labor migration trends
  **Labor productivity and productivity trends
  **Labor availability/supply
   *Prevailing wage rates
  **Skill levels available

Site Characteristics
   *Area of site and layout of physical structure(s)
   *Construction/remodeling costs and insurance
    premiums
  **Current condition
***Future resale value of site and physical
    structure(s)
   *Market price of site and structure(s)

Strategic Relevance of the Proposed Site
  †Interaction with the remainder of the
    corporation
  †Extent of engineering and management
    assistance from corporate headquarters
  †Role and status of the production facility (e.g.,
    main, satellite, or branch plant)
  †Supplied by or supplier to other company
    plants?

Taxes and Financing
  ††Property and other local taxes
  ††State income tax
  †††Tax breaks, incentives, or concessions

Transportation Service
  **Transfer economies
  ††Trucking, rail, and air freight service (cost
    structures, rates, routings, shipping and
    packaging requirements, insurance, etc.)

Utilities and Services
  **Availability, quality and price of water, sewage,
    electric, and natural gas services
  **Quality of roads, police and fire protection,
    medical facilities, and other services

*Quantifiable factor.
**Partially quantifiable factor.
***Forecast.
†Determined by firm.
††Known.
†††Negotiable.

Source: Wardrep (1985, p. 10) with modifications.

and its particular growth characteristics. (pp. 10–11)

Michael Webber (19, pp. 36–37) sees essentially three types of location decisions, each of which involves an entirely different set of considerations or locational criteria depending on the production requirements, strategies, or needs of the firm.

> *The first is the decision to build or buy a new establishment . . . (involving) starting in business or relocating . . . or building additional capacity. Location theory has traditionally concentrated on this type of decision. Second, the firm can reorganize production, by altering the products produced at its various establishments or by closing some factories and concentrating production at others (rearranging or restructuring production capacity). The third decision is the decision to close down an establishment—to reduce capacity.*

In essence, the location or relocation of a production facility or a facility's production capacity may be represented as part of a corporation's investment or disinvestment strategy. The location decisions of individual firms should not necessarily be viewed as separate from the more complex decision-making processes of the entire firm network or corporation itself, especially when that corporation is composed of multiple production units or facilities of various functions and degrees of interdependence.

Note that each firm or facility represents a collection of functions or activities to design, process, fabricate, market, deliver, support, and service its products, as part of a process that adds value to, or embodies value within, that product—the so-called **value chain**.[7] A firm's value chain may be broken down into two major sets of activities: **primary activities** and **support activities**. As discussed by Dicken and Lloyd (1990, p. 271), the five primary activities include:

---

[7]Michael Porter, *Competitive Advantage* (New York: Free Press, 1985).

---

1. *Inbound logistics*—the acquisition, handling, transport, warehousing and storing of materials/production inputs, as well as inventory control.
2. *Operations*—activities associated with the transformation of production inputs and the processing assembly, testing, and packaging of the product.
3. *Outbound logistics*—the collection, storage, and distribution of production output to market.
4. *Marketing and sales*—activities related to the diffusion of information or exposure of the product to consumers and facilitation of ordering and purchasing of products as accomplished by advertising and sales personnel.
5. *Service*—after-sale product maintenance and value retention activities.

Support activities, by contrast, include such things as

1. *Firm infrastructure*—management, financial, and legal activities.
2. *Human resource management*—activities such as recruiting, training, upskilling, and labor relations.
3. *Technological development*—research, product development, and design activities.
4. *Procurement*—the purchasing of production inputs.

Decision-making agents that plan the location of a firm must, therefore, consider how that location decision may affect any or all of these activities in the value chain at both the intra-and interfirm level: at the new facility and the already existing ones. Considerations must be made in reference to how *vertically integrated* the new firm is expected to be (i.e., how many of the five primary activities will be carried out at that facility) and how existing facilities are expected to adjust (if at all) to the addition or changes. Location decisions with respect to a given production unit could involve firms that cover the entire spectrum of activities, from firms that have only one primary activity (i.e., highly specialized units) to firms that carry out all five primary activities (i.e., highly diversified and vertically integrated production units).

As part of the corporate strategy to gain a competitive edge in the midst of changing industry structures, many location decisions must be viewed as part of an interdependent process, as firms have become sensitive to the location of other firms that provide both primary and support activities (on a contracting-out basis). The recent emergence of **manufacturing networks** in the United States, for example, and the development of sophisticated production alliances have redefined the science/art of facility location. This is particularly true for small and highly specialized businesses, which continually face new challenges and intensified competition from the larger, more efficient, and more vertically integrated corporations in the global marketplace.

According to a recent report published by the Northwest Policy Center, Graduate School of Public Affairs, University of Washington (p. i) a manufacturing network may be defined as

a group of firms that collaborate to achieve together what each cannot do alone. . . . Network cooperation may take many forms, from the exchange of strategic information to joint ventures for product development and commercialization. Initial cooperative activity usually covers such areas as employer job training, owner training, coordinated purchasing (such as employee insurance), etc. As manufacturer networks become more experienced and sophisticated, the complexity of issues tackled by the network brokers also expands. Advanced network services might include strategic planning, joint production, cooperative marketing and more detailed interaction. . . . As an economic development mechanism, networks provide numerous advantages, including: increased regional diversification, targeted approach to services and increased job creation and retention.

Manufacturing networks are viewed as a logical response to changes in the production spheres of the global economy, as firms respond with a rigid adherence to vertical integration of their manufacturing operations. Increasing size has, in many cases, meant increased inflexibility and unmanageable production schemes.

Instead, competitive advantage in today's business environment rests with firms which are flexible, quality driven, and focused on customer needs. Manufacturing networks provide a medium in which a number of firms can combine their efforts to gain that competitive advantage. (p. 1)

Location decision makers must also consider the benefits and enhanced performance aspects of the firm within a production network, something we will call **network economies** (the savings that accrue to a firm as part of a production network). The location search and site-selection processes must assess how network formation or network assistance could help the firm or corporation achieve its market and financial goals. Network integration could improve quality, enhance production capacity and productivity, and reduce costs, as well as help increase customer satisfaction and production flexibility. Cooperation among participating firms that share a common interest and the strengthening of interrelationships and linkages between those firms are part of an emerging manufacturing phenomenon known as "flexible production".

THEORIES OF PLANT LOCATION

We have been considering the role of selected individual factors in the location of manufacturing plants. When plant locations are selected, however, the decision is based on the interplay of a set of factors taken together. In order to understand manufacturing geography better, we must examine the general principles or theories of plant location because these locational principles will apply, in one form or another, to a large number of specific empirical case studies. Most location theories begin with certain simplifying assumptions as a way of controlling variables. In geographic research, such control can be achieved only by making assumptions that certain conditions are the same and then noting the effects of other variables.

Median Location Principle

To understand the median location principle, we must make the outrageous assumption that no elements of production cost will vary among alternative locations. The only cost that will be allowed to vary is the delivery cost. The plant absorbs this cost, and thus the plant wishes to select a location that minimizes its delivery cost. That location is also logically the maximum profit location. Lowest delivery cost, then, is the variable to be examined.

Consider the distribution of customer locations in Figure 10.3. The assumption is that consumers are located along a line, such as a highway or a river. There are 12 distance units and 7 consumer locations (A, B, C, D, E, F, and G). Which location will minimize the sum of the distances or delivery price to consumers? Table 10.3 summarizes the calculations, showing that a location at D, the median point, will minimize delivery costs.

A further example involves one very large urban area surrounded by several much smaller centers. Given this limited area, the median location would be within the large urban area. Thus, because the median location of consumers tends to be in large cities, such cities are likely to grow bigger by attracting new industry. Median location is a basic principle in manufacturing lo-

Table 10.3 Minimum Distance to Consumers

Consumers	Distance from D	Distance from E
A	4	5
B	3	4
C	2	3
D	0	1
E	1	0
F	6	5
G	7	6
	$\Sigma D_d = 23$	$\Sigma D_e = 24$

cation and favors places at the center of a consumer market.

Linear Market Competition

Let us next assume there are two manufacturers, Atlas and Biscuit, producing at exactly the same costs for a linear market (uniform demand for the product along the line). Again, these are outlandish assumptions, and yet all of these have a very good point. The manufacturers pay the delivery cost, and the consumer therefore buys at the lowest price. Where should the manufacturers locate? Let us first suppose, as in Figure 10.4a, that Atlas and Biscuit are located so as to divide the linear market equally. Everything is fine. Atlas, however, decides to compete with Biscuit to acquire more than half the market. If Atlas cannot reduce its production costs, as already assumed, then Atlas can only change its location. The plant will do so advantageously by moving just next to Biscuit and obtaining all of Biscuit's market except the portions to the right,

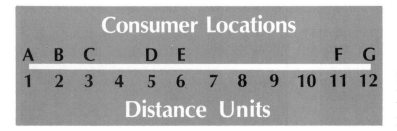

Figure 10.3 A linear market, with customer locations at *A* through *G*. Where are the mean and median locations?

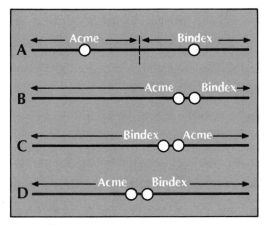

Figure 10.4 Competition in a linear market between two producers who are free to move locations at will (the ice cream vendor problem).

as shown in Figure 10.4b. (We are, of course, assuming no relocation costs.) Obviously, Biscuit will retaliate in this free-competition example by locating immediately to the left of Atlas, as in Figure 10.4c. Now Biscuit has the lion's share of the market. It should be clear that with this free competition, the two firms will hop over one another until a final competitive solution is reached, as in Figure 10.4d—the two firms clustered at the center of the equally divided market. Such a competitive solution leads to a higher average delivered price compared to the initial situation of equal spacing (Figure 10.4a). In this very simple, hypothetical example, the first set of locations results in a better welfare or societal solution, whereas the last gives a solution based purely on market forces. These solutions might be regarded as planned locations in the case of the first example and a free market or unplanned outcome in the last example.

Weber's Theory of Location

In order to explain the underlying influences on location as applied to all industries, Alfred Weber, a German location theorist, put forth a general theory of industrial location in his 1909 book, translated into English in 1929 as *Theory*

of the Location of Industries.[8] We will look in some detail into Weber's classic contribution, for the basic principles he delineated continue to hold, to one degree or another, at the present time. Weber's theory is general in that he developed it to apply to any political, cultural, or economic system. His approach was also based on a series of formal assumptions that permitted simplification of the analysis in order to single out certain location factors for examination when other factors were held constant. His overall objective was to determine the minimum-cost location for a manufacturing plant. The three major factors of location treated by Weber were transport cost, labor cost, and agglomeration.

Assumption and Definitions. Weber made five basic, formal assumptions.

1. The model is operative in a single country with a uniform topography, climate, technology, and economic system. This assumption is known as the ***uniform*** or ***isotropic plain*** assumption.

2. One finished product at a time is considered, and the product is shipped to a single market location. This assumption is clearly at variance with multiple-product plants, but it must be remembered that Weber wished to understand the general reasons for manufacturing location rather than to explain actual locations.

3. The raw materials are fixed at certain locations, which are known sites, and the point of consumption (market) is also fixed and known.

4. Labor is fixed geographically (lacks mobility) but is available in unlimited quantities at any production site selected.

5. Transport costs are a direct function of weight of the item and the distance shipped.

---

[8]Alfred Weber, *Theory of the Location of Industries* (Chicago: University of Chicago Press, 1929).

Several of the terms Weber introduced need to be defined. *Ubiquities* are materials available everywhere throughout the uniform plain at the same cost; examples might be sand and gravel in the glaciated Midwest, water in the South, or nitrogen from the atmosphere at any location. In contrast to ubiquities are *localized materials*, available only at specific locations; examples would include coal deposits, petroleum fields, and bauxite sites. Weber also made a distinction between *pure materials* and *weight-losing materials*. Pure materials are localized materials that enter to the full extent of their weight into the finished product. They lose no weight in processing. A pure material might include petroleum, for which there is almost no weight loss in the refining process. In contrast, weight-losing materials are localized commodities that impart only a portion or none of their weight into the finished product. An example would be fuel consumed in manufacturing or a material with a large waste-product component.

Transport Costs. Following Weber, we will consider the cost of transportation under two highly simplified conditions. The first examines transport cost with a single market and one source of material supply. The second situation deals with two supply sources and involves Weber's classic *locational triangle* (Figure 10.5).

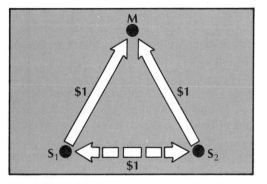

Figure 10.5 Weber's locational triangle, with one market and two sources of material supplies.

1. One Market and One Source

• If the material is ubiquitous (actually, many potential sources), then the processing will take place at the market. This location is obvious because it would make no sense to ship an ubiquitous material to a processing point other than the market.

• If the material is pure, processing may occur at the market, the material site, or any place in between. An intermediate location would entail an unnecessary additional handling cost—a cost not recognized by Weber.

• If the material is weight-losing, the processing will locate at the material source to avoid transporting waste material.

2. One Market and Two Sources

• In the first example of the locational triangle, S_1 and S_2 are the two material sources and M is the market location (Figure 10.5). Because the distances (and consequently the costs) between these three points are identical, we may assign each of the three distances a cost of, say, $1. Where will processing occur? The answer is, at the market, for the two needed materials can be shipped there at a total unit cost of $2. If processing were to locate at S_1, for instance, there would be the cost of shipping one unit from S_2 to S_1 ($1), the cost of shipping that same unit, now processed, on to the market ($1), and the cost of shipping one unit of the material from S_1, also now processed, to the market ($1). Thus, the total transport cost, if processing were to locate at S_1 or S_2, is $3 versus $2 per unit at the market.

• The situation is different and somewhat more complex when two weight-losing materials are brought together in processing. Let us assume for simplicity that there is a 50 percent weight loss for each of the two materials. Where, according to Weber, will manufacturing locate? Let the cost of transporting one unit of the weight-losing material be $2 (Figure 10.6). If a

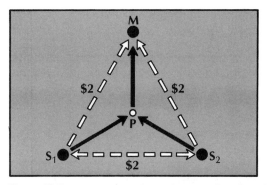

Figure 10.6 Illustrating Weber's intermediate location emphasis. The least cost production location is at *P*.

market location is selected, one would have to ship one unit of material from both S_1 and S_2 at total cost of $4. If S_1 were selected for processing, the cost of obtaining the material from S_2 would be $2. No transport cost would be charged to get the material from S_1 and the cost to transport the product to market with the 50 percent weight loss would be $2. The market, S_1 or S_2 would have the same total transport cost.

• Weber, however, was concerned with selecting the least-cost or optimum location. A second look at Figure 10.6 suggests that an intermediate location at *P* would be optimum, rather than at *M*, S_1 or S_2, where the transport cost at *P* would be less than $4. Furthermore, if one material had a greater weight-loss ratio than the other, the intermediate location for processing would be "pulled" toward the site of the greatest weight loss. Do you understand why?

Certain generalizations emerge from Weber's analysis. First, manufacturing that utilizes pure materials will never tie the processing location to the material site, and the location decision is normally made on the basis of other factors. Second, industries utilizing high weight-loss materials will tend to be pulled toward the material source as opposed to the market. The third generalization,

that many industries will select an intermediate location between market and material, is subject to considerable criticism and is referred to as Weber's intermediate-location bias. Weber's model is biased in favor of intermediate locations because he does not take into account terminal (extra handling) costs or the tapering effect of freight rates.

Labor Costs.   Weber viewed the geographic variation in the cost of labor as a "distortion" of the basic transport pattern. An area handicapped by high transport cost might nevertheless be attractive to industry because of inexpensive labor. According to Weber's argument, an industry would select the location that has the least cost when transport and labor are considered together. In other words, a tradeoff may exist between transport and labor costs, and the firm chooses the location with the least combined cost.

To determine this location, Weber introduced two concepts. One is the *isotim*, a line of equal transport cost for any material or product. An example of isotims is shown in Figure 10.7, in which the isotims are given in $1 intervals. The cost of shipping the finished product is shown by the shaded isotims. If processing was located at the material supply site, there would be a $4 transport charge to send the finished product to the market. The isotims for the material are shown by the white lines. In this example, the cost of transporting the material to the market is only $2, with the market being the least-cost location. The cost of moving the material is thus half that of shipping the finished product. If we wished to know the total transport cost at location X, we would simply add the two isotims: $2 to ship the product to market and $1 to obtain the material from the source. The cost at *X*, then, would be $3.

The second concept Weber introduced in this connection is the *isodapane*, which is a line of total transport costs. The isodapane is found by

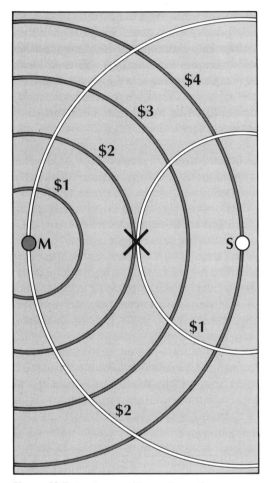

Figure 10.7 Isotims, or lines of equal transport cost, show the market (*M*) is the optimum location for production.

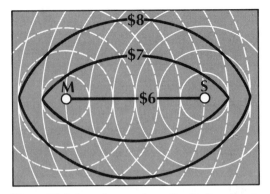

Figure 10.8 Superimposed on the isotims are isodapanes (heavy lines), lines of equal *total* transport cost.

summing the isotims at a location. Once the isodapanes are determined and we can identify the point of least total transport cost, then variation in labor costs can be considered in combination with the isodapanes. The reason for using isodapanes is systematically to introduce the labor component into Weber's locational theory.

Figure 10.8 depicts a situation with one market and one material source. The isotims have the same interval for both the product and the material, indicating equal transport cost. The least-

cost total transport cost is $6, and, as noted earlier, one can locate (with a pure material) at the source, the market, or any place between at the same $6 cost. The $6 isodapane is drawn in the bold line. The $7 and $8 isodapanes are also shown. Thus, if the labor costs at some point on the $7 isodapane were more than $1 a unit less than the labor costs along the $6 isodapane, it would make sense to locate there and substitute a $1 increase in transport costs for a more than $1 savings in labor. Isodapanes may be used not only to incorporate the cost of labor in Weber's theory but also to evaluate other spatially variable costs, such as taxes.

Agglomeration.   In addition to transport costs and such spatially variable costs as labor, Weber recognized that agglomeration may operate as a distinct location factor. Weber viewed agglomeration as the dollar savings per unit that would accrue to a plant from locating within a cluster of other plants. Specifically, Weber saw agglomeration not as producing internal-scale economies, but rather external economies (including urbanization economies). Figure 10.9 illustrates the cost of three manufacturing plants, A, B, and C, which have each independently located at their least-cost point. Around each plant is drawn a ***critical isodapane***, a line showing where the savings from agglomeration would exactly

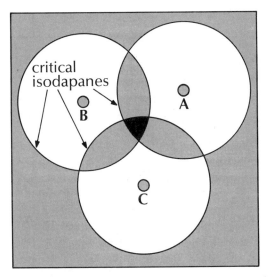

Figure 10.9 Where the critical isodapanes overlap, firms *A, B*, and *C* can take advantage of agglomeration economies.

offset the added transport cost for each firm. In other words, if each of these three firms could locate together, the agglomeration advantages would be just matched along these lines by the higher transport costs. Thus, all firms would benefit from agglomeration savings if they were to locate within the shaded triangle.

Critique of Weber.   Weber's purpose was to provide a general theory of industrial location, and in this regard his contribution has proved most valuable over the years. His work, however, has a number of shortcomings that limit its application in explaining fully actual manufacturing location. First, Weber did not effectively and realistically take into account geographic variation in market demand, a locational factor of paramount influence. Second, his treatment of transport, as already noted, did not recognize that these costs are not proportional to distance and weight and that intermediate locations necessitate added terminal charges. Moreover, transport is seldom regarded empirically as the single most important locational determinant. As in-

novations and improvements in transportation and communication technologies help to reduce the cost of shipping commodities, transporting people, and transferring information, transportation costs are becoming less and less of a localizing agent through time. Third, labor is normally quite mobile through migration and is not always available in unlimited quantity at any location. Fourth, a great many manufacturing plants obtain a large number of material inputs and produce a wide range of products for many diverse markets; Weber's theory does not easily apply to such circumstances. Finally, Weber's treatment of agglomeration was not very satisfactory, and he probably underestimated its effect.

Lösch's Economics of Location

Whereas Weber viewed industrial location largely as a result of geographic differences in the cost of producing and delivering a product, other location theorists have focused on spatial variation in sales potential. August Lösch, writing in 1939, recognized the least-cost versus maximum-sales (gross receipts) approaches to location theory. Lösch went on, in what is one of the most original works of location theory, to develop a theory based on maximum profit. He noted that "in a free economy, the correct location of the individual enterprise lies where the net profit is greatest."[9] Net profit is the difference between sales receipts and minimum costs, and the entrepreneur's solution is to find the location where these differences are the greatest. Having realized theoretically what is meant by the optimum location, Lösch wrote that it is empirically impossible to examine all points in an area to determine cost and demand and hence "the place of greatest money profit." Lösch, despite his criticism of Weber's a one-sided least-cost approach, was guilty of largely ignoring cost

[9]August Lösch, *Economics of Location* (New Haven, Conn.: Yale University Press, 1954), p. 27.

and overemphasizing demand or sales factors in a profit-maximization treatment of location theory.

Isard's Space Economy

Another major contribution to location theory was the publication of *Location and the Space Economy* by Walter Isard in 1956.[10] Isard attempted to develop a general theory of location (including industrial location) by integrating the works of von Thünen, Weber, and Lösch. Isard linked location theory to the general theory of economics through the substitution principle. In economic theory, capital can be substituted for labor, for example. Similarly, the selection of a manufacturing site from among alternative locations can be viewed as substituting expenditures among the various production factors such that the best site is chosen.

Figure 10.10 provides one simple illustration of Isard's substitution principle. In Figure 10.10*a* we have the Weberian situation of one market, C, and two material sources, M_1 and M_2. The line T to S represents a set of possible locations arbitrarily chosen at three miles from the consumption point, C. In Figure 10.10*b*, the distance from M_1 is plotted against the distance from M_2 with respect to the line T-S, referred to as the transformation line. At location T, distance from M_1 is only two miles, but seven miles from M_2. Conversely, at location S the distances are approximately four miles from M_1 and five miles from M_2. As one moves along this transformation line, distances are increasing with respect to one material site as they are decreasing for the other. If these distances are regarded as transport inputs or costs, the transport costs for one source are being substituted for the cost of the second material source.

In order to determine the optimum location along the line T to S, equal outlay lines are plot-

[10]Walter Isard, *Location and the Space Economy* (New York: Wiley, 1956).

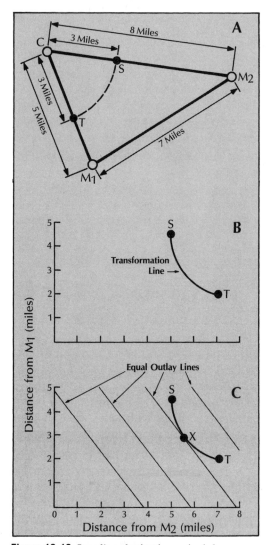

Figure 10.10 Isard's substitution principle. *Source:* Isard, see footnote 10.

ted on Figure 10.10*c*. These lines depict the costs of transporting materials from the two sources. Given the objective of determining the optimum location, the place selected will lie at the point, X, which is the lowest-cost point on the line T to S for that equal-outlay line. Therefore, based on the simple example of substituting among locations at a three-mile distance from the consumption point, the optimum location will be at X with respect to transport costs from M_1 and M_2. The results of this analysis by Isard follow Weber, except for the conceptual emphasis on substitution.

Smith's Spatial Margins

In a more recent attempt to synthesize various elements of industrial location theory, David Smith suggested a spatial margins approach.[11] His conceptual design is quite straightforward and is based on the statements of other location theorists. Recognizing the complexity of the industrial location decision, Smith began by simplifying the real-world conditions. He assumed a profit motive. He observed that processing costs vary in space as do revenues. The most profitable location will be where total revenue exceeds total cost by the greatest amount as Figure 10.11 illustrates. In Figure 10.11a, total revenue (TR) is constant over space, as shown by the horizontal line, whereas the total cost line (TC), termed the space–cost curve, increases away from point O. At point M_a and M_b, total cost matches total revenue, and beyond that distance profits are not possible. Thus, M_a and M_b represent the spatial margins to profitability, beyond which one could not produce at a profit. Point O is the optimum location; it is here that profits are greatest. Figure 10.11b shows a situation in which total costs are geographically constant, but total revenue is spatially variable. Again, point O achieves maximum profit, and M_a and M_b represent the spatial limits beyond which profit is not possible. Finally, Figure 10.11c shows spatial variation in both total cost and total revenue. Thus, total cost and total revenue may take on any combination of geographical expression. Theoretically, a point of maximum profit may be identified, as well as spatial margins to profitability.

Figure 10.11a represents Weber's approach to location theory, where cost varies but revenues are ignored or assumed to be everywhere equal. Figure 10.11b represents Lösch's assumption of

[11]David Smith, *Industrial Location* (New York: Wiley, 1981).

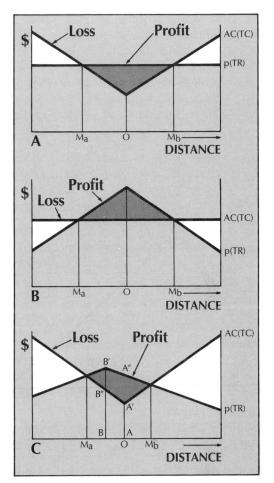

Figure 10.11 Smith's spatial margins to profitability, here illustrated in different spatial cost-revenue situations.
Source: Smith.

variable revenue over space but constant cost. In both Figures 10.11a and 10.11b, Weber, Lösch, and Smith would each identify point O as the optimum location—despite approaching the problem from different points of view.

Smith noted that a firm is free to locate anywhere within these spatial margins. For example, a firm may take noneconomic factors into account in locating away from the optimal profit site but at a location that may otherwise result in greater entrepreneur satisfaction. Furthermore, it is not empirically possible, as Lösch realized, to obtain sufficient data to map all these spatial variations. In reality, the optimal location may not be known, but any location within the spatial margins—though suboptimal—will produce a profit. Smith's model allows the incorporation of suboptimal behavior into industrial location theory and, therefore, is more in step with the increasingly recognized noneconomic factors of importance in industrial location theory.

Note also that decisions to locate a firm on the basis of profit-maximization principles have come under criticism. Michael Webber points out that decision-making agents do not usually possess enough information to be able to choose an optimal/profit-maximizing location. In addition, corporate location decisions may involve decision-making agents that have no personal stake in corporate profits (pp. 37–40).

Webber's Uncertainty Effect

Michael Webber's *Impact of Uncertainty on Location* (1972)[12] and *Industrial Location* (1984) provide some useful discussions of location theory under limited or imperfect information (i.e., uncertainty). Webber viewed uncertainty as a kind of cost that all firms share to one degree or another. Whereas classical location theory assumed perfect knowledge of alternatives and complete information, the theory of location under uncertainty brings us a stride closer to reality because actual firms simply have to operate with educated guesses about alternative and future conditions. Uncertainty affects industrial location through distance costs, external economies, and scale economies.

The greater the uncertainty, the greater the reduction in plant size as corporations are unwilling to invest large amounts of capital in an operation for which the likelihood of a successful outcome is in considerable doubt. Only a "sure

[12]Michael Webber, *Impact of Uncertainty on Location* (Cambridge, Mass.: M.I.T. Press, 1972).

bet" will lead to huge investments; otherwise, a smaller-scale project may be selected, which, if unsuccessful, will not result in massive losses. Uncertainty, which varies among industries, placing limitations on plant size, prevents manufacturing plants from operating at their technical optimum size and efficiency. Webber points out that *"The problem of uncertainty is particularly acute for new location decisions. The impact of uncertainty depends on the amount of capital committed by the decision and the ease with which the decision can be revoked"* (p. 38).

Uncertainty also varies over the spatial economic system, tending to increase with greater separation from the market. Price variability rises with distance from the market, resulting in more conservative production decisions and lower returns. Increased distance from the supplier, as well as from markets, leads to increased stock inventory as a result of uncertainty, for uncertainty in material flow can be compensated by storage.

Uncertainty makes external economies more important than would be the case under an economic system with perfect knowledge. New firms have more uncertainty than older firms, are therefore smaller, and must then seek to locate in or near large cities to obtain necessary external services. Proximity to services reduces uncertainty, and external economies are related to the cost of distance. The societal impact is that firms tend to locate nearer to one another than would otherwise be the case, with a high degree of industrial concentration in the large urban areas.

According to Webber (p. 39), firms may be encouraged to seek the profit-maximizing location, yet with imperfect information and, hence, uncertainty "the expected outcome of a location decision must be distinguished from the actual outcome." In other words, a clear distinction must be made between *ex ante* and *ex post* evaluations. Given that information is costly to acquire and process, Webber argues that maximum profit locations are virtually unobtainable and that location decisions are usually carried out with an underlying objective to obtain a satisfactory level of corporate profit. This type of decision-making behavior is referred to as **satisficing**, as opposed to the more traditional profit-maximizing or **optimizing** frameworks that assume perfect information. As discussed by Dicken and Lloyd (pp. 272–274), uncertainty may also be introduced through *production environment pressures*—forces exerted on a firm or production unit which emanate from any of the three following sources:

1. Competitors: both existing and potential, that is, known rivals or new entrants.

2. Groups with bargaining power: large suppliers of materials or large purchasers of finished products that exert leverage on the firm solely on the basis of the size of their transactions.

3. Regulators: agencies or governing bodies that impose regulations, restrictions, and legislative actions such as taxation, safety requirements, supervised entry into the industry, and so on, and ultimately influence such factors as wage levels, work conditions, production requirements and technologies, and terms of employment.

PLANT LOCATION IN PRACTICE

In the locating of manufacturing plants, several theoretical as well as practical considerations must be taken into account. Often the theoretical features of plant location involve macroscale decisions, such as in what part of the country the plant should locate or whether the location will be metropolitan or nonmetropolitan. Microscale decisions involve selection of one particular site from among several. Typically, macroscale decisions are made first; that is, the region or areas are selected, and then the specific site is determined.

One conceptual model, the ***product cycle model***, may be used to illustrate how theoretical and practical considerations blend together in the location decision. The product cycle model holds that manufactured products typically go through three stages or phases in their life cycles. Phase one, or the *initial stage*, is characterized by the early development of the product and further refinement and improvement of it. The second phase, known as the *growth stage*, is defined by the rapid growth to satisfy large market demand. Mass production methods are introduced, and a growing number of firms enter the market to produce the product. The last phase, the *mature stage*, is characterized by stable but slowed levels of production. Production technology has become standardized, and the number of firms producing the product will decline.

At each of these three stages, different factors of production are especially important. Similarly, at each stage, different kinds of locations are optimal. In the initial stage, the two most important production factors will be (1) scientific and engineering technology and (2) urbanization economies. Both factors favor a metropolitan location. Most scientific and engineering technology is to be found in the large metropolitan areas. Large cities are believed to have greater urbanization economies than small cities. Therefore, the optimal location for firms producing products in the initial stage will be large metropolitan areas. Certainly, metropolitan areas in industrial economies have been favored locations for manufacturing, and the early industrial history of the United States was associated with manufacturing in the cities of the traditional Manufacturing Belt.

During the growth stage, the two most important production factors are management and capital. With many firms in the market, the competitive edge will go to firms that are efficiently managed and have the capital resources to invest in the appropriate technology for mass production. Typically, the optimum locations associated with the mature stage are in the suburbs or near large metropolitan areas. Clearly, in the U.S. Manufacturing Belt, manufacturing spread from the largest cities to intermediate and smaller cities located nearby.

The mature stage requires unskilled labor and continued capital investment. Because the product has become standardized, there is little need for scientific and engineering know-how. The importance of management is reduced in the less competitive market. As capital is relatively mobile, the factor that influences optimal location in the third phase is unskilled, cheap labor. This labor typically will be found in nonmetropolitan areas, often in the peripheral regions of a country, such as the U.S. South.

One explanation for the recent growth of manufacturing in the South, as provided by the product cycle theory, is the region's large quantities of inexpensive, unskilled, and largely nonunionized labor. The leading state with new manufac-

turing facilities in the United States in recent years has been Texas, followed by North Carolina and Florida, with New York, Illinois, California, and Louisiana not far behind.

One way firms adjust to the product cycle changes is by establishing branch plants, often in nonmetropolitan areas in the mature or standardized stage. Figure 10.12 shows the location of the headquarters of branch plants in Georgia. Although Georgia is the leading state for corporate headquarters of branch plants located within the state, the role of other states, especially New York, is considerable. Thus, a significant proportion of Georgia's manufacturing base is externally controlled, leading to a condition known as a **branch plant economy**. Such

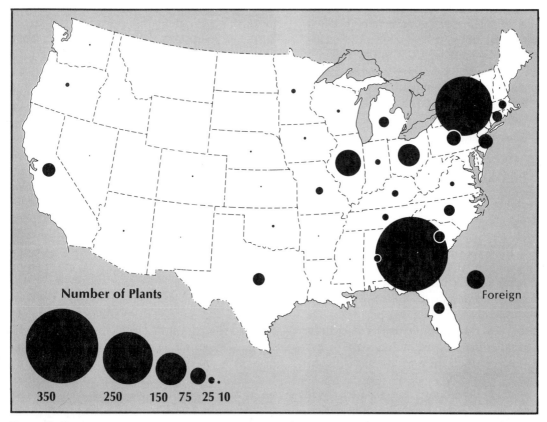

Figure 10.12 Headquarters of branch plants in Georgia (in number of plants).
Source: Wheeler and Park.

an economy is by definition externally controlled and results from nonmetropolitan manufacturing in the third stage of the produce cycle. External control increasingly characterizes the world economy, which is becoming ever more interdependent.

SUMMARY

This chapter examines the economic geography of manufacturing from the point of view of the manufacturing establishment making a locational decision. The focus is on the factors that go into the decision to locate and on certain attempts to formulate theories of location. The next chapter treats manufacturing from a regional perspective and considers the location of many plants in different industries in an area. Whereas this chapter views manufacturing from the angle of a single firm or plant, the next chapter looks at manufacturing as one views a region in which industry has located. Just as, for the manufacturing plant, there are generalizations, principles, and theories of location, there are likewise models and principles for regional manufacturing structure and change.

FURTHER READINGS

Dicken, P., and P. E. Lloyd. *Location in Space: Theoretical Perspectives in Economic Geography* 3rd ed. New York: Harper Row, 1990.

Greenhut, Melvin L. *Plant Location in Theory and Practice: The Economics of Space*. Chapel Hill: University of North Carolina Press, 1956.

Isard, Walter. *Location and Space Economy*. Cambridge, Mass.: MIT Press, 1956.

Karaska, Gerald, and David Bramhall, eds. *Locational Analysis for Manufacturing*. Cambridge, Mass.: MIT Press, 1969.

Lonsdale, Richard E., and H. L. Seyler. *Nonmetropolitan Industrialization*. New York: Wiley, 1979.

McGregor, John R., and Robert H. Maxey. "The Dal-
ton, Georgia, Tufted Textile Concentration." *Southeastern Geographer* 14 (1974), pp. 133–144.

Miller, E. Willard. *Manufacturing: A Study of Industrial Location*. University Park.: Pennsylvania State University Press, 1977.

Moriarty, Barry M. *Industrial Location and Community Development*. Chapel Hill.: University of North Carolina Press, 1980.

Northwest Policy Center. *Entrepreneurial Strategies: Readings on Flexible Manufacturing Networks*, Seattle: University of Washington, 1992.

Nourse, Hugh O. *Regional Economics*. New York: McGraw-Hill, 1968.

Peet, Richard. "Relations of Production and the Relocation of United States Manufacturing Since 1960." *Economic Geography* 59 (1983), pp. 112–143.

Smith, David M. *Industrial Location: An Economic Geographical Analysis*. 2nd rev. ed. New York: Wiley, 1981.

Stafford, Howard A. "Environmental Regulations and the Location of U.S. Manufacturing: Speculations." *Geoforum* 8 (1977), pp. 243–248.

Taylor, Michael. "Industrial Geography." *Progress in Human Geography* 8 (1984), pp. 263–274.

Wardrep, Bruce N. "Factors Which Play Major Roles in Location Decisions." *Industrial Development* 154 (1985), pp. 8–13.

Watts H. D. *The Branch Plant Economy: A Study of External Control*. London: Longman, 1981.

Watts, H. D. *Industrial Geography* New York: Wiley, 1987.

Webber, Michael J. *Impact of Uncertainty on Location*. Cambridge, Mass.: MIT Press, 1972.

Webber, Michael J. *Industrial Location*. Beverly Hills, Calif.: Sage, 1984.

Weber, Alfred. *Theory of the Location of Industries*, trans. C. J. Friedrich. Chicago: University of Chicago Press, 1929. (originally published as *Uber den standort der Industrien*, Tübingen, 1909.)

Wheeler, James O., and Sam Ock Park. "External Ownership and Control: The Impact of Industrial Organizations on the Regional Economy." *Geoforum* 15 (1984), pp. 243–252.

Wood, Peter A. "Industrial Geography." *Progress in Human Geography* 6 (1982), pp. 576–583.

CHAPTER 11

Manufacturing: Regional Patterns and Problems

———— ◇ ————

Life is the continuous adjustment of internal relations to external relations.

—HERBERT SPENCER

INTRODUCTION

When many entrepreneurs act individually and independently in locating manufacturing plants, they create a regional pattern of industrialization. Such a pattern may be highly clustered in one place or in several places, such as large urban areas. The pattern may be spaced more or less evenly over the region, or it may be spread linearly along a river, a highway, or a mountain range suddenly rising from a plain or plateau. Or the distribution of the manufacturing plants within a region may not reveal any real pattern at all, appearing as a jumbled, virtually random set of plant locations. How does one describe these regional patterns of manufacturing, and how do these patterns change over time as industrial regions mature or as manufacturing diffuses to other locations? What is the role of government in the regional pattern of industrial location? And what is the nature of regional problems arising from too little or too much manufacturing activity in a region? What role does manufacturing play in regional economic growth and development? These questions are addressed in this chapter.

THE IMPORTANCE OF MANUFACTURING

Many regional analysts contend that manufacturing activities are being displaced or rendered obsolete by white-collar services and high tech in the "postindustrial" economy. The once-thriving urban manufacturing corridors of the United States, for example, have experienced major shifts in their employment profiles away from heavy industry and toward services. A relatively small and shrinking percentage of the U.S. labor force is directly involved in manufacturing activities (slightly less than 16 percent), while services continue to employ a large and increasing percentage of people (now accounting for over three-fourths of the U.S. labor force).

The shift of regional economies toward a service orientation is, in part, a reflection of the changing composition of U.S. production. Consider the fact that in 1990, manufacturing accounted for only 17 percent of the U.S. gross domestic product (GDP), down from 28 percent in 1965.[1] Services, by contrast, accounted for 59

---

[1]GDP, or gross domestic product, refers to the value of all final goods and services produced domestically by a national economy in a given year.

percent of GDP in 1965, a figure that rose to 70 percent by 1990.[2] Producer services alone, the fastest growing sector of the U.S. economy, account for approximately one-quarter of the gross national product (GNP).[3]

Explosive growth in services and new technology sectors have combined to transform regional economies in ways not imagined just a few decades ago. Financial and consulting services, product maintenance agreements, extended warranties, increases in consumer income and spending, and significant employment growth in the public sector are just a few of the reasons for the sectoral shift to services and the relative decline of manufacturing. The intensification of intercorporate competition and related increases in research and development (R&D) expenditures, advertising and promotion budgets, and consumer financing have contributed greatly to the rise of producer services.[4] These changes have prompted a challenge to the traditional viewpoints on manufacturing as the urban economic base. Although growth in services and new technology industries facilitates economic transactions, stimulates regional production, and generates new employment opportunities, questions do arise concerning the long-term ability of such activities to sustain economic growth.[5]

High-tech industries (characterized as those with a high proportion of R&D expenditures or a large share of employees with advanced or scientific degrees) and services have been hailed as modern-day replacements for manufacturing. Stephen Cohen and John Zysman suggest, however, that the large majority of services are complements to manufacturing rather than substitutes or successors.[6] Since high tech is associated primarily with the design and development of producer goods rather than consumer goods, Cohen and Zysman contend that high tech must "gravitate toward state-of-the-art producers." Hence, highly competitive regional manufacturing centers that show mastery of product design and production technology are more likely to establish and sustain high tech.

The symbiotic relationship between manufacturing and high tech has been largely confined to metropolitan areas and rural areas adjacent to metropolitan areas. The phenomenon of high tech in urban and rural settings alike, however, is mostly a response to the locational tendencies of high-tech firms and the persistent dominance of existing high-tech concentrations,[7] and not necessarily a case of evolutionary succession. Amy Glasmeier and others suggest that the growth of high-tech industries and R&D facilities is more likely to occur at locations that are close to large metropolitan markets where suitable supplies of highly skilled or technical labor are

[2]Data from the World Bank's World Development Report 1991, 1992 (Oxford: Oxford University Press, 1991 and 1992, respectively).

[3]GNP, or gross national product, refers to the total value of all final goods and services produced by the national economy at home and abroad in a given year.

[4]See T. M. Stanback, P. J. Bearse, T. J. Noyelle, and R. A. Karasek, *Services: The New Economy* (Totowa, N.J.: Allanheld & Osman, 1981); and T. J. Noyelle and T. M. Stanback, *The Economic Transformation of American Cities* (Totowa, N.J.: Rowman & Allanheld, 1984).

[5]For discussions on services as stimuli, consult D. I. Riddle in *Service-Led Growth: The Role of the Service Sector in World Development* (New York: Praeger, 1986), pp. 1–26; see also W. B. Beyers, M. J. Alvine, and R. Johnson, "The Service Sector: A Growing Force in the Regional Export Base," *Economic Development Commentary* 9 (1985), pp. 3–7; P. Daniels, *Service Industries: A Geographical Appraisal* (London:

Methuen, 1985); and T. J. Noyelle's *New Technologies and Services: Impacts on Cities and Jobs* (College Park, Md.: University of Maryland Institute for Urban Studies, 1985). For a critique of service-led growth in Florida, see T. J. Fik, E. J. Malecki, and R. G. Amey, "Employment Trends for a Service-Oriented Economy," *Economic Development Quarterly* 7 (1993), pp. 358–272.

[6]See Stephen S. Cohen and John Zysman, *Manufacturing Matters: The Myth of the Post-Industrial Economy* (New York: Basic Books, 1987), pp. 1–27 and pp. 259–263.

[7]As discussed by E. J. Malecki in an article entitled "Industrial Location and Corporate Organization in High Technology Industries," *Economic Geography* 61 (1985), pp. 345–369.

readily available.[8] Notwithstanding the ongoing debate on what constitutes the contemporary regional economic base, we contend that the prosperity of a regional economy is highly dependent on that region's ability to control production in both high-tech and traditional manufacturing sectors.

The augmentation of service and high-technology sectors is also a direct outcome of intercorporate competition among manufacturers. It is, therefore, logical to argue that a shift of resources out of manufacturing into services and high tech could ultimately erode a region's industrial wealth and power base. Maintaining a competitive advantage in manufacturing is a desirable goal for several reasons. If a region loses its competitive edge and abandons the production of a certain type of commodity, the region stands to lose more than just the jobs associated with the loss of that industry and those industries linked to it. As R&D expenditures decline, the region will also lose its production know-how. It must also, therefore, forego future opportunities to exploit design improvements on existing product lines and the benefits associated with innovations in that and related industries. In other words, the loss of a particular manufacturing sector prohibits a region from competing in the production and sales of products from that sector. More importantly, it also precludes that region from realizing the spinoffs and benefits associated with future product development and sales of next-generation products with yet unforseen commercial potential.

Manufacturing not only adds value to products by changing their form, but also helps define the types of *linkages* (contacts and flows of materials and information between interdependent economic agents) found throughout the production or value-added sequence. The strength and number of linkages are directly proportional to the degree of export orientation. For instance, a region's employment base is more likely to expand if its manufacturing activities are associated with the sale of products in markets outside the production region. The outward flow of exportable commodities and the inward flow of dollars returning to producers from the sales of those commodities in external markets produce a regional multiplier effect. Creation and expansion of regional employment opportunities and economic growth are part of a cumulative process whereby manufacturers produce, export, and sustain those industries that supply various production inputs or support services. Portions of export revenues are used to cover local labor costs (in the form of wages), money that will filter into the local economy and recirculate as workers and their families purchase goods and services and, in turn, support other producers and service industries within the region.[9] The greater the ex-

The reconstructed Iron Bridge at Coalbrookdale is widely recognized as the symbol of the Industrial Revolution. From this site of the first iron bridge, built in the eighteenth century, the process of building iron bridges spread remarkably.

[8]As presented by Amy K. Glasmeier in *The High-Tech Potential: Economic Development in Rural America* (New Brunswick, N.J.: Center for Urban Policy Research, 1991), pp. 159–193 (Chapters 8 and 9); and Susan L. Bradbury and Edward J. Malecki, "R&D Facilities and Professional Labour: Labour Force Dynamics in High Technology," *Regional Studies* 26 (1992), pp. 123–136.

[9]Consult Chapter 6 of Peter Dicken and Peter E. Lloyd's *Location in Space: Theoretical Perspectives in Economic Geography*, 3rd ed. (New York: Harper & Row, 1990), pp. 219–252.

port orientation of manufactured products or the final value of exports from a region, the greater the share of value added retained by that region and the more likely that region is to experience economic and employment growth due to industry expansion. In addition, the greater the retained value added, the greater the implied regional economic base multiplier effect.

REGIONAL PATTERNS AND PROCESSES

Cycle Theory

John H. Thompson has suggested that industrial regions progress through a sequence of stages over time.[10] Although such a consistent sequence may be noted for many regions, there are numerous exceptions, and by no means do regions inevitably follow the sequence about to be outlined here. Moreover, even when industrial regions do progress through a typical change cycle, they do not do so at any necessarily consistent rate. Nevertheless, it is instructive to consider the *regional cycle theory* of industrial change.

The cycle theory maintains that once an industrial area is established, it goes through a regular sequence of change involving *youth, maturity*, and *old age*. (Note the distinction between the *regional cycle theory,* which refers to regions, and the *product cycle model* discussed in the previous chapter, which relates to manufactured products and where they are made.) Each of these three stages brings with it a different set of problems and a different competitive position. The industrial youth stage witnesses a period of experimentation and rapid growth. Markets are typically expanding rapidly, and the relative locational advantages of the region are suddenly being recognized. Investment capital rushes in. New technology is either imported or developed,

spurring further growth. The vigorous growth attracts managerial expertise. The youthful industrial region has the clear-cut competitive advantage of being able to produce at a low cost and to market over a wide geographic area.

During the second stage, maturity, the industrial region achieves a dominance over other regions. Managerial personnel, because of their know-how, may be "exported" to other areas. Competition becomes increasingly severe, as other regions vie for pieces of the manufacturing pie. To meet competition from other areas, ***branch plants***—subsidiaries of the original firm—are located in the other areas, and plant managers and other supervisors are transferred from the original plant. Still, the mature industrial region is able to maintain comparative locational cost advantages.

In the old age stage, these cost advantages are largely lost. Markets have significantly shifted, new and cheaper sources of raw materials have become available, and adequately skilled labor has been found in other regions at a lower cost. Buildings and machinery are now obsolete. Taxes have shot up, and competitive land uses are encroaching on the plant site, making expansion impossible. Congestion is often a problem. Those with top managerial skills may be attracted away to other kinds of employment, leaving a number of smaller family-run establishments in which entrepreneurial know-how has lagged.

Thompson has also suggested that the New England area (comprising the states of Connecticut, Maine, Massachusetts, New Hampshire, Rhode Island, and Vermont) provides a good example of a region that has gone through the industrial cycle from youth to maturity to old age. The Industrial Revolution in the United States started in New England, and the region grew vigorously during the early 1800s. As Thompson notes:

The most favorable localities in the Northeast experienced unusual manufacturing growth

[10]John H. Thompson, "Some Theoretical Considerations for Manufacturing Geography," *Economic Geography* 42 (1966), pp. 356–365.

and large cities began to evolve. Transport nets into the Midwest and South were being established, but up to 1880 a manufacturer in Woonsocket, Lowell, or Troy did not have to contend much with competition from the Midwest or South. The wave of industrial spread was moving forward, but hadn't reached these areas. They were still largely beyond what might be termed the industrial frontier. Few places had the locational advantages of the Northeast. It might be said to have been at that time in the stage of vigorous industrial youth.

In the ensuing years as manufacturing continued to grow rapidly in the Northeast, entrepreneurs, management people, and even foremen, who had learned their business there, began to be "exported." Northeastern companies moved or established branches elsewhere and new industrial areas began to open up in other parts of the country. Population shifts also occurred and accompanying these shifts was a change in the geography of markets. World War I found the Northeast a strong, successful manufacturing area, but one which was in the midst of a competition battle with other more rapidly expanding industrial regions. It had industrial inertia, traditional managerial knowhow, the country's most skilled labor force, and still reasonably good access to national markets. It was in a competitive struggle all right, but it was doing well industrially. It might be said to have been in the stage of industrial maturity.

By the 1920s and 1930s population and market shifts had been extensive, the transportation net was efficiently serving the entire nation, and new sources of industrial raw and processed materials became available. Many of the Northeast's earlier locational advantages in the geography of markets, labor, transportation, and power, too, had disappeared. To stay with the cycle analogy, the Northeast was at that time taking on the symptoms of industrial old age and the following major problems appeared:

(1) Labor costs became relatively high. Older experienced individuals who made up a large part of the factory payrolls demanded more pay, shorter working hours, and less input of work. Union pressures were greater than in more youthful competing areas. (2) Land occupied by factories became surrounded by the urban land uses of cities. It cost more and there was little available space for expansion. (3) Taxes, including real estate, state income, and workers' compensation, were high by comparative standards. (4) Buildings and equipment had grown old and obsolescent. (5) Many products, long manufactured and in demand in the national market, were by this time difficult to sell in competition with new products developed elsewhere. (6) In some instances, most often among the smaller establishments owned and operated by local families, management quality and know-how had not kept pace with those of younger industrial areas elsewhere. (pp. 357–358)

Manufacturing Within the Urban System

Industrial activities are unevenly located within a group of cities. Such a group of urban centers is often referred to as an urban system if the centers are located relatively near one another and are functionally related through industrial linkages or interaction patterns (see Chapter 6). Since industrialization forms an important basis for urban growth, large cities or metropolitan areas obviously will have a substantial manufacturing base compared with smaller cities. The introduction of industrial jobs into a community will create additional employment, as indicated in earlier discussions.

Large cities are attractive to many manufacturers because such cities have large local markets. Large cities also have better access to the surrounding region, especially other large cities, and to the national market, because large cities are better served by various transportation connections (interstates, railways, and air links).

Many industries locate in large metropolitan areas to serve national markets and to take advantage of the superior transportation linkages. Large cities are also pools of relatively skilled labor, which is essential for certain kinds of manufacturing. Finally, large cities offer convenient business services, warehousing facilities, access to a great variety of partially processed goods, and relatively quick and inexpensive communication linkages.

Similar arguments hold true at the global scale as well. Large cities in the global urban system continue to hold tremendous advantages over smaller cities in their ability to attract manufacturing. As the world economy continues to change in response to the increasing mobility of capital, the intensification and diversification of international trade, the geographic expansion of producer services, and the concentration and centralization of those services in urban areas, manufacturing will likely continue to gravitate toward locations near or within large international urban centers.[11]

In general, large urban areas provide the greatest locational advantage for manufacturing by reducing uncertainty in the location decision-making process. Large urban areas are able to provide many localization and urbanization economies. Localization economies include cost savings that arise from proximity to a wide variety of producer services, production inputs, information sources (as they pertain to the behaviors of consumers and rivals), and potential clientele (the market for manufactured goods). Urbanization economies include production cost savings that accrue from access to physical and transportation infrastructure and diverse urban labor markets.

Smaller urban centers or towns have few of these advantages. Naturally, the local market is smaller, the town is almost invariably less well

connected with the transportation network, and the variety of opportunities found in the larger city do not exist. On the other hand, a smaller center may have certain advantages. First, the cost of labor will typically be lower. As a result, manufacturers able to use less sophisticated labor may be attracted to smaller centers to reduce cost. The outcome is that smaller centers normally have different kinds of industries than the large metropolitan areas, with the smaller centers tending to be slow-growth industry; that is, the industry generates little population growth in the community. Second, smaller centers will usually have manufacturing that is oriented more toward raw materials. A good example is agricultural processing. These materials need to be broken down by weight before they are shipped a great distance or in some cases may be perishable. Manufacturing based on local raw materials, of course, reflects the local economy, such as the type of agriculture, mining, or forestry.

Diffusion of Manufacturing

Examining regional patterns of manufacturing over time will help us to recognize the rate and direction of change. Another way of saying this is that manufacturing often diffuses or spreads out. Such a *diffusion process* is quite complex, seldom being as simple as the diffusion that occurs when one throws a rock in a pool. After all, we have just seen that manufacturing is attracted differentially by the size of cities, and certainly the locational advantages of one place do change over time, as suggested by the cycle theory. No two regions, when studied over time, will display the same changing patterns of manufacturing spread. And yet these regions may have certain features in common.

A fundamental characteristic of manufacturing diffusion is that it normally spreads from a point or points. Usually, a point is an existing settlement or a raw-material site (that soon becomes a settlement). One kind of manufacturing

---

[11]See P. W. Daniels, *Service Industries in the World Ecocomy* (Oxford, UK: Blackwell, 1993), pp. 113–142.

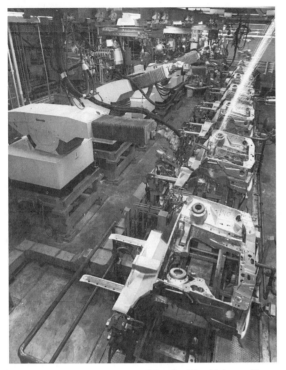

Robots welding front assemblies for Ford Motor Company, Wayne, Michigan.

attracts others, as people are drawn to the location. Manufacturing, when mapped over a period of time, appears to "spill over" from this initial location and diffuse over the landscape in some manner. The spread will be faster in some directions than in others, just as water flows fastest where the slope is steepest. In like manner, manufacturing spread may encounter barriers and be unable to spread in those areas very rapidly. Barriers to manufacturing may be physical, such as a swamp or mountain range, or cultural-political, as along a political boundary between two countries. Manufacturing diffusion, which may proceed in one direction during one era, may reverse itself during another time period. The outward diffusion process may, in fact, be redirected toward an earlier pattern of concentration of manufacturing at one or more locations.

MANUFACTURING REGIONS OF THE UNITED STATES

As manufacturing accelerated in both absolute and relative significance in the United States in the latter part of the nineteenth century, an increasingly concentrated location pattern became evident. Although manufacturing during the early history of the country was largely clustered along the East Coast, and was especially associated with large port cities, it spread into the Midwest with the opening of the Erie Canal and later the railway. From about 1880 until World War II, the overall location of U.S. manufacturing maintained a fairly stable and concentrated pattern that expanded mainly at the periphery of the concentration. In fact, so striking was this pattern that in geographic studies prior to World War II, as well as into the 1960s, it became common to use the term the **American Manufacturing Belt** or **Rustbelt** (Figure 11.1) To be sure, different economic geographers debated exactly where they thought the Belt was properly located (should Kansas City be included or not?). Nevertheless, it was quite clear that the preponderance of American manufacturing productivity took place in the northeastern quarter of the United States and the southern fringe of Ontario in Canada.

The classic delimitation of the American Manufacturing Belt ran something as follows: it extended from Boston to Montreal to Toronto in southern Ontario, and across southern Ontario through the southern half of Michigan's Lower Peninsula and into the southern half of Wisconsin, reaching as far west as Minneapolis. Thence it cut southward through eastern Iowa as far south as St. Louis, and then it extended eastward through Louisville and Cincinnati, through southern Ohio to south of Pittsburgh, and on eastward to the vicinity of Baltimore and Washington, and then northward to include the major cities of the East Coast back to Boston. Included within this Belt was the great majority of American manufacturing production.

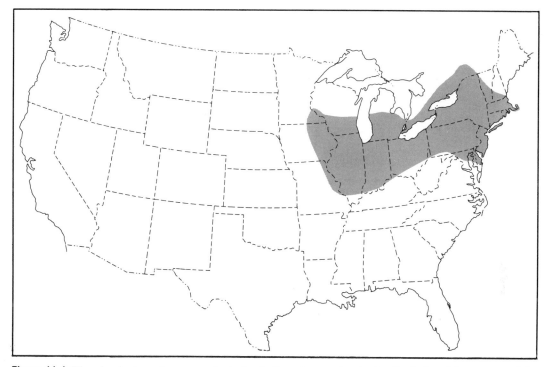

Figure 11.1 The classic American manufacturing belt no longer dominates the industrial structure of the United States and Canada, as it once did.

New York was, without question, the single leading metropolitan area in manufacturing production as measured by value added by manufacturing.[12] Chicago was second. Regional concentrations stood out within the American Manufacturing Belt. The most notable concentration was that within the Megalopolis running from Boston to Washington. Another concentration ran from Montreal to Windsor in Canada, including Buffalo and Rochester, New York. Still another was the iron and steel cluster focused at one end on Pittsburgh and at the other on Cleveland. The Detroit area merged with this iron and steel cluster, as well as the Canadian concentration, and in fact formed the nucleus of yet

another region associated with automobile manufacturing, in which many large- and medium-sized cities produced various components for the automotive industry. At the western edges were Minneapolis and St. Louis, as already mentioned. Chicago, with its associated concentrations in Milwaukee to the north and Gary, Indiana, at the southern tip of Lake Michigan, constituted a large industrial complex within the Belt.

Changing Manufacturing Patterns and Trends

Several important changes have occurred in the pattern of American manufacturing since World War II. Indeed, the term *American Manufacturing Belt* is no longer appropriate to describe the distribution of American manufacturing. Journalists have coined the term **Sunbelt** to refer to the growth of population and the economy in the

[12]Carol L. Jusenius and Larry C. Ledebus, *Documenting the "Decline" of the North*, Economic Development Research Report (Washington, D.C.: U.S. Department of Commerce, June 1978).

southern and western portion of the country, often reserving the word ***Snowbelt*** for the colder, northern area (comprising the old Manufacturing Belt). Immediately after World War II, people generally became aware of the rapid population growth in California and Florida. Population figures between 1960 and 1970, however, revealed that rapid growth occurred not only in areas in these two states, but also in many other parts of the so-called Sunbelt. During this decade, population increase was especially rapid in the larger metropolitan areas whereas growth was much slower in several of the smaller cities.

During the 1970s, the contrasts between the Sunbelt and Snowbelt became even more noticeable, as many of the metropolitan areas of the Northeast lost population or experienced only modest increases. This period also witnessed a movement away from large cities in general—in contrast to the previous growth of the large metropolitan areas—and into rural areas at the metropolitan fringe.

Primarily as a result of these national changes in population, a major shift also occurred in manufacturing location, leading to the erosion of the Manufacturing Belt. The Snowbelt has grown at a significantly slower rate in industrial employment than the South and West in general. Between 1977 and 1982, the western states showed the largest percentage increase in manufacturing employment. Manufacturing employment increased 20 percent in the mountain states of Montana, Idaho, Wyoming, Colorado, New Mexico, Arizona, Utah, and Nevada during this period, and increased 13 percent in the Pacific states of Washington, Oregon, California, Alaska, and Hawaii. In contrast, the New York metropolitan area, for example, lost 75,000 manufacturing jobs between 1980 and 1985, but increased its total employment by over 215,000, virtually all of which was in the service sector. Although there has been some migration of manufacturing firms from the North to the South, such relocation has not been the primary reason for the growth of manufacturing in the South.

Manufacturing is both following population to the South, in which case the growth of population spurs manufacturing increase, and, as a primary job creator, attracting more population to the South. The main reason for the relative decline of manufacturing activity in the North has been the closing (going out of business) of firms, not outmigration. From 1969 to 1974, for example, manufacturing firms were being established in the South at almost twice the rate of those in the North, but these were not relocating firms. In fact, both the North and the South experienced about the same "death" rate of manufacturing firms, but the "birth" rate was much higher in the South. The rate at which manufacturing firms closed in the North was approximately twice the rate that industrial establishments opened for business in the North.

Nonetheless, U.S. manufacturing can be characterized as having gone through a state of relative decline over the last few decades. Stagnation of various manufacturing sectors and attrition (due to foreign competition) are only partly responsible for this trend. The subtle increase in manufacturing employment has been largely overshadowed by employment gains in other sectors of the U.S. economy (e.g., services). Consider, for example, that manufacturing employment rose only one-third of 1 percent from 1970 to 1990 (accounting for 19,676,600 and 19,741,600 total jobs, respectively), while the total number of people employed in the U.S. economy increased by 52.8 percent over the same 20-year period (from 89,752,500 to 137,160,200 total jobs).

Despite the relative decline of manufacturing in the traditional Rustbelt areas, Sunbelt states have experienced significant growth in manufacturing sectors. The Rustbelt-to-Sunbelt shift is attributable to such factors as regional variations in business climate (which favors the South and the Midwest), the implied shifts in market potential (due to Snowbelt–Sunbelt migration), and favorable labor-cost locations that are predominantly associated with the existence of "right-

Table 11.1   Location Quotients for U.S. Manufacturing Employment by State, 1970, 1990

State	LQ(1970)	LQ(1990)	Difference	State	LQ(1970)	LQ(1990)	Difference
Alabama	1.079	1.359	0.280	Montana	0.392	0.408	0.015
Alaska	0.251	0.387	0.136	Nebraska	0.560	0.743	0.182
Arizona	0.579	0.713	0.133	Nevada	0.160	0.262	0.101
Arkansas	0.991	1.374	0.383	New Hampshire	1.295	1.208	−0.087
California	0.820	0.933	0.112	New Jersey	1.304	0.993	−0.310
Colorado	0.550	0.694	0.144	New Mexico	0.254	0.427	0.173
Connecticut	1.462	1.224	−0.23	New York	0.981	0.836	−0.144
D.C.	0.129	0.156	0.026	North Carolina	1.375	1.584	0.209
Delaware	1.226	1.225	−0.000	North Dakota	0.174	0.353	0.178
Florida	0.515	0.546	0.031	Ohio	1.405	1.339	−0.065
Georgia	1.040	1.075	0.035	Oklahoma	0.569	0.746	0.177
Hawaii	0.288	0.242	−0.045	Oregon	0.899	1.013	0.113
Idaho	0.603	0.876	0.272	Pennsylvania	1.365	1.168	−0.197
Illinois	1.223	1.096	−0.127	Rhode Island	1.277	1.310	0.033
Indiana	1.445	1.473	0.028	South Carolina	1.327	1.410	0.083
Iowa	0.794	1.026	0.232	South Dakota	0.257	0.616	0.358
Kansas	0.634	0.894	0.260	Tennessee	1.221	1.350	0.129
Kentucky	0.889	1.066	0.177	Texas	0.695	0.799	0.103
Louisiana	0.572	0.661	0.088	Utah	0.572	0.869	0.297
Maine	1.164	1.078	−0.085	Vermont	0.940	1.069	0.128
Maryland	0.742	0.546	−0.196	Virginia	0.790	0.824	0.033
Massachusetts	1.129	1.022	−0.106	Washington	0.766	0.959	0.193
Michigan	1.405	1.403	−0.001	West Virginia	0.905	0.830	−0.075
Minnesota	0.880	1.092	0.212	Wisconsin	1.204	1.406	0.201
Mississippi	0.945	1.483	0.538	Wyoming	0.224	0.290	0.065
Missouri	0.953	1.035	0.082				

LQ(year) = [SMEmp/STEmp] / [NMEmp/NTEmp], where S = state; N = Nation; M = Manufacturing; T = Total; and EMP = Employment (for a given year).

to-work'' laws, which prohibit compulsory union membership. In addition, land and industrial building costs have tended to favor the South.[13] Most Sunbelt states have also offered tremendous tax advantages and tax breaks to attract industry. In any event, the shifting manufacturing core has had profound effects on interregional wage disparities in metropolitan areas. During the 1980s, wage growth slowed significantly in all sectors, but especially hard hit were wages in union and blue-collar (manufacturing) sectors in

the Rustbelt. By contrast, this period saw a considerable strengthening of real wages in the South.[14]

Dramatic geographic shifts in manufacturing employment have occurred in the United States since the late 1960s. To highlight these shifts, Table 11.1 shows "location quotients" of U.S. manufacturing employment by state for the years 1970 and 1990. The location quotient is an index that describes whether a small geographic unit or region (e.g., a state) has greater, equal, or less than its share of a particular activity (e.g., man-

[13]See discussions pertaining to the U.S. economy in Chapters 7, 8, 9, and 10 of H. D. Watts, *Industrial Geography* (New York: Wiley, 1987) and discussions of labor cost as a location factor in K. Chapman and F. Walker, *Industrial Location*, 2nd ed. (Oxford, UK: Basil Blackwell, 1991), pp. 44–51.

[14]See D. P. Angel and J. Mitchell, "Intermetropolitan Wage Disparities and Industrial Change," *Economic Geography* 67 (1991), pp. 128–146.

ufacturing employment as a percentage of total employment) in comparison to some larger geographic unit or region (e.g., the nation). If a location quotient equals one, it indicates that a smaller geographic unit has exactly the same share of a particular activity than does the larger geographic unit. If a location quotient is greater (less) than one, it indicates that the smaller geographic unit has more (less) than its share of a particular activity in comparison to the larger geographic unit.

The data in Table 11.1 are summarized in Figure 11.2. The map highlights two interesting geographic patterns. First, manufacturing growth

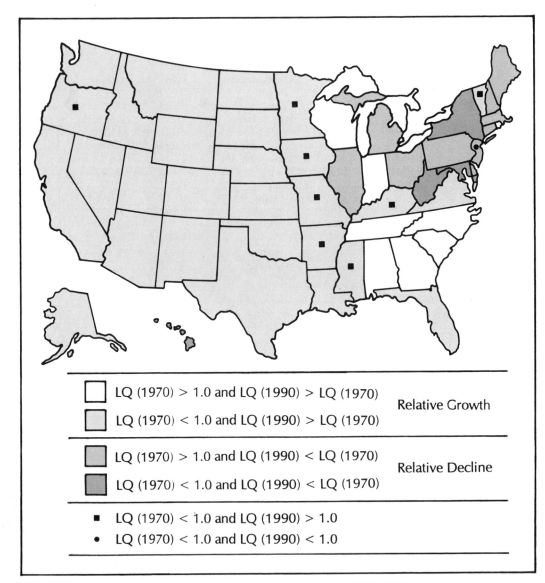

Figure 11.2 Changes in U.S. manufacturing employment location, 1970–1990.

has been largely concentrated in areas that are peripheral to the Rustbelt. Particularly strong is the relative growth of manufacturing in the ***New Southern Manufacturing Belt*** (NSMB). This belt is centered about the states of Tennessee, North and South Carolina, and Georgia (as shown by the cluster of dark-shaded areas just south of the Rustbelt). Second, states that have had dramatic turnarounds in manufacturing employment (as indicated by "+" signs) are peripherally located just west of the Rustbelt and northwest of the New Southern Manufacturing Belt. Note that these states are located along the Mississippi River basin—an area that provides a high degree of accessibility to both national and international markets. These patterns are also highly consistent with both regional cycle theory and a spatial diffusion process. The youthful status and vigorous growth of the NSMB, as well as the increase in production costs in the now mature Rustbelt, are responsible for the relative shifts and redistribution of manufacturing employment.

Figure 11.3. shows various regional comparisons of the percentage share of U.S. manufacturing employment for the years 1970 and 1990.

Notwithstanding regional employment shifts in manufacturing from the traditional core to peripheral locations, the Rustbelt continued to hold over 41 percent of U.S. manufacturing employment in 1990. This figure is comparable to the total percentage of combined U.S. manufacturing employment in the South, including California and Texas (see states in dark-shaded and cross-hatched regions).

The emergence of the New Southern Manufacturing Belt has also been attributed to investment capital transfers. The increasing mobility of capital and the subsequent proliferation of ***multinational organizations***—firms or companies that produce within two or more nations and do business across international borders—are part of the global transnationalization process of industrial location. Direct foreign investment and the subsequent location of foreign manufacturing plants (branch plants or subsidiaries) in the production cost-competitive environments of the South increased markedly during the 1980s. The states of Tennessee, North Carolina, and Georgia each absorbed 50 or more branch plants from 1978 to 1987. The majority of these facilities are associated with the production of high-value-

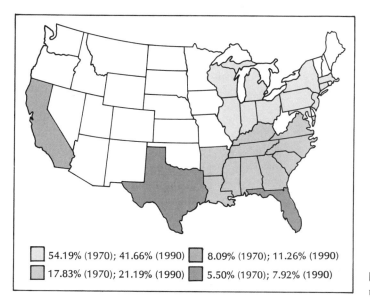

☐ 54.19% (1970); 41.66% (1990)	☐ 8.09% (1970); 11.26% (1990)
☐ 17.83% (1970); 21.19% (1990)	☐ 5.50% (1970); 7.92% (1990)

Figure 11.3 Percentage share of U.S. manufacturing employment, 1970–1990.

added products such as industrial machinery, electronic devices, motor vehicles, and transportation equipment.[15]

Although foreign-owned manufacturing plants have offered employment opportunities and spinoffs to linked industries, such operations do not ensure that profits will be reinvested within the host nation (in this case the United States). Profits from the sale of manufactured goods in both the United States and abroad (from production facilities located within the United States) are commonly expropriated back to the investing nations such as the Netherlands, Canada, Germany, the United Kingdom, and Japan (the top five investing nations). Many of these plants are located in low-wage, right-to-work states where wages and benefits to workers are small in comparison to those found in regions with considerably higher percentages of union membership. In addition, many of these plants are involved in the assembly of final products whose component parts may or may not be of domestic origin. Hence, manufacturing employment opportunities from direct foreign investment tend to yield cumulative multiplier effects that are relatively low in comparison to those typically generated by high-wage industries that are domestically owned, operated, and linked to other domestic industries (i.e., those that retain the greatest amount of value added at each stage of production). Nonetheless, capital transfers in the form of branch plants have recreated manufacturing jobs in the South at a time when jobs were being lost due to the effects of foreign competition and rising production costs in the old manufacturing core.

In addition to the emergence of multinationals and direct foreign investment transfers, Allen Scott has elaborated on a new and important trend that is transforming the geography of manufacturing in both North America and Europe.

This phenomenon, as part of the technological and institutional structure of production, competition, and capital accumulation in the contemporary capitalist space-economy, is known as *flexible production*.[16] Flexible production represents the recent pursuit of greater flexibility among small production units or firms and the search for external economies in the spatial organization of industry and industrial linkages. It has given rise to agglomerations of small firms in geographic areas that were previously nonindustrialized. Meric Gertler writes:

Recent times have seen an intensification of firms' desires to adopt certain practices in the productive sphere of the economy. These include: (i) a more flexible use of workers and machines; (ii) more flexible inter-firm relations (vertical disintegration, subcontracting, alliances, and the like); (iii) more flexible relations within the market, driven by intensified competition and a consequent shortening of product cycles (resulting in a greater diversity of products being produced, and a need to cut time to market for new products); (iv) a reduction in the amount of unrealized capital tied up in inventories; (v) changes to social institutions to foster more flexible employment relations; and (vi) the breaking down of previous barriers to the mobility of capital between sectors and between places, through the deregulation and restructuring of many products, service, and capital markets. (p. 260)

Labor market processes are viewed as central to the renewed tendencies toward industrial agglomeration in regions engaging in flexible production. Flexibility is achieved through vertical disintegration of the production process, as pro-

---

[15]Jan Ondrich and Michael Wasylenko, *Foreign Direct Investment in the United States* (Kalamazoo, Mich.: W. E. Upjohn Institute for Employment Research, 1993).

[16]Allen J. Scott, *New Industrial Spaces* (London: Pion, 1988); see also the review of Scott's work and critique by Jamie Peck, "Labor and Agglomeration: Control and Flexibility in Local Labor Markets," *Economic Geography* 68 (1992), pp. 325–347; and discussions in Peter Dicken, *Global Shift* (New York: Guilford Press, 1992), pp. 115–118.

ducers externalize many of the functions previously performed within the firm. As production becomes more specialized and the division of labor more pronounced, a complex web of interdependencies within the production system develops and intensifies. The end result is a dense, high-integrated, and self-supporting production network with a vast array of interorganizational transactions among producers (linkages), and a unique set of labor market and community relations that give rise to a cooperative social structure. Furthermore, flexible production involves the use of information technologies and controls in production to permit rapid switching from one part of the production process to another and allow for a diverse production output. The final output can then be tailored specifically to meet the requirements of individual customers.

Flexible production regimes provide a stark contrast to the rigid, entrenched production processes and social relations observed in the era of Fordist mass production. *Fordism* may be defined by the period in which production output was controlled by the development of the assembly-line process and large-scale production units (roughly spanning the early 1900s to late 1970s). Traditional Fordist-type automation was geared primarily toward high-volume output of a standardized product, taking advantage of scale economies to drive down the average cost of production. It typically involved the use of machines that performed a single production task.

In contrast, post–Fordist flexibility permits different products to emerge from the same assembly line, as producers utilize machines that are capable of performing a multitude of tasks. This arrangement allows firms to operate efficiently over a wide variety of scales, and to turn out small batches of uniquely designed products at a fairly low cost. Unlike the large-scale production facilities of the Fordist era, flexible manufacturing complexes are usually comprised of small-scale production units. Flexible production typically appears in localities with little or no prior history of industrialization and organized labor

activity. As a result, flexible production is associated with low-labor-cost regions or locations with flexible labor market conditions (as determined by the movement away from or absence of labor negotiations or collective bargaining agreements), the presence of a multiskilled labor force and associated reductions in job demarcation, and the deployment of temporary workers in response to fluctuations in labor input requirements.

As Scott maintains, flexible production can be found in numerous sectors including (1) revivified craft and design-intensive industries that focus almost entirely on the production of consumer goods such as shoes, furniture, sporting goods, jewelry, ceramics, textiles, apparel, and machine parts and tools; (2) high-tech industries and the many linked suppliers and subcontractors; and (3) an expanding set of services aimed at promoting efficiency in production (e.g., business and financial services). Flexible production systems, though found in diverse locations, are typically at some distance (socially or geographically) from the high-cost/wage and congested centers of Fordist mass production. In other words, flexible production is associated with a greater locational preference to form and occupy new industrial spaces, away from the old industrial spaces of the dominant manufacturing core. This represents a major shift in regional investment "from traditional working-class communities to alternative production sites with a very different cultural and political character" (Scott, p. 14). Take for example, the emergence of clustered high-tech industries in various new growth centers of the politically conservative business climates within the U.S. Sunbelt.

Although flexible production regimes have actively evaded areas with unionized labor and unfavorable corporate tax structures, as producers are able to choose from a wide array of locational alternatives at any given time, no one proven location strategy is known to exist. As noted by Ash Amin, "the key elements of the successful industrial district are highly place specific"

(p. 31). The search for new economies and new forms of control in production may be viewed as nothing more than a basic survival strategy of firms as they face and respond to intensified competition and new market signals. Nonetheless, flexible labor practices and production, task specialization, and industrial networks of small agglomerated firms with less rigid technological arrangements may well be facilitating enhanced efficiency, product innovation, greater productivity, and reduced transportation costs.[17]

New growth centers and production complexes based on flexible production have emerged in numerous geographic areas around the globe, particularly those that have been largely insulated from Fordist industrialization and the historical experience of organized labor movements. These areas include the large portions of the U.S. Sunbelt, craft industry centers in Denmark, southern Germany, northeast and central Italy (also known as the Third Italy), the Jura region of Switzerland, and central Portugal, and the labor-intensive (sweatshop-oriented) jewelry and clothing industries in world cities such as New York, Los Angeles, Toronto, and Paris—flexible production centers that rely on the recent major waves of immigration for cheap and abundant labor.

The flexible production movement has not only led to the relocation and restructuring of firms and linkages and changing industrial patterns, but it has also given birth to new ways of management. The notion of *"just-in-time"* (JIT) production is a philosophy that defines how flexible manufacturing systems should be managed. It is rooted in the belief that individual firms and subcontractors in a manufacturing system must work under the realization that they are essential parts of an interconnected network. To be truly flexible, production units must develop a network view of their identities. This realization will enable them to increase market share and profits

by acting in accordance with one underlying objective: enhance customer satisfaction through the availability of options to meet the needs of a diverse and ever-changing market, with an assurance of product quality and value, and prompt delivery times of products at intermediate and final stages of production. The JIT system of production is essentially designed to eliminate wasteful operations that do not contribute to the value-added process. JIT production management schemes, pioneered by the Toyota Motor Corporation, helped the Japanese automotive giant penetrate and expand regional and world markets.[18]

Location of Industrial Corporate Headquarters

In 1920, the headquarters of the 500 industrial firms with the greatest assets were almost entirely located in the historical American Manufacturing Belt.[19] Specifically, the Manufacturing Belt controlled 90 percent of the assets of these 500 industrial corporations. In fact, two-thirds of the assets were controlled from locations within Megalopolis and 40 percent from New York City alone. Such an intense concentration resulted from the origin and growth of many firms at earlier times in these leading port and river cities of the Manufacturing Belt. John R. Borchert concluded that "the pattern reflected an earlier set of economic locations, mainly mercantile, preserved or enhanced by a set of large corporations."

The locational pattern of assets controlled from the 500 largest industrial headquarters changed somewhat from 1920 to 1971 (Figure 11.4). The shifts, however, were not nearly so great in headquarters locations as in the pattern of manufacturing productivity. A considerable degree of inertia has kept many headquarters lo-

[17]Ash Amin, "Flexible Specialization and Small Firms in Italy: Myths and Realities," *Antipode* 21 (1989), pp. 13–34.

[18]See G. J. R. Linge, "Just-in-Time: More or Less Flexible," *Economic Geography* 67 (1991), pp. 316–332.
[19]John R. Borchert, "Major Control Points in American Economic Geography," *Annals of the Association of American Geographers* 68 (1978), pp. 214–232.

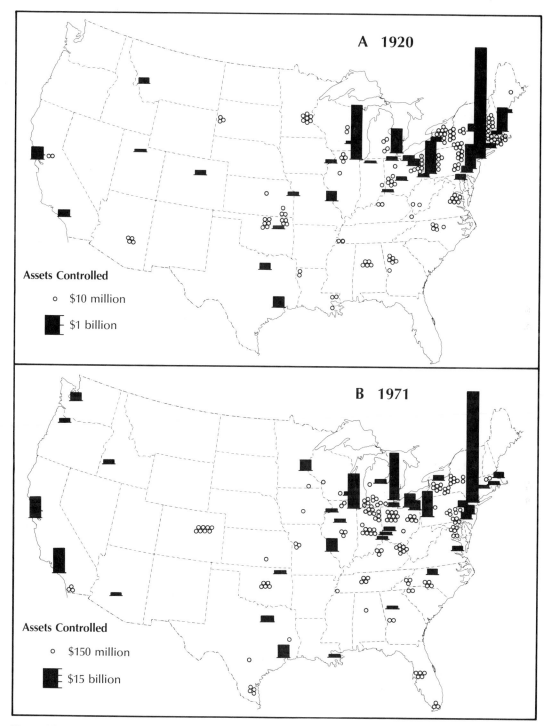

Figure 11.4 Headquarter locations of the 500 largest industrial corporations in 1920 and 1971.
Source: Bochert, see footnote 19.

cations basically unchanged, even though the actual labor force employed with the assets and the value added by manufacturing have shifted rather dramatically to the South and West. Headquarters locations have grown in the southern Piedmont of the Carolinas and Georgia and in various metropolitan areas in the South and West (Atlanta, Houston, Dallas, Phoenix, Los Angeles, San Francisco, Portland, and Seattle). Within the historic American Manufacturing Belt, the Midwest has gained over the past few decades at the expense of Megalopolis. And within metropolitan areas, some relocation of headquarters has also been occurring from downtown to suburban locations. Especially characteristic is the movement out of Manhattan in New York City into surrounding suburban fringes.

John Rees has examined the relocation of manufacturing firms that moved to the Dallas–Fort Worth metropolitan area.[20] Between 1971 and 1976, the number of manufacturing firms with a net worth over $1 million headquartered in Dallas–Fort Worth increased by 25 percent. Rees's sample of 100 firms in this metropolitan area showed that 69 were "born" locally and that the remaining 31 were the result of relocations. Up to approximately 1960, manufacturing headquarters relocation to Dallas–Fort Worth reflected movement from generally smaller cities and commonly from within the region (Figure 11.5). After 1960, there was much greater attraction of manufacturing headquarters from outside the region, especially from very large metropolitan areas such as New York, Chicago, and Detroit. Initially, headquarters were spawned locally as manufacturing developed in the Dallas–Fort Worth area. Second, headquarters began relocating "up" the urban hierarchy from small regional centers to Dallas–Fort Worth. Finally, and increasingly since 1960, Dallas–Fort Worth

has been attracting from the national level the relocation of manufacturing headquarters representing firms with higher and higher net worth. As Rees (p. 345) noted: "Thus, the relocation pattern that emerges over time is initially a neighborhood diffusion effect up the urban hierarchy that was replaced during the rush of relocations in the 1960s and 1970s by a non-local, inter-regional movement generally down the urban hierarchy." This recent movement is in response to the growing market potential within the region. This process of industrial change relates to the cycle theory, as discussed earlier in this chapter.

The 1980s witnessed a decline of the spatial concentration of corporate headquarters away from the large urban metropolises of the North (e.g., New York City—the national hub) and a proliferation of these facilities in other large cities that were experiencing rapid population growth. Despite the decline, New York City retained a dominant position as a national center for corporate headquarters. Large urban areas, mostly outside the traditional manufacturing belt (e.g,. service-oriented centers of the Sunbelt), continued to attract corporate facilities due to existing infrastructure, urban amenities (cultural and recreational), large and diverse labor pools, and the presence of educational and research institutions. Firm relocation strategies, along with mergers and acquisitions, also played a significant role in the dispersal of corporate headquarters.[21]

Government Influence on Regional Manufacturing Patterns

The government has always been an important factor in the manufacturing plant's location decision, and it is certain that this influence will be

---

[20]John Rees, "Manufacturing Headquarters in a Post-Industrial Urban Context," *Economic Geography* 54 (1978), pp. 337–354.

[21]See S. R. Holloway and J. O. Wheeler, "Corporate Headquarters Relocation and Changes in Metropolitan Corporate Dominance, 1980–1987," *Economic Geography* 67 (1991), pp. 54–75.

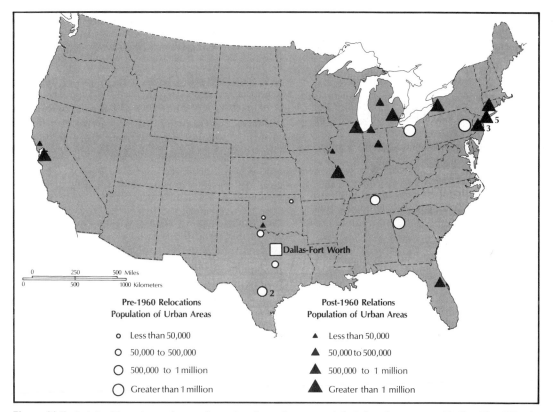

Figure 11.5 Original locations of manufacturing firms that moved their headquarters to Dallas-Fort Worth. *Source:* Rees, see footnote 20.

even greater in the future. In socialist or planned economies, the government, of course, directly decides what will be manufactured and where, although these decisions are constrained to a certain extent by the economic realities of procuring, producing, and distributing materials. In a country such as the United States, however, the government has an indirect role in industrial location and will be of increasing influence in the future. Such government action, whether at the federal, state, or local level, either encourages or prohibits the development of new or expanded industry in an area.

One of the most basic ways in which government affects the location of industry is through government contracts with manufacturing plants and through government procurement of indus-

trial products. What a governmental agency chooses to buy, be it a carpet for a new office building or a squadron of aircraft, has considerable implications for the growth and success of a particular manufacturer and the lack of success of others. The carpet manufacturer sells only a small portion of output to government and will be only slightly affected as a result. The defense contractor may need to hire or lay off a large number of workers depending on whether or not a specific contract is secured. In the latter case, the role of government spending may have regional economic impact as well.

The federal government in the United States is also involved in efforts to revive distressed areas through a variety of programs, from construction of public works to grants and loans to state and local governments. All of this activity affects industry. The Appalachian Regional Commission oversees expenditure of federal funds within portions of the 13 states comprising the region. Significant investment has been made in highways, which in turn influences the suitability of the region for manufacturing. A large number of other multistate, federal, state, and local agencies pursue policies that have an influence on industrial location decisions.

Perhaps the classic example of a federal program that had unforseen consequences for manufacturing location was the construction of the more than 40,000 miles of interstate highway across the country and through and around its metropolitan areas. The interstate system brought about profound changes in national growth and development, as it gave metropolitan areas located in the system accessibility advantages. These advantages were immediately translated into transport cost savings for manufacturers. Thus, certain regions and metropolitan areas were favored indirectly through federal investment in a facility of considerable importance to the location of industry. Even within metropolitan areas, industrial decentralization was accelerated as manufacturers left the older city center for more spacious settings at the periphery along accessible interstate routes.

Government policy and action can affect the regional development of industry in several other ways. One way is through differential taxation, although it is generally recognized that the tax rate is seldom the most significant factor in the location decision. (Taxes simply do not constitute a large share of the total cost of manufacturing.) Another way in which government may affect industrial location is by assisting national industries against foreign competition through subsidy or through import barriers. Yet another kind of government action, though often overemphasized in its importance, is the role of state industrial development boards and chambers of commerce in attracting industry. Finally, operating at the local level are a series of zoning regulations that restrict industry from certain areas and channel it toward other locations.

REGIONAL INDUSTRIAL DEVELOPMENT PROBLEMS

Because any country will display unequal levels of industrialization and growth from region to region, some areas will inevitably lag and be perceived as regions with problems. Exactly how these regional problems will be perceived and defined will depend on societal or governmental attitudes, usually in comparison with other parts of the country and with existing levels of technology. The general problem of economic development was treated in Chapter 3; here we wish to focus on development problems that specifically relate to industrialization.

David M. Smith has identified three types of problem regions.[22] One is the ***underdeveloped region*** in which industrialization is either lacking or exists at a very backward level. The Appalachian region of the United States is one example; Brazil is another, though at a national scale. At the global level, the large majority of nations in sub-Saharan Africa could be classified as underdeveloped regions. Resources within this type of region are not being fully utilized, and developmental capital is scarce. As a result, income is low, and purchasing power (market forces) does not attract industrial investment. Other conditions, such as dense and interconnected transportation network of skilled industrial workers, are lacking, further discouraging industrial development. Frequently associated with underdeveloped regions, again as noted in Chapter 3, are low educational level, limited technology, poor standards of health and medical care, and a generally low standard of living.

An underdeveloped region differs from a ***depressed region*** in that the depressed area had

---

[22]David M. Smith, *Industrial Location: An Economic Geographic Analysis* (New York: Wiley, 1981).

achieved a relatively high level of industrial development but now suffers from depressed growth. The Ruhr in western Germany is an example. Unemployment may be high, as manufacturers close down operations or reduce their production. These conditions are often the result of competition from other regions, as new markets open up at distant locations, making competitive pricing difficult. Costs, such as labor, may rise to the point that lower-cost labor areas become more competitive and advantageously located. The region may experience a depressed economy because of the shutdown or slowdown of a single large manufacturer, of a single major industry, or of several industries. Whatever the case, the result is a reduction in per capita income and consequent purchasing power. Because of the multiplier effect, a cutback in basic employment activity will bring about a downturn in supportive, nonbasic activities, resulting in further unemployment. In some instances, a depressed region may recover from its economic plight rather quickly; in other examples, the recovery period may be quite long and the economic adjustments very painful.

A third type of problem region identified by Smith is the *congested region*. Such a region is at the opposite extreme from the underdeveloped region, as the congested region has too much development in the sense that diseconomies occur (see Chapter 7). The transportation system has become clogged; the intensity of land use is very great (high land rent); great strain is placed on resources such as water supply, fire and police protection, and sewage disposal; and other environmental problems may exist. As a result of these problems, the cost of manufacturing increases, making these regions less and less advantageous. In extreme cases, congested regions may evolve into depressed regions, especially if new markets or ample resources exist elsewhere to attract industrial investment away from the congested region.

Once problems of underdeveloped, depressed, or congested regions have been identified, some

solution may be posed by governmental policy and planning.[23] One policy, sometimes referred to as the *national demand approach*, asserts that competitive market forces operate so that in the long run there will be an optimum spatial distribution of industrial production. Following the notion of the national demand approach, we see that it makes no sense to intervene governmentally. A region is depressed because it is not competitive, and noncompeting regions do not deserve intervention and assistance. After all, some other region will be growing and will be benefiting. Migration will redistribute population, creating new markets, which will attract manufacturing, and so on. The policy of doing nothing is simply a policy embracing a belief in this national demand approach, with the faith that all is well—if not now, then in the future.

A much more commonly accepted viewpoint is the *theory of planned adjustment.* This approach involves governmental intervention in the industrial economy precisely because competitive market forces do not lead to an optimal spatial distribution of manufacturing activity. The United States, along with industrialized countries in general, follows the planned adjustment approach, and, of course, the socialist or planned economies go several steps further. Whereas the national demand approach focuses strictly on economic issues, the planned adjustment viewpoint takes into account social, environmental, political, and even military factors. These factors may be deemed to be more important than purely economic considerations. Policy decisions must be made, for example, between federal assistance to highways in congested Megalopolis and in underdeveloped regions of Appalachia, with direct implications for manufacturers in each of the two regions.

In Chapter 3, the growth pole theory of economic development was discussed. The role of

[23]Gordon C. Cameron, *Regional Economic Development: The Federal Role* (Washington, D.C.: Resources for the Future, 1970).

industrial activity at the growth pole is fundamental to the spatial pattern of economic development within the region as a whole. Thus, the economic area may be divided into the core region, containing the growth pole, and the peripheral region, which has less population and lower per capita income. Various centripetal forces work to maintain the viability of the core region, such as in the historical American Manufacturing Belt. At the same time, other forces of a centrifugal type induce industrial expansion in the peripheral regions, such as in the U.S. South.

Herbert Giersch has proposed a theory relating the effect of political boundaries on the spatial distribution of manufacturing production.[24] He assumed that transportation costs were proportional to distance, à la Weber. Like von Thünen (see Chapter 13), he posited a large plain encircled by a desert, which acts as a total barrier to trade beyond the circular plain. Initially, Giersch also assumed an equal spatial distribution of resources, population, and manufacturing production units over the plain.

In Giersch's model, the lower the costs of transportation and the greater the economies of scale, the larger will be the market areas of the industrial producers and the fewer will be the number of producers. Over time, the location at the center of the plain becomes more favored, because of transportation cost advantages and consequent production-scale economies. These advantages cumulate over time, leading to a dominant agglomerative center (core region) of industrial activity and a much less dense and less favored peripheral area near the desert border. With the accumulation of capital for growth and the recognized locational advantages of the central location, manufacturing in Giersch's model undergoes a redistribution from a spatially even pattern to the highly clustered one.

If instead of one large plain, as Giersch initially

[24]Herbert Giersch, "Economic Union Between Nations and the Location of Industries," *Review of Economic Studies* 17 (1949–1950), pp. 87–97.

assumed in his model, the plain becomes divided by national boundaries that restrict trade, the agglomerative advantages will not be allowed to develop as fully at the center of the plain. Instead, several much less industrialized centers will develop in each of the countries. In turn, the elimination of national boundaries as barriers to trade will favor the agglomeration centrally located in the plain. On the other hand, retention of national borders will be advantageous to industrial areas located peripherally within the plain but centrally within national borders. The application of the Giersch model fits well with industrial Europe (p. 91).

The locational consequences of the formation of a European Union, for example, can now be described by the following statement: The abolition of barriers to inter-European trade and to inter-European movement of factors will weaken the deglomeration effect of national agglomeration and will thus enforce international, or more precisely, inter-European, agglomeration. It will strengthen the attractiveness of the highly industrialized center for both labor and capital. Towns and regions with artificial advantages due to national agglomeration will become disadvantageous. On the other hand, particular regions near the industrial center, which have suffered under the depressing influence of national borders, will gain.

Regional Impact of Multiplant Corporations

In the major industrialized economies of the world, manufacturing activity is controlled more and more by large corporations. These corporations may not only be quite diversified in what they manufacture, but they also may be geographically fragmented because they produce in multiple plants spread throughout a country or the world. (That is, they may involve multinational corporations.) Securing materials for manufacture may be highly complex geographically, for items produced by one level of a particular plant may be shipped by the corporation for further manufacture by the same corporation at a different plant.

As a result, multiplant firms may make locational decisions on a somewhat different basis than firms with a single plant. Multiplant firms are able to spread their risks by producing at several locations (see Chapter 10). If labor problems, for example, occur at one plant site, production may be increased at another plant location with little effect on the corporation, depending on labor laws. On the other hand, the negative effect on the regional economy may be considerable. A corporation, for instance, may stand to lose 100 units of production per day at location A because, let us say, of an assembly-line malfunction. Even if plant B produces the same item at a higher cost, it makes sense to shift as much production from A to B as possible, assuming that a market exists for the items produced.

With the worldwide growth of corporations, it is increasingly common for the manufacturing plant to be located far from the corporate headquarters controlling the production decisions. Quite often, these decisions are not made on the basis of a single plant's locational advantages or shortcomings, nor on that of the community's or region's. Rather they are made on the basis of the external firms' objectives and their tradeoffs. There are several reasons why manufacturing activity within a region may be controlled and directed from headquarters beyond the region.[25] First, an indigenous manufacturer may relocate his headquarters in another region. One example is the manufacturer in a small urban center near Dallas who moves his office to Dallas to take advantage of business services not provided in the small center. Second, regional manufacturing growth may occur more rapidly in firms that are externally controlled than among the indigenous plants, giving a differential advantage to extra-

regional locations. Third, external control of a region's manufacturing may increase because of a faster rate of growth in the establishment of branch plants—having headquarters in other regions—than among local manufacturing starts. Finally, external control may increase simply through acquisition and merger, whereby extra regionally headquartered firms buy up indigenous manufacturing plants.

What impact does external control have on a region's manufacturing? The answer depends, according to Peter Dicken, on the "actual or potential clash of interests between the goals of multiplant business enterprises, many of which now operate on a global rather than a national scale, and the interests of the local communities." Thus, external control may lead to either positive or negative impact. In some cases, external capital may, through the multiplier effect, create economic growth in a region that otherwise lacks capital for industrialization. Local resources may be tapped, for instance, to stimulate the regional economy, which may eventually lead to increased per capita income.

Dicken summarizes other examples in which external financial and decision-making control of a region's manufacturing have harmful effects on the region.

Decisions regarding the plant, its scale, type of operations and even its continued existence, are made elsewhere. The plant's connections with local suppliers of inputs, particularly of business services, may be either severed or at a lower level than might be the case if the plant were an autonomous unit. These two elements, the integration of the plant within a much larger multiplant organization and the nature of its local linkages, may produce undesirable side-effects on the region in question. One such side effect is the leakage of some locally generated income via profits remitted to the head office region. Another is the loss of business to local suppliers. The removal of high level functions and the reduced use of local inputs may, in turn,

[25]Peter Dicken, "Enterprise and Geographical Space: Some Issues in the Study of External Control and Regional Development," *Regional Studies* 19 (1976), pp. 401–412.

attenuate the region's occupational ladder, less- ening higher level career opportunities and leading to the out-migration of potential entre- preneurs or professional and executive workers. Such losses may be reinforced either by the clo- sure of the plant, if its continued existence ceases to fit overall corporate needs, or by the substitution of capital for labour and the shift towards the employment of lower skilled work- ers. In the longer term, there may be a general decline in the level of regional income and pos- sibly a lessening of the region's attractiveness for further investment either by local entrepre- neurs or outside investors. (p. 405)

Again, whether or not external control of a re- gion's manufacturing is beneficial depends on the degree to which local-regional interests coincide with external corporate decisions. Many com- munities apparently believe that the advantages of attracting industry to their industrial parks outweigh any harmful effects of external control. On the other hand, with certain **footloose indus- tries** (those having little investment in plant and a set of production costs that do not vary much geographically), a community may find that when the five-year tax break they gave to attract the manufacturer expires, the manufacturer picks up and rather suddenly goes elsewhere.

U.S. PATTERNS OF MANUFACTURING

Different types of manufacturing industries se- lect different kinds of locations. The result is a spatial pattern of production that reflects the net effects of the various factors of production (Fig- ures 11.6 and 11.7). Some industrial patterns show a strong orientation to material inputs, as with tobacco manufacturing in the states of North Carolina, Virginia, and Kentucky. Lumber and wood products also show the influence of material sites (compare the Pacific states with those of the Great Plains). Yet another example of the effect of material source on location is in petroleum and coal products manufacturing.

Manufacturing that is usually located in met-

ropolitan areas includes printing, publishing, and a wide variety of instruments. Transportation equipment manufacturing, reflecting Detroit's long-standing role, is heavily concentrated in Michigan and also in California because of Cal- ifornia's large market demand and great distance from the Midwest. The spatial patterns of textile manufacturing suggest the important role of low- cost labor in the South. It is interesting to com- pare the maps in Figures 11.6 and 11.7 to deter- mine which are similar and which are especially different. How similar are the maps of primary metals and fabricated metals? What explains the map of food and kindred products, population or agriculture regions? Or is it both?

Commercial Biotechnology

Commercial biotechnology firms represent a new and distinct kind of manufacturing activity. Bio- technology uses living organisms or their parts to create or modify products, such as improving plants and animals and developing microorgan- isms for particular uses. Commercial biotechnol- ogy firms began forming in the United States in 1976 and have grown rapidly in number (Figure 11.8). In stark contrast to, say, textile manufac- turing with its orientation toward low-cost labor, commercial biotechnology firms have extremely high labor costs, with a high percentage of the employees having Ph.D. degrees. Biotechnology firms are highly localized. They are typically as- sociated with major universities in or near large metropolitan areas which offer labor agglomer- ation economies and local infrastructure, such as the Boston to Washington axis (including New York, Philadelphia, and Baltimore), Chicago, San Francisco and environs, and southern Cali- fornia (Los Angeles and San Diego). Empirical findings also suggest that federal and state reg- ulations, taxes, product marketing capabilities, and sources of R&D funding are leading factors in determining biotech company growth.[26] Table

[26]See Peter Haug and Philip Ness, "Industrial Location De- cisions of Biotechnology Organizations," *Economic Devel- opment Quarterly* 7 (1993), pp. 390–402.

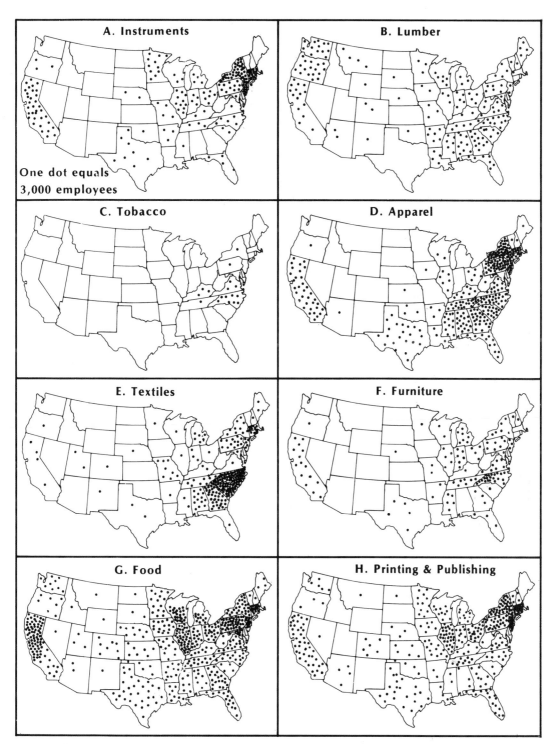

Figure 11.6 The spatial distributions of employment, by state, of varioius kinds of manufacturing.

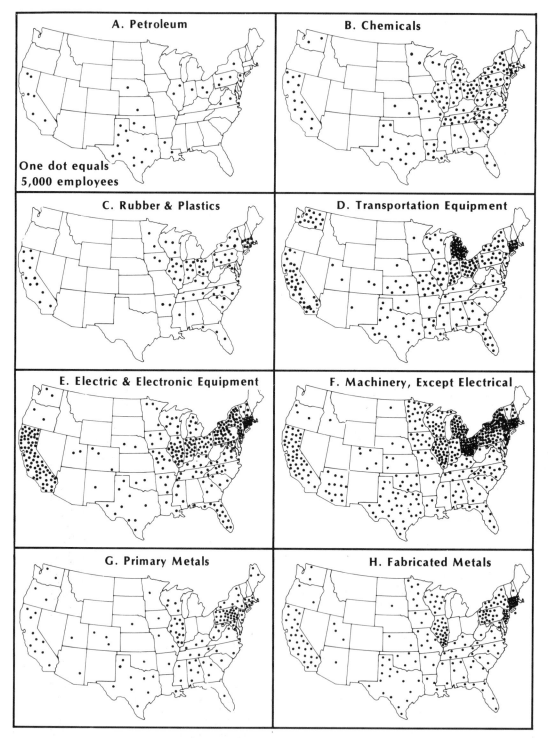

Figure 11.7 The spatial distribution of employment, by state, of various kinds of manufacturing.

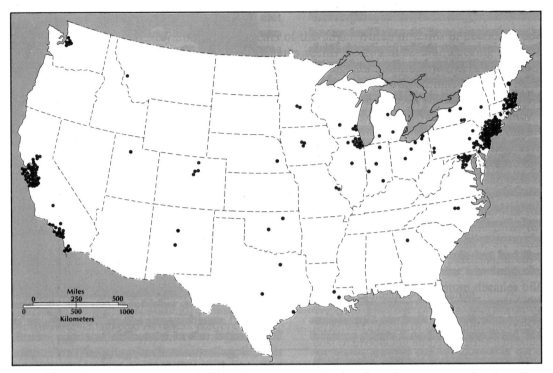

Figure 11.8 The location of commercial biotechnology firms, showing clustering near selected metropolitan areas.

11.2 provides regional employment data for the major biotechnology concentrations in the United States for the year 1990, which correspond to the regional clusters shown in Figure 11.8.[27]

It is projected that commercial biotechnology will have a great impact on society and the world economy. For those metropolitan areas, as well as those countries, with biotechnology firms, this fast-growing activity will likely act as an export base, that is, exporting technology and importing dollars. The widespread applications in biotechnology are just beginning to be appreciated. The industrial applications of biotechnology to pharmaceuticals (the production of such proteins as

insulin, interferon, and human serum albumin, antibiotics, and vaccines) is only beginning, with enormous medical potential. Biotechnological applications in animal and plant agriculture promise significant results, especially in plant growth and change, as world population continues to expand. Other areas of application include chemistry, the environment, energy production, and bioelectronics. Biotechnology firms will play a key and growing role in the economy of those metropolitan areas, regions, and countries that attract this new technological expertise. Currently, the United States is the world leader in commercial biotechnology, but Japan is likely to become the major competitor in the near future, for the Japanese government has targeted biotechnology for funding its commercial development.

[27]Ibid., p. 393.

Table 11.2 Employment in U.S. Biotechnology Concentrations (1990)[a]

Regional Concentration	Biotechnology Employment	Percentage of U.S. Biotechnology Employment
San Francisco Bay area	12,456	25.0
New York-Tri State area	9177	14.1
Boston area	5492	11.0
Washington, D.C. area	4343	8.7
San Diego	3329	6.7
Greater Seattle	2183	4.4
Los Angeles/Orange County	2102	4.2
Iowa	1440	2.9
Philadelphia	1041	2.1
Ohio	1005	2.0
Minnesota	998	2.0
St. Louis area	987	2.0
Texas	885	1.8
Utah	736	1.5
Georgia	714	1.4
Indiana	710	1.4
Colorado	621	1.3
Illinois	513	1.0
Other regions	3227	6.5
Total	49,825	100.0

[a]As adopted from Haug and Ness (1993), p. 393.

WORLD MANUFACTURING PATTERNS

As is true of other distributions of human activity, manufacturing is most unevenly scattered over the earth (Figure 11.9). In general, the world pattern of manufacturing corresponds with the distribution of economic development levels (see Chapter 3), since manufacturing investment and productivity are major ingredients in a region or country's economic development. Even though manufacturing typically occupies a small site and represents a small amount of the total land use of a region or country, the importance of manufacturing to the economy, as we have already seen, is very great indeed. At the global level, manufacturing is the driving and dominant force behind both international production and trade.[28]

[28]Peter Dicken, *Global Shift: The Internationalization of Economic Activity* 2nd ed. (New York: Guilford Press, 1992), Chapter 2, pp. 16–46.

The world distribution of manufacturing shows several rather distinct concentrations of activities. One of the largest is associated with the United States and southeastern Canada. A second large world concentration is in Western Europe, especially in England, France, Belgium, the Netherlands, Germany, Switzerland, and northern Italy. Various manufacturing outliers are found in the Scandinavian countries to the north, in Spain to the south, and, most importantly, in the countries of Eastern Europe, notably Poland. Russia has several manufacturing concentrations, especially the Moscow region. The Ukraine, the Volga, the Urals, and western Siberia also have important concentrations. Finally, Japan constitutes a major manufacturing region, running from Tokyo to Osaka.

Many other areas of the world have important concentrations of manufacturing, at least on a local level. These areas, however, do not stand out on a world scale. As examples, manufacturing is

Inside the Braviken Paper Mill in Nonköping, Sweden. At one end of the paper machine, logs are shredded into wood chips; at the other end, the machine spins out a continuous sheet of paper at 60 miles per hour.

found in major cities of the People's Republic of China (an area likely to develop rather rapidly in importance), in India, in Australia, in selected areas of Latin America (Brazil, Argentina, and Mexico in particular), and, to a lesser extent, in metropolitan areas of Africa.

Notwithstanding the uneven geographic distribution of manufacturing as an economic activity, the bulk of manufacturing value added remains highly concentrated in three geographic regions which comprise the *economic triad*—the three dominant production and investment sources and sinks in the world economy. The economic triad is composed of a North American contingent (the United States and Canada), Japan, and a Western European contingent (whose big players include Germany, France, the United King-

dom, and Italy). These mature, industrialized, market-based economies hold the vast majority of wealth, technological know-how, and production capacity in the world. Together they form the manufacturing core of the world economy. Excluding the production regions of Russia and China (formidable in their own right), the economic triad accounted for approximately 75 percent of the world's total manufacturing value added in the mid-1980s.[29]

Outside of several significant manufacturing regions in Eastern Europe, nations in two regions account for a large share of the remain-

[29]K. Champ and D. F. Walker, *Industrial Location* (Oxford, UK: Basil Blackwell, 1991), Chapter 10 (pp. 193–223).

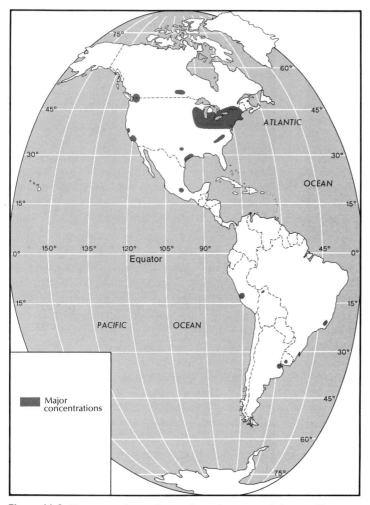

Figure 11.9 Concentrations of manufacturing around the world.

ing percentage of manufacturing value added: the rapidly industrializing nations of East Asia and Latin America. Of the two, the East Asian group has been far more successful in terms of promoting export-based manufacturing. This success is easily explained by their broad-based view of *economic nationalism*—a national commitment to economic growth and development as the primary goal and requirement for national security in an uncertain and potentially hostile

international environment. East Asian nations have been able both to take advantage of the expansion in international trade throughout the last three decades and to attract multinational corporations in their attempt to meet national economic development objectives. In contrast, the role of the state and its concerns about foreign economic (as opposed to political) domination in Latin American nations have promoted a more narrowly based view of economic nation-

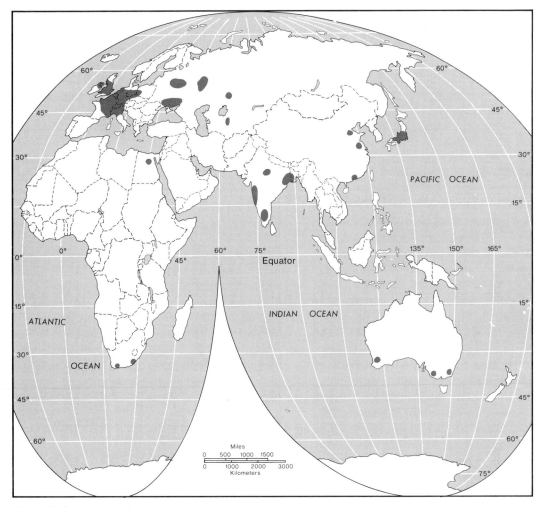

Figure 11.9 (continued)

alism (one rooted in the suspicion of exploitation).[30]

[30]See Christopher Ellison and Gary Gereffi, "Explaining Strategies and Patterns of Industrial Development," Chapter 14 of G. Gereffi and D. L. Wyman, *Manufacturing Miracles: Paths of Industrialization in Latin America and East Asia* (Princeton, N.J.: Princeton University Press, 1990), pp. 368–403; and also Albert Fishlow, "Latin American Failure Against the Backdrop of Asian Success," *Annals of the American Academy of Political and Social Science* 505, pp. 117–128.

Global Change and Shifts

Peter Dicken highlights three major changes that occurred between 1963 and 1987 within the seven dominant nations that comprise the economic triad. First is the substantial decline of the United States as a world leader of manufactured products. In 1963, the United States was responsible for approximately 40 percent of the world's manufacturing output. By 1987, its share had diminished to just under 25 percent, a position that is increasingly challenged by overseas competitors (mainly Japan). The United States is still, however, considered a center of gravity for global production. Second was the uneven and wildly fluctuating performance of the Western European nations during the period in question. Third, and more strikingly, was the stellar performance of Japan, a nation that experienced an average of 13.6 percent growth in manufacturing output during the 1960s (two and one-half times greater than that of the United States). Japan's share of world manufacturing output increased from just over 5 percent in 1963 to almost 20 percent by 1987.[31]

Still other nations stand out in terms of their phenomenal economic growth over the last two decades. Much of this growth has been directly tied to growth in manufacturing sectors and the expansion of the export base. These nations have been aptly labeled Newly Industrializing Countries or NICs. They continue to capture an increasing share of world exports. NICs held 12.4 percent of world exports in the mid-1980s, a dramatic increase over the mere 4 percent in the early 1960s. Of all the NICs, distinct geographic groups emerge, three of which share a similar locational attribute (an Asian connection).

The most prominent group of NICs is the so-called *four tigers* of the Pacific Rim—South Korea, Taiwan, Singapore, and Hong Kong. These nations have consistently exhibited double-digit growth rates in manufacturing output, steady increases in manufacturing exports, and GDP growth rates that far exceeded the world average of 3.1 percent during the 1980s.[32] Their success story has been largely mirrored, albeit to a lesser degree, by several other NICs within the same immediate geographic region—namely, the *four pussycats* of the Pacific Rim—Malaysia, Thailand, Indonesia, and the Philippines. Lastly, India (as a center of gravity for a potentially emerging Indian Ocean Rim) has exhibited impressive growth in its manufacturing base, with increasing average annual manufacturing production growth rates over the past three decades. India continues to upgrade its position as a destination for direct foreign investment partly due to its advantageous geographic location and its cheap and abundant labor force.

The recent integration of the coastal areas of China into the world economy has helped elevate China's economic development status: it now represents a significant manufacturing core within the Pacific Rim. Very few world economic analysts would dismiss the notion of China as a major player in the global economy come the next century. Perhaps China could best be described as the sleeping saber tooth of the Pacific Rim. Despite its population size and growth, it recorded a GDP per capita growth rate of 6.6 percent from 1985 to 1990, far outpacing the developed market economies, which recorded an average GDP per capita growth rate of only 2.5 percent over the same time period.[33]

Manufacturing-for-Export and Economic Growth: Some Empirical Evidence

The importance of establishing a manufacturing export base as a means to promote economic growth in developing regions is easily understood when we consider some recent empirical evidence. Table 11.3 provides a summary of the average growth rates in GDP for groups of developing economies classified by their export orientation from 1985 to 1990.[34] Note that nations characterized as exporters of manufactured goods demonstrate substantially higher eco-

---

[31]Dicken, *Global Shift*, pp. 22–23.

[32]Ibid., p. 26; and World Bank, *World Development Report 1991* (New York: Oxford University Press, 1991), pp. 206–207 and pp. 230–231.

[33]*Global Outlook 2000* (Washington, D.C.: United Nations Publications, 1990), p. 72. Note that "developed market economies" refer to the United States and Canada, the nations of Southern and Western Europe (excluding Cyprus, Malta, and former Yugoslavia), Australia, Israel, Japan, New Zealand, and South Africa.

[34]Ibid., p. 11.

Table 11.3 GDP and GDP per Capita (GDPPC) Growth Rates of Developing Nations [a] by Export Orientation

Orientation	Growth Rates, 1985–1990 [b]	
	GDP	GDPPC
Petroleum-exporting nations	1.3%	−1.3%
High-income oil exporters	1.5%	−2.5%
Primary commodity exporters	2.0%	−1.1%
Major exporters of manufactured products	4.9%	+3.0%

[a]Developing nations, as defined by the United Nations in *Global Outlook 2000*, include the whole of Latin America and the Caribbean, Africa (other than South Africa), and Asia (excluding China, Vietnam, North Korea, Mongolia, and Japan).
[b]At 1980 dollars and exchange rates.

Source: Global Outlook 2000 (UN, 1990), p. 11.

nomic growth rates than do nations engaged in either the export of primary-sector commodities (fuels, minerals, and agricultural commodities) or petroleum. Although all groups listed experienced positive growth rates in GDP from 1985 to 1990, only those nations classified as major exporters of manufactured goods (in this case Brazil, the Four Tigers of the Pacific Rim, and China) were found to have both positive GDP and GDP per capita growth rates. By contrast, exporters of primary-sector commodities and petroleum-exporting nations, showed negative GDP per capita growth rates during the same period. These figures suggest that the benefits of more moderate economic growth in association with a nonmanufacturing export base were largely reversed by population growth.

THE GLOBALIZATION OF PRODUCTION

Several forces of change have led to the restructuring of production activities in the world economy. These forces continue to influence and reshape patterns of manufacturing:

1. "transnationalization" of capital—the increase of the propensity for capital to flow across international borders;

2. proliferation of "multinationals" or transnationalized firms and the subsequent globalization of production systems (where the stages of production and subsequent value added is spread across many regions);

3. the emergence of "global capitalism" as the prevailing economic system (as opposed to a system driven by regionally concentrated manufacturing);

4. "flexible" production;

5. increasing foreign direct investment;

6. "trade liberalization" (lessening barriers and restrictions in the flow of commodities and services across international boundaries); and

7. the reemergence of "regionalism"—processes which tend to promote the organization of alliances and/or agreements that are instrumental in the formation of regional or continental trading zones or blocs to enhance the transnationalization process and promote trade on a restricted geographical basis.

The growth of global product markets and emerging markets in developing regions and the acceleration of a global production network has been aided by the transnationalization of capital and multinationals. As emerging markets in developing nations continue to grow and the demand for aircraft, communications and electrical equipment, computers, locomotives, construction supplies, and transport vehicles, etc. continues, production and export possibilities increase as firms and production go global. Industries like robotics, fiber optics, lasers, advanced semi-conductors, satellite networks, plastics and synthetic materials, energy technology, and precision machinery continue to expand globally, reshaping both the production landscape and the nature of flows and linkages. Despite the globalization phenomenon, increasing polarization of the world economy, regionalization of trade, and uneven economic development have left many regions without a globally competitive manufacturing base.[35]

Further Readings

Borchert, John R. "Major Control Points in American Economic Geography." *Annals of the Association of American Geographers* 68 (1978), pp. 214–232.

Cameron, Gordon C. *Regional Economic Development: The Federal Role*. Washington, D.C.: Resources for the Future, 1970.

Chapman, Keith. "Corporate Systems in the United Kingdom Petro-Chemical Industry." *Annals of the Association of American Geographers* 64 (1974), pp. 126–137.

Chapman, Keith. *Industrial Location*. 2nd ed. Oxford, UK: Basil Blackwell, 1991.

Cohen, Stephen S., and John Zysman. *Manufacturing Matters: The Myth of the Post-Industrial Economy*. New York: Basic Books, 1987.

Collins, L., and D. Walker, eds. *Locational Dynamics of Manufacturing Activity*. New York: Wiley, 1975.

Dicken, Peter. "The Multiplant Business Enterprise and Geographical Space: Some Issues in the Study of External Control and Regional Development." *Regional Studies* 10 (1976), pp. 401–412.

Dicken, Peter. "A Note on Location Theory and the Large Business Enterprise." *Area* 9 (1977), pp. 138–145.

Dicken, Peter. *Global Shift: The Internationalization of Economic Activity*. 2nd ed. New York: Guilford Press, 1992.

Dicken, Peter., and P. E. Lloyd. *Location in Space: Theoretical Perspectives in Economic Geography*. 3rd ed. New York: Harper & Row, 1990.

Dunning, J. H. *The Globalization of Business: The Challenge of the 1990's*. New York: Routledge (1993).

Feller, I. "Invention, Diffusion and Industrial Location." In L. Collins and D. F. Walker, eds. *The Locational Dynamics of Manufacturing Activity*. New York: Wiley, 1975, pp. 83–107.

Fik, T. J. *The Geography of Economic Development: Regional Changes, Global Challenges*. New York: McGraw-Hill (1997).

Gertler, Meric S. "Flexibility Revisited: Districts, Nation-States, and the Forces of Production." *Transactions of the Institute of British Geographers* 17 (1992), pp. 259–278.

Gibb, R. "Regionalism in the World Economy," in *Continental Trading Blocs: The Growth of Regionalism in the World Economy*, Gibb, R. and W. Michalak eds., New York: Wiley (1994), pp. 1–36.

Gibb, R., and W. Michalak. *Continental Trading Blocs: The Growth of Regionalism in the World Economy*. New York: Wiley (1994).

Giersch, Herbert. "Economic Union Between Nations and the Location of Industries." *Review of Economic Studies* 17 (1949–1950), pp. 87–97.

Glasmeier, Amy K. *The High-Tech Potential: Economic Development in Rural America*. New Brunswick, N.J.: Center for Urban Policy Research, 1991.

Glick, L. A. *Understanding the North American Free Trade Agreement*. Boston: Kluwer (1994).

Hall, Peter, and Ann Markusen, eds. *Silicon Landscapes*. London: Allen & Unwin, 1985.

Hamilton, F. E. I., ed. *Spatial Perspectives on Industrial Organization and Decision-Making*. New York: Wiley, 1974.

Hamilton, F. E. I., ed. *Contemporary Industrialization: Spatial Analysis and Regional Development*. London: Longman, 1978.

Hamilton, F. E. I., ed. *Industrial Change: International Experience and Public Policy*. London: Longman, 1978.

Haug, P., and P. Ness. "Industrial Location Decisions of Biotechnology Organizations," *Economic Development Quarterly*, 7(1993) pp. 390–402.

Jusenius, Carol L., and Larry C. Ledebur. *Documenting the "Decline" of the North*. Economic Development Research Report, Department of Commerce: Washington, D.C., June 1978.

Krugman, P. R., and A. Venables. *Globalization and the Inequality of Nations*. Cambridge, Mass.: National Bureau of Economic Research (1995).

Michalak, W. "The Political Economy of Trading

[35]Fik, T. J., *The Geography of Economic Development: Regional Changes, Global Challenges*. New York: McGraw-Hill (1997), Chapter 8 (pp. 437–532).

Blocs," in *Continental Trading Blocs: The Growth of Regionalism in the World Economy*, Gibb, R. and W. Michalak eds., New York: Wiley (1994), pp. 37–72.

Michie, J., and J. G. Smith eds. *Managing the Global Economy*. Oxford: Oxford University Press (1995).

Norton, R. D., and J. Rees. "The Product Cycle and the Spatial Decentralization of American Manufacturing." *Regional Studies* 13 (1979), pp. 141–151.

Pred, A. *City-Systems in Advanced Economies: Past Growth, Present Processes and Future Development Options*. New York: Wiley, 1977.

Rees, John. "Manufacturing Headquarters in a Post-Industrial Urban Context." *Economic Geography* 54 (October 1978), pp. 337–354.

Sachar, A., and S. Oberg eds. *The World Economy and the Spatial Organization of Power*. Brookfield, Vermont: Gower (1990).

Schott, J. J. "Trading Blocs and the World Trading System," *The World Economy* 14, (1991), pp. 1–17.

Scott, Allen J. *New Industrial Spaces*. London: Pion, 1988.

Semple, R. K. "Recent Trends in the Spatial Concentration of Corporate Headquarters." *Economic Geography* 49 (1973), pp. 309–318.

Shambaugh, D. ed. *Greater China: The Next Superpower*. New York: Oxford University Press (1995).

Smith, David M. *Industrial Location: An Economic Geographic Analysis*. 2nd rev. ed. New York: Wiley, 1981.

South, R. B. "Transnational Maquiladora Location," *Annals of the Association of American Geographers* 80 (1990), pp. 549–570.

Stoddard, E. R. *Maquila: Assembly Plants in Northern Mexico*. El Paso, Texas: Texas Western University Press, University of Texas at El Paso (1987).

Storper, M., and A. J. Scott. *Pathways to Industrialization and Regional Development*. London: Routledge (1992).

Thompson, John H. "Some Theoretical Considerations for Manufacturing Geography." *Economic Geography* 42 (1966), pp. 356–365.

Townroe, P. *Planning Industrial Growth*. London: Leonard Hill Books, 1976.

Watts, H. D. *Industrial Geography*. New York: Wiley, 1987.

PART FIVE

Energy

CHAPTER 12

The Economic-Geography of Energy

◇

In . . . the long history of humanity . . . traditional belief was that to survive, people had to fight nature: people were weak and nature was hostile. It is only since the conquest of fossil energy that things have changed and that to survive, people have to protect nature instead of fight it.

—BASED ON JACQUES COUSTEAU, 1979, *THE OCEAN WORLD*
NEW YORK: ABRADLE PRESS, P. 210.

INTRODUCTION

What is this commodity we call energy? Common definitions of energy are: (1) the capacity to do work; and (2) power efficiently exerted. But in an organized society energy transcends the physics terminology because the use of energy changes the human-environmental interaction. In this chapter we focus on the consequences to our economic landscape from energy's intimate involvement in every segment of the nation's economic geography and from its centrality to the creation of what most of the nation's residents have come to accept as a high quality of life. This chapter analyzes energy production and consumption both at the international and U.S. national scale. Three principal themes are developed in this chapter:

- *Location and spatial distribution* What kind of energy resources are there? Where are these resources located? Who uses these resources, and where do they use them? Where should energy production facilities, such as nuclear power plants and nuclear waste facilities, be located?

- *Spatial allocation and movement* How is the energy transferred from where it is produced

to where it is consumed? How do these energy transportation networks affect industrial location?

- *Futurism* What will be the energy resources of the future? How will society and economic geography adjust to a depletion of the earth's nonrenewable resources?

As is true of other geographic phenomena, the characteristics and effects of energy differ by scale of analysis. In this chapter, the information on energy is divided according to geographic scale: international, national, and local. Because the energy which the end-user consumes at the local level is a result of a myriad of decisions at the national and international levels, those issues that arise on the international scale are important at national and local scales as well. Thus, although the present work has scale that is discrete and linear (from small scale to large scale), any constraint on its organization is more a function of having to write within a printed textbook medium than it is of adhering to reality: scale should be recognized as being more like a three-dimensional hologram with local, national, and international considerations all affecting one another. For example, cascading downward in scale, we have world trade in energy and energy politics affecting the nation's economy, which influences the objectives of the nation, which in turn affects our individual lifestyle.

ENERGY IN THE INTERNATIONAL ARENA: TRADE AND GEOPOLITICS

Energy and technological change are the primary components of economic development. Energy shapes, and is shaped by, changing technology. In order to sustain a high standard of living and a high rate of economic growth, people in technologically advanced economies have come to expect and depend on the easy availability of inexpensive energy. The control of energy and per capita utilization has even been used to rank a nation's overall stage of economic development. Because most nations aspire to sustained and high levels of economic development, the mastery of energy and the geopolitics of energy are center stage to each nation's foreign policy.

Energy geopolitics have led nations to adopt foreign policies that would be viewed as intolerable if applied to the nations' own residents. Contrary to the democratic values that a nation's residents may personally have, the quest to safeguard the supply of energy and its energy transportation networks has been considered sufficient reason for the support of foreign governments whose despotic leadership act only in the interest of a few power elite.

International energy geopolitics can define national energy policy because what transpires in the international arena quickly translates into the affecting nations' economies and populist temperament. For example, because of the Arab oil embargo in 1973 and 1974, strategic petroleum reserves (SPR) were established. In 1977, the equivalent of just one day of petroleum imports was stored in the SPR. The SPR increased to 115 days in 1985. However, since 1985 the SPR

has declined to 81 days.[1] The number of days' equivalent of imports in the SPR can be interpreted as a measure of perceived security from disruption of linkages to foreign suppliers and the importance of this security. Decline in the SPR is evidence of the decision makers' belief that disruptions in the international flow of petroleum is either unlikely or that the United States can correct disruptions in linkages within 81 days.

World Energy Overview

Worldwide primary energy production in 1997 was 365 quadrillion Btu's, an increase of over 25% compared to 1978 production.[2] Primary forms of energy include the conventional fossil fuels of coal, crude oil, as well as hydropower and nuclear power. A Btu (British Thermal Unit) is the amount of energy required to raise the temperature of one pound of water from 39.2°F to 40.2°F.[3] One-quadrillion Btu's is 45 million short tons[4] of coal, 170 million barrels of crude oil, or 28 days of U.S. petroleum imports. Electricity is a secondary source of energy since it is manufactured from other energy sources: heat to drive a steam-turbine comes from the primary forms of energy. In 1986, the then U.S.S.R. surpassed the U.S. as the world leader in energy production. In 1996, Russia produced 12 percent of the world's energy. China became the world's third largest

[1]The principal statistical source used throughout this chapter is the *Annual Energy Review*, Energy Information Administration, annual volumes.

[2]U.S. energy production by contrast was 61 quadrillion Btu's in 1978 and 70 quadrillion in 1996.

[3]One Btu is the equivalent of about 0.25 food calories. Five-hundred Btu's are the equivalent of a 5-ounce glass of table wine. One-million Btu's is equivalent to 90 pounds of coal, 120 pounds of oven-dried hardwood, or 8 gallons of automobile gasoline.

[4]Two thousand pounds is a short ton, 1.102 short tons is a metric ton, and 1.120 short tons is a long ton; 6.65 U.S. barrels is a short ton, and 1.25 short tons is an average cord of dry hardwood.

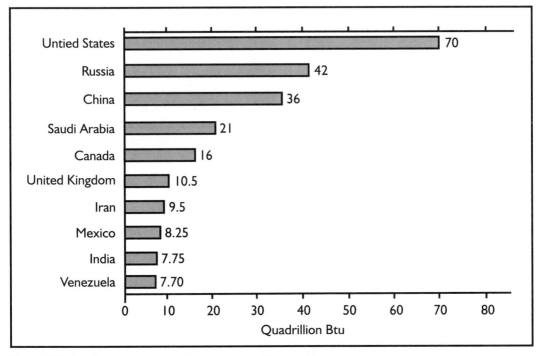

Figure 12.1 Leading energy producing countries of the world.

energy producer in 1982; its 1996 energy output was 35 quadrillion Btu's or nearly 10 percent of the total world production. The U.S., Russia, and China together account for 42 percent of total world primary energy production. Figure 12.1 shows world primary energy production by top producing countries for 1996.

The production of energy is not evenly distributed among world regions. Figure 12.2 shows primary energy production by world region. The Western Hemisphere leads other large geographic divisions of the globe in primary energy production. Excluding the United States and Canada, the remaining countries of the Western Hemisphere added only 7 percent to world production. Including the United States and Canada, the Western Hemisphere accounted for nearly one-third of world production of energy in 1996. Eastern Europe and Russia accounted for about 15 percent. The Far East and Oceania accounted for about 16 percent. The Mideast ac-

counted for only 13 percent, and the African continent for roughly half that amount.

The top three energy producing world regions increased primary energy output at similar rates during the 1990s. The same period saw Africa and Western Europe maintaining steady levels of production of primary energy. In comparison,

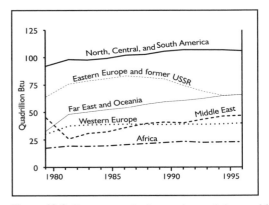

Figure 12.2 Energy producing regions of the world.

the Middle East appears quite volatile in production, beginning a significant decline in 1979, but in the late 1980s and 1990s, increasing production slightly faster than the rate shown for the other top world energy-producing regions.

In the Western Hemisphere, the greatest percentage increases over the least decade have come from Mexico and Canada. The United States is the largest producer and exceeded in absolute terms the increase in primary energy produced by either Mexico or Canada. One might speculate that Mexico's ability to produce energy was a compelling argument for the United States to include Mexico in NAFTA (the North American Free Trade Agreement).

Dominant World Energy Source: Location and Spatial Distribution

The dominant primary source of energy in the world is crude oil and natural gas. In 1996, 60 percent of world primary energy was attributable

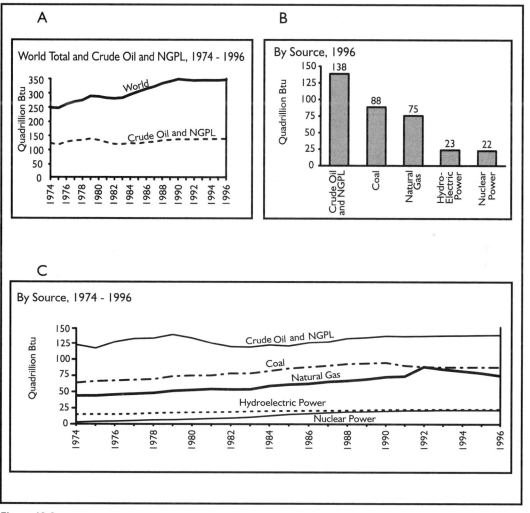

Figure 12.3 Primary sources of world energy produced.

to crude oil and natural gas; coal followed behind with 25 percent. Far less significant in world primary energy production is hydroelectric power and nuclear power, each with less than 1 percent of the share of total world primary energy production. For the past half-decade, crude oil, natural gas, and coal have increased at roughly the same linear rate. Hydroelectric power appears to have reached a steady state of energy production. Nuclear power production continues a modest increase. Primary sources of world energy are shown for 1996 in Figure 12.3.

World Crude Oil

World Petroleum Production. Worldwide, crude oil is the dominant primary source of energy because, per Btu, it is less expensive to transport than its nearest competitor, coal. For over the past decade, the United States has been steady in its production of crude oil, while Russia has leveled off from its high rate of growth when it was the core of the Soviet Union. Saudi Arabia has been very volatile since 1973. OPEC has attempted to act as a cartel to manipulate the world price of crude oil by restricting the amount of crude oil each member nation can produce. As is characteristic of all voluntary cartels, however, there is a strong incentive to cheat, and cheating has been commonplace among all the OPEC countries, but especially among Kuwait and the United Arab Emirates. OPEC's crude oil production increased steadily until 1973–74, when supplies were withheld for sale. In the early 1980s, OPEC output experienced a dramatic decrease.

Of the approximately 62 million barrels of crude petroleum produced worldwide per day, over 40 percent is produced by OPEC (Table 12.1). The leading producing country in the world is Saudi Arabia, accounting for more than 13 percent of the world production, followed by the United States (10 percent), and Russia (9 percent). In addition to Saudi Arabia, other leading OPEC producers are Iran, Venezuela,

Table 12.1 World Petroleum Production, 1996

World Regions	Millions of Barrels per Day
North America	12
Central and South America	5
Western Europe	5
Eastern Europe and Russia	7
Middle East	19
Africa	7
Far East and Oceania	7
OPEC	26

Nigeria, Indonesia, and Iraq. Leading non-OPEC producers besides the United States and Russia are China, Mexico, and the United Kingdom.

The Middle East leads the world in known oil reserves (Table 12.2). Russia accounts for only 5 percent of known world reserves of crude oil. The United States possesses less than 4 percent of known crude oil reserves; combined, the United States, Canada, and Mexico control only 10 percent of known world crude oil reserves. The entire Western Hemisphere harbors only 16 percent of known reserves. Western and Eastern Europe, along with Russia, control 7 percent of known world reserves of crude oil. Africa, the Far East, and Oceania together control 11 percent. Instead, five Middle Eastern countries (Saudi Arabia, Iraq, Kuwait, Iran, and United

Table 12.2 World Petroleum Reserves, 1995

World Regions	Percentage of World Total
North America	4.0
Latin America	12.4
Europe	2.6
Russia	4.8
Middle East	65.7
Asia and Australasia	4.5
OPEC	76.7
World	100.0

Table 12.3   World Petroleum Consumption, 1996

World Regions	Millions of Barrels per Day
North America	21.0
Central and South America	4.0
Western Europe	14.8
Eastern Europe and Russia	6.6
Middle East	3.5
Africa	2.2
Far East and Oceania	16.0

Arab Emirates) together control 64 percent of the known world crude oil reserves.

World Petroleum Consumption and Diversification.

The United States is the leading petroleum consumer, consuming over 30 percent of the total world production in 1990, followed by Germany with 12.3 percent and by Russia and Japan with 8 percent each (Table 12.3). Industrialized North America, Europe, and Japan are the leading consumers.

How is it determined which nation or region will buy or sell from another? The geographic distribution of oil reserves plays a role in who supplies crude oil. But Russia with fewer known reserves supplies more crude oil than Saudi Arabia with the largest known oil reserves. Hence, many geographical considerations help explain the world crude oil market. A geographer's first

expectation is for a country to have a bias to import from the nearest supplying place and thereby minimize shipping charges. Evidence supporting such distance bias can be found in the form of the United Kingdom (UK) selling nearly 70 percent of its crude oil exports to neighboring continental Western European countries. But international trade in crude oil is more complex than the geographer's measure of the friction of distance. Besides distance, long-standing friendly contact networks explain the trade between the UK and Western Europe, which was reinforced after the formation of the European Economic Community (EEC). Because there is a risk that contracts may not be filled, there is a bias against trade reliance with historically unfriendly or politically unstable regions.

Diversifying produces benefits. When mistrust exists, emanating from a history of conflict between countries, the supplying and consuming nations will tend to reduce their dependence on one another. Unlike Britain's reliance on Western Europe (the EEC) as customers, Mexico sells a smaller 45 percent of its primary energy production to its nearest neighbor, the United States. In other words, Mexico may trade with other countries because its decision makers prefer not to become wholly dependent on the changing whims of U.S. politics and trade policy.

Diversification is fundamental to understanding the economic geography of global energy

Table 12.4   Import and Export Dependence for U.S. and Its Major Crude Oil Supplying World Regions

	Middle East	Africa	Central & South America	Far East & Western Oceania	Canada & Europe	Mexico
% Of All U.S. Imported Oil From Given Region	0.211	0.213	0.151	0.066	0.080	0.259
% Of Exported Oil Going to U.S. From Given Region	0.101	0.261	0.500	0.197	0.144	0.618

Source: Energy Information Administration, *1989. Annual Energy Review*, 1989. Table 110: International Crude Oil Flows, 1987; p. 253.

Table 12.5 Import and Export Dependence for Japan and Its Major Crude Oil Supplying World Regions

	Middle East	Africa	Central & South America	Far East & Eastern Oceania	North Europe	America
% Of All Japan Imported Oil From Given Region	0.6803	0.0052	0.0016	0.2583	0.0003	0.0544
% Of Exported Oil Going to Japan From Region	0.2145	0.0042	0.0035	0.3923	0.0004	0.0797

Source: Energy Information Administration, 1989. Annual Energy Review, 1989. Table 110: International Crude Oil Flows, 1987; p. 253.

markets. An oil-importing country that purchases its entire imports from only one country would yield political and price leverage to the exporting country. Conversely, if an exporting country were to rely entirely on one customer, then the exporting nation would be in the undesirable situation of the consumer dictating terms of price as well as exerting considerable political influence over the exporting nation.

The United States is diversified from where crude oil is purchased (Table 12.4). In like manner, the Middle East is diversified from where it sells its crude oil. Just as the OPEC cartel may at times influence the world price of oil by restricting crude oil supplies, so too the United States, being the world's largest importer of crude oil, has a powerful leverage position. Of all crude oil exported in the world, 19 percent ends up in the United States. Canada has allowed itself to be placed in a monopsonistic or single-buyer relation with the United States; a staggering 98% of Canadian exported crude oil ends up in the United States. Because of proximity, the United States can offer the best price to Canada. But the same could also be said for the United States' southern neighbor, Mexico, which sells less than half of its crude oil exports to the United States. Mexico is more diversified by selling 30 percent of its exports to Western Europe and 12 percent to Japan. The inclusion of Mexico

in NAFTA should reverse this policy leading to greater dependence of Mexico on the U.S. energy market.

Japan is most heavily dependent on the Middle East as shown in Table 12.5, followed by nearby Far East and Oceania[5] Japan's economic geography is precariously positioned, with 68 percent of its crude oil coming from the turmoil-prone Middle East. On the one hand, Japan may be a greater energy risk taker than the United States. On the other hand, Japan may reason that its risk is quite low, believing that the United States will not tolerate disruption in the flow of crude oil from the Mideast, thereby reducing its own vulnerability.

World Coal

The United States leads the world in known recoverable reserves of coal, followed closely by Russia, as shown in Figure 12.4. This does not place the United States into an important leverage position as a seller of primary energy because, per Btu, bulky coal is more costly to transport long distances. Figure 12.5 shows the top

---

[5]Principal nations exporting crude oil in the Far East and Oceania are Australia, China, India, Japan, North Korea, New Zealand. Japan imports crude oil but then exports some of the refined finished product.

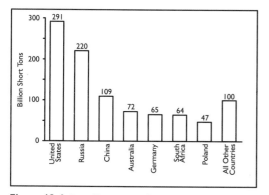

Figure 12.4 Leading countries of the world in coal reserves.

coal-producing countries. The former communist countries have been short on foreign exchange currency and have, therefore, placed a greater emphasis on exploiting their indigenous energy resources. The United States has nearly three times the known reserves of coal as does China, but China is the world's leading producer of coal.

Although coal per Btu is expensive to transport, at the same time it is often inexpensive to

mine. Australia is the world's leading exporter of coal; in 1989, it exported nearly 2,800 trillion Btu's of coal, followed by the United States with 2,200, and South Africa with 1,000. Japan, the world's leading importer of coal, imported 2,800 trillion Btu's of coal in 1997. South Korea was second with only 750 trillion Btu's imported. Japan imported 40 percent of its total coal imports from Australia, 18 percent from Canada, and 10 percent from the United States.

World Nuclear
The United States is the top generator of nuclear power with 30 percent of world production. France is second with 16 percent. Japan trails with 12 percent, followed by Germany at 7 percent and Russia with 5 percent. Since the beginning of commercial nuclear power in the United States in 1957 when there was only one operable unit, its nuclear energy production increased at a geometric rate to 110 operable units in 1989. The phenomenal rise of nuclear energy production did not continue during the 1990s; 1989 was the first year since 1957 that the percentage of

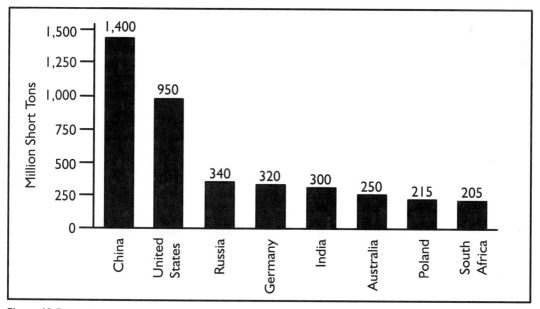

Figure 12.5 Leading coal producing countries of the world.

total electricity produced by nuclear facilities declined in the United States. Nuclear energy as a percentage of all U.S. energy produced increased, however, from 8.8 percent in 1990 to almost 10.0 percent today.

Some nuclear power plants have nearly completed their expected operating life. Others have been closed or are significantly limited in power-generating capability, such as the Three Mile Island (TMI) nuclear generating facility in Pennsylvania that experienced a near meltdown in March 1979. The owners of TMI are seeking to have customers pay the costs of the accident until the year 2014. The unit operated only four months. Excluding the cost of replacement and the original construction, the cost of dismantling and disposing of the damaged unit alone will exceed $195.6 million.

The notoriety of Three Mile Island, the meltdown of the nuclear power plant in Chernobyl, Ukraine, and the acknowledged clouds of radiation that have been allowed to be expelled from the Hanford Nuclear Weapons Facility in the Pacific Northwest have contributed to the rise of barriers to the construction of new nuclear power facilities.

THE NATIONAL ARENA: LOCATION AND SPATIAL DISTRIBUTION

U.S. National Overview

In the United States today, coal leads all other sources of primary energy (see Figure 12.6). Coal is followed by natural gas and then crude oil in total primary energy production. Twenty-nine percent of all primary energy produced goes into the production of the dominant secondary form of energy, electricity.

Which sectors of the U.S. economy are the leading consumers of energy? Until the early 1980s, energy consumption by industry was greater than the combined consumption of commercial and residential sectors. More recently,

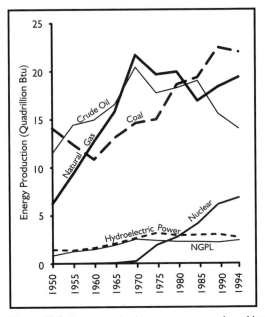

Figure 12.6 Sources of primary energy produced in the United States.

primarily because of air conditioning,[6] these sectors have been consuming the same amount, with transportation lagging somewhat behind (see Figure 12.7). In 1995, industry consumed 29.61 percent of energy produced, commercial and residential consumption was 29.47 percent, while 22.15 percent was consumed by transportation. The residual 18.77 percent was largely waste from the production and distribution of electricity!

In 1957, the United States passed into a new

[6]Without air conditioning, the high-rise urban skyline would not be possible. Air conditioning is regarded as part of the requisite milieu of phenomena that initiated the post World War II economic development of many cities in the Sunbelt. Without it, many of the manufacturing processes now carried on in the Sunbelt could not be performed. The temperature, and in the Southeast the temperature combined with high humidity, would be insufferable to many without air conditioning. Air conditioning brought with it a change in the "front-porch" conversational South to that of sealed houses radiating the hum of the air conditioner.

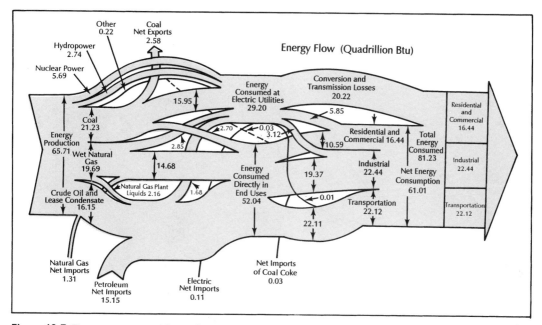

Figure 12.7 Energy consumed by major sectors of the U.S. economy.

era of increasing reliance on foreign energy sources (Figure 12.8). Liberal policy makers responding to the 1973–1974 embargo of oil exports to the United States by Arab nations questioned whether this energy transition made the United States too vulnerable.

Liberal policy supports platforms favoring greater use of energy resources that the nation controls; this translates into the nation increasing the exploitation of raw materials located in the United States and into greater emphasis on (1) those sources of energy that use native raw materials and (2) reduction of energy waste. Here the aspiration of self-reliance in energy comes into conflict with another liberal national goal: preserving natural landscapes and reducing the nations' environmental pollution.

A conservative counter-position is that the greater the mutual interdependence created through trade, the more peaceful the relations among trading partners. In this line of reasoning, trade in energy is viewed as no more or less im-

portant than trade in automobiles or corn: the least expensive energy is purchased by the end-user regardless of origin. Cheaper energy is more desirable than expensive energy. A strong national defense with high worldwide visibility is important to safeguard energy transportation networks and thereby contributes to the internal stability of energy-supplying countries: without a military presence and a quick response, energy geopolitics can lead to the closing of energy transportation networks or the cessation of energy production in supplying nations. This is in conflict with another conservative principle that market prices reflect true costs of production and that neither production nor consumption should be subsidized.

In the late 1990s, the United States is importing more energy than at any other time in its history, over 22 quadrillion Btu's, even higher than in the 1970s when the OPEC energy crisis was in full swing. As a reaction to the events of the 1970s, the United States greatly curtailed its re-

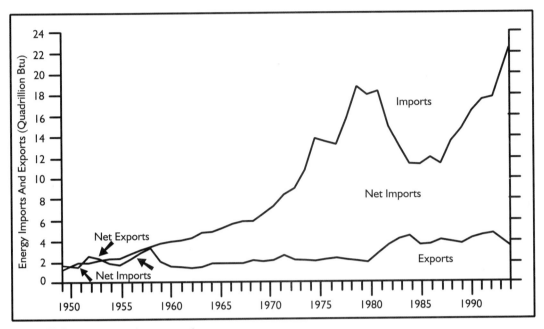

Figure 12.8 U.S. energy imports and exports.

liance on foreign energy sources in the late 1970s and early 1980s. Since 1985, the United States has experienced a dramatic rise in the net import of energy, with rising imports and a relatively constant level of exports (Fig. 12.8).

U.S. Electrical Power: Secondary Energy

Electricity is a secondary form of energy because other primary forms of energy are consumed for its production. Coal, natural gas, and petroleum are examples of primary sources of energy; their energy may be used directly without being converted to electricity.

Several problems are associated with the use of electricity—a secondary form of energy—in lieu of the direct consumption of primary sources. Most significant of these problems is the inefficiency of converting from a primary power source such as coal or natural gas to the secondary form. Energy loss is the difference between total energy input and the total sold to end-use consumers. Sixty-seven percent of energy is lost

in steam-electric power plants—which in the United States are mostly fueled by coal, nuclear or petroleum—in the thermodynamic conversion of heat energy into mechanical energy to turn the electricity-generating turbines; 9 percent is lost in transmission and distribution; 5 percent is lost in electricity that the steam-electric plants themselves use.

Another problem associated with electricity is the inability to store electrical power reserves, thereby requiring that generating facilities maintain large surplus generating capacity to meet daily and seasonally fluctuating peak load demands. Figure 12.9 reveals the typical seasonality of consumption of energy by the residential and commercial sectors. Because natural gas is a primary source of energy, it is generally less expensive per Btu; thus, it is commonly used for heating in cold-climate regions. Heating particularly by natural gas is the major contributor to the large cycles shown in Figure 12.11. Electricity consumption has cycles of consumption that are the inverse of natural gas. The warm months of

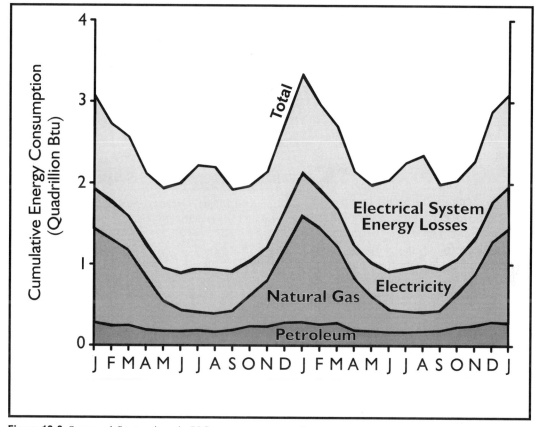

Figure 12.9 Seasonal fluctuations in U.S. energy consumption.

June, July, and August are the peak periods of electricity consumption, primarily because of air conditioning.

Of the 3,000 billion kilowatt-hours of electricity produced in the United States during 1994, about 56 percent was produced from coal-fired steam turbines, 21 percent from nuclear power-fired steam turbines, 10 percent from natural gas-fired steam turbines, 8 percent from hydroelectric power, 3 percent from petroleum (distillate fuel oil, residual fuel oil, including crude oil, jet fuel, and petroleum coke), and less than 1 percent from geothermal, wood, waste, wind, photovoltaic, and solar thermal energy. Figure 12.10 traces the sources of energy that have been used in the production of electricity since 1949. Coal

and nuclear power are the major primary energy sources for the production of electricity in the United States; both have gained in total share of electricity produced. In 1979, coal was responsible for 48 percent of electricity production from coal. Between 1979 and 1994, the share of electricity production from coal increased by 40 percent while nuclear power increased by 66 percent. Total electricity generated increased by 27 percent during the same period.

Hydropower, though a renewable source of power, has had a declining proportion of electricity produced since midcentury. The best dam sites have been used up, silting is threatening the continuation of existing facilities, and tougher environmental and safety laws have added to construction costs. In addition, droughts have shown hydropower to be an unreliable power source unless significant excess capacity is maintained. In 1979, hydroelectric power accounted for almost 13 percent of total electric production, and by 1994 had been reduced to 8 percent.

Figure 12.11 shows the location of nuclear-generating facilities in the United States as of 1995. Nuclear electricity producing facilities are clustered along the East Coast, industrial Midwest, and the California/Arizona population corridor. Other primary sources of electrical power production in the United States are mapped in Figure 12.12. As shown earlier in this chapter, on a per Btu basis, coal is expensive to transport; hence, coal-fired electricity tends to be most heavily concentrated in Appalachian and Midcontinent coalfields. The map in Figure 12.12 demonstrates the relatively low transferability of

Bonneville Dam, Oregon, a renewable resource, generating hydroelectric power.

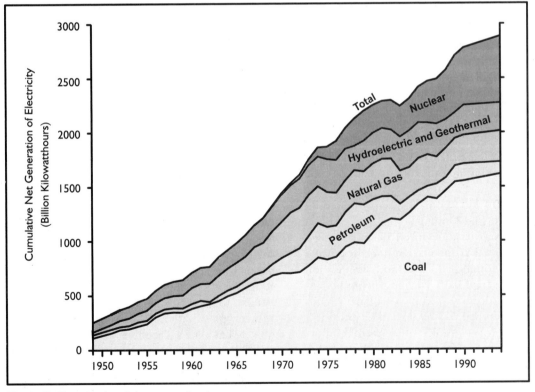

Figure 12.10 U.S. electricity generation by energy source.

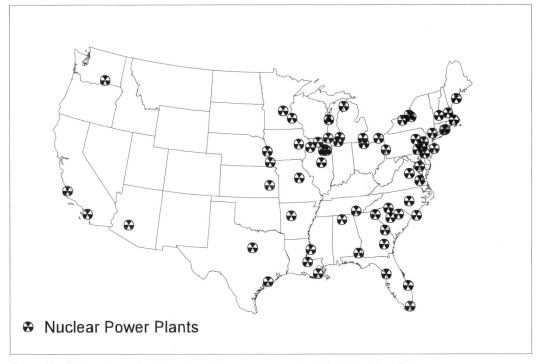

☢ **Nuclear Power Plants**

Figure 12.11 Locations of nuclear electricity generating plants in the United States.

coal energy, with much of the power generation in these regions being located near the mouths of coal mines or along waterways, such as the Ohio River, where transport costs per mile are cheapest.

The pattern of locating coal-fired power facilities near coal mines holds even in the Tennessee valley where locally mined coal is so cheap and efficient for power generation that it surpasses hydroelectric production by the Tennessee Valley Authority. Hydroelectric power generation remains important only in the Pacific Northwest's Columbia basin, with its massive Bonneville, Grand Coulee, and other dam facilities. Coal-fired power plants already supplement the shrinking proportion of water power in the Tennessee Valley Authority district and in the United States' and Canada's huge Niagara Falls hydroelectric joint venture at Niagara Falls. Petroleum-generated electricity is concentrated in a small number of areas, but where it is found, production occurs in large quantities. The major area for petroleum-based electricity production is New York–southern New England, whose huge power complexes were forced to turn to cleaner-burning petroleum after stricter air pollution laws were enacted in the late 1960s; this contributes to the nation's dependency on imported energy. Because of its proximity to Texas and the nearby crude oil transportation links, Florida depends on petroleum based electricity production. Natural gas-produced electricity is localized in the Gulf and Southern Plains regions, with pipelines extending that fuel dominance as far north as Denver and Omaha and as far west as Los Angeles and San Francisco.

Technological change has enabled the power plants to become larger, and greater voltages of high-power electricity transmission lines enable energy to be economically transported for hun-

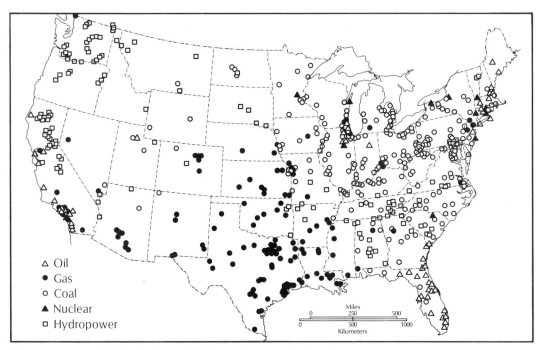

Figure 12.12 Spatial distributions of U.S. electricity production by source.

dreds of miles. This has allowed mine-mouth electricity generation such as that at the Four Corners region where the states of New Mexico, Colorado, Utah, and Arizona converge. Electric power is transmitted from there to Los Angeles and Phoenix. Long-distance energy transmission reduces power plant emissions in metropolitan airsheds and permits the use of cheaper land and possibly cheaper labor. The main problem and inefficiency associated with transporting electricity over long distances is the loss of power.

The New York City blackout in 1965 demonstrated the advantages of an interconnected nationwide electrical power grid. The first regional interties were created over 70 years ago when the states of Pennsylvania, New Jersey, and Maryland decided to form a common power pool in 1927. After World War II, such regional pools were common in every densely populated part of the country. By the late 1960s, remaining areas were being incorporated and the first nationwide interlinkage became possible in 1976 with the

completion of the Stegall, Nebraska, facility that tied together the eastern and western power grids. Energy planners view a high-capacity nationwide electrical network as highly desirable because power can be instantly shunted to wherever it is in the highest demand, thereby making available for consumption the surplus capacity that must be built into each electric generation facility.

Massive consumption of electricity has already been identified as a leading source of the nation's fuel wastage and low overall energy efficiency. Electricity production is also often beset by the difficulty of keeping generating capacity abreast of huge consumer demands for power. One major cause is that energy planners, with the blessing of government policy makers, simply placed too many eggs in the nuclear basket. Thus, when nuclear power encountered widespread political and public opposition in the late 1970s—in the form of overlooked construction, waste-disposal, and safety problems—electric utilities were caught without contingency plans to revert to conventional sources of power to handle increasing rates of consumption.

U.S. Primary Energy: Coal, Crude Oil, Nuclear Overview

The predominant sources of the United States' primary energy are the conventional fossil fuels (coal, crude oil, and natural gas). Over 85-percent of the United States' energy resource production originates from fossil fuels. Because conditions necessary for the production of fossil fuels have not been everywhere the same on our planet, fossil fuels are sporadically located. Thus, to understand the economic-geography of energy, the location of the fuels must be known.

U.S. Coal. In 1982, coal surpassed natural gas and crude oil as the major form of energy production in the United States. In 1997, 90 percent

of coal produced was consumed by electric utilities, and roughly 10 percent of all U.S. coal production was exported in 1996. Over 38 percent of U.S. coal exports went to Canada, Japan, and Italy in 1994. Canada, purchasing 15 percent of U.S. coal exports, is the largest single consuming nation, followed by Japan, which purchases 14 percent of all U.S. coal exports.

The geographic distribution of U.S. coal resource deposits is shown in Figure 12.13. Coal's low value by weight makes for a strong distance bias that shapes the geography of coal usage: end-users tend to be located near the coal source and decline with distance away from the coal region. Thus, the producing regions are also the dominant coal consumers, and relatively little coal reaches areas distant from major coalfields (such as the northeastern, West Coast, and southcentral states). The Appalachian and eastern Midcontinent states are the largest consumers: this area uses more than twice as much coal

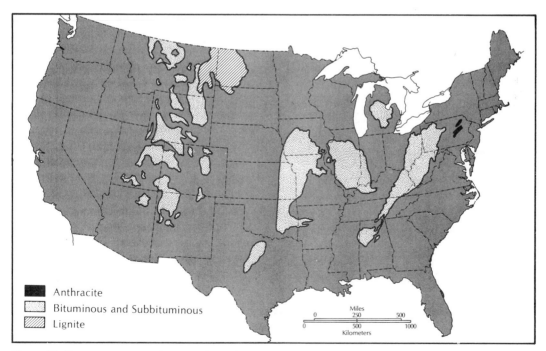

Anthracite
Bituminous and Subbituminous
Lignite

Miles
0   250   500
0   500   1000
Kilometers

Figure 12.13 Spatial distribution of U.S. coal reserves.

as any other region. The oil- and gas-rich Gulf and southern Plains states consume the least coal.

Three major concentrations of American coal are mapped in Figure 12.13 (1) Appalachia, extending northeast from western Alabama to eastern Pennsylvania; (2) Midcontinent, an arc stretching north from central Texas into Iowa and then southeast through Illinois into the western portions of Indiana and Kentucky; and (3) the West, a broad swath extending southwest from the northern Plains through the central Rockies into Arizona's Colorado Plateau. Together, these three regions account for more than 97 percent of annual U.S. coal production.

In 1990s, Appalachia produced about 42% of the nation's coal; Interior Fields 16 percent; and West, 42 percent. Appalachia's coal production declined in part because the Federal Clean Air Act of 1970 restricted the burning of high-sulfur coal; this type of coal accounts for roughly 80 percent of Appalachia's steam-grade bituminous reserves. Thus, because of the Federal Clean Air Act, and at the expense of Appalachia, the West has expanded production greatly since 1970 and in 1996 accounted for 42 percent of U.S. coal production.

Most of the Midcontinent coal region's production is found in central and southern Illinois, southwestern Indiana, and western Kentucky. Like Appalachia, Midcontinent coal is overwhelmingly of the high-sulfur content variety. Bituminous-grade deposits are always lower in quality there than in Appalachia. However, Midcontinent coal lies in near-surface seams, allowing cost-saving strip-mining. This accounts for the region's relative stability in coal production.

Western coal tends to be of mediocre quality. The West also has huge supplies of thick-seamed, strippable, low-sulfur coals. Nearly two-thirds of U.S. coal energy is in the West. Recent advances in reducing the cost of transporting coal have proven a mutual gain for both the West's coal-producing regions and the coal-consuming midwestern manufacturing Belt States. Within the western coal region, two producing areas dominate. The first is the Fort Union formation of the northwestern Plains, the nation's biggest contiguous fossil fuel deposit, which underlies western Dakota and eastern Montana and Wyoming (Figure 12.13). At least 1 trillion tons of largely strippable subbituminous and lignite coal are available, meaning that *coal from the U.S. Fort Union formation alone contains an energy content surpassing all of Saudi Arabia's remaining petroleum*. The other, more remote producing area is located in northeastern Arizona–northwestern New Mexico. Much of its lower-grade sub-bituminous coal is being converted into electricity at the mine mouth for long-distance transmission via high-voltage lines to serve the Los Angeles–Phoenix corridor.

Western coal production, however, is beset by problems. Conflicts have arisen over the use of the region's limited water supplies. Farmers and urban development groups compete with energy producers for limited water resources. Coal-fired power plants consume up to six tons of water for each ton of coal burned. The controversy has been heightened by proposals to consume more water in coal-slurry pipelines, which ship a mixture of crushed coal and water much like a crude oil pipeline. More is written on the coal-slurry pipeline later in this chapter.

Coal Transportation in the United States: Spatial Allocation and Movement. The principal coal carrier in the United States is the railroad. Foremost among cost-reducing rail technologies is the unit-train (UT), an innovation introduced in the 1960s. UTs are essentially rolling conveyer belts composed of 100 high-speed hopper cars that shuttle constantly between coalfield and market center. UTs employ automatic loading and unloading methods, speeding turnaround time. Evidence is that UT technology requires only two-thirds of the number of hopper cars required by traditional rail technology to maintain the same volume of throughput.

UT technology has especially benefited the

Energy Transport

The construction of a new facility to tap an energy resource brings about a chain of interactions that changes the relationship between the energy supply and end-user, prices, and new competitive positions between the different energy sources.[7]

   The energy supplier needs to transport the energy to the end-user. Transportation solutions are sought that maximize the volume of transportable energy, minimize the cost of moving the energy to the end user, minimize in-transit energy losses, and nowadays also minimize the likelihood of being litigated against because of some environmental problem or other hazard. Should that medium be continuous such as a pipeline, or noncontinuous involving a set of nodes and linkages such as a rail line or barge? The answer usually depends on the size of the energy source and its projected life span, the size and regularity of consumer demand in different market areas, the value-by-weight of the fuel to be carried, and scale economies attainable in the transportation process itself.

[7]See: Gerald Manners, *The Geography of Energy* (London: Hutchinson University Library, 1964), p. 45.

northern Plains coalfields, offsetting their situational disadvantage and making Wyoming–Montana subbituminous coal competitive in the Midwest and distant coal markets. The success of UT technology has brought maximum capacity usage on some Midwestern rail lines, so it is unlikely that UT transport can keep pace with increasing energy demands. For example, it is estimated that if all future Pacific Northwest power stations were to be coal-fired plants, mile-long UTs would be forced to make hourly hauls across the region by the end of this century. A switch to ever-heavier loads in speedier UTs is certain to hasten widespread deterioration of railroad railbeds that will cost billions to strengthen or replace.

   Coal is also transported by water, particularly the Mississippi and Great Lakes basins. Water transport is most economical where distances exceed 300 miles and where barges several hundred feet in length can be accommodated. Highway transport of coal is more flexible but is uneconomical for hauls exceeding 100 miles. Highway

transport is used within the dispersed coalfields of Appalachia, where it is not feasible to lay rails to serve the smaller mines.

   A controversial postwar transport medium is the slurry pipeline. Water is added to coal in a 50–50 mixture and pumped through a pipeline. The technology was perfected in the 1950s, with the opening of the 100-mile Ohio Pipeline, which

A coal-slurry pipeline, where coal dust and water are mixed and pumped, Utah.

was closed down in 1963 after the federal government allowed railroad coal-haulage rates to drop. Subsequently, the Peabody Coal Company in 1970 opened a more successful 18-inch-diameter underground pipeline. It was to carry 5 million tons of coal slurry annually from the Black Mesa fields of northeastern Arizona 300 miles west to the Mojave, Nevada, power station on the Colorado River.

The 1000-mile Gillette (Wyoming)–White Bluff (Arkansas) slurry pipeline has provoked great controversy. The pipeline was opposed by two interest groups, the railroad companies and environmental activists. Railroads are opposed because of the economic threat to their coal-carrying business. The environmentalists argued that scarce water resources in the semiarid West do not permit the luxury of diverting limited supplies for piping away with coal. (However, water use in a coal slurry pipeline is modest in comparison to water consumed as coolant in new western thermal electricity-generating plants.) Delays and legal uncertainties have affected other projects such as the Montana–to–Houston coal slurry pipeline that was canceled in 1984.

U.S. Coal Future. The United States' vast coal reserves cannot quickly be tapped to increase their contribution to the national energy-supply budget. Air pollution laws mandate compliance with the 1970 Clean Air Act; there has also been legislation to limit the sale of leases to develop new coal-mining operations. Development of western coal supplies has been slowed by environmental opposition to strip-mining and local water use, and by the low energy prices of the middle to late 1980s. In the East, new health and safety standards for coal miners add to the costs of coal recovery, making deeper mines unprofitable to develop as long as real prices do not increase significantly.

Coal is unlikely to be the elixir of U.S. energy independence in the near future. In New England, the region most heavily reliant on imported petroleum, the total switchover to coal by industry and public utilities would reduce annual crude oil consumption by only 7 percent. Government policymaking reflects the above described conflicting ideological agendas: the Department of Energy encourages while the Environmental Protection Agency discourages rapid development of new coal sources.

U.S. Crude Oil. Oil and natural gas accounted for 65 percent of U.S. energy consumption in 1995; of that amount, about 10 percent went into electric power production. Motor gasoline accounted for two-thirds of all petroleum products supplied. While the importance of oil is slowly being displaced by coal, in total energy consumed, still the oil age will not soon come to an end in the United States.

Oil drilling is feasible down to the 20,000-foot level, the "floor depth" beyond which oil is transformed by great pressures into gaseous hydrocarbons. American oil-producing regions are mapped in Figure 12.14. The major new North Slope oilfield of northern Alaska did not begin producing until the late 1970s. The Gulf Coast field arcs northeastward from the Mexican border beyond the Mississippi Delta into southwestern Alabama and extends an average 200 miles inland as well as dozens of miles offshore into the floor of the Gulf itself. The second oilfield in the Midcontinent district stretches northeastward from the Permian basin of southeast New Mexico–northwest Texas through Oklahoma and into central and eastern Kansas. The third is the Appalachian field, a crescent extending southwest along the western flanks of the Appalachian Plateau from northwestern Pennsylvania through the upper Ohio valley, west across Kentucky, and then finally north into eastern Illinois. The last of the major regions is found in California, running north from Los Angeles almost to San Francisco and from the San Joaquin Valley west into the Pacific's narrow continental shelf. Three smaller discontinuous oil districts are also evident in Figure 12.14: the Prairie, encompassing northern Montana–northwest

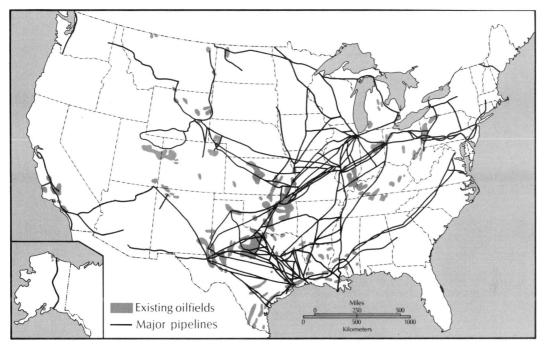

Figure 12.14 Spatial distribution of U.S. petroleum production and pipelines.

North Dakota, eastern Wyoming, and western Nebraska–northeast Colorado; the Rocky Mountain, consisting of northwest Wyoming, northeast Utah, and northwest New Mexico; and two East Lakes concentrations in western Michigan and northeast Indiana–northwest Ohio–southeast Michigan.

Foreign dependency on petroleum will not decline in the near future. Of all petroleum products consumed in the United States during 1995, 65 percent were imported. OPEC was the source for 50 percent of these imports, Hence, about a quarter of total petroleum products consumed in the United States came from OPEC, down from 60% in 1990 and down from 73% in 1980.

Crude oil extraction is one of the most costly methods for recovering energy. Drilling and pumping to depths of 10,000 feet or more, both on land and offshore, are visible operations using complex technology. Refining and distillation of crude into its various end products are even more expensive processes than extraction; a drilling rig

costs more than $3 million, and a moderate-sized refinery costs at least a quarter of a billion dollars. Yet, there are more than 250 refineries in the United States and Puerto Rico. Because crude and refined oil are about equally expensive to transport over long distances, refineries may locate at oilfields, at markets, or at intermediate sites. In practice, few large refineries are found in oilfield areas. The Gulf coast is an exception because of the huge agglomeration of petrochemical industry there. Intransit refinery locations also exist; refineries in the Caribbean process crude imports flowing to the United States from Latin America, Africa, and Saudi Arabia.

Because of the market-oriented location of most refineries, 75 percent of all crude oil is shipped by pipeline, in contrast to 33 percent of all refined petroleum products being piped to consumers. Most refined petroleum products are shipped to end-users via local tank-truck deliveries. Crude oil pipelines must be amortized over 20-year period to break even. The United States has a vast and still growing 250,000-mile pipeline network that daily moves more than 10 million barrels of crude and refined petroleum among major source and consumption points. The current state of pipeline technology is best illustrated by the Trans-Alaska facility, the largest private construction project in history, which opened in 1977. The $9 billion Trans-Alaska Pipeline runs 800 miles south from Prudhoe Bay on Alaska's Arctic North Slope to the winter-warm port of Valdez on Alaska's southern coast. The 48-inch-diameter pipeline was completed in three years and soon thereafter attained its initial carrying capacity of 1.2 million barrels per day (more than 10 percent of the nation's entire pre-existing pipeline capacity).

U.S. Natural Gas. Natural gas supplied 30 percent of the nation's energy in 1989, a figure that remained almost unchanged since 1982. 14.5 percent was converted into electric power and 75 percent was consumed directly. Of the amount consumed directly, industry and household-commercial users each consumed slightly less

than half of the output, with the small residual utilized by the transportation sector.

During the decade 2000–2010, the transportation sector may consume an increase in natural gas: it burns cleaner and is less expensive per mile driven than petroleum motor fuel. However, the storage tanks are heavy and bulky limiting natural gas as a practical vehicle fuel only for short-distance vans. United Parcel Service is converting a portion of its fleet of delivery vans to natural gas. Natural gas is relatively inexpensive to transport over long distances, thereby allowing a wide dispersion of natural gas energy users. Gulf coast and Southern Plains states are major producers of natural gas; there natural gas is substituted for the expensive-to-transport bulky coal for the production of electricity.

At a large scale of resolution, natural gas fields in the United States tend to coincide with the spatial distribution of oil fields (Figure 12.14). However, seldom is natural gas actually found at the same site as crude oil. The Gulf Coast and Midcontinent regions together contain the lion's share of American gas production. (The states of

The 600-mile, above-ground Alaska pipeline, here shown in the white, frozen tundra, brings black liquid gold (oil) to U.S. motorists.

Oil slick on beach in Wales, with rescued bird in foreground.

Texas and Louisiana alone account for 71 percent of national output, and Oklahoma–New Mexico–Kansas an additional 20 percent). The Gulf gas-producing area extends further inland, with the largest fields found in coastal Louisiana west of the Mississippi Delta, northwest Louisiana–northeast Texas, and the lowest portion of the Rio Grande valley. Midcontinent gasfields are concentrated in the Panhandle–Hugoton district of northwest Texas–northwest Oklahoma–southwest Kansas, the Anadarko basin of eastern Oklahoma and Kansas, and the West Texas–southeast New Mexico Permian basin. Appalachian gasfields cover an extensive portion of that region's heart, although their output is modest when compared to the two leading producing areas. Three minor petroleum regions are Prairie, Rocky Mountain, and East Lakes. The sizable San Juan gasfield of northwestern New Mexico is a noteworthy exception because it occurs together with both oil and major coal deposits. To transport the U.S. supply of natural gas to its customers, over 1 million miles of natural gas mains and pipes are in operation (Figure 12.15), a system more than four times the size of the nation's oil pipeline network.

Despite heavy use of natural gas, an advertisement of the American Gas Association has pro-

claimed that "There's Still Twice as Much Gas Underground as We've Used in the Last 50 Years." It claims that untapped reserves lie beneath every state, with the possible exception of Minnesota, Wisconsin, Vermont, and New Hampshire. That optimism appears to be justified by reports of several natural gas discoveries made since 1975 in places as diverse as central Louisiana's Tuscaloosa Sand formation, southwest Wyoming's Overthrust Belt, and the Appalachian ridge-and-valley section of central Pennsylvania. Perhaps the most spectacular recent natural gas strike is the huge gasfield discovered in conjunction with oil exploration on Alaska's North Slope.

The search for new natural gas deposits has expanded to offshore areas, which accounts for about 25 percent of American natural gas production (versus 10 percent for crude oil). Unlike crude oil, foreign imports of natural gas are not expected to increase beyond 5 percent of all gas produced in the United States because gas must be liquefied under enormous pressure for trans-oceanic shipment, a very costly and extremely dangerous endeavor.

U.S. Nuclear Power.   Most nuclear-generated electrical power occurs at sites remote from

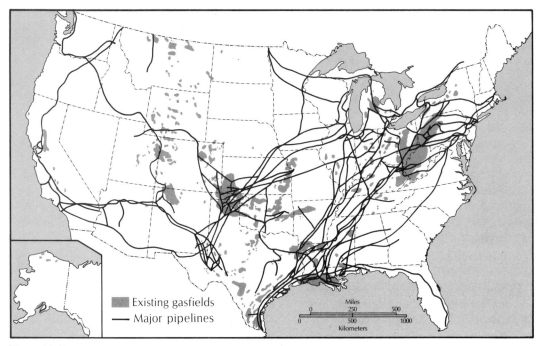

Figure 12.15 Spatial distribution of U.S. natural gas production and pipelines.

heavy concentrations of population; notable exceptions are facilities in Minneapolis, New York, Rochester, Chicago, and Hartford. So much controversy has arisen over the safety of nuclear power facilities and the disposal of spent nuclear fuel that the future of nuclear facilities is highly uncertain.

Atomic energy was once touted as the most promising source of cheap and unlimited power. The construction of nuclear generating facilities supposedly marked the end of the fossil fuel age, just as the transition to electricity usage marked the end of the age of the steam engine as a direct source of power.

Nuclear fission, the process now used to harness atomic energy, involves the splitting of heavy atoms, such as those of uranium (**U**), in order to release and capture the internal energy that held the atom together. Nuclear fuel-quality uranium (**235U**) is rare, occurring as less than 1 percent of the world's uranium-ore deposits. Until the 1978 opening of Australia's vast northern "yellowcake" lode, it was thought that only enough fuel-grade uranium was available worldwide to fuel several hundred reactors. American supplies of **235U** are considered adequate for national requirements, with deposits located in New Mexico and smaller deposits in the north-central Rockies. In the unlikely event that nuclear power significantly expands in the United States during the next decade, it will be necessary to develop breeder reactors that manufacture more nuclear fuel than is consumed. However, breeder reactors produce weapons-grade surplus plutonium (**239U**). Public sentiment opposes the construction of such breeder reactors because of the threat of terrorist activity.

Alternative Sources of U.S. Energy

Identifying and developing nonfossil fuel alternative energy systems is as essential as devising new methods to reduce waste in energy. What will be the energy resources of the future? Financial support of pure and applied research increased as fuel prices skyrocketed through much of the 1970s and early 1980s. However, as a result of the stable energy prices from the middle 1980s to the late 1990s, research and development funds have plummeted. This is regrettable, since we have seen the supply of energy and its prices can be quite volatile. A successful R&D program for reducing waste and identifying new energy sources can occur only if it is sustained over the decades.

Wood.   In 1987, 5 million households relied on wood as their main heating fuel, each consuming an average of 4.7 cords; 17.4 million households depended on wood as a secondary heating fuel, each consuming an average of 1.1 cords. Total energy produced by wood in 1987 for all economic sectors was 2437 trillion Btu's. The South led all other regions of the United States in the consumption of wood energy, while the Northeast fell behind the other regions.

As recently as a century ago, most U.S. energy was obtained from the burning of wood (Figure 12.16). In the 1880s, coal surpassed wood for the first time. In the post–World War II era, energy transition again occurred. Crude oil exceeded coal in 1952, and natural gas exceeded coal in 1958.

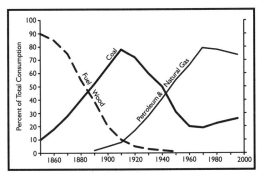

Figure 12.16 U.S. fuel-use patterns since the middle of the nineteenth century.
Source: U.S. Bureau of Mines and the Federal Energy Administration.

Solid Waste (Refuse).   In 1995, energy from solid waste (garbage) was 15 percent that of wood. As with wood, the South led other regions in refuse to energy conversion.

Environmentalists support the reduction of refuse placed in landfills, but this alternative energy source has been heavily criticized. Dioxins may form in the cooling plume of gasses from the chimney of the solid waste to energy incinerators; dioxins in very minute quantities are known carcinogens.[8] The ash that results from the burning of solid waste is one third the volume of the original material. The chemical composition of the ash is such that the ash should be treated as hazardous. Hazardous components of the ash include high concentrations of heavy metals that can easily pollute the aquifer. Heavy metals get into the solid waste by such innocent sources as the ink in the color comics in Sunday newspapers.

Geothermal Energy.   Geothermal energy is created by taking advantage of tectonic forces. The earth's crust is composed of many plates: friction from the collision of these plates results in heat. Heat is present near the surface where these plates pull apart, and it is also present in the deeper mantle, coming to the surface in what are thought to be convection currents in the molten rock. The Hawaiian Islands and Yellowstone are thought to have been formed as the result of such upwelling molten rock. This heat can be exploited for the production of geothermal energy; heat can be used to produce steam to spin turbines that produce electricity.

[8]Thrall G., 1987. "Solid Waste Technology and Its Impact upon Local Land Use and Land Values," in Cynthia Valencic (ed.), *There is No Away: Proceedings of the Interdisciplinary Conference on Waste Reduction, Reuse and Disposal Alternatives*, March, 1986; University of Florida Law School, Gainesville FL, and the Legal Environmental Assistance Foundation, Tallahassee FL.

Geologic heat sources were successfully tapped as long ago as the 1890s, when the city of Boise, Idaho, built a hot-water pipe network that is still in use. Geothermal energy production has increased rapidly since 1960 but still accounts for less than one-half of one percent of all U.S. energy produced.

Potential geothermal locations in the western United States are shown in Figure 12.17. Many eastern states contain geothermal potential, especially those in a broad arc of the Atlantic coastal plain stretching northeast from southern Georgia to New Jersey. This physiographic province is known to be underlain by numerous hot granitic formations, and the eastern seaboard's first geothermal well was drilled in 1979 on Maryland's outer Chesapeake Bay shore.

Solar Energy.   The kilowatt-hours produced with photovoltaic modules has doubled every five years since 1980. Consumer goods, residential use, and communication represent over 60 percent of photovoltaic module users. With the module's high expense of production, low yield of energy per unit space, reliance on sunshine, and high cost or inadequate energy storage, at present it is impractical as the main source of household energy. Most research dollars have been spent in the United States on technology for centrally produced energy systems (such as nuclear) rather than dispersed energy systems (high-power photovoltaic modules). For all these reasons, no suburban houses will in the near future be energy self-reliant with shingles replaced with photovoltaic modules.

Also relying on direct radiant energy from the sun are solar thermal collectors. Eighty-five percent of solar thermal collectors sold in the United States are used to heat swimming pools. Solar light and heat energy received at the earth's surface is another nonfossil fuel alternative. That energy supply is free, unlimited, effectively inexhaustible, and low-polluting. Yet progress in tapping solar energy to date has only been modest, and enormous technological and economic problems await solution before solar power can contribute meaningfully to the nation's energy budget. The most important problem concerns dilution of the sun's energy available at the ground. Although the United States receives about 15 times the solar energy it needs to replace all fossil fuels, with the technology available today as much as 7 percent of the nation's surface would have to be used for solar collectors to recover that energy.

Wind Energy.   Unequal heating of the earth's surface produces air masses of varying density. The atmosphere moves to reduce pressure differences, producing wind. Where winds occur regularly, they can be harnessed as an energy source, as Dutch farmers have demonstrated with their windmills for many centuries. Some view wind as cheap and inexhaustible future alternative to fossil fuel energy. The nationwide distribution and spatial variation of available wind power is mapped in Figure 12.18. The central and western Great Plains comprise by far the most promising region (its farmers have also made much use of windmills over the past century), particularly near the Rocky Mountain front range along the western edge of the Plains where katabatic winds, resulting from the gravity drainage of cold, heavy air masses spilling out of the highlands, can often sharply reinforce the speed of airflows for hundreds of miles to the east.

The Future of U.S. Energy

If an energy crisis does exist and is intensifying, a large majority of Americans have remained unpersuaded. The recent past, as we have observed, has been a period of high energy usage—especially in waste-prone electricity—in which yearly consumption has increased. Most energy conservation has been a response by businesses to higher fuel prices. There is a myth that great numbers of households are changing to renewable energy sources such as wood; this component of the back-to-nature movement is just a

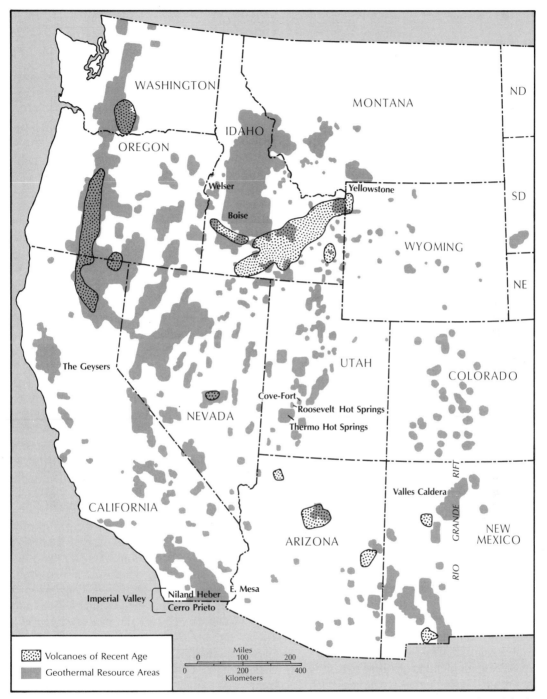

Figure 12.17 The distribution of known and potential geothermal deposits, and recent volcanic activity in the western United States.
Source: After Walter Sullivan, "Seeking Energy Out of the Volcanic Past: Geothermal Drillers Looking for Reserves of Boiling Water." *The New York Times*, November 25, 1977, pp. D-1, D-2.

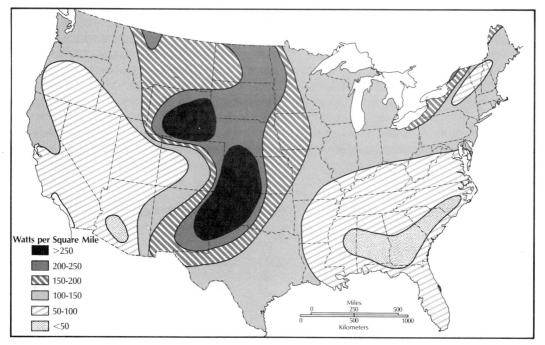

Figure 12.18 Average annual wind power available in the United States.
Source: William W. Eaton, *Solar Energy* Washington, D.C.: U.S. Energy Research and Development Administration, 1976.

fabrication of the well wishers. Indeed, public opinion soundings consistently report widespread apathy and skepticism of pronouncements that a worsening energy supply situation is at hand.

Although the nation faces a number of energy problems, these do not add up to a crisis. The term *energy-crisis* is a mainstream media catchphrase that explains nothing and yet still manages to create an incorrect impression. The label *crisis* implies the existence of a pervasive, unified, and chronic energy supply problem, a perception that is nearly the exact opposite of the truth. The United States is not confronted with a single interconnected energy dilemma attributable to the imminent exhaustion of energy resources. Each energy source faces a set of separate problems, which in the near term does not include impending supply depletion. *It is important to note that the United States has become dependent on foreign suppliers not because domestic petroleum has*

been depleted, but because it has been considerably cheaper to import foreign supplies than to develop indigenous oil reserves. Instead, among the real problems we face are the environmental impacts of energy extraction, transport, and use, and the real cost to the nation from the international geopolitics of energy.

The popular perception of a unified and chronic "energy crisis," then, is a distortion of reality. However, the expensive conversion to lower-quality and more inaccessible fuel reserves has signaled the end of the era of cheap U.S. energy supplies. Naturally, people prefer to pay a lower price rather than a higher price; but there is every indication that Americans are prepared to pay much higher energy prices, especially for gasoline and electricity, than they have hither to experienced paying. It was also demonstrated earlier that although the prices of gasoline and electricity have risen sharply within the memory of most Americans, total energy expenditures

The windmill farm at Altamont Pass near Livermore in the California coastal range southeast of San Francisco.

still account for a smaller proportion of median family income than they did in the 1960s when energy was widely held to be inexpensive. Low-income and moderate-income households do suffer as the price of energy increases.

Still, the possibility of more expensive energy is expected to affect gradually individual life-styles. The impact on the location of certain economic activities because of higher production costs is also anticipated to continue to widen during the 1990s, prompting highly dependent energy-dependent industries to continue shifting operations to energy-rich regions and nations.

Energy geopolitics is at the forefront of international relations. The economies and societies of developed nations will increase their dependence on nonrenewable energy sources. Although these sources are for the moment plentiful, their supply is concentrated within a few regions of the planet. The concentration on the

one hand, and the dependence on the other, will ultimately give the balance of influence over to those who control the energy sources. Transporting petroleum from the other side of the planet further increases the United States vulnerability to sustained energy supplies. The United States has demonstrated through its past actions that access to energy supplies and the unhindered transport of these supplies is paramount in its international policy.

U.S. energy supplies are adequate currently, but the picture in the decades following the year 2000 may be different. No matter how much more energy can be obtained from known and as yet undiscovered domestic fossil fuels, these nonrenewable resources are in finite supply and will eventually become exhausted, perhaps during the twenty-first century. Energy strategy must recognize this approaching depletion and plans must be made for alternative sources of energy.

Development of nonfossil fuel alternatives is certain to require substantial expenditures of time and money. It is therefore important to invest in research now. To buy enough time to develop these alternative energy sources, we must now embark on major conservation efforts despite widespread public skepticism. This can extend the time before remaining fossil fuels are depleted. Such a strategy will more likely ensure the continuation of both a high quality of life and political independence from foreign powers.

SUMMARY

This chapter surveys the topical issues of energy at world, national, and local levels. Dealing with the geopolitics of international energy flows adds an additional complication to an already complex set of energy issues. It is important to remember that the United States has not become dependent on foreign-suppliers because domestic petroleum has been depleted. Rather, it is because it has been considerably cheaper to import foreign supplies than to develop indigenous oil reserves. The problems addressed in this chapter will remain the foremost issues well into the next century.

The economic geography of energy is a topic that requires a worldwide description and documentation of where the sources of energy are to be found. The same for the consumers of energy. Because consumers and producers are seldom at the same location, we also need to document the energy transportation network. The theories used by economic geographers are central to explaining the flow of energy and the energy consumed. This chapter has presented an overview of the production and consumption of energy in the world and, in more detail, the United States. The present and future problems that confront energy users are outlined, the major theories summarized, and important data on energy reviewed. A thorough examination of data, as well as a synthesis of the data and theory, allows us to anticipate what the future may hold. With this knowledge, we can hopefully make better judgments about our energy future.

The issues presented in this chapter on the economic geography of energy will be among the most vital challenges all nations have ever faced. Their solution and the manner in which the solutions are obtained will influence the character of international relations and will determine the type of society and environment in which we and future generations will live.

Further Readings

Anderson, J. *Oil: The Real Story Behind the Energy Crisis*. London: Sidgwick and Jackson, 1984.

Berry, Brian J. L., Edgar C. Conkling, and D. Michael Ray. *The Global Economy in Transition*, 2nd ed. Upper Saddle River, N.J.: Prentice-Hall, 1997.

Calzonetti, Frank J., Barry D. Solomon, eds. *Geographical Dimensions of Energy*. Boston: D. Reidel, 1985.

Calzonetti, Frank J., and Mark S. Eckert. *Finding a Place for Energy*. Washington, D.C.: Association of American Geographers, 1981.

Cuff, David J., and William J. Young. *United States Energy Atlas*, 2nd ed. New York: Free Press, 1986.

Cutter, S. L., H. L. Renwick, and W. H. Renwick. *Exploitation, Conservation, Preservation: A Geographic Perspective on Natural Resource Use*, 2nd ed. New York: Wiley, 1991.

Manners, Gerald. *The Geography of Energy*, 2nd ed. London: Hutchnson University Library, 1971.

Mounfield, P. R. "Nuclear Power in Western Europe: Geographical Patterns and Political Problems." *Geography* 70:315–327.

Pierce, William P. *Economics of the Energy Industries* Belmont, Calif.: Wadsworth, 1986.

Pryde, Philip R. *Nonconventional Energy Resources*. New York: Wiley/V. H. Winston, 1983.

Rees, J. *Natural Resoruces: Allocation, Economics and Policy*. New York: Methuen, 1985.

Ruedisili, Lon C., and Morris W. Firebaugh, eds. *Perspectives on Energy: Issues, Ideas, and Environmental Dilemmas*, 3rd ed. New York: Oxford University Press, 1982.

Turner, Bille Lee II, ed. *The Earth as Transformed by Human Action: Global and Regional Changes in the Biosphere Over the Past 300 Years*. New York: Cambridge University Press.

PART SIX

The Geography of Agriculture

CHAPTER 13

The Spatial Organization of Agriculture

◇

*I hope that the reader who is willing to spend some time and attention on my work
will not take exception to the imaginary assumptions I make at the beginning because
they do not correspond to conditions in reality, and that these assumptions will not be
rejected as arbitrary and pointless. They are a necessary part of my argument,
allowing me to establish the operation of a certain factor, a factor whose operation we
see but dimly in reality, where it is in incessant conflict with others of its kind.*

*This method of analysis has illuminated—and solved—so many problems in my
life, and appears to me to be capable of such widespread application, that I regard it
as the most important matter contained in all my work.*

—JOHANN HEINRICH VON THÜNEN, 1826

INTRODUCTION

Only 5 million Americans—2 percent of the nation's total population—live on farms today. Only about 1 million Americans have farming as their principal occupation. Although the number of households that are farm owners is comparatively small, the contemporary farm has become a business relying on advances in complex technology. In 1990, the total value of farm implements and machinery was $91.7 billion: $18,200 in total farm capital for every farm resident.[1] In 1995 there was $86.9 billion in farm machines and equipment. Between 1990 and 1995 there was then a decrease of almost $5 billion in farm capital investment. Still, this capital investment has contributed to increasing farm productivity, which has resulted in farm operators in 1994 having average incomes of $44,140.[2,3]

To the geographer, the study of agriculture is more than how the soil is cultivated, how food crops are raised, and how livestock are bred. These topics are important but fall more within the domain of the agricultural engineer and agronomist.

Geographers are motivated by a quest to *describe and document* the spatial patterns of the agricultural landscape. The geographer then seeks to *explain* the spatial regularity of agricultural land use and the connections between agriculture's use of land and the happenings in other sectors of the economy and environment.[4] To the economic geographer the explanation for the spatial regularity of land-use patterns is based on consequences of competitive market behavior: which producer or sector will attain the

[1]U.S. Department of Agriculture, Economic Research Service, *Economic Indicators of the Farm Sector: National Financial Summary,* Table 1104: Farm Machinery and Equipment: 1970 to 1990, 1992.
[2]Data from U.S. Department of Agriculture, *Agricultural Sta-*

tistics 1997 (Washington, D.C.: U.S. Government Printing Office, 1997).
[3]U.S. Department of Commerce, Statistical Abstract of the United States, Table 1092: "Average Income to Farm Operator Households: 1991–1995," 1996.
[4]G.I. Thrall, 1995 "Stages of GIS Reasoning," *Geo Info Systems.* (Volume 5, number 2 [February], pp. 46–51.)

right to use the land, where, and how changing prices and technology will affect the ability to compete at particular locations. Human survival depends on the steady availability of food. This food must be produced somewhere. The geographer *predicts* how the spatial distribution of food production changes as a result of some change in the economy or society and how such changes are expected to be manifested in agricultural land-use patterns. The geographer draws on all this information to make *judgments*. Decisions made by individual land users, national policy makers, and world policy makers affect the availability of food that you and others sharing the world with you eat, the quality of the environment, and the general well-being of the global society.

This chapter introduces the principles of agricultural land use and its spatial patterns; the next chapter applies the concepts introduced here by detailing the actual spatial patterns of contemporary American agriculture. The general theory is presented before the documentation and description of the agricultural landscape because we want the reader to anticipate how actual patterns of agricultural land use are expected to behave. Observing that one's expectations are confirmed reinforces the value and role of general theory.

HISTORICAL GEOGRAPHY OF THE FARM IN AMERICA

The farm household is on the same technological footing with urban businesses of comparable size. The contemporary farm has become a capital- and technologically-intensive business. Accessing data via microcomputers from the family farm is today an equal part of the daily routine as milking the cow. For those who choose farming as their occupation, the farm is capable of generating reasonable incomes and can provide a high quality of life. From the viewpoint of the American farm household, the lower crime rate and lower cost of living in rural areas places them ahead in attainable welfare of urban households with comparable levels of job skills.

A Wisconsin farm with various outbuildings, rolls of hay for winter feeding, and, of course, the house at left.

Still, the long-term financial outlook for the agricultural sector is not secure. In the 1980s, farm businesses generally faced high and quickly changing interest rates, rising prices for equipment, dramatic swings in the price of the energy to run the machines to produce the agricultural output, and high costs for chemical fertilizers and insecticides that can despoil rural environmental quality. In the 1990s, interest rates stabilized at comparatively moderate to low levels, but, new, perhaps greater problems face the farmer. Today there is greater awareness of the lingering deleterious effect of pesticide residues on food. Decades of heavy use of pesticides have resulted in their cumulative buildup in the soil and ground water. Environmental problems stemming from the farmers' naive and short-sighted application of advanced technology have brought new uncertainty to today's business farm.

Changing and uncertain market conditions lead to land values that fluctuate widely from year to year. As a result, the largest asset that farmers have—their land—is often undesirable as collateral for loans necessary to finance the farm business on the yearly cycle from planting to harvest. Each year it is uncertain if there will be an international demand for the surplus produced over domestic consumption. And if there is international demand, the federal government may intercede and prohibit agricultural output from being sold to those countries willing to buy.

While these swings occur on a daily basis by way of the agricultural futures market (similar to the stock market but for promised agricultural output), the farmer has only two important decisions to make each year, the timing of which is determined by the season and weather: what to produce (plant) if anything, and whether to expend funds to harvest the product. The timing of the farmer's decisions and the vagaries of the futures market seldom coincide, making it impossible to make an optimal decision. Consequently, the farm and the rural centers that serve the farm are caught in a pendulum that swings between "farm crisis" and moderate prosperity.

The ratio of persons living on American farms versus persons living in urban areas is declining, but at a much lower rate than was the case between 1945 and 1970 (see Figure 13.1). From 1900 to World War II, the number of persons living on farms had reached a maximum of about 30 million persons. At the same time, the relative share of the total U.S. population living on farms had been declining since 1790; by the 1870s, half of the U.S. population lived in cities. In the post–World War II era up to 1970, the number of persons living on farms declined by 70 percent. In 1945, roughly 25 percent of the U.S. population lived on farms, declining to about 2 percent today.

Persons living in rural areas do not necessarily live on farms, but their occupations are often linked to farming and other primary industries, or to industries that provide the support network for farms. The proportion of the total U.S. population living in rural areas has declined since the United States industrialized in the mid-1800s (Figure 13.2). The share of people living in urban versus rural population is an index of the relative health of urban versus rural economies in the respective regions. The ***urban transition*** is the change from a high-population concentration in rural areas to a preponderance of population share working or living in urban areas; it is a record of past regional development. A region has completed the urban transition when the rural share of the population has gone from 100 percent to less than a quarter. Completing the urban transition may be a prerequisite to further regional development.

The Northeast preceded other U.S. regions in the urban transition from a 90 percent share of population residing in rural areas in 1800 to a 20 percent share since 1950. The urban transition began in the Northeast in about 1820. In the north-central region, the urban transition began in about 1840, followed a decade later by the West. Half of the population in both north-central and western regions was urban by 1915. The South lagged behind the other regions, with

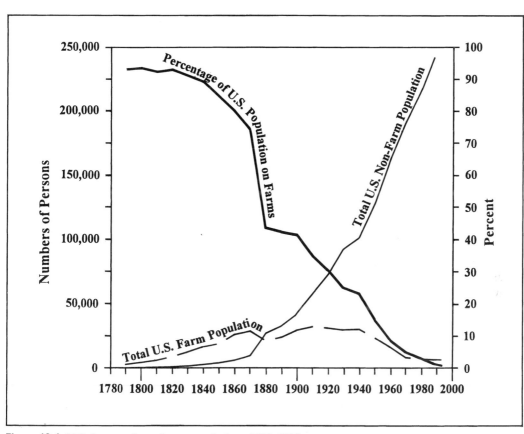

Figure 13.1 U.S. farm and nonfarm population, 1790–1900.

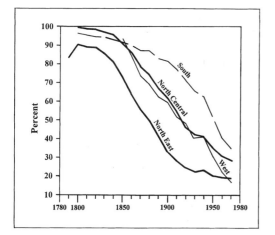

Figure 13.2 The proportion of total U.S. population living in rural areas.

50 percent of its population still rural in 1950. The rise of the "southern-Sunbelt" regional economy parallels the South's urban transition. In this context, the rise of the regional economy of the South can be thought of as a laggardly urban transition, falling behind the other regions of the nation but inevitably catching up to the nation's average.

HISTORICAL GEOGRAPHY OF FARMING IN THE WORLD

About 10,000 years ago there began a turning point in the history of human settlement. In the Eurocentric cradle of civilization, the Middle East where roughly today Iraq and Iran lie, a series of events are hypothesized to have started the Western Agricultural Revolution. Passive adaptation to the environment through hunting and gathering was replaced by active utilization of the resources at hand in the surrounding environment. In quick succession a variety of animals and food plants were domesticated for the first time. Neolithic humankind thereby gained the upper hand over the physical habitat. By domesticating plants and animals, surpluses could be produced, enabling people to advance beyond a subsistence level of existence.

Neolithic society changed since it no longer had to spend all its energy and time in search of sufficient food to survive. We do not fully understand why or how the transition occurred from a nomadic hunting and gathering to a sedentary pastoral society. One hypothesis is that the early population discovered that implements could be made to process otherwise inedible wild foods into edible foods: pottery could be used for the fermentation of readily available but inedible hard wild barley into a primitive beerlike slurry. Pottery for fermentation can be difficult to transport, but either by accidental or purposeful distribution of a portion of the gathered grain about a cache of pottery, the plant could in effect be made to come to where the pottery was.

By tending plants, yield increases. On the one hand, people became more restricted in their movement. On the other hand, domestication allowed a controlled and steady supply of food, perhaps more food than a single family unit required. As domestication diffused to more and more people, and as humankind became more secure in the ability to produce surpluses, occupational divisions of labor developed.[5] Nonagriculturalists began to specialize in the production of simple goods and services, such as pottery, that were exchanged for food produced by these early farmers. The surplus of agricultural pro-

duction allowed nonfarmers to engage in manufacturing handcrafted goods and performing services such as trade.

For reasons discussed in Chapter 8, there prevailed geographic forces leading people to concentrate at nodes central to the nearby farming population. The first urban settlements, what we today know to be low-order places, thereby came into existence.[6] Over 3000 years ago larger centers were created as movement improved, spawning the beginnings of a regional central-place hierarchy. First, there came many small settlements, then a few intermediate-sized places, and afterward a smaller number of larger places. The largest places were farthest apart, whereas the smaller places were closer together, nested within the domain of the larger places. The largest places became the earliest city-states. As trade grew, these city-states thrived. Since the hinterlands surrounding the city-states were necessary for their survival, these hinterlands were jealously protected.[7] The early state was thereby formed. With the state there came rules specifying the relationship between the new urban inhabitants and the state, how people in the higher density environment of the city were to relate to one another, and even how competing states were to relate to one another. These rules helped establish the principles of the world's great religions and the basis for many of the conventions that today we accept as law.

Civilization, agriculture, and the city are closely linked in cause and effect. The first civilizations grew out of the revolution in agriculture of domesticating plants and animals; the technological change in agriculture was necessary for the growth of cities. Indeed, the words *civiliza-*

---

[5]For more on spatial diffusion see Richard Morrill, Gary Gaile, and Grant Thrall, *Spatial Diffusion*, Vol. 10, Scientific Geography Series (Newbury Park, Calif.: Sage, 1988).

[6]For more on the theory of central places see Leslie J. King, *Central Place Theory*, Vol. 1, Scientific Geography Series (Newbury Park, Calif.: Sage, 1984).

[7]For more on calculating the extent of hinterlands around central places, see Kingsley E. Haynes and A. Stewart Fotheringham, *Gravity and Spatial Interaction Models*, Vol. 2, Scientific Geography Series (Newbury Park, Calif.: Sage, 1984).

tion and *city* have the same root. The economic geographer is interested in the linkage between agriculture and the city; this relationship is generalized in Figure 13.3 as an abstraction or model.

A *model* is an idealized representation of reality in order to demonstrate certain properties.[8] The model presented in Figure 13.3 is of the spatial division of labor within a simple, self-sufficient economic system comprised of an urban center and its complementary surrounding hinterland. The center's secondary and tertiary functions serve the rural tributary area. In turn, the rural tributary area supplies the urban economy with the surplus food and raw materials it needs to assemble the complete range of economic goods. Such economic interaction across space is central to an understanding of agricul-

tural land use in both ancient societies and the modern world. Before examining that dimension, particularly agricultural land use in America, we need to know more about the role of modern agriculture in the space-economy of today.

AGRICULTURE IN MODERN SOCIETIES

Unlike manufacturing and services, agriculture is an economic activity that is highly geographically dispersed. There are three reasons for this high dispersion: (1) agricultural productivity is not the same everywhere for the same type of produce; (2) agriculture competes with other land users—including urban and recreational land users—for the use of land; and (3) the markets where agricultural products are sold are geographically dispersed.

The intensity of agricultural land use can be measured in a variety of ways. The labor-to-land ratio calculates the person-hour inputs per unit land area. The capital-to-land ratio calculates the total expenditure in equipment and other built fixed facilities averaged over the farmed area. And the ratio of the value of output to land area measures the revenues or profits for each areal unit.[9] Regardless of which measure of intensity is used, agricultural intensity in absolute terms is generally low when compared to most secondary

Figure 13.3 A simple, self-sufficient economic system showing the spatial divisions of labor in production between an urban center and its rural hinterland. The arrows indicate two-way complementary trade between the two components, which enables each to assemble the full range of primary, secondary, and tertiary products.

[8]Peter Haggett, *Locational Analysis in Human Geography* (London: Edward Arnold, 1965), p. 19.

[9]The great nineteenth-century economist, Alfred Marshall, believed that land has area and density, and is a complement to capital and labor, and that there was a certain application of capital and labor to the acre that would yield the highest return. See A. Marshall, *Principles of Economics*, 8th ed. (London: Macmillan, 1996), p. 447. A normative and heuristic theory explaining why such ratios map as they do and how they relate to productivity has been advanced by G. I. Thrall, "Production Theory of Land Rent," *Environment and Planning A* 23, (1991), pp. 955–967. From an empirical viewpoint, also arguing that such ratios can be a measure of productivity, is the work of M. S. Fogarty and G. A. Garofalo, "Urban Spatial Structure and Productivity Growth in the Manufacturing Sector of Cities," *Journal of Urban Economics* 23, (1988), pp. 60–70.

Tractor pulling plough with barn and house in background.

and tertiary activities. Nevertheless, agricultural land-use intensity does differ markedly between locations depending on the crop, the technology used in the production of the crop, and the particular location of the farm.

Because farm production is so highly dispersed, long-distance geographic relationships are more important to agriculture than to other economic activities. Incentives to minimize the farm-to-market distances are great. Transportation costs can be reduced with increased proximity to market. We saw in Chapter 5 that transport plays a leading role in the functioning of the space-economy. Today American agriculture is so dependent on efficient long-distance transportation that a short disruption in railroad or trucking operations can be disastrous. Consequently, over the centuries spatial regularities of striking notability and persistence have arisen as agricultural land users compete with one another for proximity to the market.

Proximity to the market can result in less damage to the product. The fewer miles are traveled, the less chance there is for the product to be damaged. The product can get to the market faster if it is produced near to the market, translating into less spoilage. Technology that addresses these problems is a substitute for market proximity. Advanced processing technology extends the shelf-life of the product. Advanced processing is so prevalent today that double the number of people are employed in food processing than in actual farming. Biotechnology, through which products such as tomatoes are genetically altered to be more resistant to damage through bumping and jarring, reduces the need to locate near the market. Customers may complain that the tomato is rock hard, but that hardness allows the tomato to be transported thousands of miles, at low cost, with no damage to the fruit.

Substantial annual funds are spent on the development of such technology. Indeed, the School of Agriculture plays an important part in research and education in the American university. In 1970, the federal government spent $600 million on agricultural research and related services; in 1980, $1.4 billion, and in 1996 an estimated $2.731 billion.[10] There is a close tie between agriculture and industry as well. The agroindustry is highly sophisticated. In fact, the sophistication of the marketing end of the food production sequence is second to none. The agroindustry is also vertically integrated: every enterprise that the food comes into contact with—from farm to placement of the food on the shelf at the grocery store—may be owned by a single corporation. The distribution arm of the industry uses highly efficient nationwide distribution channels to speed the flow of finished products into the hands of the final supermarket or grocery store customer. At the farmer's end of the production chain, advanced technology via sophisticated mechanization is changing the agricultural industry as well. (This topic is explored more fully in the following chapter.) Machines have steadily replaced manual farm labor. In 1900, 42 percent of the American population lived on farms; by 1942, this figure had dropped by half to 21 percent; in 1957, the number had halved again to 10.5 percent; in 1967, only 5.5 percent of the total population lived on farms; and today it is less than 2 percent.[11] While the labor-to-land ratio has declined dramatically, the capital-to-land ratio has risen in compensation.

The trend to substitute capital for labor, or to purchase higher levels of technology, is partly responsible for the farmer's enduring economic problems. Because the producing unit is small and their competitors many, individual farmers exert no control over the market price they will receive for their goods. Yet, farmers commit themselves to long-term indebtedness to pay for expensive tractors and combines. Farmers must

The Erie Canal, built in 1825 before railroads became dominant, became the main route for agricultural items from the midwest to ship to New York and manufactured items from New York to ship to the Midwest.

make their production decisions by planting time, months in advance of when they will sell in a market whose conditions are unknown. Hence, the price they receive for their product may not be sufficient to pay the debt. Moreover, once planted, their crops are at the mercy of variable weather. Geographers' research on agricultural decision making has established that profit-seeking behavior has its upper limit and that once a predetermined level of income satisfaction is attained, farmers will not pursue further profits.[12] Therefore, in making their decisions on what technology to adopt and when and what to produce, farmers seek to minimize risk and usually rely on strategies that were successful in past years. They seek a reasonable return beyond their expenditures; the profit motive in farming therefore has an upward bound. However, to attain income sufficient to keep farmers in the business, farmers must master managerial, legal, meteorological, and other skills. The increasing skill

[10]U.S. Department of Commerce, *Statistical Abstract of the United States*, 116th ed., Table 517: Federal Receipts, by Source, and Outlays, by Function (Washington, D.C.: U.S. Government Printing Office [GPO], 1996).

[11]U.S. Department of Commerce, *Historical Statistics of the United States: Colonial Times to 1970*, (Washington, D.C.: GPO, 1990). U.S. Department of Agriculture, *Agricultural Statistics* (Washington, D.C.: GPO, 1970, 1989).

[12]Julian Wolpert, "The Decision Process in Spatial Context," *Annals of the Association of American Geographers* 54 (December 1964), pp. 537–558.

requirements necessary to survive as today's farmer are primarily responsible for the present decrease in the full-time farming population. Often, those who possess these advanced skills can achieve much greater personal income—with lower risk—when engaged in urban-centered occupations. This issue will be covered again in the next chapter in a discussion of the family farm versus the corporate farm.

The economic geographer is interested in the spatial dimension of farming. The earliest geographic characteristic of organized human agricultural activity was the setting aside of land to be used exclusively for agriculture. Such areal specialization has endured for 10,000 years and has become highly refined in recent centuries as farming technology has advanced. What is produced where has a persistence and does not change, even though short-term market conditions change. Different crop and livestock systems require differing levels of specialization of labor and capital; such specialization itself can keep a region specializing in a particular product and retard the diffusion of that crop from being farmed elsewhere. Earlier chapters dealt with the merits of an interdependent set of specialized producing regions, and these efficiencies apply particularly well to the geography of modern agriculture. With this in mind, we are ready to proceed with the locational analysis of agriculture in developed societies.[13] After an introduction to the agricultural location process, our presentation will focus on the early nineteenth-century writings of Johan Heinrich von Thünen (1783–1850), who is considered to be the founder of modern location analysis.[14]

[13]More specifically, North America, Europe, Australia–New Zealand, and the central and southern margins of the South American continent. The argument will be developed for the United States but can be applied to these other areas as well.

[14]Johann Heinrich von Thünen, *Der Isolierte Staat in Beziehung auf Landwirtschaft und Nationalokonomie*, 2nd ed. (Stuttgart: Gustav Fischer, 1926), reprinted 1966. English translation *von Thünen's Isolated State*, P. Hall, ed. translated by C. M. Wartenberg (Oxford: Pergamon Press, 1966).

INTRODUCTION TO THE AGRICULTURAL LOCATION PROCESS

The study of geography and related spatial disciplines involves a hierarchy of process and procedure.[15] The process of geography includes five stages:

Stage 1: *Documentation and description* of the landscape.

Stage 2: *Explanation and analysis* of the phenomena documented in Stage 1.

Stage 3: *Prediction.*

Stage 4: *Prescription or judgment.* (That is, a decision is made based on the presentation of information from the earlier stages.)

Stage 5: *Management and implementation.*

When a geographer first begins to explore spatial phenomena, the phenomena are initially visualized using maps. Maps assist our visual interpretation and improve our intuitive understanding of the spatial distribution and interrelationships among phenomena. In other words, a map provides a "bird's eye view" of the phenomena being investigated. Exploratory maps are intended to assist our understanding of the data. Unfortunately, those without appropriate training in geography end the process of geography with the Stage 1 exploratory descriptive approach to geography. Indeed, those without training may believe that the portrayal of data on a map is all that a geographer does. Actually, this is just the starting point (Stage 1) of the process of geographic reasoning. Relying solely on description and intuition will lead to an uncritical and perhaps erroneous acceptance of the "facts."

Explanation and analysis (Stage 2) is a necessary mark in the hierarchy of stages. The pio-

[15]The four-step approach was first expressed in Grant Ian Thrall and Susan Elshaw Thrall, "Commercial Data for the Business GIS," *Geo Info Systems* 3, No. 7 (July/August, 1993), and further developed by Grant Ian Thrall, "Stages of GIS Reasoning" *Geo Info Systems*, Volume 5, No. (2) 1995, pp. 46–51.

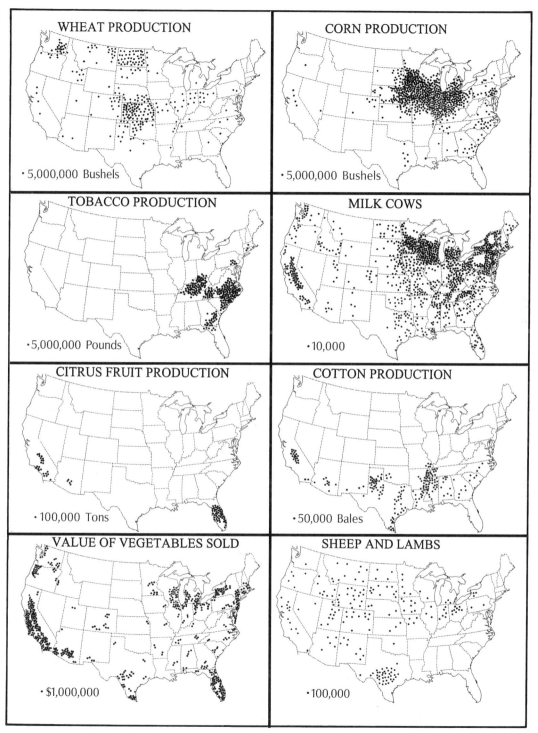

Figure 13.4 The distribution of eight major U.S. agricultural activities.

neering agricultural land-use theory of von Thünen is detailed in the later sections of this chapter. His theory allows us to explain the pattern of agricultural activities that arise. His theory is robust in that it allows us to anticipate (Stage 3) what will happen if market conditions change. Such knowledge is invaluable and a prerequisite for making decisions and rendering judgment concerning spatially distributed phenomena (Stage 4). Finally, implementation or management (Stage 5) recognizes the importance of managerial action with the spatial information. Von Thünen was motivated to produce his great land theory so that he could apply the information to better manage his estate.

The process of geography requires drawing a map of the phenomena to be studied. Figure 13.4 illustrates the geographic distributions of several major American agricultural products. These maps reveal a significant spatial pattern: each agricultural product is clustered within one or several regions. But to *understand* why the particular agricultural location patterns arise as they do, we must proceed to a Stage 2 analysis, which *explains* two things: (1) what causes the concentration of farming activities; and (2) what forces determine the overall allocation of specialized crop- and livestock-producing regions within the United States? In the discussion that follows, both questions will be answered.

Agriculture is a primary economic activity linked directly to the biophysical environment. Thus, natural influences must be considered in any analysis of what agricultural products are produced where. Every farming activity is constrained by environmental conditions of temperature, precipitation, soil quality, altitude, and related physical variables that must be satisfied in order for production to occur.

A hypothetical example is illustrated in Figure 13.5. Crop A can be grown wherever a certain soil type (region X), rainfall (region Y), or temperature regime (region Z) exists. Crop A can therefore be produced anywhere in regions X, Y,

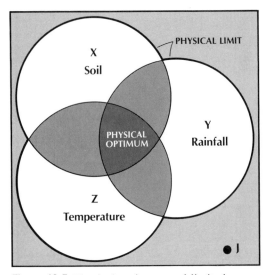

Figure 13.5 Physical optimum and limits in a normative setting for Crop A in Regions X-Y-Z.

and Z, whose outer boundaries circumscribe the ***physical limit*** beyond which the crop cannot be raised (such as location J). Within the possible production area, the most favorable locations for crop A are those where beneficial environmental conditions overlap, especially at the core of region X–Y–Z, where all three variables coincide and comprise the ***physical optimum*** for the crop in question.

A less abstract example in Figure 13.6 shows how the optimum-limits concept might operate in the case of cotton in the southeastern United States. The physical limits of cotton are as follows: to the north, the 200 frost-free-day isoline prevents production beyond the 37th parallel; to the west, cotton may be raised without irrigation until the 20-inch isohyet is reached at about the 100th meridian in central Texas; and to the southeast and south, too much rainfall in the harvest months excludes cotton from peninsular Florida and the Mississippi Delta. Within this region, which closely approximates the Old Cotton Belt, physical optima are situated where concentrations of soil of superior quality and natural

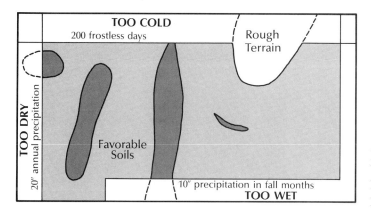

Figure 13.6 Physical optimum and limits in a more empirical setting: cotton in the southeastern United States. *Source:* After Harold H. McCarty and James B. Lindberg, *A Preface to Economic Geography*, Englewood Cliffs, N.J.: Prentice-Hall, 1966, p. 220.

productivity occur in the prairies of eastern Texas and Oklahoma, the so-called Black Belt of central Alabama, and especially along the floodplain of the lower Mississippi from southernmost Illinois downriver to northern Louisiana.

The physical optimum-and-limits model is helpful in considering the hypothetical extent of farming activities, but there are few real applications of this model. Modern irrigation, fertilization, and other agricultural technology allow the extension of physical limits to include formerly unfavorable areas when expected rates of return are perceived to exceed the economic and social costs of such an investment. More importantly, the physical optimum-and-limits model cannot help confront a situation that is frequently encountered in the United States where several crop and livestock systems are suited for the same environment. Because the natural environment of Iowa could equally well support wheat, dairying, fruit, vegetable, and several other kinds of food production, we must turn to nonphysical forces in order to explain Iowa's predominantly corn/hog/beef cattle agriculture.

An alternative model is the ***economic optima-and-limits*** model. In this case (Figure 13.7), the optimum becomes the zone of greatest profit, and the limit becomes the ***economic margin*** at which net income is the minimum required to keep a farmer from switching from crop A to a more profitable alternative. In order to understand the geography of economic optima, we need to develop a formal theory of the spatial distribution of the location of the phenomena agriculture. Von Thünen created the model presented here. While the subject of geography has existed for several thousand years, the systematic study of the subdiscipline of economic geography had not emerged by von Thünen's time. Because his work is a precursor to much modern economic geography reasoning, economic geographers today claim him as an early pioneer in the development of the subdiscipline. A testimony to his insight is that his analysis remains applicable to the spatial arrangement of food production in both developed and developing countries today. His model has also provided the starting

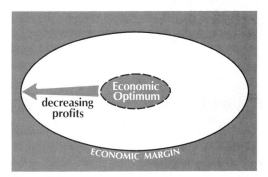

Figure 13.7 Economic optimum and limits for Crop A.

point for contemporary studies of the spatial organization of land use in the urban built-environment.[16]

VON THÜNEN'S LOCATION THEORY

The main idea of von Thünen's location theory, or model of commercial agricultural systems, is as follows: if environmental variables are held constant, then the farm product that achieves the highest profit will outbid all other products in the competition for location. The competitive position of a crop or livestock activity (namely, how high the bidding needs go to secure a desirable site) will depend on the level of return anticipated from producing at the particular location. A product with a high expected return and therefore high rent-paying ability will be able to outbid a product with a lower profit level and, therefore, a relatively modest rent-bid ceiling.

Not all commercial farms are rented from landlords (although tenant farming relationships are common throughout the world and are increasing throughout the United States). Still, the notion of rent is valid for landowning farmers as well. In a very real sense, landowning farmers pay rent to themselves by choosing to farm their own land because they forgo the rental income they might otherwise receive if a tenant worked the land for them. If a landowner–farmer earns an annual return of $40,000 by working his own land, as opposed to the $22,000 income a tenant would pay him to do the same farming, the landowner, who could also earn an outside annual income of $35,000 by managing a fast-food outlet full time at a nearby freeway interchange, is making the "sacrifice" or incurring an *opportunity*

cost of $17,000 (where $17,000 = $35,000 + $22,000 − $40,000) by choosing to farm his own land. Von Thünen was the first to propose the idea of opportunity cost; he had done so in an endeavor to derive a general theory of how labor wages are determined.

By carefully compiling economic data on different farming activities on his own large estate *Tellow* in northeastern Germany, von Thünen was able to determine the relative rent-paying abilities of each major agricultural product. Of course, the technology and agricultural products he managed in the early nineteenth century were different from those of today. But there are sufficient similarities to allow the analysis to be updated for our purposes. Moreover, his explanation was truly general, allowing his explanation approach to be applied to most contemporary agricultural situations.

Following von Thünen's reasoning, we may rank contemporary agricultural activities by rent-paying ability in the decreasing order listed in Table 13.1. With a caveat to be explained shortly, von Thünen reasoned that any one of these farming systems could outbid those of lower ranking if they should happen to be competing for the same land. For example, if vegetable, dairy, and wheat farmers were all interested in a plot of farm land put up for rent, the landlord, whose motive is to secure the highest possible income from her property, would rent the land to the vegetable grower, whose profit expectations would enable her to offer a higher rent-bid than either the dairy or the wheat farmer.

Table 13.1 Illustrative Hierarchy of Agricultural Crops

1. Truck farming (fruit and vegetables)
2. Dairying
3. Mixed crop and livestock farming (Corn Belt agriculture)
4. Wheat farming
5. Ranching (yearlings often sold to feedlots of mixed crop and livestock farming)

---

[16]For example William Alonso, *Location and Land Use: Toward a General Theory of Land Rent* (Cambridge, Mass.: Harvard University Press, 1964). Richard Muth, *Cities and Housing: The Spatial Pattern of Urban Residential Land Use* (Chicago: University of Chicago Press, 1969). Grant I. Thrall, *Land Use and Urban Form: The Consumption Theory of Land Rent* (London: Routledge/Methuen, 1987).

To demonstrate the geographic pattern of agriculture that emerges from such economic competition, von Thünen constructed the world's first spatial model of the human landscape. We have already seen several elementary spatial models in this chapter. Each of these models is an abstraction of reality. Components of reality that are important to the reasoning are retained in the model, while all else is either assumed not to be important or to take on stereotypical forms. Von Thünen assumed that the environment of the landscape could be described as summarized in Table 13.2. The rationale for his three assumptions is very similar to what was described in Figure 13.3. Moreover, what today we call assumptions in von Thünen's day and locale fairly well described the landscape surrounding his estate *Tellow*. In many ways, these assumptions are reminiscent of the isotropic plain discussed in Chapter 8 in connection with central-place theory; however, the two surfaces are not identical. On the central-place surface, population and income are dispersed evenly, whereas von Thünen's surface has densities that decrease as distance from the central town increases. It was von Thünen's intent to isolate distance from a single market center so that accessibility would become the dominant explanatory force for creating the geographical arrangements of agricultural production that he observed.

The geographic setting is now established, and the motivation of those making decisions in the farming sector is also known. These streams of reasoning can be put together to trace the process whereby agricultural activities are allocated on the landscape.

The single urban center and undifferentiated landscape of von Thünen's model landscape is portrayed in Figure 13.8*a*. Where are the most desirable farming locations situated? For every farmer, regardless of the crop or livestock type raised, the answer is indisputable: as close as possible to the central market. The market is the destination for agricultural goods produced throughout the region.

Next, assume that *all the land* in the heretofore undifferentiated landscape is placed on the auction block *at the same time*. The myriad of vegetable, dairy, mixed crop-and-livestock, wheat, and cattle-ranch land users eagerly submit their rent-bids to the landowners. All these actors prefer to purchase the right to use farm land near the market. Recall from Table 13.1, however, that the vegetable farmers have a **higher relative rent-paying ability near to the market** than their competitors; hence, at the auction the vegetable farmers will outbid all the others. The vegetable producers will thereby acquire the right to farm the land adjacent to the market. Since the undifferentiated landscape presents no advantages to being on a particular side of the market, the land users will distribute themselves circularly around the center so as to minimize their distance to the town.

The bidding continues after vegetable farmers are accommodated. Since dairy farmers rank next highest in rent-paying ability, they will successfully outbid the remaining contestants for locations in the next most accessible zone. Dairy farmers, too, arrange themselves in circular fashion. There arises a definite formation of concentric rings of different land uses circumscribing the market (Figure 13.8*b*). The remaining agricultural systems can be arranged concentrically around the market center in the same fashion, according to their competitive economic positions. The completed pattern of production rings is shown in Figure 13.8*c*.

Table 13.2   Assumptions for von Thünen's Landscape

1. *Homogeneous*, containing a flat land surface, identical climate, and soil conditions throughout.
2. A *uniform transportation surface* on which movement costs increase equally with distance in every direction.
3. A *single urban market* at the center whose needs are entirely supplied by the surrounding agricultural hinterland, which itself has no trade with the outside world.

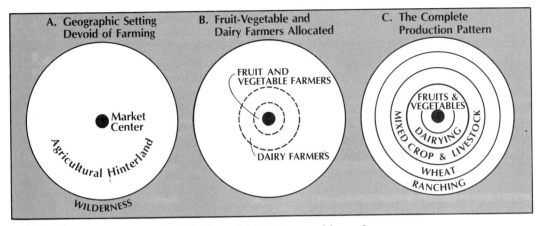

Figure 13.8 Von Thünen's Isolated State model in its stages of formation.

Developing von Thünen's model in this manner allows us to see that the spatial order of production centers on the central market. What is produced in each zone of land use, and its areal extent, depend on the competition among producers of the various agricultural products and the location of the central market. For each individual producer, the amount of rent they can bid depends on the relative net income per unit area derived from each type of farming. This in turn can be thought of as the difference between the farmer's gross profits and total production expenditures, averaged over the land area of the farm. Geographers refer to this net land income as ***location rent***. Location rent may be formally defined as the income above the farmer's opportunity cost for a unit of land in excess of that threshold level of earnings at which the land would be transferred to some other use. This same concept is also sometimes called ***economic rent***, although this term is best reserved for those situations where neither location nor space is an issue. The term *location rent* is preferred to economic rent when its magnitude depends on the location of the parcel relative to other parcels and the market center. The concept of location rent is summarized in Figure 13.9.

The lower portion of the gross income bar (Figure 13.9) consists of ***transfer earnings***, the minimum return (coverage of expenses plus the lowest acceptable profit) required to keep the land user (tenant farmer) from changing over to an alternative land-use activity. Transfer earnings are the same as the notion of the ***economic margin of production***. Above the economic margin is income derived from the location advantage of the site—in other words, the land unit's location rent. It is important to distinguish between the term *location rent* and the more com-

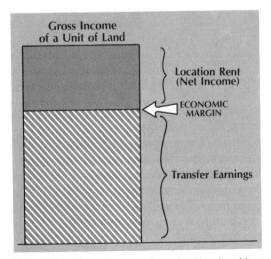

Figure 13.9 Gross income of a unit of land and its component parts: transfer earnings and location rent.

mon usage of the term *rent*. In the vernacular, rent is a payment by a tenant to a landlord for the right to use the landlord's property; it is properly referred to as **contract rent**. Location rent will always be written out in full in this text so as not to confuse the two terms.

Location rent is a measure of the competitive position of a particular type of land use within the larger farming system. The concept is most meaningful when we compare how location rent differs between types of agricultural products and locations. This is done below in the formal presentation of von Thünen's general theory. Location rent serves to allocate to a site the so-called highest and best use among competing types of agricultural land use. In this model, the driving force that leads to location rent differing from one site to another is the distance the site is from the central market. Several distance relationships that characterize the economic geography of von Thünen's hypothetical landscape are worth exploring further.

Land Values. For reasons very similar to the intraurban land-value surface discussed in Chapter 7, competition by agricultural land users for the locations with better access (nearer) to the central market bids up the value of land. Land values become so high that only those producers who yield the greatest location rents can afford it. A distance-decay relationship and inverted cone is revealed, with land values declining as distance from the central peak increases. The location advantage of proximity to the market is reflected in higher land values; as accessibility declines, so do land values.

Land-Use Intensity. In direct response to the land-value pattern, land-use intensities also decline with increasing distance from the center. Producers on farm land with better access to the central market must use that land intensively to produce high enough revenues to afford to locate there. This results in high person-hour inputs per unit area of land for central farms, thereby re-

quiring large hired-labor forces. (Hired farm workers often reside in town, and so their commuting distances are minimized.) Farm size is another indicator as to the intensiveness of agricultural production; farm size generally increases with increasing distance from central markets. High land prices encourage farms to be comprised of fewer acres. Thus, in the inner zones, financing may be difficult to obtain on a scale necessary to support large farm operations. Relatively less expensive capital (such as chicken sheds) will therefore substitute for relatively more expensive land. The lower value of outer farm land permits the more lavish or extensive use of agricultural space. Because both the cost of land and farm size change with changing accessibility to the market, aggregate location rent per farm can be fairly constant across the landscape. For example, the aggregate location rent for a 50-acre vegetable farm in the inner production ring can be roughly equivalent to a 1000-acre ranch in the most peripheral zone.

Transportation Costs. The small variation of per-farm aggregate location rent across the Thünian zones is a result of site cost decreasing at approximately the same rate as transportation costs increase (Figure 13.10). High land values near the market are in a sense payments for savings

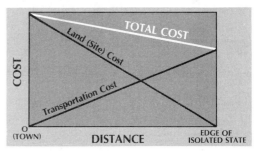

Figure 13.10 Increasing transportation costs graphed against declining land costs in the Isolated State. Total cost at any location is derived by summing site and transport costs. Note the gentle gradient or total costs that contributes to generally constant per-farm incomes across the Thünian zones.

in product-movement costs. Moreover, inner-ring farming is distinguished by the production of goods that do not easily withstand long-distance transportation. Highly perishable commodities such as fruits, vegetables, and dairy products share this low transferability. This relationship is underscored by what we will see shortly as a comparatively steep location-rent gradient for truck gardens. (Refrigeration, can-

ning, and freezing technology were, of course, unknown in von Thünen's early nineteenth-century era.) Particularly bulky commodities are also not easily transferable. The original Thünian model contained forestry (in its second ring) near to the market because heavyweight wood used for fuel and construction was expensive to transport. By the second half of the nineteenth century, cheaper rail transportation, the substitution

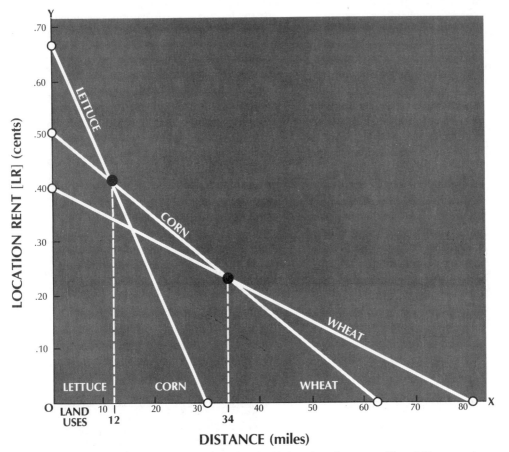

Figure 13.11 If we remember that the crop with the highest location rent will outbid competitors at each location, lettuce is seen to be dominant from zero to 12 miles from the market center (to the point where its location rent curve intersects the one for corn). Beyond this point corn exceeds lettuce's location rent and will dominate from 12 to 34 miles, at which distance it crosses below the location rent cure for wheat; wheat, in turn, will be raised from 34 miles out to the edge of the agricultural area at a distance of 80 miles.

To this point we have considered only a one-dimensional production sequence along a straight-line route (*OX*) from the central town to the outer margin of the Isolated State.

of other building materials for wood, and the replacement of wood with other sources of energy (see Chapter 12) brought an end to zones of forests near the city, relegating them instead to remote tracts of land. Transportation then shapes the geographic pattern of economic activity, a distributional influence exerted and heightened in the case of commercial agriculture through the Thünian location-rent mechanism.

Von Thünen was one of the first to adopt the "new math" of his era, calculus, and to apply that mathematics to a problem of the social sciences. He was a pioneer in the use of data for the verification of his normative theory. Von Thünen's innovative research method was similar in composition to what we would today call computer simulation. Indeed, much of the approach to social science thought today (certainly, logical positivism) can be traced back to von Thünen's general method of analysis as its precursor. His contribution to modern thinking in the social sciences stands without parallel. His general approach became diffused through its adoption by the leading scholars of the generations that followed him, and by their adoption of his general method in their own work.[17] Von Thünen's application of his general method to his own land-use theory became generally accessible only in the early 1950s when Edgar S. Dunn published his interpretation in English of von Thünen's reasoning.[18]

Von Thünen is no exception among the greats whose reasoning in time is recognized to have contained an error. The beauty of using mathematics over mere verbalization to express concepts or hypotheses is that when an error is made the error can often be corrected irrefutably. Dunn found an error in von Thünen's treatise and corrected it. Recall from the discussion above that a caveat was to be presented to von Thünen's general theory: once the hierarchical ranking of farming systems was established, such as that listed in Table 13.1, those of lower ranking would always be outbid by those of higher ranking should both happen to be competing for the same land. Instead, Dunn correctly reasoned that since location rent changed by a different amount for each agricultural product with distance from the central market,[19] then at some locations a lower ranking farming system could indeed outbid a higher ranking farming system, even though positive rents were bid by the higher ranking farming system. What may appear as a marginal location for the higher ranking system may be the most advantageous location that the lower ranking system could afford. Therefore, Dunn argued, a lower ranking system may outbid the higher ranking system at some locations. To clarify this reasoning, we now present Dunn's interpretation of von Thünen's general theory.

Von Thünen's General Theory of Land Use

The following is von Thünen's general theory as corrected by Dunn. Location rent is the difference between total revenues and total costs per acre. Total revenue is the product of yield per acre and the market price of the agricultural product. Total cost is the product of the yield per

---

[17]The great economist Alfred Marshall wrote in his *Principles of Economics* (1890) at the end of the nineteenth century that "I have long ago forgotten Cournot; and I may be wrong. But my impression is that I did not derive so much of the substance of my opinions from him as from Von Thünen. Cournot was a gymnastic master who directed the form of my thought. Von Thünen was a bona fide mathematician, . . . , he was a careful experimenter and student of facts and with a mind at least a fully developed on the inductive as on the deductive side. . . . And I loved Von Thünen above all my other masters. Professor Fisher has cared for Cournot. I wish that someone would care for Von Thünen."

[18]Edgar S. Dunn, Jr., *The Location of Agricultural Production* (Gainesville, FL: University of Florida Press, 1954).

[19]This is because the slopes and intercepts of each location rent curve for each product are usually different. The rate at which land rents decline with distance from the market (the slope) and the maximum land rent a producer of a product is willing to pay (the intercept) depend on the numerical values unique to each product. The numerical values are market price, cost of production, freight rate, and amount produced.

acre and the per unit cost of production, less the cost of shipping the yield to the market. In other words,

$$LR = Ep - Ea - Efk \qquad (13.1)$$

which rearranged is

$$LR = E(p - a) - Efk \qquad (13.2)$$

where

LR = location rent per acre
E = yield (bushel) of agricultural product per unit of land (acre)
p = market price per bushel of agricultural product
a = cost of producing each bushel of product, including the land user's opportunity cost
k = distance (miles) product is shipped from farm to central market
f = freight rate per bushel per mile

Each crop has its own yield, market price, cost of production, and freight rate. A system of three competing crops will be explained, but the method is valid for any number of agricultural activities. The equation once rearranged is a straight line, with slope Ef and intercept $E(p - a)$. Knowing this, we can easily graph the location-rent curve for each crop as a straight line. This is done by solving for the horizontal and vertical intercepts of each line. Set LR equal to 0 in Equation (13.2) and solve for the intercept on the horizontal or distance axis; the resulting equation for the intercept is

$$k^* = (p - a)/f \qquad (13.3)$$

k^* is interpreted as the outer range that producers are willing to bid for the right to use agricultural land to produce their product. Beyond k^*, transportation costs become so high as to leave the tenant farmer with insufficient revenues to cover their other costs; hence, they are not willing to pay positive rents beyond k^*. To solve for the intercept on the vertical axis, set k equal to 0 in Equation (13.2) and solve for LR^*:

$$LR^* = E(p - a) \qquad (13.4)$$

LR^* is interpreted as the rent-bid to be paid by the tenant farmer at the market where there are no transportation costs. Because in von Thünen's model, rent declines with distance from the market to counter the greater transportation costs outward from the central market, then LR^* is the maximum rent-bid by producers of the particular product. Therefore, land rents are highest at the central market and decline with decreasing accessibility.

Recall from the discussion concerning the above caveat that von Thünen believed that higher ranking agricultural products would always be outbid by those of lower ranking (Table 13.1). In the above mathematical terms, higher ranking agricultural products would have greater values for LR^*. However, this ignores the fact that each crop type will also have a different value for k^* in Equation (13.3) and a different slope $(-Ef)$. In other words, the straight-line bid-rent curves can intersect because each crop type has differing values for their negative slopes and differing maximum values at the market. The land will be rented to the tenant who is willing and able to pay the highest amount to use the land at a particular location. Hence, if the land-rent curves intersect, then the higher ranked agricultural product will outbid the lower ranked inward of the location where their land rents are equal. Outward of that location, the lower ranked will outbid the higher ranked. Assume there are two crops i and m. The location of transition from crop i to m, $k^{**}_{i,m}$, can be determined by setting the land-rent curves for the two competing crops LR_i and LR_m equal and then solving for $k^{**}_{i,m}$.

$$LR_i = LR_m \qquad (13.5)$$

$$k^{**}_{i,m} = \frac{[E_i(p_i - a_i) - E_m(p_m - a_m)]}{(E_i f_i - E_m f_m)} \qquad (13.6)$$

The algebraic steps sufficient to derive Equation (13.6) from (13.5) are given in Table 13.3.

Table 13.4 presents example numerical values

Table 13.3   Derivation of Location of Agricultural Market Transition

LR_i	$=$	LR_m
$E_i(p_i - a_i) - E_i f_i k^{**}_{i,m}$	$=$	$E_m(p_m - a_m) - E_m f_m k^{**}_{i,m}$
$E_i(p_i - a_i) - E_m(p_m - a_m)$	$=$	$E_i f_i k^{**}_{i,m} - E_m f_m k^{**}_{i,m}$
$k^{**}_{i,m}(E_i f_i - E_m f_m)$	$=$	$E_i(p_i - a_i) - E_m(p_m - a_m)$
$k^{**}_{i,m}$	$=$	$[E_i(p_i - a_i) - E_m(p_m - a_m)] / (E_i f_i - E_m f_m)$

that can be substituted into the equations for the two intercepts. The bottom rows of the table include the solutions for the intercepts for each crop and the location of market transition from one crop type to another.

Try substituting the numerical values from Table 13.4 into the equations to derive k^*, k^{**}, and LR^* for each of the three illustrative crops. For example, $k^*_{truck\ garden} = (63-45)/3$, and $LR^*_{truck\ garden} = 300(63-45)$, and $k^{**}_{truck\ garden,\ dairy} = [300(63-45) - 200(45-25)]/[(300)(3) - (200)(2)]$.

The crop that can afford the highest location rent can outbid competitors. Producers of truck gardens outbid producers of other crops from the

Table 13.4   Example Agricultural Parameters and Solutions

Parameter	Truck Garden	Dairy	Wheat
E	300	200	100
p	$63	$45	$30
a	$45	$25	$10
f	$3	$2	$1

Derived Terms	Numerical Solutions		
k^*	600 miles	1000 miles	2000 miles
LR^*	$5400	$4000	$2000

$k^{**}_{dairy,\ truck\ garden}$ = 280 miles
$k^{**}_{truck\ garden,\ wheat}$ = 425 miles
$k^{**}_{wheat,\ dairy}$ = 667 miles

Note: Freight rate f is given in units per hundred miles. Hence, f must be divided by 100 before calculating k^* and k^{**}.

market center out to 280 miles. From 280 to 667 miles, dairy producers outbid the competition. From 667 miles to 2000 miles, wheat producers outbid producers of the other crops for the right to use the land. Within a 280-mile radius of the market center, producers of corn and wheat are willing to bid a positive location rent for the right to use land there. But lettuce producers bid the greatest amount, thereby demonstrating that at the particular location they are the so-called highest and best use; they aren't everywhere, however. Consider once again the caveat noted earlier in this chapter. Even though in Table 13.1 the truck garden's lettuce ranks in the hierarchy of crops above corn and wheat, and even though in Figure 13.11 lettuce producers bid a positive location rent between 12 and 30 miles over this range, corn producers are willing and able to bid a higher location rent than lettuce producers. Indeed, Figure 13.11 shows that even wheat producers are willing and able to outbid lettuce producers over some locations.

It is conventional in such discussions to express the general ideas on a one-dimensional ray OX extending from the central market to the outer margins of the market area. This is known as analysis using *relative spatial location*. That is, we have considered some activity occurring 280 miles from the market without regard to direction. Indeed, as noted earlier, the homogeneous landscape assumption will bring about competition by the producers of the various crops identical for every direction about the central market. To make the analysis three dimensional so that we can portray the results on a map (absolute spatial location), rotate the horizontal axis 360°

around the stationary vertical axis OY (Figure 13.12). By adding the third dimension, the previously seen concentric-ring pattern of crop production zones is derived.

Von Thünen carried the analysis of Figure 13.12 a significant step further toward realism by drawing on some of the potential of analysis using absolute spatial location. He allowed the parameters for each crop to differ by direction about the central market, and he included additional and competing central markets on the landscape, each with its own set of numerical val-

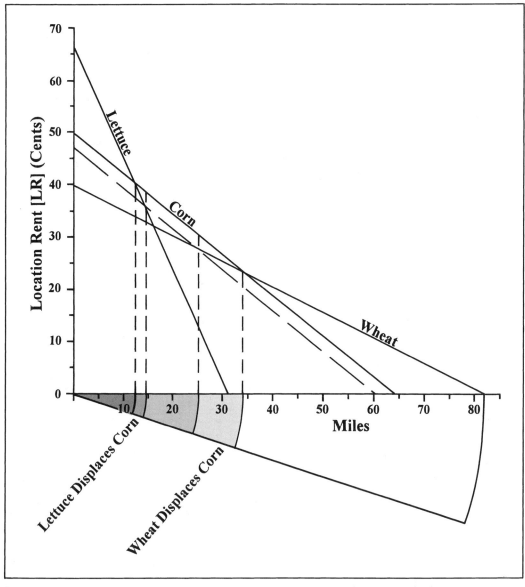

Figure 13.12 We add the areal dimension and thereby elicit the familiar concentric-ring pattern.

ues for the parameters. He then asked the question "what if?" What if a particular parameter of Table 13.4 changed while the values of the other parameters were held constant? Alternative landscape patterns could then be "forecast."[20]

What If? Say corn price decreases by 10 percent. Economists would use their normative model of supply and demand to analyze what the expected consequence would be from the price decrease. The economists' normative model would indicate that because price has declined, suppliers will be willing to offer fewer dairy products for sale on the market. The normative model will give the general trajectory of what is expected to happen. Such models can also be referred to as *heuristic* because they tell "a story" as to what the general trajectory of events are expected to be. However, if an exact numerical answer is required, not just a trajectory, how much will quantity offered on the market decrease? Then the economist must apply statistical (econometric) methods to derive the answer.

The economic geographer, when analyzing the same phenomena, would instead ask the question: *where* will the decrease in corn production occur that results from the decrease in corn prices? Using von Thünen's normative spatial model, an economic geographer's answer can be computed by first observing that the price of corn p is included in both the distance intercept k^* of Equation (13.3) and the location-rent intercept LR^* of Equation (13.4). As p decreases then, so do k^* and LR^*. However, p is absent from the slope Ef of Equation (13.2), meaning that the slope of the location-rent curve does not change. Hence, the decrease in the price of corn results in a parallel shift downward and to the left of the location-rent curve for dairy as shown in Figure 13.12. The expected trajectory is that agricultural producers shift out of corn and instead produce lettuce or wheat: lettuce producers increase their areal extent outward, while wheat producers increase their areal extent inward. Spatial-statistical methods that economic geographers have developed can be used to forecast where these changes will actually occur.

You can create your own numerical simulation by recalculating the breaking points between truck garden, dairy, and wheat with the same parameters as in Table 13.4, except for a 10-percent lower price of dairy. Compare these numerical results to those with the higher price of dairy. Draw maps for each set of parameter values. How do the two maps differ, and where do they differ? Similarly, evaluate the following economic-geography problem. What would happen if the cost of transporting wheat were to decrease by 20 percent while the values for all other parameters in Table 13.4 remained the same? Derive your results first using von Thünen's normative model, and then recalculate the breaking points for Table 13.4. Compare these numerical results to those with the original transportation cost. How do the two hypothetical landscapes differ, and where do they differ?

EMPIRICAL APPLICATIONS OF THÜNIAN LOCATION THEORY

Von Thünen realized that his normative/heuristic model of land use could be applied to forecast the pattern of land use on his estate *Tellow*; then, by comparing forecasted results to actual spatial patterns, the accuracy of the model could be determined. Indeed, he can be considered the first social scientist to empirically calibrate such a

---

[20]Von Thünen was the first to conceptualize this normative way of structuring thought. Computer simulations and the spreadsheet of the microcomputer are commonplace today, but it is to von Thünen that we owe gratitude for such a powerful method of reasoning. It is this contribution—interestingly, not his application of this method of reasoning to create his theory of agricultural land use—that he considered to be his greatest intellectual accomplishment and to which he was referring in his quotation at the head of this chapter.

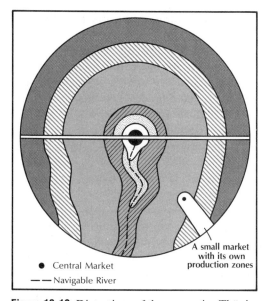

Figure 13.13 Distortions of the normative Thünian zonation with transportation and single-market assumptions relaxed. *Source:* After Michael Chisholm. *Rural Settlement and Land Use.* London: Hutchinson University Library, 1962, p. 29.

model. The type of reasoning he pioneered is now an important methodology for many social scientists known as logical positivism. He introduced the empirical dimension to his heuristic framework by systematically removing the spatial constraints with which he had begun his agricultural location analysis.

One of his findings is depicted in Figure 13.13, where the assumptions of a uniform transportation cost surface and a single central market are suspended. A navigable river connection from the town into the hinterland is added, thereby distorting accessibility in favor of the water route; movement is cheaper and faster along the water route than in any other direction. The effect of low-cost transportation networks then is demonstrated by this normative model to "pull" the rings of similar land use outward along the low-cost network. (Note that the economic mar-

gin of ring 2 in the river sector is more than three times the distance from market than its counterpart in the upper half of the diagram.) The normative model also clearly shows what can be expected from a competing outlying market center: the production zones oriented to the main market leap over the space claimed by the secondary center. The same kind of interruption would have occurred if the second market's area were occupied instead by some obstacle that prohibits farming (for example, a swamp or small mountain range). Heuristic models are useful, for they can improve our understanding of what would result when there is a change in the environment.[21]

Von Thünen's general theory and its application to the landscape surrounding his estate represented a major step in human reasoning. However, the economic geography of his time differs considerably from the conditions of the contem-

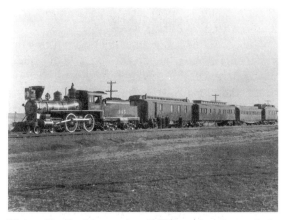

Union Pacific locomotive (1870) and rail cars help open up the western United States by linking Chicago and San Francisco.

[21]Two examples of other heuristic models developed by economic geographers are Walter Christaller, *Central Places in Southern Germany*, translated by Carlisle W. Baskin from *Die Zentralen Orte in Suddeutschland.* (Englewood Cliffs, N.J.: Prentice-Hall, 1966), and Grant Thrall, *Land Use and Urban Form.* (London: Routledge/Methuen, 1987)

porary world. Although the Thünian system is highly ordered via the pedagogic principles that shape the system, an observer may still not recognize how it can apply to our complex world. Isolated city-states surrounded by impenetrable wilderness? Horse-and-buggy transportation? The Germany of 150 years ago? How can this possibly add to our understanding of the spatial organization of land use for the contemporary agricultural sector? Answering this question is imperative; otherwise we lose sight of our mission to understand the geography of the economy that surrounds us. Up to now, we have been concerned only with establishing the logic of the Thünian location theory. We must now shift from concepts and principles to a consideration of the changing empirical form of the von Thünen model by directly examining its present relevance for understanding the spatial organization of American agriculture.

During the past 150 years, there have been sizable changes in agricultural land use and the economy with which it interacts. The most important of the changes have been improvements in transportation technology; these improvements now permit a space–time convergence of distant places, thereby expanding the scale of possible economic organization. In von Thünen's day, heavily loaded horse-drawn carts moved to market at the rate of about one mile an hour. A journey from the wilderness edge to the market center[22] would require more than two full days, without pauses for rest. Therefore, the truest measure of economic distance in the Thünian model—the absolute mileage beyond which farming was simply too far from the market and could no longer yield location rent—is in terms of a 50-hour *time–distance*. If that 50-hour time–distance radius is constant as a Thünian farming system evolves, what would be its territorial extent today? Considering the continental

United States with its present-day rail and truck agricultural-transport system, that radius equals the east-west extent of the nation, assuming ground speeds of 60 mph over a distance of 3000 miles (a movement rate consistent with express freight timetables).

With the establishment of the coterminous United States as a contemporary laboratory in which to search for Thünian processes, where is the "supercity" needed to focus such a macroscale model? In his writings, Geography professor Peter Muller has proposed that such a supercity can be found in the Megalopolis conurbation of the United States, which extends along the northeastern seaboard from Washington, D.C., to Boston. In the earlier part of this century, the Megalopolis's locational pull was dominant in American economic life. Certainly, with the rise of Los Angeles, Dallas–Fort Worth, and other significant secondary cities such as Atlanta, Megalopolis is no longer the dominant force it once was. Nevertheless, the words written in 1961 by one of the foremost students of Megalopolis, Jean Gottmann, still ring true.

There are many other large metropolitan areas and even clusters of them in various parts of the United States, but none of them is yet comparable to Megalopolis in size of population, density of population, or density of activities, be these expressed in terms of transportation, communications, banking operations, or political conferences. Megalopolis provides the whole of America with so many essential services . . . that it may well deserve the nickname of "Main Street of the nation." And for three centuries it has performed this role, though the transcontinental march of settlement has developed along east-west axes perpendicular to this section of the Atlantic seaboard.[23]

---

[22]Von Thünen gave this radial distance as 50 miles (Hall, *Von Thünen's Isolated State*, p. 157).

[23]Jean Gottmann, *Megalopolis: The Urbanized Northeastern Seaboard of the United States* (New York: Twentieth Century Fund, 1961), pp. 7–8.

Muller's interpretation of a normative macro-Thünian model for the United States, anchored by Megalopolis, is shown in Figure 13.14. Its utility for explaining the national pattern of agricultural production is demonstrated as follows.

We begin again by relaxing the normative assumptions of the Isolated state model, but this time with the realization that empirical irregularities will be complex in the sophisticated economic space of the present-day continental United States. However, because we are concerned only with the overall organizational framework of farming regions at a high level of spatial generalization, the search is not complicated: if macro-Thünian processes have shaped the production pattern, then empirical response to them will be easily discernible. The main task is to set up the investigation by cataloging physical-environmental and economic-empirical irregularities in order to derive an appropriate map of the expected real-world spatial pattern.

Environmental variables, as pointed out in connection with the physical limits model, are only a general locational constraint and play a passive role in shaping the distribution of modern commercial agriculture. In the human-technological context, the employment of artificial irrigation, chemical fertilizers, and the like allows farmers to overcome most environmental barriers if it is profitable to do so. Nevertheless, because physical factors vary considerably throughout the vast 3 million-square-mile territory of the continental United States, it should be expected that the orientation to Megalopolis will be tempered accordingly. Temperature regimes vary with latitude, from year-round growing seasons along the subtropical southern rim to short, cool summers along the Canadian border in both the Northeast and Northwest. Precipitation tends to decline from east to west, rising again between the Sierra Nevada–Cascade Mountain Range and the Pacific littoral; the key

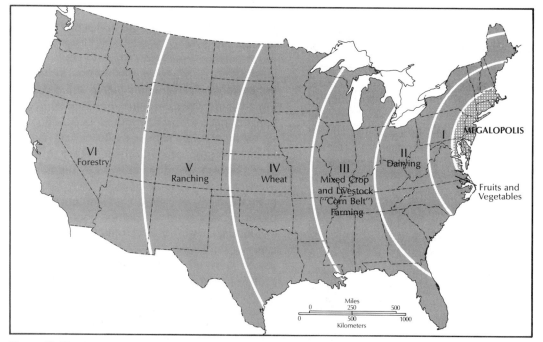

Figure 13.14 The macro-Thünian model for a normative United States, focused on the megalopolis national market.

rainfall boundary separating humid from semi-arid areas (which require irrigation for many crops) is the 20-inch isohyet, which will be included in our empirical map. Soil variability is also noteworthy, and we will identify areas of outstanding natural fertility (as before in the case of southeastern cotton and its physical optimum). Extreme topography is also important, largely as a constraint for most types of farming; major mountain ranges are noted as well as heavily glaciated areas whose soil profiles are unusually shallow.

Three kinds of economic empirical irregularities can be anticipated to influence the national Thünian pattern: transportation biases, distant concentrations of production that appear inconsistent with his model, and secondary markets.

Transport or market accessibility biases are particularly important (as we already know from von Thünen's own early empirical application) because they shape geographic distance as measured by freight movement and time costs within the total macrogeographic system. From the discussion of American transportation evolution at the beginning of Chapter 5, it will be recalled that a bias in favor of east-west movement across the North developed in the nineteenth century and persists to this day. That bias may in fact be localized to a corridor of "bundled" rail and highway routes that constitutes *a national transportation axis* stretching inland from central Megalopolis through both Pennsylvania and upstate New York and then as a single route west to San Francisco via Cleveland, Chicago, Omaha, Denver, and Salt Lake City.

Outlying concentrations of farming may also "disturb" the Thünian system if they possess superior agricultural advantages. Areas with year-round growing seasons, such as Florida and southern California, are examples. Historical inertia may also be a contributing factor: the remote state of Idaho began its distinctive potato production before competing regions arose and has been able to withstand later challenges to its initiative and prominence. However, the key to

A truck carrying milk to market.

success in the distant producing areas that appear to "beat" the von Thünen system is outstanding local economic organization. High-speed transportation and shrewd ability to capitalize on long-haul economies to minimize shipment rates are crucial for survival and must be supported by the nurturing of unique specialization advantages and self-contained agglomeration economies that keep local production costs to a minimum. California's Sunkist association of citrus growers is a good example of the business acumen necessary to compete in a national market a continent away. Its managers orchestrate the smooth flow of fruit from orchard to railyard to guarantee the full loading of long eastbound freight trains at highly predictable intervals, so that California oranges can sell at prices competitive with Florida's in New Jersey supermarkets.

Although Florida and California can success-

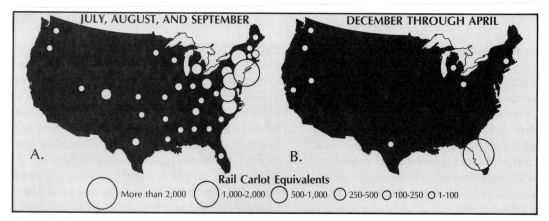

Figure 13.15 Sources of cucumbers sold in 46 U.S. and Canadian cities, 1963–1965 average. Note the radically different supply areas for winter and summer months. *Source:* After Sidney R. Jumper, "The Fresh Vegetable Industry in the U.S.A.: An Example of Dynamic Interregional Dependency." *Tijdschrift voor Economische en Sociale Geografie* 60 (September–October, 1969), p. 314.

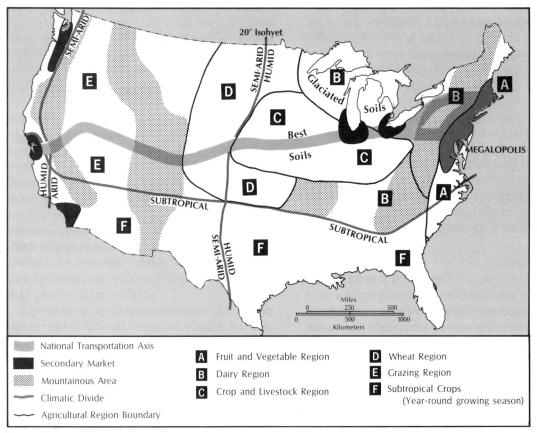

Figure 13.16 The expected spatial pattern of American agricultural organization, allowing for empirical disturbances at the national scale.

fully compete against each other in Megalopolis, they are unable to succeed when competition arises from producing areas adjacent to the national market. This is demonstrated in Figure 13.15, which shows what happens when northeastern states can temporarily produce their own fresh vegetables in the warm season: transport savings and comparative locational advantages achieved by Megalopolis truck farmers sharply curtail the long-distance flow of cucumbers in the summer months (Figure 13.15*a*) whereas in the winter remotely produced cucumbers dominate the Megalopolis market (Figure 13.15*b*).

Secondary markets, as we know, can also disrupt the Thünian pattern. Two other large U.S. conurbations may be noted in this regard: the midwestern "chipitt" (Chicago–Detroit–Cleveland–Pittsburgh) and the Californian "San–San" (San Francisco–Fresno–Los Angeles–San Diego) urban concentrations. Although their populations are large enough to affect macroagricultural spatial organization, we do not

anticipate that these influences will be major, for neither comes close to the "Boswash" northeastern Megalopolis in size or in national economic dominance.

We may now assemble our knowledge of agricultural location principles together with these national empirical irregularities into a single map that describes the expected macro-Thünian pattern (Figure 13.16). With this map as predictor, let us compare and evaluate its consistency with the actual pattern of American farming regions, which is mapped in Figure 13.17 (compare also with the maps of individual crops in Figure 13.4).

Comparison of the anticipated and actual macro-Thünian patterns shows obvious spatial correspondence between them. The east-to-west sequence of agricultural regions in the northern United States accords particularly well with our expectations, and we may conclude that the response to economic distance from the dominant Megalopolis market conforms to what we would expect of the nationwide distribution of farming

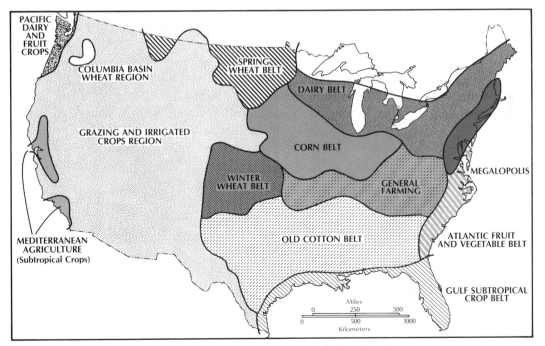

Figure 13.17 The actual geographical arrangement of U.S. agricultural regions.

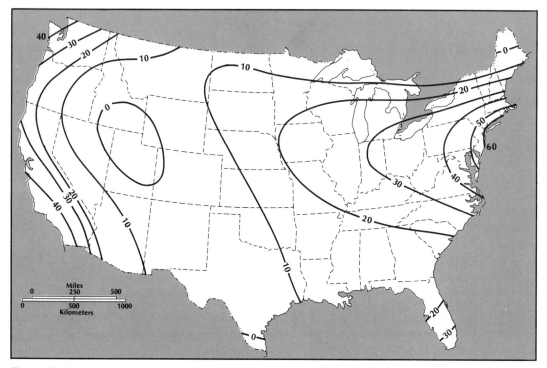

Figure 13.18 The net-income-per-acre surface for the United States in 1964, mapped with a contour interval of $10. *Source:* After Peter O. Muller, "Trend Surfaces of American Agricultural Patterns: A Macro-Thünian Analysis." *Economic Geography* 49 (July 1973), p. 237.

systems. Producing regions lying outside of the fruit–vegetable/dairying/Corn Belt/Wheat Belt/ grazing sequence can be explained by anticipated empirical disturbances. Physical factors largely account for the eastern general farming region (miscellaneous and generally low-grade farming in scattered basins and valleys) that largely occupies the central Appalachian Upland and Ozark Plateau and the widely dispersed irrigated croplands of the semiarid Far West. The outlying concentrations (largely high-value fruit and vegetable specialty crops) of the subtropical Gulf and southern Pacific coasts are consistent with our expected map and, in a very real sense, represent discontinuous outliers of the innermost market-gardening (or truck-farming) production ring that cannot feed Megalopolis and the rest of the nation for most of the year. The smaller farm-

ing regions of the Pacific Northwest can be interpreted in similar fashion. In the Southeast, the old Cotton Belt (most cotton is now raised in the Southwest) increasingly contains high-value crops appropriate to its regional position.

Geographers have verified the existence of the U.S. macro-Thünian pattern. Limited data availability, especially transport-rate information, prevent direct empirical testing of the Thünian–Dunn location-rent formula for individual agricultural activities. However, a surrogate variable for location rent—net income per acre—has been examined for the nation at the county level of data aggregation. Mapping these data in Figure 13.18 clearly shows the overriding macro-Thünian influence in shaping this income surface. Other recent work has more clearly established the important historical dimension of the macromodel. Consideration of this supplementary approach will deepen our understanding of the temporal dynamics of the agricultural location process.

DYNAMIC AGRICULTURAL LOCATION THEORY: THÜNIAN ANALYSIS IN TIME–SPACE

The macroscale application of the classical Thünian model to interpret the contemporary spatial structure of American farming regions implies a sequence of intermediate stages whereby the original-scale Thünian landscape was transformed into a nationwide agricultural system. As transportation improved in the nineteenth century, allowing constant expansion in the geographic range of agricultural goods, one may visualize the concomitant westward enlargement of the macro-Thünian production zones as a series of spreading concentric ripples of the kind that emanate from the point where a stone is thrown into water. Simultaneously, Megalopolis rapidly coalesced as a combined national and international marketplace. This was a result of both massive internal urban growth and increasing command of American foreign trade as this country began to compete in the international food-export market. Sharply rising agricultural demands within the Megalopolis market, reinforced by steadily shrinking movement costs and time–distances, fueled the deeper penetration of food-supply regions into the continental interior. The leading edge of this national commercial farming system was the American frontier. As the frontier swept toward the Pacific, rural areas left in its wake experienced the progressive westerly migration of more and more intensive farming as illustrated by the movement of the Wheat Belt across Wisconsin between 1850 and 1890 (Figure 13.19).

It is useful to trace the evolution of the nationwide Thünian system parallel with the development of the various dominant modes of transportation, because the American agricultural system depends so heavily on long-distance transportation. (The various transportation eras were set forth in Chapter 6. (Chapters 5 and 6 should be reviewed at this point.)

The pre-1825 *Local Era,* prior to the coming of the railroad, was one of short-distance movement by waterway and interior overland roads. Each major urban center on the northeastern seaboard was responsible for supplying its own food from the local hinterland, the hinterland corresponding to the production pattern and spatial extent of the classical Thünian model.

The transition or phase shift from local to broader regional spatial organization occurred during the *Trans-Appalachian Era* (1825–1865). The arrival of cheap long-distance rail transportation after 1830 greatly reduced per-mile movement costs, and the rail lines that penetrated the Central Lowlands permitted time–space convergence to occur between the Northeast and Midwest. As a result, food production in the North during this period was characterized by *spatial integration* in which a near-national set of more specialized producing regions emerged, dominated by a large-scale geographic division of labor, international agglomeration economies, and increasing interregional trade. At the same time, isolated local seaboard markets greatly expanded, merged all but their most immediate farming hinterlands, and were well on their way toward forming a national agricultural marketplace (trends generalized in Figure 13.20b). We may again use the "spreading ripples" analogy to describe these growth patterns: if three stones are thrown into calm water near one another, their splash ripples will quickly coalesce to form a single set of concentric pulsations that spread outward to cover a large area. Although several larger-scale agricultural regions had emerged by 1850, the macro-Thünian system was not yet complete. High-speed railroads linking the Great Plains, Far West, and much of the South with the rest of the nation had still not incorporated many potential farming areas, as the Wisconsin maps of Figure 13.19 remind us. Nevertheless, the

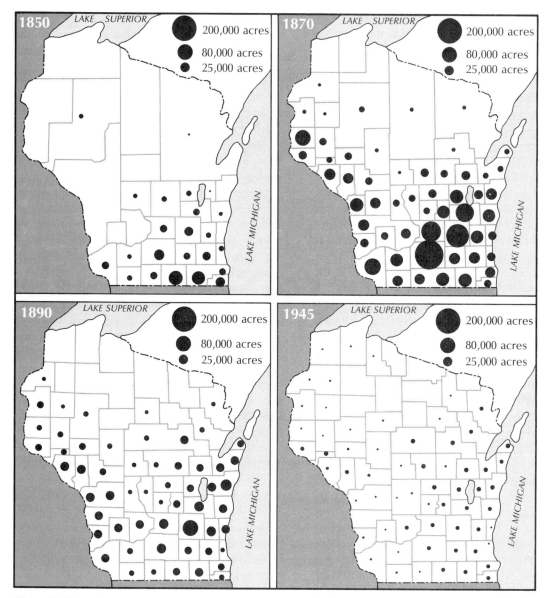

Figure 13.19 Wheat migrates west with the American frontier through Wisconsin eventually to become established in the Great Plains. *Source:* After *A Century of Wisconsin Agriculture.* Wisconsin Crop and Livestock Reporting Service, Bulletin No. 290, 1948.

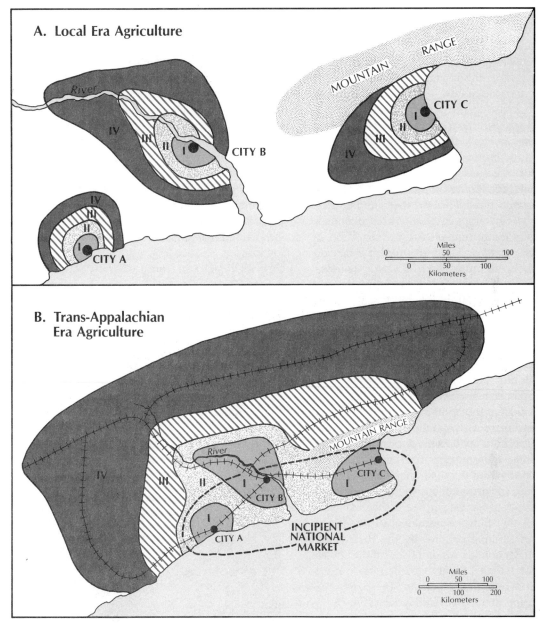

Figure 13.20 Generalized macro-Thúnian patterns for the first two transport eras. Observe the growing orientation of farming to the emerging national market.

United States had passed through its takeoff stage of development during this transport era, and abandonment of local in favor of national production was diffusing rapidly from the northeast quadrant of the country by the eve of the War Between the States.

The era following the War Between the States and the First World War was one of *Railroad Dominance* and saw the achievement of a nationwide food production system, geographically focused on the now consolidated Megalopolis national market. Transcontinental rail transportation became possible after 1869, and further time–space convergence resulted from higher-speed railroading, thanks to the innovation of steel tracks that were able to support a heavier rolling stock and much more powerful steam locomotives. Large-scale areal specialization and sophisticated regional interdependence, abetted by railroad network expansion that stressed interconnecting linkages, dominated late-nineteenth-century production. These new farming regions were clearly evident after 1875; the macro-Thünian patterns was first confirmed by the German land economist Engelbrecht in 1883.[24] This third transport era also encompassed the nation's drive to economic maturity whereby industrial technology became widespread. In the agricultural sector, industrialization launched an agrarian revolution in which machinery steadily enhanced farm productivity (a movement that still persists today as we will see in the next chapter). Mechanization became indispensable for a number of farming systems by the turn of the century, most notably wheat raising in the central and northern Plains. Countless other innovations improved agricultural efficiency, the most spectacular being the refrigerated boxcar, which initiated the long-distance transportation of highly perishable commodities.

The fourth (and current) stage of agricultural-transport evolution began in 1920 and might be called the *Competitive Era*. Other modes, particularly intercity trucking, have increasingly challenged the railroads, although rail continues to be the primary mover of farm commodities at the national level. Postwar railroading has been plagued by network curtailment, the mid-1970s' cutback of freight lines in the Northeast being an especially dramatic example. Present policy seems to be one of preserving only the highest-priority linkages. With each freight-line closure, truckers make additional inroads. With the completion of the nonmetropolitan segments of the nation's interstate freeway system, the day may soon come when more agricultural goods are hauled from farm to market by highway than by rail.

With changes in transportation conditions, the macro-Thünian system has also been modified since its emergence a century ago. Before discussing that subject, however, we will briefly review the four stages of agricultural development just discussed and their larger implications for economic regionalization in space and time. This summary is presented within the context of Janelle's model of spatial reorganization, which is diagrammed in Figure 13.21.[25] A continuous pro-

Fresh flowers are transported around the world by air. Here, fresh flowers are being loaded in Bogota, Columbia, for shipment by air.

[24]T. H. Engelbrecht, "Der Standort der Landwirtschaftsweige in Nordamerika," *Landwirtschaftliche Jahrbücher* 12 (1883), pp. 459–509.

[25]Donald G. Janelle, "Spatial Reorganization: A Model and Concept," *Annals of the Association of American Geographers* 59 (June 1969), pp. 348–364.

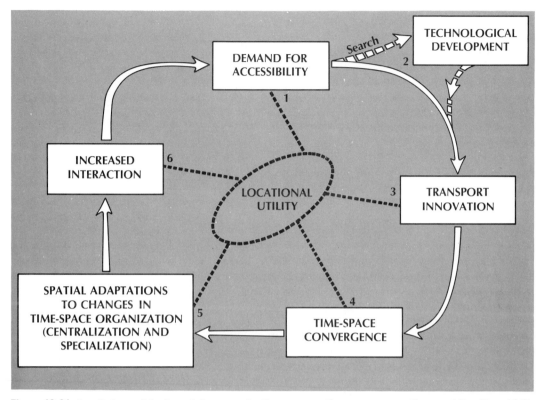

Figure 13.21 Janelle's model of spatial reorganization as a continuous process. *Source:* After Donald G. Janelle, "Spatial Reorganization: A Model and Concept," *Annals of the Association of American Geographers* 59 (June 1969), p. 350.

cess is involved that works to maximize locational utility or efficiency at each growth stage (in this case, the agricultural region). Demand for better access (1) begets technological development (2) which results in transport innovation and (3) events occurring during the Local Era, which culminated in the appearance of the railroad. The railroad propels time–space convergence (4) in the Trans-Appalachian Era, which results in the centralization and specialization (5) as well as the increased interaction (6) of the Railroad Dominance Era (and, to a lesser extent, the Competitive Era). With ongoing network pruning today, some farmers are again returning to the initial demand-for-accessibility stage, which is being met by truckers. Perhaps this newest trend will once again unleash a whole new spatial reorganization cycle.

THÜNIAN LOCATION THEORY IN THE LATE-TWENTIETH-CENTURY WORLD

Macro-Thünian distance relationships have strongly shaped American agricultural development since colonial times, and they continue to be felt (as observed in Figure 13.16). Our introductory presentation of location theory should not be expected to explain fully an agricultural space as complex as that of the United States in the late twentieth century. New forces have emerged since the macro-Thünian system was achieved 100 years ago, including transportation changes (already discussed), population shifts toward the West and South (note the West Coast secondary market in Figure 13.16), and institutional changes such as the rise of larger-scale farming (discussed more fully in the following

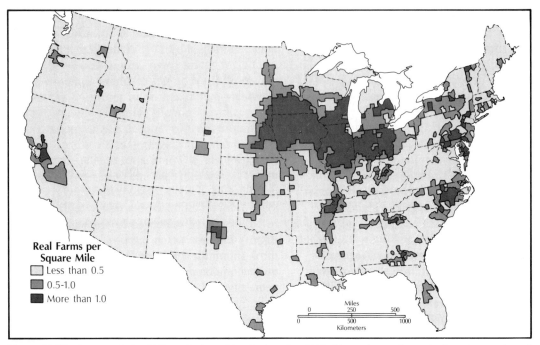

Figure 13.22 A map of the U.S. agricultural implosion for 1964. Note that truly agricultural counties of greater than 0.5 "real" farms (possessing gross incomes of more than $10,000 from the sale of farm products) are strongly associated with the national transport axis and its eastern seaboard and Mississippi Valley tributaries. *Source:* After John Fraser Hart, "A Map of the Agricultural Implosion." *Proceedings of the Association of American Geographers* 2 (1970), p. 69.

chapter). The net result of these and other modifications is the relaxation in the overall national geographic infrastructure. This effect is counterbalanced by farmer conservatism and location inertia effects (see Chapter 1), which ensure the persistence of the macro-Thünian landscape. Distance from market as an organizing spatial framework is still important today at the nationwide level; this geographic reality will become even more significant if fuel prices rise. Thünianstyle agglomeration also perseveres as an active contemporary agricultural location process, especially the internal and external economies concentrated along the national transport axis (Figures 13.16 and 13.18). This trend is underscored by Hart's evidence of an agricultural "implosion" whereby less rewarding farm land is abandoned in favor of greater concentration on more productive land, much of the latter lying within this broad east-west corridor (Figure 13.22)[26]

Empirical evidence of Thünian spatial systems is also widespread beyond the United States. Figure 13.23a shows the macroscale pattern of agricultural intensity for the European continent, which is sharply focused on the conurbation ring-

[26]John Fraser Hart, "A Map of the Agricultural Implosion," *Proceedings of the Association of American Geographers* 2 (1970), pp. 68–71. An alternative hypothesis to John Fraser Hart, of the same phenomenon, is that Thünian rent surfaces predominate when the economic geography of the landscape is young. After the development of competing destinations and of several competing and efficient transportation media, Ricardian rent surfaces predominate. In the Ricardian world, location is not important, while land productivity is the most important determining factor for land value and land utilization.

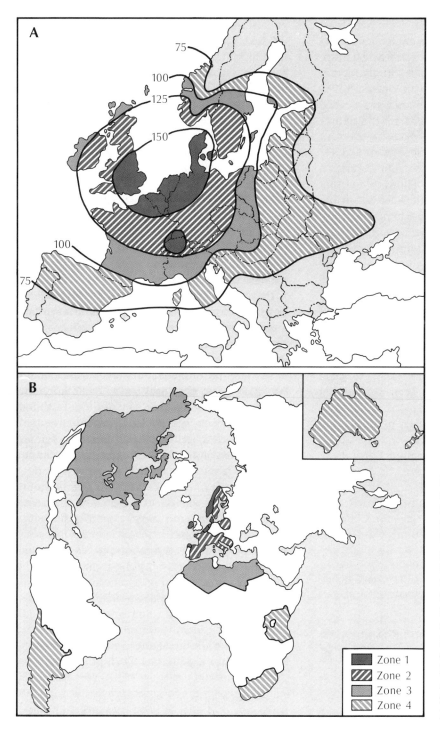

Figure 13.23 Other large-scale Thünian systems, showing macrogeographical patterns of agricultural intensity for Europe (A) and the entire globe (B). Zone 1 represents the highest level of agricultural intensity, with zone 4 the lowest. *Source:* After Samuel Van Valkenburg and C.C. Held, *Europe*, 2 rev. ed. (New York: Wiley, 1952), as depicted in Michael Chisholm, *Rural Settlement and Land Use* (London: Hutchinson University Library, 1962), pp. 108, 99.

ing the southern margin of the North Sea, from London and Paris to Copenhagen. By combining the American and European patterns and proceeding to a yet greater level of spatial aggregation, one can even perceive (in Figure 13.23b) a global-scale Thünian system focused on the "world metropolis" that borders the North Atlantic Ocean.[27]

Thünian distance relationships can also be discerned at the national level in smaller developed countries such as Uruguay. Allowing for that nation's empirical irregularities, Ernst Griffin discovered that the expected Thünian pattern accorded nicely with the actual intensity of agricultural land use.[28] Continuing down the level-of-generalization continuum from mesoscale to microscale, Thünian influences are often observed to shape farming at the local level.[29] Moreover, local agricultural production in the less developed world, where technological conditions are more comparable to those of von Thünen's day, may even exhibit spatial structures reminiscent of von Thünen's landscape. Ronald Horvath found just such a pattern for the area surrounding Addis Ababa, Ethiopia. Of particular significance was his discovery of an expanding transportation-oriented eucalyptus forestry zone in its classical inner position beyond the vegetable production area.[30]

Returning to the United States and the notion of a spatially expanding urban market, Robert Sinclair detected some interesting effects on production in the innermost agricultural land in the path of metropolitan encroachment.[31] Spreading urbanization appears to influence agriculture several miles in advance of the builtup frontier because farmers realize they cannot compete against the coming much-higher location rents earned by urban land uses. Thus, metropolitan expansion is perceived as a displacement threat in the affected inner rural zone, and this is reflected in the spatial behavior of farmers. Those closest to the urban frontier feel most threatened and keep their agricultural investments minimized. These investments rise with distance from the frontier to the outer edge of this zone of anticipation, where the specialized agriculture of the region takes over. Figure 13.24a diagrams the sequence of uses within this zone of rising value for agriculture as distance from V increases: OV is the area occupied exclusively by urban land; farming activities V–W–X–Y of increasing intensity are found beyond the frontier; and crop Z is the regional speciality in accordance with the macro-Thünian system.

Sinclair postulated four types of farming, which correspond to uses V–W–X–Y, and these are seen in the four inner zones of Figure 13.24b (The fifth zone—specialized feed-grain livestock or Corn Belt agriculture—is the wider regional specialty beyond the belt of expanding urban influence.) Proceeding outward from the beginning of Sinclair's Zone 1, they are (1) urban farming, a hodgepodge of small producing units, scattered through the already subdivided outer suburban environment, which favor poultry-keeping, greenhouses, mushroom-raising, and other building-oriented uses; (2) vacant and temporary grazing, where farmers leave much land empty to sell to urban land speculators at the most opportune moment and allow grazing only under short-term leases; (3) transitory field crop and grazing, a transitional agricultural type dominated by farm uses, but with definite anticipation

[27]See John T. Schlebecker, "The World Metropolis and the History of American Agriculture," *Journal of Economic History* 20 (June 1960), pp. 187–208.

[28]Ernst Griffin, "Testing the Von Thünen Theory in Uruguay," *Geographical Review* 63 (October 1973), pp. 500–516.

[29]See Michael Chisholm, *Rural Settlement and Land Use: An Essay in Location*, 3rd rev. ed. (London: Hutchinson University Library, 1979), pp. 33–62, 106–129.

[30]Ronald J. Horvath, "Von Thünen's Isolated State and the Area Around Addis Ababa, Ethiopia," *Annals of the Association of American Geographers* 59 (June 1969), pp. 308–323.

[31]Robert Sinclair, "Von Thünen and Urban Sprawl," *Annals of the Association of American Geographers* 57 (March 1967), pp. 72–87.

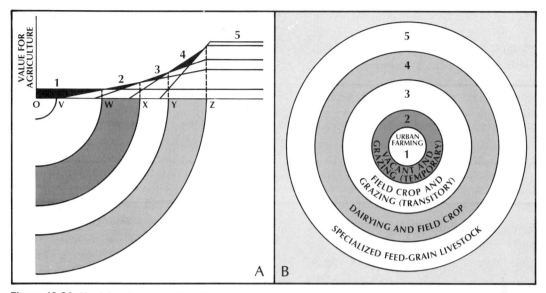

Figure 13.24 Sinclair's inverted Von Thünen model for the zone of anticipated urban encroachment: distance relationships (A) and theoretical land-use sequence (B). *Source:* After Robert Sinclair, "Von Thünen and Urban Sprawl," *Annals of the Association of American Geographers* 57 (March 1967), p. 80.

of near-future displacement, expressed by little investment beyond the short term; and (4) dairying and field crop farming, wherein farmers begin to shift to more extensive agriculture with a view toward encroachment in the foreseeable future.

SUMMARY

Almost two hundred years ago, Johann Heinrich von Thünen demonstrated that the geographic pattern of agricultural land use was highly regular and predictable. He first described the pattern of land use within and surrounding his own large estate. Based upon his descriptions he next formulated a hypothesis to explain the geographic pattern. His hypothesis was that the higher the cost of transportation, the lower the amount a tenant farmer would be willing to pay to use the land. He expressed his hypothesis using clear and unambiguous mathematics. He reasoned that by placing reasonable numerical values into his mathematical formulation he could closely predict actual land values and land uses. Among his general conclusions was that land values decline with increasing distance from the market center; and that land values and land uses change as the various costs of production, transportation, and prices of agricultural commodities change.

Today, the cost and technology of transportation has had a dramatic effect upon the agricultural land use patterns that one would expect by applying von Thünen's logic. Agricultural land use patterns that are evident surrounding market centers are thought to be historic remnants of a bygone era, or the result of administrative institutions whose existence brings about a persistence to the historic patterns of land use. At the scale of the continent and the globe we now can observe von Thünen-like market forces and patterns of land use.

The von Thünen logical framework has been important in the evolution of our thinking of how land values and land uses come about in the modern city. Indeed, von Thünen's general theory of land values and land uses has been important in the evolution of thought as to how land values and land uses within cities arise. By analogy, in an urban environment, we expect that land values (per unit such as per acre) will increase with increasing access to important destinations such as places of shopping and work.

Thünen's location theory provides a general framework for analyzing the spatial organization of agriculture. With this foundation in mind, Chapter 14 will examine the geography of contemporary agricultural regions in the United States. As you read about agricultural land use in the next chapter and elsewhere, keep von Thünen's theory of land use and general method of reasoning in mind and draw on it to anticipate and explain the spatial patterns you observe.

Further Readings

Chisholm, Michael. *Rural Settlement and Land Use: An Essay in Location.* 3rd rev. ed. London: Hutchinson University Library, 1979.

Dunn, Edgar S., Jr. *The Location of Agricultural Production.* Gainesville: University of Florida Press, 1954.

Ewald, U. "The Von Thünen Principle and Agricultural Zonation in Colonial Mexico." *Journal of Historical Geography* 3 (1977), pp. 123–133.

Found, William C. *A Theoretical Approach to Rural Land-Use Patterns.* London: Edward Arnold, 1971.

Griffin, Ernst. "Testing the Von Thünen Theory in Uruguay." *Geographical Review* 63 (October 1973), pp. 500–516.

Grotewold, Andreas. "Von Thünen in Retrospect." *Economic Geography* 35 (October 1959), pp. 346–355.

Hall, Peter, ed. *Von Thünen's Isolated State: An English Edition of "Der Isolierte Staat"* by Johann Heinrich von Thünen, Carla M. Wartenberg, trans. London: Pergamon Press, 1966.

Hall, Peter. "Introduction." In Peter Hall, ed., *Von Thünen's Isolated State.* Carla M. Wartenberg, trans. London: Pergamon Press, 1966, pp. xi–xlvii.

Harvey, David W. "Locational Change in the Kentish Hop Industry and the Analysis of Land Use Patterns." In R.H.T. Smith et al., eds., *Readings in Economic Geography: The Location of Economic Activity.* Chicago: Rand McNally, 1968, pp. 79–93.

Harvey, David W. "Theoretical Concepts and the Analysis of Agricultural Land-Use Patterns." *Annals of the Association of American Geographers* 56 (June 1966), pp. 361–374.

Horvath, Ronald J. "Von Thünen's Isolated State and the Area Around Addis Ababa, Ethiopia." *Annals of the Association of American Geographers* 59 (June 1969), pp. 308–323.

Jackson, Richard T. "A Vicious Circle?—The Consequences of Von Thünen in Tropical Africa." *Area* 4 (1972), pp. 258–261.

Jackson, Richard T. "Some Observations on the Von Thünen Method of Analysis: With Reference to Southern Ethiopia." *East African Geographical Review* 8 (April 1970), pp. 39–46.

Johnson, Hildegard B. "A Note on Thünen's Circles." *Annals of the Association of American Geographers* 52 (June 1962), pp. 213–220.

Jonasson, Olof. "Agricultural Regions of Europe." *Economic Geography* 1 (October 1925), pp. 277–314.

Jones, Donald. "Rent in an Equilibrium Model of Land Use." *Annals of the Association of American Geographers* 68 (1978), pp. 205–213.

Jones, Donald. "Monopsony and Plant Location in a Thünen Land Use Model." *Journal of Regional Science* 28 (1988), pp. 317–327.

Jones, Donald, and J. Krummel, "The Location Theory of Animal Populations: The Case of a Spatially Uniform Food Distribution." *The American Naturalist* 126 (1985), pp. 392–404.

Jones, Richard C. "Testing Macro-Thünen Models by Linear Programming." *Professional Geographer* 28 (November 1976), pp. 353–361.

Jumper, Sidney R. "The Fresh Vegetable Industry in the U.S.A.: An Example of Dynamic Interregional Dependency." *Tijdschrift voor Economische en Sociale Geografie* 60 (September–October 1969), pp. 308–318.

Katzman, Martin T. "Industrialization, Agricultural Specialization, and Frontier Settlement in South-Central Brazil, 1940–70." *Development and Change* 6 (October 1975), pp. 25–49.

Kellerman, Aharon. "The Pertinence of Macro-Thünian Analysis." *Economic Geography* 53 (July 1977), pp. 255–264.

Kellerman, Aharon. "Agricultural Location Theory 1: Basic Models." *Environment and Planning A* 21 (1989a), pp. 1381–1396.

Kellerman, Aharon. "Agricultural Location Theory 2: Relaxation of Assumptions and Applications." *Environment and Planning A* 21 (1918b), pp. 1427–1446.

Leaman, J. Harold, and Edgar C. Conkling. "Transport Change and Agricultural Specialization." *Annals of the Association of American Geographers* 65 (September 1975), pp. 425–432.

Lemon, James T. *The Best Poor Man's Country: A Geographical Study of Early Southeastern Pennsylvania.* (Baltimore: Johns Hopkins University Press, 1972 (paperback edition published by the Norton Library, 1976).

Lozano, Eduardo E. *Location and Regions: Agricultural Land Use in an Integrated Economy.* Cambridge, Mass.: Harvard University Laboratory for Computer Graphics, Geography and the Properties of Surfaces Series, Paper No. 12, 1968.

Morgan, W. B. "The Doctrine of the Rings." *Geography* 58 (1973), pp. 301–312.

Muller, Peter O. "Trend Surfaces of American Agricultural Patterns: A Macro-Thünian Analysis." *Economic Geography* 49 (July 1973), pp. 228–242; *Professional Geographer* 25 (August 1973), pp. 239–241.

O'Kelly, Morton. "Equilibrium in a Two-Crop Model With a Low-Cost Transportation Route." *Environment and Planning A* 21 (1989), pp. 385–396.

Peet, J. Richard. "The Spatial Expansion of Commercial Agriculture in the Nineteenth Century: A Von Thünen Interpretation." *Economic Geography* 45 (October 1969), pp. 283–301.

Peet, J. Richard. "Von Thünen Theory and the Dynamics of Agricultural Expansion." *Explorations in Economic History* 8 (1970–1971), pp. 181–201.

Schlebecker, John T. "The World Metropolis and the History of American Agriculture." *Journal of Economic History* 20 (June 1960), pp. 187–208.

Sinclair, Robert. "Von Thünen and Urban Sprawl." *Annals of the Association of American Geographers* 57 (March 1967), pp. 72–87.

Symons, Leslie. *Agricultural Geography*, 2nd rev. ed. Boulder, Colo.: Westview Press, 1979.

Tarrant, John R. *Agricultural Geography: Problems in Modern Geography.* 2nd rev. ed. New York: Wiley/Halsted, 1980.

Thrall, Grant Ian. "Production Theory of Land Rent." *Environment and Planning, Series A* 23:955–967.

Thrall, Grant Ian. *Land Use and Urban Form*, London: Routledge/Methuen, 1987.

Visser, Sent. "On Agricultural Location Theory." *Geographical Analysis* 14 (1980), pp. 167–176.

CHAPTER 14

Contemporary American Agriculture: Regions and Trends

—————◇—————

The use of a certain area of the earth's surface is a primary condition of anything that people can do; it gives them room for their actions; it determines their distance from, and in a great measure their relations to, other things and other persons. It is this property that distinguishes land from all other things, and is the foundation of much that is most interesting and most difficult in the economic sciences.

—ALFRED MARSHALL, 1890

INTRODUCTION

The principles of agricultural location introduced in the preceding chapter provide the conceptual organization around which an empirical analysis can be built of the economic geography of U.S. farming. The following survey of the economic geography of U.S. agriculture is divided into two parts: (1) an overview of the major producing regions of the United States examined within the context of the geographic Thünian framework, followed by (2) an overview of the nation's changing agricultural trends.

OVERVIEW OF THE MACRO-THÜNIAN LANDSCAPE OF THE UNITED STATES

The Thünian framework provides an understanding of the spatial organization of food production. The present analysis applies the Thünian framework in order to identify and then explain the behavior of the major landscape trends at the nation's geographic scale; Figures 13.17 and 13.18 should be used as a guide to this part of the chapter. To organize the analysis

around the Thünian logic, look for the spatial behavior of land value, observe where land values conform to what is anticipated within the context of the Thünian model, and explain why they diverge when the spatial behavior does not conform to what is anticipated.

Average farm land prices for representative states by agricultural region between 1970 and 1989 are shown in Table 14.1; agricultural land values in 1989 are mapped in Figure 14.1. The overall spatial trend depicted in the table and map conform closely to the Thünian sequence of land values and farm products relative to the national market. The robust model can be refined by relaxing several implicit assumptions of the Thünian framework: (1) Consider the lesser but important other urban markets, such as the "San–San" San Francisco–San Diego corridor on the West Coast and the "Chipitt" Chicago–Pittsburgh urban belt in the Midwest. (2) Consider special circumstances of weather, such as in California's multiseason central valley and the subtropical climate of Florida. (3) Consider urban encroachment where agricultural land values may be more a reflection of investment by land

Table 14.1 Farm Real Estate: Average Value per Acre of Land and Buildings, 1970–1996

(1) Agriculture Type	(2) Example State	(3) 1970	(4) 1986	(5) 1992	(6) 1996	(7) Average Yearly % Change 1970–1986	(8) Average Yearly % Change 1986–1992	(9) Average Yearly % Change 1992–1996
Fruits and vegetables								
	New Jersey	1092	3913	6710	8172	15%	10%	4%
	Maryland	640	1887	2530	3826	11%	5%	10%
	California	479	1571	2157	2404	13%	5%	2%
	Florida	355	1435	2033	2306	18%	6%	3%
Dairying								
	Wisconsin	232	711	865	1175	12%	3%	7%
	Vermont	224	1180	1223	1534	25%	1%	5%
Corn belt								
	Illinois	490	1143	1536	2064	8%	5%	7%
	Iowa	392	841	1153	1442	7%	5%	5%
	Ohio	399	1013	1396	1989	9%	5%	8%
Wheat								
	Kansas	159	387	460	553	8%	3%	4%
Ranching								
	Colorado	95	357	400	558	16%	2%	8%
	New Mexico	42	134	212	258	13%	8%	4%

Source: U.S. Department of Agriculture, *Agricultural Statistics, 1997* (Washington, D.C.: GPO, 1997), Table 9-12, p. IX–8.

investors than they are proportional to the average agricultural returns to the land. Other considerations will be added later.

The general Thünian trend from east to west is clear in Figure 14.1. Land values descend with distance from the northeastern Megalopolis, but generally at a lower rate along the path to Chicago than in the less urban southwesterly direction. Land values reach a minimum in the mountain and desert states and then rise with proximity to the West Coast San–San urban market. The long and narrow Florida peninsula with its "Mojak" (Miami–Orlando–Jacksonville) urban corridor and high-valued citrus crops behaves as a Thünian outlier in the far Southeast.

Among the greatest increases in average agricultural land values have been those in areas adjacent to Megalopolis, including New Jersey and Maryland. Columns 7, 8, and 9 of Table 14.1 shows that the average yearly percentage increase in land values during the past quarter century. Increases since the inflationary middle 1970s through early 1980s have generally moderated for all regions. Those states nearby Megalopolis have generally experienced the greatest increase. Less rapid increases have occurred in the more distant dairy state of Wisconsin and the Corn Belt states of Illinois and Ohio, with the least increases being in the wheat state of Kansas and the ranching state of New Mexico. Recreation and urbanization in Colorado is largely responsible for the increases in Colorado being larger than New Mexico.

Considerations for Adjustments to the Thünian Theme

In addition to land costs noted in Table 14.1 and Figure 14.1, other high-cost inputs per unit area are necessary for successful farming. These investments include considerable outlays for buildings, labor, machinery, seed, fuel, fertilizers, and chemicals. Robert McNee has likened the farmer

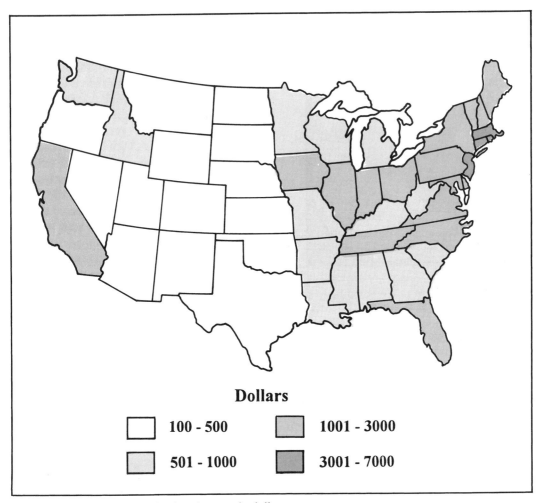

Figure 14.1 Agricultural land values by state in dollars per acre.

to a manufacturer who assembles raw materials and transforms them into specialized finished products.[1] Figure 14.2 itemizes the components of farm production expenses averaged across all categories of U.S. agriculture.

Declining numbers of legally employed farm workers, coupled with unionization and federal laws that have raised the minimum housing stan-

dards for migratory farm workers, have added to the real cost of farm labor. In response, farmers are substituting relatively lower cost farm machinery for manual labor.

In 1910, there were 3.4 million hired farm workers in the United States; by 1951, there were 2.2 million; and by 1970, the number had declined to 1.2 million.[2] In 1996 there were 598

---

[1]Robert B. McNee, *A Primer on Economic Geography*, Primer Economics Series (New York: Random House, 1971), p. 160.

[2]U.S. Department of the Census, *Historical Statistics of the United States* (Washington, D.C.: GPO), Table K 174–183, p. 467.

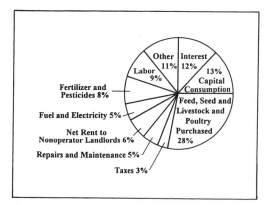

Figure 14.2 Farm production expenses for U.S. agriculture.

thousand paid farm workers in 49 states. At the same time, capital used on farms has had a dramatic increase. The adoption of the farm tractor typifies the changeover to the highly mechanized farm.[3] In 1910, there were 1000 farm tractors on U.S. farms; this figure had risen to 3.7 million in 1951 and to 4.8 million in 1970. The number of tractors have remained nearly constant since 1970. While U.S. farms have become saturated with such machinery, resulting in small yearly increases in tractors and related machinery today, the cumulative effect is to make the modern farm reliant on mechanization. The chicken-broiler industry is one example of the "farm-factory" with high capital requirements; they can be found in the southern portion of the Atlantic Belt, from Delaware down the coast to Georgia (see Box).

The tomato is an example of a truck-garden crop that is now completely automated. Biotechnology is used to breed tomatoes to be machine-harvestable by emphasizing its growth uniformity, resiliency during handling, and ability to last up to a month on the vine without deterioration in ripeness. Once picked by the mechanical harvesters, these tomatoes are mechanically loaded into large bins for final au-

tomated packing. This technology has more than tripled tomato yields and eliminated most hired labor jobs on tomato farms.[4] This technological change is part of the controversy between organized farm hired labor and their employers. Much of the expense for agricultural research and development is paid for by federal and often state governments; the federal government spent $2.7 billion on agricultural research and related services in 1996 alone. These funds come from general federal and state tax revenues, contributed to by all taxpayers, including hired agricultural labor. Unions representing organized farm hired labor are, of course, opposed to general tax revenues subsidizing the research and development of technology designed specifically to eliminate their jobs.

The mechanization trend has fostered greater agricultural specialization because machines are optimized to work on single crops only; their great expense requires that they be used as frequently as possible. Specialization then makes the agricultural land use of a region more homogeneous. Instead of a land user purchasing harvesting equipment for his sole use, several land users may form a cooperative to purchase the equipment collectively. That also means that each land user must produce the same crop for several years to pay for the harvest equipment. Or a retail business may rent out specialized equipment. Still, there must be sufficient land users in close proximity that require the same type of machinery to make such retail enterprises worthwhile; that is, the *threshold* requirements must be met. Therefore, before land users switch to a new crop, there must be sufficient threshold demand by other land users to acquire the capital inputs needed for the new crop. Establishing such ***agglomeration economies*** is an impediment to any individual land

[3]Emilio Casetti and R. Keith Semple, 1969. Concerning the testing of spatial diffusion hypotheses *Geographical Analysis*, 1, 254–259.

[4]Raymond E. Webb and W. M. Bruce, "Redesigning the Tomato for Mechanized Production," *Science for Better Living: 1968 Yearbook of Agriculture* (Washington, D.C.: GPO, 1968), pp. 103–107.

Chicken Broiler Production: Industrialized Agriculture in Action

Typical of today's ultraspecialized and industrialized market-oriented agriculture is the production of *chicken broilers*, which in recent years has become spatially separated from egg farming. This type of poultry raising has always been symbiotic with intensive fruit-and-vegetable farming: weight loss and perishability of fresh-killed birds necessitate locating near Megalopolis, and linkages between the two farming systems have always been strong (chicken droppings are a prized variety of natural fertilizer). Broiler production is now dependent on sophisticated management techniques and factorylike methods. Whereas more than 200 small companies controlled production in the largest broiler region (Delmarva Peninsula) at the end of World War II, only about 10 remain, and all are structured around high-volume scale economies. Assembly-line manufacturing complete with conveyor belts dominates, and rapid turnovers are assured because the newest breed of broiler bird requires only seven weeks from hatching to maturity. Highly scientific procedures are widespread: chicken diets are fully computerized, and complex drugs are used routinely both to prevent disease and to accelerate growth. Increased vertical integration of broiler production is removing control of the operation from farmers, who supply buildings and labor but are provided with chicks and feed by outside managers in return for the security of a guaranteed price.* These recent changes also encourage

Each of these broiler houses is the seven-week home of 16,000 chicks in Oconee County, Georgia. Automatic-feed silos and watering and cooling systems help bring the chicks to an average 4.2 pounds, at which point they are harvested, processed, and packed for shipment to places as far away as California.

*John Fraser Hart, *The Look of the Land* (Englewood Cliffs, N.J.: Prentice-Hall, 1975), p. 196.

farmers to concentrate on other crops, thereby relegating chicken-raising to more of a sideline pursuit.

One of the best known integrated broiler companies is Perdue, Inc., of Salisbury on Maryland's eastern shore; its owner, Frank Perdue, is familiar to millions of easterners through television and radio commercials about his yellow-skinned, high-quality chickens (how many Americans know the brand name of Holly Farms, the nation's largest company?). Perdue orchestrates the entire production cycle from hatchery through processing and marketing. More than 800 Delmarva farmers supply the company with about 2 million broilers each week, and Perdue has expanded its processing operations into mainland Virginia and North Carolina in an effort to keep pace with the demand for its products. Among the company's other resources are a feed mill and a genetic research facility that operates on an annual budget of around $500,000. Undoubtedly, Perdue is in the vanguard of large-scale corporate operators who are revolutionizing broiler production, part of a nationwide movement (as will be seen later in this chapter) that is helping to transform other agricultural regions as well.

user's switching over to a new crop. This process discourages change and contributes to persistence in type of agricultural land use. Similarly, a farmer may be forced to abandon the production of a particular crop because other nearby farmers have already switched over to an alternative land use. The land user may be able to plant the crop but for lack of equipment may not be able to harvest it. This last occurrence forces changeover from agricultural use to urban use at the expanding urban periphery.[5]

Related to the role of specialized machinery in promoting uniform land use within a region is the array of specialized service personnel required to support the modern factory-farm. Today's farmers require the services of experts in their particular production line—not only machinery repair personnel, but also plant biologists, agronomists, economic forecasters, soil chemists, product handlers, and marketers. Marketers are especially vital because an intricate system of interme-

diaries—from auctioneers to packagers to wholesalers—now dominates the marketing chain for every mass-produced crop. What emerges for each such product is a growing *service complex* of specialists, without which farmers cannot cost effectively get the yield from their land to the market. An equally significant *agglomerating force* is the growing linkage between farmers and the food-processing industry. These ties are being strengthened by the proliferation of *contract farming* in which processor and farmer enter into a written agreement before planting, whereby the entire yield will be purchased upon harvesting for a predetermined price. Both parties benefit in these arrangements: the farmer is guaranteed a customer and an acceptable price, and the processor is assured of a supply at a set price that is not subject to fluctuation. These contracts influence agricultural production and consequently the land-use pattern in the vicinity of the contractor's factory.

The themes established in the opening paragraphs of this chapter will continue throughout as we evaluate in greater detail the various agricultural regions of the United States within the context of the Thünian framework. The appli-

[5]For a discussion of innovation and willingness to adopt, see Richard Morrill, Gary Gaile, and Grant Thrall, *Spatial Diffusion*, Vol. 10 of Scientific Geography Series (Newbury Park, Calif.: Sage, 1988).

cation of this framework will begin at the doorstep of the Megalopolis market and proceed inland through regions of generally decreasing agricultural intensity. From east to west, the macrogeographic regions are fruit-vegetable truck gardens, dairying, crop-livestock, wheat, and ranching zones. The discussion ends with an examination of the residual producing areas of national importance which was mapped in Figure 13.17.

Truck Gardens and Chicken-Broiler Factory-Farms

Megalopolis Truck Gardens. A testimony to contract farming and its visual effect on the agricultural landscape can be found in southern New Jersey and along highways connecting Philadelphia to the Atlantic shore. Roadside stands that were formerly overflowing with tomatoes now stand empty because the tomato crop is sold in advance to Campbell's, Hunt's, and other manufacturers. Farming areas within the Atlantic Belt increasingly concentrate on single products. Figure 14.3 shows the resulting distribution of production. Production is most heavily clustered along the coastward margin of Megalopolis. The upstate New York fruit-and-vegetable region (which includes the famous Finger Lakes winemaking complex) and potato farming in Aroostook County of northernmost Maine can be considered outlying extensions of the Atlantic Belt, with each possessing locally favorable agricultural *site* conditions as well as a desirable *situation* resulting from easy access to seaboard metropolitan centers.[6]

Von Thünen's normative heuristic theory leads us to anticipate that highly intensive agriculture will prevail on small farms. This is indeed the case throughout the Atlantic Fruit-and-

[6]It is to Alfred Marshall that we owe a debt for the concept of site versus situation value. See Alfred Marshall, *Principles of Economics*, 8th ed. 1946 (London: Macmillan, 1890), p. 441.

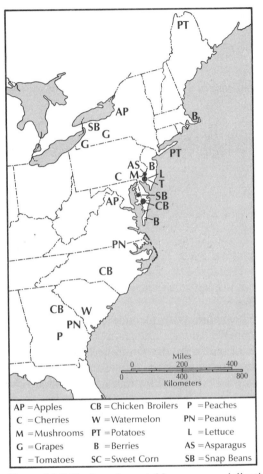

AP =Apples	CB =Chicken Broilers	P =Peaches
C =Cherries	W =Watermelon	PN =Peanuts
M =Mushrooms	PT =Potatoes	L =Lettuce
G =Grapes	B =Berries	AS =Asparagus
T =Tomatoes	SC =Sweet Corn	SB =Snap Beans

Figure 14.3 Fruit-and-vegetable crop specializations in the Atlantic Belt and its East Coast outliers.

Vegetable Belt; farm sizes of 50 acres or less are normal for this region. As shown in Table 14.1, agricultural land prices have increased more in this region than in any other agricultural region of the United States. Part of this increase could have been anticipated using the normative Thünian framework: as market conditions for produce strengthen, then agricultural land values for those products will rise. There has also been increased competition from other uses of land, including using agricultural land as a hedge against inflation. Investors purchase farm property at prices greater than can be justified for agricultural reasons alone; the premium they pay is akin to insurance that their wealth will not lose value through inflation. These investors then attempt to manage the farm in such a way as to have the sale of farm produce cover as much as possible the mortgage payment. While revenues from farm produce cannot cover the mortgage, still this strategy forces the investor to adopt the highest possible intensity of land use and serves to reinforce the Thünian sequence of land use. (This theme is evaluated further in Figure 14.15 later in this chapter.)

High-value fruit and vegetable cultivation has traditionally been the most market-oriented farming system and continues to dominate agricultural activity located closest to the national market. Because of the Appalachian barrier to the west and glaciated areas associated with short summers to the north, the fruit–vegetable region has been deflected southward along the Atlantic coastal plain and into the broad valleys of the Piedmont from Cape Cod to eastern Georgia (Figure 13.17). As we saw in the previous chapter, this region formed in the nineteenth century as the expanding inner food-supply zone of the Megalopolitan cities, and then it coalesced into a single market-gardening belt (Figure 13.17). During the last few decades, motor trucks permitted this zone to expand west and north into the more hospitable valleys and basins of northern Appalachia and New England, and especially southward into the Carolinas where less expensive labor contributes to lower production costs than in the Northeast. *Truck farming* then typifies much of the region near Megalopolis today. The development of interstate highways and competition from urban land uses push this type of land use further westward.

California's Outlying Truck Gardens. California's role as an outlier of Thünian inner-ring fruit-and-vegetable farming was mentioned in the preceding chapter. The statewide trends in its average agricultural land values are listed in Table 14.1.

The agricultural land market of California has been subject to the rapid urban growth of San Francisco–Palo Alto, Los Angeles–Orange County, and San Diego, constituting the so-called San–San corridor. Moreover, conversion from agricultural to urban land financed by wealth from the entertainment industry has been closely linked since the inception of the movie industry in California. Much agricultural land at the present San–San urban periphery is owned by famous entertainers. They allow the display of their name as part of the sales promotion of the property, such as Lawrence Welk Drive at the urban interface between San Diego and Riverside. The abundant supply of investment money from the entertainment industry helps support the value of agricultural land in the path of urban development, at a rate that could not be sustained from agricultural returns alone.

A period of peak urban land values during the middle 1980s has been followed by the recent saturation of the urban housing market of California and a temporary downswing in the urban land-value cycle. The demand for developable agricultural land also declined in the late 1980s; this is partly responsible for the low rate of increase in agricultural land prices in the rightmost column of Table 14.1.

California's comparative advantage in agriculture lies in the length of its growing season, which makes it the nation's largest and most varied agricultural producer. Efficient long-haul transportation—both truck and rail—compensate for California's distant position relative to the eastern Megalopolis market; the state's high-value farm produce now often moves by air freight. Within California, superior organization of farm production and collection by trade associations such as Sunkist further ameliorates locational disadvantages, as do internal agglomeration economies achieved by clustering similar crop production and their supporting service complexes. Much of California's farm products are purchased by processors and then marketed as canned or frozen foods. Although the "tyranny" of distance from Megalopolis can largely be overcome by exploiting local comparative advantages, the West Coast still is not competitive in distant northeastern markets when that market's local producers offer summertime fresh vegetables (Figure 13.15).

Geographic factors operating in California give rise to internal areal specializations of agricultural land use (Figure 14.4). Because of the urban development of the coastal San–San corridor, most of the production today is concentrated in the Central valley, which is fed by the San Joaquin and Sacramento rivers, and in the arid Imperial valley in the southeast corner of the state, which is irrigated by heavily federally subsidized Colorado River water. Besides the same truck crops grown in the East, the arid climates of the Central and Imperial valleys in southern California also permit citrus fruit production. Periodic droughts make for public awareness that water is critically important to California's agriculture and urban growth.[7] The availability or lack of water may determine California's future competitive agricultural position. As international trade increases with those agricultural products in which the state now enjoys a comparative advantage, for lack of water the state may lose its market as distributors look to producers close by in Mexico, further abroad in South America, and even in Southeast Asia. With the reduction in barriers to trade with Mexico by NAFTA it is expected that Mexico will become a major competitor with California in agricultural products.[8]

Other Truck-Garden Outliers.   At the national scale (Figure 13.17), several additional fruit-and-vegetable-producing outliers also exist, and these regions merit our further attention.

The subtropical Gulf coast (the coastal strip of Florida, Alabama, Mississippi, Louisiana, and Texas) has also developed as an outlier for fruit-and-vegetable farming. As the citrus groves of California's Los Angeles and Orange counties succumbed to urban development, Florida growers benefited by capturing a 75-percent market share of oranges and grapefruit. Like California before it, rapid urbanization in Florida will transfer Florida's share of the market to other states on the Gulf of Mexico and especially to foreign producers. The Mississippi Delta and the Texas

[7]A drought in 1977 caused Los Angeles to impose mandatory rationing. In 1991, severe drought again made the water management district consider mandatory cutbacks as much as 31 percent. Droughts place agricultural versus urban land users into direct confrontation. Such confrontation will become more intense as California's population increases from 1990 to the end of this decade by more than 25 percent. A *Los Angeles Times* poll taken in January 1991 placed water shortage ahead of education and marginally behind crime and drugs, as the most important problem facing California. Excessive urban population growth was considered by 45 percent to be the cause for the water shortage, while 5 percent considered waste by agriculture as the cause. Most considered desalination and reclamation of waste water as the cure for the water shortage.

[8]NAFTA is the North American Free Trade Agreement.

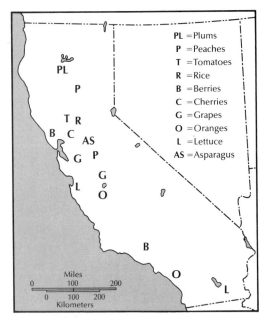

Figure 14.4 Fruit-and-vegetable crop specializations within California.

coast, which have specialized in sugar and rice production and insignificant local-specialty crops such as hot peppers, may move to higher-valued citrus production.

Other scattered outliers, such as Idaho's potato production, exist for the same reasons as those in California and the Gulf coast region. Also worth mentioning is the fruit belt that lines the eastern shore of Lake Michigan, which specializes in truck crops for the Chippit megalopolis. Other large interior metropolises have spawned local market-oriented truck farming, which is pursued as a side operation (to the prevailing regional specialty) on a few spare acres. Numerous examples of managerial success have shaped the nearby agricultural landscape, such as a local truck-crop processing enterprise succeeding in the national market and going into high-volume manufacturing. The massive canning and frozen product division of Le Sueur, Minnesota's Green Giant Company, supports a crescent of vegetable raising from the Red River of the north in western Minnesota southeast through that state into east-central Wisconsin.

In the northern tier of Megalopolis, as urban land values soared during the past decade, many residents responded by "underinvesting" in the expensive housing markets of cities such as Boston and instead allocated their income to attractive weekend retreats in Vermont. This push effect from Boston and the pull of the attractive rural amenities of Vermont have made that state one of the fastest growth regions of the nation, with prices increasing for agricultural land in anticipation of future housing development.

Florida is presently receiving over 1000 new migrants per day, a number equal to adding a city the size of Tampa to the landscape each year. A large portion of migrants to Florida are persons retiring from northern regions of the East and Midwest who are attracted by the warm climate of the southern part of the state. South Florida's climate also makes that part of the state favorably suited for truck gardening and citrus production. Competition with urban land development

drives the already high Thünian outlying truck-garden land values of Florida even higher. This is clearly evident in Table 14.1.

The Dairy Belt

Dairying claims agricultural space on the inland side of Megalopolis because, unlike intensive fruit-and-vegetable farming, the production of milk and its derivatives does not require high-quality cropland. Dairy farming has become largely a feeding operation; locally grown hay and other forage crops are viewed as inexpensive adjuncts to supplemented feed imported from the Corn Belt. Location near metropolitan markets is important for fresh milk production, but, with refrigerated trucks, fresh milk production can range outward many hundreds of miles. Less perishable dairy goods, such as butter, cheese, and evaporated milk, can engage in a national market.[9] The nation's Dairy Belt stretches in a broad arc from Maine and Vermont to Minnesota, dipping into central Appalachia alongside the national market in its eastern portion, and is associated with glaciated terrain north of the Corn Belt in its western Great Lakes segment (Figure 13.18).

The spatial organization of the Dairy Belt is consistent with Thünian location theory, not only in its regional position but also in its internal zonation of production. Close to urban markets we expect to find (and the normative model is supported by our finding) production of fluid grade-A milk sold in nearby population centers. However, as distance from these markets increases, dairy farmers shift to producing lower-grade and lower-priced milk for processing into cream, cheese, butter, ice cream, and condensed

[9]Less perishable dairy goods can even compete in an international market as well. New Zealand can be considered in a far extensive Thünian zone with regard to the combined massive population agglomeration that borders the north Atlantic Ocean: U.S. Megalopolis to the west and the London–Paris–Berlin crescent to the east. New Zealand relies heavily on cheese exports to this market.

and powdered milk. Because of the distribution of markets within Megalopolis, fluid-milk production is concentrated in the eastern half of the dairy region, with western Dairy Belt fresh milk limited to supplying the local needs of the nearby midwestern metropolises. Most of the dairying in the more remote Great Lakes–upper Midwest portion of the Belt is therefore engaged in producing milk that will be processed further. Beyond the relatively small fluid-milk zone along the northwestern rim of the Chipitt urban corridor lies first a cheese zone in Wisconsin and then a zone of butter production in southern Minnesota. Cheese is the more market-oriented of the two, since 10 pounds of milk are required to produce 1 pound of cheese, whereas the ratio for butter is 20 to 1. Therefore, even with milk production intended for further processing, the production by type of further processing follows a regular Thünian spatial arrangement.[10]

Milk, in addition to being perishable, is bulky, with a low value per unit of weight; this encourages the concentration of creameries, condensaries, and other manufactured-milk industries in the outer margins of the Dairy Belt. This trend toward production at the periphery is further reflected in farm-size patterns within the Dairy Belt: northeastern farms range between 50 and 150 acres, whereas those in the cheese and butter zones west of Lake Michigan average closer to 200 acres. The zonation of milk/cheese/butter specializations emerged in the nineteenth century. These zones expanded outward in a manner as would be expected in a dynamic Thünian model with decreasing transportation costs and increasing competition with land for urban use after the War Between the States (recall Figures 13.1 and 13.2 on relative population concentrations of urban versus rural). As the zones expanded outward, a once nationally important cheesemaking area in upstate New York disappeared as it was displaced westward into central Wisconsin.

Fluid-milk production is most heavily concentrated in the rugged Appalachian uplands west of Megalopolis. Although land quality and the cool humid climate here are not conducive to high-yield cropping, conditions are satisfactory for dairy farmers who through their actions reveal their preference to trade off inferior *site* factors for an excellent *situation* relative to the market. Because of the nature of the product, the spatial organization of fresh-milk marketing is heavily regulated by federal, state, and local agencies in order to ensure compliance with rigid sanitary and health standards. In general, milk is supplied from hinterlands, or **milksheds,** which overlap in the Northeast where metropolitan areas are often bunched together (Figure 14.5). The geographic range of a milkshed, with allowances for topographical constraints on farming density, is very much a function of city size: The milkshed of Madison, Wisconsin, with a population of 170,000 extends out less than 10 miles. But the 8 million people of New York City have spawned a supply zone 400 miles in radial extent. The federal government's role is vital, too, because its administrators determine both the price paid by milk distributors to farmers, and the number and location of collecting stations authorized to receive milk bound for a certain market.[11]

Thus, government regulation limits competition between urban markets. For example, the areal extent of the milkshed for New York City (Figure 14.5) is a result of space–price discrimination: Distributors of southeastern Pennsylvania milk licensed to ship the product to New York City are allowed to offer higher farmgate prices than are distributors who are licensed to ship milk to Philadelphia. Distributors of milk to Philadelphia are then not competitive with New York City distributors. This forces Philadelphia distributors to purchase milk farther afield toward Pittsburgh and deeply into the coastal areas

[10]John W. Alexander, *Economic Geography* (Englewood Cliffs, N.J.: Prentice-Hall, 1963), p. 132.

[11]Loyal B. Durand, Jr., "The Major Milksheds of the Northeastern Quarter of the United States," *Economic Geography* 40 (January 1964), p. 14.

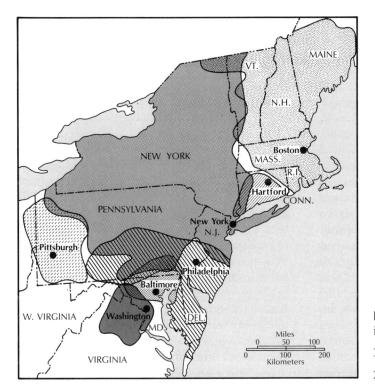

Figure 14.5 Major metropolitan milksheds in the northeastern United States. *Source: After Jean Gottmann, Megalopolis.* New York: Twentieth Century Fund, 1961, p. 230.

of Delaware, beyond a range that distributors to New York City need venture.

Pennsylvania also offers one of those instances where a special circumstance can alter the normative Thünian mapping: competition in this part of Pennsylvania is heightened by industrial demands for fresh milk by the Hershey Chocolate Corporation, which annually consumes 50 million gallons (the output of 50,000 cows), guaranteed by contract. Applying the reasoning presented thus far on the normative Thünian model, how may the Hershey Chocolate Corporation affect the agricultural land-use and land-value surface?

Within each milkshed, the product moves in a vertical hierarchy from farm to consumer. Fleets of refrigerated tank-trucks operated by milk-marketing associations and urban dairies make daily rounds to each dairy farm to collect milk from their bulk storage tanks. This milk is shipped to regional milk-collecting stations. In the larger markets, this milk may be transshipped to facilities at the suburban ring of the market metropolis. There the milk is packaged and shipped to the retail outlets. Milk transportation is accomplished entirely by truck. As a result, production facilities and sometimes whole milksheds are heavily oriented toward interstate highways. Off the main arteries, well-kept all-weather local roads are necessary to allow constant truck access to dairy farms. A spinoff of the dairy industry is the highly efficient backroad snow removal in areas such as upstate New York.

More than any other American agricultural region, the Dairy Belt continues to be dominated by small family farms. The typical modest farmstead centers around the dairy barn, where milking operations take place, and its adjacent milk house, to which the product is piped for storage and cooling in bulk tanks to await collection. Surrounding fields are used to graze cows, with the best land used for raising forage grasses and grain. In the past, grain crops were grazed or harvested before ripening for ensilage, but even traditional dairy farmers increasingly rely on imported feed and let their own crops grow to maturity for use during the winter. As feed prices rise, Corn Belt grains are being replaced with by-products of other agriculture commodities that before were disposed of, such as citrus pulp from Florida. Unlike fruit-and-vegetable farming, dairying labor costs are kept low by using family members to supply most of the substantial person-hour inputs. When hired labor is employed, its utilization is planned very carefully. More significant are the investments in milking and storage equipment that are necessary to meet rigid health and sanitation regulations. These and other investments in automated and scientific farming have paid off in rising efficiencies in milk production. Between 1960 and 1980, milk output per cow more than doubled to 15,000 pounds, which contributed to a 25-percent decrease in the number of dairy cows.

Dairying is not immune to the national trend toward larger-scale farming. Dairy Belt farmers have persisted in their way of life, but this, too, may succumb to production costs rising faster than farm revenues. Factorylike feedlot operators have been successful in the South and West. These high-capital-intensive farms treat cows as producing machines; large numbers of cows are concentrated in massive walkthrough milking barns. These facilities provide minimal living and exercise spaces for the animals. Feedlots are beginning to penetrate the eastern Dairy Belt, where they function much like chicken-broiler farms; often, investors will hire a farm family to perform the daily operations, but control of the dairy falls to the investors. Dairy feedlots require small acreages compared to traditional dairy farms; investment shifts out of land into capital, thereby raising the capital-to-land ratio.[12] Residual land where dairy feedlots are predominant

have comparatively low agricultural value because the residual tracts may be partitioned into small acreages, making it difficult to attain agglomeration economies for alternative types of agriculture. These residual lands are often farmed for low-grade feed to supplement higher grade feed imported from the Corn Belt.

Outside of the Dairy Belt, fluid milk is either trucked in over great distances or is produced locally. The milkshed of Gainesville, Florida, with a population of 120,000 comes largely from feedlots of the nearby Suwannee River Valley; that milkshed also serves the more distant Jacksonville, Florida, market. Suwannee River Valley milk is supplemented with milk as far away as southwestern Georgia and southeastern Alabama. Long-distance shipment of milk has been made possible by the completion of interstate highways. Regular tank-truck runs of up to 2000 miles have brought milk from Minnesota and Wisconsin to urban markets in the Deep South and the Southwest.

Long-distance shipment of milk, however, is usually not competitive with the new factorylike feedlot operations that serve local markets. These drylots are typified by milk production in metropolitan Los Angeles, which has no remaining farm land. Despite complaints from neighbors, dairies there operate in the midst of suburbia at extremely high animal densities: 50 cows per acre is not unusual, and most farms own at least 400 cows versus about 100 cows per farm in the Dairy Belt.[13] Needless to say, the stench can extend a great distance, and manure removal can be a significant cost of milk production. It is ironic that noxious feedlots have coexisted in the high-population concentrations of Los Angeles, but are prohibited from operating in the rural county that surrounds Gainesville, Florida, forcing the dairy industry through zoning to locate in

---

[12]Market forces will force producers to adopt particular capital-to-land and labor-to-land ratios; for discussion and proof see G. I. Thrall, "Production Theory of Land Rent," *Environment and Planning A* 23 (1991), pp. 955–967.

[13]John Fraser Hart, *The Look of the Land* (Englewood Cliffs, N.J.: Prentice-Hall, 1975), p. 95; Howard F. Gregor, "Industrialized Drylot Dairying: An Overview," *Economic Geography* 39 (October 1963), pp. 299–318.

adjacent Suwannee County. Even in rural Suwannee County, the feedlots are highly controversial, more because of their threat to ground and river water pollution than because of their odor.

Milk intended for further processing and for the West Coast market comes mainly from the Willamette–Cowlitz–Puget Lowland in western Oregon and Washington. This Pacific Northwest dairy region (see Figure 13.17) is humid, yet mild enough to support lush pastures year-round. Milk yield there is so great that the region has become both the dominant western cheese-and-butter supplier and an important contributor to the national supply of condensed and powdered milk.

The Corn Belt

The midwestern Corn Belt is the best-known farming region in the United States, and its agriculture is the most productive and highly developed in the world. The region is located where the macro-Thünian model tells us to expect it: beyond the fluid-milk production zone, stretching west from central Ohio through Indiana, Illinois, and Iowa to the edge of the Great Plains in eastern Nebraska and South Dakota (Figure 13.17). By no coincidence, the national transport axis also forms the Corn Belt's central spine, for accessibility to markets is critically important, not only for Megalopolis but also, on a grander scale, for foreign markets via the Mississippi and the international seaport of New Orleans, as well as the Great Lakes ports and the St. Lawrence Seaway. Moreover, good transportation is a necessity within the Corn Belt because of intraregional crop and livestock ties as well as linkages to local agricultural processors. As a result, the region possesses one of the most extensive and efficient rural rail-and-highway networks in the nation.

As discussed in Chapter 13, the Corn Belt farming system consists of integrated crop-and-livestock raising whose final product is high-

quality beef and pork; the nation's **Meat Belt** may be a more accurate appellation for the Corn Belt region. Corn and other crops are cultivated intensively for livestock feed and occupy about four-fifths of the agricultural space within the belt (compared to half that proportion throughout the rest of the United States). Beef cattle and hogs, which supply about 80 percent of the Corn Belt's agricultural income, are clustered at high densities on feedlots where they are fattened for several months prior to sale for slaughter. This is another example of a production system in which agricultural raw materials (corn and other livestock feeds) are locally concentrated and converted into a more valuable product (corn-fed beef and pork).

The Corn Belt region has advantages that make it particularly well suited for large-scale agriculture. Because it is the bottom of an ancient inland sea, the Midwest's surface is largely flat, making it ideal for both farm machinery operation and local transport development. Deep fertile prairie soils are high in organic content and permit great crop yields. The region's weather varies little from year to year and is ideal for growing corn. Agricultural experts for the Federal Reserve Bank of Chicago have written:

For top corn yields, there should be plenty of moisture in early spring, followed by a warm dry spell in the first half of May so that the corn can be planted about that time. In June the critical requirement is plenty of warm weather to give the crop a fast start. Corn "blooms" in July, and this is the critical month for rainfall. For best results there should be at least three inches of rain in that month. August and September, and the latter months should be fairly dry. Killing frost should not come until after September has been discarded from the farmer's calendar.[14]

[14] Federal Reserve Bank of Chicago, *Annual Report 1954, Including a Perspective on Midwest Agriculture, 1954,* pp. 8–9.

For the same reasons as truck-farming regions are becoming more specialized, the trend toward specialized agricultural production is affecting the Corn Belt. Traditional farm-level interdependence between crop and animal raising has given way since 1970 to specialization by subregion in either cash grain or feedlot livestock production. Cash grain production is becoming concentrated in eastern Illinois, Indiana, and northwestern Ohio, whereas feedlot operations are becoming concentrated in the western portion of the Corn Belt, in Iowa and northwestern Illinois. The eastern cash grain subregion grows in importance as feed demands rise both within and beyond the Corn Belt. This is also the case for other feed crops raised in rotation with corn (in order to restore soil nutrients and avoid erosion), such as oats, alfalfa, hay, and especially soybeans. The versatile soybean is a multiple-use commodity. It enriches soils and fattens livestock. This highly nutritious, protein-rich food ingredient is used in a wide variety of products from vegetable oil to cholesterol-free artificial bacon. Soybeans are an important raw material in the manufacturing of plastics, lubricants, antifreeze, and paints. Corn is also a multiple-use commodity (oils, starches, cereals, liquor, plastics). As demand by industry for both crops grows, linkages tighten between cash grain farmers and local manufacturers.

Productivity in the eastern subregion of the Corn Belt is further enhanced by the constant increase in mechanization. The greater the level of mechanization—namely, increased capital and therefore higher capital-to-land ratios—the larger will be the farm size. Also, the larger the size of the farm, the greater number of faster machines are required to handle the larger yield and to provide adequate coverage of the land. These machines are expensive and must be used as many hours per day as possible. "Forty acres and a mule" gave way to farms of a quarter-section (160-acres) in size; they in turn have yielded, as shown in Figure 14.6, to the current average size

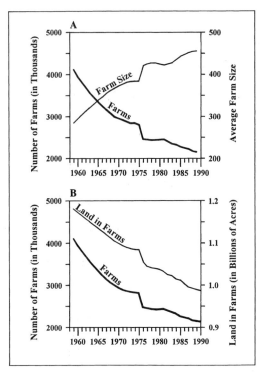

Figure 14.6 Trends in U.S. farms, farm size, and land in farms.

of 456 acres. Figure 14.6 is a graphic illustration of the changing farm size from 1959 to 1996. As large numbers of farm producers with the same motivation attempt simultaneously to increase their landholdings with nearby acreage, land prices increase.[15] Examples of increases in agricultural land prices are given in Table 14.1.

The trend for U.S. farm sizes shown in Figure

---

[15]It is expected in such perfectly competitive spatial-production systems to have land prices rise to that level that leaves the producer with the same return on her investment that prevailed before the technological change. The producer that does not adopt the new technology cannot provide output at a price that will both lead to the sale of the product and provide a normal return to the producer. This process ensures that producers that remain are all using the same and most efficient technology. For further discussion and proof, see Thrall, "Production Theory of Land Rent," pp. 955–967.

14.6 supports the above presentation.[16] The total number of farms declined by an estimated 45 percent over the 35 year period from 1959 to 1989 (−32 percent before 1976, and −13 percent from 1976 through 1989). Over the same period, total land used in farming declined by over 14 percent. The average size of the nation's farms increased by 34 percent.

The western Corn Belt subregion centered around Iowa specializes in the raising of beef cattle and hogs. Most steers are purchased at age one to two years from western ranches in the Grazing Belt, where the animals have foraged for themselves on semiarid grassland. Yearling steers are moved onto feedlots of the Corn Belt where they spend several months in fattening. Farmers who have traditionally combined feedlot operations with grain production choose a feeding period to coincide with the October–April winter suspension in cropping. The trend in Iowa is to switch over to specialize in full-time feedlot operations. Because feedlot operations represent a more intensive use of land than crop raising, as the changeover takes place, application of the Thünian model would lead to a prediction that agricultural land values rise. Evidence in support of this trend would, of course, be further confirmation of the validity of the Thünian model and of the notion that new regional livestock specialization crowds out land uses yielding a lower location rent. Indeed, Table 14.1 bears this out. A sample of rank ordering of land values among states listed in the table by agricultural region conforms to what would be expected in a Thünian system. The rank order from highest to lowest reveals that the rank generally declines with both lesser intensity of agricultural land use and distance from Megalopolis.

Competition has forced cattle raisers to adopt

recent technological advances that use land more intensively and achieve greater ***economies of scale*** (abandonment of joint products in favor of concentration on a single activity, year-round operations, bigger herds, larger facilities, import of bulk quantities of feed from other specialized farmers, and greater mechanization to reduce labor costs). The number of person-hours invested per pound of meat produced has been more than halved since 1950.

As economies of scale have increased the yield in cattle production, so too has specialization in corn grain production resulted in steadily increasing yields of corn (see Figure 14.7). Corn yield per acre steadily increased after 1900. Recall from the previous chapter that the farm population had reached its zenith by World War II. The period between 1951 and 1970 then coincides with declining farm populations (Figure 13.1) and decreasing employment of hired farm workers, greater use of machinery as evidenced by the 29.7 percent increase in farm tractors between 1951 and 1970, as well as advances in chemical pesticides and fertilizers. The rise in

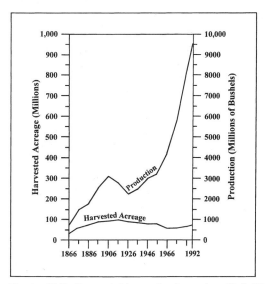

Figure 14.7 Corn yield trends since the Civil War. *Source:* U.S. Department of Agriculture.

[16]The abrupt kink of Figure 14.4 occurring in 1976 is attributable to estimating methods being reported by the U.S. Department of Agriculture from 1959 to 1975, differing from those between 1976 and 1989.

yield since 1980 is due mainly to specialization and biotechnological advancements in corn seed. Figure 14.7 shows that acres planted in corn reached a zenith during the same period as farm population reached its maximum; the decline in the number of acres planted in corn mirrored the decline in farm population, presently dipping below the acreage planted in the 1890s. Still, fewer people involved in harvesting fewer acres of corn can create more corn output. Figure 14.7 demonstrates that total corn production has increased regularly since the 1930s and reached a record high in 1985. Because the market could not absorb the 1985 bumper corn harvest and also sustain high corn prices, corn prices fell in 1986–88. It is in response to the fall in corn prices and the shift to land uses that could generate greater location rents (such as feedlot operations) that total corn output declined in the late 1980s.

The increase in farm land intensity as measured by the increasing ratio of harvest output to acres of farm land used is expected to have produced an upward movement in Corn Belt agricultural land prices. Again Table 14.1 bears this out.

As Corn Belt meat production becomes more concentrated in the western subregion, so does the raw-material-oriented meatpacking industry. Competition for access to the supply markets has brought the meatpacking industry out from the now defunct Chicago stockyards. Meatpacking is now dispersed throughout the western Corn Belt, particularly in urban areas surrounding Iowa.

Meatpacking has also outmigrated from Chicago to the important outlying regions of cattle production. As the West Coast market has grown, a mini-cattle-fattening region exists on feedlots of the arid Imperial valley in southeastern California. Cattle on farms in California account for about 5 percent of the nation's total. Cattle production for slaughter has been an important agricultural product in north Florida since the time of the Spanish occupation and,

later, during the War Between the States. Cattle on farms in Florida is equal to that of Alabama, Arkansas, Georgia, Mississippi, Indiana, Ohio, and North Dakota. Each of these states represents between 2 and 3 percent of the nation's total; each state individually exceeds Wyoming in cattle on farms. Texas is the leading state in the nation for cattle on farms, with about 12 percent of the nation's total and with highest concentrations in the eastern and southwestern part of the state. The meatpacking industry's facilities are now distributed in each of these cattle production locales.

The Wheat Belts

Recall from Chapter 13 the discussion on the difference between the economists' normative heuristic model of supply and demand, and the economic geographers' location analysis. The economists' normative model was designed to answer the question concerning the trajectory of price and quantity change following some perturbation in the economy. Instead, the economic geographer when analyzing the same phenomena would ask *where* the perturbation in the economy would be felt and how it would be felt, *at that location*. Perhaps no other example more clearly exemplifies this than the economic geography of wheat production.

Beyond the Corn Belt/Meat Belt lies the Thünian wheat production zone of the Great Plains, where agriculture is characterized by large farms exceeding several hundred acres, relatively low land values, and low output per acre. There are two distinct long-standing divisions of the Wheat Belt—spring wheat in the northern Plains and winter wheat in the central and southern Plains (Figure 14.8). The fine boundaries as shown in Figure 14.8 should be recognized as fluid approximations of wide transitional zones in which one farming system gradually gives way to another. Recall that the division of the Corn Belt into Corn Belt and Meat Belt is the result of market situation forces and specialization. Instead,

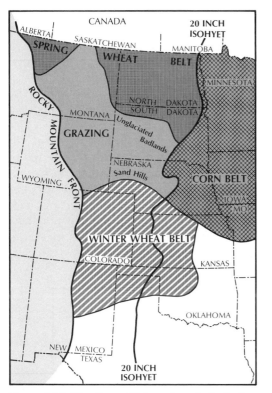

Figure 14.8 The Great Plains wheat belts in the context of climate and physiography.

the Wheat Belt is divided into further parts solely for physical geographic reasons: climate, topography and soil: (1) The rugged terrain in western South Dakota's badlands limits the use of farm machinery; (2) bad soil conditions of the Sand Hills of central and northwestern Nebraska limits wheat production; and (3) temperatures are too low for winter wheat north of its boundary (Figure 14.8) and summers too hot for spring wheat south of the boundary that demarcates Winter and Spring Wheat Belts. Precipitation is also very important, especially along the east-west axis. In addition to market situation forces of the Thünian sequential rings, on the boundary of the Spring Wheat Belt and the Corn Belt to the east is the critical 20-inch isohyet boundary. This boundary marks the transition from a humid to a semiarid climate. The minimum annual mois-

ture required by high-yielding Corn Belt crops is about 20 inches of precipitation. (This isohyet is mapped in Figure 14.8.) The average position of the 20-inch isohyet is subject to considerable fluctuation from year to year because rainfall in the Plains is highly variable. Because of these physical geographic reasons, as well as the consequential uncertainty over steady output in the zone lying between Spring and Winter Wheat Belts, east-west railroads avoided this zone. With reduced access to eastern markets, the next less intensive land use, grazing, has been established there.

Wheat is among the most transferable of food commodities both in terms of low movement costs and ability to withstand extensive handling and long storage periods. Wheat is often shipped as a backhaul cargo in empty oil tankers returning to Third World petroleum-supply ports. Wheat farming is almost totally mechanized and is thus well suited to areas of low rural-labor density. Environmentally, wheat is a sturdy dryland crop, closely related to the natural prairie grasses it has displaced.

Higher-yielding **winter wheat** is raised in Kansas–Oklahoma–eastern Colorado where winters are mild enough to support the high evapotranspiration rates and dry-spell probabilities of the southern Plains summer. The winter wheat crop is planted in the cool, moist fall months, is induced to flower by winter's lower temperatures (it can withstand short periods of hard freeze), blooms in the early spring, and is harvested in May and June. Since World War II, production has shifted from monocultural to a mixture of winter wheat with grain sorghum. Grain sorghum was introduced from arid Africa and can grow where annual rainfall is as low as 10 inches. It is raised and exported as a feed crop whose nutritional value almost equals that of corn.

The **spring wheat** of the Dakotas, north-central Montana, and the adjacent Canadian prairie provinces is planted in early spring to achieve as great a growth as possible before the high summer temperatures. Spring wheat has lower yields than winter wheat, but can survive more arid conditions. The Spring Wheat Belt is also no longer monocultural, with dryland rye, barley, and flaxseed (for linseed oil); the Red River valley of North Dakota also has irrigated soybean and potato production.

Dry farming has enabled the Wheat Belt to expand into the more arid western margins of the Plains, including northern Montana. This cultivation method lets fields lie fallow during alternate years so that they may accumulate moisture, which is protected by constant weeding and keeping idle fields covered with straw to prevent wind erosion. In the Winter Wheat Belt, *center-*

pivot irrigation now irrigates many fields by a rotating pipe mounted on motorized towers, with water supplied from a pumping station located at the center. Nebraska quadrupled its total wheat output within five years of the introduction of this form of irrigation in the mid-1970s. With the investment in irrigation equipment, higher-valued crops can replace wheat.

Clearly, the Plains environment makes for risky agriculture. Western explorers referred to this dry plateau as the Great American Desert. Thus, in spite of the region's fertile soil, frontier expansion and displacement of indigenous people leapfrogged over the Plains to the more hospitable Pacific coast. Drought hazards are caused

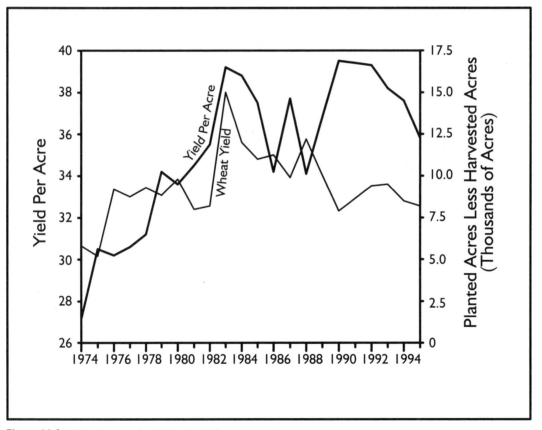

Figure 14.9 Wheat acres planted and yield per acre.

by moist air from the south and the need to over-come the predominant west-to-east airflow to penetrate into the central and northern Plains. Wind presents a constant threat of soil erosion in the subhumid area, as evidenced by the Dust Bowl eras of the 1930s and 1950s, and serious dust storms in the mid-1970s. After the 1930s Dust Bowl, farmers learned to plant trees on the windward western edges of their fields to act as windbreaks.

Figure 14.9 shows the difference between wheat acres planted and wheat acres harvested; both bad economic conditions and changing government regulations can encourage a farmer to decide not to harvest his planted field. More likely, environmental damage reduces the number of acres harvested, bringing great uncertainty to the returns to be made from farming in this region.

Adding to the environmental risk of agricultural production in the Great Plains is the risk produced by widely fluctuating prices for bushels of wheat. The environmental risk leads land users to overplant, so that if yields are low they will still receive adequate revenues. Overplanting without accompanying environmental damage leads to bumper crops and depressed prices. To smooth these cycles, the federal government initiated programs that guarantee the farmer will receive floor prices on each bushel of wheat regardless of what the market price is. Early in the 1970s, wheat prices had risen sharply in response to rising foreign demand (only about 40 percent of U.S. wheat is consumed domestically). This was the period of the first major Soviet purchase of American agricultural products since the inception of the Cold War. When wheat stocks purchased by the government through its price support program declined, the U.S. Department of Agriculture allowed production to increase; wheat acreages harvested jumped from 47.3 million in 1972 to 68.9 million in 1975. By 1977 (see Figure 14.10), the wheat boom had ended. Harvests remained high, but reduced foreign demand and bumper wheat harvests elsewhere in

the world caused the 1974 price of over $4 per bushel to plummet to $2 during 1977.[17] By 1995 farm price for a bushal of wheat had returned to the $4.00 range.

The decline in market prices for wheat caused farmers to shift their production to other crops. As a result, wheat yield declined in 1977. The reduction in wheat yield then caused wheat prices to rise. The higher prices led farmers to shift production back into wheat. The greater wheat output caused market prices to tumble again from 1982 through 1986. Such cycles as just described (see Figure 14.10) do not favor the geographic stability of wheat regions. The level of risk can be translated into a production cost. When the risk is high, the cost of production when averaged over several seasons is higher.

The cost of production shown in the Thünian framework of Equations (13.1) through (13.4) is subtracted from location rent, exactly countering market price for the final product. In other words, high risk translates into high cost of production which decreases location rent. Thus, strong cycles as evidenced in Figures 14.9 and 14.10 lead to lower location rent and consequently to contraction of the geographic area of the high-risk agricultural product. Cycles of Wheat Belt contraction and expansion occur along the western fringe of the Wheat Belt. When prices rise, farmers earning lower location rents can "move up" to wheat production.

The Winter and Spring Wheat Belts are among the most mechanized agricultural regions on earth. Central Kansas farms average about 620 acres, South Dakota farms average more than 1100, and farms in Montana are in excess of 2500 acres. Machinery investments are large, but these costs are spread out over large acreages. At the same time, land values as shown in Table 14.1 are lower than those in the regions discussed earlier. The low land values allow land users to

---

[17]Most wheat farmers claimed that their breakeven income near the end of the 1970s was from $2.50 to $3.00 per bushel. The federal price support was then $3.30 per bushel.

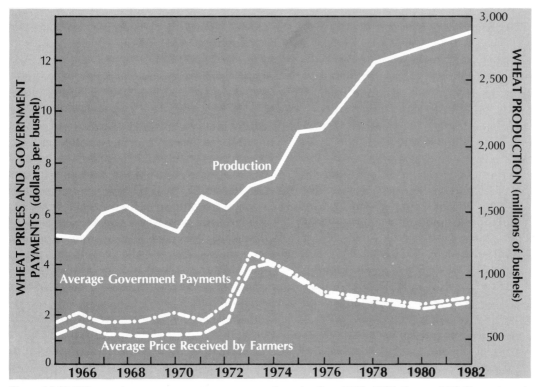

Figure 14.10 Wheat prices, governemnt payments, and production, 1965–1982. *Source:* U.S. Department of Agriculture.

farm large acreages, which reduces the overall average capital-to-land ratio.

Harvested grain begins its marketward journey when trucks collect the contents of the farmer's wheat storage bins and transport them to a local elevator situated next to a main rail line. From there trains carry the grain to terminal elevators located together with flour mills; milled flour is then distributed by rail to national markets. Midwestern cities are efficient sites for flour manufacturing because they are flow collection points on the marketward side of the Wheat Belts. Half the product's weight is lost during milling, making raw-material-oriented manufacturing-in-transit at break-of-bulk points desirable. To reduce milling costs, milling operations are agglomerated in a few large cities. Kansas City and Minneapolis are two leading examples.

They have a location advantage because several east-west railroads converge there and because their location on the Missouri and Mississippi rivers, respectively, gives them access to the international seaport of New Orleans.

Only one other wheat-producing region is nationally prominent: the winter-wheat Palouse Hills in the central Columbia River basin of eastern Washington State (see Figure 13.18). Its situation makes it uneconomic to transport wheat to the Northeast: the Plains Wheat Belts act as an intervening supply opportunity for Megalopolis. Palouse wheat is therefore sold to West Coast markets; as much as 80 percent is exported to Japan and other Pacific Rim customers. Intensive cultivation is required for wheat farmers to survive such a remote location. Despite the need for dry farming in this semiarid country, wheat output per acre is higher here than in Kansas.

We have learned the important role of transportation cost in shaping the agricultural landscape; decreasing transportation costs can extend the intensive margin of production outward along the corridors of lower cost. As agriculturists take advantage of changing transportation technology and infrastructure, the cities that depend on that commerce can flourish or die. No city better characterizes this cycle than Buffalo, New York. Commerce in wheat transportation and Buffalo's important location in the North American water transportation network brought about its growth. Buffalo became one of the leading fresh water ports on the Great Lakes. Wheat was transported by barge from railheads at Duluth and Chicago through Lake Huron and Lake Erie to Buffalo. The wheat was offloaded in Buffalo back onto rail with direct connections to the Megalopolitan seaboard cities. In the earlier Canal era, the wheat would have been offloaded from lakegoing vessels onto smaller barges pulled through the Erie Canal. Today the Welland Canal joins Lakes Erie and Ontario by cutting across the Canadian Province of Ontario; it allows oceangoing ships to travel directly from Lake Huron through the St. Lawrence Seaway onto ports of the world, thereby bypassing Buffalo. A recurring theme is that what has given Buffalo its wealth and *joie de vivre* soon leaves it. Toledo, Ohio, now surpasses Buffalo in tonnage shipped through its port.

Grazing and Irrigated-Crops Region

The outermost Thünian agricultural ring in the continental United States is the Grazing Belt. Most of the Grazing Belt consists of dry grassland on high plateaus (including the northwestern Great Plains). Mountain ranges break up the Grazing Belt into dry grassland plateaus of the southwestern and northwestern Great Plains, and the intermontane plateau lying between the Rocky Mountains and the Sierra Nevada and Cascade chain to the west.

Reflecting the Spanish heritage of much of this region, farms are generally referred to here as ranches. It is the combination of large size and low intensive use of the land that distinguishes a ranch from a conventional farm. Ranch sizes are large and can occupy several thousand acres, giving rise to extremely low measures of land-use intensity: low capital-to-land ratios, labor-to-land ratios, and output-to-land ratios. It has already been shown that this most extensive of farming systems has a close symbiotic relationship with the Corn Belt; in the Grazing Belt, young beef animals are bred for subsequent fattening on Corn Belt feeder lots. To a lesser extent, sheep and lambs are also grazed, along with young cattle for their meat and wool. Aridity and inferior land quality combine to support only modest annual growth of the dry grasses of this region. It is not uncommon for a single animal to require the vegetation of 100 acres of rangeland.

Location rents in the Grazing Belt are the lowest in the nation, often below $1 per acre. Low production costs per acre and highly transportable animal products allow the region to survive economically. With current technology, it is not desirable to increase the level of intensive use of the land, for it is presently grazed near its carrying capacity. Even alpine meadows above the tree line are used for grazing during summer. Overgrazing will retard the growth of vegetation in subsequent seasons and heighten wind erosion.

At several places in the grazing region, irrigated-crop farming occurs. Water is supplied either from concentrated surface flow or from deep subsurface aquifers. Some of the larger scattered pockets of intensive agriculture appear like remote desert oases. One of the largest is the Colorado Piedmont at the base of the Front Range of the Rockies, north of Denver. It is served by mountain streams and the Big Thompson project, whose tunnels transport water beneath the Continental Divide. Irrigation allows the production of sugar beets in the Colorado Piedmont; also, beef-cattle feedlots allow Denver to be an important meatpacking center. Irrigation of the Snake River plains of southern Idaho allows for potato production. Through one of the nation's most sophisticated irrigation networks, the Wasatch Front, east of Utah's Great Salt Lake, can produce a variety of valuable crops. The Humboldt Valley of northern Nevada possesses both irrigation water and a good situation to the market via the main San Francisco–Salt Lake City railroad and highway. Irrigation of southern Arizona's Gila basin supports both an expanding animal-fattening feedlot industry and a robust cotton industry.

Interspersed with ranching throughout much of the Grazing Belt is *lumbering*. Some economic geographers locate forestry as the outermost Thünian ring. Recall from Chapter 13 that lumber production was displaced from an inner position in the original Thünian scheme following the introduction of long-distance rail transportation and alternative fuel sources in the mid-nineteenth century. Lumbering in the continental United States is concentrated in the mountainous Cascades of Oregon and Washington, the Sierra Nevada, and the Rocky Mountains. Lumbering is also an important agricultural product in the less populated areas of the Deep South where large unprofitable plantations have turned to "tree farming." Lumbering gives rise to localized sawmill and paper-making industries, which is an important addition to the economic base of small towns in these regions.

The natural amenities of the mountain region of Colorado is attracting more intensive recreational uses of land, thereby displacing ranching and lumbering. Colorado's Vail ski resort which following the second World War was a sheep ranch, has become world renowned as America's premier winter resort. Vail's mild summer climate, mountain trails, scenic beauty, and golf courses have also contributed to its attraction as a summer resort. Mountainous Vail is a model of good urban planning, creating a compact city that encourages walking and concentrations of exciting high-order retail activities. This all adds

to land values soaring to levels equal to those of the larger American cities. New Mexico also has incipient ski and golf resort developments like those that began in Colorado in the early 1970s. Retirement households from the western portion of the United States and Canada are increasingly choosing New Mexico and Arizona (instead of more costly coastal southern California) as their destination, as Florida has long attracted midwestern and northeastern retirees. Nearby California retirees can exchange their relatively higher priced real estate for much less expensive smog-free New Mexico retirement havens, with the bonus of also acquiring sizable bank accounts in the transaction.

The Remaining Agricultural Regions

The only farming areas left to be discussed in our regional survey are located in the Southeast: the General Farming Region and the Old Cotton Belt (see Figure 13.17).

The General Farming Belt that straddles the rugged central Appalachians and Ozark–Ouachita uplands west of the Mississippi permits little agricultural activity. Poor quality land is found throughout, and commercial farming is restricted to small scattered valleys and several fertile pockets such as the Kentucky Bluegrass basin. Landowners here are seeking to increase land values by building self-contained recreational and retirement communities. The Appalachians are potentially appealing as an intervening opportunity for otherwise Florida-bound tourists and retirees. In like manner, the Ozark–Ouachita uplands has potential as a significant destination for inhabitants of the Mississippi River basin. However, the potential development of this region has been lessened by a history of poor urban planning.

The original location of cotton in the Southeast follows what would be expected from the macro-Thünian model. Cotton is a subtropical crop that earns a location rent equal to that of Corn Belt crops. Climatic conditions required for cotton production deflected the crop southward and away from the Megalopolis national market center (see Figure 13.6). The old Cotton Belt still produces one-third of the nation's cotton, but, since World War I, cotton has been replaced by more profitable agricultural activities.[18]

"King Cotton" in the Southeast began to decline after World War I when black farm laborers began to outmigrate to northeastern and midwestern industrial cities. As the traditional supply of cheap labor dwindled, cotton producers were forced to mechanize. Many of the plantation owners who chose to mechanize faced financial ruin from repeated boll weevil scourges. The boll weevil was controlled by the late 1920s, but by that time many land users had already switched to alternate crops such as peanuts. Reinforcing the shift away from cotton was the federal government's Agricultural Adjustment Act of 1933. The intent of those who designed the act was to increase the price of bailed cotton through federal price supports and acreage controls. The effect was that land users concentrated cotton production on their best land and cultivated it more intensively; yields from harvested acreage increased and total cotton production rose. Federal agricultural policy makers responded by rolling back allowed acreages, leaving many small operators with such small allotments that they abandoned cotton production altogether.[19]

Federal price support policies encouraged land users in other regions to enter cotton production. In the Southwest, federally subsidized irrigation projects made high cotton yields possible where land and other production costs were half those in the Southeast. The labor-poor Southwest had early on adopted the strategy of substituting mechanization for labor. Today over 50 percent

of the nation's cotton is produced in a zone that extends west from the Texas Panhandle through southern Arizona into California's San Joaquin valley (Figure 13.4). As the boll weevil was to the Southeast, the lack of water may ultimately lead to a shift in production to less-water-consuming agricultural crops. Stiff competition from highly versatile synthetic textiles may lead to a decline in the areal extent of cotton production. The result is that cotton production in the Southeast has contracted to fall only within its physical optimum (Figure 13.6). This is the region of the Mississippi River Delta, which extends from the confluence of the Ohio River and the Mississippi River to central Louisiana.

The remainder of the Old Cotton Belt, however, contains several types of agriculture that have made the modern South agriculturally diversified. Several highly intensive truck crops are produced in the region (Figure 13.17) such as Vidalia onions; there are also concentrations of poultry factory-farms and peanut farms. Soybean production has increased in the Delta, especially alongside cotton. Forestry has been adopted on many old plantations. As touched upon in the section detailing the Corn Belt, beef-cattle raising in the Old Cotton Belt supplies about one-third of the Corn Belt's imported feeder animals. High concentrations of land used for pasture are found in the southeastern corner of the Old Cotton Belt. There feed for calves and yearlings is supplemented by accessible citrus pulp and other fruit residues from nearby Florida.

Like cotton, tobacco has been displaced southward from the national market. Climate is a less constraining factor in tobacco production than it is in cotton production. Cotton will grow well in both subtropical and midlatitude climates. Remnants of tobacco production could be found through the 1970s along the southern Connecticut River valley and in the Pennsylvania Dutch country which lies to the west of Philadelphia. The soil, climate and administrative skills of Connecticut tobacco farmers have allowed them to continue to compete on the world market with

[18]John Fraser Hart, *The South*, 2nd rev. ed. New Searchlight Series (New York: D. Van Nostrand Co., 1976); Merle C. Prunty, "Some Contemporary Myths and Challenges in Southern Rural Land Utilization," *Southeastern-Geographer* 10 (November 1970), pp. 1–12.

[19]Hart, *The South*, pp. 35–36.

high valued cigar wrapper. Tobacco was initially grown in the Chesapeake Bay area before the American Revolution. Concentrations of tobacco production today are found in southeastern Virginia, eastern North Carolina, and the Kentucky Bluegrass basin.

AGRICULTURAL TRENDS AND PROBLEMS IN THE LATE-TWENTIETH-CENTURY UNITED STATES

This section begins with an overview of two institutional issues: (1) agribusiness and corporate farming, and (2) international trade in agricultural products as it affects the United States as both a food exporter and a food importer. Next we examine the substantive issue of (3) agricultural land–price inflation, cycles, and the widening gap of agricultural land values versus land rents. The chapter concludes with (4) a point of view on possible futures for U.S. agriculture in the twenty-first century.

Agribusiness and Corporate Farming

The first part of this chapter provided a rationale for why farms are the size they are and why the location-specific level of agricultural intensity has arisen for the region. Small farms are viewed as being comparatively inefficient. It is a mistake to view the trend toward bigness as resulting from a takeover of much of the farming sector by large absentee corporations.

Column 7 of Table 14.2 reveals that for 1992, almost 50 percent of farms had less than $10,000 in gross value of sales. The table also reveals that less than 0.8 percent of all farms make revenues in excess of $1,000,000. Thus, in terms of numbers of farms, the small family farm is strongly entrenched on the U.S. landscape.

It is a myth, then, that the small family farm has vanished, to be replaced by the large corporate farm, Table 14.2 reveals that in 1992 almost 18 percent of farms had gross sales exceeding $100,000 and 6.5 percent over $250,000. Those 6.5 percent of the largest farms also exceeded an

Table 14.2 Farms—Number, Acreage, and Value of Sales, by Size of Sales: 1992

Value of Products Sold	Farms (1,000)	Acreage		Value of Sales		Percent Distribution		
		Total (mil.)	Average per farm	Total (mil. dol)	Average per farm (dol.)	Farms	Acreage	Value of sales
Total	1,925	945.5	491	162,608	84,459	100.0	100.0	100.0
Less than $10,000	907	123.5	136	3,043	3,357	47.1	13.1	1.9
Less than $2,500	423	55.7	132	411	972	22.0	5.9	0.3
$2,500-$4,999	232	26.9	116	836	3,605	12.1	2.8	0.5
$5,000-$9,999	252	40.9	162	1,797	7,132	13.1	4.3	1.1
$10,000 or more	1,019	822.0	807	159,565	156,623	52.9	86.9	98.1
$10,000-$24,999	302	81.8	271	4,841	16,039	15.7	8.7	3.0
$25,000-$49,999	195	91.4	477	6,967	35,662	10.1	9.7	4.3
$50,000-$99,999	188	133.9	713	13,517	71,990	9.8	14.2	8.3
$100,000-$249,999	208	228.0	1,094	32,711	156,958	10.8	24.1	20.1
$250,000-$499,999	79	130.9	1,666	26,914	342,653	4.1	13.8	16.6
$500,000-$999,999	31	80.6	2,598	20,953	675,368	1.6	8.5	12.9
$1,000,000 or more	16	75.5	4,751	53,663	3,377,175	0.8	8.0	33.0

Source of tables 1076–1078: U.S. Bureau of the Census, *1992 Census of Agriculture*, vol. 1.

average of over 1666 acres in size and accounted for over 31 percent of all farm land. Although the small family farm remains a significant presence in the United States, it is the few corporate farms that own the largest tracts of agricultural land and have the largest revenues. The significant scale economies they can achieve also makes the largest farms the most profitable.

The concentration of production onto larger farms, such as that which was discussed above as occurring in the Corn Belt, is almost entirely a movement toward bigger family farms. Which are the corporations that own the largest farms that also generate the largest sales? Over 80 percent of all corporate farms are family operations. The reasons for the shift to large farms were discussed above. Advantages of incorporation include better financing, limited liability, numerous tax benefits, and fewer inheritance problems.[20]

The only states in which large absentee-owned corporations control a sizable share of farm land can be found along the perimeter of the nation. Florida, Texas, and California share reasons for corporate ownership: (1) all were former Spanish colonies in which the land-tenure tradition encouraged huge plantation-like holdings; (2) the great distance from the national market in these states required enormous capital investments, large-scale economies, and organizational expertise to overcome this geographical handicap; and (3) the dominance of specialty crops such as citrus fruits lends itself through vertical integration to outside control by big companies. Most farm corporations, however, began as family operations, assembled large-scale family-owned businesses, incorporated, and then were sold. Eventually, many passed into foreign ownership. A corroborating map of foreign ownership is displayed in Figure 14.11. It reveals high concentrations of foreign ownership at the perimeter of the nation, declining toward the interior.

Agriculture and U.S. Foreign Trade

In the post–World War II era, food exports have accounted for 10 to 25 percent of annual production. The United States supplies 80 to 90 percent of the world's exported food, accounting for over half of the world's export grain alone. Unfortunately for American farmers, foreign demand fluctuates as much as 30 percent from one year to the next. Foreign demand depends on may factors, including competitive foreign production, foreign income, and the value of U.S. currency on international money exchanges. Figure 14.12 shows that the value of total U.S. agricultural exports increased from the 1970s through 1981, and then began a cycle of decline through 1986 when an upswing began. The line in Figure 14.2 for "% of All Exports That Are Agricultural" is comparatively flat, while the line for "Total Agricultural Exports" is strongly cyclical. This means that agricultural exports closely mirror the behavior of the U.S. exports of all commodities. In 1974, roughly 25 percent of all exports were agricultural, declining to about 12 percent in 1988. Thus, while exports in 1988 were up 66 percent from 1974 levels, other sectors of the economy were exporting more, thereby decreasing the agricultural share by half.[21]

Developed countries purchased almost half of the $35 billion in U.S. agricultural exports in 1988; roughly 40 percent went to less developed countries, and the remainder was sold to centrally planned countries. Apart from a variation of about 3 percent in agricultural products sold to centrally planned countries, these proportions have remained relatively stable since the late 1970s.[22] Japan and Canada are the largest purchasers of U.S. agricultural produce. Japan pur-

[20]Ibid., p. 90.

[21]U.S. Department of Agriculture, *Agricultural Statistics* 1997 (Washington, D.C.: GPO, 1989), Table 15-11, "Foreign Trade"; p. 506.
[22]Ibid., 1997, Table 15-11 "US Agricultural Exports," pp. xv–11.

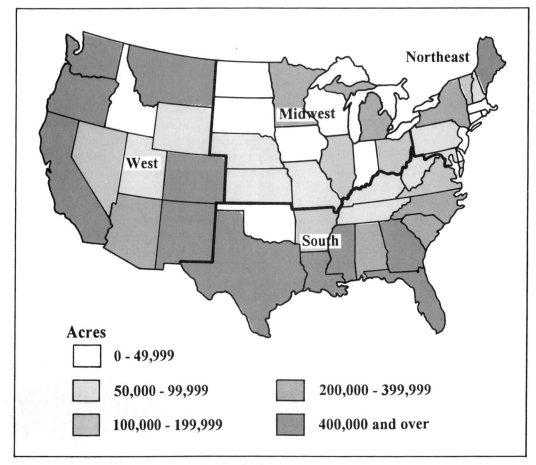

Figure 14.11 Foreign ownership of U.S. farm land.

chased over $9.2 billion dollars in sales in 1994, and Canada over $5.3 billion dollars in 1994. Mexico accounted for over $4.1 billion. In 1994 the leading US agricultural exports were feed grain, followed in order by wheat, oilseed, and feeds and fodders.

The United States is also a major importer of agricultural products. Over the past decade, the value of agricultural imports has risen by 50 percent. In 1988, there was a $14 billion surplus of exports over imports of agricultural goods, and in 1994 there was a $16 billion surplus. The leading countries from which the United States imports agricultural products are Canada, followed

in order by Mexico, Indonesia, Brazil, Colombia, Netherlands and Italy. The leading agricultural product imported in 1994 was fruits and nuts and vegetables, followed in order by bananas, coffee, cocoa, and meat.

Trends in Agricultural Land Values and Their Widening Gap with Land Rents

The gap is widening between what agricultural land sells for versus what it can receive in rent. As this gap grows, many who presently own agricultural land and use it for farming will either leave the industry or become tenant farmers.

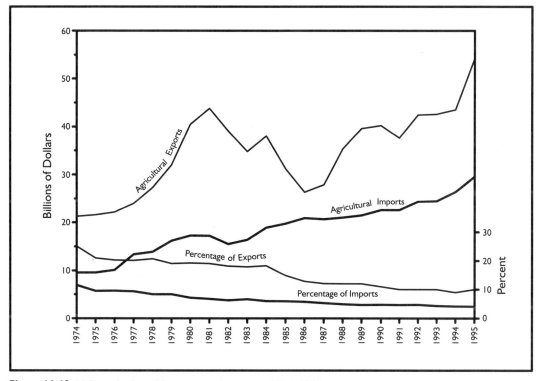

Figure 14.12 U.S. agricultural imports and exports, 1974–1995.

The average price of what agricultural land has sold for is shown in Figure 14.13. Table 14.1 documented change in agricultural land values from the 1970s to the middle 1990s. Beginning in 1985 (Figure 14.13), average agricultural land values declined; by the end of the decade, they were again increasing.

When agricultural prices decline, the short-term winners are the large incorporated farms with considerable assets. Such owners can take advantage of short-term swings in land prices to assemble ever-increasing acreage at relatively low prices. Small farmers are at a disadvantage when agricultural land values turn downward because they depend on the value of their land as collateral to obtain funds to purchase equipment, seed, fertilizer, and so on, for the present season. A downturn in land prices coupled with a downturn in commodity prices leaves the small farmer in the perilous position of needing to refinance loans with devalued collateral. Many small farmers are forced to sell to the large corporations.

Figure 14.14*a* shows the percentage change in agricultural land values between 1982 and 1989 by state. Agricultural land surrounding Megalopolis increased by as much as 145 percent. The rapid urban growth states of Florida and Georgia increased by 2 percent and 11 percent, respectively. However, where urban land use does not significantly compete with agricultural land use, land values declined. Thus, the Delta states, Northern Plains, and Great Lakes states witnessed a 40 percent decline in agricultural land values.

Evidence has been presented in this and in the previous chapter that agricultural land values follow the expected Thünian distance decay: as distance from the central market increases, land val-

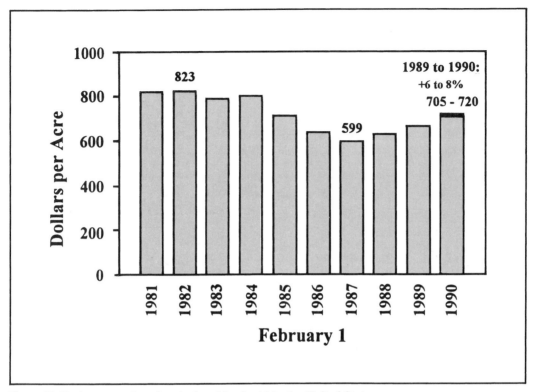

Figure 14.13 Average price of agricultural land sold in the United States.

ues decline. This chapter has also offered an explanation of why exceptions to this rule occur. The discussion, however, has used numerical values of what agricultural land sells for from a willing seller to a willing buyer. What about the large market of agricultural land rent: a contract for payment for the right to use acreage for one or several seasons without change of ownership? Agricultural land contract rent follows a pattern that also conforms to the Thünian reasoning, with the same modifications as required to explain the special outliers noted above (see Figure 14.14*b*).

Figure 14.14*b* shows average yearly cash rents for cropland per acre. As expected, rents are relatively high in the densely populated Mid-Atlantic Megalopolis states. They decline with distance from Megalopolis and then increase with proximity to the fast urban growth Georgia/Florida markets. As with land values, the "Chipit" urban/industrial corridor commands land rents that are among the highest agricultural rents in the nation—particularly in Iowa whose agricultural rents reflect the gains noted above from feedlot operations. The values in brackets in Figure 14.14b are for irrigated land.

If agricultural land values were a straight reflection of the expected returns to agricultural use, then agricultural land rent and agricultural land value should be a constant proportion of one another: each year's rent should cover the principal and interest costs prorated over the lifetime of the mortgage. To determine what multiple land value is of land rent, divide land value by the yearly rent of land; the average ratio of land value to land rent by state for the continen-

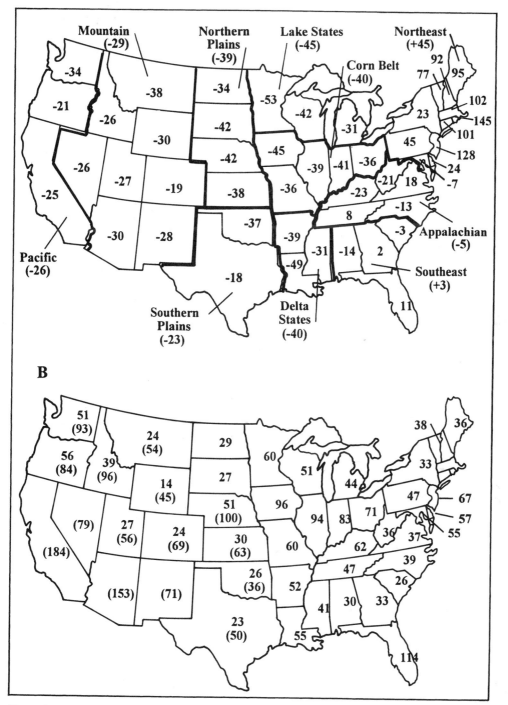

Figure 14.14 Changes in the percentage of agricultural land values by state, 1982–1989; and agricultural land contract rent by state.

Source: U.S. Department of Agriculture, *Agricultural Statistics, 1989.* (Washington, D.C.: GPO, 1989), Table 38. And U.S. Department of Commerce, *Historical Statistics of the United States, Colonial Times to 1970* (Washington, D.C.: GPO, 1975), Table K 502–516.

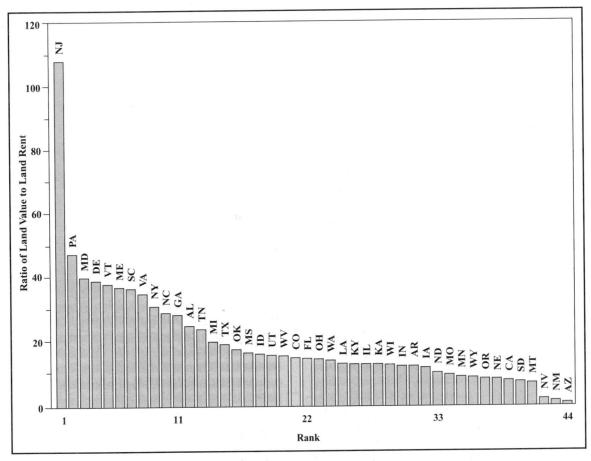

Figure 14.15 Ratio of land value to land rent by state.

tal United States is 20.32. This means that, on average, 20.32 years of rent is required to pay for one acre of land, and this does not include the cost of seed, fertilizer, equipment, and labor!

Mapping the land value to land rent can aid interpretation of the ratio of land values to land rent. This ratio is derived by dividing the values of the map in Figure 14.1 by those for the same state of Figure 14.14*b*. The rank ordering of the resulting ratio is shown in Figure 14.15.[23]

[23]This analysis is from Grant Ian Thrall, "The Agricultural Land Value to Land Rent Ratio," Department of Geography, University of Florida, 1991, mimeograph.

The highest ratio of land value to land rent is found in the Northeast Megalopolis: New Jersey followed by Delaware, Maryland, and Pennsylvania, and then the nearby states of Maine and Vermont. The ratio is 108 in New Jersey, which means that 108 years of rents are required to purchase an acre of agricultural land. The ratio declines with increasing distance from Megalopolis. The highest ratios are in those states where intensive nonirrigated agriculture is dominant. The lowest ratios are in those arid irrigated lands of Arizona, New Mexico, and Nevada; the ratios for these states are not comparable to those of the other states since the calculations used rents for irrigated land while nonirrigated agricultural land is used elsewhere. Montana has the lowest ratio among nonirrigated states; seven years of rent are required to purchase one acre of agricultural land.

Part of the explanation for the wide gap between land value and land rent in the Northeast lies in the steady, virtually guaranteed market for the truck-garden product produced there. This low long-term risk translates into higher land values. Conversely, the high long-term risk of the Wheat Belt translates into lower land values, while land rents are proportional each season to lower risk expectations concerning the coming year's market and output. Another part of the explanation for the gap in land values and land rents is the involvement of land investors in agricultural land markets, driving northeastern agricultural land values higher than would be justified by returns from mere agricultural land use.

The greater the gap between land values and land rents, the more difficult for the land user to enter into agricultural production. In addition, the greater the gap, the more tempting it is for the land user to sell the farm to land investors. Some land users leave agriculture, while others may rent the land back at low rates from the new landowners.

A GLIMPSE AT FUTURE AMERICAN AGRICULTURE

The uncertainty of the market for agricultural products, heightened by the wide gap between land values and land rents in most parts of the nation, may make the agricultural industry appear to be unhealthy and rapidly coming to an end. Agriculture may appear to be noncompetitive with urban industry and urban incomes. For many farm families that is true. However, the wide land-value, land-rent gap in heavily agricultural states is a signal that many investors see a strong future in the farming industry. And the rural and agricultural way of life remains a lure for many households.

What will the nation's farming be like in the next century? On the not so bright side to the producer, foreign competition—with lower-cost labor and lower-cost land—will become a more active player in the U.S. agricultural market than it has in the past. Free trade with Canada and Mexico will heighten this changed role especially as a consequence of NAFTA.[24] On the bright side to the U.S. producer, the nation's lead will come from anticipated technological breakthroughs, including better methods to prevent wind and water erosion; crop hybrids that increase yield; and hybrids whose characteristics offer greater nutritional value and resistance to pests, salt, and drought. Improvements in long-range weather forecasts will enable land users to better choose what to plant and when to place the soil in fallow. Technology is advancing for desalinization of seawater for use by urban centers; this innovation will eventually be transferred to low-cost irrigation. Modular energy systems, including solar panels, will reduce the dependence of farmers on off-farm energy sources. To be internationally competitive, farming will be forced to become a mirror more of technologically advanced urban-based firms than of the nineteenth-century homestead. The distinction between the farm business and the urban business will become blurred.

Further Readings

Andrea, Bernd. *Farming Development and Space: A World Agricultural Geography*. Howard F. Gregor, trans. Berlin and New York: de Gruyter, 1981.

de Blij, Harm J. *Wine: A Geographic Appreciation*. Totowa, N.J.: Rowman & Allanheld, 1983.

Bickel, Blaine W. "Revolutions in American Agriculture." *Monthly Review*, Federal Reserve Bank of Kansas City, June 1972, pp. 3–9.

Ebeling, Walter. *The Fruited Plain: The Story of American Agriculture, 1865–1980*. Berkeley: University of California Press, 1979.

Fite, Gilbert C. *Cotton Fields No More: Southern Ag-*

[24]NAFTA, North American Free Trade Agreement.

riculture, 1865–1980. Lexington: University Press of Kentucky, 1984.

Food—From Farm to Table: 1982 Yearbook of Agriculture. Washington, D.C.: U.S. Government Printing Office, 1982.

Furuseth, Owen J., and John T. Pierce. *Agricultural Land in an Urban Society*. Washington, D.C.: Association of American Geographers, Resource Publications in Geography, 1982.

Grigg, David B. *The Dynamics of Agricultural Change: The Historical Experience*. New York: St. Martin's Press, 1983.

Hart, John Fraser. *The Look of the Land*. Englewood Cliffs, N.J.: Prentice-Hall, 1975.

Hart, John Fraser. *The South*, 2nd rev. ed. New Searchlight Series. New York: D. Van Nostrand Co., 1976.

Heiser, Charles B., Jr. *Seed to Civilization: The Story of Food*. 2nd rev. ed. San Francisco: W. H. Freeman, 1981.

Knight, C. Gregory, and R. Paul Wilcox. *Triumph or Triage: The World Food Problem in Geographical Perspective*. Washington, D.C.: Association of American Geographers, Resource Paper 75-3, 1976.

Kollmorgen, Walter M., and George F. Jenks. "Sidewalk Farming in Toole County, Montana, and Traill County, North Dakota." *Annals of the Association of American Geographers* 48 (1958), pp. 209–231.

Kollmorgen, Walter M., and George F. Jenks. "Suitcase Farming in Sully County, South Dakota." *Annals of the Association of American Geographers* 48 (1958), pp. 27–40.

Mealor, W. Theodore, Jr., and Merle C. Prunty. "Open-Range Ranching in Southern Florida." *Annals of the Association of American Geographers* 66 (September 1976), pp. 360–376.

Miller, Thomas A., et. al. *Economics of Size in U.S. Field Crop Farming*. Washington, D.C.: U.S. Department of Agriculture, Economics and Statistics Service, Report No. 472, July 1981.

Parsons, James J. "Corporate Farming in California." *Geographical Review* 67 (July 1977), pp. 354–57.

Problem-Solving Approaches and Analytical Methods in Economic Geography

———— ◇ ————

You know my methods. Apply them.
—SIR ARTHUR CONAN DOYLE

APPLIED ECONOMIC GEOGRAPHY

Applied economic geography simply refers to the application of geographic concepts and methods of analysis to practical problems. The problems may not necessarily be viewed by everyone in the same way, and the problems may certainly not be seen by all from a geographic perspective. Yet our many societal, economic, and environmental problems may be approached by examining them as they exist in geographic space, for in many instances a cause or solution, or both, may be recognized when the problems are broken down into their spatial components.

Often the problems in applied economic geography are thrust on one by the day-to-day operation of society and the economy. These are real problems in the sense that they call for actual and often immediate solutions. An airport, because of aircraft noise, is leading to a decline in residential housing values in an area adjacent to the facility; what can be done? Funds have been awarded for a new regional hospital; where should it be located? Or a bypass is to be built around a medium-size city; which of several alternative routes should be selected?

Problems in applied economic geography dif-

fer from the kinds of research problems in theoretical economic geography, which may involve hypothetical situations, unrealistic assumptions, or greatly simplified conditions. Therefore, there is often the tendency to see theoretical approaches as in conflict with the approaches of applied economic geography. Such a tendency, however, is not only unfortunate; it is actually downright erroneous. Applied economic geography should be seen as complementary to theoretical or conceptual approaches.

First, it would be extremely difficult to render meaningful solutions to applied problems in economic geography without a solid conceptual foundation. For example, the airport noise problem leading to lowered residential housing values should be considered within the context of land-rent theory, even though one would not wish to propose a solution on such strictly theoretical grounds. Rather, it is the ideas, relationships, and interdependencies—derived from a conceptual base—that are necessary for useful and significant solutions to real-world problems. The planner who attempts to locate the regional hospital without recognition of the distance minimization principle would likely propose a hopelessly unworkable location. And yet the distance minimization principle is clearly not the only conceptual element the planner should take into account in such a location decision.

Applied economic geography is not only supported and strengthened by its derivation of concepts and principles, but the problems of interest and significance in theoretical economic geography are also defined and made meaningful by the nature of actual, real-world issues and problems. Hence, the applied and the theoretical perspectives are legitimate equals in the field of economic geography, and advances in one affect developments in the other.

Much of applied economic geography is learned by doing. One cannot learn to drive a car only by attending lectures on driving; one must also drive to learn. To reach successful solutions, one must (1) perceive the problem in its totality, along with the implications of the problem and its possible solutions; (2) have the necessary factual data or information base to analyze the problem; (3) have the proper analytic skills to attack the problem in order to shed more light on it and understand the relationships involved more clearly and fully; and (4) be capable of communicating solutions to others through written, oral, and graphical means. This chapter considers in turn each of these steps in the problem-solving process.

DEFINING THE PROBLEM

Defining a research problem is the most fundamental step in arriving at a solution to that problem. A well-defined and carefully articulated statement of the research problem implies a need for the kind of data that will have to be gathered to address the problem, as well as a direction to be taken in the methodological analysis and procedures that will be required to answer the questions raised in the problem statement. A carefully thought-out, clearly stated, and crisply conceived statement of a research problem may

be taken up by a different researcher or research team and carried on to completion. Again, the point is that if the statement of problem is carefully developed and presented, other steps in the research process are in large part also specified. On the other hand, a vaguely conceived and fuzzy statement of a research problem may suggest many quite different directions to its solution, as well as leading to a variety of results. The importance of a detailed and logical statement of the research problem holds both for theoretical economic geography and for applied research in the field. In a day-to-day sense, the consequences of a nebulously stated and poorly conceived research proposal in applied economic geography could be quite serious in that solutions might be proposed that are not relevant to the actual research problem at hand.

A first and basic step in defining a research problem, especially in applied economic geography, is to understand the **background conditions** that have led to the need for research to focus on the solution to the problem. How one achieves an understanding of these background conditions will, of course, vary widely from one situation to another. The main point to keep in mind in attempting to reach this understanding is to recognize that the particular issue being addressed is a component of several other issues or processes that impinge in some fashion on the central issue being defined.

A second step in the process of problem definition is to **decompose the problem** into its components and attempt to specify how these components interrelate with one another. Which components of the problem are salient and which are minor? Some research problems in applied economic geography are composed of many elements that are interrelated in complex ways. Others are simpler and more straightforward.

These two steps, understanding the background conditions and decomposing the problem, may be viewed in a **systems approach.** Although a "systems approach" may connote a theoretical perspective, such an approach is essential to clear problem formulation. In defining any problem, a researcher goes through the process of understanding the background conditions and decomposing the problem, whether consciously or not. If the researcher is not conscious of these processes, the background conditions, for example, may simply be assumed and the decomposition process may be haphazard at worst and poorly thought-through at best.

One may conceptualize the internal and external forces relating to problem definition. The ***internal features*** of the applied research problem include several identifiable components and the functional relations among these components. The ***external forces***—that is, those elements that are external to the problem but that impinge on it—represent the background conditions that must be taken into account in undertaking to solve the problem. The researcher thereby sees that the research problem does not exist in isolation but rather is part of ever larger problems. Lack of understanding of how the specified research problem fits into the larger system may easily lead to misspecification of the problem.

To take a particular example, imagine a simple locational problem in applied economic geography in which one wishes to determine the site for a public building—say, a library. The internal factors in this case are very simple in that one must know something of the size of the facility (how many books will be housed, how much study space), the amount of funding allocated for the purchase or construction of the facility, and the amount of space needed for parking vis-à-vis the building space and also the fact that the facility will obviously have to be located within the political administrative unit funding the project. These are examples of constraints internal to the locational problem.

The question of external constraints or background conditions is much more complex in this example. One must consider adjacent land uses, centrality to population to be served, perhaps lo-

cations to other libraries, the spatial patterns of land rents, any environmental impacts, and traffic generation and street and intersection capacities. Overlooking these and other background conditions could well lead to a very poor locational choice for the facility even though the internal components of the problem are properly specified.

DATA REQUIREMENTS

Once the research problem is precisely identified, it follows that particular kinds of data or other information will be needed in order to reach a solution to the questions posed. It is, once again, important to remember that a properly specified problem will virtually pinpoint the nature of the information and data that will be necessary. A general difficulty with studies in applied economic geography is that the necessary data sources may not already exist, making data collection or compilation mandatory. In most research undertakings, the appropriate data may not be found in a single source even if census material is to be used. Field interviewing or field mapping may be necessary. These means of obtaining data can be very costly and time-consuming, but there are many instances when they are the only feasible ways of obtaining data to address a particular problem. Air photos or satellite imagery may be used in certain instances and with great advantage. Other research will entail the use of historical and archival records. Many governmental agencies compile various kinds of data and other useful information; some practical experience in the local community will normally be most valuable in learning where to find the needed kinds of information. Data requirements for a study seems to be an obvious part of any research investigation. It should be always kept in mind, however, that the data used must be appropriate to the questions asked in the research problem, or the suggested solutions may be both inappropriate and useless, as well as wrong.

DATA ANALYSIS

Once data have been collected, the next logical step is to undertake some analysis of the data with an eye toward reaching a solution to the research problem. This section, after providing a brief background statement, presents several elementary analytic procedures easily used in applied economic geography to help solve a wide range of problems. The particular analytic procedure to be utilized will, of course, depend on what questions have been asked. The decision of the appropriate analytic technique may also depend on the nature of the data collected.

Data are often classified as one of three basic types. First and most basic are data at the ***nominal scale***. Nominal data provide the number of observations that fall into different categories where one cannot array the categories in any order of magnitude. An example of nominal categories might be male and female; north, south, east, and west; and automobile, truck, bicycle, and feet. Whereas the nominal scale does not allow one to rank the categories in terms of importance, the ***ordinal scale*** does permit a ranking by order of magnitude, but it is not possible to determine how much greater one item is compared with another. One might rank, from 1 to 5, five sections of town in which he or she might prefer to live. Such a ranking does not indicate whether section 1 is preferred twice as much as section 2, or only half again as much. Such a ranking of data without knowledge of the interval between the ranks is known as ordinal data. ***Interval data*** provide more detailed information, inasmuch as the actual interval or distance between objects is known. Here we are referring to such measures as feet or meters, weight in pounds or grams, income in dollars or marks. Interval data, being more exacting, are generally to

The making of maps and graphs has become almost totally automated by many highly sophisticated software packages.

be preferred although in many instances it is difficult to impossible to establish actual interval units. How does one, for example, meaningfully measure isolation in geographic units? Can an isolation index developed for a city be equally applied in a rural setting? Solutions to such questions can be found only after establishing certain rather arbitrary measurement rules.

Locational Indexes

A large number of locational indexes have been developed and utilized in studies in applied economic geography. One of the most basic and widely used indexes is the ***location quotient,*** which is a ratio of ratios. The location quotient is appropriate when one wishes to map relative distributions. For example, if one wished to know the distribution of professional workers among zones within an urban area in comparison to total workers, the location quotient would provide such information. For purposes of illustration, one may take a very simple example. Suppose the city is to be divided into five areas. In area 1 there are 5 professional workers, in area 2 there are 10 professional workers, and so on (Appendix Table 1). We will suppose there is a total of 100 professional workers in all of the five areas. By dividing the total professional workers (100)

Appendix Table 1   Data for Computing the Location Quotient

Areas	Professional Workers (X_i)	Total Workers (N_i)
1	5	100
2	10	50
3	15	150
4	25	250
5	45	450
Sum	$\Sigma X_i = 100$	$\Sigma N_i = 1{,}000$

into the number in each of the five areas, we will obtain the proportion of professional workers in each of the five areas.

Next, we examine the number of total workers in each of the five areas. In area 1 we have 100 total workers, in area 2 we have 50, in area 3 we have 150, and so on. For computational convenience, there are 1000 total workers in the city. One may thus calculate the proportion of total workers in each of the five areas (Appendix Table 2).

Thus, we have calculated two ratios. The first will be the numerator in the formula for the location quotient—that is, the proportion of professional workers in each area. The second will be the denominator, the proportion of total workers in each area. If we then divide the proportion of total workers for zone 1 into the proportion of professional workers in that area, we derive a location quotient for that area. In the

Appendix Table 2   Steps in Computing the Location Quotient

Area	$X_i/\Sigma X_i$	N_i/Σ_i	Location Quotient
1	0.05	0.10	50
2	0.10	0.05	200
3	0.15	0.15	100
4	0.25	0.25	100
5	0.45	0.45	100

example at hand, we would divide 0.10 into 0.05, and, by convention, multiply by 100, obtaining a location quotient for area 1 of 50. For area 2, we divide 0.05 into 0.10, then multiply by 100 to get a quotient of 200. For area 3, we divide 0.15 into 0.15, then multiply by 100 to obtain a location quotient of 100.

In area 3 it is clear that there is the same proportional distribution of professional workers as there is of total workers. Thus, a location quotient of 100 indicates that the two proportional distributions are identical. In area 1, with a location quotient of 50, there are fewer professional workers than "expected." In area 2, where the location quotient is 200, there are twice as many professional workers as "expected." Therefore, a map of location quotients shows areas of relative concentrations of a sub-group as well as areas in which that subgroup is not strongly represented.

In terms of a formula, let X represent any subgroup, such as professional workers. N will stand for the total group, or total workers in our example. The subscript i will refer to any particular area. The summation sign, Σ, indicates that the values for X or for N have been summed for all areas i. Thus:

$$LQ = \frac{X_i/\Sigma X_i}{N_i/\Sigma N_i} \cdot 100$$

The location quotient is easy to calculate and provides useful information on relative distributions. One may compare professional workers and service workers by compiling maps of location quotients for the two groups. Such information might prove useful in locational decisions as to where to locate particular kinds of institutional facilities in urban areas. Another common use of the location quotient is for examining relative distributions of manufacturing industries. One may be interested in the relative distribution of employment in the textile industry by state or metropolitan area in comparison to total employment. Any time a total or group can be broken down into subgroups or subcategories and the data are mappable, one may potentially employ the location quotient to assist in understanding relative distributions.

A second locational index is the *index of dissimilarity*. Whereas the location quotient compares the relative spatial distribution of a subcategory with the category, the index of dissimilarity compares the proportional distributions of two subcategories. The proportion of professional workers in a city may be compared with the proportion of service workers. The index values range from zero, indicating identical proportional distributions, to 100, reflecting a totally opposite spatial distribution.

Again, the index of dissimilarity is easily calculated. For each of several areas, one finds the proportion of, say, professional workers in an area, based on the total number of professional workers. If X_i is the number of professional workers in area i, then $X_i/\Sigma X_i$ is the proportion of these workers in area i, where ΣX_i is the total number of professional workers in all of the areas. Likewise, $Y_i/\Sigma Y_i$ is the proportion of, say, service workers (Y). For every area i, one subtracts the absolute value (ignoring plus and minus signs) of one proportion from the other, that is $|(X_i/\Sigma X_i) - (Y_i/\Sigma Y_i)|$, where the vertical lines refer to taking the absolute value. These absolute differences are then summed for all areas divided by 2 to avoid double counting and multiplied by 100 (by convention to express the index in whole numbers). Thus:

$$\text{ID} = \sum_{i=1}^{N} \frac{|(X_i/\Sigma X_i) - (Y_i/\Sigma Y_i)|}{2} \cdot 100$$

How does one interpret the index of dissimilarity? Suppose we have information on the number of professional workers (X), sales workers (Y), and service workers (Z) for a number of areas within a metropolitan area. We wish to know how the spatial distributions of these three groups are proportionally dissimilar. Are professional workers more similar in their spatial distribution to sales or to service workers? In Ap-

Appendix Table 3 Hypothetical Values of Index of Dissimilarity

Workers	Professional (X)	Sales (Y)	Service (Z)
Professional (X)	—	17	43
Sales (Y)		—	30
Service (Z)			—

pendix Table 3 we have hypothetical values of the index of dissimilarity for these three groups. The value of the index comparing professional (X) with sales workers (Y) is 17, indicating that 17 percent of the workers would have to move to other areas for the worker proportions to be identical. The table also shows that professional workers are more similar to sales workers than they are to service workers in their relative spatial distributions. Typically, one may wish to make a great many comparisons among groups, such as a comparison among 20 industry types, a number of ethnic population groups, or sales volume among retail types in different shopping centers.

An index closely related to the index of dissimilarity is the *index of segregation*, its name derived from the application of this index to studies of residential segregation. The index of segregation combines features of the location quotient and the index of dissimilarity. Like the former, it treats a relationship between a subcategory and the category itself; like the latter, it measures the degree to which two proportional distributions are spatially similar. The index of segregation provides a single statistic that summarizes the relationship between, say, professional workers and total workers. The location quotient on the other hand gives a comparison on an area by area basis. Both the index of dissimilarity and the index of segregation generalize the spatial distributions in terms of a single number.

The formula for these two indexes is very similar. The index of segregation (IS) may be found by following:

$$IS = \sum_{i=1}^{N} \frac{|(X_i/\Sigma X_i) - (N_i/\Sigma N_i)|}{2} \cdot 100$$

In fact, the only difference is that the term $(Y_i/\Sigma Y_i)$ is replaced by $(N_i/\Sigma N_i)$ where N refers to the total number as in the location quotient. If a value of, say, 25 is calculated for the index of segregation between professional and total workers, one may interpret that 25 percent of professional workers would have to relocate in a different area in order for professional workers to have the same proportional distribution as total workers. Thus, the index of segregation may be used if one is interested in a single number that generalizes the proportional spatial differences among subcategories with the category. The index of segregation, therefore, has the same interpretation as the index of dissimilarity, and the range in its value is also from 0 to 100.

The final locational index discussed here is the **Lorenz curve**. The Lorenz curve is really just a graphical representation of the index of dissimilarity. It may be used to show the degree of areal concentration or to compare several distributions for degree of similarity. The Lorenz curve may be used to compare several variables in one region, one variable in several regions, or changes in one (or more) variable or variables in a region over time. Its advantages are that it is intuitive, graphical, and easy to compute. It is especially appropriate to use when other techniques are not applicable as when one is analyzing extremely asymmetrical statistical distributions.

There are five steps in calculating the Lorenz curve. Assume data for two variables, X and Y, for each of several areal units. To what extent do the variables reflect similar spatial distributions? One would first calculate a ratio of X/Y for each areal unit. Appendix Table 4 shows some hypothetical data and calculated results for a highly simplified situation in which there are only four areal units, $a,b,c,$ and d. For further simplicity, we have set the totals for the two variables at 100 each. We see that areal unit a, for example, has a value of 25 for variable X, corn production, and 50 for variable Y, wheat production. Thus, the Y/X ratio for area a is 2.0.

The second step in finding the Lorenz curve is simply to rank the Y/X ratios from lowest to highest for each of the areal units. In our example, location b has the lowest ratio and location a has the highest value. The third step is to compute the percentages for each variable for each areal unit, a computation easily accomplished, for the denominator is 100 in each case. The fourth step is to cumulate these percentages for the areal units in the order of the ranking of the ratios (step 2). The only remaining step is then to plot on a two-dimensional diagram four points (one for each areal unit) and to connect those points to form a line known as the Lorenz curve (Appendix Figure 1).

Had the spatial distributions of the two vari-

Appendix Table 4   Calculating the Lorenz Curve

Area	Y/X Ratio	Area	Ranked Ratio	Area	Y	X	Cumulative Lorenz Value Y	Cumulative Lorenz Value X
a	2.0	b	0.5	b	.20	.40	20	40
b	0.5	c	0.6	c	.10	.15	30	55
c	0.6	d	1.0	d	.20	.20	50	75
d	1.0	a	2.0	a	.50	.25	100	100

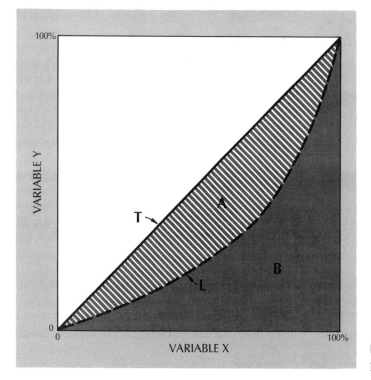

Figure A.1 The Lorenz curve, showing departures from a spatially even distribution.

ables, X and Y, been identical, the line formed would have been T, as shown in Appendix Figure 1. We use T to emphasize that this is the *theoretical* curve against which one may measure departure. T is the "expected" distribution, and L is the actual, computed Lorenz curve indicating just how far from the "expected" the relationship between the two variables is. Said yet another way, the Lorenz curve measures the degree of deviation from an "even" spatial distribution.

Look again at Appendix Figure 1: the area between line T and line L is labeled A, which is the extent of deviation from the "even" spatial distribution.

Look again at Appendix Figure 1: The area between line T and line L is labeled A, which is the extent of deviation from the "even" spatial distribution. The area in the figure labeled B, lying to the right of line L, represents the remainder of the space in the diagram. With a moment's thought, it should be clear that one may calculate a ratio that will indicate the degree of deviation from the theoretical spatial distribution

$$D = \frac{A}{A + B}$$

where D is the measure of deviation, A is the actual deviation, and $A + B$ is the maximum level of deviation possible. Clearly, one may plot several Lorenz curves and calculate several D values for comparison. Values of D range from 0 up to 1, where 1 indicates maximum deviation ($b = 0$).

The Lorenz curve is a useful descriptive, graphical measure that may be employed in a number of situations. As with most indexes, the effect of areal boundaries is critical. Moving a boundary slightly one way or another may well mean a significant shift in values from one area to another as especially would be the case with highly variable spatial distributions.

A Measure of Concentration

A number of measures may be used to measure concentration. The one examined here is an *entropy* measure, derived from information theory, where it indicates the degree of disorder or uncertainty in a system. The measure has a range from zero, maximum concentration, to unity (1.0), maximum dispersal. Certainty is related, in information theory terms, to the degree of spatial concentration.

Consider a map of an area subdivided into, say, counties or small units of area. In each of the counties there are people or some other distribution. The economic geographer wishes to know whether the distribution is dispersed or concentrated. The entropy measure is, therefore, appropriate.

The first step is to calculate the proportion of the population in each county such that the sum of the proportions equals 1.0. The second step is to apply the following entropy formula to the county proportions.

$$H = -\Sigma Pi \; \ln Pi$$

where H denotes absolute entropy, Pi refers to the proportion of population in county i, and $\ln$ refers to the natural logarithm. Computationally, one finds the natural logarithm of Pi and multiples that value by Pi. The products for all countries are summed to obtain H, the absolute entropy measure. In order to allow comparisons among different spatial distributions, one needs to calculate a *relative entropy* statistic.

$$G = H/\ln k$$

where G is relative entropy and k is the number of categories, or counties, in our example. If G equals zero, then all the population will be in a single county. If G equals unity, then each county will have the identical population numbers.

Appendix Table 5 provides an example of two sets of data for which relative entropy is calculated. A glance at data set I reveals a rather evenly spaced or dispersed pattern of population among the five counties. In contrast, data set II shows a highly concentrated pattern, with 96 percent of the population in a single county. For example, the population in county 1, data set I, is 10, which translates into a proportional value, Pi, of 0.1. When the natural logarithm of 0.1 (i.e., -2.303) is multiplied by 0.1 (Pi), the value is -0.230. The values for all counties are summed to yield H, or 1.577. Because there are five counties ($K = 5$), the denominator in the equation for G is 1.609. Not surprisingly, G equals a high value, 0.967 for data set I. For data set II, however, the G statistic is 0.139, indicating a much more concentrated pattern.

Measures of Association

Various measures of *spatial association* may be employed in data analysis, depending on the na-

---

Appendix Table 5   Calculating Relative Entropy

Counties	Data Set I			Data Set II		
	Population	*Pi*	*Pi* ln *Pi*	Population	*Pi*	*Pi* ln *Pi*
1	10	0.1	−0.230	1	0.01	−0.046
2	20	0.2	−0.322	1	0.01	−0.046
3	20	0.2	−0.322	1	0.01	−0.046
4	20	0.2	−0.322	1	0.01	−0.046
5	30	0.3	−0.361	96	0.96	−0.0392
	100	1.0	−1.557	100	1.0	−0.233
	$G = 1.557/1.609 = 0.967$			$G = 0.223/1.609 = 0.139$		

ture of the data and the goals of the researcher. It may be helpful to think of spatial association in a simplified way as a comparison of two maps. One map shows the distribution of wheat production on the Great Plains, and the other depicts the distribution of precipitation in the same area. How similar are the two maps? One may be able, through visual inspection, to determine that the two maps are or are not generally similar. The degree of similarity or spatial association will be very difficult to determine precisely through visual means, however. Two different observers might well examine the maps and come away with different evaluations. As a means of avoiding such subjective interpretations of spatial association, several quantitative measures have been developed and applied.

One of the simplest and basic measures is the *coefficient of areal correspondence* (A_c). This coefficient is able to use data at the nominal scale, where there are two categories such as the presence or absence of some phenomenon. Consider two maps, one showing the areal extent of land classified as more than 10 percent in slope and the other showing the extent of land classified as severely eroded. To what degree do the two maps overlap? If land in slope is designated as A and severely eroded land is referred to as B, we will want to know the extent to which A and B overlap or, in more common mathematical terms, the *intersection* of A and B ($A \cap B$). We will also need to know the area covered by either A or B. The area covered by either A or B is the union of A and B ($A \cup B$). The coefficient of areal correspondence (A_c) may then be calculated by dividing the intersection A and B by the union of A and B.

$$A_c = \frac{A \cap B}{A \cup B}$$

The range of the coefficient is from 0, indicating no areal correspondence, to 1.0, in which there is perfect correspondence between the two distributions. If the coefficient is, say 0.60, then 60 percent of the area containing A and B (total

of A and B) contains both A and B together (AB). The coefficient of areal correspondence can be very useful when appropriately applied to nominal data.

Another interesting measure of spatial association is Tinkler's *coefficient of association for binary data*.[1] Again, this coefficient assumes the use of nominal data in which values are either 0 or 1, as with the presence or absence of something. One may take an example from transportation. Suppose we have 50 major urban centers in the southeastern United States (1 to 50). A measure is taken to determine if there is a direct link between each of these 50 centers via the interstate highway systems (X). If there is a direct link between center 1 and 2 for interstate highways, enter a *1* in matrix X. If there is not a direct link between the same centers by rail, enter a *0* in matrix Y. When both matrix X and matrix Y have been completed, one may wish to determine the degree to which the two matrices (or the two transportation networks) are similar. Needless to say, visual inspection of networks of any size and complexity would make such a determination exceedingly difficult.

The next step is to count the number of coincident pairs, (0–0) or (1–1), in the two matrices. If there is a highway and a rail link between centers 1 and 2, it is defined as a coincident pair (1–1). Similarly, if there is no link in either case, they have a coincident pair (0–0). A noncoincident pair occurs when there is either a highway or rail link but not both, (1–0) or (0–1). One then simply counts the number of coincident pairs and, using the simple formula that follows, calculates the coefficient of binary association

$$C_a = \frac{2P}{N} - 1$$

where P = the number of coincident pairs and where N = the total number of pairs in the matrix.

---

[1]The term *binary* simply refers to values of 0 or 1.

The coefficient ranges in value from 0 to ± 1.0. A value of 1.0 would of course indicate that the two transportation networks were identical. A value of −1.0 would show that every time there is a highway link, there is not a rail link (and vice versa). A value of 0 would mean that there was no relationship between the two networks and that these spatial arrangements were randomly laid out.

Yet another measure of spatial association is **point biserial correlation**. This measure is appropriate when one areal distribution is recorded at the internal scale and the other distribution is scored on a nominal scale having only two values. It might be that one is interested in how the volume of retail sales varies between grocery stores that are located (1) in large shopping centers and (2) in nonshopping center sites. The variable retail sales is thus measured in dollars of retail sales (interval scale), and the second variable [location in (1) or not in (0) a shopping center] can take only one of two values. The hypothesis might be that higher grocery retail sales will occur in stores in shopping centers than in isolated locations. The technical procedure of computing point biserial correlation is as follows:

$$R_p = \frac{\overline{Y}_1 - \overline{Y}_0}{S_y} \cdot \sqrt{\frac{N_1 N_0}{N(N-1)}}$$

This at first rather complex-looking formula is actually quite simple and straightforward. R_p is the correlation coefficient. The average or mean retail sales value is calculated both for grocery stores located in shopping centers ($\overline{Y}_1$) and not in shopping centers ($\overline{Y}_0$). The symbol S_0 is used

as a measure of the degree of variation in retail sales, technically known as the standard deviation.[2] Thus, the difference in retail sales between the two types of store locations is found by simple subtraction, with the difference divided by the amount of variability from store to store in retail trade. This term, then, is multiplied by a factor that controls for the number of stores being analyzed, where N stands for the total number of stores being studied and where N_1 refers to the number of stores in shopping centers and N_0 to those not in shopping centers. The details of the statistical computations need not delay us here except perhaps to note that the second term in the equation is expressed in square-root form. A value of 0 would indicate no association between retail sales and location; a value of 1.0 would indicate a perfect positive relationship.

Many other examples of situations could be listed in which point biserial correlation is appropriate. No attempt will be made here to cover testing for statistical significance; for further discussion, one may consult various statistical textbooks widely available.

When there are data at the ordinal scale—that is, rank-order data—one may appropriately measure spatial association with **Spearman's rank-order correlation**. Take as an example an estate consisting of a large number of fields. During one year wheat is grown in each of the fields; during a second year all fields are planted in corn. The question is whether the yields per acre are similar for the two crops for the two years. Because the data are not normally distributed in a statistical sense—that is, do not form a normal, bell-shaped curve—one cannot use "regular" correlation analysis and must then rank order the fields by average yield per acre. In this instance, Spearman's rank-order correlation is appropriate.

Spearman's rank-order correlation takes values ranging from 0, no relationship, to ±1.0, a perfect relationship. A positive coefficient indicates that the ranking of fields by wheat yields is identical with the ranking of fields by corn yields.

---

[2]For those interested, the standard deviation is computed by squaring each difference between a given retail sales volume and the overall mean of that sales volume, then summing these squared values, dividing by $N-1$ (where N is the number of stores), and taking the square root of the quotient. The formula is

$$S_y = \sqrt{\Sigma \frac{(y - \overline{y})^2}{N-1}}$$

A perfect negative association would mean that the highest ranking field in wheat yield would rank lowest in corn yield and that the second-highest-ranking field in wheat yield would rank second lowest in corn yield, and so on for all ranks.

The Spearman rank-order correlation is very simple to calculate. Appendix Table 5 lists eight fields and the rank order of wheat yields and corn yields for each field. A first step in computing the rank-order correlation coefficient is to find the differences in the ranks for each field and then to square these differences (thereby removing minus signs). In this example, field A ranks first in wheat yield and third in corn yield. When one subtracts corn-yield rank from wheat-yield rank, the result is -2. When squared, the value of course becomes 4. The sum of the differences in rank, column d, will be zero, as positive and negative values will cancel out. The sum of the squared differences, Σa^2, will naturally be positive.

Having determined the sum of the squared differences, one can easily compute R, the rank-order correlation coefficient

$$R = 1 - \frac{6\Sigma d^2}{N(N^2 - 1)}$$

where N is the number of observations, that is, number of fields. The value 6 is a constant. In this example (Appendix Table 6), Σa^2 equals 18

and N equals 8. The reader should verify that R equals 0.79, indicating a strong positive correlation. The value of R derived may be tested for statistical significance, but this discussion lies beyond the scope of this introduction to applied geographic analysis.

Rank correlation has the advantage that it can be quickly and easily computed. It may be used with data that are not normally distributed. It is also appropriate when one has only data by ranks rather than data at the interval scale. Finally, if one has interval data that may not be as precise or accurate as a measurement at the interval scale would imply, it might be better to rank order the data and apply rank correlation than to use some other technique.

One other correlation technique will be briefly mentioned, **Pearson's Product Moment Correlation**. The purpose of this discussion is merely to suggest conceptually how this correlation coefficient may be used in geographic analysis, not to demonstrate its computational solution, which is normally carried out by computer analysis.

Take the case of two variables or attributes measured at several locations or places. One variable might be of value of farm products sold per acre. This is the variable in which the researcher is interested; that is, he or she wishes to understand why this variable varies in magnitude or value from place to place in the study area. Because the spatial distribution of the value of farm products sold is what is being investigated, this variable is referred to as the **dependent variable**. The first question the researcher asks is why this dependent variable differs from place to place in the study area. One logical reason might relate to the level of farm inputs, that is, amount of fertilizer used, labor costs, and cultivation costs (gasoline, weed spray). This second variable, farm inputs, is thus used to "explain" the reason for the spatial variation in the dependent variable. This explanatory variable is then referred to as the **independent variable**. Correlation then proceeds to determine if the independent variable is indeed independent, or unrelated, with respect to the dependent vari-

Appendix Table 6 Computing Rank-Order Correlations

Fields	Wheat Yield	Corn Yield	d	d^2
A	1	3	-2	4
B	2	2	0	0
C	3	1	2	4
D	4	4	0	0
E	5	7	-2	4
F	6	5	1	1
G	7	8	-1	1
H	8	6	2	4
			$\Sigma d = 0$	$\Sigma d^2 = 18$

able. Again, the correlation coefficient ranges from ±1.0.

In the present example one would expect a positive correlation: when value of farm products sold is high, the level of farm inputs will also be high. Careful examination of the relationship between the two variables in different parts of the study area may reveal certain areas in which the farm-inputs variable overpredicts or underpredicts the dependent variable. Thus, an area with very poor soils might require higher levels of farm input (fertilizer) to achieve a given level of sales than is typical of the study area in general (underprediction). Conversely, a richly endowed part of the study area might require fewer farm inputs.

A single independent variable may then not be sufficient to account for all the variations in the dependent variable, and other independent variables, such as soil quality, may need to be added to the analysis. The selection of other independent variables to be added must be guided by commonsense understanding of the problem under study, as it is, of course, possible to add nonsense variables that might, based on random chance, "explain" (but only in a statistical sense) the variation in the dependent variable. As with any technique, correlation analysis is subject to *GIGO,* "Garbage In and Garbage Out." One example would be a correlation between wheat yields in Kansas and the number of cattle in India: if there were a statistical correlation, it would have no meaning or causal connection.

This discussion has not more than scratched the surface of the rich vein of data analytic tools and procedures available to the economic geographer involved in applied research. Those who wish to employ these and other analytic techniques would need to develop an understanding that goes beyond the scope and space of this introductory book.

DATA REPRESENTATION

Having looked briefly at data requirements for studying resource problems in applied economic geography and having examined some selected data analysis techniques, we turn to the issue of data representation. Data representation, as used by a geographer, may be viewed as having two components: (1) verbal and (2) graphical. No matter what kind of study has been carried out in economic geography, the results of the effort must be communicated in some way to the appropriate audience. Verbal communication may be written or oral, and further discussion of verbal representation of data and analytic results is beyond the scope of this chapter. Suffice it to note that verbal presentation, in whatever form, is a vital part of the problem-solving approach. Without lucid, organized, and comprehensible verbal communication, even the most useful data and technical results will obviously be greatly weakened, if not rendered meaningless.

Graphical representation of data and data analysis is equally critical. "A picture is worth a thousand words," and a map or graph is nothing more than a simplified picture of a segment of reality. A map communicates a vast amount of information in an extremely simplified manner. For many maps, it would, in fact, take more than a thousand words to record precisely every detail on the map such that one could redraft the map from the verbal description. Maps are communication devices, and just as one learns how to use language in written and oral form, it is necessary to learn the fundamentals of cartography to read and draw maps. Again, the comments here are offered as a backdrop and guide to students interested in problem-solving approaches to applied economic geography.

APPLIED GEOGRAPHY AND EMPLOYMENT OPPORTUNITIES

One of the major shifts occurring in economic geography and indeed—all geography over the past decade—is the much greater emphasis on what has variously been called applied or nonacademic economic geography. We prefer the term *applied* because academic geographers can and do carry out studies in applied economic geography. One reason for this shift in interest is that the academic marketplace for geographers has become tighter and, at the same time, many nonacademic employers have come to recognize the capabilities and backgrounds of economic geographers. As employers in government, business, and planning have experienced what economic geographers can do with their substantive background in locational analysis and with their technical expertise in such areas as computer analysis (including graphics), cartography, statistics, field methods, and remote sensing, employment opportunities have rather suddenly opened up. We are now experiencing a "second-generation" effect whereby previous graduates in economic geography have moved up the employment ladder into supervisory positions, and these supervisors, being geographers themselves, are hiring other economic geographers. Future trends appear good for the well-trained and informed economic geographer to pursue various careers in applied geography.

One question relating to applied economic geography involves the nature of educational preparation. Should undergraduate, as well as graduate, education for those interested in applied geography careers be technical and specialized or substantive and broad? Although one may, no doubt, find people who would argue for either extreme, it would seem that those most successful in obtaining employment in applied geography, as well as in advancing rapidly, are those who combine a solid substantive background in locational analysis with a strong technical understanding. One must be competent in both content and techniques. A person who is highly trained in one or more geographic techniques but who lacks knowledge of the content of economic geography will not make a good applied geographer because she will have little content to apply. Conversely, a person knowing content but not appropriate geographic techniques will not know how to go about applying geographic knowledge. A middle road seems the most reasonable and valuable.

Many untapped employment opportunities lie ahead for applied economic geography. In countries such as Russia and Sweden, applied geography is far ahead of its position and contribution in the United States. In such countries, geographers are directly involved in governmental research in everything from monitoring fish counts in lakes with pollutants to the location of new urban settlements. As geography matures in the United States and the issue of the visibility of geography outside academe becomes less of a problem, applied economic geography should significantly expand and contribute to a wide variety of societal, policy, and environmental issues. As J. Russell Whitaker, president of the Association of American Geographers, stated in his presidential address in a somewhat different context in 1954, "The way lies open."

Further Readings

Carter, James R. *Computer Mapping: Progress in the 80s*. Washington, D.C.: Association of American Geographers, 1984.

Cuff, David J., and Mark T. Mattson. *Thematic Maps: Their Design and Production*. New York: Methuen, 1981).

Dent, Borden. *Principles of Thematic Map Design*. Reading, Mass.: Addison-Wesley, 1985.

Haggett, Peter, Andrew D. Cliff, and Allan Frey. *Locational Analysis in Human Geography*. 2nd rev. ed. New York: Halsted Press, 1977.

Hodler, Thomas W. "Do Geographers Really Need to Know Cartography?" *Urban Geography* 15 (1994), pp. 409–410.

Isard, Walter. *Methods of Regional Analysis*. Cambridge, Mass.: MIT Press, 1960.

Lewis, Peter. *Maps and Statistics*. New York: Wiley, 1977.

Monmonier, M. S. *Computer-Assisted Cartography: Principles and Prospects*. Englewood Cliffs, N.J.: Prentice-Hall, 1982.

Natoli, S. V. *Careers in Geography*. 3rd rev. ed. Washington Association of American Geographers, 1983.

Norcliffe, G. B. *Inferential Statistics for Geographers*. New York: Wiley, 1977.

Peucker, Thomas K. *Computer Cartography*. Washington, D.C.: Resource Paper No. 17, 1972. Association of American Geographers.

Robinson, Arthur H., Randall D. Sale, Joel L. Morrison, and Phillip C. Muehrcke. *Elements of Cartography*. 5th ed. New York: Wiley, 1984.

Sabins, Floyd F., Jr. *Remote Sensing: Principles and Interpretation*. San Francisco: W. H. Freeman, 1978.

Shaw, Gareth, and Dennis Wheeler. *Statistical Techniques in Geographical Analysis*. New York: Wiley, 1994.

Silk, John. *Statistical Concepts in Geography*. London: George Allen & Unwin, 1979.

Stoddard, Robert H., *Field Techniques and Research Methods in Geography*. Dubuque, Iowa: Kendall/Hunt, 1982.

Taylor, D. R. Fraser, ed. *The Computer in Contemporary Cartography*. New York: Wiley, 1980.

Taylor, D. R. ed., *Graphic Communication and Design in Contemporary Cartography*. New York: Wiley, 1983.

Taylor, Peter J. *Quantitative Methods in Geography: An Introduction to Spatial Analysis*. Boston: Houghton Mifflin, 1977.

Teicholz, Eric, and Brian J. L., Berry. *Computer Graphics and Environmental Planning*. Englewood Cliffs, N.J.: Prentice-Hall, 1983.

Tinkler, K. J. "A Coefficient of Association for Binary Data." *Area* 3 (1971), pp. 31–35.

Unwin, David. *Introductory Spatial Analysis*. New York: Methuen, 1981.

Whitaker, J. Russell. "The Way Lies Open." *Annals of the Association of American Geographers* 44 (1954), pp. 231–244.

Wrigley, N., and R. J. Bennett, eds. *Quantitative Geography*. London: Routledge & Kegan Paul, 1981.

Yeates, Maurice. *An Introduction to Quantitative Analysis in Human Geography*. New York: McGraw-Hill, 1974.

ILLUSTRATION AND PHOTO CREDITS

Chapter 1

Page 3: Courtesy James Wheeler.

Figure 1.2: Reproduced by permission from the *Annals of the Association of American Geographers*, Vol. 64, 1974, p. 9, Figure 3, Edward J. Taaffe.

Figure 1.6: Reproduced by permission from the *Annals of the Association of American Geographers*, Vol. 54, 1964, p. 6, Figure 1, Brian J. L. Berry.

Page 10: Philip & Karen Smith/Tony Stone Images/ New York, Inc.

Page 15: Courtesy General Motors Corp.

Chapter 2

Page 21: Greg Probst/Tony Stone Images/New York, Inc.

Page 24: Courtesy Louis De Vorsey.

Page 26: Jack Spratt/The Image Works.

Page 31: Michael Dwyer/Stock, Boston.

Page 32: Courtesy Catherine L. Brown.

Chapter 3

Page 36: Keith Wood/Tony Stone Images/New York, Inc.

Page 40: Owen Franken/Stock, Boston.

Page 42: Michael Siluk/The Image Works.

Figure 3.11: Reproduced from Allan Pred, *Spatial Dynamics of Urban Industrial Growth*, Cambridge, M.I.T. Press, 1966, p. 25.

Page 52: Courtesy Catherine L. Brown.

Chapter 4

Page 57: Courtesy James Wheeler.

Page 62: Demetrio Carrasco/Tony Stone Images/New York, Inc.

Page 68: Courtesy Metro Toronto Convention & Visitors Association.

Page 72: George Holton/Photo Researchers.

Chapter 5

Figure 5.6: Reproduced by permission, *Growth and Change*, Vol. 18, 1987, p. 52, Figure 4, James S. Fisher and Ronald L. Mitchelson.

Page 85: Hans Schlapfer/Tony Stone Images/New York, Inc.

Figure 5.9: Reproduced from Edward J. Taaffe, Richard L. Morrill, and Peter R. Gould, *Geographical Re-*

view, Vol. 53, 1963, with the permission of the American Geographical Society.

Page 88: Mitch Wojnarowicz/The Image Works.

Page 97: Rhoda Sidney/The Image Works.

Figure 5.17: Reproduced from the *Annals of the Association of American Geographers*, Vol. 59, 1969, p. 352, Figure 4, Donald G. Janelle.

Chapter 6

Page 108: Ted Clutter/Photo Researchers.

Page 112: Rob Nelson/Black Star.

Figure 6.5: Reproduced from *Modern Transport Geography*, Belhaven Press, 1992, p. 209, Figure 11.2, Yehuda Hayuth.

Page 116: Courtesy The Boeing Corporation.

Page 124: James Sugar/Black Star.

Page 125: Courtesy Federal Express.

Chapter 7

Page 131: Mark Segal/Tony Stone Images/New York, Inc.

Page 132: Courtesy Wal-Mart Stores.

Figure 7.2: Reproduced from *Urban Geography*, Vol. 13, 1992, p. 344, Figure 3, B. Ó hUallacháin and N. Reid.

Figure 7.3: Reproduced from the *Professional Geographer*, Vol. 41, 1989, p. 166, Figure 2, James O. Wheeler and Ronald L. Mitchelson.

Figure 7.4: Reproduced by permission of *Lund Studies in Geography*, Alan Pred, 1967.

Figure 7.5: Reproduced by permission of *Economic Geography*, Vol. 46, James B. Kenyon, 1970, p. 12.

Figure 7.6: Reproduced from *Urban Geography*, Vol. 14, 1993, p. 282, Figure 1b, Paul Waddell and Vibhooti Shukla.

Figure 7.7: Reproduced by permission of the American Academy of Political and Social Science and Chauncy D. Harris.

Page 147: Jagdish Agarwal/The Image Works.

Page 148: Glen Allison/Tony Stone Images/New York, Inc.

Figure 7.8: Reproduced by permission of the American Geographical Society, *Geographical Review*, Vol. 80, 1990, p. 374, Figure 1, James O. Wheeler.

Figure 7.9: Reproduced from the *Professional Geog-*

rapher, Vol. 45, 1993, p. 37, Figure 2, Daniel Z. Sui and James O. Wheeler.

Chapter 8

Figure 8.1: Reproduced from W. Christaller, *Central Places in Southern Germany*, translated by C. W. Bakin, Englewood Cliffs: Prentice-Hall, 1966, p. 61.

Figure 8.3: Reproduced from Brian J. L. Berry and Allan Pred, *Central Places Studies*, Regional Science Research Institute, 1961, p. 17.

Figures 8.5, 8.6, and 8.7: A. Losch, *Southern Economic Journal*, 1938.

Figure 8.8: Reproduced from the *Annals of the Association of American Geographers*, Vol. 59, 1969, pp. 396–398, Figures 2, 3, Gerald Rushton.

Page 162: Courtesy James Wheeler.

Figure 8.9: Reproduced by permission of the Department of Geography, Indiana University, Monograph Series, Vol. 3, *A Space Preference Approach to the Diffusion of Innovations: The Spread of Harvestore Systems Through Northeast Iowa*, 1971, Figures 38, 54, pp. 64, 92, David De Temple.

Figure 8.10: Reproduced from *Urban Geography*, Vol. 9, 1988, p. 14, Figure 4, William Wyckoff.

Page 165: Beringer-Dratch/The Image Works.

Page 166: Courtesy Metro Toronto Convention & Visitors Association.

Figure 8.12: Reproduced from *Location, Location, Location*, Methuen, 1987, p. 231, Figure 8.5, Ken Jones and Jim Simmons.

Page 169: Courtesy James Wheeler.

Figure 8.14: Reproduced from Brian J. L. Berry, *Geography of Market Centers and Retail Distribution*, Englewood Cliffs: Prentice-Hall, 1967.

Figure 8.15: Reproduced from *Economic Geography*, Siyoung Park, Vol. 57, 1981, Figure 6, p. 122.

Page 173: Gregg Adams/Tony Stone Images/New York, Inc.

Chapter 9

Figure 9.1: John S. Adams, *Annals of the Association of American Geographers*, 1970. Reproduced by permission from the *Annals of the Association of American Geographers*, Volume 60, 1970, p. 56, Fig. 15.

Page 178: Courtesy J. C. Nichols Company.

Figure 9.2: Reprinted from *Urban Geography*, Rodney A. Erickson, Vol. 4, 1983, Figure 1, p. 96.

Page 183: Jim Pickerell/Tony Stone Images/New York, Inc.

Page 184: Courtesy Henry N. Michael.

Page 185: Courtesy Patricia Ulmer.

Figure 9.3: Peter O. Muller, *The Outer City: Geographical Consequences of the Urbanization of the Suburbs* (Washington, D.C.: Association of American Geographers, Resource Paper for College Geography Number 75-2) 1976, p. 41, Fig. 10. Reprinted by permission.

Page 187: Eric Neurath/Stock, Boston.

Page 188: Courtesy Union Carbide.

Figure 9.5: Arthur Getis, *Proceedings of the AAG*, Association of American Geographers, 1969, p. 57, Fig. 1.

Figure 9.6: Arthur Getis, *Proceedings of the AAG*, Association of American Geographers, 1969. Reproduced by permission from the *Proceedings of the Association of American Geographers*, Volume 1, 1969, p. 57, Fig. 2.

Figure 9.7: Arthur Getis, *Proceedings of the AAG*, Association of American Geographers, 1969. Reproduced by permission from the *Proceedings of the Association of American Geographers*, Volume 1, 1969, p. 57, Fig. 3b.

Figure 9.8: Arthur Getis, *Proceedings of the AAG*, Association of American Geographers, 1969. Reproduced by permission from the *Proceedings of the Association of American Geographers*, Volume 1, 1969, p. 57, Fig. 3a.

Figure 9.9: Arthur Getis, *The Journey from Work and the Critical Isochrone*, Rutgers University, Department of Geography, 1970. Reprinted by permission, Rutgers Geography Discussion Papers Series.

Chapter 10

Figure 10.1: Reproduced from Charles Kiester, M.A. thesis, University of Georgia, 1972.

Page 206: Courtesy James Wheeler.

Page 209: Michael Dwyer/Stock, Boston.

Figure 10.4: Reproduced from J. Friedmann and W. Alonso, eds. *Regional Development and Planning*, Cambridge: M.I.T. Press, 1964, p. 80.

Figures 10.5, 10.6, 10.8, and 10.9: Reprinted from A. Weber, *Theory of the Location of Industries*, translated by C. J. Friedrick, Chicago Press, 1929. Copyright © 1929 by the University of Chicago Press. All rights reserved.

Chapter 11

Page 228: Courtesy Louis De Vorsey.

Page 232: Courtesy Ford Motor Company.

Figure 11.4: Reproduced by permission from the *Annals of the Association of American Geographers*, Vol. 68, 1978, p. 219, Figure 3, J. R. Borchert.

Figure 11.5: Reproduced by permission of *Economic Geography*, Vol. 54, J. Rees, 1978.

Page 253: Courtesy the Braviken Paper Mill.

Chapter 12

Page 274: Collins/The Image Works.

Page 279: Phil Degginger/Tony Stone Images/New York, Inc.

Page 282: John Lawlor/Tony Stone Images/New York, Inc.

Page 283: Ben Osborne/Tony Stone Images/New York, Inc.

Page 289: Courtesy Robert L. Thayer, Jr.

Chapter 13

Page 293: Cameraman/The Image Works.

Page 298: Andy Sacks/Tony Stone Images/New York, Inc.

Page 299: Antman Archives/The Image Works.

Figure 13.6: Harold H. McCarty and James B. Lindberg, *A Preface to Economic Geography*, © 1966, p. 220, Fig. 11.2. Reprinted by permission of Prentice-Hall, Inc., Englewood Cliffs, New Jersey.

Figure 13.13: Michael Chisholm, *Rural Settlement and Land Use* (London: Hutchinson Publishing Group, Ltd., 1962), p. 29. Redrawn by permission.

Page 314: Granger Collection.

Page 317: Comstock, Inc.

Figure 13.15: KNAG Committee for Publications, Uithoorn, The Netherlands, 1969. From Sidney R. Jumper, "The Fresh Vegetable Industry in the U.S.A.," *Tijdschrift Voor Economische en Sociale Geografie*, 60(Sept.-Oct., 1969), p. 314.

Figure 13.18: Reproduced by permission from Peter O. Muller, "Trend Surfaces of American Agricultural Patterns: A Macro-Thünian Analysis," *Economic Geography*, 49 (1973), p. 237.

Figure 13.19: Reproduced courtesy of Wisconsin Crop and Livestock Reporting Service, from *A Century of Wisconsin Agriculture*, Bull. No. 290, 1948.

Page 324: Timothy Ross/The Image Works.

Figure 13.21: Reproduced by permission from the *Annals of the Association of American Geographers*, Volume 59, 1970, p. 350.

Figure 13.22: Reproduced by permission from the *Proceedings of American Geographers*, Volume 22, 1970, p. 69.

Figure 13.23 (top): Samuel Van Valkenburg and C. C. Heid, *Europe*, New York, John Wiley, 2 rev. ed., 1952. Reproduced by permission of Mrs. Marianne Van Valkenburg Carey.

Figure 13.23 (bottom): Redrawn by permission from Michael Chisholm, *Rural Settlement and Land Use* (London: Hutchinson Publishing Group, Ltd., 1962), p. 99.

Figure 13.24: Reproduced by permission from the *Annals of the Association of American Geographers*, Volume 57, 1967, p. 80.

Chapter 14

Page 336: Courtesy James Wheeler.

Figure 14.5: From Jean Gottmann. *Megalopolis: The Urbanized Northeastern Seaborad of the United States*, Fig. 66, © 1961 by the Twentieth Century Fund, Inc., New York. Reproduced by permission.

Appendix

Page 368: Courtesy James Wheeler.

AUTHOR AND SUBJECT INDEX

GEOGRAPHICAL INDEX